The Washington Senators, 1901–1971

To my wife,
who had confidence,
and to my mother,
to whom I promised this,
many years ago.

This book is
also dedicated to
the men who
played baseball for
the Washington Senators.

The Washington Senators, 1901–1971

by TOM DEVEAUX

McFarland & Company, Inc., Publishers

Jefferson, North Carolina, and London

Acknowledgments: I wish to thank my parents for their help and support over the years — you have my love and gratitude always.

The following people have been helpful in providing much-appreciated encouragement, advice, tangible assistance, or just a sympathetic ear along the way: my sister Angela, my friend Claude, Leo Squires, Gilles Deveau, David Copp, James Cypher.

My thanks to W. C. Burdick of the Baseball Hall of Fame for his enthusiasm and support for this project.

And last but not least, thanks to my wife Janet, who wants the world to know that she hates baseball — despite that flaw, I love you. Thank you for understanding why I needed to devote so much time to the Washington Senators.

The present work is a reprint of the library bound edition of The Washington Senators, 1901–1971, *first published in 2001 by McFarland.*

LIBRARY OF CONGRESS CATALOGUING-IN-PUBLICATION DATA

Deveaux, Tom, 1956–
The Washington Senators, 1901–1971 / by Tom Deveaux.
p.   cm.
Includes bibliographical references and index.

ISBN 0-7864-2359-5 (softcover : 50# alkaline paper) ∞

1. Washington Senators (Baseball team : 1899–1960).   2. Washington
Senators (Baseball team : 1961–1971).   I. Title.
GV875.W3D48   2005
796.357'64'09753 — dc21   2001031289

British Library cataloguing data are available

Cover photograph: Walter Johnson *(Library of Congress, LC-USZ62-77759)*

Manufactured in the United States of America

*McFarland & Company, Inc., Publishers
Box 611, Jefferson, North Carolina 28640
www.mcfarlandpub.com*

CONTENTS

But I continue to sit back with my ever-lastin' frown
For my childhood ended when the Senators left town.
— *Thomas Ponton*

Show me a hero and I will write you a tragedy.
— *F. Scott Fitzgerald*

PREFACE

There is available an ample supply of books on the subject of baseball statistics. This one does not intend to add to that list, but instead to provide an unbroken account of the history of the Washington Senators during their tenure in the American League.

Of course, no baseball book can do without statistics, and those in this book were gleaned from *Total Baseball* and MacMillan's *The Baseball Encyclopedia*. These two references do at times differ. When discrepancies were noted, the benefit of the doubt was given the player in question except in more noteworthy instances, which are explained in the text. If a particular stat does not concur with one of the sources, it will match the other.

I am grateful to the authors of all the resources I've had at my disposal. I would like to highlight the contemporary works of Henry Thomas and James R. Hartley, which describe in greater detail, respectively, the period spanning Walter Johnson's career, and the history of the second Senators franchise. A complete bibliography appears at the back, along with appendices outlining the Senators' year-by-year history, the final career stats of all Hall of Famers who played even one game for Washington, and the list of the players drafted by the original 1961 expansion Senators.

It should not be left unsaid, in case it should be perceived that certain performances are at times belittled, that every player mentioned in this book made it to the major leagues. Each one of these men — who played, incidentally, at a time when the love of the game seemed to matter a lot more than it does today — is therefore in my eyes a kind of hero.

INTRODUCTION

On October 7, 1924, a day which would become known as "Goslin Day" in baseball circles, my grandfather celebrated his 23rd birthday somewhere in New York City. It would be a fairly safe bet that he spent some time with his pals from down home — Nova Scotia, Canada. These were prohibition times, but the boys had their own still and my grandmother once confided to me that "Thomas used to go to these places they called speakeasies." One thing is sure, my grandfather wasn't at the Polo Grounds on that particular fall day in 1924. He told me he saw Jack Dempsey fight at Madison Square Garden, but that he never once went to a big-league ballgame.

Had I been alive and in New York on my grandfather's 23rd birthday, there is no doubt in my mind that I would have been at the Polo Grounds. There I would have seen Goose Goslin, himself only a year older than my grandfather, go 4-for-4 with a home run to lead the Washington Senators to an easy win over the hometown Giants in the fourth game of the World Series.

I think I know I would have been there because some things are just meant to be. On the day I was born, a Thursday in early September in the midfifties, one might have expected a full slate of games in the major leagues. That day, however, was a travel day for most teams, and only two games were played. One of those involved the Washington Senators, at a time when the club was the league doormat — one of the worst clubs to represent the capital in any era. On that day, the Senators won.

It was only about ten years later that this baseball club, or actually a different club with the same name, became important to me. As a youngster, I became conscious of a home run hitter named Frank Howard, who was taller and bigger than any other player. It seemed obvious to me that as a direct consequence of his size, Howard hit home runs farther than anyone I'd ever heard of. I became a fan of the Washington Senators. To this day, I remain one.

1901–1909: First in War, First in Peace

The creation of the Washington Senators had everything to do with the actions of a man so vain as to be considered totally unable to take a back seat to anyone. That man was Byron Bancroft "Ban" Johnson, who is recognized, and rightly so, as the driving force behind the formation of the American Baseball League in 1901.

A year earlier, the only existing major league, the National, had reduced its number of teams from twelve to eight. Among the teams dropped was a franchise in Washington, which was banished along with outfits operating in nearby Baltimore, as well as in Cleveland and Louisville. The Western League, organized in 1894 by ex–newspaper reporter Johnson, quickly moved to absorb two of those cities, displacing its St. Paul team to Chicago and its Grand Rapids, Michigan, ballclub to Cleveland.

Despite its presence in other cities which were already major population centers, the Western League continued to function as a minor league at the turn of the new century. This meant that league president Johnson and the team owners, which included future Hall of Famers Connie Mack at Milwaukee and Charles Comiskey at St. Paul, agreed to abide by the National Agreement. This was a pact stipulating that the National League was the only "major league," and that other associations had to honor the reserve clause included in all National League player contracts. In other words, the pirating of major-league players was a no-no.

As mentioned, Ban Johnson did not have the temperament of a man who liked to be dictated to. Arrogant and humorless, he loved attention — it was said of him that he would be moved to make a speech at any place where more than two people were seen gathered together. For 1901, the Western League adopted the name American League and Ban Johnson decreed that the National Agreement would no longer be respected. There would be a second, independent major league with new eastern clubs established in Washington, D.C., Baltimore, Boston, and Philadelphia. Four members were retained from the Western League — Cleveland, Chicago, Detroit, and Milwaukee (shifted to St. Louis after just one year). "The American League," Johnson grandly predicted, "will be the principal organization of the country in a very short time. Mark my prediction!"

In 1900, the National League had in place a salary limit of $2,400. This did not represent much money even then, and the American League was able to take advantage of that situation right away. Of the 182 players in the new league in 1901, 111 were National League expatriates. Likely the best among all of those was Napoleon "Larry" Lajoie, otherwise known as "the Frenchman," from Woonsocket, Rhode Island. Nap, a second baseman with the Philadelphia A's, led the new league in every important offensive category in 1901, finishing with a batting average of .422.

Ban Johnson had a chance to demonstrate his ingenuity at the beginning of the following year when, after Lajoie had played in the season opener, the Commonwealth of Pennsylvania sought to intervene in the battle between the major leagues. The state's ruling was that Lajoie and two other former members of the National League Phillies would have to return to that team. Johnson managed to circumvent the court decision by having Lajoie and one of the two others, Bill Bernhard, transferred to the Cleveland club so they wouldn't have to play in Philadelphia anymore. Whenever the Cleveland team journeyed to Philadelphia, Lajoie and Bernhard enjoyed a holiday elsewhere.

Lajoie was by no means the only star the upstart league had been able to pry away from the National League. Among the others were future Hall of Famers Cy Young, Eddie Plank, and Joe McGinnity, pitchers, and catchers Wilbert Robinson and Roger Bresnahan. The American League also welcomed playing managers John McGraw and Jimmy Collins, both third basemen. It came as no surprise when the American League met with immediate success. The new loop outdrew the National League, and this also held true in cities in which both leagues held franchises — Chicago, Philadelphia, and Boston.

On the field, Charles Comiskey's Chicago White Sox took the pennant by four games over Boston. Chicago's winningest pitcher was one Clark Griffith, whose 24–7 record earned him the best winning percentage of any pitcher in the league. His five shutouts tied him with Denton True "Cy" Young, a 34-year-old icon who still had many of his best years ahead of him. The Washington Nationals came in sixth in the eight-team circuit. While "Nationals" was the officially adopted nickname of the ballclub, the team was also referred to as the "Senators" from the very beginning, as that had been the name of

the city's preceding major-league entry, which had ceased operating in 1899.

While not a winning club, this first Washington squad did distinguish itself as the best in the league defensively in 1901. Shortstop Billy Clingman stood out by leading all players at his position in number of assists and fielding percentage. Among the pitchers, rookie Casey Patten, who would remain with the Senators for seven years, won 17 and lost just ten. As a group, Washington's pitchers allowed the fewest walks in the league. It was on the offensive side of the ledger that the club was weakest. Despite the efforts of first baseman Mike Grady, who finished third in the league in homers with nine and led the league in home run percentage, the Nationals wound up second from the bottom in offense. The lack of punch was what cost them a higher place in the standings.

Before the season was out, Ban Johnson managed to live up to his shortened first name. He banned 31-year-old first baseman Burt Hart of Baltimore for life. Hart, incensed at being called out when he tried to stretch a double into a triple, had hurled a glove at umpire John Haskell, and had then punched the official. Two days later, when manager Hugh Duffy of the Milwaukee Brewers cold-cocked an umpire, nothing was done. Duffy, one of baseball's best players since he'd begun his career in the major leagues 13 years earlier, might have gotten the benefit of the doubt from Ban Johnson that poor Burt Hart did not.

When the 20th century dawned, Washington, D.C., already had a modern electrically driven railway system which made the capital the showpiece of American cities. Washington had doubled in population since the Civil War and had indeed come a long way since the French minister De Bacourt had described it half a century earlier as "... a desolate spot where living is unbearable." The streets were by now well lit, and there were already more than 180 miles of paved roadways.

Washington's image in the baseball world, however, was something else entirely. Going back to 1884, no Washington professional team had so much as even finished in the first division, and this despite the fact that in some years, the city fielded teams in more than one league.

Nonetheless, Washington's place as a hotbed of baseball in America is irrefutable. At the beginning of the Civil War, regiments camped in the city had played baseball. A local club known as the Washington Nationals faced the 71st New York Guards regiment on the grounds of the White House as early as 1861. The following year, President Abraham Lincoln had arrived in a black carriage drawn by two black horses to take in a game on a Washington circus lot. President Lincoln and his young son Tad had sat in sawdust left over from the circus and cheered from their vantage point near the first base line.

Lincoln was probably the first of many U.S. presidents who were great baseball fans. There is a wonderful story of his love for the game which appeared in literature produced to commemorate baseball's centennial year in 1939. A delegation of the Republican National Committee called on Lincoln at his home in Illinois, at a time when he was still a country lawyer. Lincoln happened to be playing baseball at the time, and asked the delegation to wait until he'd had his turn at bat. Only after he had taken his swings was the delegation able to inform Lincoln that he'd won the Republican nomination for the U.S. presidency.

It is recorded that after the Civil War ended, President Andrew Johnson, who had succeeded the slain Lincoln, was among 6,000 fans who witnessed a game in the capital city between the renowned Brooklyn Atlantics and the Philadelphia Athletics. President Johnson was a true lover of the game, as evidenced by the fact that he ordered the Marine Band to play at all Saturday baseball games on the Ellipse, a lot located behind the White House.

In 1870, a former Union soldier named Michael Scanlon, who had learned the game after joining the army as a 15-year-old, realized that baseball had gained sufficient popularity in Washington for a buck to be made. Scanlon built a 500-seat ballpark and charged 25 cents admission. A year later, the wooden structure became the home park for the Washington Olympics when they became a charter member of the National Association.

Two separate Washington clubs dropped out of the National Association, which itself lasted just five years. There were more unsuccessful attempts to maintain teams in the even more short-lived Union Association and in the American Association. In 1886, the well-established National League accepted Washington into its fold, but four years later the club, which had played its games at a playing field known as the "Swampoodle Grounds," was expelled, never having finished higher than seventh. The National League was preparing for its fight with the upstart Players' League, and gave Washington's place to the Cincinnati Redlegs.

Six years later, a reprieve came in the form of a National League transfer of the Philadelphia club to Washington. Owners George and Jacob Earl Wagner, associates of the Armour meat-packing firm, were true incompetents. They disbanded a local board of directors and proceeded to sell nearly all of the team's best players, but were still able to make money. One ploy was to use pitcher Win Mercer on Tuesdays and Fridays. Mercer was strikingly handsome, so Tuesdays and Fridays were designated as "Ladies' Day."

There was a sad footnote to the life of Win Mercer, a daring player who twice won 20 or more for Washington in the late 1890s and who pitched for the Nationals in their first American League season of 1901. Given to bouts of depression, Mercer had discovered a tonic—gambling. The riskier the bet, the happier he became. He secretly borrowed from the treasury of a team of big leaguers with whom he had been touring California, and accumulated a huge debt of $8000, which he couldn't possibly repay. After another losing day at the horse track in Oakland, Mercer took his own life on January 12, 1903, leaving behind letters which contained an epitaph—"A word to friends: beware of women and a game of chance."

In eight seasons in the National League, the last eight years of the 19th century, the Washington Senators were not able to climb higher than sixth in the standings. After the team placed 11th in the 12-team league in 1899 (the infamous Cleveland Spiders were last, setting a record for ineptitude which endures to this day, winning just 20 games and losing 134), the National League purchased the Washington club from the Wagners. The brothers had raped the franchise and made a quarter of a million dollars in the process.

Deprived of professional ball for a year, Washington hit the big time again in the American League. Ban Johnson was successful in convincing the owner of the Kansas City club, Jimmy Manning, to transfer his new franchise to the Capital. Although the Nationals finished sixth at 61–73 (see Appendix A for year-by-year records) under Manning, who managed the team himself, there was no doubt that he, unlike the despised Wagners, was doing his darndest to build a winner. The American League had amassed a fund to help its owners pirate players from the National League ranks, and Manning took full advantage of it. He had a plan — to go after top-ranked players, but to limit his roster to just 13 or 14 spots in order to keep his payroll under control.

One of the first players signed was Smiling Al Orth, known as the "Curveless Wonder." Orth changed on his fastball so well that he didn't need a curve, amassing over 200 wins in a long career. He was also a fine hitter, ranking in the top ten of all time, with 389 career hits. Orth was pilfered from the National League Phillies' roster, as were pitcher Happy Jack Townsend, a hard thrower with control problems, and Harry Wolverton, a third baseman who had hit .309 for the Phils in '01.

The biggest news by far, however, was Manning's acquisition of outfielder Ed Delahanty, again from the Philadelphia Phillies. Known affectionately as the "Only Del" for his batting prowess, Delahanty was one of five baseball-playing brothers from Cleveland who eventually made it to the big leagues. By now 34, the handsome Delahanty had dominated every important hitting category at one time or another during his impressive career, once even leading in stolen bases. He was coming off a banner .354 season with the Phillies.

In 1899, Delahanty had smashed the magical .400 barrier for the second time in his career, leading the National League with a .408 mark. In 1895 and '96, he had batted .399 and .397. No mere singles hitter, Delahanty, also known as "Big Ed" (the record shows he weighed 170 pounds), had paced the National League in slugging in four of his 11 years in that circuit.

One can imagine the baseball fever in Washington, D.C., then, in the spring of 1902. One of the most unbelievable sagas in Washington baseball history, and indeed in the whole history of baseball — the saga of Big Ed Delahanty's signing — was beginning to take shape. The excitement generated as a result of Delahanty's signing was curbed, however, by the abrupt departure of Jimmy Manning. Manning had tried to sign Brooklyn's Wee Willie Keeler (nicknames were pretty commonplace back then!), still famous today for "hittin' 'em where they ain't." When Manning tried to access the league fund to sign the two-time batting champ, Ban Johnson refused, thinking it wise to take a wait-and-see approach. Delahanty had been signed for the astronomical sum of $4,000, and Johnson wanted some return on that investment before Manning was again allowed to dip into the league coffers. Manning, enraged, sold his shares in the Washington baseball club, and left town.

The new manager would be Ban Johnson's own man, a longtime baseball man by the name of Tom Loftus. Although he'd appeared in only nine big-league games, Loftus had started as a professional player a quarter of a century earlier with the Peoria Reds, a famous team which numbered among its members future Hall of Famer "Old Hoss" Radbourn, and future stars Bill and Jack Gleason and Jack Rowe. From Peoria, as a 22-year-old, Loftus had gone on to captain a team in Dubuque, Iowa, which had featured a brilliant young first baseman named Charlie Comiskey.

Tom Loftus was an expert on the rules of the game and was recognized as an astute businessman. By taking over the Nationals, he became the only man to manage in four different major leagues. At the end of the 1902 season, a prosperous one for the Washington entry, team president Fred Postal was so impressed with Loftus's part in the franchise's success that he rewarded the manager with a 25 percent share of the ballclub.

The club's new management was more appreciative of the fans. A man by the name of E. Lawrence Phillips was hired to roam the stands during games to announce lineups, thus becoming the forerunner of the modern-day public-address announcer. The games were played at League Park, also known as National Park, located at 14th Street and Bladensburg Road NE. The National League Senators had previously played in the 6,500-seat bandbox between 1892 and 1899.

As might have been expected, Ed Delahanty and the three others who had come from Philadelphia were bound by the same Supreme Court ruling which had ordered Nap Lajoie returned to the Phillies. The Senators' attorney, Wilton J. Lambert, assured the players, however, that the ruling only applied to Pennsylvania and that all they had to do was stay out of that state. So like Lajoie, the four got to enjoy some leisure time whenever the Senators played in Philly. They would go to the racetrack in New York, where one day Ed Delahanty placed an ostentatious $20 bet on a long shot, and won $500.

When Ed Delahanty, so effortless in his movements as to seem lackadaisical, had made his jump to the American League, there were jokes that the Washington heat would make him so lazy that he'd need cold showers before and after games! But Big Ed did not disappoint Washington's "bugs" or "cranks" (as fans were then known) in his first season in the capital. He won his third major batting championship with a .376 average, and for the fifth time led his league in slugging, and this by a wide margin over Nap Lajoie. Del's ten homers and 93 ribbies placed him in the top five in the A.L. in both categories.

Despite Big Ed's accomplishments, and the performance of Smiling Al Orth, who straight-balled his way to 19 wins, and of Casey Patten, who again won 17, the new-look Senators fell one game below their previous year's finish. While the club had improved dramatically on offense, the wholesale changes had involved sacrifices in the field. Having retained only third baseman Bill Coughlin and catcher Boileryard Clarke from among the previous year's regulars, the Senators went from best to next-to-last in defense. The pitching staff was the worst in the league, and even Orth and Patten had high earned run averages.

There was a corresponding slide in attendance for Nationals' games in 1902, and the figure of just over 188,000 was one of the league's lowest. Rumors of a franchise shift to Pittsburgh became so widespread that team president Fred Postal saw fit to issue a public denial. When the season ended, Ed Delahanty nevertheless requested and obtained from Postal an advance of $600 on his next season's salary. It was well known that Win Mercer was by no means the only ballplayer with the gambling bug. Truth was, it was a way of life for many ballplayers. Ed Delahanty had a reputation of being among the best players at making a kill at the racetrack — he was a man who knew how to ride a winning streak. In New York, though, he hit a string of bad luck, and wired Postal for more funds. He got a check for $1,000 in the mail.

At this time, rumors were widespread in newspapers on the eastern seaboard that Delahanty would be jumping to the National League. There were reports that Phillies manager Billy Shettsline had handed Del a blank two-year contract for the player to fill out, and had given him a wad of cash containing $3,000. Whenever asked by newspapermen, Del kept denying that there was any truth to the rumors. He even took it upon himself to wire Senators manager Loftus, telling him about everything that had happened. Delahanty emphasized that the Senators had always treated him well, and that he would stick with them. Shortly afterward, Big Ed returned to Washington for the horseracing season at the Benning racetrack.

It was at Benning that Delahanty ran into John McGraw, the "Little General" who had been the first manager of the A.L.'s Baltimore franchise. McGraw hadn't lasted long. As arrogant as Ban Johnson, and a good deal more aggressive in his demeanor, McGraw had jumped back to the National League's New York Giants at midseason, 1902, following repeated run-ins with Johnson. It would later come to light that it was during the Benning racing season in late 1902 that McGraw made Ed Delahanty an offer that the star ballplayer of the Washington Nationals, increasingly pressed for funds, was not able to refuse.

Delahanty signed a deal with the Giants which historians have pegged at $6,000 a year. Del had insisted on getting most of his salary, about $4,000, in advance. Furthermore, he would be paid no matter what — whether he was injured or could not play in Philadelphia because of the court injunction, he would not be penalized monetarily.

While all this was transpiring, Ban Johnson was busy with an idea which would spawn the most storied and glorious franchise in baseball history — the New York Yankees. Johnson had decided that his league's doormats, the Baltimore Orioles, would be moved to New York, where he'd determined the junior circuit needed a franchise. At the same time, the elimination of the Orioles would be good for the Senators, improving Washington's market position because of the proximity of the capital to Baltimore.

While visiting New York to seek a site for a new ballpark, Johnson was approached by a group of men while dining at the Criterion Hotel on the evening of December 11, 1902. The men were owners of National League teams, and one of them was Garry Herrmann of the Cincinnati Redlegs, a friend of Johnson's since the days when both had been newspapermen in that city. The National League owners wanted to arrange a conference with the American League in order to reach a settlement in terms of what to do about more than a dozen players who had signed contracts with teams in both leagues.

This was a most curious development, since less than two years before, the National League owners had decreed they would not

meet with Johnson "until hell froze over." A Chicago writer, Cy Sanborn, in discussing the proposed conference and the amount of time it had taken the Nationals to come around, penned the sardonic observation that "there have been no cablegrams from the lower regions to the effect that his Satanic Majesty was learning to skate, yet ... the old leaguers were falling over each other to get to Johnson."

The January meeting between the magnates from both leagues did indeed restore peace to baseball. More importantly for Washington, it brought back Ed Delahanty. Ban Johnson had gone into the talks determined that Delahanty would not be allowed to leave, and Del was one of nine players awarded to the American League. Seven other contract jumpers were allotted to National League clubs. Del got the news in New Orleans, where he'd been frequenting racetracks and enjoying the nightlife with his young wife. He wired New York to indicate he would abide by the ruling. That was before Ban Johnson informed him that he would have to turn his advance salary back to the Giants. Del pointed out that, because of advances already received from the Senators and his advance from the Giants, when all would be said and done, it would actually cost him $100 to play for Washington in 1903. He threatened to retire instead.

Delahanty remained in New Orleans as spring training was about to begin, still proclaiming to reporters and friends that unless he could play for the New York Giants, he would play for no one. Some doubt was cast upon this declaration, if only because of the fact that Delahanty had actually wired the Senators to request that his uniform and equipment be forwarded to New Orleans so that he might be able to practice with teams that would be training there.

In correspondence to John McGraw, Delahanty vowed to join the Giants at their spring site in Savannah, Georgia. On the way there, he was talked out of it after running into an old friend, Bill Armour, who happened to be the manager of the Cleveland ballclub. Delahanty wired Fred Postal in Washington and requested a meeting with Tom Loftus. The Senators at this time were, for reasons of poverty or thrift, the only big-league team which didn't train in the South. On his way to Washington, a train wreck on Del's path derailed his plans once more.

Delahanty was in Washington for two and a half weeks before anything was resolved. He spent time at the racetrack, of course. He admitted to manager Loftus that even if he had wanted to return the money the Giants had given him for signing, as demanded by the league and the Senators, he would not have been able to do so because he didn't have it. He also felt that Loftus didn't want him on the team, because he wasn't being allowed to practice with the Senators. Finally, the two worked out a solution — the ballclub would deduct half of the $4,000 advance Delahanty had received from his 1903 salary, and the other half the next season. To a reporter, Delahanty proclaimed, "I will try to please my former friends here, and if any of them feel sore against me, I will attempt to make them forget all about it with that trusty bat of mine."

On Opening Day 1903, the players were taken in special open carriages to American League Park, or National Park, the Senators' home since their most recent incarnation in 1901. They followed a marching band into the park and lined up on the field. There never being a dearth of politicians in Washington, a few speeches were heard as well. The grandstand and the bleachers were overflowing onto the field. Loud cheers greeted each of the players as, one by one, they made their way to home plate to receive presents. An overweight Ed Delahanty accepted a large horseshoe made of roses.

This was the first game in the storied history of the New York Yankees, then named the Highlanders. Working against the Senators' Smiling Al Orth was another man with a cheery nickname — "Happy Jack" Chesbro, a 20-game winner over the course of the last two seasons who was famous for wetting the ball. Ironically, Al Orth would end up getting traded to the Highlanders the following

season and learning the spitball from Chesbro. There is a great anecdote concerning Chesbro's spitter. While pitching for the Pirates a few years earlier, some Philadelphia players had impounded the game balls and smeared horse manure all over them. They dared Chesbro to lick those balls, and his reply was that, to win a ballgame, he'd do anything! What neither the Senators nor anyone else knew on this day was that Chesbro was just one year away from winning an incredible total of 41 games in a single season, a record which has stood the test of time through to the modern era.

On this particular day, April 22, 1903, Happy Jack and Smiling Al Orth were engaged in a close game. With the score knotted at one and a man in scoring position in the fifth, who should step to the plate but Ed Delahanty. He tagged a spitter into left field, easily scoring the run. Al Orth pitched the whole game — this was the custom back then, a custom that would be upheld for several decades yet. Even in that era, Tom Loftus was known as a manager who would almost never replace a pitcher. Before a partisan crowd of 11,950, Orth beat the Highlanders 3–1 on this day. All was well at League Park — the "cranks" once again felt that Ed Delahanty was one swell guy.

This newfound tranquillity didn't last long — less than a week in fact. Word got out that Delahanty had accepted terms to play for Denver of the Western League. As on so many previous occasions, this turned out to be just hearsay. In fact, Delahanty had inquired about playing for Denver while he had been waiting things out in New Orleans in early spring. Big Ed eventually cleared his name by proclaiming that when he had come to terms with manager Loftus, he had had no more intention of leaving the club than he had of jumping off the Washington Monument.

On the day Delahanty made that statement, the Senators were trounced 11–1 by New York. Only when Del made a barehanded catch of a ball about to fall safely in the last inning was he finally able to smile. There was more reason to smile in Washington early in this 1903 season. A split of four games with New York was followed by two wins out of three versus the Boston Puritans, destined to become league champions and to represent the American League in the first World Series.

On April 29, 1903, the Senators departed on a month-long road trip that would spell disaster. Washington lost six of the first seven games and fell to the bottom of the standings. In New York, Ed Delahanty had been spotted by a writer, weaving down the street, obviously drunk. His wife was ill, and Del subsequently went to Philadelphia to visit her on an off day.

After more losses in Boston, the Senators went into Philadelphia, where Delahanty appeared on a ballfield for the first time in two weeks. Batting just .227, he singled and doubled and was cheered on by the indulgent fans. But he also dropped a flyball and the Senators were annihilated 19–5. In the newspapers, the Nationals were accused of "stupid playing." Tom Loftus called his team "ladylike," implying that they had no fight and never contested umpires' decisions. The pitching was lousy and there were all kinds of injuries. Al Orth had to fill in at shortstop and his pitching suffered as a result.

There was bickering as well. In a 13–11 loss to the A's in which Casey Patten surrendered 19 hits, Jimmy Ryan (a 40-year-old centerfielder!) and rightfielder Kip Selbach let a flyball drop between them and then started screaming at each other. Ryan complained to Loftus that he had no faith in Selbach, and Selbach insisted he wanted to be moved to left field, his true position. All of these events were foreshadowing one of the darkest days in the history of baseball.

From Philadelphia, the troubled Washington ballclub headed for what was until the late 1950s the westernmost baseball stop, St. Louis. Big Ed Delahanty got five hits in 15 at-bats but came up with a bad back. He was still carrying too much weight and had been favoring a sore leg. The *Washington Star* printed that Delahanty looked like "a fat man escaped from a circus." Sent up as a pinch hitter a few days later in Cleveland, Delahanty

grounded out feebly. Loftus had seen enough, and decided to send the future Hall of Famer to Mount Clemens, Michigan, where Big Ed would be able to partake of the hot baths and hopefully get himself back into playing shape.

At this point, the Senators had won just six of their last 23 games. When Delahanty next saw Loftus he was informed that Selbach would man left field from then on. Del would have to be content with playing in right. There was a tremendous argument, but Del backed down ... again. The next day, May 29, the Senators dropped a 7–2 decision to Big Bill Dinneen, the eventual hero of the upcoming World Series, and the Boston Puritans. Del homered, his first of the season, and also singled cleanly. It didn't improve his disposition, though. He didn't seem to be making much of an effort in the field.

Six days later, on June 4, the Senators dropped their eighth in a row, 9–1, to the St. Louis Browns. Delahanty was hitting well, having raised his average above .300. His fielding, however, was atrocious, and what's more, Big Ed still didn't seem to care. The Senators lost another one before finally starting to turn things around, handing the Browns a 10–0 pasting as Big Ed singled and doubled twice. Cleveland came next on June 7, and Delahanty outhit Nap Lajoie 7–6 over the three games, all won by Washington.

Pitcher-manager Clark Griffith's Highlanders were still mired in seventh place at this point, and Ban Johnson was distraught, feeling it imperative that New York field a strong team to compete with the National League Giants. The Giants had stunned most observers by fighting for the lead in the other league. Griffith needed not just a good player, but one who might be able to grab some headlines from the controversial McGraw. Ed Delahanty was just the man he needed. Tom Loftus was apparently on the verge of agreeing to a trade. Big Ed heard about it and became hopeful. In fact, he became downright joyful, so much so that he went on a tear, getting 11 hits in 20 at-bats. This, unfortunately for him, canceled all talk of a trade.

When the Senators left Washington for

St. Louis on the evening of June 17, they had another modest streak going, having won three in a row. In his excellent book *July 2, 1903*, Mike Sowell states that Ed Delahanty was wearing some expensive jewelry on this night, and his teammates found out that all the rings, pins, and diamonds didn't belong to him at all. He was showing them off for a Washington jeweler, who trusted him to sell some of them for him. On the way to St. Louis, however, Del drank heavily and, according to Sowell's research, told some of the others that he had taken out a policy on his life. His mood soured, and he spoke of death.

Delahanty's rantings were not taken seriously by his teammates, as they were all well acquainted with his personal difficulties. The other players also suspected marital problems, and that Big Ed was jealous of his wife. Later, some of them might have remembered a remark that Sowell writes Delahanty had made a couple of years previously, when there had been discussion about a man who had committed suicide by drowning. Del had apparently said at that time, "Only a coward would drown himself."

On the fateful date of July 2, 1903, "Scranton Bill" Coughlin, the Senators' third baseman, sought out Delahanty to return a diamond ring Del had let him wear on their just completed western trip. Coughlin may have been the last teammate to see Delahanty. The slugger disappeared, and it was discovered later that he had written his wife to tell her that he would arrive at New York's Grand Central Station early the next morning, one day ahead of the team.

On the trip to New York, Delahanty's actions were bizarre. Impeccably dressed in a stylish blue suit, he smoked in the sleeper car even though it was against the rules. He annoyed other passengers by continually ringing the call bell, and he broke a glass case containing a firefighting axe. The last straw came when he playfully yanked the ankles of a woman asleep in an upper berth of the sleeper car. The train was stopped at a small station at Bridgeburg, on the Canadian side of the Niagara River, just across from Buffalo. At

10:45 p.m., the miscreant in the blue suit was told by the conductor to get off the train.

In a statement not filed until the next morning, a railroad night guard, Sam Kingston, reported having been startled when he had met a man walking along the span above the river at about 10:55 the previous night. At this spot, there was no footwalk and no railing, just a train track. The sidebeams were a good foot and a half wide. When he had shone his lamp in the stranger's face, Kingston said he had been threatened with words like "Keep that light away, or I'll knock your lights out!"

Later on in the day, when Sam Kingston was interrogated by police, he added another detail to his story — that the stranger smelled strongly of liquor. A tough man of about 60, Kingston stated he had grabbed the stranger by the collar but had stumbled in doing so. The guard said his own foot fell between the railroad ties, and before he could pull himself back up, the man was gone. Then, he heard a splash.

Yet again, the bridge guard later changed his story, insisting there had been no physical confrontation at all, and that the stranger had just ignored him and kept on walking — right off the bridge. Whether he was pushed, or stumbled due to drunkenness, Big Ed Delahanty fell to his death. Frank Delahanty, the ballplaying brother who later became a lawyer, was convinced that Big Ed had only intended to jump the Washington ballclub, and not from a bridge. Ed, Frank maintained, was going to join the New York Giants, which would have reignited the war between the two major leagues.

Whatever happened, Washington had lost an irreplaceable baseball player. Ed Delahanty and his career batting average of .346, fourth best in all history, were permanently enshrined in the Baseball Hall of Fame in 1945. To this day, he remains the only man to have won batting championships in both major leagues.

Only a month after Delahanty's death, the Washington team was in serious disarray. Club president Postal was threatening to quit, having had enough of the constant badgering by manager Loftus, who wanted more cash to acquire players. Ban Johnson rushed to Washington to see what could be done to avert a crisis. Charles Jacobson, the team vice-president and a prominent Washington banker, offered to buy the club, but would not agree to assume the Nationals' bad debts, estimated at around $12,000 at the time. So Johnson stepped in and bought the team himself for $15,000, and also took on the existing bills. It became clear for the first time that the Senators were league-controlled, although this had long since been the case (for instance, dipping into league coffers in order to buy players). One of Johnson's first decrees was to make it clear that Loftus would not return.

By March of the next year, Johnson had succeeded in unloading the club to local interests comprised of a half dozen men headed by a baseball writer turned promoter, William Dwyer, and Thomas C. Noyes, a member of the family which published the wealthy Washington *Evening Star*. Tom Loftus was still around, claiming that he would be the manager and that if, as rumored, the Senators were able to acquire St. Louis Cardinals' star Patsy Donovan, then Donovan would move in as a player only. Management waited until a week before opening day and then sacked Loftus. In St. Louis, Donovan was seeking his release, claiming the Redbirds owed him $3,600. While an arbitration board pondered the case, the Senators named veteran catcher Malachi Kittredge as their new manager.

Patsy Donovan was awarded to Washington in late April, but even at that juncture it was already too late. The Nats had lost their first 13 games, a dubious record not eclipsed by any major-league club until the 1988 Baltimore Orioles came along and lost their first 21. When Donovan arrived, the Nationals stood at a pitiful 1–16. The club felt repercussions at the gate, as Washington fans had little confidence — only 3,000 had turned out for the opener. In 1904, the club went on to post what would stand as the worst record in its history — 38 wins and 113 losses. While attendance was up all over the league, only 132,344 showed up in Washington. As for Bill

Dwyer (who now realized the problem was the ballclub itself and not the deposed Kittredge), he promptly gave up on his nascent career as a baseball administrator.

Happy Jack Townsend's nickname was put to a severe test with the Senators of 1904 — he finished with a record of 5–26. Rookie Beanie Jacobson hardly fared better, at 6–23. A 32-year-old veteran with the alliterative name of Davey Dunkle brought an end to his career with a 2–9 slate. Long Tom Hughes went 2–13 after being acquired from the Highlanders in an ill-advised trade for Al Orth. The swap, engineered the previous January, hurt the club immensely, as Orth would win 18 games in '05 and lead the National League with 27 wins in '06. On the bright side, a young first baseman by the name of Jake Stahl was developing into a fine hitter and leader — his .261 average led the club, which, like a crippled horse, came in dead last in an eight-team race.

The Washington franchise became much more stable when, on the last day of January, 1905, Thomas C. Noyes accepted the club presidency, which he would retain for 15 years. In a reorganization of the club's stock, Washington businessmen took majority control of the club, with the American League retaining the rest. Jake Stahl, just turned 26 at the beginning of the season, was installed as manager. Stahl came from a wealthy family and was college-educated. He played baseball solely for the love of the game. By mid–May, he was the toast of the town, having guided the Nats to the top of the league. The Senators clung to the first division until midway through the campaign and then waned when Stahl became ill, compounding a shorthanded situation due to injuries to a number of other players. Two veteran outfielders, Charley Hickman and John Anderson, became solid contributors following their purchase for $5,000. Long Tom Hughes turned things around and won 17 games.

Prior to the start of the '05 season, the new owners had attempted to put the club's recent history behind it by inviting baseball fans to submit their suggestions for a new name. "The Nationals" was selected as most acceptable, but did not truly take. The name was ill-suited in the first place, as it suggested a National League team, and merely represented an oddly nostalgic longing for the bad ballclubs of the 1880s and 1890s.

Fans and reporters alike, in Washington and elsewhere, continued to call the team the Senators and to nickname the team the Nats. It would be 50 years, however, before "Senators" would become the official team name. For our purposes, we shall henceforth refer to the club alternatively as the Senators, as it was generally known throughout its existence, and also as the Nationals, the official name throughout most of its existence, but a term less in vogue at certain times than at others.

Lousy by any name, the team ended up seventh in 1905, winning 64 games. However, the Nats avoided banishment to the league basement, and for this the players were awarded a reported bonus of $1,000, which they shared among themselves. The darkest stretch of the season came over the final two days of August and the first of September, when Washington dropped three consecutive doubleheaders, all to the New York Highlanders. Following an off day, the Highlanders swept consecutive twin bills against Philadelphia and Boston to set a major-league record of five doubleheader sweeps in just six days.

There was bad news for the Senators even before the 1906 season got under way. In March, rapidly developing shortstop Joe Cassidy died of typhoid fever at the age of 23. The season began on a positive note on the field, however, with the Nats streaking to the league lead early in the season. Eventually, Washington came in seventh once again.

The highlight of the season came in late August when the Senators brought an end to the 19-game winning streak of the "hitless wonders," the Chicago White Sox. This White Sox squad eventually won the pennant despite maintaining a .230 team batting average, the worst in the league by far. On the other hand, this was the deadball era, when low-scoring games were par for the course and teams were content to scratch out two or three

runs and hope to win. The White Sox took the '06 World Series in six games from their crosstown rival Cubs despite hitting just .198 in the fall classic.

For their part, the Senators won nine fewer games in 1906 than in the previous year. On a brighter note, veteran Lave Cross had come from the A's to reinforce the infield at third, and rookie catcher Howard Wakefield hit .280. Jake Stahl's dismissal at the end of the year rated as something of a surprise, as he could hardly be blamed for the club's lackluster performance. The new manager would be Joe Cantillon — "Pongo Joe" as everyone called him — a former umpire with a reputation for being better at starting fights than quelling them. Cantillon did not come cheap — he reportedly earned $7,000 a year for three years, plus 10 percent of the profits.

For Jake Stahl, his dismissal was nothing compared to another misfortune which befell him at the same time. His older brother, Charles "Chick" Stahl, player-manager of the Boston Pilgrims, committed suicide. Chick drank four ounces of carbolic acid in a hotel room in West Baden, Indiana. His last words, to teammate Jimmy Collins, were, "Boys, I couldn't help it; it drove me to it." Nearly 80 years later, it came to light that what had driven Chick, a married man, "to it," was that he had been about to father a child by a woman who was not his wife.

Known for his quick temper from his days as a brawling umpire, it follows that Joe Cantillon, the Senators' new manager, was not particularly known for taking much guff from players. In his book *The Washington Senators*, Shirley Povich tells of one incident which had occurred back when John McGraw had still been in the American League at Baltimore. McGraw had yelled insults at Cantillon over the course of a particular afternoon. Cantillon told Clark Griffith, the playing manager of the White Sox, to pick McGraw off first base the first chance he had to throw there. Griffith obviously balked while moving toward first, but Cantillon nonetheless called McGraw out. When Griffith tried the same move on another runner later in the game, Cantillon unabashedly reminded him that the McGraw pickoff had been a personal favor, and that from then on, Griffith would have to obey the rules.

At one time a saloon operator in Chicago, Cantillon had more recently had success managing at Milwaukee in the American Association. Another incident demonstrating his toughness arose, according to Povich, when Cantillon had sent in a pinch hitter for George Stone, then the A.A.'s leading hitter. When Germany Schaefer, hitting .380, complained on Stone's behalf, Cantillon put in a pinch hitter for Schaefer as well. With the Washington Senators, Cantillon's term was less than a success: an eighth-place finish in 1907, seventh in '08, and a return to the basement in 1909.

A familiar refrain began to be heard during the first decade of the 20th century in ballparks throughout the American League. It played on the Washington club's position at the bottom of the heap during four of the seven seasons from 1903 to 1909. Writer Charles Dryden had penned the disparaging verse: "Washington—first in War, first in Peace, last in the American League." While the derisive little chant would come to lose its base in fact with the passage of time, it would nevertheless shape an enduring image in the psyches of baseball fans in rival American League cities. For the moment, however, Pongo Joe Cantillon was about to play a pivotal role in ensuring better days ahead for this downtrodden franchise.

The baseball gods were indeed smiling down upon the Washington Senators on the day in 1907 when catcher Cliff Blankenship broke his finger. Joe Cantillon wanted to get some use out of the disabled Blankenship and decided to dispatch him on a scouting assignment. For some time, Cantillon had been receiving letters from a traveling salesman who raved about a young man not yet 20 years old who was burning up the Snake River Valley League with his pitching arm. In mid–June, one of these letters told Cantillon that this boy's pitches were so fast, you couldn't see them, and that only the boy knew where the pitches were going. The proof of that was that

if he didn't, "there would be dead bodies strewn all over Idaho." The boy's name was Walter Johnson.

Initially, Johnson hadn't even been the main focus of Blankenship's scouting mission. The Senators already had their eye on Clyde Milan, a 20-year-old outfielder with Wichita of the Western Association. An esteemed judge of baseball talent, Joe Cantillon had spotted Milan when the Senators had played Wichita during a spring exhibition game on their way home from training camp in Galveston, Texas. There is little doubt that Blankenship's scouting trip was the most successful of its kind in all of history. Milan was signed for $1,250 and would become the team's best outfielder for the next 14 years. During all that time, his roommate would be Walter Johnson.

Clyde Milan said years later that Blankenship had at the time resented being sent on what he called a "wild goose chase" just to see "some palooka" who was striking out everybody in Weiser (pronounced "weezer"), Idaho, in a semipro league. The punk, Blankenship opined, probably wouldn't be worth a dime. His mind changed quickly on the day he arrived in Weiser to see the local team play against the league's Caldwell entry. Johnson was easy to recognize, as Blankenship had already gotten a description from the locals, who had told him of his long arms and plowman's walk. Johnson was also easy to recognize as a real prospect—he pitched 12 innings but lost the game due to an error after two were out.

For years, the story went that Blankenship had drawn up a contract right then and there on a piece of meat wrapper, but this was not the case. Johnson had insisted that he be given another two weeks to finish the season at Weiser, and then he would come to Washington, but only if he could get his father's permission. He did, but then the cautious lad had another proviso for Blankenship—that if he failed to make the big club, the Senators would also pay for his return fare home to Fullerton, California. He had asked for $250, but Blankenship had only $100 for him.

Walter joked years later that he never was able to find out who had gotten the change. Nonetheless, the Washington Senators got their tall, gangly boy with the golden arm. This youngster would become a pillar for the struggling franchise — not just *its* greatest player, but quite likely the greatest pitcher in American League history.

The Senators were in New York when Joe Cantillon got a telegram from Cliff Blankenship telling him that Johnson, "the fastest pitcher since Amos Rusie," had been signed to a contract. This was relayed to the baseball writers, and the *Washington Post* correspondent, noting that he didn't know yet whether Johnson was left- or righthanded, heightened expectations by writing that Johnson had pitched 75 innings in the Idaho State League without allowing a run. He had struck out 166 batters in 11 games, about 15 strikeouts per game.

It later came to light that the Senators may indeed have been very fortunate to snare Walter Johnson, the strapping lad of 20 years, of mostly British stock, who looked Scandinavian and was nicknamed "Swede" as a result. Earlier that spring, the National League's Pittsburgh Pirates could conceivably have signed him if they had agreed to shell out nine dollars for train fare from Weiser to Hot Springs, Arkansas, where the Pirates were training. Pittsburgh manager Fred Clarke was told of the youngster's prowess by a friend who had been tipped off by an umpire working in the Idaho League. The Pirates were about to break camp, and Clarke decided there was no time to look at any more prospects.

In 21 seasons with the Senators (10 of them with second-division clubs), Johnson would go on to win 417 games, second to only Cy Young on the all-time list. Of those wins, 110 were by shutout, and of those, 38 were by a 1–0 score, far and away an all-time record. Pitching for the Senators would entail disappointment, too — 65 of Johnson's losses would be by shutout, 26 by 1–0 scores (both all-time records as well). His other accomplishments would include earning five wins, three of which were shutouts, in nine days in 1908; the

recording of 16 straight wins in 1912; and a run of 56 scoreless innings in 1913, when he posted a 36–7 record and a 1.09 earned run average.

Born into a farm family in Humboldt, Kansas, on November 6, 1887, Walter Perry Johnson first moved west in the spring of 1902 when his folks decided to try their luck in the oil fields of California. After school and during summers, he had driven a team of horses for his father and never did play baseball on a sustained basis until he got to California, when he was into his 15th year. By the time Cliff Blankenship found him toiling in the semipro leagues of southwestern Idaho, Walter already had his signature windup down pat.

Johnson stood straight up on the mound and employed a windmill motion with which he rotated the ball in a circle. He would swing his arm behind him as far as it would go before springing forward with an easy delivery employing a motion that was neither sidearm nor underarm, but somewhere in between. Davy Jones of the Tigers, the first man ever to bat against Johnson in a major-league game, told Lawrence Ritter in *The Glory of Their Times* that the youngster's arms were "like whips," and "absolutely the longest arms I ever saw."

Walter Johnson was not to become a great success overnight. While the speed of his fastball was a surefire asset, he was susceptible to being victimized by the bunt, which he hadn't learned to field yet. Barely more than a year before joining Washington, he had been handed his release by the Tacoma club of the Northwestern League. After he had done well in Idaho, Tacoma tried to get him back for a healthy $350 a month: top pay in the minor leagues in 1907. Indicative of the young man's high moral character, though, he would not return to a team which had not given him what he considered a fair chance. Now, having played only at a level inferior to that of the Northwestern League since Tacoma let him go, he had somehow landed in the best league in the world, albeit with a last-place club. He was, as he'd admit years later, as nervous as he could possibly be.

By the time Joe Cantillon finally entered Walter Johnson in a game, on August 2, 1907, the city of Washington was rabid with baseball fever brought on by all the talk in the papers of this young man's fastball. More than 10,000 fans packed American League Park for the first game of a doubleheader against the Tigers, the best-hitting team in the league and the eventual pennant winners. These were the Tigers of Ty Cobb, then just 20 years old, the most ferocious of players who will likely forever remain baseball's all-time batting champion. The Tigers also featured outfielder Sam Crawford, who hit more triples than any player in history, and a bevy of other solid hitters.

Crawford would later tell Lawrence Ritter for *The Glory of Their Times* about Joe Cantillon coming over to the Detroit bench prior to this game and boasting that Washington was going to show the Tigers a "great big appleknocker today," who had what the oldtimers called "a swift," a remarkable fastball, and that the Detroit players had better be ready. Pongo Joe Cantillon, Sam Crawford remembered, was a great kidder, but he wasn't kidding anyone on that day.

By all accounts, many fans were surprised by Johnson's sidearm delivery and sweeping underhand motion. He sure didn't move like a fastballer, and yet there was no doubt in the minds of the witnesses that day that his pitches were really moving. The record shows that he gave up just six hits, three of which were bunts; two of these were by Cobb, who felt that bunting was the only counter to the incredible speed of Johnson's hard one.

Following one of Cobb's bunts, another moved him all the way up to third, from where he scored. Johnson was removed by Cantillon for a pinch hitter in the eighth inning with the Senators trailing 2–1. The game was eventually lost 3–2, but Walter Johnson was on his way. The great Ty Cobb would admit later in life that the Tigers had known on that very day that they had encountered the most powerful arm ever turned loose in a big-league ballpark.

For the record, Johnson's catcher for his first big-league outing was Mike Heydon, a 33-year-old vet who would fashion a .179 career batting average. Heydon would catch the first three of Walter's games, after which Jack Warner, a 35-year-old who had caught the New York Giants' Christy Mathewson during some of his best years, returned to action following an injury. It was Warner who advised Johnson to take up another pitch, and Warner marveled at how quickly the lad was able to master the change of pace.

Walter Johnson would recount many years later how he'd been the greenest rookie one could ever imagine. He had noticed how the fans had laughed when the Tigers had bunted him all over the place, and he recalled missing the bus back to the hotel after the game. That evening, he had been approached by a man on the sidewalk who had told him that he was a big man in this city already — so much so that a hotel had already been named after him. The man had pointed across the street, and there was the "Johnson Hotel." Johnson said he had believed him; that's how green he had been.

After that first game, Tiger manager Wild Bill Donovan gushed that within two years, Johnson would be greater than the best pitcher of the day, Christy Mathewson. Surprisingly, however, Donovan mentioned to Joe Cantillon that he thought Johnson had mixed in some spitballs, which were then legal, with his other pitches. This had in fact not been the case.

Five days after Johnson's debut, manager Cantillon gave him the ball again, and the first of 417 wins was registered. The big boy went all the way, and gave up no hits between the first and ninth innings in a 7–2 Senators romp over a strong Cleveland Indians ballclub, breaking a seven-game Washington losing string. Johnson gave up two hits in each of the first and last innings and twice struck out Elmer Flick, a career .315 hitter and eventual Hall of Fame inductee who had won the batting championship two years earlier. A number of the following day's newspaper accounts pointed out that some of the Cleveland hitters had seemed a little shy facing Johnson's unusually rapid fastball.

Although Johnson had pitched two games for the Nationals, he was still without a contract. When $350 a month was dangled in front of him, he declined. This was the same amount he'd been offered a few months earlier by minor-league Tacoma, and perhaps Walter was still wondering where the extra $150 he had requested for train fare had gone. He held out for $450, and on August 8, following the Cleveland game, Joe Cantillon acceded to his wishes, doubtless getting more than a little concerned about the potential of losing the young phenom to a preying competitor.

Johnson was made to feel less satisfied six days later when he lost 1–0 to St. Louis, the first of 26 such heart-rending losses in his career. He had held the Browns, one of the A.L.'s weaker clubs, to six hits, but lost when second baseman George Nill made a mental blunder. Johnson had thrown to second, but Nill hadn't covered the bag and the throw had gone into the outfield. In his next game, against Cleveland on August 20, the Nats again failed to score for him and he lost by shutout (as mentioned, there would be an unbelievable 65 of these shutout defeats over the course of his career). In offering words of consolation following the St. Louis game, manager Cantillon mentioned that from then on, Walter could expect to take his regular turn, and the idea sank in for the young man that he had arrived as a major-league baseball player.

Walter Johnson would come to be known as "The Big Train," and was so named by famed sportswriter Grantland Rice because of the speed of his peerless fastball. "Barney" was his other nickname, and that one originated with contemporary auto racer Barney Oldfield, who had reached speeds of 60 miles per hour. Johnson purchased a two-cylinder motor car, his first vehicle. He later told of being stopped for speeding immediately following the purchase, not two blocks from the car dealership. Teammates Clyde Milan and Germany Schaefer were along for the ride, and the mischievous Schaefer told the police officer that Johnson was Barney Oldfield in the flesh. When Walter began showing a propensity for striking people out, the nickname "Barney" stuck. Within a year, the battle cry around the league was that when you were facing Johnson and you saw his arm go up, you swung!

In early September 1907, Walter Johnson pitched two great games. On September 7, he turned in a 1–0 gem at Boston, the first of his 38 career shutouts. A second straight whitewash followed five days later at New York. When the '07 season wound down, the rookie's earned run average for 110⅔ innings was 1.88, fourth best in the league. Of his first 12 big-league starts, he had completed 11, two of which were shutouts. His unimpressive 5–9 record was a sad reflection of the team he was with, and also an omen of more misfortunes. Five of Johnson's losses were by one run. In the seven seasons from 1905 to 1911, Washington was never to rise above seventh place.

The Senators came in dead last in 1907 with an awful 49–102 slate, a full 11 games out of seventh spot, and a staggering 43½ games behind pennant-winning Detroit. For Joe Cantillon, this was a pretty inauspicious debut, to say the least. The powerful Tigers went on to the first of their three straight American League pennants but would lose the World Series to the Chicago Cubs. In this season, at age 20, the great Ty Cobb, a maniacal competitor, began a string of 12 batting championships in 13 years. But Cobb would never again participate in a Series after 1909, and would never be part of a World Championship club during his whole 24-year career.

It didn't look like the 20-year-old Johnson would ever be part of a great club either, as long as he was with the Washington Senators, but already there was a feeling that the Kansas strongboy would be around for a long time. In 1908, Johnson was given 29 starts and parlayed them into a 14–14 record in an improved, but nonetheless seventh-place, ballclub. His ERA dropped even further to 1.64, again fourth best in the league, and, in his sophomore year, he placed fifth in strikeouts.

Washington's 17½-game improvement in 1908 was also due to the fact that only two regulars from the previous year's team were held over — Ed Delahanty's brother Jim at second base, and Otis Clymer in the outfield. Of the five Delahantys in professional baseball, Jim was to have the second-best career and would last 13 years in the pros, amassing a creditable .283 career batting average.

To further reinforce the middle of the infield for 1908, a 27-year-old shortstop named George McBride was brought in from Kansas City of the American Association, and he would provide stability for a good decade. McBride was the league's premier defensive shortstop during his time. He led the American League at fielding his position four straight years between 1912 and 1915, and led in double plays six years between '08 and '15. His offensive credentials were something quite different. For players with more than 5,000 at-bats, McBride holds the record for the lowest career batting average (.218), and slugging average (.264), testimony to the superior defensive skills which kept him in the game long enough to attain such an ignominious record.

Clyde Milan took over in center field on August 19, 1907, stealing the job away from three-year vet Charlie Jones. Milan would remain a fixture for 15 years. Late in '07, Washington's owners sold swift outfielder John Anderson to the White Sox, thereby annoying many fans. Anderson had led the team in hitting with .288 and had tied for the league lead in stolen bases in '06. It would take a while for Milan to blossom at the plate, and he'd bat just .239 and .200 over his first two full seasons.

The man who would become known as "Walter Johnson's catcher," Charles "Gabby" Street, also joined the Senators, his contract having been purchased from San Francisco of the Pacific Coast League. Street, who would manage the St. Louis Cardinals to a World Championship in 1931 (the same year he sent himself up to bat as he approached his 49th birthday), was just 25 when he joined Washington after having appeared in only 45 National League games. Nineteen hundred and eight and 1909 would be his two busiest seasons in the majors, but he would bat just .206 and .211, assuring himself of a more regular

place "riding the pines" for another two seasons in Washington.

Gabby Street is associated with baseball lore because of his connection to one particular incident. In Washington, D.C., the prospect of catching a ball dropped from the 555-foot-high Washington Monument was always a hot topic. Made of Maryland white marble and shaped like a hollow shaft, the structure had been erected to commemorate the first president, George Washington. The government had begun building it in 1848, but it wasn't completed until 1884 due to delays caused by the Civil War and other political wrangling. When it was finally finished, it offered a breathtaking view of the city from a vantage point at the top of an iron stairway of 898 steps.

In 1894, a catcher named Pops Schriver had attempted to catch a ball dropped from the top of the monument. Some said Schriver was successful on the first try. Other accounts said it never happened at all. It seems certain that other old-time catchers, Charlie Snyder and future Hall of Famer Buck Ewing, were not successful. Outfielder Paul Hines met with the same result. So Street, a Southerner who earned his nickname "Gabby" for obvious reasons and who may have been baseball's precursor to Ted Turner as "The Mouth of the South," became determined to give it a try. The idea came about because two well-to-do Senators fans had been discussing the topic and had made a $500 bet. They then prevailed upon Street to settle their wager. Things were done right this time, unlike in 1894 when police had had to shoo Schriver and the interested onlookers away from the site. Formal permission for the attempt was obtained from the superintendent of parks.

On the morning of August 21, 1908, the two bettors, Preston Gibson and John Biddle, climbed to the top of the Washington Monument with a basketful of baseballs and a wooden chute designed to slide the balls beyond the wide base of the structure. Street was in street clothes. Signals were given from above, but the first ten balls which came down caromed off the base of the monument. Gibson then discarded the chute and threw the balls out. Finally, on the 15th try, Street made the historic catch. It was completed with both arms high above his head, as if he'd caught a foul pop. There the similarity ended. The impact drove the mitt that caught Walter Johnson's fastball almost down to the ground, but Gabby held on.

It was reported at the time that mathematicians had calculated that Street's hand had resisted 300 pounds of force. Street said afterward that he hadn't caught sight of the ball until it was halfway down. The toss previous to the one he had caught had hit the tip of his mitt, and he knew at that moment that he was risking breaking his arm if he didn't catch the ball cleanly. The ball had dropped an estimated 504 feet. This would stand as the record for all mankind until 1930, when Charles Hartnett, the Chicago Cub catcher, coincidentally also nicknamed "Gabby," would catch a ball dropped from the Goodyear blimp from an altitude of about 550 feet. On the same afternoon that he'd completed his oddball stunt, Gabby Street caught a 3–1 Walter Johnson victory over the Detroit Tigers.

The Senators were reasonably competitive in 1908; for Walter Johnson, though, this was the season during which he became a national hero. First, however, he had to contend with an operation in late February for the removal of an abscess located behind his right ear. The operation was a serious one, and his family had feared for his life. Johnson survived but was in considerable pain for several weeks afterward. He missed all of spring training as a result, and didn't join the club until June 6, nearly two months into the season.

Johnson's record was 1–6, largely because of a lack of offensive support, when, on July 28, he struck out 15 Browns in St. Louis to earn a 2–1 win in 16 innings. With that game, in which Walter recorded his highest strikeout total to date, he undertook a string of 11 wins in 13 decisions. Then, over four glorious days in early September, the 21-year-old accomplished a feat not seen before or since.

The chain of events began innocently

enough when on Friday, September 4, 1908, Johnson pitched a six-hit 3–0 shutout against Jack Chesbro and the New York Highlanders. On the following day, the New Yorkers' chagrin, not to mention surprise, can only be imagined when they again saw Johnson warming up on the sidelines. It should be pointed out that in 1908, Big Ed Walsh of the White Sox led the league in games started with 49, the rough equivalent of a start every third game.

Only three pitchers had made the road trip for the Senators, as the mound corps was beset by injuries, and Joe Cantillon had asked Walter prior to the first game of the four-game set in New York whether he could start three times in a row. The Big Train would later confide that Cantillon had been able to placate him time and again in the same way — Walter would ask the manager for an extra seating pass to a game for a friend, and Pongo Joe would surprise him with half a dozen. When the manager unexpectedly asked him to pitch, Walter couldn't turn him down because, he explained, his friends were always after passes.

Going the route for a second straight day, Johnson gave up just four hits and shut out the Highlanders again, 6–0. Now there was talk that Walter might not only start three games in a row, but get a shutout in all of them. The *Washington Post* reported that manager Cantillon had joked that maybe Johnson would pitch again Monday. The city was mad about Walter and the sports pages were jammed with stories about him. There was no chance that he would get three shutouts on consecutive days, however, since the third day was the Sabbath day. It would be another ten years before baseball could be played in New York on Sundays.

On the Monday, September 7, 1908, there was to be a doubleheader in New York. It must have occurred to Johnson that he might start, but if so, likely not in the first game. While warming up with Gabby Street, it became apparent there was no one else getting ready. Johnson reportedly looked at Joe Cantillon, received a nod from the manager, and when he got back to the dugout after just a few easy tosses, told Cantillon, "It's all right with me if it's all right with you."

Barney then went out and tossed a third shutout at the Highlanders in just four days. He showed no sign of tiring during the course of the game. In fact, he yielded just two hits, having improved each game as he'd gone along. (He had given up six hits on Friday and four on Saturday.) He walked no one and struck out five, beating Jack Chesbro again despite taking one of Chesbro's spitballs in the ribs in the third inning. Furthermore, from Monday to Monday, the Big Train had made four mound appearances, having pitched 4⅔ innings against Boston on the previous Monday.

Following the third shutout in a row, W.W. Aulick wrote in the *New York Times* of September 8, 1908: "We are grievously disappointed in this man Johnson of Washington. He and his team had four games to play with the champion [*sic*] Yankees. Johnson pitched the first game and shut us out. Johnson pitched the second game and shut us out. Johnson pitched the third game and shut us out. Did Johnson pitch the fourth game and shut us out? He did not. Oh, you quitter!"

After the third straight whitewash, Cantillon must have thought it was time to rest his 20-year-old prodigy. Johnson came out again on Thursday, three days later, and edged the A's and their ace Eddie Plank 2–1. He said after this particular game that he did not deserve the victory, an early sign of his humble disposition. Over the years, Walter would consistently credit his teammates for his own well-deserved successes.

On the day following the victory over Eddie Plank, young Johnson was asked to start again because sore-armed Charley Smith was unable to take his turn. Again, the Big Train went all the way, for his fifth victory in nine days. Throughout his lengthy career, Walter Johnson would display tremendous stamina. According to team trainer Mike Martin, the effortlessness with which he threw a ball, which Johnson himself felt was a result of his use of the sidearm delivery, could be compared to the energy a normal human expends in snapping his fingers.

Following a three-inning shutout performance in relief two days later that saved the last game of the Philadelphia series, Johnson finally lost on September 18. He gave up just three hits, but lost a 1–0 decision to Big Ed Walsh* (the league's top winner at 40–15 in '08) and the White Sox on a tenth-inning bunt. This setback ended a string of five wins for the rising star. In acquiring those five wins, Barney had allowed just five runs in 58 innings.

Two days later, Johnson faced Rube Waddell of the St. Louis Browns. Waddell was baseball's real "rebel without a cause." A great pitcher, he drove managers insane wherever he played. Seemingly as innocent and erratic as a child, Waddell would miss time at the ballpark to chase fire engines or to just go fishing. Sportswriters would come to talk of Walter Johnson's fastball in the same breath as Waddell's, who had thrown very hard for Connie Mack's A's beginning in 1902. That is, he had until he injured his arm while horsing around with teammate Andy Coakley prior to the start of the 1905 World Series, which the A's lost in five games, mainly because of Christy Mathewson's "three golden eggs"—three shutouts in the first ever best-of-seven World Series.

Rube Waddell's arm was never quite the same after the fall of '05, but he still had plenty left when he faced the Senators in September '08. He struck out 17 Nats and was the winner over Walter Johnson, who struck out nine. The Big Train had pitched seven complete games for the Senators, with a save thrown in for good measure, within 17 days, and Joe Cantillon did not give him a break until the end of the campaign, which must not have come too soon for poor Walter. He

---

*Roughly two years later, on August 24, 1910, Ed Walsh would collaborate with his battery mate, Billy Sullivan, to re-enact Gabby Street's stunt at the Washington Monument. Walsh would hurl 23 baseballs at speeds estimated at around 110 miles an hour. Sullivan would catch only three of them.

had indeed earned his forthcoming salary increase of $800, to $3500 for 1909.

The 20-year-old destined to become the greatest righthander of all time had truly arrived. Just out of his teens, Johnson was already getting about 60 letters a day from fans across the country. He was answering all of them, succinctly explaining to reporters who asked that if there were folks who were kind enough to write to him, then the least he could do was write them back.

Barney finished with a record of 14–14 on a team which won just 67 games against 85 losses, and which was spared a second consecutive last-place finish only because the New York Highlanders were atrocious and won just 51 games. The Senators had little else to boast about, except perhaps a catcher who could catch baseballs dropped from skyscrapers. Financially, the club had profited from Johnson's presence to the tune of a 15 percent dividend to stockholders.

While the team's new infusion of talent seemed to bode well for 1909, there would be no improvement. It would be the worst year of Walter Johnson's career. He came down with a nagging cold while training in Galveston, Texas, and didn't get his strength back for two whole months. He lost 18 pounds and didn't make an appearance until April 24 in New York. The Nats were shelled 17–0 by the weak Highlanders club, and when Barney got off to an 0–5 start, there was talk that he might have been a one-year wonder, so regularly was he being hit hard.

On June 11, Johnson showed signs of his old self, stopping the Tigers 1–0 on a four-hitter, after which an anonymous Detroit player reportedly told the *Detroit Press* that if Walter Johnson was a member of the Tigers, he would never lose a game. When Barney beat New York on June 29 to even his record at 8–8, Joe Cantillon was offered what New York newspapers were calling a "fortune," $30,000, for Johnson and his catcher, Gabby Street. Joe Cantillon was widely quoted as saying that if he had sold those two, he may as well have gotten rid of the entire team. Sadly, he was right.

Despite missing six weeks due to his cold and, later, because of arm miseries, Johnson placed second in the league in strikeouts (164), innings (296), and fourth in complete games (27). But this was the only season among his first ten in which his earned run average rose above two runs per game (2.22). He won just 13 and lost 25 for a Washington club which had pretty much disintegrated. Big Ed Delahanty's brother Jim had a bad year at the dish, following up a .317 season with .232 before being sent to Detroit for Germany Schaefer, a reliable hitter and accomplished baserunner, in an exchange of second basemen (the Senators also got catcher Red Killefer).

A regular player with the great Tiger teams since 1905, Schaefer, who like Rube Waddell was one of baseball's more renowned zany characters, had once caused a change in baseball's rules. After stealing second with a man on third, he was not able to coax a throw from Cleveland catcher Nig Clarke. So on the next pitch, Schaefer went back to first so that he could try again. He did, this time drawing a throw which allowed the winning run to score. As a result of Schaefer's unexpected maneuver, it would become illegal to run in the wrong direction on the basepaths.

Three months prior to obtaining Schaefer, the Senators had dealt for pitcher Nick Altrock in order to attempt to bolster their sorry pitching staff. Altrock was a 20-game winner three straight years (1904 to 1906) for the White Sox. (As in many other cases, different sources differ on the exact number of wins he had for each of these years — *Total Baseball* attributes only 19 to him for 1904.) Altrock had built a career on pitching with his noggin. He also was the best-fielding pitcher of his time, and indeed still holds a number of fielding records for pitchers. He also had a deadly pickoff move, and had once won a game in relief without having thrown a single pitch toward the plate. He had gotten out of a jam by picking a man off first, and his club had then won the game in the bottom of the inning.

Altrock had just been released by minor-league Kansas City, and he won just one game for the Washington Nationals. Nevertheless, he and Schaefer served double duty for the beleaguered ballclub. Beginning in 1912, they would form a comedy act on the coaching lines which endured until Schaefer was given a scouting job by his old friend John McGraw of the Giants. Altrock then teamed up with Al Schacht, a young pitcher with the Senators in 1919 who got a sore arm and gave up playing in 1921. Privately, Altrock and Schacht hated each other and didn't speak off the field during the last seven years of their professional association. On the field, however, they did develop about 150 pantomime routines to entertain baseball fans.

While Schaefer was the pioneer when it came to comedic showmanship, it was Altrock who was the real talent of the comedy duo — he was a master juggler and mime. The two would wear clown faces and engage in merry devilment. Altrock may not have endeared himself to the umpires: from the Nationals' coaching box, he would at times mimic an arbiter's every move. His second partner, Al Schacht, took his comedy seriously and made of it a vocation. He would sever the relationship with Altrock to start his own career as the "Clown Prince of Baseball." For 25 years, Schacht donned a clown costume and a battered hat to regale fans across America with pantomime and anecdotes, always ending the season with a booking wherever the World Series was being played.

Schacht's first such engagement was at New York on the occasion of the World Series. At this time Rudolf Valentino was starring in a hit picture called *Blood and Sand*. In it, the heartthrob battled and finally killed a bull and made love to a beautiful maiden. For the purposes of Schacht's performance, the bull would be a runaway goat, whose services he had enlisted by roping it and stuffing it into a taxi for the trip to the ballpark. Abetted by cabbage, which bought the goat's cooperation, and by Altrock, who played the role of the maiden, Schacht's pantomime made a huge hit with the crowd.

Comedy was indeed what the Washington ballclub was best at in 1909; it slipped to only 42 wins in 152 games. The highlight of

the season was a scoreless, 18-inning tie with the Detroit Tigers on July 16. Ed Summers pitched the whole way for the Tigers, and he permitted just seven hits and one walk until, mercifully, the game was called because of darkness. Bill "Dolly" Gray, who had won 58 games over the two previous years in the Coast League but who had to endure an ugly 5–19 rookie season in the majors, started but did not finish for Washington. In this game, ironically, Tiger greats Ty Cobb and Sam Crawford both went 0–for–7. But the Senators, who had sunk to the darkness of the league basement in June, remained there.

The 1909 Nationals still hold records for fewest runs scored in a season (380) and the most times shut out in one season (29). They finished an unbelievable 56 games behind the first-place Tigers and 20 games out of seventh. Indicative of the meager support he received, Walter Johnson set a league record for shutouts lost in a season (10), and a major-league record for shutouts lost in a month (5, in July) on the way to posting his poor 13–25 ledger. Apart from Johnson and Gray, the other starters, Bob Groom — who like Gray had been a star in the Coast League, winning 49 games over the previous two seasons — and Charley Smith, fashioned respective records of 7–26 and 3–12. An embarrassed Tom Noyes went so far as to offer to resign from his position as club president, but his proposal was rejected by the board of directors.

Pongo Joe Cantillon was fired at the end of the season, having guided the Nats to one seventh-place and two eighth-place finishes during his abbreviated regime. It took the Senators so little time to find a replacement that Cantillon was to become known as the manager who had been fired but had not left a vacancy. League president Ban Johnson had listed Cantillon in his bad books ever since Pongo Joe had taken the Senators' managing job without consulting him — Ban Johnson had had the Boston managerial job in mind for his old umpire. In 1908, Cantillon had gotten into further hot water with Johnson by participating in exhibition games involving ineligible players.

Now that Cantillon was on his was out because of the poor quality of his ballclub at Washington, the league president stepped in and suggested the hiring of Jimmy McAleer, most recently the manager of the St. Louis Browns who had finished an awful seventh in 1909. The affable McAleer had finished out of the second division only three times in eight years with the Browns, so although Washington was becoming known as a burial ground for managers, he couldn't afford to be choosy. The marriage was consummated, and the former stylish outfielder of the Cleveland Spiders took over the helm of the Washington Nationals for 1910.

1910–1919: The Big Train and the Little Ballclub That Could

On April 14, 1910, Walter Johnson took the mound for the season opener for the Senators. This was the first of 14 times he would do so in his 21-year career. The opening game was also historically significant because William Howard Taft, the 27th President of the United States, threw out the first ball and became the first President to inaugurate a baseball season. In April of the previous year, President Taft and Vice-President James Sherman had made an appearance at a Nationals game, the first time a U.S. President had shown up at a ballgame in the city since Benjamin Harrison had back in 1892. The tradition of the ceremonial first pitch is one that would be followed from 1910 onward.

Prior to the presidential toss, new manager Jimmy McAleer had urged a shy Walter Johnson to volunteer to catch the ball. Walter had responded that he was sure the President had not come to the ballgame just to play catch. Gabby Street was enlisted as the official receiver, but then for some reason apparently known only to President Taft, the President turned and threw the ball to Walter Johnson instead. A member of the presidential party who had overheard Johnson's remark to McAleer had interpreted it for President Taft in such a way that the President understood

that Walter had backed out of the ceremony because he was too bashful. For Johnson, the baseball became the first in a collection signed by various presidents which he would accumulate and treasure. This was only the beginning of what was going to be quite a day for the Big Train.

The initial excitement was somewhat tempered when Secretary of State Charles Bennett, sitting in the presidential box with Taft and Vice-President Sherman, was skulled by a line drive fouled off the bat of Frank "Home Run" Baker of the A's. There was general confusion until Bennett waved to attendants to indicate that he was not in need of first aid. President Taft was quite a fan of the grand old game. While visiting St. Louis less than three weeks later, he shuttled between the stadiums in which the Browns and Cardinals were playing simultaneously, in order to appear nonpartisan and not to offend anyone. In contrast to the way history portrays him, baseball showed President Taft to be something of a consummate politician.

Of his 14 opening-day starts, Walter Johnson would win eight of them, an incredible seven by shutout. This one was the first — a one-hit 3–0 masterpiece against the Athletics in front of 12,000 partisans. The no-hitter was lost in the seventh inning when right-fielder Doc Gessler, never known for his prowess with the glove, got tangled up with a fan at the edge of the roped-off outfield and dropped the ball. Gessler, who hit .259 and .282 as the Nats' regular rightfielder in 1910 and '11 before retiring at age 30 to become a physician, apologized to the Big Train. He need not have.

Walter Johnson never, ever, noted errors behind him. He also never spoke of any lack of offensive support behind him. Nor did he ever complain about the vagaries of umpires and the effects their calls might have had on his fate. Johnson was also a rare specimen in the rowdy early years of the century in that he was genuinely concerned about the safety of batters. The fact that he hit a record 205 batters during the course of his career seems illogical.

Throughout this season, if for no other reason, Washington fans would have something to cheer about. The 22-year-old Big Train lived up to every expectation that he had produced with his incredible performances during September 1908. On the seventh-place 1910 Senators, Johnson's record was 25–17, with a pair of one-hitters and a pair of two-hitters. He was the league's dominant pitcher, leading in strikeouts, innings pitched, and complete games.

Despite an ordinary start for the fourth straight year, and standing at 2–5 and later 13–14, Johnson won 12 of his last 15 decisions. In late August, he struck out 38 batters in three games, a record which stood for 64 years, until broken by Nolan Ryan in 1974. In his very next start following that stretch, Barney struck out three consecutive lefthanded pinch hitters on ten pitches.

It seemed that Jimmy McAleer played a role in turning Walter Johnson around in 1910. From then on, the Big Train could count on being a starting pitcher only, and not having to drive himself to the point of exhaustion with frequent relief appearances. Also, with McAleer, Walter would be given normal rest time between starts. McAleer also offered advice from an opposing manager's viewpoint —

he felt that Johnson could be beaten whenever he began to rely too heavily on his curveball. The tip proved invaluable.

Walter Johnson's 1910 ERA was a minuscule 1.35, and for a while it was thought that his 313 strikeouts had established a new all-time mark. He had indeed shattered Rube Waddell's mark of 302 set in 1903, but it was later found that Waddell had registered 349 K's in '04. Amazingly, the editor of the *Spalding Baseball Guide* refused to heap any praise upon the Nats' wunderkind. Among other things, it was written that Johnson "made a better record than he did in some other years, but there is still room for improvement in his pitching … he lacks that control which is necessary to place him with the leaders in the Base Ball world." Yet, Johnson was considered enough of an asset that, just after the 1910 World Series, won by Connie Mack's A's, there were rumors flying about that he might be traded for Ty Cobb who, two months shy of his 24th birthday, had just won his fifth consecutive A.L. batting title. When asked about the rumor, Tigers president Frank Navin expressed the opinion that Washington would never consider trading Walter Johnson for anyone, even Ty Cobb.

The Big Train was something of an idler on the mound, meaning he never gunned for strikeouts. He was of a humble nature, and there was evidence that he was the kind who had no use for records and was content to just win, without regard for how that was to be accomplished. This may never have seemed so true at this early stage of his career as in the anomalous July 8 game at St. Louis. Barney struck out the first seven men he faced and eight of the first nine. However, buoyed by a large lead when the Nats scored ten runs for him in the fifth inning, he didn't take the trouble to strike out anyone else among the anemic Browns over the course of the rest of the game.

Johnson's 25–17 record, marking the only time in history a pitcher has gone from 25 losses to 25 wins in one year, would certainly have been enhanced if he had had better backup. Only the quick Clyde Milan and the defensive whiz at shortstop, George McBride, excelled. Milan established himself as a base-stealing menace by swiping 44 bases and hitting .279 in a league that, as a whole, hit just .243 in 1910. McBride, however, was consistently a weak hitter, finishing at .230.

The new third baseman was Kid Elberfeld, the "Tabasco Kid," a former star shortstop with the New York Highlanders who, at 35, was, needless to say, not a kid anymore. Elberfeld didn't help much, batting .251 with just about the worst fielding average among the league's starting third basemen. Without Walter Johnson, the Senators would have been hardpressed to stay in front of the Browns, and this was in a season when St. Louis won just 47 games. To compound matters for the embattled Nats, Johnson's personal catcher, Gabby Street, was injured for long stretches and it caused Walter to ease up on his fastball. In Street's absence, the Nats tried four nondescript catchers in his place, including one carrying the ultimate anonymous moniker of John Henry who would manage to stick around in a part-time role until 1917.

The Senators dropped into seventh place on the last day of the 1910 season. On the business end, home attendance had increased while the league's had decreased because of a 24½-game improvement in the standings. Jimmy McAleer agreed to manage again, this time inking a two-year contract.

Team president Tom Noyes was summoned to Atlanta by a jittery McAleer, who did not relish starting a new season without his two most valuable commodities, who were threatening to hold out for more money. Noyes quickly gave Clyde Milan what he was asking for, and offered to raise Walter Johnson's pay to $6,500. Barney made what was a characteristic speech for him, and told Noyes, "Nothing doing." When Johnson showed he meant it by catching the next train to his father's dairy farm in Coffeyville, Kansas (Walter also raised purebred birds and won prizes at county fairs), the Washington media and fans became riled. Accused of stinginess, and amid rumors that he was considering trading Johnson to Detroit or Philadelphia, Tom

Noyes steadfastly held to his position that Walter Johnson would be the highest-paid pitcher in the league if he accepted the Senators' offer.

The stalemate over money between the Big Train and team president Noyes had resulted in manager McAleer ordering Johnson to leave training camp because of his refusal to sign. The league's best pitcher had been asking for $7,500 a year, and eventually he did settle for a three-year arrangement at $7,000 per. Because of the holdout, Johnson lost the opening-day starting assignment to southpaw Dolly Gray, who was embarking on a season in which he would go 4–14, 5.06.

Not only was Walter Johnson not present for the 1911 opener, but Washington's shabby wooden ballpark wasn't there either. Except for a small bleacher section, it had burned down 18 days before. There was considerable scrambling to erect a concrete and steel structure. Somehow, it was ready for baseball on April 12, despite the fact that wooden forms were still protecting drying concrete. The only box seats were for the President of the United States. The dimensions of League (or National) Park would change little in the years to come. From left to right they were established at 407–421–328. The right-field distance was reduced to 320 feet in 1926. The right-center field scoreboard was 41 feet high, and it mushroomed to an unreasonable 56 feet in 1946 when enhanced with the omnipresent sign advertising the "National Bohemian" beer company. Needless to say, this ballpark would be the kiss of death to would-be home run hitters.

When he did make his first start, on April 15, Walter Johnson again brought attention to his unusual talents. On this particular day, he turned the trick of striking out four Red Sox batters in the same inning. Even more unlikely, Boston scored during the inning. Washington catcher Eddie Ainsmith missed the third strike on the second strikeout. Larry Gardner stole second when Johnson fanned future Hall of Famer Harry Hooper, and then scored on a double by Tris Speaker, another Hall of Famer to be. ("Spoke" happens to hold the all-time record for doubles — 792 according to *Total Baseball,* but it's been 793 for so long that the number has become synonymous with Speaker.)

Despite another slow start, Walter Johnson would win 16 of his last 20 decisions and put together a record of 23–15 for 1911, leading the league in complete games and placing in the top three in most of the other important categories. Of the club's other pitchers, only Bob Groom, at 13–16, won more than nine games in 1911. The Senators, meanwhile, were regressing, ending the season 3½ games behind the previous year's pace. From mid–May on, they stayed in seventh place. Germany Schaefer, playing first base, had his one good year for Washington, batting .334, and Clyde Milan continued to improve, increasing his average to .315 and his stolen bases to 54, which ranked second in the league behind Ty Cobb. Manager McAleer, who had been a great outfielder himself, loved Milan, but he did not approve of his nonchalance in catching the ball with one hand.

By the end of the '11 season, Gabby Street had lost his number one catcher's job to Eddie Ainsmith, for whom the Senators had paid a reported $3,500 to his Lawrence, Mass., club the previous fall. Walter Johnson, who worked regularly with Ainsmith now, was supportive, and indicated that Ainsmith did the best job of catching his fastball whenever the Big Train's control was a little off. The muscular receiver preferred light padding in his mitt; not only would he use that mitt to catch the world's fastest pitcher, but at times he would catch a high Johnson fastball barehanded just for the fun of it!

In mid–September, the Senators were surprised to find out that Jimmy McAleer, who had a year left on his contract, was relinquishing the managerial reins. McAleer had just purchased a partnership in the Boston Red Sox along with Robert McElroy, who would be succeeded as secretary to league president Ban Johnson by a Chicago railroad man named William Harridge. The departure of McAleer launched a long era in the history of the Washington Senators. By the end of October, the Senators had their replace-ments — Clark Calvin Griffith, the renowned player-manager, was returning to the league he had helped get off the ground.

Clark Griffith's life began 31 years before the founding of the American League, in which he had had a leading organizational role along with Ban Johnson and Charles Comiskey. Griffith first saw the light of day on the morning of November 20, 1869, in Vernon County in southwestern Missouri, about 15 miles from the Kansas border. His parents had come from Illinois on a covered wagon train bound for the more fertile Oklahoma panhandle.

Griffith's father, Isaiah, came from proud Colonial Virginia stock and his mother was the descendant of one of the original purchasers of Nantucket, Mass., in the midseventeenth century. Isaiah Griffith decided to leave the wagon train early and had staked out 40 acres to farm. He quickly turned to hunting for a living, supplying railway companies with food for their workers. Two-year-old Clark was orphaned when his father was accidentally shot by his neighbor's teenage son, who had mistaken him for a deer. Clark's mother, bearing a fifth child at the time, had to take to the fields herself, and set an example of courage that would last young Clark a lifetime.

During the first years of her widowhood, the men of the community pitched in to help Clark Griffith's mother plow the fields. Their home became a focal point of the community, and very often a gathering place. By the age of ten, Clark's brother Earl was stalking game with a shotgun. Clark, six years his junior, soon followed Earl as a provider for the family. As a 10-year-old, he was making his own traps and catching coon, skunk, and possum for very good pay — up to $1.25 per hide. At 11, he hired himself out to a local farmer, chopping corn and doing chores all summer long. His pay at the end of the summer was two little pigs.

Much later in life, Griffith — who had by then met U.S. presidents, been a pitching star in the major leagues, owned a big-league club, and been elected to the Hall of Fame — insisted that his greatest thrill in life had had nothing to do with any of those accomplishments. He instead told *Washington Post* reporter Shirley Povich about an experience he'd had in the company of his proudest possession as a child, his dog Major. The dog had been half bulldog, half hound. In Griffith's estimation, purebred hounds were too lazy to make excellent coon hunters. Clark had trained Major to bark only twice if he was on to something. The usual modus operandi was for Major to chase their bounty up a tree, where Clark would climb and shake limbs until the animal would lose its grip. Major would take over on the ground and bring an end to the proceedings. On this one occasion, Clark noticed that Major was having an awful time of finishing his job. When he got back down, he clubbed Major by mistake before finally subduing the coon. While walking home, he met a farmer who told him that what he had over his back wasn't a coon at all, but a wildcat. When Clark got in better light, he saw that the farmer was right, and that he actually had licked a wildcat that was as heavy as he was at the time, about 60 pounds.

At age 13, Clark Griffith became sickly, a victim of malaria, then prevalent in the Missouri lowland country. His mother was advised to move him out of the area, which she did. Resettled with relatives in Bloomington, Illinois, Clark, who had been the mascot of the local Stringtown, Mo., team, got more serious about baseball. The sport had been invented only about 40 years earlier — this was at a time when the batter needed seven balls for a walk, and a strikeout was achieved even if the catcher, who was the only player who wore a glove, caught the ball on a bounce. The Illinois climate worked wonders for Clark's health, and at 16 he had already earned a local reputation in Bloomington, hometown of big-league pitching ace Charles "Old Hoss" Radbourn.

In 1888, Griffith signed to play for Bloomington, which held a franchise in the Inter-State League of the era. He lost his first start in bizarre fashion — he gave up just five hits but himself committed five of his team's

ten errors. Nonetheless, he did become the top pitcher in the league, and at age 18, Clark Griffith was already about to get his big break. An exhibition game was arranged with Milwaukee of the superior Western League. As the winner of that game, Griffith was offered a $225-a-month salary with Milwaukee, and his professional career took off. He joined a team which featured Jimmy McAleer, who 23 years later would create a vacancy with the Nationals that would bring him to the capital and alter the face of baseball in Washington, D.C.

By the end of the following season, Griffith was the best pitcher Milwaukee had, finishing the season with a record of 25–11. Charles Comiskey, then managing the major-league American Association's St. Louis Browns, signed him, starting Griffith on a protracted tour that would include seven big-league stops. He won 14 games as a rookie for the Browns in 1891, but then was traded to the Boston Americans for a pitcher named Jack Easton who would win just five more games in the major leagues. Now a teammate of future Hall of Famers Hugh Duffy, Mike "King" Kelly, and Dan Brouthers, Griffith went 3–1 and played on a pennant winner. However, the seven games he pitched in for Boston were his last for the team. The American Association disbanded, and for 1892, the National League would be the only game in town.

Griffith had developed a sore arm at the end of the previous season, and no National League team bid for his services, so he found himself back in the minors at Tacoma, Washington. He rehabilitated his arm and had great success at Tacoma. His team was so strong, though, that the league ended up disbanding as a result. The Tacoma players hadn't been getting a paycheck for weeks anyway, so from there Griffith persuaded several of his teammates to follow him to Missoula, Montana; the townspeople there had offered to pay them Tacoma salaries to represent their team in the Montana State League, an outlaw association which pirated players from wherever it could. Missoula was a wild mining town full of gambling joints and saloons crowded along the one main street. In this atmosphere, Griffith became a hero, but it wouldn't be enough for a man who had already tasted the rewards of playing in the best leagues.

There were no offers coming Clark Griffith's way in 1893 either, so he headed for the west coast, where he joined Oakland of the tough Pacific Coast League. The star second baseman at Oakland was young Joe Cantillon. Again, Griffith was victimized by the instability of the minor-league baseball of the times. Unpaid for several weeks, he led an insurrection against the Oakland owners. The players refused to take the field for a game at San Francisco, and this precipitated a chain of events that led to the disbanding of the entire league.

Griffith had become close friends with Cantillon, and the two drifted up the California coast where they found work as, of all things, actors in a traveling vaudeville show. Griffith put his frontier background to good use, playing the part of an Indian who was shot, twice a night, by the six-shooting Cantillon. In late August, the young pitcher got his reprieve when the major leagues beckoned. James A. Hart, who had signed Griffith to his first contract with Milwaukee, had become president of the National League club at Chicago. Hart needed pitching help for his hapless Colts, and telegraphed Griffith, who proved of little use. Starting but two games, he was hit solidly. The 23-year-old righty made two relief appearances, one of them in Washington, his first appearance in the city where he would leave his most indelible mark.

At the end of the season, Griffith really began his trek toward fame when he perfected the pitch which became known as the screwball, which he later claimed to have invented. While playing exhibitions in California, Griffith had pitched too often and had again felt soreness in his arm. He started experimenting with different grips, hoping to develop a slow pitch that would spare his arm and fool batters at the same time. He discovered that if he released a curve outside his middle finger, rather than between the index and the thumb, the ball would break away

from a lefthanded hitter. He also expanded his repertoire by scuffing baseballs and otherwise tampering with them to produce all sorts of weird effects.

In 1894, Clark Griffith got his first taste of success with Cap Anson's Chicago Colts, winning 21 and losing just 11. His curve was mild compared to what the great Christy Mathewson would be able to muster a decade or so later, but by the age of 25 it had already earned Griffith the nickname "The Old Fox," which would stay with him for life. This was a tribute to his "smarts" as a pitcher — Griffith knew hitters' weaknesses and pitched to them. He knew how to tamper with the ball, had good control, and could make the ball deviate from a straight path. In one celebrated incident, he fooled Washington batter Kip Selbach (with whom he had been arguing during the at-bat) with an underhand pitch. Selbach took a prodigious cut, but struck out before the ball even got to the plate. Pitching with his head, the Old Fox upped his record to 25–13 in 1895.

Not everything about Clark Griffith was admirable. By the late nineties, he had acquired quite a reputation as a rabble-rouser. When things did not go so well for him on the mound, he would bait the umpires. It reached the point where arbiter Thomas Lynch was moved to promise that he would bring charges against Griffith should he persist in using the type of language he had already heard him use on the ballfield.

Griffith won more than 20 games for Chicago over six straight seasons, and in 1898 he led the National League in ERA, with 1.88, while recording a sparkling 26–10 record for the second-place Colts. Following a mediocre campaign in 1900, however, Griffith decided to cast his lot with the fledgling American League. True to the word he had given to cofounders Ban Johnson and Charles Comiskey, he began a feverish raid of National League clubs, singlehandedly delivering 39 of the 40 National Leaguers he had promised to sign. The one man he was not able to convince to come over to the new league was likely the world's best player at that time — the

"Dutchman," the reigning 26-year-old National League batting champion, Honus Wagner of Pittsburgh.

For his own Chicago White Sox, Griffith had acquired pitcher Jimmy Callahan and infielder-outfielder Sam Mertes from the crosstown Cubs, star outfielder Fielder Jones of Brooklyn, and catcher Billy Sullivan from Boston. So equipped, the White Sox beat out the Red Sox by four games in the American League's first pennant race. Aside from managing the club, the 31-year-old Old Fox was 24–7 on the mound, leading the league in winning percentage, and tying the future immortal, Cy Young, who was then 34, with five shutouts.

The top hitter was Fielder Jones, who rewarded Griffith's doggedness in pursuing him by placing third in the league in hitting with .340. To sign Jones for the White Sox, Griffith had plodded through three miles of knee-deep snow. So crafty was the dogged Old Fox that prior to the 1902 season, he borrowed money from Phillies majority owner Tom Shibe in order to sign star catcher Ed McFarland, one of Shibe's own players.

Griffith played a key role in the George Davis incident, one of the most celebrated battles in the war between the two major leagues. A talented shortstop and batsman (belatedly elected to the Baseball Hall of Fame in 1998), Davis, as a nine-year veteran of the New York Giants, was another who jumped to Griff's White Sox for the 1902 campaign. Unhappy with his salary under the penurious Charles Comiskey, however, Davis would decide to return to the Giants the following year. Peace was declared between the leagues early in the '03 season, and Davis, following deliberations involving owners from both leagues, was awarded to Chicago, although he didn't want to return there.

Later on in the summer, the National Leaguers tried to accommodate George Davis with an illegal scheme engineered by N.L. president John Brush that would have enabled the shortstop to rejoin the New York Nationals. After having played just four games for the Giants under Brush's advice, Davis was served with an injunction. He hired John Montgomery Ward, a lawyer who at one time had been a talented player and driving force in the formation of the Players' League in 1890. That ill-fated loop, which had operated just one year, had been set up as a result of a backlash on the part of the National League players, who had revolted because of the miserliness of N.L. owners.

Ward's representation of Davis had serious repercussions for his own career because, years later, Ban Johnson opposed and effectively quashed Ward's attempt to become president of the National League. As for Davis, he had his case thrown out and was ordered to report to Comiskey's Chicago Americans, which he finally agreed to do, for 1904. In his one season under Griffith with the White Sox back in '02, Davis had led all shortstops in fielding and had hit a robust .299. So it can be safely said that the White Sox were happy to have him back, despite the circumstances.

For 1902, Connie Mack's A's had added Rube Waddell and finished five games ahead of Jimmy McAleer's Browns. Griff's White Sox had finished eight out, and his own performance declined as well — his ERA took a nosedive to 4.19, well above the league average of 3.57. At this point in Griffith's career, he seized an opportunity created when Ban Johnson became convinced that the American League needed a club in New York City. Johnson suggested that Griffith be named manager and, offer accepted, the two set out on another player raid.

They hit the Pittsburgh Pirates particularly hard, stealing pitchers Jack Chesbro and Jess Tannehill for their Highlanders for 1903. Chesbro, then still in his midtwenties, was coming off two terrific seasons with the Pirates. Tannehill, 28 years old and four times a 20-game winner already, had led the National League in ERA in '01, and in winning percentage with a 20–6 slate in '02. Griffith and Johnson also snared catcher Jack O'Connor, third baseman Wid Conroy, and outfielder Lefty Davis from Pittsburgh. Thirty-one-year-old Wee Willie Keeler, still "hittin' them where they ain't," came over from Brooklyn and hit .318, fifth best in the loop.

The Highlanders had needed a place to play in New York, and a location had been chosen at 168th and Broadway. Military artifacts were discovered by workmen during the construction of what would become known as Hilltop Park. The site had been a battleground through which George Washington had led his charges during the Revolutionary War. With their new team and new park, the Highlanders came in fourth in 1903, a full 17 games behind Boston. Thirty-three-year-old Clark Griffith rang up a record of 14–10, with a very respectable ERA of 2.70. The team finished ten games over .500 and was popular with the fans, despite the fact that the Giants had a contending club in the other league.

The Highlanders were even more competitive the following year, and battled the Red Sox right down to the wire. On the last day of the season they were in a position to win the pennant, but needed to win both ends of a doubleheader with the Red Sox. Jack Chesbro had developed a dandy spitball which had earned him 14 straight wins and his still-standing record of 41 victories. With a man on third and two out in the ninth inning of a game knotted at two runs, Chesbro uncorked a wild pitch that blew New York's chances for the pennant.

Outside of a strong second-place finish in 1906, the Highlanders were mediocre throughout the rest of Clark Griffith's tenure. By late June, 1908, they were dead last and in the throes of the worst streak of their brief history. Over the years, a great deal of animosity had developed between Griffith and the club's owners. Following his ejection during a game in Philadelphia, there was reprisal from Highlanders owner Frank Farrell. Clark Griffith had had enough, and he tendered his resignation.

Garry Herrmann, owner of the Cincinnati Reds, was the first to offer Griff a job, which was initially to scout for the Reds. Soon, Griffith was back on the bench, where he managed the Reds for three full seasons, 1909–11. He had only an average club with the Reds, but was well paid and was being offered another contract for 1912. But as early as 1908, when it had been rumored that Joe Cantillon would be leaving the Senators, the Old Fox had been keeping a close eye on the situation in Washington.

Griffith was a longtime friend of Thomas Noyes, the newspaper publisher, who was still the chief stockholder in the ballclub. The Senators approached Griffith during the 1911 World Series. Through Edward Walsh, an insurance broker who was a director of the team, a meeting was set up with the stockholders. At this meeting, held at the Commercial Club near the White House, Griffith was informed of the group's intention to double the club's capital stock, from $100,000 to $200,000. The injection of fresh financing had been rendered necessary due to the cost of construction of the new ballpark the previous spring.

Now coming upon his 42nd birthday, Clark Griffith had thoughts of becoming a stockholder himself. Having pitched for 16 years in the majors and been a manager for 11, he undoubtedly considered the fact that only he, of the three main founders of the American League, had yet to achieve the kind of financial success enjoyed by Ban Johnson and Charles Comiskey. Even his old teammate, Jimmy McAleer, was becoming an owner at Boston. Although he couldn't afford to back himself up financially, Griffith made an offer to buy as large a piece of the team as the stockholders were willing to sell. The deal fell through when many of the stockholders tried to jack up the share price to turn a quick profit.

Then, Griffith's pal, club president Tom Noyes, and Edward Walsh offered to sell their shares to Griffith for what they had cost them. They also drew their partner, Ben Minor, in on the same deal. Noyes was suggesting selling their combined 1,200 shares at $12.50, and that Griffith should also shell out the $15 per share the other stockholders wanted for another 800 shares. A total of 2,000 shares would give Griffith a tenth interest in the Washington Senators and also, more impressively, make him the largest single shareholder in the club.

Griffith turned his energies toward finding the money to do the deal. Ban Johnson had promised a $10,000 loan when Griffith had first heard of the Washington possibility, but now Johnson balked. Relations between the two became strained as a result. Clark Griffith got no support from Charles Comiskey. The Chisox owner told him he would be crazy to sink any money into a club located in "that baseball graveyard" known as Washington.

Griffith nonetheless proceeded to give Noyes all of his own cash assets, an amount of $8,000. He needed $19,000 more, and Noyes agreed to wait two weeks for it. Years before, the Old Fox had invested in a ranch at Craig, Montana. His elder brother Earl had been running it for him, and now it was Griffith's salvation. The First National Bank of Montana consented to a $20,000 mortgage on the ranch. Griffith rushed back to Washington with the cash, and signed a three-year contract on October 27, 1911, which would pay him the grand sum of $7,500 a year. Thus began the career in Washington of the man whose name was to become synonymous with Senators baseball.

In acquiring part ownership of the team, Clark Griffith had a stake in the greatest young talent in the game, the man with the golden pitching arm, Walter Johnson. The rest of the components of the team which was set to take the field for 1912 were less than confidence-inspiring, but Griffith had changes in mind with some new faces. This ballclub, coming off a seventh-place finish, would perform at a level which would greatly surpass all expectations.

Clark Griffith wanted a young team to replace the previous season's 64–90 entry. The regular lineup he was about to assemble would stay together for four years. Only the reliable George McBride at shortstop, a .235 hitter in 1911, and centerfielder Jesse Clyde "Deerfoot" Milan, who had just completed his .315 campaign and was stealing nearly as many bases as the great Cobb, were retained as regular position players.

Griffith got rid of Walter Johnson's catcher, Gabby Street, insisting that the two youngsters the Nats already had, John Henry and Eddie Ainsmith, would fill the bill between them. He also cut loose a pair of sidekicks from his Highlander days, infielders Wid Conroy and Kid Elberfeld. All told, Griffith released or sold ten players — veteran outfielders Jack Lelivelt and Doc Gessler, and pitcher Dixie Walker (whose two sons would one day become stars in the National League), were among those set adrift.

To replace them, Griffith brought in youngsters. Eddie "Kid" Foster, 24, would play third and Ray Morgan, just 20, second. Morgan would supply a dependable brand of second base for this ballclub for seven years, and hit .238 as a rookie and .254 for his career, spent entirely in Washington. At 25, Clyde Milan would anchor an outfield also featuring 22-year-old holdover Clarence "Tilly" Walker, 21-year-old rookie Howard Shanks, and an older newcomer, Danny Moeller, 27, a fleet outfielder who had last appeared in the big leagues with the Pirates in 1908. The 1912 pitching staff wasn't deep — the bulk of the work would go to Walter Johnson, Bob Groom, and Tom Hughes.

The righthanded Groom, a wild 27-year-old fastballer, had completed his third season, and had suffered right along with the Senators, having had that dismal 6–26 rookie season despite a respectable 2.87 ERA. That year, 1909, Groom had lost 19 straight, an unenviable mark since tied, but still a record for a rookie. Following his 13–17, 2.76, showing in 1910, he had then relapsed to 13–16, 3.82, in '11.

Bob Groom was an inch taller than the 6'1" Long Tom Hughes, so named for his height in an age when people didn't generally grow to be as tall as they do nowadays. Hughes had jumped to the A.L. in 1902 following a 21-loss rookie campaign with the Chicago Cubs in 1901. By '03, he was winning 20 for the world champion Boston Pilgrims. His career had been spotty since, but he'd won 16 in '05 and 18 in '08 for the Senators. Long Tom was, however, coming off a disappointing 4–11 year, and was 33 years old in 1912.

At this time, the Nationals also signed a

young pitcher named Joe Engel, a Washington boy who was the son of the owner of one of Clark Griffith's favorite saloons. Griffith was introduced to the strapping 18-year-old by the boy's father, took one look at him, and invited him to spring training. Thus began a 36-year career during which Engel would serve first as player, and later as scout, and eventually as director of the farm system. For his promotional skills at the minor-league level, Engel would eventually merit the title "Barnum of the Bushes."

Griffith convened the players in the spring of 1912 at Charlottesville, Virginia, but the weather was particularly uncooperative. The players were kept busy shoveling snow for the better part of two weeks, and the Nats got off to another bad start. With the club sitting at 17–21 at the end of May, Clark Griffith's new regime was already being labeled a flop by the press. The Senators' directors did not want to spend any money, and Griffith was desperate for a good first baseman. Again, club president Noyes came to his rescue and lent him $12,000. Griffith put down the cash, along with some part-time players, to acquire 24-year-old Charles "Chick" Gandil, who had been tearing up the International League with the Montreal Royals.

Chick Gandil's name lives in baseball infamy because in 1919, he was to become a kingpin in the so-called Black Sox scandal, the black mark left on baseball as a result of players conspiring with gamblers to fix the World Series. In fairness to those players, they had been held in servitude by penny-pinching owners like Charley Comiskey, who had amassed fortunes at their expense. In the minds of these mostly uneducated young men, deceit was the only way they could get what was rightfully theirs.

The accused White Sox players, including superstar slugger Joe Jackson and Chick Gandil, who was fingered by many as the ringleader on the players' side, were never convicted in court — some of the documents which may have incriminated them somehow went missing. The eight players were nonetheless turfed out of baseball by the new Commis-sioner, Kenesaw Mountain Landis, and banned forever from any organized play under the umbrella of the National Association. The autocratic Landis vowed to clean up baseball so that it wouldn't lose its foothold as "America's Game."

In 1912, Chick Gandil was just the tonic the Washington Nationals needed. The effects of his joining the club were felt immediately. Beginning with a Decoration Day double-header sweep of the Red Sox in Boston (Walter Johnson won the second game with a 5–0 whitewash), the Senators did not lose a game for three weeks. They rattled off 16 victories in a row, all on the road, a feat which would remain an American League record until 1984.

Following a heroes' welcome in Washington, President William Howard Taft threw out the first ball on June 18, compensating for the opening day he had missed due to the *Titanic* disaster and the death of his aide and friend Archie Butt, who was among those who had perished. The Senators won for the 17th straight time, 5–4, in a barnburner with the Athletics, setting a league record. The party ended the next day when the A's swept a doubleheader and, for good measure, inflicted the same punishment the day after that. This didn't faze the Nats, who then embarked on another long winning streak, this one lasting ten games.

It was during this period that Griffith developed the famous "run-and-hit" play, which mainly featured the 5'6½" Eddie "Kid" Foster, who was very adept at placing his hits. Griffith insisted Foster was even better than the former crony he had just let go, Willie Keeler. Instead of employing the hit-and-run, then already in vogue, it was assumed that with Kid Foster at the plate, any Senators baserunner would be going, so skilled was Foster at placing the ball where he wanted.

Foster hit .285 in his rookie year and led the league in at-bats, an accomplishment he would replicate three more times. Not only was he a complete player, but he had great endurance as well, missing no games in four of his first five seasons in Washington. Danny

Moeller had been purchased along with Foster from the Rochester, N.Y., minor-league club, and he was also a prize catch, batting .276 in what turned out to be his one solid year in the majors.

Walter Johnson went two months without losing. After the end of May, the Senators spent most of the season in second place. Bob Groom won 24 games. Clyde Milan stole 88 bases to lead the league (25 more than runner-up Eddie Collins), and batted .306 to lead the club. With his 88 steals, Milan set the then all-time record, besting by five the mark Ty Cobb had established the previous year. In the Nats' 14th straight win, in early June, Deerfoot Milan pilfered five bases, including home plate, over a span of just three innings in Cleveland.

Clyde Milan was the Nats' second bona-fide star, a fielder in the class of Cobb and Tris Speaker. Jimmy McAleer, likely the best outfielder of his time, had taught him how to play an even shallower center field than the great Speaker. Milan was durable as well, appearing in the outfield in 511 consecutive games from 1910 to 1913. Chick Gandil, an outstanding fielder, made enormous contributions, batting .305 and driving in 81 runs in 117 games after coming over from Montreal. Kid Foster was also distinguishing himself as a fielder at the hot corner.

Naturally, though, the team's top performer in 1912 was again Walter Johnson, who broke the 30-win mark for the first time. His slate was 33–12,* and he led the league with a 1.39 ERA. The Big Train held the opposition to a pathetic .196 batting average, and in this regard, Johnson would do better in just one other season over his 21-year career: 1913. The 1912 season marked the beginning of Walter Johnson's most glorious era.

One player who passed through Washington in 1912 was 24-year-old lefthanded pitcher James "Hippo" Vaughn, acquired on waivers from the Yankees in late June. Only 2–8 with the woeful Highlanders, Vaughn went 4–3 for the Nats. Had the Nationals kept him, Washington would have had a pitcher who, beginning in 1914, was destined to win more than 20 games for the Chicago Cubs four times, and whose lowest win total in a span of seven years would be 17.

The 6'4" Hippo, nicknamed for his running style rather than his size, would become best known for pitching a nine-inning no-hitter against Cincinnati on May 2, 1917. This was all the more remarkable because Fred Toney of the Reds also pitched a no-hitter, still a unique occurrence in baseball history as the 21st century dawned. In the tenth inning of the historical game, Vaughn gave up a clean single to Larry Kopf, who then made it to third on a dropped pop fly. The next batter was Jim Thorpe, later a member of the Professional Football Hall of Fame, who in 1950 would be voted greatest American athlete of the half-century. Thorpe hit a bouncer toward Vaughn, who threw to the plate, but not in time to catch the runner sliding in.

With a 10–2 six-inning verdict over the New York Highlanders on the eve of Independence Day, Walter Johnson began a string of performances that would make the 1912 season a memorable one in baseball history. On one day's rest, Walter delivered the best relief performance of his life. With one out and two on, he took over for Joe Engel in the fourth inning. Shortstop McBride, a slick man with the glove, made a miscue which let in the tying run. Then the game went on, for 12 more innings, until the Nats finally brought a run across. Walter Johnson had surrendered three hits and no runs in 12⅔ innings. From then on, the wins continued to pile up for a club that was clicking, always supplying the great one enough runs to win. On August 16, following a relief win over Ed Walsh and the White Sox the previous day, Johnson faced

---

Macmillan's The Baseball Encyclopedia, *and Warner Books'* Total Baseball, *inspired by the Society for American Baseball Research (SABR), have differed on many statistical totals, and this is one. SABR credits Johnson with 33 wins for this season, and 417 for his career, rather than the 416 long held as the true figure. For the most part, Macmillan's 1981 tome has been employed as a source for this book, with this case and the one concerning Johnson's 1913 ERA, described later herein, being notable exceptions.*

only 29 men, the second time he'd done so in 1912. The result was a 4–0 one-hitter during which only two balls were hit to the outfield and the last 19 batters to face him were all retired.

With Clark Griffith directing the show from the dugout, Johnson was back to doing quite a bit of relief duty, appearing 13 times in that role over the course of the season. Walter did not cherish relief work, and he did not hesitate to speak candidly whenever the subject was broached. The Big Train termed relief pitching a "disagreeable experience," strong words for the young man, because relief was often unexpected and, for him, more taxing than pitching a whole game. While Johnson decidedly didn't like being drawn into a situation where there was usually no margin for error, he never turned down an assignment, of course.

On August 20, Barney pitched 8⅔ innings of relief in the first game of a doubleheader and beat the Indians 4–2; it was his 15th consecutive win, which broke Jack Chesbro's 1904 record. In the second game of the August 20 doubleheader, big 21-year-old righthander Jay Cashion, enjoying his only decent season in the big leagues, took the focus off Johnson for the moment when he no-hit the Indians to earn a 2–0 shutout in a game called after six innings. Three days later, with an 8–1 conquest of the Tigers, Walter Johnson brought his season record to 29–7 by winning his 16th in a row. He set this record in 51 days, nearly averaging a win every three days — a truly amazing accomplishment, considering that as often as not, he had no more than two days' rest between starts.

Under modern rules, Johnson would not even have been docked with the defeat which was to bring the streak to an end. In relief of Tom Hughes in the seventh inning of the August 26 game at St. Louis, he came in with the score tied and men on first and second. These runners, back in 1912, were not considered the responsibility of the pitcher who allowed them to get there, namely Hughes. Johnson struck out Burt Shotton of the Browns, but then threw a wild pitch and allowed a single through

the infield by reserve outfielder Pete Compton which scored both runs.

The matter spurred quite a controversy at the time. Ban Johnson ruled that Johnson was indeed the pitcher of record because he'd allowed the baserunners to move up on the wild pitch. The Senators sought out National League president John Heydler, hoping a differing opinion might carry some weight with their league's prexy. Heydler indeed backed the Senators' contention, but Ban Johnson would not budge. Walter Johnson's reaction? He thought it would have been unfair to charge Tom Hughes with a loss just so his own streak could be extended. The topic became moot when Walter lost his next game. Characteristically, though, Johnson blamed himself for allowing the two runs which had severed his skein of victories. Paradoxically, but logically, he would years later express favor for the rule which would have spared him and baseball a good deal of controversy back in the summer of 1912.

On August 21, 1912, in the same week in which Johnson's streak was broken, club president Thomas Noyes died at age 44 following a four-day illness. Having served nearly eight years as chief officer, he would not be around to enjoy the thrill of finishing out of the second division for the first time. Noyes had given Clark Griffith his support in building the team. The Senators' attorney, Ben Minor, from whom Griffith had also bought shares, was elected president of the club. With Minor, Griffith would find out that things would work a little differently — from now on, he would have to get his decisions approved.

On September 6, 1912, Walter Johnson faced the ace of the Boston Red Sox, Smokey Joe Wood, before a crowd of 30,000 at Fenway Park. When asked to compare his own fastball with Wood's, the modest one had once replied, "Listen my friend, there's no man alive who can throw harder than Joe Wood." Wood, for his part, later in life told Lawrence Ritter for Ritter's wonderful *The Glory of Their Times* that Walter Johnson had been the only pitcher he'd ever hit against who, whenever he swung and missed, left him no clue as to whether he had swung over or under the ball. Back on June 26, the two had engaged in quite a battle, won by Boston 3–0, in which Wood had allowed three hits and Johnson four.

Clark Griffith, showman that he was, had really stirred the pot for this matchup. Ironically, Joe Wood at this point was only three wins short of Walter Johnson's all-time record of 16 consecutive victories. The Old Fox gave the word to the press that Red Sox manager Jake Stahl had been holding Wood back for the easiest opponents. Griffith made it clear that when the Nationals came to Boston, Wood would have to face Walter Johnson, and that Johnson would be held back until such time as Wood was ready to pitch. To make sure there was no mistake about there being a challenge issued, the Old Fox said that Wood was going to be considered to be nothing more than a true coward if he didn't start against the great Walter.

If ever there was a game which fulfilled its promise, this was the one. Wood was in trouble in four different innings and the Big Train got by unfettered until the sixth. Alas, this was the year of the Red Sox, and with two out, back-to-back doubles courtesy of Tris Speaker and Duffy Lewis brought in the game's only run. Speaker's double into a roped-off area would have been an out had there not been an overflow crowd. Lewis' hit was really a pop fly at the foul line that Danny Moeller got his glove on but couldn't hold.

For the record, Smokey Joe Wood did go on to win two more games to tie the Big Train's record, but he failed to break it. There was indeed not a lot to choose between the outstanding performances rendered by Johnson and Wood in 1912 — Johnson's ERA (1.39) and strikeouts (303) were better, whereas Wood led in complete games (35) and shutouts (10). Walter held the opposition to the .196 composite average already mentioned; Wood limited batters to .216. Wood won 34 and Johnson, with an inferior offensive alignment backing him, 33. Gracious sportsman that he was, Johnson, covering the World Series for the *Boston Herald*, predicted that Joe

Wood would not lose a game. He did, but won three as the Red Sox took the Series in seven over the New York Giants, making a world champion of ex–Washington boy-manager Jake Stahl.

The 1912 edition of the Senators had gotten to within four games of the Red Sox, a team which eventually won 105 games, still that franchise's best single-season output. Washington slipped back and by the tail end of the season found itself having to fend off the A's for second place. On September 26, following two rainouts which now magnified the importance of the remaining games of this series with the A's, Walter Johnson was called upon to relieve Tom Hughes. With one out and two men on, an error and a wild pitch allowed the A's to tie the score.

In the ninth, with Johnson very fast but a little wild, Senators catcher Rippy Williams, substituting for Eddie Ainsmith who was out of the lineup because of a broken finger, missed one of Johnson's hummers, the ball actually nicking umpire Billy Evans' ear. Evans had seen enough, or rather not enough, and immediately called the game because of darkness.

There was a popular but likely apocryphal yarn which well illustrates Walter's blinding speed. In the latter stages of a game, with darkness looming and two strikes on the batter, catcher Eddie Ainsmith had urged Walter to fake a windup because the batter was going to swing at anything (nothing, even). Ainsmith planned to pound his mitt in an attempt to fool the umpire into thinking the ball had actually arrived. The ruse worked and the umpire called strike three. The batter of course disagreed. He bellowed that the unpitched ball had been at least a foot wide!

On the day following Billy Evans' close call, Johnson relieved Bob Groom in the ninth and pitched ten shutout innings, prompting Eddie Collins, a future Hall of Famer, to comment that he had never known Walter to have thrown any faster. The Nats finally made Johnson a winner in the 19th. Barney's 33rd victory of an amazing year on the last day of the season, October 3, at New York, clinched second place for Washington, 14 games behind Boston, and a game ahead of the defending champions, the Philadelphia Athletics.

These lofty heights, achieved with 91 wins, were all the more exciting for the cranks who followed the Washington club, because their team had never before even finished higher than sixth. Clark Griffith's ballclub had earned an infusion of about $100,000 into the operation in a single season. According to Shirley Povich in *The Washington Senators,* the board of directors' only complaint was that the ballclub was using too many baseballs, at a cost of a whopping $1,400 for the year! An improvement of more than 50 percent in gate receipts over 1911 earned Griffith election to the board of directors at the end of the season. Interestingly, in what we can only surmise must have been conceived as a show of generosity by the owners, each stockholder was declared eligible to buy two reserved seats for opening day, 1913 — as long as they did so, mind you, before a late–March deadline.

Right off the bat, the 1913 edition of the Washington Senators set out to show that the previous year's performance had not been a fluke. President Woodrow Wilson agreed to tend to the opening ceremonies, thus lending credence to Clark Griffith's dream of having the President in the ballpark to usher in each new season. The Old Fox was also lobbying to have the first game of each season always played in Washington. In the 1913 season opener on April 10, the newly named New York Yankees, formerly Highlanders, encountered the same old Walter Johnson, who beat them 2–1. The Big Train permitted a run in the first inning, and then shut them out the rest of the way. More than a month would pass, over a span of eight games, before he would allow a run again.

Exactly a week following the opener, the Senators played the Highlanders in the first game ever at the Polo Grounds. The event was timed with "Chance Day," in honor of the new Yankees manager, Frank Chance, who was inheriting a last-place team which would escape the basement in this season by a mar-

gin of a single game. The Senators put a considerable damper on the Polo Grounds festivities, coming away with a 9–3 decision at day's end.

Clark Griffith's "little ballclub," as he'd gotten into the habit of calling it, again finished second in 1913, by 6½ games. The A's, however, had been ahead by double digits until the last week of the season. This 96–57 Philadelphia team featured a pitching staff which included a couple of future members of the Hall of Fame — Eddie Plank and Chief Bender. Jack Coombs was taking a regular turn, and rookies Herb Pennock and Bullet Joe Bush, both of whom would attain stardom, were starting to contribute. The pride of the A's was the infield, then widely referred to as the "$100,000 Infield," which included Stuffy McInnis, Eddie Collins, Jack Barry, and Frank "Home Run" Baker.

On the "little ballclub," even by the standards of the time, there was not much offensive firepower. Clark Griffith came to a conclusion that rocked the baseball world. With Walter Johnson capable of winning at nearly every turn and the Nats a viable contender along with the A's and Naps (as were called the Indians, named after their star player, the affable Napoleon Lajoie), Griffith was desperate for more hitting. Barely a week into the season, he claimed to have made the Detroit Tigers an overture he felt they couldn't possibly refuse. The *New York Times* printed it — Washington had tendered an astounding $100,000 bid for Ty Cobb.

According to Griffith, he had written a check and passed it to Tigers owner Frank Navin with the stipulation that he be allowed two weeks to cover it. In return, Washington wanted the one-and-only Cobb, at once the most prolific and most combative position player in the league, winner of six straight batting crowns and on his way to extending the string to nine (eventually, 12 in 13 years). Navin must have thought Griffith was joking, but for the public record, he never did confirm whether the offer had even been made, let alone considered. If the proposition ever really was dangled in front of Navin, his astonishment might have been minimal compared to that of the members of the Senators' board of directors. The Old Fox was ready for them.

Griffith's plan, according to writer Shirley Povich, had been to sell 100,000 one-dollar tickets to fans who could use them for whatever game they wished. After all, there were always empty seats at League Park. The fans would support this, thought Griffith, since it was obvious that the team was now very good and just a step away, as the saying goes. Newspapermen dismissed the rumors of an imminent deal, reasoning that no player, even Ty Cobb, could possibly be worth $100,000. Besides, they wondered, where would Washington get the money? The whole situation eventually dissipated when nothing happened. Just as well for Clark Griffith, who was likely spared what seemed like an oncoming confrontation with the club's directors.

The 1913 Senators, sans Ty Cobb, were another excellent club nonetheless. They won 90 games, just a two-game aggregate short of the previous year's standing. They were the best draw in the league, what with the Altrock-and-Schaefer comedy team supplementing an alert ballclub. And then there was also one of the top attractions in all of baseball, the lightning-fast Walter Johnson.

The Big Train's roommate, Clyde Milan, followed his 88-stolen-base season with 75 more, enough to comfortably outdistance both Cobb and Eddie Collins for his second consecutive title, the only two of his career. Danny Moeller stole 62 bases, runnerup to Milan in the league, and catcher Eddie Ainsmith got into the act with three steals in one inning and 17 for the season. The club's 287 stolen bases was tops in the A.L. and fell just one short of tying for best in the league's short history. More impressively, the mark of 288 established by the 1910 New York Highlanders remained unbroken for two-thirds of a century before being shattered by the Oakland Athletics in 1976 (341).

Walter Johnson was again superb, so much so that this was probably the greatest of all his seasons. For once, he had gotten off to a fast start, and not just any fast start but the fastest ever. Walter this season held opposing batters to an unbelievable .187 batting average and .217 on-base percentage, both bests for his entire career. His 36–7 record would represent career highs in terms of wins and winning percentage. His league-leading 1.14 ERA would also remain his best. The 11 shutouts Barney recorded led the league and would also endure as the most for him in a season.

Johnson put together three long victory streaks, emerging as the winning pitcher in ten, fourteen (over a period of more than two months), and then seven games in a row at various times. Lanky rookie Joe Boehling, an astute purchase Griffith had made from the Richmond Battleaxes, went 17–7 with a very sound 2.14 ERA. Boehling would win 12 in each of the following two years for the Nats before dropping out of baseball and then returning for a lengthy stint as a minor leaguer. The Senators led the league in strikeouts for the second straight year, and in shutouts. They were also tops in stolen bases for a second straight year.

To emphasize just how dominant 25-year-old Johnson had become, in 1913 he had an astonishing, and heart-breaking, five one-hitters. The St. Louis Browns earned the title of being Johnson's "jinx team," breaking a surreal string of scoreless innings during the course of a 10–5 Washington victory on May 14. In this game, Johnson passed the record of 53 consecutive scoreless frames, previously held by Jack Coombs. The Big Train, who had had his string of 16 consecutive wins interrupted by St. Louis the previous summer, struck out six Brownies in the first three innings, firing nothing but fastballs. Coincidentally, the batter Walter retired in the first inning to set the new mark was Pete Compton, the same Pete Compton who had broken Barney's win streak less than nine months earlier.

Finally, with one out in the fourth, Gus Williams doubled and Del Pratt singled to bring a run home for the Browns, the first Johnson had surrendered in 55⅔ innings, the equivalent of more than six full ballgames. It is interesting to note that the one out Walter got in the fourth inning, oddly enough, is not officially part of the streak. The modern way of calculating is bizarre to say the least — it is such that outs in innings in which the streak is broken don't count. Hence, for years, the record was considered to be 56 innings.

In either case, the accomplishment stood as the major-league record for 55 years, until broken by Don Drysdale in 1968, the so-called "Year of the Pitcher." Drysdale's record of 58⅔ was later topped by another Dodger, Orel Hershiser, who bumped the mark up to 59. While Drysdale no longer owns the National League record, Walter Johnson's record of 55⅔ still stands as the American League standard, and it was the record of which Walter was proudest.

In his next start following the end of the streak, on May 18 at Detroit, the only run off him was a steal of home by Ty Cobb, and the Nats pulled out a 2–1 victory. Sportswriter Grantland Rice, in a poem written in tribute to the Big Train, wrote, "How do they know what Johnson's got? Nobody's seen it yet."

A big man for his time, measuring 6'1" and weighing in at 200 pounds, Walter Johnson, at 25, was a model of endurance, as he led the league in complete games and still put in 11 appearances in relief. He had won ten straight to start off the year, and after winning five of the next 11, embarked on his 14-game win skein. It began on June 27 with a 2–0 three-hitter over the A's. On July 3, Walter provided some justification to those who wanted to dub him an "artful loafer" — one who would only bear down when he had to. The Big Train yielded 15 hits in 15 innings, nevertheless blanking the Red Sox 1–0 and establishing the still-standing major-league record for most hits allowed while pitching a shutout. Later in the month, on the 25th, he struck out 15 while pitching 11⅔ innings of shutout ball in a 15-inning tie with the Browns.

Eight days later, the Big Train had his day. On August 2, 1913, the date marking the sixth anniversary of his big-league debut, he was presented with a silver loving cup and nearly $700 in cash collected from the gath-

ered admirers. President Woodrow Wilson was not only present for Walter Johnson Day, but as excited as anyone there, cheering as loudly as the staunchest of fans.

Johnson's 14-game winning streak this year ended in Boston on August 28, and ironically it coincided with what Walter later said had been his best performance to date. A single in the second inning by Steve Yerkes resulted in Boston's only baserunner through 8⅔ more innings. Twenty-six up and 26 down until Yerkes again singled, sharply to center. The ball went right through the wickets of the usually adept Clyde Milan and allowed Yerkes to take third. Yerkes eventually scored and Johnson, who'd given up three hits, no walks, and had struck out ten in 10⅓, was a 1–0 loser for another of the record 26 times by that score during his career.

Following this particularly tough defeat, according to Clark Griffith, Johnson had tears in his eyes. Griffith would tell this story when he was trying to impress upon someone the kind of man Walter Johnson was. While heartbroken, Johnson responded to a teammate who had mentioned it was a shame to waste such a performance by losing on an error. Johnson reminded the player that Zeb (his nickname for Milan) didn't miss too many out there.

Some other footnotes to this season involved games with the Boston Red Sox. Just a couple of weeks after Johnson's early-season heroics, on Decoration Day, May 30, 1913, outfielder Harry Hooper of the Red Sox (Hall of Fame, 1971), hit home runs to lead off both games of a doubleheader. This had never happened before, and would not occur again in the big leagues for another 80 years.

One of the strangest games in baseball history took place on October 4. With nothing at stake, Clark Griffith, nearing his 44th birthday, decided to pitch an inning. The game was a farce, the players padding their averages and the umpires allowing four outs in one inning. Walter Johnson, who'd pitched his 12th shutout five days earlier for his 36th victory, played center field, but relieved in the ninth and permitted a double and a triple, and two runs.

Those final two runs account for the difference in Walter's final reported earned run average for the season. For more than 70 years, his ERA for 1913 stood at 1.09. When it was discovered that the results of the 1913 travesty had been left out, history was rewritten and Barney's ERA was bumped up to 1.14. As a result, when Bob Gibson came along 55 years later and posted a 1.12 ERA, he passed Johnson's record, unbeknownst to anyone at the time, for the best ever ERA in a single season.

Johnson's 1913 year was one of the best any pitcher ever enjoyed, arguably the most dominant by anyone. For it, he was awarded the Chalmers Award as the Most Valuable Player of the American League. Prior to the second game of the World Series, he was presented with a Chalmers luxury sedan and took the vehicle around Shibe Park for a test ride. The game which followed was one of the great games in the history of the World Series, with Christy Mathewson and Eddie Plank engaged in a scoreless tie through nine innings. The Giants won with three runs in the tenth, but it was the A's who took the Series in five games, their second conquest of the Giants in three years.

The threat of the First World War hovered over and then descended upon the United States in 1914, but the little ballclub remained intact and reached first place for one day, on June 7, only to fall back to third by the end of the year, behind the A's and Red Sox. The Nationals were just about as good as the previous year, but as a team did not lead in any category except the number of strikeouts by the pitching staff.

Walter Johnson, now making $12,000 a year (which represented a $5,000 raise on his expired three-year pact and as much money as Ty Cobb had made in 1913), was still himself, but things did not go his way on many occasions. Barney wound up with a 28–18 record despite a golden 1.72 ERA He pitched more innings, 372, than in any other year of his career. He led the league in wins, games (51), complete games (33), strikeouts (225) and shutouts (9). The baseball player who had put the Washington Senators on the map was by

now widely recognized as the best pitcher baseball had ever known.

Again in 1914, the Senators lacked hitting, particularly from a power standpoint. Deerfoot Milan hit .295, best on the team, but missed 40 games after sustaining a broken jaw on July 17 as a result of an outfield collision with Danny Moeller in Cleveland. Only third baseman Eddie Foster, at .282, excelled offensively. There were an inordinate number of low-scoring losses, making it impossible for Walter Johnson in particular and the team in general to remain successful for any extended period. There were a crushing 11 1–0 losses, three absorbed by Johnson.

The infield was composed of a bunch of crackerjacks, so the pitchers had great support from that standpoint. In this season, infielders Morgan, McBride and Foster led the league in double plays at their respective positions. The other infielder, first baseman Chick Gandil, was also a slick gloveman, but his batting slipped to .259 from .318 in '13. The Senators batted .244 as a unit, below the league average, and barely crawled into third, losing a full nine games off their record of the preceding year.

While gathering war clouds dampened the spirits of baseball partisans all over the country, there was still at least some fun to be had at the old ballpark. Cleveland outfielder Jack Graney had a bull terrier named Larry who served as the team's mascot. Larry was also acrobatic and did tricks to entertain the fans at all big-league venues. This was all well and good until Larry refused to give up the game ball to the umpire, Big Bill Dinneen, at League Park. Back then, fans, let alone dogs, had to return balls batted into the stands. Larry's obstinacy was not appreciated, and he was banned from attending any more Washington games by no less an authority than League president Ban Johnson.

As if the news from overseas wasn't gloomy enough, from Coffeyville, Kansas, came another ominous threat during the following winter. The rebel Federal League, an offshoot of a players' revolt against penurious owners, had formed the previous year. As had been the case when the American League was organized a decade and a half earlier, players now had some bargaining power — they were able to shake off the shackles of baseball's reserve system and accept more money from a competing league for their services.

In the midst of this more advantageous environment, from a players' standpoint, Senators president Ben Minor hit upon the bright idea that Walter Johnson would have to take a cut in pay. His 28–18 did not warrant a $12,000 salary, and Minor resolved to write to his star hurler to address the matter. Clark Griffith nearly had a coronary and begged Minor not to do this. The Old Fox knew that the Chicago Federals were making a bid for Johnson's signature on a contract, and knew that Minor's ultimatum would be the straw to break Barney's back. Minor mailed his letter anyway. Johnson wrote back in mid–November, 1914, stating that he was looking for nothing less than $16,000 a year for three years, plus a $6,000 a year signing bonus.

Ben Minor believed rumors that the Federal League was about to go under, and that Walter Johnson was going to have to play by his rules. Minor wrote back that he could pay $12,500 only, for one, two, or three years. That is what Johnson really didn't like; he would not have anyone dictate terms of his contract. Then the Chicago Federals offered the Big Train $17,500 a year and his $6,000 bonus; Walter signed, on December 3, 1914.

Clark Griffith initially reacted in anger, claiming the Nats were going to sue the star pitcher "to the end of the earth" for breach of contract. The signing, the worst thing that could have happened to the American League, let alone the Washington Baseball Club, had immediate repercussions. League president Ban Johnson arranged the sale of Philadelphia's Eddie Collins to the White Sox so the league could have a marquee player to counter the Big Train in Chicago.

It is ironic how incensed Griffith had been with the great pitcher. He himself had of course once jumped leagues and raided National League clubs at the turn of the century. The time had come for the Old Fox to live up

to his sobriquet. He enlisted the help of Fred Clarke, manager of the Pittsburgh Pirates, who happened to be a friend of his and who lived near Independence, Kansas, not far from where the recalcitrant pitcher lived. This was the same Fred Clarke who had once been too busy to give young Walter Johnson a tryout. On behalf of the Washington owner, Clarke now reminded Johnson, just turned 27, of his obligation to baseball and particularly to the fans of Washington.

There was only one thing to do, according to Clarke, and he soon had Walter in tears. It was arranged that he would meet Clark Griffith summarily. At that meeting, Johnson agreed to sign for Minor's $12,500. Walter got the Old Fox's word that he would do everything in his power to get the best pitcher in baseball a big increase after that. This is what happened, and Johnson was very satisfied the following year to sign a five-year agreement, good through the 1920 season, at $16,000 per.

For the moment, however, there was still for Clark Griffith the problem of paying Walter Johnson the $6,000 bonus he had been promised by the Chicago Federals. To match that, Griff approached Ban Johnson and tried to sell him on the importance of retaining Walter Johnson in the American League. The league's "emergency fund" had grown to nearly a half a million dollars, and surely, Griffith pleaded, this was an emergency. Despite the league's healthy resources, Ban Johnson initially turned him down.

Charles Comiskey was reportedly with Ban Johnson while the league prexy discussed the matter with Griffith over the telephone. Johnson, exasperated, asked to confer with Comiskey. Griffith impressed upon the tightwad owner that if Walter Johnson headed for Chicago, that would be formidable opposition for his White Sox. Then Comiskey agreed to cover the $6,000, and the deal was finally done. Johnson turned the bonus over to his brother Earl, who wanted to buy a garage back home in Coffeyville, Kansas.

The squabble over the contract was humiliating for Walter Johnson, as was related in the April 1915, issue of *Baseball Magazine*.

In the detailed article, the letter Johnson had received from Nationals president Ben Minor was reprinted in its entirety. In the ten pages it took to explain why he had signed with the Federals, Walter admitted he had broken his contract with the Chicago outfit only because he felt that *that* would be less serious than the harm he would do to baseball in Washington, D.C. Damned if he did, and damned if he didn't, he had been humbled more than he ever could have been by actually playing the game he excelled at.

It's worth noting that it was at this time that the nickname Big Train originated. Bud Milliken wrote in the *Washington Post* that the "Big Train" had been prevented by "a storm" from getting to spring training on time, an allegorical reference to the pitcher's absence. Milliken reintroduced the moniker a couple of weeks later, and it got picked up by other writers. Still, it would be nearly a decade before it would be universally adopted.

Clark Griffith himself got a new contract prior to the opening of the 1915 baseball season, although it wasn't for the five-year term he'd been seeking. It was for a reported $10,000 a year for three years, an increase from $7,500 a year. On the ballfield, he was contemplating changes. Chick Gandil was irresponsible, but got his hitting back on the beam with .291. But Griffith had been patient long enough with Howard Shanks and Danny Moeller in the outfield. On a scouting trip to Buffalo in search of some help, Griff made a discovery that would instead bolster the infield for a long time to come. He was at first only interested in Charlie Jamieson, an outfielder who in fact turned out to be a blue-chipper, except not before the Senators let him get away on waivers in 1917.

The Buffalo owner, David Harum, was talked not only into giving up Jamieson, but throwing in a first baseman named Joe Judge for an extra $500. Griffith thought Judge could hit, and that he was obviously a great fielder—a natural ballplayer. A son of Irish immigrants and raised in one of the roughest sections of New York City, Judge would be a regular in the Washington lineup for 15 years.

Nineteen fifteen was quite a remarkable year for players breaking into the major leagues — most noteworthy were Rogers Hornsby, George Sisler, Joe Judge, and another Washington player who would become another piece of a championship puzzle for the Nationals.

An industrious businessman, Clark Griffith had cultivated friendships with baseball men everywhere, and he kept an eye on developing minor-leaguers. He formed allegiances with owners, and in the spring of 1915, he loaned some money to the Petersburg club of the Virginia League. That loop folded, and in lieu of cash, Griffith was persuaded to take a promising young pitcher instead. The pitcher, Edgar Charles (Sam) Rice, would be converted into an outfielder without much power, but who could place the ball and who had the speed and instinct to steal bases and cover an enormous amount of real estate. Sam Rice would be good enough to make the Hall of Fame. He and Joe Judge would be teammates for 18 years, a record which would stand until broken in 1996 by Alan Trammell and Lou Whitaker of the Detroit Tigers.

Sam Rice was already 25½ years old by the time he first appeared in a game for the Nats on August 7, 1915. (He relieved in a 6–2 loss to Chicago, one of his nine appearances before the idea of his pitching was abandoned the following year. The rightfielder behind him in his debut was Walter Johnson, subbing for the injured Danny Moeller.) The reason for Rice's late start in baseball remained a secret for 70 years. The truth was that he had shown up for a tryout three years earlier at Galesburg, Illinois, leaving a wife and two children behind in Indiana. A number of days later, while Rice's wife and children were visiting his parents in Morocco, Indiana, a tornado struck their farm. His wife, children, parents, and sisters were all killed.

Rice drifted for about a year after that, and then joined the navy. He became a star pitcher and, after seeing actual combat in Mexico, returned to pitch for Petersburg of the Virginia League during furloughs. He did so well that Clark Griffith thought it fit to accept his contract from the Petersburg owner as repayment of the old debt. Edgar Rice got a new name right then. Clark Griffith forgot Rice's given name and told a newspaper reporter that he thought it was Sam, and the name stuck.

In 1915, the Senators slipped down another notch in the standings, finishing fourth despite a slightly improved record of 85–68. Walter Johnson again led the league in a host of pitching categories and logged a 27–13 slate on his way to recording ten straight seasons with 20 or more wins. He improved his ERA to 1.55, just short of Joe Wood's league-leading 1.49. As it had been in 1912, the Senators' pitching staff was the A.L.'s best, recording a 2.31 ERA in a league which averaged 2.94. This was still the era of slap hitting, and the New York Yankees led the league with a grand total of 31 home runs.

Nineteen fifteen was also the year Ty Cobb reclaimed the stolen-base title with his career best 96, which stood as the majors' record until broken 47 years later by Maury Wills. The Senators did distinguish themselves on the basepaths in the July 19 game. They stole eight bases in one inning, the first, against Detroit, with Steve O'Neill the unfortunate catcher involved. Moeller, Milan, McBride, and Eddie Ainsmith, a fast runner for a catcher, all swiped two each. Ainsmith by this time caught only Walter Johnson — he contended his hands needed several days to recover from the beating they took when Barney pitched.

Of note in 1915 was the August 22 game at Detroit, an 8–1 win, when the Nationals managed to score without recording a single official at-bat in the inning, the only time this has been done in major-league history. Following walks to Chick Gandil and Merito Acosta, Rip Williams moved the baserunners ahead with a sacrifice bunt. George McBride hit a sac fly to score Gandil, and Acosta was then picked off second base.

The presence of Joe Judge precipitated the departure of Chick Gandil, who was sold to the Indians in February 1916. Later in the season, Danny Moeller and pitcher Joe Boehling were traded to the Indians for outfielder Elmer Smith and third baseman Joe Leonard, neither of whom was to make a big splash in Washington. Smith would be sold back to the Indians less than a year later and would enjoy a fine 10-year career.

Walter Johnson beat the Yankees 3–2 in 11 innings on Opening Day, April 12, the third opening-day win over the Yankees for Johnson. (The Yanks would beat the jinx two years later with a 6–3 decision at National Park.) After a good start, the Senators tailed off and finished 76–77, good enough for only seventh place in a very tight field, 14½ games behind the champions, the Red Sox.

Clark Griffith's own standpat stance was starting to impact on his team's performance. This was not as serious as what was happening in Philadelphia, however, where Connie Mack, after winning the World Championship in 1913 and reaching the World Series again in 1914, had sold off his stars. In '16, the A's sank to an incredible 54½ games behind the pennant-winning Red Sox; they won just 36 games and lost a whopping 117.

Boston had a southpaw who was now providing worthy opposition to Walter Johnson as the league's best pitcher. While Johnson, with his easy whiplike sidearmer, remained overpowering in 1916 — leading in wins (25), strikeouts, complete games and innings pitched — he also lost 20 games for the second time in his career. Thirteen of those defeats were by a single run, and four were of the disheartening 1–0 variety. Meanwhile, the big raw youngster of the Red Sox, George Herman "Babe" Ruth, led the American League in earned run average, starts, and shutouts (nine, still the single-season league record for a lefthander).

Ruth would also establish a dominance over the Big Train when the two were the pitchers of record. Ruth would win the first six matchups, including a 13-inning barnburner. Within a few short years, however, American League batters would be rejoicing when Ruth would be converted into the greatest offensive phenomenon ever to grace a baseball diamond.

The Senators' offense took another step backward in 1916, putting the Nats in that regard pretty much on a par with the pathetic A's at the bottom of the league. In a case not unlike Ruth's, the Nats were taking notice of the hitting skills of pitcher Sam Rice. Washington third baseman Eddie Foster, for one, was convinced that Rice, with his flat stroke, should give hitting a try. Rice himself became convinced he should when pitcher George "Hooks" Dauss of the Tigers, a notoriously weak hitter, banged a game-winning triple off him.

Given some time in the outfield, Sam Rice hit .299 in nearly 200 at-bats and was on his way to his Hall of Fame induction in 1963. A model of consistency over 19 years with the Senators, Rice would never hit below .294. (He played one final year with the Indians in 1934 and hit .293 at age 44.) He was the classic contact-type hitter who practically never struck out; he did so only 275 times in 20 years. He had no power but hustled enough to hit a good number of doubles and triples; his career high in homers was six, and his lifetime total 34. Of Sam Rice's 33 round-trippers as a Senator, not one in 19 years was hit over the fence at home, testimony to National Park's disheartening dimensions.

Attendance was down in Washington in 1917, where wartime seems to have had a particularly sobering effect. The Senators lost over $40,000 and could not have stayed afloat without the support of the men who sat on the board of directors. The franchise continued to operate because of loans the directors were able to personally underwrite. On the field, things were nearly as grim. The club climbed to fifth in 1917, but actually dropped two games off the previous year's pace.

Sam Rice led the offense, cracking the .300 mark during his first full season as a hitter and finishing at .302. George McBride, the regular shortstop since 1908, was replaced adequately by Howard Shanks, an outfielder with the Senators since 1912. Shanks' substitute in the outfield was Mike Menosky, from a place called Glen Campbell, Pa., who hit .258. Joe Judge improved from a .220 hitter

as a rookie to .285 in his sophomore year at age 23, but in July he broke his leg as a result of a sliding mishap.

Clyde Milan managed to improve to .294 after an off year in '16, and was joined by his brother Horace, who had been brought up for a second cup of coffee. Between the '15 and '17 seasons, Horace Milan got 32 hits in an even 100 at-bats, for a cool .320 career average frozen forever in time.

An interesting aside to the 1917 season, especially in light of the inevitable emancipation of baseball players still more than a half-century away, were the efforts of Senators catcher John Henry. Henry had become involved in the Base Ball Players' Fraternity, and tried to convince his reticent teammates to join in a united front which would seek to obtain better wages and playing conditions. League president Ban Johnson promised to crush Henry and all others of his ilk.

Henry, in no way intimidated, proclaimed that Ban Johnson had no power to drive him out of the American League, and that the prexy was obviously trying to make him the "goat" in the midst of an embarrassing situation. If the league president insisted on picking on him because he was a friendly fellow, well-liked by teammates and owners alike, that was okay with Henry. Ban Johnson, Henry declared, was "crazy for power." The rebellion died down, however. After being forced to accept a $1,200 cut on his salary of $4,600, Henry, a .190 hitter in '17, was unceremoniously sold right out of the league to the Boston Braves, where his career ended after just 102 more at-bats.

For a change, the Washington team had some arms. Clark Griffith thought he had died and gone to heaven. According to longtime coach Al Schacht, Griff's system of working his pitchers would keep everyone on edge right up until warm-up time, about 20 minutes before a game began. Nobody knew for sure until then who would be pitching. His choice finally made, Griff would call the pitcher's name and toss him the ball. In 1917, he had more choices than in years previous.

For the first time since the birth of the

Federal League and the corresponding departures of Long Tom Hughes and Bob Groom, Walter Johnson had the support of a group which could log some innings. Four starters besides Johnson pitched 205 or more innings: "Grunting Jim" Shaw, so named because his grunts could be heard up in the stands when he pitched, Bert Gallia, Doc Ayers, and George Dumont. A fifth, Harry Harper, went 11–12 with a 3.01 ERA. Dumont was particularly unlucky, with his better than average 2.55 ERA earning him nothing better than a 5–14 record.

Johnson was again the mainstay, ringing up a 23–16 mark and a 2.30 ERA. His fastball was still good enough for him to lead the league in strikeouts, and he had eight shutouts. His best game of the season came on August 6, four days following his tenth anniversary with the Nats. The 1–0 11-inning victory at the expense of Eddie Plank and the St. Louis Browns turned out to be the last game of Plank's illustrious 17-year career. He retired a week later, attributing his demise to stomach problems. In reality, the future Hall of Famer, who'd won 20 or more seven times for strong Philadelphia A's teams and 21 two years earlier in the Federal League, had had enough of playing for a team as lousy as the St. Louis Browns.

The league's top pitcher in 1917 was Eddie Cicotte of the White Sox, who would be among the banned Black Sox three years later. Cicotte, a tricky righthander with phenomenal control, led the league with 28 wins and a 1.53 ERA. Over at Boston, 22-year-old Babe Ruth won 24. Ruth played a bit part in the Senators' best-remembered game of 1917. On June 23, the young Babe became enraged when umpire Brick Owens awarded ball four to Washington's lead-off batter, Ray Morgan. Ruth threatened to punch Owens if the umpire ran him out, so Owens promptly did exactly that. Ruth cocked his fist but thought better of taking his threat any further — Brick

Owens had a reputation of being able to handle himself. Into the fray came Ernie Shore, a four-year veteran like Ruth who would later be a teammate of the Babe's during his heyday with the Yankees. Ray Morgan was quickly erased when he tried to steal second base. Ernie Shore then proceeded to pitch a perfect game, retiring 26 Senators in a row.*

Crippling to baseball at this time was the reality of war and the government's refusal to yield to Ban Johnson's pleas for draft deferments for baseball players. On May 23, 1918, baseball was shocked to learn that Secretary of War Newton D. Baker's "Work or Fight" order meant that all able-bodied men of draft age either had to enlist or otherwise engage in work considered essential for the war effort. Washington catcher Eddie Ainsmith, granted a deferment earlier, was now ordered to sign up, and his became the test case on which the fate of the game depended. On July 19, War Secretary Baker announced that baseball was not adjudged to be an essential war activity.

League president Ban Johnson shocked everyone by announcing that the season would end, and suddenly, in just two days. By now, the owners had had enough, and Clark Griffith stepped into the breach. Griffith was friendly with the Secretary of War. Even though the war was dragging on, Griffith was able to convince Newton Baker to allow baseball players, who were in shape anyway, to do military drills prior to games, with baseball bats instead of weapons no less. In Washington, young Assistant Navy Secretary Franklin D. Roosevelt led some of these drills.

Griffith obtained assent from War Secretary Baker for baseball to continue until Labor Day, with an extra two weeks allotted for the World Series. No doubt riding a patriotic wave, Griff reciprocated by sponsoring a fund-raising drive which netted $100,000 to buy baseball equipment for servicemen in Europe. The first supply of gear reportedly ended up

---

*This went into the books as a no-hitter, after some hedging by league president Ban Johnson. Later, it was removed from the list of genuine perfect games, not to mention no-hitters, because Shore had not retired the requisite 27 batters for nine full innings of work.

at the bottom of the Atlantic, sunk by a German U-boat.

Sam Rice, Mike Menosky, veteran Doc Lavan, and catcher Val Picinich were unable to avoid enlistment before the end of the 1918 season, which saw the Senators pull up third after what was for them a 128-game schedule. Rice, despite previous service in the navy, was drafted into the army and played in only seven games while on furloughs. Clyde Milan hit .290, and another outfielder, old-timer "Wildfire" Frank Schulte, who had seen even better days with the Cubs, chimed in with .288.

Doc Lavan, a one-year player for the Senators, hit .278, but led all A.L. shortstops in errors with 57. He had come to the Nats after a fall from grace at St. Louis, where Browns owner Phil Ball had accused him and second baseman Del Pratt of intentionally playing less than their best in a game against Chicago. Lavan and Pratt sued Ball, seeking $50,000 for slander. Clark Griffith was instrumental in getting the matter settled out of court, and then purchased Lavan's contract. By January 1919, however, Lavan, who'd committed an abominable 75 errors for the Browns in 1915, was sold by Griffith and once again landed in St. Louis, but this time with the Cardinals, where he would continue his error-prone ways, twice leading National League shortstops in miscues.

Walter Johnson shaved over a run a game off his earned run average, and with a minuscule 1.27 reclaimed the ERA title he had not won since 1913. At 23–13, he was tops in wins in the big leagues for 1918 and led the majors in strikeouts with 162, his lowest number among the eight league-leading totals he'd had to date. Incredibly, he finished every single game he was in: 29 starts and ten relief appearances. Always a good hitter, he was getting even better, batting .267 in 150 official at-bats and playing four games in the outfield, which he'd also done three years earlier.

On May 7, 1918, Babe Ruth homered off Walter Johnson at League Park, the first of his ten career dingers off the great one, although Barney prevailed in this game, 7–2. The day

before, Ruth had appeared in the lineup for the first time at a position other than pitcher or pinch hitter, in a game at New York. He had hit a home run in that game, and Yankees owner Jacob Ruppert had wanted to buy Ruth's contract from the Red Sox right then and there.

On May 9, Walter Johnson picked up a win by pitching the tenth inning, and Ruth, the starter that day who'd gone all the way for Boston, was the loser. It was the last official matchup between the two, as Ruth was soon going to be an everyday player exclusively. He hit his last homer of the year against the Senators on September 27, although the Nats swept a doubleheader from the Yankees that day. Almost exactly nine years hence, the Babe would make even bigger headlines versus the Washington Senators.

Walter Johnson's durability was being put to the ultimate test in 1918. Two days after defeating Ruth, he shut out Jim Bagby and the Indians (the league's best-hitting team in 1918) by a 1–0 score. In his next start on May 15, he pitched the longest shutout in history. It took 18 innings before the Nats finally scored a run courtesy of a wild pitch by Claude "Lefty" Williams, another who would become implicated in the Black Sox scandal. Johnson gave up ten hits and a walk and fanned nine.

There were an extraordinary number of long games for Walter as the season wore on. While teams would play 17 percent fewer games in '18, the Big Train pitched exactly three fewer innings (325) than he did the previous year. On July 25 at St. Louis, he took another 1–0 decision, this one slightly shorter than the one in mid–May, in 15 innings.

Ten days later, on August 4, the Big Train pitched his second-longest game of the season, not to mention ever, going 17⅓ innings only to lose 7–6 in a bizarre contest on a scorchingly hot day in Detroit. He faced a career-high 64 batters, giving up 16 hits and eight walks. Eleven innings intervened between the sixth and seventh Detroit runs, both driven in by Ty Cobb. Of Johnson's 88 career extra-inning decisions, an astonishing 15 took place in this season. Barney completed nine of them, including five which went 13 innings or longer.

Walter Johnson was the one bright spot for the club early in the season, and the Nationals were struggling to stay out of seventh place as late as June. Following a two-week slump in July, the club was hot from then on and finished within four games of the Red Sox and first place, the best showing for the Washington franchise to this point.

Nineteen nineteen was not so successful. Despite some good elements — solid bat production from the outfielders, and strong pitching performances from Johnson and Grunting Jim Shaw — the Senators sank to seventh, their lowest standing in ten years. Johnson, who began the season with a 1–0 13-inning whitewashing of the A's, his record fifth opening-day shutout, won 20 for the tenth straight year. It was an even 20, against 14 defeats. His dwarflike 1.49 ERA led the majors for the second year in a row, and is particularly remarkable considering 1919 was a year of much-increased hitting, with the league ERA shooting up nearly half a run per game to 3.21. Five of Barney's seven shutouts were by 1–0 scores, and he led the league in strikeouts for the eighth year in a row. On July 24, at Washington against the A's, he had his best inning ever, striking out the side on nine pitches.

In another of the many memorable games of his career, Johnson hooked up with spitballer Jack Quinn on May 11, the first ever legal Sunday baseball game in New York. Walter labored for 12 scoreless innings, retiring 28 consecutive batters and allowing only two hits, pitching to just one batter over the minimum. The game was called off prematurely at 6 P.M., due to New York owner Jacob Ruppert's misinterpretation of the new Sunday law, with the score still 0–0.

Of note is that in this particular game, rookie George Halas was fanned twice by the Big Train. Halas, later to become owner and longtime coach of the Chicago Bears football team, went 0–for–5 in this game, and 2–for–22 for his entire big-league career. These 12-inning shutouts on the part of both Johnson and

Jack Quinn were not, however, the biggest story in baseball on May 11, 1919. Over in the other league, Hod Eller of the Cincinnati Reds spun a no-hitter against the St. Louis Cardinals.

Walter Johnson's best years had coincided with the decade now ending. He had led the league in strikeouts nine times during the period, and in shutouts and complete games six times. His 265 wins during the decade represented 35 percent of Washington's victories. Now 32, Johnson was supplanted as staff workhorse by Jim Shaw, who logged more innings and appearances than any pitcher in the league. For all of his superior work, though, Shaw finished with a 16–17 slate. While the Washington pitching staff was third-best in the league, the offense lacked punch and Clark Griffith was determined to get some. Clyde Milan and Eddie Foster had slowed down. In finishing seventh, the Senators together hit fewer home runs (24) than Boston's young Babe Ruth (29).

In the boardroom, Clark Griffith found out that some of the directors had ideas that were quite different from his own in terms of what steps needed to be taken to improve the ballclub. With the dismal seventh-place showing, there were now calls for the Old Fox's hide. But this baseball team had become too important to Griffith. It occurred to him that if he could somehow gain control of the team, then, quite naturally, he couldn't be fired.

Connie Mack had once introduced Griff to William Richardson, a wealthy grain exporter from Philadelphia. With backing Griffith was able to obtain from Richardson, he walked into the Metropolitan National Bank and got the loan for $87,000 that allowed him and Richardson to purchase about 85 percent of the team. They paid $15 a share, a terrific bargain as it would turn out. Taking over as majority owner and president, Griffith was granted the right to speak for Richardson's holdings as if they were his own. To signal his new status as owner, president, and manager of the Washington Senators, League Park, or National Park, was renamed Griffith

Stadium and it was at this time that the stands stretching from the infield to the foul poles were made into double-deckers.

Clark Griffith was finally in a position to bring his little ballclub to unprecedented heights during the course of the free-wheeling decade that lay ahead.

1920–1929:
THE TRIP TO THE TOP

Very early in 1920, the baseball world was rife with rumors that eight members of the Chicago White Sox, acclaimed by most pundits as the majors' best team, were possibly guilty of having thrown the 1919 World Series in what would become known as the "Black Sox Scandal." Among the players believed involved were Joe Jackson, one of baseball's premier hitters, as well as star infielders Buck Weaver and Swede Risberg, and veteran pitchers Ed Cicotte and Claude "Lefty" Williams. Most of these players were bound by a common repugnance of their team's owner, and for a couple of their prominent teammates — second baseman Eddie Collins (who made twice as much money as Joe Jackson and who wasn't particularly supportive of his teammates' pleas for better salaries), and combative catcher Ray Schalk, a Collins supporter.

The players of this era were being paid a menial wage in comparison with the revenues they were generating for the owners of major-league clubs. Charles Comiskey's White Sox were a case in point. Comiskey would blatantly cheat his players out of their money — he sidelined Cicotte for a few games so that his ace would have no chance of getting a bonus for reaching 30 wins. Commie treated his friends in the press with lavish spreads of food and drink, but his players were given flat wine to celebrate the winning of the 1919 pennant. The players lashed back.

Chick Gandil, the rookie sensation of the upstart 1912 Washington Senators, who'd come to Chicago by way of Cleveland, was the contact man for the players. Through Gandil's connections with a former failed Washington pitcher named Sleepy Bill Burns (6–11 with the Senators in '08), the players, some no doubt more guilty than others, decided to throw some games, and indeed the whole Series, in return for financial compensation. The cash was to have been supplied by runners associated with New York crime kingpin Arnold Rothstein.

Following a bizarre two weeks of testimony in the courts, the players were found not guilty on August 2, 1921, largely because they had been brought to trial in order to determine whether they had conspired to defraud baseball and the White Sox. Since profits were way up in 1920, the game had hardly suffered, the jury reasoned. The damage to baseball's credibility, however, had been done.

The National Commission, the triumvirate which included the two league presidents and which was dominated by Ban Johnson, had ruled the majors from 1903 to 1920. It had failed to eradicate gambling from the game, however, and to achieve that goal several clubs had called for a supervisory office. The only man for the job of commissioner would be Kenesaw Mountain Landis, a judge who had won the owners' gratitude back when the Federal League was in operation, in competition with the major leagues, in 1914 and '15.

When the Federal League had brought an anti-trust suit before Judge Landis, he had stalled for so long that eventually the lawsuit became a moot point. The Federals went under, and Landis never had to make a ruling. The owners had, in no small part due to Landis's dawdling, been able to retain their monopoly status. They never considered anyone else for the commissioner's post, even though Landis accepted the appointment only under the strict condition that he be granted complete autocracy.

Thus it would be until Landis's death in 1944: he ruled with an iron hand, with no public criticism of his decisions by anyone affiliated with the big leagues permitted or tolerated. He banned 15 players from the game, and at one particular time had a grand total of 53 professional ballplayers on his ineligible list. Of the eight Black Sox banned by him, Buck Weaver may have been the least guilty. Weaver indeed continued to declare his innocence for the rest of his life. He had batted .324 in the 1919 World Series and had made sensational plays. The great Joe Jackson, an illiterate man who many believe was aware of what was going on but not an actual participant in the scheme, had batted .375 in that World Series.

Landis held firm and rejected the ballplayers' entreaties for reinstatement, and most of them did apply. The majority of the players had admitted during their trial to collusion with gamblers, and this is what Landis contended could not be tolerated. Yet, a few years later, when evidence mounted against two superstars, Ty Cobb and Tris Speaker, he dismissed a case against them that was much more solid than the one against the disgraced Black Sox players.

Somewhat lost in the midst of the unfolding Black Sox saga was the fact that on January 5, 1920, George Herman Ruth was sold to the New York Yankees by the Boston Red Sox. A brutish man-child, Ruth had slugged an astounding 29 homers in '19. (In 1918, he had tied for the major-league lead with only 11 home runs.) Red Sox owner Harry Frazee, more interested in promoting broadway plays than in the fortunes of his baseball team, let Ruth go for $100,000 and a $300,000 loan to finance more of his productions. This was twice the highest price previously paid for a player. Four years earlier, when Frazee had first taken over the Red Sox, his ballclub was a much higher priority, and he had made public a bid of $60,000 for the services of one Walter Johnson.

It would be Babe Ruth, and not Commissioner Landis, who would be the true savior of baseball. Surely, there was nothing phony about Ruth's blasts. The Babe would change the game. He'd been a pitcher in the big leagues for six years when the Yanks made the decision that he was just too good a hitter to be wasting any time on the bench. The beneficiary of a juiced-up baseball, Ruth pounded 54 homers in a mere 458 official at-bats. His style set the tone for the next two decades. Teams would come to rely more and more on the home run as a weapon, reducing the emphasis on scratching out runs with the 'savvy' game of walks, bunts, the hit-and-run, and the stolen base.

However, it was neither the Yankees nor the incumbent White Sox (whose best players had yet to be barred from the game) who came out on top in the American League in 1920. The Cleveland Indians, spearheaded by playing manager Tris Speaker (.388) and a lineup which included only one hitter who averaged below .292, finished two games ahead of Chicago and three in front of the Yankees. The Indians accomplished this despite losing their shortstop as a result of the only fatality in history associated with the playing of the game at the highest level.

During a game against the Yankees, the Indians' Ray Chapman was struck on the head by a ball thrown by Carl Mays, a pitcher known to have a mean streak. He died in hospital 12 hours later. It is significant that Mays threw with a submarine type of delivery which froze Chapman. The man behind the plate for the Yankees that day was a young Muddy

Ruel, who would become a member of the Senators for 1923. Ruel felt his pitcher was blameless, and that Chapman had simply lost sight of the ball. He would be forever haunted, though, by the sight of Chapman struggling to get back up on his feet. The Indians replaced their very capable shortstop, who was hitting .303 at the time of his death, with a first-year professional from the minor leagues who went on to play his way into the Hall of Fame — Joe Sewell.

The Washington Nats, in the middle of the pack offensively, featured the worst pitching staff in the league and finished sixth in 1920, 29 games behind the Indians. Clark Griffith's skills in recognizing talent were beginning to show results all the same. The previous year, Griff had nearly signed Pic Traynor, a future Hall of Famer then at third base for the Pirates. The management of the Portsmouth club of the Virginia League had apparently doubled the price on Traynor despite an earlier agreement.

In the fall of 1919, Griffith was more fortunate. Both he and Joe Engel went to Buffalo to scout an infielder who played for a shipyard team in Baltimore and who had been highly recommended to them by Joe Judge. In the doubleheader they witnessed, this player, Stanley "Bucky" Harris, had an outstanding day at the plate, and did so with two fingers taped together because one was broken — Harris wasn't going to miss a chance to show what he could do. Needless to say, Bucky Harris was signed, and as a rookie in the big leagues in 1920 he hit an even .300 and fielded reliably.

There is no telling what 32-year-old Walter Johnson might have accomplished in 1920 had he been at the top of his game. The Senators provided plenty of runs, but the Big Train responded with the worst campaign of his career. Afflicted with a sore arm after more than two weeks of rail travel while training in the South, he missed a season-opening assignment for the first time since 1911. He would wind up a disappointing 8–10. On May 14, he did register the 300th win of his career, a 9–8 decision over the Tigers, but kept alternating

good performances with bad throughout the season. Not one Washington starter had better than a .500 record — Tom Zachary logged the most innings and charted the best mark on the staff, 15–16. A Quaker who farmed tobacco in his native North Carolina, Zachary's smooth delivery would bring 15 or more wins to the Nats in three of the next four years.

In apparent defiance of all logic, it was during this troubled season that Walter Johnson threw the only no-hitter of his entire career. It was July 1, at Fenway Park in Boston, on his son Walter, Jr.'s fifth birthday. Johnson, Sr., had in fact been detained that day because the young lad was feeling ill. The 13-year vet struck out ten and only five balls were hit beyond the infield. There were no walks, but it was not a perfect game. In the seventh, Bucky Harris missed what was by all accounts a soft grounder off the bat of future Hall of Famer Harry Hooper, who led off the inning for the Red Sox. Had that not happened, Johnson would have pitched the third perfect game in modern baseball history (since 1901) up to that time. The others had been authored by Cy Young, in 1904, and Addie Joss, in 1908.

The Big Train's best game of the year until then had been his previous start, a three-hit, no-walk masterpiece in a 7–0 pasting of the Athletics, who thereby lost their 18th straight game. Johnson required only 72 pitches, and it was all over in just one hour and 18 minutes — the most efficient game of his career. The win was the seventh in a row for the Nats and moved them past the Red Sox and into fourth place. But following the no-hitter in his next start, there were no more heroics in store for Walter, who was plagued by a sore arm for the rest of the year.

In a way, Bucky Harris was heroic in Johnson's no-hit game as well, as it was he who drove in the game's only run, and Joe Judge saved the day in the ninth when, after Johnson had struck out two pinch hitters, the dangerous Hooper pulled a liner that Judge leaped for and caught cleanly off the ground. In no position to get to first in time to outrace Hooper, Judge had to relay to Johnson. The Big Train came in all right, and caught Judge's relay to nip Hooper. For extra theatrics, Johnson caught the ball with his bare hand.

Walter's arm hurt so much after this game that he was not able to make his next start, the second game of a doubleheader, which was to follow a morning game against the Yankees at Griffith Stadium. Clark Griffith had advertised that Walter would be pitching, and he was hard up for someone to put out there as an emergency replacement. Asking for conscripts, he chose among the volunteers a grass-green rookie named Al Schacht. A New Yorker, Schacht would later write that he had sent Clark Griffith several letters in the past, in the manner effectively employed by Ty Cobb about 15 years earlier. Schacht, who had simply signed the letters, "A. Fan," had begged Griff to scout a young phenom named Al Schacht.

We wouldn't be telling this story, naturally, if Schacht hadn't beaten the league's best offensive team that day. Babe Ruth, who would lead the league with his unbelievable total of 54 home runs, was the first to get a hit off Schacht — in the fourth inning. Schacht came away with a seven-hitter and a 9–3 win, and needless to say, his pitching skills and penmanship earned him a tidy contract from Griffith for 1921. In this way began a playing career cut short by a sore arm, but followed by his very long run as a baseball comedian.

Widely recognized as the "Clown Prince of Baseball," Schacht became a full-time baseball comic in 1921, teaming up with Nick Altrock, coach and resident clown. The two revived some of the routines Altrock had first performed with Germany Schaefer. Eventually, Schacht would strike out on his own, touring major- and minor-league ballparks across America. His act, part pantomime and part anecdotes, got him bookings at 25 World Series and 18 All-Star games. During World War II, he would tour Europe, Africa and the Pacific theater with the USO.

There was nothing comical, however, about the Washington Senators' future prospects. With the sure-handed Joe Judge and Bucky Harris, and the brilliant centerfielder Sam Rice now in place as pillars he could build

on, Clark Griffith already had an imposing offensive team in 1920. Judge hit .333. While he would record a .298 average for his career, he excelled even more as a fielder. Small physically at 5'8" and about 155 pounds, the nonetheless graceful first baseman, who excelled at the 3–6–3 double play, led or tied the league in fielding at the first base position six times over his career (still an American League record).

When he retired, Joe Judge held the lifetime fielding average record for first basemen (.993) for more than 30 years. As a hitter, he was hardly a slouch, crashing the .300 barrier in nine full seasons. The 30-year-old Rice and the veteran Clyde Milan were also outstanding contributors in 1920, batting .338 and .332 respectively. Rice was following in Milan's footsteps, leading the league with 63 stolen bases. The Senators were tops by far in that department.

Clark Griffith's 34 years in a major-league baseball uniform came to an end after the 1920 season. The administrative workload during his one year as president and manager, as it related to scouting, making player deals, and overseeing the club's financial affairs, proved to be too much. To lessen the burden, Griff chose a trusted friend as on-field manager, a strategy he would in future resort to again and again. The 51-year-old turned to longtime shortstop George McBride, his field captain of six years, to whom he had often delegated authority when he'd been away on scouting trips. Griffith used to tell his players that if McBride saw fit to fine anyone while he was away, it would go double when he would get back.

McBride had an improving squad on his hands, and was able to guide the Nats to an 11½-game improvement in the standings. They finished fourth, only a half game behind the Browns, but a full 18 games back of the Yankees. Babe Ruth arguably had the best season of his entire career in 1921, and that's saying something. Ruth had the kind of season only he has ever had in baseball history: 59 home runs, 171 RBIs, a .378 batting average, and an awesome .846 slugging percentage in

540 at-bats. It would remain his career best (Babe also had 540 at-bats in 1927, when he produced 60 homers, 164 ribbies, a .356 average, and slugged at .772.)

By contrast, the Senators in 1921 hit only 42 homers as a team. In fact, the Babe on his own hit more homers than any entire team except the Browns and the last-place A's. On May 7 of this season, Ruth slammed a drive toward center field off Walter Johnson; it was believed to be the longest ever in Washington up to that point.

The Nats' pitching staff did rebound — an indication that the previous season had been something of an aberration. Walter Johnson, recovered from the bout with his sore arm, took on double the workload and won 17 games. Though visibly slowed, he still led the league in strikeouts, dismissing batters back to the bench on as regular a basis as in '18 and '19, when he had been the league's top pitcher. On September 5 of this season, Johnson fanned seven Yankees, thereby breaking Cy Young's standing record of 2,796 (a figure later adjusted slightly upward at 2,812, and then back down to an even 2,800).

Clark Griffith was taking more measures toward building a championship-class ballclub out of his Senators. He had solid offense and defense particularly at first base with Joe Judge, at second with Bucky Harris, and in right field, where Sam Rice had taken over. The pitching was probably as good as the Nats had ever had, with Tom Zachary and George Mogridge complementing Walter Johnson as starters. Mogridge was a tall, friendly lefty whose past history had not foretold the consistency he would bring to Washington's pitching staff. Obtained from the Yankees in a deal involving outfielder Braggo Roth, who'd hit .291 in his one year with the Nationals, Mogridge would average 16 wins a season over the next four years.

On the lookout for the left-handed slugger the Senators sorely needed, Griffith learned that the Columbia club of the Sally (South Atlantic) League was willing to part with a hard-hitting 20-year-old outfielder who just happened to hit lefty. Griffith sent Joe Engel to scout the outfielder, but nothing came of it.

While playing golf in nearby Baltimore about a month later, Griffith learned from a Baltimore Oriole stockholder that Orioles owner Jack Dunn, who had been the man who signed Babe Ruth to his first professional contract, was about to pay $5,500 for a Sally League outfielder. Griffith knew Dunn would not part with such a huge sum easily so, as the Old Fox enjoyed retelling later on, he remarked to his Baltimore golf partner at the time that "whatsisname" sure seemed to be the answer for Jack Dunn's lineup. Griffith snapped his fingers, feigning frustration at being unable to recall the player's name. He got the name — Leon Goslin, the same player Joe Engel had scouted earlier.

Engel was on the next train to South Carolina to better Jack Dunn's offer. Goslin was reportedly hit on the head by a fly ball in the one game Engel witnessed, but he also smacked three homers. For Goslin, this would pretty well set the trend for a primarily good-hit-no-field type of career. Nicknamed "Goose" (not so much because of his name as for his frantic arm waving whenever he chased a fly ball), Goslin signed Engel's contract and would become the franchise's greatest slugger.

Here was a line-drive hitter with enough power to frequently drive the ball for home runs, as well as for numerous doubles and triples. Goslin would carve himself a niche in the Baseball Hall of Fame with a .316 career batting average and .500 slugging percentage. He would drive in 100 or more runs 11 times. It would be understating the point to say that the reported $6,000 purchase price for Goose Goslin was money well spent by Clark Griffith. This was quite a notable deal, especially in light of the fact that with Griffith, when there was money involved in a transaction — and there often was — it was usually going into his pocket. The Old Fox described his situation best, and he said it frequently: he never knew what morning the sheriff was going to knock on his door and tell him *he* was taking over.

Later on in the 1921 season, with Blackie

O'Rourke not hitting or fielding adequately, the eagle-eyed scout Engel went on a hunt for a shortstop. In Peoria, Illinois, he was impressed with the talents of a young 20-year-old named Ossie Bluege. But Bluege had been noticed before, and the Philadelphia Athletics had decided not to sign him after he had injured his knee while still in negotiations with them. Joe Engel's approach was a novel one — he challenged Bluege to a race. When Bluege beat him handily, the deal was closed the very same night. Bluege, a serious type and an outstanding gloveman, would last 18 years in a Washington Senators uniform.

George McBride, who himself had worn Washington colors for 13 years as a player, didn't make it through a full year as manager. He was struck in the face by a thrown ball while hitting grounders to his infielders. One side of his face remained paralyzed, and he suffered a nervous breakdown. He retired at the end of the season, but would eventually return as a coach with the Tigers under Ty Cobb. McBride would also live to the ripe old age of 92.

After McBride's terrible accident in August, 34-year-old Clyde Milan, who batted .288 in 112 games in his player's role, took over. Milan, by now in his 15th year with Washington, guided the club to its 80–73 finish. The Nats had four .300 hitters in '21— Sam Rice registered a .330 mark, catcher Patsy Gharrity .310, Howard Shanks .302, and Joe Judge .301. Shanks led the league in triples and had by far the best campaign of a 14-year career. The squad as a whole, however, managed .277, which, during the high-powered age of the '20s, wasn't that great. The Senators were next to last in batting; the Yankees hit more than three times as many home runs. In relation to these numbers, it should also be considered that the league batting champion, Harry Heilmann of Detroit, hit .394; his teammate, Ty Cobb, was second with .389.

On September 24, 1921, one of the more celebrated incidents involving the tempestuous Cobb occurred following a game at Griffith Stadium. The Nats won 5–1, and Tyrus was in a rage because of two calls made by umpire Billy Evans. When challenged by Cobb, Evans,

normally a refined type, accepted, and the two had it out under the grandstand in front of fans, players, and even Cobb's son, Ty, Jr. There was a considerable amount of blood, but the maniacal Cobb got the best of it. The incident was reported to Commissioner Landis by the game's other umpire, George Hildebrand. Cobb earned a suspension, but was allowed to continue managing the Tigers.

Top man on the Senators' 1921 pitching staff was not Walter Johnson, but George Mogridge, who made good use of a befuddling mixture of off-speed offerings. Mogridge was the workhorse and top winner at 18–14, and Walter Johnson went 17–14 with an inflated 3.51 ERA, up considerably from 1.49 just two years earlier.

Erratic throughout this season, Johnson settled down and won five of his last six starts. One of those victories was a 1–0 whitewashing of the Browns in which he faced the minimum 27 batters for only the second time in his career. While the great pitcher's era of sheer dominance had come to an end, his career was by no means over. He still led the majors in strikeouts, and there were two 20-win seasons three years off in the future.

For third base for 1922, to replace Howard Shanks, Griffith got Donie Bush, who'd been the Tigers' regular shortstop since 1909. The idea was to get Bush to spell Shanks at third and Blackie O'Rourke at short, as the dark-featured Canadian hit only .234 as the regular. Shortstop was Griffith's main concern and in the first month of 1922, he decided to make a pitch for veteran Roger Peckinpaugh, a 31-year-old who had been the best in the league at the position for years. What the bow-legged Peckinpaugh may have lacked in grace, he made up for in range and strength.

The regular Yankees shortstop since 1914, "Peck" had been traded to Boston in another sensational, money-saving deal engineered by the Red Sox's Harry Frazee on December 20, 1921. (Everett Scott, "Bullet Joe" Bush and "Sad Sam" Jones were sent to the Yankees.) Money, however, had not been the only motivation behind that particular deal. Babe Ruth disliked Yankees manager Miller Huggins, and wanted to have Peckinpaugh named manager of the New York club, for which Ruth had now completed his first season. The Yankees had obviously decided not to grant Ruth the power of deciding who his immediate superior was going to be.

In any case, Peckinpaugh became a Red Sox in name only. He'd been on their roster for all of three weeks, obviously never even suiting up for them. On January 10, 1922, he was moved to Washington by Frazee, who had been tempted to accept cash from Griffith. Frazee had thought better of that, however. He was the most unpopular man in Boston, having already expelled, in addition to Bush, Jones, and Scott, the likes of Waite Hoyt, Herb Pennock, and Wally Schang. Then, of course, there had been the kid called the Babe. If cash wouldn't do in an exchange for Peckinpaugh, though, Clark Griffith had no star player he could part with.

It was Griff's inside knowledge which ultimately enabled him to get Peckinpaugh for the Senators. The A's had a fine young third baseman named Joe Dugan who had begun showing decent power as a 24-year-old the previous season. But there was a problem with Dugan, for which he had earned the nickname of "Jumping Joe." He often got homesick and would jump the ballclub, without notice, to return to his hometown of Boston to visit family and friends. Now if Griffith could get Dugan from Connie Mack, he could probably turn right around and send him home for good.

Clark Griffith's complex strategy to acquire Roger Peckinpaugh succeeded, but it cost him dearly. Griffith surrendered three players, including incumbent shortstop Blackie O'Rourke, and outfielder Edmund "Bing" Miller who had hit .288 with the Senators in '21, his only season in Washington. In Miller's case, Washington made a mistake. Over the next nine years, his lowest batting average as a regular in Philadelphia would be .299. But at the time of the trade, what hurt Griffith the most was the $50,000 check he ultimately had to write Frazee in order to get Peckinpaugh for his ballclub.

To add insult to Griffith's financial injury, Peckinpaugh was late arriving for spring training at Tampa, Florida, in 1922. When he did arrive, he announced he had a sore back and that, by the way, he would not play unless he got a better contract. While Peck did come into the fold by opening day, Ossie Bluege ended up playing shortstop, and playing remarkably well, during spring training. In one game against the Phils, Bluege and Bucky Harris combined for six double plays. Bluege was still a year away from a full-time big-league job, but he earned some time as a utilityman and then was dispatched to Minneapolis, where he hit a healthy .315. The new Peckinpaugh-Harris-Judge combination would become one of the most lethal rally-killing trios in history. As Clark Griffith so succinctly put it, whenever the ball was hit in the direction of any one of those guys, everybody was out.

The sensation of the spring, however, was the young slugger, Goose Goslin. His defense was still suspect at this point in his career, but he was knocking the ball around with authority against big-league pitchers. Goslin had an abundance of confidence. The previous September, when he had made his big-league debut, he had hit the ball hard off White Sox ace Red Faber. Faber was completing a 25-win season, the third of his career with more than 20 wins up to that point, and on his way to the Hall of Fame. After Goslin scored and got back to the bench, Joe Judge remarked that he never thought he would have seen the day the Nats would have a healthy lead against Red Faber. Goslin, on the other hand, said he doubted this Faber fellow was actually any good at all.

Cockiness was already getting Goslin, who loved to live the good life, in trouble. He got fined before he ever got paid. One night, two weeks into 1922 spring training, he stayed up and won big money gambling. He went directly from the craps table to the breakfast table, only to run into his furious manager, Clyde Milan. Escorted to his room, Goslin was told to rest and that Milan would return to talk to him in an hour. When Milan showed up again, he found nothing but an open window.

Nevertheless, Goslin ended up being the club's only .300 hitter, as 1922 unfolded into a poor year for the Nationals. While the pitching improved marginally, the Nats were again next-to-last in hitting.

The keystone combo of Harris and Peckinpaugh was the main asset, setting a then major-league record for double plays with 168. On the other side of the coin, third base remained a trouble spot, and the Nats had too little power overall. They fell to 69–85 and, after just one year at the helm, Deerfoot Milan gave up his managing job, having found the work decidedly unsatisfying. He'd been beset by stomach problems all year, brought on by nonstop worry about his sixth-place charges. In Walter Johnson's opinion, his best friend was too nice a guy, and some players had taken advantage of him. Milan's batting average, as an occasional insert in the lineup, had plunged from .288 to .230. He would never play again in the big leagues, although he would hit over .300 in the following two years as a player-manager in the minors.

Walter himself was still a key factor, more effective than he'd been the previous year, finishing at 15–16, but his 2.99 ERA was good for fifth in the league and still more than a run better than the league average. He had, however, stood at 9–3 at one point and had been particularly effective during the latter part of June. On the 28th, Barney pitched a third consecutive shutout to beat the Yanks 1–0 at Griffith Stadium. He gave up just seven singles, two to Babe Ruth. His poor finish was primarily due to the lack of offensive support he got from the sixth-place team behind him. George Mogridge won 18 for the second straight year, again leading the club, and Tom Zachary, the minister's son who had served overseas with the Red Cross in World War I, chipped in with 15 victories.

Requiring a tougher taskmaster to replace Clyde Milan as field boss, Clark Griffith had to look no further than the veteran Donie Bush, still a fireplug despite his fading on-field skills. There was also the new catcher, Herold "Muddy" Ruel. A practicing attorney in the off seasons (in later life, he became assistant to

Commissioner Happy Chandler), Ruel had an average arm, but his quickness, ability to handle pitchers, and uncanny ability to deliver the clutch hit would become trademarks. He was obtained from the Red Sox, but earlier had been let go by the Yankees in a deal Miller Huggins later identified as the worst move he'd ever made.

Muddy Ruel was about to realize the baseball dream of his boyhood days, when he'd always made a special effort to attend games which had featured Walter Johnson at Sportsman's Park, in his hometown of St. Louis. His goal had been to someday catch the great righthander, and now he would. However, only the most hopeful of Washington fans could have fantasized at this point that among position players, Ruel was the last important piece to be added to a championship ballclub.

Accompanying Ruel to Washington in the trade with Boston was Allan Russell, a rubber-armed reliever still privileged because of the fact that he could throw the spitball. When the pitch was banned in 1920, Russell was one of those permitted to continue throwing the spitter until retirement, since it was his bread-and-butter pitch — the baseball was the bread, and a substance called "slippery elm" the butter. Russell contributed ten wins and led the league in saves with nine in 1923. He was one of the very first career relievers in baseball, and his 40 relief outings in '23 represented the greatest degree of relief specialization to that point in major-league history.

Further brightening the outlook in the capital at the end of the 1923 season was a big Texan named Fred "Firpo" Marberry. Raised on a Texas cotton farm, Marberry was mean on the mound. Unlike Allan Russell, he disliked working out of the bullpen. So anxious was he to get into games that on many occasions, when the manager was headed out to talk to a starting pitcher in trouble, Marberry would come barreling out of the bullpen without waiting for a signal to do so.

Fred Marberry was something of a precursor to the likes of Al Hrabosky, the "Mad Hungarian" of later years — the type of pitcher who would stomp and fume and glare menacingly at batters. Once, having had his ears verbally assaulted by the Yankees' bench, Marberry challenged the whole lot of them, and yelled to their big guy, Babe Ruth, that he would gladly oblige him first and that the Babe would need "all the help he could get." There was dead silence — no one wanted any part of this farmboy. Marberry won all four of his 1923 decisions and was going to become an invaluable part of the ballclub.

Ossie Bluege was moved to third and, finally given the chance to play fairly regularly, provided extraordinary fielding at the position. A quiet, expressionless type, Bluege played the shallowest third base in the league, enabling him to cut off more hits with his lightning reflexes. Clark Griffith would for years to come enjoy promoting Bluege as the best third baseman he'd ever seen. Bluege would become known particularly for his live arm, which often cut runners down as they were just getting out of the batter's box. The rookie hit only .245, but the other new man in the lineup, catcher Ruel, delivered a lusty .316. The reliables did not disappoint — Rice with .316, Judge .314, and Goslin .300 with 99 ribbies.

Nemo Leibold, a speedy slap hitter, chipped in with a .305 average in 95 games as the regular center fielder after being acquired in May for the waiver price from — who else — the Red Sox. Leibold had also been a member of the infamous Black Sox, but had been unaware of the sinister plan harbored by some of his teammates during the 1919 World Series. His arrival in the capital enabled Sam Rice to return to right field, his preferred position, which he had vacated to make room for Clyde Milan back in 1920 when Milan had been slowing down.

Walter Johnson hurt his left knee while striding, on May 20, in St. Louis. The incident eventually led to the dismissal of coach George Gibson. It had been Gibson's idea that the way to get the kinks out of Walter's leg was to have him chase fungoes every day. When the strategy backfired, Gibson was replaced with the old pitching great, Jack Chesbro. Chesbro wasn't around long, replaced as third-base coach before the beginning of the next season by Al Schacht, the ex-pitcher and funnyman with the hangdog look.

Schacht had called Clark Griffith on a promise the Old Fox had made three years earlier, on the occasion of another Walter Johnson injury. Back on July 5, 1920, when Barney was to have started one of the games of a doubleheader at home versus the Yankees but had been unable to come out, Schacht had saved the day, as mentioned, before a large crowd that the owner would have been loath to disappoint. When he volunteered, Griff had promised Schacht a job forever if he went out and won the crowd over, and of course, he did. There was no question that the Clown Prince of Baseball was no clown when it came to baseball know-how, and now he would be reaping his reward on the coaching lines.

Walter Johnson's early-season leg injury slowed the 35-year-old icon for most of the rest of the 1923 campaign. But then he had another strong finish, winning both ends of a doubleheader for the only time in his unbelievable career, at St. Louis on September 17. Nine days later, he won another of his 38 career 1–0 decisions over the White Sox. In the last game of the year on October 5, in the epitome of a strong finish to a season, the power of the Big Train was fully in evidence. In beating the Red Sox 4–2, Walter struck out 12, the highest total for the year in the American League. Added all up, his record amounted to 17–12, 3.48, highly creditable considering the injury and slow start. He led the league in only one major category, strikeouts, with a modest 130.

While showing improvement, Washington wasn't quite able to elevate itself above .500 in 1923, winding up at 75–78. The club did, however, vault itself out of the second division, where it had spent the whole season, making it to fourth place with a victory over the Browns on the last day of the campaign. (In the National League, Rogers Hornsby of the Cardinals went 3-for-5 in the last game to finish at .401, becoming the first to crash the .400 barrier in that league since Ed Delahanty had done so for the Phillies of 1899.)

Attendance for the year was down nearly

100,000 from the previous two years, although the figure of 360,000 was still a 50 percent improvement over the level of 1919, when Clark Griffith had taken over the club. The Old Fox was plowing some of the profits back into the stadium which now carried his name, and increased seating by some 13,000. There was a new concrete-and-steel stand along the left field line which lent a makeshift appearance to the place, as its roof was higher than the one covering the infield stands. Renovations were undertaken on the clubhouses, and the field was resodded — the Griffith Stadium infield now had the reputation of being the best in the world.

Would Clark Griffith's *club* ever be the best in the world? The fans of Washington were those for whom the cry of "Wait 'til next year" was beginning to take on a distinctly hollow ring. The city was the only one in either major league to have never experienced a championship season, and that in nearly 50 years of professional baseball. Griff definitely thought he had better horses than the record showed. He was going to make another change at manager. He and Donie Bush hadn't hit it off that well anyway. Out with Bush, and in with a new man.

That new man was, by all accounts, totally in shock after receiving a letter from Griffith while on a golf vacation in Tampa during the first days of 1924. The new field marshal would be none other than the shortstop, just turned 27, Bucky Harris. Harris was the youngest regular player on the team, but he apparently had no qualms about taking the job.

Instructed by Griffith to call him by long-distance telephone as soon as he got his letter, Harris recovered from his initial surprise and tried to reach the boss. The connection was bad, and while Bucky could hear Griffith, Griff couldn't hear him. Exasperated, Griffith hung up. Harris then scooted over to a telegraph office and gave the clerk the considerable sum of $20, instructing him to send a telegram right away, and to repeat it every hour over the course of the following four hours.

Harris's telegram stated that he was ready to take on the additional responsibility and do no less than win Washington's first American League pennant. Bucky Harris would secure a place among the most important personages in the history of the Washington Senators and a spot in the venerable Baseball Hall of Fame in Cooperstown, New York. For a while, though, his hiring as Washington field boss would be known as the "Old Fox's Folly."

Harris was astonished at being named manager because he thought he was in Griffith's doghouse at the time the position was offered. During the winter of '23–24, Bucky had planned on earning some extra money by playing professional basketball. In late December '23, at a New Year's Eve dance at a ritzy Washington hotel, he sported a black eye received in a basketball game. Griffith's secretary was there, and word got back to the old man, who fined Bucky.

This happened just after Harris had signed his player's contract for 1924 for $7,000. Although Harris had signed, like many players back then he was truly unhappy with the arrangement. What choice did a player have? It was either sign, or be black-balled out of baseball.

Griffith's negotiations with Harris had been based on the possibility that he could somehow obtain the great Eddie Collins from the White Sox to play second base. In that event, he hoped that Harris would be able to adjust to third base. When Harris was summoned to his office so Griffith could order him to stay away from basketball permanently, he was also asked if he would play third if Collins could be acquired. When the plan fell through, not only was Harris still the second baseman, he was also the manager.

Bucky Harris was born in New York State but raised in Pittston, in the same Pennsylvania mining country from which Christy Mathewson, Hughie Jennings, and the pitching Coveleski brothers hailed. Harris was from a mining family and he himself toiled underground at the age of 12. He earned his nickname working as a breaker boy, separating slate from coal as it came down chutes.

Half a dozen years later, but three years before the Nats came calling in Buffalo, Bucky Harris was already in the Detroit Tigers' training camp as a 19-year-old, interacting with the likes of manager Jennings, Ty Cobb, Sam Crawford, Harry Heilman, and his future manager in Washington, Donie Bush. When Harris first appeared at the Tigers' camp at Waxahachie, Texas, in mid–March 1916, he must have been disappointed to discover that Jennings, who had scouted him back home, had had an attack of blood poisoning and was in hospital in Oklahoma. Harris never even got a chance to hit during his first two weeks in camp. As was customary in a less-sensitive age, he was shunned by the veterans and told to take a hike whenever he got ideas about stepping into the batter's box. He didn't even stand out in the field — he had never in his life played on anything even remotely similar to the smooth grass infield at Waxahachie.

Later that year, Hughie Jennings did ask Harris to report to Muskegon, Mich., of the Central League, where he hit just .185. The following season, Jennings found Bucky a spot at Norfolk of the Virginia League. Three weeks later, America entered World War I and the league folded. Harris fired off letters to every professional club he knew of, and latched on with Reading of the New York State League because of a misunderstanding. Manager George "Hooks" Wiltse, formerly an accomplished big-league pitcher and five-time pennant-winner with the Giants, asked his players if anyone had ever heard of this Harris kid. Pitcher Bill Donahue said he had — that Harris had been his teammate in the Canadian League and that he was a good fielder who might hit enough. Donahue had actually been thinking of Harris's brother Merle, and was just trying to help out an old pal.

When the error was discovered, Bucky begged for a chance anyway, and made good. The following season he was promoted to Buffalo, where Hooks Wiltse reappeared as manager. Bucky didn't stay, but instead skipped to the Baltimore Drydocks' team, a club which had three major leaguers at the other infield positions — Joe Judge of the Senators at first, Dave Bancroft at short, and Frank "Wildfire" Schulte at third. This shipyard team whipped the Baltimore Orioles of the International League in exhibition matches in 1918.

Harris was forgiven by Buffalo and offered $300 a month for 1919 — more than double the salary he'd earned at Reading less than two years earlier. When his average got up in the .280s, he was dispatched on an off day to try out for the New York Giants. Reporting to John McGraw, he got on the field and showed what he could do, taking batting and fielding practice and, by all accounts, did rather well. McGraw never said another word to him, though, and the next time they spoke was during at the 1924 World Series. The Giants passed up on Harris again later, picking pitcher Rosy Ryan to complete an earlier deal with Buffalo.

Just before Clark Griffith joined Joe Engel to evaluate Harris at Buffalo, a line drive had shattered the middle finger of Bucky's throwing hand in three places. While Griff was sold on him, so were, by then, the Giants and the A's. Harris was told by Buffalo management that he would be sold, and that he could control his destiny by deciding where he wanted to go. Aware that the Giants had Larry Doyle and an up-and-comer named Frank Frisch, and that the A's had finished last for four straight years since their 1914 pennant year, Harris chose Washington.

The Senators had finished a respectable third the previous year and Hal Janvrin was the second baseman Bucky Harris would have to compete with. Clark Griffith purchased Bucky's rights for something variously reported at between $2,000 and $5,000, and Hal Janvrin was included in the deal. Harris broke into the big leagues against the Yankees, and in his second game drove in two runs, but later pulled a boner that cost Walter Johnson and the Senators the game. It was the 13th inning, and Harris called outfielders Milan and Rice off a fly ball hit into shallow right-center field. He proceeded to drop the ball, letting the winning run score. Harris would never forget what happened next. As he shuffled off the field, Walter Johnson had been waiting for him so he could put his arm around him and tell him not to worry about it, that such things happen to everyone.

Then followed the events that led to his hiring as manager. Bucky Harris hit .300 as a rookie in 1920, .289 in '21, slipped to .269 in '22 but teamed up with Peckinpaugh to become a stalwart defensively, and hit .282 with 23 stolen bases and 13 triples in 1923.

In years to come, Harris would promote the notion that there were really only two things a good manager had to know: when to change pitchers, and how to get along with his players. At spring training '24, Bucky showed he had a grasp of that philosophy very early on by employing a novel approach among big-league managers — one brought on by necessity, as he was being asked to lead a bunch of former teammates, most of whom were older than he was. He informed his players in clear terms that he was not going to tell them how to play baseball. He implored them to simply make him a good manager. Walter Johnson and Joe Judge, good leaders of men, had been approached by him already, and they had pledged their allegiance.

Harris relaxed bed checks and invoked the honor system during spring training at Hot Springs, Arkansas. He turned the comradeship he had had with his teammates to his advantage. On one occasion, on his way back east from Hot Springs with the main squad, he plotted with his underlings to get even but good with the team's resident clown, the comedic buzzsaw, Al Schacht. Harris hatched a plan designed to bring the prankster to his knees. Schacht was a real ladies' man, and when Bucky and the rest of the team reached Orlando, Florida, he told Schacht that there were a couple of fine-looking southern ladies who were going to be catching up with them later on in the week. And ... they wanted to meet Al Schacht.

Intrigued, Schacht asked a number of questions. One of them was whether these ladies were single. Harris said that indeed they were, that both women were applying for divorce so there was nothing to worry about.

Harris also reassured Schacht by telling him that he, manager of a big-league ballclub, knew what he was doing and was not about to get himself involved in any sort of scandal. On the appointed day, Schacht eagerly went looking for Harris at the team dinner, reminding him of the date they had for that evening. Harris encouraged Schacht to spend a few dollars, for a bottle of liquor and some oranges for the ladies.

They were chauffered along a lonely side road before coming to a cottage nearly completely secluded in a thickly wooded area. Schacht paid for the cab too; Bucky fumbled for money in his pockets, then humbly let the Clown Prince cover the tab. When they got to the door, to Schacht's very sudden dismay, a man answered their knock and Schacht saw and heard a gun. He also saw Bucky Harris go down, and then did what might have come naturally to anyone — he ran. He ended up making his way on foot five miles along a desolate stretch of road, back to where he and Bucky had been driven from.

Along the way, cold and fear-stricken, Schacht wondered if Bucky had died. He considered going back, but thought again. The Clown Prince, recounting the incident in his book *Clowning Through Baseball*, wrote that he walked back with his hat pulled over his eyes and his collar turned up on an exceedingly dark night. Hardly any cars went by. It did occur to him, for perhaps a minute of that time, that the whole horrible thing could have been a hoax, a big setup, but no, that was just his irrational mind racing away, he thought.

When he finally arrived back where the team was staying, a number of players were waiting for him at the doorway to the residence. One of them remarked that he looked a little pale, which drew some laughs. Schacht instinctively decided to laugh too, and then there was an uproar. Then he understood that he'd been had. He found out that half the team, including the great Walter Johnson, had been hiding in the bushes observing the goings-on back at the cottage. For years, Schacht heard taunts like "Hey, Al, how's Tampa Margie?" Al Schacht may have been a clown, but no one ever accused him of being stupid. On that day, he said later, he found out that the stage had lost a great actor when young Bucky Harris had decided to take up baseball.

This is the type of relationship that Harris cultivated with his players, and his enthusiasm also would help in earning the respect of key guys like Walter Johnson, Roger Peckinpaugh, George Mogridge, and Joe Judge. The Nationals would be a group of highly committed and combative ballplayers in 1924. During the early weeks, though, there were no real signs that this would be a very special season. Right off the bat, the burdensome term "Griffith's Folly" was used, but only by certain baseball writers; when the Senators sank to the second division, the phrase gained currency.

Then something happened. All the key men started clicking on all cylinders. Harris was playing well, not at all affected by his double duties. His partner Peckinpaugh was rebounding from a mediocre 1923, and he and Harris were again formidable as a double-play duo. All of a sudden, veterans Johnson, Rice, and Judge were simultaneously enjoying their best periods of sustained good play in years. The scholarly Muddy Ruel, credited with coming up with the term "tools of ignorance" to describe the equipment worn by catchers, was again solid at the plate and behind it. The rookie reliever, Firpo Marberry, was so effective that he would set a new record for relief appearances. On June 19, Griffith made a pickup that may have seemed inconsequential at the time, but which would prove of great value over the course of the season. Righthander Curly Ogden, just 23 years old but sore-armed, was claimed on waivers from the Philadelphia A's. This was perceived as a nonevent at the time because Ogden's career record in the majors to this point was 2–9, and his 1923 ERA had exceeded six runs per game.

Curly Ogden's arm made a remarkable recovery, for which Senators trainer Mike Martin received much of the credit. It was a recuperation to the tune of eight straight victories as a starter down the stretch in 1924,

including three shutouts for Ogden, a former reliever. But how he suffered! Following each start, he would pace the floor in his hotel room, clutching his arm, convinced he wouldn't be able to pitch again. Mike Martin made sure he always did, and the story of Curly Ogden would be one of those that would make this good team a great one.

Every team in the top half of the league, including the Nats, had a taste of first place during the first half of the campaign. Wid Matthews, a small, peppy player in center field hit .359 during his first three weeks after joining the club on June 5, but by the end of the season, Matthews would become Clark Griffith's chief concern. Matthews had led the entire league in outfield errors as a rookie with the A's in '23, and his hitting soon began to tail off. Later renowned as a scout, Matthews hit .302 for the Senators in 1924, but he'd been getting most of his hits by pulling the ball into short right field. When defenses began adjusting, his success as a hitter diminished greatly.

Griffith wanted someone with prowess at the plate who would be more surehanded between Goose Goslin and Sam Rice. Nemo Leibold, now 32, would not fill the bill, as his defensive skills were merely average at best. Scout Joe Engel was ordered to scan as far and wide as he had to in order to find a center fielder. The field got narrowed down to two players: Billy Zitzmann, of Newark, and Earl McNeely, of Sacramento. On Engel's recommendation, Griffith went to Buffalo to see Newark's Zitzmann, who had previously appeared in the big leagues briefly, and would resurface with Cincinnati the following season. The Old Fox was unimpressed.

Scouting McNeely would mean a lot of time and expense. Deciding he couldn't waste another two weeks in the heat of a pennant race, Griffith decided to rely on Engel's word and purchased McNeely, sight unseen. He did talk Sacramento down from the original publicized asking price of $75,000 to $35,000. In order to get McNeely, Griff also gave up three lesser players, including loaning Wid Matthews for the rest of the season. (Matthews' big-league career would end following ten games with the Nats in 1925.) The fiery Matthews was a fan favorite, but Clark Griffith could not have guessed the popular outcry which resulted from the move.

The Old Fox tried to back out of it, but it was too late. His hesitation had more to do, however, with McNeely's condition when he reported to the Nats than with Wid Matthews' box-office appeal. When McNeely joined the team, Clark Griffith reportedly greeted him at the club's Chicago hotel with a tongue-in-cheek comment to the effect that he was finally coming face to face with the man he'd paid so much money for. Griffith extended his hand, but McNeely was unable to take it. He told Griffith that he'd hurt his shoulder the previous week and that he couldn't raise his throwing arm above his hip. Griffith hit the proverbial roof. Right away, he was on the phone to Commissioner Landis, demanding that the deal be canceled. But the deal stood. Barely given enough time for proper introduction to his new teammates, McNeely began asserting himself, batting .394 in his first ten games. In 45 games to the end of the season, he hit .330, and he had the range and speed of a top-flight center fielder. In a tight pennant race, Earl McNeely would make a difference for Washington.

Fast approaching age 37, Walter Johnson made it known to Griffith following his contract signing in January that 1924 would be his last year. The Big Train intended to buy the Vernon (Los Angeles) franchise of the Pacific Coast League. At spring training, though, Walter had discovered that his arm was totally pain-free for the first time since 1920. There had been a knot above his elbow which had gotten smaller in size each year since then. Now, it was gone. When the Nats faced the New York Giants in a preseason game, the National League champions' shortstop, Travis Jackson, commented that if Walter Johnson had ever been faster, he was glad he'd been in kindergarten at the time.

On opening day, doubt that the Big Train was all the way back evaporated. With President Calvin Coolidge presiding and pro-

viding Johnson with another autographed presidential baseball, Barney shut out the A's 4–0 before the home crowd. The Big Swede would have his best campaign of the past five years, and toward the end, on August 25, he would no-hit the St. Louis Browns in a game shortened to seven innings because of rain. This would be Barney's league-leading sixth and last shutout of the season, the 107th of his career. Would the Big Train really retire? (Hint: the record shows he had six more shutouts left in him.) Certainly, Johnson's excellent 23–7 performance in 1924 militated against that. As well as in shutouts, Barney was also tops in the A.L. in wins (23), games (38), strikeouts (158) and ERA (2.72).

While Walter was solid all year, the club had floundered at first. Those who had dubbed Griffith's hiring of Harris "Griffith's Folly" definitely had the upper hand by mid–May, as the Nats were cowering in the depths of the second division. On May 23, Walter Johnson pitched one of the great games of his career, facing 28 batters and striking out 14 in blanking Chicago 4–0 on one measly hit and one measly walk. He tied a league record by striking out six in a row. By this stage of the new season, the Big Train already had four shutouts.

Within a couple of weeks the Nats were back at the .500 level, prompting Babe Ruth to quip that he'd never seen a team turn things around so quickly. In late June, the club was red hot and built a four-game lead by month's end. By now, one of the nation's foremost sports scribes, Grantland Rice, was writing about how most Americans, if they could vote for such a thing, would want to see the Senators win the pennant. If only, many felt, Walter Johnson could finally make an appearance in one World Series before calling it quits.

Johnson told the editors of *Baseball Magazine* that he longed for the days when his arm had been able to bounce back on a daily basis. Now he preferred to pitch every four days. If he could do now what he could then, he said, he knew that he would have even more success, considering the quality of the teams which had usually backed him up in the past.

But Walter Johnson was not one to get too caught up in reverie, and he proclaimed himself still good enough to help a contender like this edition of the Washington Senators.

The club lost five in a row in the smothering heat of St. Louis and dropped back behind not only the Yankees, but the Tigers as well. It was Johnson who broke a six-game losing streak for the club on August 7, keeping the Nats in the race. Washington regained second spot by taking four of five from the Tigers at home. Johnson was extraordinary on the 17th, giving up four hits, no walks, and getting the side out in order in seven of the nine innings. He struck out Ty Cobb to end the game, which the Nationals won handily, 8–1.

From now on, Walter told Bucky Harris, he wanted the ball every third day. He would do anything he could to bring a pennant to Washington, and told the skipper he didn't care what the consequences were for his arm. If he ended up knocking himself out of action and missing a World Series, then so be it. This was Walter Johnson.

Punctuated by Barney's rain-shortened no-hitter against the Browns on the 25th, a nine-game winning streak ensued. Following the seven-inning masterpiece, George Sisler, the Browns' star hitter, commented that he thought the Big Train had looked very much like his old self. Any hitter, Sisler thought, would have considered it an accomplishment just to make contact.

The Nats had pulled even with the murderous Yankees. New York, turbopowered by Ruth, was outslugging every team in the league at this point. Bob Meusel and Wally Pipp were on their way to producing 120 and 113 runs respectively. Their pitching staff included great names like Waite Hoyt, Herb Pennock, and Bullet Joe Bush. Their receiver was Wally Schang, one of baseball's best catchers throughout his long career with outstanding teams in New York and Philadelphia.

Over the last four days of August, the Nats were to play the Yanks a single game each day at one-year-old Yankee Stadium. In the opening match, Babe Ruth socked a pair of

home runs and Bob Meusel another, but that wasn't enough for the Yankees to reclaim first place. The Nats slaughtered the pitching of Herb Pennock, Goose Goslin hit for the cycle, and Washington scored eight in the eighth, prevailing 11–6. All of a sudden, the Senators were in first place. What's more, the New York fans had cheered Washington's victory unabashedly. It became obvious on this day that the nation truly stood behind the capital's team, and everyone knew why.

When Walter Johnson struck out Babe Ruth to end the first inning the following day, there was bedlam. Barney was good enough on this day to keep New York off the scoresheet for seven innings, working out of a bases-loaded jam and two situations with baserunners on the corners. Twice he snuffed out potential rallies by striking out the dangerous Bob Meusel with two men on. All the while, his mates were amassing a healthy lead off Joe Bush. Goose Goslin, who would end up eclipsing Ruth, Meusel, Pipp, and the rest, to lead the league in runs batted in (129, to go with a .344 average), was on a tear. He went 3–for–4 with a home run and scored three times. Washington won again, the final score 5–1.

In the eighth, everyone got a scare when Johnson reached for a Wally Schang liner and had the ball glance off his pitching hand. Bucky Harris decided not to take a chance and immediately pulled the living legend from the contest. One writer described the ovation that followed as the loudest ever accorded any baseball player in New York City.

The third game was a setback, particularly since the Nats got 11 hits off Waite Hoyt, while Curly Ogden gave up just five. The Yankees won 2–1. The finale was a classic. George Mogridge, who would finish the season at 16–11, 3.76, got into plenty of trouble early but held New York to two runs until the eighth, when Firpo Marberry came in to relieve. Joe Judge hit one of his three homers this season, off Sam Jones, setting up some tenth-inning heroics by Sam Rice, who doubled to drive in two runs for a 4–2 decision. Rice led the league in hits (216) and at-bats, and hit .334. The pesky Nats had taken three out of four; within four weeks, their 13–9 overall record against the Yankees in this campaign was to prove of the utmost significance.

Anyone would have thought the Washington Senators were already winners of the pennant when they pulled into Union Station in Washington that same night, one half-game up on the Yankees. With 8,000 admirers mobbing them, the players were escorted by police through an exit normally reserved for the President of the United States. President Coolidge himself would get caught up in the spirit, inviting the entire team to the White House on September 5 to congratulate the boys personally on their valiant fight for the A.L. flag. The President, still mourning the sudden death of his 16-year-old son two months earlier, told the players it was going to be quite a thrill to be able to root for Washington in the World Series. Indeed, the mood of the entire nation was such that the Senators were heavy sentimental favorites to make it to the World Series for the first time.

Walter Johnson had been a star for 18 years with nothing to show from a team perspective. What irony if he could win on a club managed by a man who would become the youngest ever to direct a team to a league championship. Bucky Harris was himself aware of the widespread favoring of the Nats, a sentiment he thought was shared by players on opposing teams. The boy manager felt that the White Sox were the only team in the league who would prefer to see the Yankees take the pennant again. He had his intuition confirmed by outfielder Nemo Leibold, who had formerly played for Chicago. Although Harris instructed his troops to cut down somewhat on the cruel taunts that usually emanated from the dugout of his spirited team, he also let them know that if they were playing the White Sox, they were free to take their best verbal potshots.

The Senators were to end the season on the road, with a three-week road trip starting September 8. Walter Johnson won 8–4 that day at Philadelphia, his tenth win in a row and 20th of the year. Taking three of four in Philly, the Nationals moved on to Detroit,

where Johnson decisioned rookie Earl Whitehill, a future Washington player. The victory was coupled in the newspapers the following day with news that Barney had been named the league's most valuable player for 1924, getting 55 of a possible 64 votes. The Nats, however, lost the last two games of the Detroit series and were now only three games up on the Tigers. Worse still, the feared Yankees had now caught up with them, with both teams at 82–59.

The Senators swept three games at Cleveland, where they had lost seven of eight games in their first two visits. Fans cheered wildly for Walter Johnson when he took the middle game 3–2 on September 17. On the 19th, the Nats ran the score up to 9–0 before the Browns even got up to bat in stifling St. Louis heat. But the Yankees were keeping pace, and Bucky Harris decided to call upon his 36-year-old ironman on just two days' rest. The strategy didn't work, and Johnson was kayoed in the first inning. Five pitchers gave up 18 hits, but the Nats managed 18 safeties of their own and nearly pulled it out. Goose Goslin homered in the top of the tenth inning, his second of the day, but Washington blew the lead in the bottom of the inning and lost 15–14 when Firpo Marberry, who could have opted for an easy play at the plate, threw wildly past second base instead.

On September 21, the Senators won when the game was called in the seventh because of rain, and with the Yankees having lost two straight in Detroit, the Nats were now two ahead. A three-game series began against the hated Chisox the next day. With Harris urging his Nats to insult the White Sox and *then* beat them, Walter Johnson won his 13th consecutive game, his 23rd victory of the season. Playing 20 games over .500 during the last month of the season, the sizzling Nationals swept Chicago. But the Yankees, champions of the world and winners of the pennant by 16 games in 1923, could not be shaken off. While the Nats were sweeping Chicago, the Bombers were doing the same to Cleveland, so Washington could do no better than hang on to its slim lead. Everything would be decided back east after all.

Ahead by two games with four left to play, the Senators might have seemed, on the face of it, to have had a slight advantage — their last four games would be contested at Fenway Park against last-place Boston. But the Yankees' opponents weren't much better. They were to face the Athletics, fighting for sixth place, in Philadelphia. The Senators quickly dispensed with half their advantage when Walter Johnson's consecutive-win streak was broken at 13 in a 2–1 heartbreaker on September 26, despite the fact that Boston fans were openly rooting for the Senators. In the same game, Sam Rice's team-record 31-game hitting streak (broken by Heinie Manush in 1933) was brought to a halt. At the same time, New York was pounding the A's, 7–1. Once again, Johnson was struck on the arm, this time by a pitched ball on the elbow. Earl McNeely had a bad game, and the rookie admitted to being downright scared about what could happen to the Nats' World Series prospects.

The following day, George Mogridge gave up four runs in the first inning, and disaster lurked and seemed imminent. Bucky Harris brought in Fred Marberry, Allan Russell, and Tom Zachary, who held the Red Sox to just one more run the rest of the way. The Senators won the game, 7–5. At one point, the Boston fans jeered their pitcher, Howard Ehmke, for striking out Roger Peckinpaugh in a key situation. When the news came that a Bullet Joe Bush wild pitch had cost New York a 4–3 decision in Philadelphia, the Nats had their two-game lead back. More importantly, with two games left in the season, the worst the Senators could do was to finish the season in a dead heat atop the standings.

On a Sunday off-day, which arose from baseball's adherence to the so-called blue laws which banned playing on the Sabbath day — the Nationals had time to contemplate the prospect of doing no worse than going into a play-off with the Yankees. That play-off was not in the cards. On the Monday, September 29, Zachary and Marberry teamed up in a 4–2 win over Boston. The offensive hero was Wade Lefler, a 28-year-old refugee from the Eastern

League whose big-league experience up to then had consisted of one solitary at-bat. Lefler had driven in the only run in the 2–1 loss the previous Friday and, pushed into a crucial situation by Harris in this game, delivered a three-run double to determine the outcome. In all, Lefler went 5–for–8 for the Nats, including three doubles, before disappearing into eternal obscurity with the enviable career major-league batting average of .556.

The Yankees were rained out in Philadelphia, although it made no difference. The improbable had finally happened. The Washington Senators, last in the league in home runs, had fought off Goliath and were the new champions of the American League. There were tears in Walter Johnson's eyes — he kept his head down as he made his way to the clubhouse from the bullpen. There were many tears in the clubhouse following the game, including some shed by Clark Griffith and Bucky Harris, who was hoisted up on the shoulders of Johnson and Nick Altrock and paraded around the clubhouse in celebration of what he had been able to achieve up to this point. Washington baseball fans finally had a champion.

When Babe Ruth found out that Washington had won its game and the pennant, he began rousing his teammates in a Philadelphia hotel. He added to the cheerlessness of an already gloomy day by shaking his teammates out of their slumber to announce that not only were they sleeping, they were now also dead.

First in War, first in Peace, and now first in the American League, the Senators were honored with a victory parade when they got back to the capital — open cars, police escort up Pennsylvania Avenue ... the whole nine yards. The end of the line was the White House, where the ballclub was welcomed by President Calvin Coolidge, who promised to be on hand for the first game of the World Series at Griffith Stadium between the Senators and the New York Giants. The truth is that President Coolidge had absolutely no affinity with baseball — he found the game a bore. Mrs. Coolidge, however, was a great fan of the game and just loved the Senators.

Three days later, on October 4, 1924, "Silent Cal" and his wife became the first President and First Lady to attend a Series opener. Secretary of State Charles Hughes, as well as the Secretary of War and the Speaker of the House were also in place in the presidential box. The United States Army Band entertained during the pregame ceremonies, and a military guard paid homage to the colors. Political and military bigwigs of all stripes had shown up for the occasion. To top things off, Walter Johnson and Roger Peckinpaugh were awarded shiny new automobiles.

A week before the World Series, syndicated columnist and future American icon Will Rogers, who ranched about 40 miles from the Johnson family spread in Coffeyville, Kansas, wrote that if Walter Johnson had played for John McGraw's New York Giants all these years, he would have had to be incompetent to have lost even a single game. Johnson, Rogers declared, could be sure that he carried more good wishes than any man, let alone athlete, who'd ever entered any competition in the entire history of America. After a "diligent search" of 150 years, Rogers wrote, Washington had finally found an honest man.

Nonetheless, since Walter Johnson had waited this long for his first World Series, he now had a platform for exposure that the Series could not have provided previously. The world was changing at a pace like never before. The automobile was now affordable to most Americans — the Ford Model T sold for $260 brand new. The first coast-to-coast airplane flight had taken place in 1923. By now, the radio receiver was commonplace in the average home. This World Series would be broadcast live over the airwaves of WRC in Washington, which had opened as the city's first radio station that summer. The previous year the Series had been broadcast in its entirety for the first time by the team of Graham McNamee, who'd given up a professional singing career to become a radio announcer, and sportswriter Grantland Rice. By the spring of 1925, all the Nats' road games would be broadcast on station WRC.

Two days before the Series began, Wal-

ter Johnson and Bucky Harris both spoke into a radio microphone for the first time. The gratitude they expressed to their fans across the country, and their promise of a World Championship victory, were broadcast across the nation over the NBC network. Western Union had strung 75,000 miles of cable to scoreboards in cities across the U.S., and wire services were available in approximately 200 other locations.

The day would be perfect if America's darling, Walter Johnson, could get his team off on the right foot with a victory over the Giants in the Series opener. We get an idea of the type of opponent the Nats were up against when we consider that six of their members are today enshrined in the National Baseball Hall of Fame. Those players are Bill Terry, George Kelly, Frank Frisch, Travis Jackson, Ross Youngs, and Hack Wilson. Both Terry and Wilson were rookies, and Terry had seen limited action during the season due to Kelly's incumbency at the first-base position.

Ross Youngs had just won the National League batting title with a .356 average, the eighth straight year he'd batted over .300. George Kelly was tops in RBIs in both major leagues in 1924, with 136. Long George, who was 6'4", had the agility of a cat around the first base bag, and he could play the outfield, and even second base in a pinch. Team captain Frank Frisch was a recognized superstar, one of the acknowledged all-time best at second base. He'd hit .328 for the season and had tied for the league lead in runs with another of the great second basemen, Rogers Hornsby of the St. Louis Cardinals, who had hit .424, a mark never matched during the entire century.

Among the other regulars were the 18-year-old lead-off hitter, third baseman Fred Lindstrom, who would hit .311 for his career, and Emil "Irish" Meusel, Yankee Bob Meusel's older brother, who would post a .310 career mark. Needless to say, the Giants, who took the pennant by a mere 1½ games over the Dodgers, had far and away the best offense in the National League in 1924. They were participating in their fourth straight World

Series — they had won two of the three previous Series, all against the Yankees, but their most recent memory was of a six-game defeat in 1923. They were led by the wiliest and toughest of baseball men, the antagonistic John McGraw.

Washington catcher Muddy Ruel would say years later that the Giants had seemed like a confident bunch on the other side of the diamond during the 1924 World Series. Apart from their offensive firepower, they had the reputation of being better defensively than any club in the American League. With John McGraw glowering at them all the while, it would have been easy for the Nats to have felt intimidated. But, as Ruel put it, those Washington Senators were a tough bunch too, and they wouldn't go down without a hell of a fight.

New York had no Walter Johnson or Firpo Marberry, and in Goose Goslin the Nats had a man with incredible power, a man who put as much into his swings as Babe Ruth. The proof was that when he missed, the Goose would do a pirouette which was pretty much just like the Babe's. But it was hard to deny that the Giants had more good hitters, and had more depth in starting pitching, and with only three days' rest following the end of the regular season and a World Series game scheduled every single day, these factors could turn out to be keys in determining the outcome. There was also the nagging fact that the Giants were taking part in their fourth consecutive World Series. On the Washington side, only Roger Peckinpaugh and Nemo Leibold had ever played in the postseason. Nevertheless, oddsmakers were calling it pretty much a toss-up, and the Nats were favored to take the first game, what with Bucky Harris having promised to start Walter Johnson.

Umpire Billy Evans was of the opinion that at one time Walter Johnson could have won a World Series by himself, reasoning that a team from another league would not have had time, in one week, to adjust to Walter's legendary blazing fastball. However, when Evans came into the clubhouse prior to the start of the first game to get some baseballs autographed for friends, it was obvious to him

that Walter Johnson, arguably the greatest pitcher in history, was very nervous. It had taken him 18 years to make it this far, the longest wait ever, incidentally, until Joe Niekro made it after 21 years, with the Minnesota Twins in 1987.

Walter Johnson admitted to Babe Ruth on the morning of the opener that he could hardly avoid the jitters, considering that everyone was expecting him to come through, everyone right up to and including the President of the United States. The first game, incidentally, would be only the second World Series game witnessed by the chief executive, President Wilson having been privy to the proceedings at a game in Philadelphia back in 1915.

Another sidebar to the 1924 World Series was the patching up of the strained relationship between two baseball legends, Ty Cobb and Babe Ruth. Cobb had recently been quoted as saying that he had gotten a real kick out of seeing the almighty Yankees fall to the Senators. The Babe had sarcastically commented to the press that Cobb, who would be doing some newspaper reporting of the Series, was probably also coming to Washington to collect some of the gate receipts as well, considering the impact he had had on deciding the pennant. Christy Walsh, ghostwriter for many a baseball star who purportedly analyzed ballgames but were in fact nowhere near the ballpark, somehow tricked Ruth and Cobb into the same cab. The two made up, acting like best buddies as they watched the proceedings from the press box throughout the week of the World Series.

While the Senators' first Series participation grabbed all the headlines, the Giants had been getting more than their share of ink. As their lead over Brooklyn dwindled in the late stages of the season, it had been alleged that Jimmy O'Connell, a spare outfielder with the Giants, had offered Philadelphia's shortstop, Heinie Sand, a sum of $500 if Sand would agree not to bear down too hard. When Sand reported the incident to his manager, Art Fletcher, the matter was brought to the attention of Commissioner Landis. The bribery plot was traced back to Giants coach Cozy Dolan, and both Dolan and O'Connell were eventually forever banned from organized baseball as a result.

With the uproar from fans queuing for tickets plainly audible beyond Griffith Stadium's walls, the Nats practiced inside, in private, for two days prior to the start of the Series. Bucky Harris wanted it that way. He had his charges working on squeeze plays, bunting drills, and defensive positioning and execution. Temporary bleachers had been set up in left field to accommodate the anticipated overflow crowd, and they had an influence on the outcome of game one.

George Kelly's homer in those stands in the second inning was particularly galling, as it fell just beyond Goose Goslin's outstretched glove at the three-foot barrier. In the fourth inning, rookie Bill Terry reached the seats on the fly with a homer that would normally have been easily caught. Walter Johnson was on his game, though, and struck out the side in that inning. Travis Jackson became his fifth consecutive strikeout victim to open the fifth. Joe Judge, a .324 hitter during the season, got the Nats' first hit off veteran southpaw Art Nehf of the Giants in the fourth, and in the sixth Earl McNeely broke the ice by doubling to left and coming around following consecutive ground-ball outs by Harris and Rice.

In the eighth, with the Giants still ahead 2–1, Ross Youngs doubled down the left field line with one out. He moved to third on a groundout, the second out, and Bill Terry was walked intentionally. Terry attempted to steal second, the idea being that if Ruel threw to second, he might make it and Youngs could come in on the second part of the double steal. But Ruel gunned the ball to third, and Youngs, who had strayed one step too far, was out. In the top of the ninth, with two out, pitcher Art Nehf singled to right with Hack Wilson on second. Sam Rice charged the ball, scooped it up cleanly and relayed it about five feet up the line so that Ruel was able to jam it right into Wilson's neck. The crowd of 35,000-plus was delirious.

The place was abuzz but the score still stood at 2–1 when the Senators came up in the bottom of the ninth. After Judge struck out, Ossie Bluege, the regular third baseman since early June who'd batted .281 for the year, singled to left. Roger Peckinpaugh followed him with a resounding double into left field to score Bluege. The ovation lasted several minutes, and hundreds of hats and cushions had to be cleared away from the field. President Coolidge was smoking cigars, constantly jumping out of his seat, and giving every indication that he was having the time of his life. When play resumed, Art Nehf got the last batters in the order, Muddy Ruel and Walter Johnson. Johnson had at this point pitched five scoreless innings, and Harris wanted to keep him in.

In the last of the tenth, with one out, Harris and Rice connected for consecutive singles. After Goose Goslin popped to short, Joe Judge hit the ball a ton, but it was caught in deep right by Ross Youngs. Johnson, who'd given up a single to Frank Frisch in the tenth, set the Giants down 1–2–3 in the 11th frame. Nehf similarly disposed of the Nats in the bottom of the inning.

The Big Train started the 12th by yielding a free pass to catcher Hank Gowdy. Then pitcher Nehf sent a low liner into center. Earl McNeely hesitated and then decided to come charging in. He got hold of the ball all right, but his knee hit the ground abruptly and the ball was knocked loose. When he tried to recover, he saw that Gowdy had stopped halfway between first and second. In his haste, McNeely threw wildly and the ball nearly ended up in the Giants' dugout. Gowdy took third and Nehf second. John McGraw then summoned pitcher Jack Bentley to hit. With a 16–5 ledger during the season, achieved almost exclusively as a starter, Bentley had also hit a respectable .265 in 98 at-bats. In 1923, he had hit .427, a major-league record for pitchers. Although his acquired middle name was "Needles," Jack Bentley was a big man. At one time, he amassed a record of 41–5 in three seasons with the Baltimore Orioles, the team Babe Ruth had played for in the minors. In 1922, Bentley also hit .349, earning widespread acclaim as the "next Babe Ruth." A Maryland native, he had broken into the majors with the Senators as an 18-year-old back in 1913, but had only a 6–9 record to show for four seasons. He then played in the minors for six years before resurfacing with the New York Giants in 1923.

With no one out, Walter Johnson decided to walk Bentley intentionally. Next, Frankie Frisch, one of the best second basemen ever, grounded to Harris, who relayed accurately to Ruel to force Gowdy out at the plate. The next batter was outfielder Ross Youngs,* a hitter of note. Youngs singled sharply to score Nehf. George Kelly then drove a long fly to left, bringing in a second run. The nightmare inning finally ended when Johnson got rookie Lewis Wilson to fly to left. (This was "Hack" Wilson, who in 1930 would set a still-standing major-league record of 190 RBIs in a single season.)

The bottom of the 12th, if anything, would prove even more electrifying. Bucky Harris had decided Walter Johnson had had enough. If this game was any indication, the Series could go long and Harris wanted to make sure his main guy would be in good form later on. The first Washington batter, reserve first baseman Mule Shirley, pinch hitting for Johnson, wound up on second base after Giant shortstop Travis Jackson muffed his fly ball. After McNeely flied out, manager Harris singled home Shirley. Sam Rice then also singled, sending Harris all the way to third. Unfortunately, Rice, hoping to avoid a double play which might have ended the inning, and in keeping with the baseball axiom that you don't make the first or third out on the basepaths, decided to try to stretch his hit into a double. He didn't make it. Two men out — with Harris on third.

Goose Goslin, the man who'd come through all year, did not do so on this occasion. He hit a slow roller and George Kelly, now playing second, came up with it barehanded. Harris had crossed home plate when

umpire Bill Klem called the Goose out, and the Nats were going to contend that Harris's run had beaten the relay to first. Goslin, Harris, Nick Altrock and Joe Judge screamed blue murder and followed Klem off the field. President Coolidge walked right by Judge and Klem, who were still arguing, and went totally unobserved by the pair.

The frustrated Goslin, who had left men in scoring position three times in this game, called Klem "Catfish," a nickname everyone knew Klem couldn't stand. In fact, Klem would never forgive Goslin, even years later when the Goose tried to apologize. The bottom line, though, was that Walter Johnson had thrown 165 pitches in his very first World Series game, but all for naught. As things turned out, however, this enthralling game would not be as crucial as another 12-inning 4–3 ballgame that was still six days in the future.

Bucky Harris chose 15-game winner Tom Zachary, who'd had one of his finest years and recorded a 2.75 ERA, to start the second game. For the Giants, it would be another lefty to follow Art Nehf. Jack Bentley, the pinch runner in the 12th inning the previous day, would get the call. John McGraw wanted to counter Washington's best batsmen, Goslin, Rice, and Judge, lefthanded hitters all, who'd hit .344, .334, and .324 respectively during the season.

The Nats struck quickly. After Zachary yielded two singles but got out of the top half unscathed, Rice singled to center with two out in the bottom of the first frame and immediately stole second. He needn't have bothered because Goose Goslin then hammered a Bentley offering over the wall and into the bleachers in right. The third lefthanded hitter, Judge, followed with a single, beating out a slow roller to first. So much for McGraw's lefty strategy for the time being, but Judge was erased for the third out on a force-out following a Bluege grounder.

There was no more scoring until the fifth.

---

*Consistently among the league leaders in hits, doubles, triples, and batting average during a brief career, Youngs died three years later at the age of 30, of Bright's disease, a terminal kidney ailment.

The Senators had threatened in the third, with both Harris and Judge having drawn walks and Harris having made it as far as third, but Judge had been caught trying to steal second. Tom Zachary was terrific, allowing only a single to Ross Youngs following his shaky first inning. With two away in the fifth, the Senators' boy manager came through with just his second home run of the season. He crushed a Bentley offering into the left-field bleachers, and the Senators led 3–0.

After an uneventful sixth, the Giants finally got on the board in the seventh. Zachary walked the first batter, George Kelly, and Irish Meusel followed with a single through short, moving Kelly over to third. Hack Wilson then bounced into a double play, scoring Kelly. The next three half-innings went 1–2–3. Zachary gave up only his third walk of the game, but also his third in four innings, to Frank Frisch to open the ninth. After inciting Ross Youngs to pop to short, Zachary surrendered a single to Kelly. Sam Rice's relay from right was bobbled and by the time the ball got to the plate, Frisch, a very aggressive player, had beaten a close play and had made it all the way around. The next batter was Irish Meusel, and he forced Harris to make a great fielding play and was thrown out.

With Kelly advanced to second, the barrel-chested Hack Wilson (5'6", 195 pounds in his prime) singled to right to drive the last nail in Zachary's coffin, and Kelly scored the tying run. Firpo Marberry, who'd led the A.L. with 15 saves on his way to his 11–12, 3.09, 1924 showing, was summoned from the bullpen to get the last out, which he did promptly, striking out Travis Jackson. The deflated enthusiasm of the partisan crowd was quickly regained in the bottom of the ninth inning. Joe Judge walked on four pitches — none of which came near the strike zone — to lead off. Ossie Bluege sacrificed by bunting to Bentley. Roger Peckinpaugh then struck his second double in two days, and the Senators had the first World Series win of their history.

These first two games were hotly, and evenly, contested. For the Nats, there was no time to bask in the day's victory. The cities of New York and Washington were in close enough proximity that the third game could be played the very next day at New York's Polo Grounds.

Roger Peckinpaugh suffered a charley horse on his game-winning hit and would have to be replaced. Harris would have liked to substitute Tommy Taylor for Bluege at third, moving Bluege to short. Taylor, however, was wearing a splint on his throwing hand, due to an injury he attributed to a fall down some steps. It was believed the real story was that he'd belted someone in the head on the night the Nats had sewn up the pennant in Boston. Instead of using Taylor, Harris had made the decision to start Peckinpaugh, who was in so much pain that he had to come out in the third inning. Harris then had to station the broad-shouldered Ralph Miller, an inferior fielder, at third. Miller had played in the field in only three games during the regular season, and these at second base.

Firpo Marberry, who'd gotten the last out the previous day, got the call from Harris. "Handsome Hugh" McQuillan, the Giants' perennial third starter, would be his mound opponent. Things did not go well for Marberry, as he yielded five hits, two walks, and three runs in the first three innings. Only one of the runs was earned. In the second, Bill Terry opened with a single. After fanning Hack Wilson, Marberry was victimized as a result of Peckinpaugh's absence. Travis Jackson hit the ball on the ground to new shortstop Bluege, whose relay to second to force Terry was dropped by Harris, who was charged with an error.

Instead of being out of the inning, Marberry was looking at men at first and second with still just one out. Hank Gowdy was the next batter. Gowdy was a World War I veteran who had, in June 1917, become the first big-leaguer to enter military service. He enlisted voluntarily, saw combat action in the trenches, and returned from the war highly decorated. Gowdy promptly delivered a sharp basehit that brought in Bill Terry. The Nationals ran Gowdy down between first and second for a second out, so there was a chance yet to get out with limited damage. Marberry next unleashed a wild pitch, and a second unearned run, which he had played a large part in bringing upon himself. The Giants scored a third run off Marberry in the third on a pair of singles and a Wilson double-play groundout, and it was 3–0 in favor of the Giants.

Hugh McQuillan was having his own problems with the Nationals, and Washington quickly got two runs back in the fourth, with Joe Judge, who had three hits and a walk on this day, supplying a double sandwiched between walks. Displaced third baseman Ralph Miller, who hadn't played the position in the majors since 1921, drove in the first run with a sac fly and, following another walk — to Muddy Ruel — McQuillan was gone, pulled in favor of another righthander, Rosy Ryan. Harris sent Benny Tate, an untried rookie catcher, to pinch hit for Marberry. The move paid off, as Tate earned a walk off Ryan, scoring a second run.

Rosy Ryan's presence in this game became even more of a factor when he strode to the plate with one out and nobody on base against new Nats reliever Allan Russell. To everyone's astonishment, including his own, Ryan clubbed a vicious home run into the upper deck of the distant right field stands at the Polo Grounds. Ralph Miller's suspect fielding skills resulted in a 5–2 Giants lead in the sixth. Miller stopped a ground ball off Gowdy's bat, but lost the handle on it. Lindstrom later doubled to bring Gowdy around.

Joe Martina,* 6–8, 4.67 in 1924, his only season in the big leagues, pitched an uneventful seventh for the Griffithmen, as the Senators were sometimes called by the writers. The Nats pulled within two in the eighth. Bluege singled with one out, was helped along when Ralph Miller walked, and then scored on an infield single by Mule Shirley, who was pinch hitting for Martina.

In the bottom of the inning, Harris brought in underarmer Byron Speece, a 27-year-old rookie righthander who had pitched well on the 21 occasions Bucky called upon him during the regular season (2–1, 2.65). Speece just didn't have any luck at all on this day. He gave up just one clean hit, to Hank Gowdy, after Travis Jackson had beaten a slow roller to first. Rosy Ryan, who pitched 4⅔ innings for the victory in this game, then grounded to Speece, bringing in the run. Speece then made a very nice play on a perfect bunt toward third by Frank Frisch, pouncing on the ball and making the play to Ruel at the plate to nip Gowdy and end the inning.

The Nats made a valiant effort in the ninth, scoring a run and loading the bases with one out. The Giants' third pitcher of the inning, Mule Watson, only 28 but making what would turn out to be his last appearance in the major leagues, got Miller to foul out to Lindstrom at third, and Ruel to ground into a force-out to wrap up the game, a 6–4 loss for Washington.

To Senators fans, game four of the 1924 World Series, on October 7, became known as The "Goslin Game." The exuberant, awkward Goose of earlier years was now one of the American League's most respected hitters, having just led the circuit in RBIs, outdistancing the likes of Babe Ruth. Ruth had dominated in that category for four of the five previous years, and would have done the same in 1922 had his season not been curtailed by injury.

A much surer fielder than he'd once been, Goose Goslin had kept the same closed stance of his earlier years, somewhat reminiscent of the lefthanded carriage later adopted by future great Stan Musial. Goslin showed only his back to the pitcher and peered at him over his shoulder. Goose had a protruding nose, and he was known to be able to joke about it. He would say that because of the way he stood at the plate, he was not able to see past his nose with his left eye. Had he been able to keep two eyes on the ball, he would have hit, he figured, around .600 or so.

The Giants wasted no time scoring first in the fourth game, as Ossie Bluege's error

---

*Martina, who won 349 minor-league games, had very bad teeth — so bad that despite his short stay in the majors, he had the honor of being named the ugliest big-leaguer of the 1920s in The Bill James Historical Baseball Abstract.

contributed to a run off lefty George Mo-gridge, the veteran who had served Clark Griffith so well since being picked up from the Yankees in '21. Following the first game, Harris had decided that Walter Johnson would not start game four — he wanted to give him one more day's rest. His first choice for this game, Curly Ogden, had sacrificed too much down the stretch — his arm was too sore — so Harris had opted for Mogridge.

Goose Goslin, who had singled off Virgil Barnes to open the previous inning, started taking matters into his own hands in the third when he came up with two on and two out. He propelled the first pitch he saw into the lower tier of the right field grandstand, bringing in McNeely and Harris, both of whom had singled in front of him. Barnes, 16–10 for John McGraw in '24, was still around when Goslin next came to bat, in the fifth inning. McNeely and Harris had again both singled in front of him, and McNeely had already counted the fourth run when Barnes uncorked a wild pitch. With one out, Goslin drove in Harris with his third hit for a 5–1 lead. The Giants were never in it, although they kept pecking away at Mogridge with single runs in the sixth and eighth frames. Until the second run, Mo-gridge (who, incidentally, struck out four times in this game) had kept the Giants off the scoresheet for four straight frames.

The Nats countered with two runs of their own in the eighth inning. Goslin led off with another single, and he and Joe Judge came home when Ossie Bluege got his third single of the day for a 7–2 Washington margin. Earl McNeely also had three hits, including a double, in this game. The Giants did reply with a run charged to Mogridge in the eighth, after Ross Youngs was given a free pass and Mogridge had been replaced by Fred Marberry. Marberry surrendered another mean-ingless run in the ninth. The Senators had themselves a 7–4 win, thanks to the exploits of Goslin, who'd had himself a 4–for–4 out-ing, including a three-run homer and four runs driven in.

The Nats had regained home-field advantage, with Walter Johnson set to go the next day in the third and last game to be contested in New York. Concerned about Ralph Miller's two errors in two days and Bluege's miscue while playing out of position at short, Johnson himself approached Peckinpaugh and urged him to play. Peck assured him that he had no mobility at all and that he couldn't play, but Johnson felt that Peck would be of value if only because his presence in the lineup would allow Bluege to return to third. Peckinpaugh did not play, however.

Game five started off with a bang when lead-off hitter Earl McNeely bashed a rocket off the lefthander, Jack Bentley. The 18-year-old rookie third baseman, Fred Lindstrom, leapt and snared the missile — a fantastic catch by all accounts. After Harris and Rice harm-lessly made outs, Lindstrom, who was to hit .333 in this, his first World Series, led off in the bottom of the inning with a single to left off Walter Johnson. Barney recovered by first getting Frankie Frisch to foul out to third baseman Ralph Miller, who was starting his second consecutive game because of Peckinpaugh's injury. Miller had played partial seasons for the Phillies back in '20 and '21, and the 1924 World Series would be his swan song. He logged only 26 official at-bats for the 1924 Washington Senators, and 11 of them came in the World Series.

The third-place hitter, Ross Youngs, flew out to McNeely in center field. Lindstrom then took off for second, but Muddy Ruel cut him down, ending the inning. After an uneventful second during which Goose Goslin's infield single was the only hit on either side, the dignified Walter Johnson approached the plate. Again he got an ovation — many New York fans had stood when he took the mound at the start of the game. Eighty percent of New York, according to Grantland Rice, was rooting for this man.

The Big Train drove the ball all the way to the left field wall, but the locomotive broke down and fell as he was rounding first. Running was not Walter's forte, and it was often said that he ran as if he was still behind the plow back on the farm. Hack Wilson pegged the ball to Frisch at second, who then relayed to Terry to intercept the Big Train. Following the out, McNeely and Harris managed to get on, but were stranded. Johnson's difficulties intensified in the bottom of the inning when Travis Jackson, the good-hitting Bentley, and Lindstrom, all singled. And it certainly could have been worse. With still just one out, Sam Rice caught a liner in right field off the bat of Ross Youngs, and then threw the ball to Johnson. The pitcher's relay to the plate caught Bentley trying to score and put an end to the shenanigans.

The Senators, down 1–0, struck right back. Joe Judge banged a single off the right field wall behind Youngs and was sacrificed to second by Bluege. Judge took third when Muddy Ruel grounded to short, bringing up Ralph Miller, 1–for–7 in the Series so far. The harried Miller came through, singling along the right field foul line. He didn't stop at first, however, and he should have. But the score was now tied.

The 12 innings Johnson had thrown in the first game of the Series had no doubt taken their toll. Having struck out 12 in that game, Johnson could come back with only three in game five. He was lucky to get out of the fourth inning without surrendering the lead, as Bill Terry had tripled to deep right with only one out. However, in the fifth, after giving up a single to catcher Hank Gowdy, Jack Bentley, the "not-quite Babe Ruth," rocked Johnson for a towering home run into the right field seats. It was estimated that the ball landed about a foot fair and a foot inside the upper-deck railing down the short right field line.

Shortstop Bluege, whom Johnson would have loved to have seen at his familiar spot at third, was in cahoots with Bucky Harris to turn a gorgeous double play to get Walter out of the inning without further damage. In the seventh, the Nats turned another defensive gem. Lindstrom and Youngs, who'd both singled, stood on the corners with two out. McGraw called for another double steal, and this time Ruel went immediately to second with his peg, stopping Youngs, the slower of the two baserunners, dead in his tracks. As Youngs

retreated and a rundown involving Harris and Joe Judge ensued, Lindstrom broke for the plate. Harris made the right decision, gunning the ball home to prevent Lindstrom from scoring before the last out was made. It was a close play, but Ruel held on to the ball and the seventh inning ended with the score unchanged.

It was not until the eighth that the Nats closed the gap. With one out and still trailing 3–1, Goose Goslin hit his third home run of the Series, this one up against the upper tier of the grandstand in right. The Goose was coming through in a major way — his infield single in the second inning was his sixth hit in a row in the World Series, a record which would still be standing at century's end. This home run also tied Babe Ruth's then record of three home runs in a single World Series. Joe Judge promptly followed Goslin's blast with a single to right to chase Bentley. John McGraw called upon Hugh McQuillan, the starter and winner in game three. McQuillan did the job, inducing both Bluege and Ruel to ground out to the infield, which got the Giants out of the inning hanging on to their 3–2 lead.

This all became academic in the bottom of the eighth, when Kelly singled and Terry was walked by Johnson. This was only the second walk allowed by Johnson on the day, but before it was over he gave up 13 hits and also hit a batter. With men on first and second, no one out, and the Giants looking to pad their lead, Hack Wilson bunted. Johnson picked the ball up but fumbled, loading the bases. The game turned on that play and the Giants pushed three runs across on a flyout, a bloop single, and Lindstrom's fourth hit of the day, for a 6–2 final.

As things turned sour for the Nats and Walter Johnson, the Polo Grounds crowd, behind Walter all day, was stunned. Is this what could befall a hero? Past his prime, the once great pitcher had not once but twice failed to make good on a shot at glory. Pressed by reporters during the train ride back to Washington, Bucky Harris defended his decision not to pull Walter from the game despite the 13 hits and only three strikeouts. Harris blared that he wouldn't have made Walter Johnson take the long walk back to the clubhouse even if it had meant winning all the games of the World Series.

When the Big Train made the trek at the end of the game, he looked particularly haggard and discouraged. In the clubhouse, Johnson lamented his second straight failure despite the fact that he would have willingly cut off his right arm to win that day. Muddy Ruel tried to boost his morale, reminding the great one that the Series was still far from over. What may have counted more was the firm advice proffered by Clark Griffith on the train ride back to Washington. Clutching Johnson's pitching arm, Griffith told him to forget about trying to help his friends find tickets for the next day's game. Walter was instructed to go right home. There may be another opportunity for him yet!

The fact remained that the Washington Senators were going home with their backs up against the proverbial wall, and their boy manager had better think of something smart real quick. Bucky Harris turned, in this time of desperate need, to Jonathan Thompson Walton Zachary, who'd won the second game of the Series and pitched to within one out of a complete game. The long-necked Southerner had made use of his elaborate handle when he had pitched in the major leagues under an assumed name. As a member of the Philadelphia A's in 1918, he had been known as Zach Walton. At the time, he had been intent on protecting his eligibility to play college ball.

McGraw's choice as starting pitcher for the sixth game was just as obvious as Harris's. He had Art Nehf ready to go. Nehf had been sitting since the 12-inning win over Johnson in game one. McGraw had kept him back one game to let him recover, and that could have been interpreted as a good move since the Giants had won the fifth contest anyway.

Five thousand fans greeted the sagging Senators at the train station upon their return to Washington, and the 34,254 fans who populated Griffith Stadium for game six numbered among them President and Mrs. Coolidge, who took their seats for the third consecutive game. The crowd's mightiest cheer was for Roger Peckinpaugh, who took the shortstop position after missing two games with a charley horse, which had caused him much pain in his left thigh for three days. Peck was saying he was ready to break a leg to get back in action. The limb was bandaged and strapped so tightly to keep it upright that Peck could hardly feel his foot touch the ground.

This game was very exciting right off the bat, as half the games had been so far. After Lindstrom led off with a bunt on which Bluege, back at his familiar position, made a nice play to throw him out, Frank Frisch crashed a solid double along the line in right. Zachary got Ross Youngs to bounce right to him and then coolly turned toward third to catch Frisch in a rundown — Youngs made it to second on the play. The crowd was immediately disquieted again when George Kelly singled off Zachary to bring in the first run. Sam Rice then had to make a fine running one-handed catch on a drive by Irish Meusel to end the first half-inning.

Zachary was never in any trouble in this game again. He allowed only five hits and just one runner to get to second the whole rest of the way. Not only were there no walks, Zachary never even got to ball three with any hitter during the entire game. But his mates weren't doing anything for him offensively. The Nats had gotten four different baserunners on in the bottom of the first inning, but Harris forced McNeely and then got himself picked off. Except for Peckinpaugh's single off Lindstrom's shoe in the second inning, the Nats went down 1–2–3 in each inning until the fifth.

Peckinpaugh singled for the second time to start things off, and then Ruel came through with the anticipated sacrifice to move him up to second. Zachary then grounded to Bill Terry, but this put Peck on third with two down. With the pressure on him, Earl McNeely, the late-season spark, drew a walk on four straight pitches. McNeely promptly stole second, Gowdy not risking a throw that could have resulted in the run coming in from third.

This brought up the boy manager, Bucky Harris, who came through for his men. His single to right brought in both runs and the Senators were up 2–1.

The Nats stayed ahead as a result of Zachary's masterful pitching on this day. In the ninth, George Kelly singled past first base with just one out. Irish Meusel then slashed a hard grounder through the box which could well have signified the beginning of the end of the Senators' hopes for staying alive. Roger Peckinpaugh had been playing the righthanded Meusel in the hole and came back toward second, leaped, made a terrific stab, and then miraculously flipped to Harris. This forced pinch-runner Billy Southworth, but Harris's relay to first conked Joe Judge on the knee. Judge went down in pain, but it turned out that he was not seriously injured and would continue. After Judge fell, everyone noticed that Peckinpaugh was also on the ground — and he wasn't moving.

Peckinpaugh was escorted from the field, bloodied and obviously in agony, his weight supported by his teammates. He would not be back during this World Series. Once again, Ossie Bluege moved over to short. With the Nats ahead, 5'8" rookie Thomas Livingston Carlton Taylor, a better fielder than Ralph Miller, was sent in to man the hot corner. This was the same Tommy Taylor who had hurt his throwing hand during the pennant-party festivities and had had it in a splint ever since. Harris, who didn't have much choice, decided to send the injured player into the fracas anyway.

With Meusel standing on first and two out, Zachary threw three pitches to rookie Hack Wilson. Wilson, who would strike out nine times in the Series, did what came naturally. Yes, Virginia, there would be a seventh game! A coin toss would determine where the deciding game of the first seven-game Series in 12 years would be played. Commissioner Landis presided, and just as they had won when a flip of the coin had decided where the Series would open, the Nats were lucky again.

If there had been some interesting developments in the first inning of several of the

games so far, they were nothing compared to the high jinks devised by Bucky Harris as the clincher got under way. Harris called upon Curly Ogden as his starting pitcher. This was the same Curly Ogden who had bombed with the A's earlier in the season and who had started 17 times for Washington in 1924. Curly Ogden of the perennially sore arm. Ogden struck out the pesky Fred Lindstrom and then walked Frank Frisch. His next move was to walk to the dugout, never to reappear.

Harris had hatched a plan which he'd revealed to Clark Griffith that morning. Going with the righthanded Ogden would incite John McGraw to start the rookie, Bill Terry, who, despite batting only 163 times during the season, was murdering Harris's pitchers. Terry had six hits in 12 at-bats, including a triple and a homer so far. McGraw generally only deployed the lefthanded-hitting Terry against righthanders.

Bucky Harris reasoned that in the first inning, he would lift Ogden and bring in lefty George Mogridge. Harris wasn't worried about Terry hitting Mogridge. If McGraw made more changes, like hopefully lifting Terry from the game, Harris would go to a righthander again — probably Firpo Marberry. Griffith gave Harris his okay for the plan, and when the manager left, Griff telephoned Walter Johnson and told him to be ready — he just might be coming in for late relief in the biggest game of his life.

Everything went according to plan, or just about, as the game got under way on the most beautiful day of the entire Series, the whole of which was played this year in particularly pleasant conditions. Ogden had been expected to pitch to the lead-off batter, Lindstrom, only, but when he got the rookie on three pitches, Harris motioned for Ogden to stay in. Maybe Curly's dead limb could bounce back for one more act of heroism, although it had given no such indication of late. Ogden walked the next man, Frank Frisch, and the strategy was then implemented.

With the lefthanded Ross Youngs batting third and due up, Mogridge was summoned. He'd been warming up out of view, under the stands. Mogridge struck Youngs out, and got Kelly to ground out harmlessly to Tommy Taylor at third, who was playing in what would turn out to be, simultaneously, his first World Series start and last major-league game. Two of the rookie's 75 official at-bats took place in the World Series.

Bill Terry grounded out to start the second and would leave the game in the sixth inning. By then, the Senators had a 1–0 lead thanks to their peerless leader, Harris, who hit a home run off screwballer Virgil Barnes for the Nats' first hit, in the fourth inning. This was Bucky's second homer of the Series; it doubled his total for the season. In a 12-year career, Bucky would hit just nine regular-season dingers. Hack Wilson, who had fallen clumsily into the temporary bleachers in left in an attempt at snaring Harris's homer, made a sensational belly slide moments later as he grabbed a sinking liner off the bat of Sam Rice.

Mogridge had been sailing along, with Lindstrom's double over Tommy Taylor's head in the fifth the only serious blow, until he got into big trouble in the sixth. Youngs walked to open the inning, and Kelly singled him to third. It was at this point that Terry was taken out of the game in favor of the righthander, Irish Meusel. Harris countered with the big, scowling righty, Fred Marberry.

Called "Firpo" (a nickname he hated) because of his resemblance to Luis Firpo, a boxer who had once knocked Jack Dempsey out of the ring, Marberry was himself knocked back by the Giants. President Coolidge had led a standing ovation as Marberry had made the trek from the bullpen to the mound. Seconds later, there were more cheers for a player who was smiling and waving back at the crowd — it was Walter Johnson, and he had left the dugout and was making his way to the bullpen.

Marberry gave up a long fly to pinch hitter Meusel to bring in the tying run. Hack Wilson then singled to send Kelly all the way to third. Then, two straight muffs in the field — one by the excellent fielder Judge at first, and the other by the displaced Bluege at

short — brought in a second run. Judge bobbled Travis Jackson's hard grounder as he tried to hurry a throw home in a hopeless attempt to get Kelly. He couldn't decide what to do with the ball, and Wilson and Jackson were both safe. Then Bluege let Hank Gowdy's roller right through the wickets, an error he would later refer to as the worst of his entire life. This scored Wilson, and pitcher Barnes then lofted a long fly to score a third run.

After Barnes retired the Nats again in the bottom of the sixth, Bucky Harris had been the only one of 19 batters to face him to even reach base. Could it be that Harris's carefully conceived plan had somehow backfired? In the seventh, the Nats' fielding showed a resurgence. Catcher Ruel reached far into the crowd to pluck out a Frankie Frisch foul. Tommy Taylor then made a great play, cutting in front of Bluege on a slow bouncer to just edge George Kelly at first. Marberry fielded a roller by Irish Meusel and applied the tag himself. The crowd was coming back to life.

Finally, in the eighth, with the Nats still trailing 3–1, there was a rally. The veteran Nemo Leibold, a reliable .293 hitter during the regular campaign, came up with one out to pinch hit for Tommy Taylor and doubled down the left field foul line. This brought up catcher Muddy Ruel. He was the author of a steady .283 bat mark during the season, but had contributed zero offense during this entire Series with an awful 0-for-18 performance. Ruel made it 1-for-19, with a base hit that nicked Kelly's glove.

Leibold stopped at third and pinch hitter Bennie Tate, a rookie with 43 major-league at-bats under his belt, was called upon to bat for Marberry. As Tate ambled to the plate, Walter Johnson was seen emerging from the dugout again, this time seemingly in more of a hurry to get to the bullpen. Benny Tate walked for the third time in his third World Series plate appearance, filling the bases. The collective hopes of nearly 32,000 fans withered, however, when McNeely lifted a benign fly to left field.

Once again, the boy manager of the Senators would have to settle the issue. He settled it in his side's favor. Harris singled sharply over Lindstrom's head, tying the score when both Leibold and Ruel raced home. In the din that resulted, some spectators burst onto the field and were quickly rounded up by police. The First Lady, Grace Coolidge, had by now worked herself into such a frenzy that she hardly ever sat down. The President, known as "Silent Cal," didn't make quite as much noise, but he did drop his cigar when the Nats tied the score.

Mule Shirley, who was in the game for Tate and who had an odd nickname for a pinch-runner, had stopped at second on Harris's hit. Manager McGraw summoned reliable Art Nehf, who'd thrown seven full innings the previous day, to pitch to Sam Rice. Rice grounded out to end the inning, but the Senators were back in it, the score knotted at three after eight.

Next came perhaps the most breathtaking moment in the history of the Washington Senators; it was perhaps the most breathtaking moment in all of baseball's illustrious story. In his deliberate, dignified gait, striding from the bench was Walter Johnson. Here was the opportunity for the 18-year veteran, participating in his very first World Series, to make amends for his two losses thus far. What a game to win!

The man many felt was the only pitcher who might have rivaled Johnson as the best of the early part of the century, Christy Mathewson, said at this precise moment in the press box that it was a shame to send Walter Johnson back into the fray — "Poor old Walter," Mathewson called him. Mathewson would later state, incidentally, that this 1924 World Series was the best he had ever seen, and he had played in four himself.

Manager Harris got the distinct impression from Walter's five warmup pitches that the big guy had his stuff. Johnson got the Giants' lead-off man, Fred Lindstrom, who'd gone 4–for–5 against him two days earlier, to pop harmlessly to third baseman Ralph Miller to start the top of the ninth. Miller had just been inserted into the game, succeeding Taylor, who had replaced Leibold — who had

started the big comeback — in the bottom of the eighth.

Frank Frisch woke everyone in spacious Griffith Stadium from their reverie with a monstrous triple over Earl McNeely's head in deepest center field, a blow of well over 400 feet. Ross Youngs was then walked intentionally, a textbook move in order to set up a double play. Walter Johnson then demonstrated to everyone that he still had that special something. Future Hall of Famer George Kelly went down on three straight swinging strikes. Heywood Broun would write in *New York World* the following day that whenever he wanted to reassure himself that the soul of man cannot die, he would remember how Walter Johnson had struck out George Kelly with one out and a man on third.

Irish Meusel, batting in Bill Terry's spot, then sent a ground ball toward 28-year-old Ralph Miller, who, unbeknownst to anyone, was, as indicated earlier, playing in his very last major-league game. Miller came up with the ball cleanly, but made a throw to first which forced Joe Judge to stretch his 5'8" frame to its limits. The Big Train was out of the inning.

With men on first and second and just one out in the bottom of the ninth, Ralph Miller hit into a double play. Walter Johnson headed for extra innings, as he'd done in the first game, and walked the first batter in the tenth, Hack Wilson. He then struck out Travis Jackson, who looked at strike three, and enticed receiver Hank Gowdy to bounce to the mound to start a double play. With one out in the bottom of the tenth, everyone's heart surged up to their throats — Walter Johnson slugged a fly to left center that looked like it had a chance to go out. It didn't, as Hack Wilson pulled it in about ten feet in front of the fence.

After Earl McNeely struck out to send the Nats down in order, Johnson allowed a lead-off single in the top of the 11th to Heinie Groh, who was pinch hitting for starter McQuillan. After Lindstrom sacrificed, Johnson fanned Frank Frisch, one of the toughest men to strike out in baseball history, who took an off-balance swipe at a roundhouse curve which moved far out of the strike zone. To this day one of the all-time best hitters among second basemen, Frisch had struck out only 24 times during the regular season, the second-highest total of his 19-year career. After again walking Ross Youngs intentionally (Youngs' fourth walk of the game), Johnson then struck out the N.L.'s top RBI man, Long George Kelly, once again. Everyone in the park went batty.

Big Jack Bentley came in to try to stop the Nats in the bottom of the 11th. One run of course, and the Nats would be World Champions. The intensity was palpable, and the crowd remained on its feet. Harris and Rice, the first two batters, both flied out — Rice hit the ball a long way, to Hack Wilson in deep left center. Goose Goslin then deposited a Texas Leaguer into right field for a double. In an odd bit of strategy, John Mc-Graw then instructed his lefthander, Jack Bentley, to put lefty Joe Judge on intentionally in favor of righthander Ossie Bluege. With Bluege up with a chance to win it, the superior-fielding Ross Youngs moved to left, and Irish Meusel went to right. The maneuver had no bearing on what happened next, as Bluege hit the ball on the ground to short, and the potential insurgence was snuffed out.

For the third straight inning, the first Giant got on against Johnson, as Irish Meusel singled to right to open the 12th, and for the fourth straight inning, the Giants would not score, as Barney mowed them down. He registered his fifth strikeout against Hack Wilson. By this point, Walter Johnson conceded later, he'd gotten it into his mind that maybe this would be his day after all.

After Miller led off the 12th with a groundout, catcher Muddy Ruel, 1–for–20 in the Series, fouled behind home plate. At this point, as Clark Griffith later put it, Giants catcher Hank Gowdy's mask came up to bite him. Gowdy's left foot came down squarely onto the mask and he tried to kick it off as he looked for the ball, which eluded him. Griffith had moved from his box seat to steps near the dugout in the eighth inning so as to be in a better position to escort President Coolidge and his wife from the stadium. When the Nats had come back to tie the game, he hadn't dared budge for fear of upsetting whatever karma might have been at work in favor of his men. He didn't move until the game ended.

With his second life, Ruel doubled past third base and down the line in left. Walter Johnson then of course came up to hit for himself and drilled the first offering to the right of shortstop. Travis Jackson, future Hall of Famer, booted it. Ruel held to his base, but the Senators were in business, with just one out and the top of the order coming up. With Earl McNeely next, the Nats expected Irish Meusel and Ross Youngs to switch places again, as the righthanded McNeely was a dead pull hitter, but they didn't.

McNeely sliced Bentley's second pitch sharply in the direction of third base, just a few feet fair. Muddy Ruel, on second with a man on first, decided to go for third right away in order to attract a tag in hopes of keeping the inning alive by avoiding a double play. The wonderful rookie, Lindstrom, stood at the ready. All of a sudden, the ball bounced way up high. It was way over Lindstrom's head … into left field!

Muddy Ruel, of all people, came bounding in all the way from second base. Irish Meusel, still in left field, had not planned on the unexpected, and this was costly. When Meusel finally got hold of the ball, with Ruel past third and on the way home, he did nothing and would get chewed out by John Mc-Graw for it on the train ride home. Bedlam ensued as the winning run of the 1924 World Series crossed the plate. In the bottom of the 12th inning, the Washington Senators had won the world championship — their first — and in front of their long-suffering home fans at that.

The field was engulfed by a sea of bodies. Walter Johnson took it all in from second base for a few seconds, and his eyes welled up with tears as he made his way through the crazed mob back to the dugout. Earl McNeely was the one who had the most difficulty making it back there. The crowd, in an enthusiastic show of its love for a hero, tore off his shirt before police could reach him and escort him to the clubhouse. The President and Mrs. Coolidge, less the focus of attention now than ever, were escorted out by the Secret Service. They passed several players on the way, including Walter Johnson. The First Couple shook hands with them and offered their congratulations.

After showering, Bucky Harris, high-strung and seemingly in a daze, was so excited that he forgot to put his clothes on. Walter Johnson came in and shook his hand, thanking him for having let him pitch. When Bucky was asked if Walter had insisted on pitching, Harris said that Johnson had been his best bet, and for anyone to have thought otherwise would have been absolute foolishness. Frank Frisch and Ross Youngs came over from the other side to congratulate Walter, whom Frisch called one of the greatest pitchers and one of the finest gentlemen ever associated with the game of baseball. In summing up the World Series for the Walsh Syndicate, John McGraw wrote that the game of baseball had been elevated by the great Walter Johnson and his ultimate triumph. The only thing better, the Little General declared, would have been for Johnson to have won the game himself— to have hit that home run which had fallen just a little short in the tenth inning.

Those who were present in the hours that followed the thriller said that Clark Griffith could do nothing to stop the tears that flowed from his eyes. He embraced all his players, thanking them and telling them how proud they had made him. Walter Johnson was so happy that, he would say years later, winning the World Series in his 18th year had hardly seemed real. He had, following great tribulation, justified his place as America's darling, redeeming himself at the 13th hour (and 12th inning), and winning his first World Series game a month before his 37th birthday. As perhaps best expressed by the eloquent Grantland Rice in *Collier's* in January 1925: "Walter Johnson had come from a lone, dejected and broken figure in the shadows of a clubhouse to a personal triumph that no other

athlete had ever drawn in all the history of sport."

Cannons, pistols, firecrackers, and the sounds of thousands of automobiles intermingled for a joyous celebration in downtown Washington. It seemed that no one wanted to miss this celebration — the fire department of nearby Cherrydale, Virginia, showed up with all its vehicles and a banner which read "Let Cherrydale Burn!" It was to be a wonderful time. For a year, the Washington Senators would stand as champions of the world. Muddy Ruel, who'd hit .095 in the World Series, insisted he didn't mind when team owner Griffith had said Ruel had taken longer than anyone he had ever seen to come around the bases with the winning run. Ruel preferred to dwell on the positives — a world championship, the role the Big Train had played, and how sweet it was to find out how sweet it was to be victorious. Then there was the matter of the winner's share of the spoils for the World Series — a check for $5,959.64 per man.

From the point of view of posterity, this would stand as one of the great World Series ever (at the time it was widely acknowledged as the most exciting since 1912), primarily because of its strange denouement ... and the unlikely triumph of a man whose career may very well place him as the greatest righthanded pitcher in all of baseball history. At the end of the day, losing pitcher Jack Bentley said it best for all of America: "The good Lord just couldn't bear to see a fine fellow like Walter Johnson lose again."

For their sheer beauty, here are the words formulated by Bill Corum, as they appeared in the *New York Times* the following morning:

> To the victor belong the spoils. When future generations are told about this game they will not hear about Barnes, or Frisch, or Kelly, or even about Harris or McNeely. But the boy with his first glove and ball crowding up to his father's knee will beg: "Tell me about Walter Johnson."

The Old Fox's Folly had paid handsome dividends, and Clark Griffith made a tidy profit of $150,000 as a result of his "little ballclub" having become a world champion. Griff directed 20 percent of that right back toward Bucky Harris, who had played and managed for $7,000 the previous year. At 27 years, 11 months, and two days, he remains, at the beginning of this new century, the youngest man to have managed a World Series winner. The new pact for 1925 called for Harris to earn $30,000 to both manage and play over three years. As the Washington Senators undertook to defend their newfound position at the top of the baseball world, Clark Griffith's generosity seemed to know no bounds.

Bucky Harris would have his work cut out for him in 1925, particularly with respect to revamping the pitching staff. George Mogridge was nearly the same age as Walter Johnson, but not nearly the pitcher. This proved true early in the '25 season, and by June, the previous year's 16-game winner had been traded to the Browns. Heading into the season, there was no guarantee on performance even in terms of Johnson. Where would the Senators end up if this was to be the season that he was to go downhill?

As for the rest of the staff, Tom Zachary was only 29, but his career already seemed to be on a downspin. He would go 12–15 with the Senators in 1925, with a mediocre 3.85 ERA. Zachary began displaying a knack for being at the wrong place at the wrong time. On May 17, he gave up Tris Speaker's 3,000th hit, albeit during a game won 2–1 by the Nats. In a little more than two years, Zachary would give up an even more historically significant hit to Babe Ruth — the Bambino's 60th home run of 1927. After a 6–9 start for the Senators in '28, he would be placed on waivers and claimed by the Yankees on August 23, becoming Babe Ruth's teammate less than a year after the Babe had slammed his 60th off him. In 1929, Zachary would go 12–0 for the Yankees, in a year when all the factors would be right — he would have a "career" year on one of the great ballclubs of all time.

The demise of George Mogridge and, to an extent, of Tom Zachary, during 1925 was discouraging for Senators supporters, for Washington's pitching staff was already riddled with uncertainties. Despite his eight wins in a row for the Nats in '24, Curly Ogden was still shaky in the early part of the '25 season, and was soon sent down to the minors. Right-hander Allan Russell was nearly 38, and not counted upon to supply very many innings. Joe Martina didn't have much left and was released. Rookies Paul Zahniser and Byron Speece didn't look promising.

Clark Griffith had won the World Series with one of the oldest ballclubs ever to win a championship, and the Nats would do so again in 1925 with a roster that was even older. A couple of weeks before Christmas, 1924, Griffith made two deals, obtaining seasoned pitchers Stan Coveleski and Dutch Ruether. A Pennsylvania coal miner, Coveleski had gotten a late start in baseball and had won 19 as a 28-year-old for the Indians in 1917. He won 22 or more over the next four seasons but was coming off a 15–16, 4.04, season with the Indians, and was nearing his 36th birthday.

The shrewd Old Fox was determined to keep patching up his club, and he'd had to part with very little for the two veteran hurlers. For Coveleski, Griff gave up Speece, of the exaggerated underhand windup, and some cash. For Ruether, who had a reputation as a troublemaker, Griffith sent some money to the Dodgers. The supposedly penurious owner even purchased the contract of Vean Gregg, who was 40 and hadn't seen the light of day in the majors in seven years. That particular move would have little impact, as Gregg would go 2–2 in 26 games before leaving the scene for good.

On behalf of the Washington Senators in 1925, Stan Coveleski, future member of the Hall of Fame (inducted 1969), went 20–5, and led the league with a 2.84 ERA, winning 13 in a row at one point. Dutch Ruether went 18–7. This tweaking of the pitching staff, coupled with Babe Ruth's famous "bellyache," which caused him to miss 64 games, was enough to keep the Yankees way out of the pennant race, which contributed to the Senators' good fortunes.

As for Walter Johnson, he had felt at first,

following the World Series conquest, that the time to retire had come, that this was the high note he wanted to go out on. He had considered buying the Vernon franchise of the Pacific Coast League. The deal had fallen through, however, and the asking price of the Oakland club, which Johnson had also looked at, had gone through the roof. Joe Engel was dispatched to the West Coast by Clark Griffith with two contracts in hand. One was for one year and the other for two, just in case Walter Johnson could be persuaded to change his mind.

When the price for the Oakland ballclub turned out to be higher than what had recently been paid for the major-league St. Louis Cardinals, Walter decided he would pitch again. Now an affluent man due to holdings in oil, real estate, and mining concerns, the Big Train was still a hard bargainer, and he negotiated with Griffith by phone from his home in Reno, Nevada, and then from Hot Springs, Arkansas. Finally, the two came to terms face-to-face at the spring training site in Tampa: a two-year contract, at $20,000 per. When Walter asked to bow out of a barnstorming tour of some southern locales so he could continue to train in Tampa, Griff refused. The boss pointed out that the Washington Senators were the South's representative in the big leagues, and that everyone wanted to see Walter Johnson in the flesh.

Barney went on to have quite a year, joining Coveleski in the 20-game winners' circle. His record was 20–7, 3.07, while allowing the fewest hits per game, registering the most strikeouts per game, and placing third in the league in ERA. Dutch Ruether's 18 victories and the stellar work of Firpo Marberry were the other positive aspects of a staff with the second-best ERA in the entire majors. There was support behind these guys — the Nats also placed second in the majors in fielding.

Here was another Washington Senators club which got everyone's attention and commanded respect, rather than derision, when it stepped onto the baseball field. The team batting average for 1925 would be .303 — Rice hit .350, Goslin .334 with 18 home runs,

World War I vet Joe "Moon" Harris .323, Judge .314, and Ruel .310. Among the position players, certainly Roger Peckinpaugh's left leg had been considered a liability when the season opened. Joe Judge was nearing his 31st birthday and was not particularly strong physically.

Griffith obtained veteran iron man Everett Scott from the Yankees to relieve Peckinpaugh, and got Moon Harris to spell Judge at first or play the outfield in case any of the shoo-ins — Rice, Goslin, or McNeely — got hurt. Harris was a 34-year-old who'd been in the majors on an on-again off-again basis for over ten years. At one point, he was banned from the majors for two years for playing in a league which operated outside the bounds of organized baseball.

The Senators team that took the field on opening day was exactly the same one that had won it all against the great New York Giants in October. Unlike the club of the year before, though, it was to discover it would no longer be the recipient of any underdog sentiment as it defended its title of champion of the American League. The Nats suffered a 5–1 loss at Yankee Stadium, with Mogridge getting the nod as starting pitcher. Babe Ruth, ailing from "the bellyache heard around the world" was noteworthy for his absence, replaced by an outfielder named Ben Paschal, who provided a reasonable facsimile of Ruth by slugging a home run.

As was customary, though, Walter Johnson got the start for the opener in Washington. It was business as usual. He opened his 19th year with a 10–1 win on April 22, with the only run off him unearned. It was noted that President Coolidge stood up at the beginning of the seventh frame, until pulled back into his seat by the First Lady. She, as the real baseball fan in the family, knew that the seventh-inning stretch was to be taken in the middle of the inning and not before.

The A's were Washington's chief opposition as the first month of the season unfolded. Philadelphia had a great new outfielder, Al Simmons, and rookie catcher Mickey Cochrane was considered a true prospect and would not disappoint. The A's second-year lefthander, Lefty Grove, was throwing bullets and would lead the league in ERA. But the Senators got off to a fine start, embroiled in a battle for first with the A's and the Indians after the first month. Earl McNeely, however, was not getting on base, and Goslin had moved over to take his spot in center. Joe Harris, a known quantity as a hitter, filled Goslin's spot in left.

At this time, the concrete wall in right-field at Griffith Stadium was raised to a 30-foot height. Reminiscent of the Green Monster, the left field wall at Fenway Park in Boston, Griffith's right field fence was seven feet shorter but five feet farther. It is recorded that Phil Todt, a young first baseman with the Boston Red Sox, hit the first home run over the Griffith fence, on May 1, 1925. By then, the A's were solidifying their hold on first place. On the 27th, Walter Johnson, the recipient of some extraordinary offensive support this season, beat the A's 10–9. It was Barney's seventh straight win, during which the Senators' bats had provided him with 60 runs. While the A's were still clinging to their lead for the time being, over the next three months the two clubs would trade places at the top of the standings.

Johnson, Coveleski, and Ruether were winning with great regularity. On June 1, Babe Ruth returned to action against Johnson and the Senators at Yankee Stadium but went 0–for–2 in a 5–3 Nats win. Less conspicuous than Ruth and Johnson on this day was another future inductee of the Hall of Fame. Twenty-two-year-old Lou Gehrig was brought up to pinch hit against Fred Marberry and began his streak of 2,130 consecutive games. It is quite a coincidence that the skein Gehrig would eventually surpass, teammate Everett Scott's 1,307 straight games, had ended the day before, when Scott had been replaced in the lineup by Pee Wee Wanninger. Within 2½ weeks, Scott would be purchased by the Senators.

On June 8, George Mogridge and catcher Pinky Hargrave were traded to the St. Louis Browns for another veteran bat off the bench, 34-year-old catcher Hank Severeid, who'd been in the league ten years before coming into his own and batting over .300 during the last four campaigns. Severeid would bat at a .355 clip in 50 games for the Senators over the remainder of the season as backup catcher. On the same day he was acquired, Goose Goslin hit three home runs, to tie the then American League record. The third shot brought in the winning runs in the 12th inning. Bucky Harris was particularly hot, and everyone in the lineup but Ruel was at better than .300.

Later in the month, on June 26, the Nationals, never lower than second in the standings, pulled into a tie with the A's for the American League lead when Goslin unloaded on rookie Lefty Grove with a three-run seventh-inning homer in a 5–3 win. Walter Johnson had shut the A's out after the third inning, in the first of three career matches between the two Hall of Famers (Johnson would win all three). Four days later, Barney spun a 7–0 two-hitter, with no walks, at Griffith Stadium against the same dangerous Athletics. Johnson had now blanked the A's, a team which would hit .307 for the season, for 15 consecutive innings.

The Big Train also equaled the A's in hits on this day. In fact, Walter would hit .433 this season, his first time over .300. On one occasion, on April 24, a Johnson pinch-hit appearance resulted in a rule change. The Big Train was in the clubhouse in the ninth inning when Bucky Harris, who'd used up all of his righthanded bats, summoned him back. The game was delayed ten minutes before Walter laced Herb Pennock's first pitch for a two-run single to win the game. In June, league president Ban Johnson announced that only players on the bench or on the sidelines could henceforth be deployed in a ballgame.

Johnson's two-hitter was the fourth win in five games against the Athletics and put the Nats in first place for the first time since early May. Dutch Ruether and Stan Coveleski were both winning nearly every time out, but the Senators were barely keeping up with the A's. The Nats lost their RBI champion, Goslin, who was suspended for the better part of a week. The Goose had lost his temper with Cleveland pitcher Bert Cole, who he thought had been throwing at him. Much more detrimental was the fact that Walter Johnson had been hit with the flu bug and wasn't getting better. He was out the entire month of July.

Thirty-five-year-old Stan Coveleski got a 13-game winning streak going until losing it to the White Sox in a blowout at the end of July. On August 2, Walter Johnson returned to the mound against the Tigers. His first appearance in over a month fell exactly on the 18th anniversary of his first big-league appearance, which had also involved Detroit. This time, though, unlike the first, Johnson won, allowing the Tigers, one of the league's stronger clubs, a measly two hits in a 5–1 Washington win.

On August 17, the Senators obtained the old Tiger outfield star, Bobby Veach, on the waiver wire from the Yankees. There can be no better indication of how good a team the Yanks were than the fact that Veach rang up a .353 batting average for them before they cut him adrift. Unfortunately, he only hit .243 for the Nats the rest of the way, and his career ended in Washington at age 37 with his career batting average resting at a cozy .310.

The Senators stayed in second place for a month, but finally, on August 20, Tom Zachary and Firpo Marberry combined for a 12-inning 1–0 shutout of the Indians. That day, the Browns beat Philadelphia, and the Nats, as it would turn out, were on top for good. Washington lost 1–0 in 11 innings the next day, but the A's failed to capitalize, getting trounced 8–2 by Chicago. The Senators demolished Detroit 20–5 on the 22nd with nine extra-base hits, including a mammoth home run by Walter Johnson. They scarcely even gave Philadelphia an opportunity to get back on top over the next six weeks.

By the end of August, Sam Rice had climbed to the top of the league batting race, a lead he would not be able to sustain. Also grabbing headlines in the baseball world was Yankees manager Miller Huggins, who announced that Babe Ruth was being suspended and fined $5,000 because of the Bambino's complete disregard for club rules. Ruth, whose bulk represented nearly twice the manager's, reportedly told Huggins that if he weighed 50 pounds more, he would have gotten a punch in the nose. Huggins shot back that if he had weighed 50 pounds more, it would have been the Babe's nose which would have been endangered.

The A's began what was to be a fatal string of losing games as August wound down. The Nats won every one of five games in a home-and-home series which began September 1 at Washington. In Philadelphia on September 7 for the traditional Labor Day doubleheader, Walter Johnson, who went 3–for–4 at the plate for the second time in a week against the A's, edged Lefty Grove 2–1 in the first game. A 7–6 Nats victory in the afternoon affair made it a horrifying 12 consecutive losses for the Athletics, and a nine-game lead for Washington.

The A's were officially eliminated and the Senators coasted to the pennant, finishing 8½ ahead of the A's, and 15 up on the third-place Browns. Walter Johnson won his 20th before a large Ladies' Day Crowd in Washington on September 11, but hurt his leg sliding six days later. Reinjured while crossing home plate when he returned to play on September 20, he would be kept on the sidelines for the rest of the regular season as the Senators awaited a second successive World Series appearance. On September 23, it was announced that Johnson had a successor as the league's Most Valuable Player — it was none other than shortstop Roger Peckinpaugh.

The oldest team in the league in terms of age of personnel had bested the franchise's 1924 record by 5½ games. Here was a team which inspired confidence as it headed into a second consecutive World Series. Granted, this year's National League champions, the Pittsburgh Pirates, were a tremendous offensive team; during the regular season, only one man, second baseman Eddie Moore, hit below .300 (.298).

Pittsburgh regulars Max Carey, Pie Traynor, and Kiki Cuyler were on a journey toward the Hall of Fame and were all bonafide superstars at this stage in their careers. Glenn Wright, Clyde Barnhart, and George Grantham were other deadly hitters. Until June 1925, these Pirates had gone 150 games without being shut out, a record which would remain unbroken until 1993. Like the Senators, the Pirates had finished 8½ games ahead of the pack in their league.

On the Washington side, it was felt that the team's experienced pitching staff might be able to effectively neutralize the Pittsburgh attack. Pittsburgh had no one of the stature of a Coveleski or a Johnson. Coveleski, however, had a sore back going into the Series. Roger Peckinpaugh was also among the walking wounded, which was reminiscent of his crippled state during the previous October's classic. Peck had rebounded magnificently this season, hitting .294 and fielding well enough to earn his MVP Award.

Hurting the most was second baseman–manager Harris, slowly recovering from a bad spike wound. Harris proclaimed that he would play, and that Walter Johnson would get the call as the starter of the first game in Pittsburgh. Among pitchers in the major leagues at this time, only the Pirates' Babe Adams, the Series hero back in 1909, was older than Johnson (by 5½ years, at that). The only other player in the big leagues older than Johnson was Ty Cobb. Bucky Harris also announced that he planned to go with his namesake, Moon Harris, who'd hit .323 in 100 games, in the outfield, rather than with Earl McNeely, who'd hit .286 with much less power than Harris.

The 1925 World Series got under way on a beautiful fall day, October 7, in Pittsburgh in front of nearly 42,000 fans in expansive Forbes Field. Walter Johnson had his fastball humming, something catcher Ruel attested to even before the game started. The curveball would be deadly accurate on this day as well, although by the late innings Walter would be relying almost exclusively on the fastball.

Barney did let one get away from him early and hit the second Pirate batter of the game, Max Carey, in the ribs with a hard one. Walter would bean Carey again in the ninth

inning, prompting the Pittsburgh star to tell his teammate and former American League star Stuffy McInnis that Johnson, who was thought of as a control pitcher, probably didn't like him very much. Carey's presence on first base in the first inning was of no consequence. Ruel cut down the 35-year-old speed merchant — who'd just won the N.L. base-stealing championship for the tenth time in 13 years — as he tried to swipe second. Johnson then fanned Kiki Cuyler, a .357 hitter in this, his sophomore season.

In the top of the second, Moon Harris connected on a curveball off the bespectacled Lee Meadows, driving the ball over the low fence in right center. Johnson would not surrender the lead on this afternoon. In the fifth, the Nats padded their margin when Harris, Bluege, and Peckinpaugh singled in succession to open the frame. After Ruel and Johnson both struck out, Sam Rice, who hit what would remain a career-high .350 during the regular season, came through with a two-run single.

Johnson allowed just five hits and a walk, surrendering a lead-off homer to Pie Traynor in the bottom of the fifth which quickly cut the lead to 3–1. The score stayed that way until the ninth, when Bluege singled in Goslin off reliever Johnny Morrison, who'd been summoned to pitch the ninth. Game one, final score 4–1, was won thanks to a performance that had been vintage Walter Johnson. His ten strikeouts and potential for two more starts had the Nats in good shape right off the bat in Pittsburgh. Walter was ecstatic, knowing that for the first time in a World Series game, he had performed up to what he knew were his capabilities. Barney called this the game of his life, and said he could not find words to express the elation he felt.

The baseball community got some bad news that same night. One of the game's early greats, the dignified Christy Mathewson, had lost his life. Matty had never fully recovered after inhaling poison gas during World War I. The players from both teams wore black armbands for game two the following day. Coveleski, his back wrapped with tape, would start for Harris. Bill McKechnie, manager of the Pirates, was like the Giants' John McGraw — a proponent of platooning his ballplayers. He would go with Vic Aldridge, another righty.

Joe Judge, a .314 hitter during the season, but with only eight homers, led off the second inning with a shot into temporary bleachers set up in right field. In the fourth, Coveleski gave up what was already Pie Traynor's second home run of the Series. It was still 1–1 in the sixth when, with two down, Ossie Bluege was hit squarely on the head by an Aldridge offering.

To run for Bluege, Harris sent out a 21-year-old youngster named Buddy Myer, who had all of eight at-bats to show for his big-league career up until then. A collegiate star in Mississippi, Myer had cost Clark Griffith $25,000 in a late-season transaction with New Orleans. Griffith could have gotten Myer for much less back in spring training, when he'd reportedly refused to sign the youngster because he didn't want to pay a $1,000 bonus. Myer would last 17 years in the majors, 15 of which would be spent with the Senators. For the moment, though, he didn't last long on the basepaths. He tried to steal second and was erased. With Bluege groggy, Myer was sent out to play third.

When the Pirates came up in the bottom of the eighth, Coveleski had allowed only a bunt single since Traynor's homer in the fourth. Eddie Moore led off the eighth with an easy bouncer which rolled up Peckinpaugh's sleeve. It was Peck's second error in two days — he had made a high throw to first in game one. After Max Carey grounded out, Kiki Cuyler slugged a two-run homer into the bleachers in right field. Clyde Barnhart then singled, and Peckinpaugh made his third error, failing to pick up a Pie Traynor roller. Although the Nats got one back in the ninth, that was all she wrote — Washington had lost the second game 3–2.

Ossie Bluege would be unavailable for the next two games, as he was being detained by doctors keeping a close watch over him at Johns Hopkins Hospital in Baltimore. It was reported by the newspapers that these doctors had never seen a skull as thick as Bluege's, and to that, they felt, the third sacker probably owed his salvation.

It rained in Washington on October 9, 1925, and game three of the World Series was put off for a day. It would be well worth the wait. When play resumed the next day for the Nats' first home game, President Coolidge and his Secretary of State, Frank Billings Kellogg, were among the many dignitaries on hand to witness the Pirates score the first run for the first time in the Series. Bucky Harris had elected to go with righthanded forkballer Alex Ferguson, 9–5 with an atrocious 6.18 ERA in '25. Twice traded during the season, Ferguson had nonetheless managed a 5–1 ledger in seven games since being acquired from the Yankees in a cash deal on August 19.

The previous year, Ferguson had been 14–17 with the hapless Boston Red Sox, but here he was starting in the World Series. He got out of trouble despite walking the first batter of the game and hitting the second one with a pitch. The Pirates scored the first run off Ferguson when, in leading off the second inning, Pie Traynor hit a low shot at Bucky Harris, who let the ball get through him and into the gap in right center for a triple. Glenn Wright followed with a sacrifice fly to left. The Senators were facing Ray Kremer, a tough man and hard drinker who had just completed the second year of a fine seven-year stretch with the Pirates. Kremer was known for destroying Pullman cars and tossing teammates' shoes out of train windows in fits of temper. He would go on to win 20 games in 1926 and 1930, 19 in 1927, and 18 in 1929.

The Senators came right back in the third inning against Kremer, with Sam Rice looping a single over second base to start things off. Bucky Harris sacrificed, and Goslin, going for more than a sacrifice, hit a shot to deep right. The catch was made, but Rice was into third easily. He scored moments later when Joe Judge doubled inside first base. The Nats nearly took the lead when Judge tried to score on a scratch hit by Joe Harris that shortstop Glenn Wright had nearly thrown into the dirt.

First baseman George Grantham, a second baseman by trade, made a major-league play, picking the peg out of the dirt and throwing Judge out at home to preserve the tie for the Pirates after three innings.

The very first batter in the top of the fourth, Kiki Cuyler, doubled to the gap in left center, and then came home on a single to left by the next batter, Pittsburgh left fielder Clyde Barnhart. Ferguson walked the next batter, and then ended up yielding an intentional pass to load the bases. Nonetheless, he muddled through without giving up another run in the inning, striking out his opposing number, Ray Kremer, to extinguish the fire. Ferguson gave up another double in the fifth, to Max Carey, but got out of the inning without further damage.

In the sixth, Roger Peckinpaugh committed his fourth error in three games and it led to another Pittsburgh run, making the score 3–1. After Pie Traynor flied to Sam Rice about 420 feet to the bleacher fence to open the inning, Glenn Wright bounced to Peckinpaugh, who made a bad relay to first. Wright eventually scored when pitcher Kremer got a base hit which took a freaky high bounce over second base. In the bottom of the inning, however, the Nats got one back very quickly when the lefty-hitting Goslin led off by pulling a home run into the right centerfield bleachers.

Alex Ferguson got out of the seventh inning, and the game, after retiring the Pirates in order for the first time. His departure was hastened because he was due to be the first batter in the next half-inning. The veteran outfielder, Nemo Leibold, took a walk and was immediately lifted for pinch runner Earl McNeely. McNeely was now strictly relegated to a reserve role due to the emergence of Joe "Moon" Harris, who was having a great Series. After Clyde Barnhart made a fine catch off a Sam Rice attempt at the left-field foul line, the Nats' peerless leader, Bucky Harris, beat out a single.

With the score 3–2 and men on first and second with just one out, the Pirates could not have been prepared for what came next.

Goose Goslin, the Nats' best slugger, swung from the heels on the first pitch and missed — the infielders were playing far back. Goslin then caught the defense by surprise, bunting along the third base line and loading the bases in the process. Joe Judge was next up, and his sac fly to center brought in McNeely with the tying run. Joe Harris was next and singled to left to put the Nats ahead for the first time in the game. The inning then ended in odd fashion when Buddy Myer got in the way of his own batted ball while outside the batter's box and was called out.

There was a much more unusual play in the eighth inning — indeed one of the more bizarre plays in all of World Series history. Firpo Marberry, pitching for the first time in five weeks and yet called upon to protect a 4–3 lead in a World Series game, began wonderfully by striking out the first two Pirates to face him. Then Pirate catcher Earl Smith slammed a monster shot to the right centerfield bleachers. Sam Rice raced to the spot, extended his glove as far as he could, and definitely seemed to get it on the ball. But Rice's momentum carried him into the bleachers, behind the fence, and out of sight. He did not immediately re-emerge, and Pirates manager Bill McKechnie came bounding out of the dugout, protesting that Rice surely must have dropped the ball. Rice only had it in his possession now, McKechnie contended, because it had been handed back to him by a fan.

The four umpires working the game conferred and after much to-do, it was decided that the catch would stand, probably because they had seen the catch and nothing else. Manager McKechnie took the matter to the commissioner's office, and did so in a manner we would not see today. He just walked over to the box where Commissioner Kenesaw Mountain Landis was sitting, and politely inquired whether he could appeal the matter. The autocratic Landis just as immediately retorted with a flat-out "no." The case was closed, and the Nats were out of the inning with their 4–3 lead intact.

Questioned by reporters later, Sam Rice

said simply that the delay behind the fence had been caused by his Adam's apple coming into contact with the hard skull of a paying customer. Commissioner Landis wanted to talk to Sam and had him summoned following the game. Sam told the judge one thing — that the umpire had called Earl Smith out. That, Landis told Rice, was precisely the answer he wanted the player to keep giving whenever that question was put to him in the future. The controversial play incited the first major rule change in the majors in five years — in the future, if a player left his feet and followed the ball into the stands, it would be a home run. This does not detract from Rice's effort, since "the catch" was the most miraculous many players professed to have seen in their lifetimes.

More confusion ensued in the bottom of the eighth ... the Senators batted out of order! When they'd taken the field in the top of the inning, McNeely had gone out to center. He had of course pinch run for Leibold, who had batted in the pitcher's spot. Since McNeely had inherited the ninth spot, it was his turn to bat following Muddy Ruel's single with one out. Instead, the pitcher, Firpo Marberry, not only batted in the ninth spot, but executed a perfect sacrifice to move Ruel ahead. Fortunately for Washington, the Pirates were also somnolent on this play. The opposition did not clue in quickly enough — by the time the play was appealed, it was too late. Sam Rice was already in the batter's box, and under the rules, what had taken place could not be negated. When Rice grounded to short, however, the whole sordid episode was rendered moot, as the Nats did not score.

There were more fireworks in the top of the ninth when, with one out, Firpo Marberry gave up successive singles and then hit Kiki Cuyler with a pitch. After inducing Clyde Barnhart to pop up in fair territory near the plate, the great Pie Traynor worked Marberry to a 3–2 count before flying out to McNeely in center. The Nats had restored their lead in the Series with a 4–3 final. An exciting game indeed, and all of its excitement was contained within two hours and ten minutes — a quick game by today's standards, but the longest of the 1925 Series to that point.

Spirits were high and buoyed even further in the nation's capital when it was announced by Bucky Harris that Walter Johnson would start the fourth game. Given the Nats' 2–1 lead in the Series, this made good strategic sense. If Johnson won, the Senators would obviously be in the driver's seat, but if he lost, he'd be available for a seventh game with sufficient rest. Johnson's opponent would be lefthanded submariner Emil Yde, who'd enjoyed a superb 16–3, 2.83 season the previous year but had slipped to 17–9, 4.13 on a pennant winner in '25. Yde would be gone from the big-league scene before the end of the 1920s, and the imminent fourth game of the World Series would prove a precursor to his demise.

Yde gave up a couple of walks in the first inning, and Johnson allowed runners to get to second and third in the second, but there were no runs. After the Big Train had retired the Pirates in order, the Nats struck in the bottom of the third. The damage they wreaked, however, would be insignificant compared to the negative impact of the play that happened next. Walter Johnson, the first batter of the inning, hit a clean single to left and the great man, trying gallantly to stretch the hit into a double, stretched a leg muscle. After the next batter, lead-off man Rice, beat out an infield single, Bucky Harris hit what might have been a double-play ball toward George Grantham at first. Grantham, who, as mentioned earlier, was really a second baseman, made a good relay but Glenn Wright dropped the ball.

The play opened the floodgates, and Goose Goslin then unleashed a huge blast into the left centerfield bleachers, a shot of well over 420 feet, his second home run of the Series. Moon Harris, the next batter, then hit one nearly as far into the bleachers in left, his second homer of an outstanding World Series for him. With the Senators suddenly up 4–0, Joe Judge coaxed a walk out of Yde, who was out of what would turn out to be his one and only World Series game after getting just seven batters out.

Johnson, who'd stayed in the game despite being bandaged after his ill-fated slide into second, pitched from the stretch but otherwise showed no ill effects the rest of the way. He gave up just four more hits through the last six innings after the incident, two of them to the infield. He'd surrendered only six singles, and walked just two, as only one Pirate reached third base all day. The 4–0 shutout had the Nats just one win away.

The Big Train had not had the usual dominance and struck out just two, compared to the ten he'd racked up while getting his first win in game one. At 37 years, 11 months, he set the still-standing record as the oldest pitcher to throw a complete-game World Series shutout. It had taken him a long time, but after 17 mostly disheartening seasons in the majors, he was now just one win away from a second straight World Championship ... no team had ever lost a World Series after holding a 3–1 lead in games.

Bucky Harris was in another quandary prior to the fifth game. It would be the final game in Washington, if not the final game of the Series. Harris, anxious to end it, was unsure whether he would go with one of his lefties, Dutch Ruether or Tom Zachary, or with his eventual choice, his best available pitcher, Stan Coveleski, who had shared with Johnson the number-one role throughout the season. Vic Aldridge would be the opposing pitcher, and Ossie Bluege, who'd been beaned by Aldridge in the second game and hadn't played since, would be back in the lineup. Bluege would double and field flawlessly.

Coveleski pitched out of a bases-loaded jam in the first inning, as game five also got off to a hectic start. The beloved Nats replied with a run. Sam Rice led off by lining a single to right. Bucky Harris, still playing with a spiked hand which affected his hitting, was able to move Rice over. Goslin then blooped a double near the left field foul line to drive in the first run. From then on, though, it was all downhill for the Senators. Coveleski surrendered a couple of walks and a single in the third, for a couple of runs. After Series star Moon Harris hit his third home run in five

games in the bottom of the fourth, the score remained 2–2 until the Pirates bunched three more singles and a walk for a couple of runs, chasing Coveleski in the seventh.

The Bucs were not to relinquish that lead, although Nemo Leibold and Sam Rice combined to bring in a run to narrow the margin to 4–3 in the seventh. Pittsburgh would win this one 6–3. Pirate shortstop Glenn Wright doubled and scored off Tom Zachary in the eighth, and drove in Clyde Barnhart with a single off Marberry, who had to come in to rescue Zachary in the ninth. Although he pitched to only two batters, Marberry aggravated the arm injury which had caused him to miss the last five weeks of the season — he would not pitch in this World Series again.

The move to go with Coveleski had backfired. The Senators still maintained a 3–2 lead in games, but Bucky Harris had a pitching rotation in disarray at this point. He had used Zachary in game five, and that had not gone well. Johnson would be held over for the seventh game, if there was one, but his injured leg was a question mark which meant this upcoming game was all the more crucial. Dutch Ruether had not pitched in the Series. Alex Ferguson had, and had done a creditable job winning the third game, giving up six hits and four walks in seven innings in his only appearance. Harris decided to go with him, despite rumors that Ferguson himself didn't think he should be the one to get the assignment.

This trepidation in the Senators' camp was quickly assuaged when, with two out in the top of the first, Goose Goslin launched a Ray Kremer pitch very deep into the rightfield stands. In the second, Joe Judge singled and was forced at second by Ossie Bluege, who then upped the score to 2–0 when Roger Peckinpaugh lined a double over the head of first baseman Stuffy McInnis. McInnis's presence since game five, which had reportedly come at John McGraw's recommendation, would later be recognized by baseball pundits as a significant move on the part of the Pirates. George Grantham had gone 2–for–14 in the Series. McInnis, a 17-year vet and longtime

A's and Red Sox star, had hit .368 following his midseason acquisition from the Boston Braves.

Pittsburgh came back in the third, with Peckinpaugh's fifth error of the Series prolonging a two-run rally. With a man on first, Peckinpaugh grabbed a high bouncer but then missed second when he tried to go for the lead man. Both runs came in on an infield single and another base hit through the box by Pie Traynor that breezed by Alex Ferguson. After that, only one man made it to first base for either side (Ossie Bluege singled in the fourth and got caught leading off first) until the top of the fifth, when Pirate lead-off man Eddie Moore hit a Chinese home run into the temporary seats in left field.

The Pirates led 3–2, and the game was uneventful the rest of the way, except for the fact that Peckinpaugh muffed another chance in the seventh, his sixth error in six games, when he threw low to first base, allowing Moore to once more get on to start an inning. Moore's homer held up as the decisive blow. The Senators had lost two in a row and there was no more margin for error, on the part of Roger Peckinpaugh or anyone else.

As had happened prior to the third game in Washington, it rained in Pittsburgh and the seventh game was postponed one day, with the decisive contest rescheduled for Thursday, October 15, 1925. It was still wet and cold, but Commissioner Landis in his infinite wisdom ordered the game played in a steady rain. It was thought that never had such an important game been played in such conditions. It was, wrote James R. Harrison in the *New York Times,* "a perfect day for water polo."

Bucky Harris' decision concerning whom to start was easier to make this time. In his statement to reporters, he announced that Washington was going to come back with the greatest pitcher the game had ever known. Walter Johnson, on three days' rest and with a sore leg, pronounced himself ready. Babe Ruth, covering the Series from his apartment in New York, thought he spoke for all American Leaguers when he said that Walter was not just respected by the players, but loved by

them. Ruth admitted he'd be rooting for a man he called the greatest character in baseball.

Vic Aldridge, who had been steady in winning games two and five, was out again for this, the big one. The Pirates certainly had momentum on their side, and the fans on their side, but it was the Senators who struck first, and struck hard, again in the first inning. Sam Rice led off with a single over second base. Bucky Harris, still hampered by the spiked hand, flew out softly to left, but Aldridge then uncorked a wild pitch, allowing Rice to take second. Aldridge was wild — he walked Goslin and then lost control of another pitch, moving the runners up to second and third. Moon Harris walked, loading the bases. Joe Judge, always selective, worked the count full and then earned a fourth ball from Aldrige, and the Nats had their first run.

Ossie Bluege was next up and singled cleanly, bringing in Goslin and precipitating Aldridge's exit. Aldridge had finally met his Waterloo and was replaced by "Jughandle Johnny" Morrison, he of the sweeping curveball. Morrison was another character on a team of characters — a heavy drinker, he would, in the two coming seasons, be suspended by the Pirates for apparently feigning illness and running off to his home in the Kentucky hills. Morrison had given up two hits and a run in one inning in a mop-up role in game one, and had allowed five hits and a walk, but no runs, in the 4–0 loss to Walter Johnson in the fourth game.

The righthanded Morrison lured Roger Peckinpaugh into batting the ball into the ground with the bases full. This was another of the strange plays in this Series. Catcher Earl Smith had apparently tipped Peck's bat, and Peck was awarded first, Joe Harris scoring the third run of the first inning. The roof caved in just a bit more for the Pirates and poor Morrison, as Eddie Moore booted a roller off the bat of Muddy Ruel, who was enjoying a much better World Series from an offensive standpoint than he had in 1924. Moore's muff brought in Joe Judge, but Morrison then fanned Walter Johnson. Despite his great season at the plate, Barney would go 1–for–11 for the Series. Sam Rice, up next, lofted a fly to left to end the inning.

The 4–0 first-inning lead held until the bottom of the third, when the Pirates came back with a vengeance. Johnson, who'd yielded two singles in the second, allowed another to pitcher Morrison, a cardinal sin, to start the third on the wrong foot. Eddie Moore promptly doubled to the fence to count Morrison, and Max Carey then singled to bring Moore in with a second run. After one out, Carey stole third and strode home easily when Clyde Barnhart dropped a single into short right center. The Senators were able to get two of those runs back immediately. After Rice and Goslin singled, the unbelievable Moon Harris, who hit .440 with three home runs in this World Series, doubled them both in for a 6–3 Washington lead.

By now, the drizzle had evolved into a steady rain and the playing field was an absolute mess. Walter Johnson, whose leg had been taped heavily prior to the game, got through the fourth okay, and his arm felt fine. There were three harmless flies to left following McInnis's lead-off single in the bottom of the fourth. Groundskeepers brought, as was customary, loads of sawdust onto the field to soak up the water when it rained heavily. Walter Johnson kept filling his cap with the stuff, to bring back to the mound. By the end of the game, wrote Robert Burnes years later in *Baseball Digest,* Walter appeared to be covered in oatmeal.

By the fifth inning, it was pouring, and the Pirates, behind by a serious margin of 6–3, were desperate to close the gap. Max Carey, who'd doubled in the first inning without result, opened the fifth with a double to right center and scored on another double, by Kiki Cuyler. Johnson then mowed the Pirates down, three at a time through the rest of the fifth and sixth. Commissioner Landis, exposed to the elements in his box seat during the whole game, reportedly told Clark Griffith sitting next to him that he was calling the game off at the end of the sixth. Griffith told the commissioner he shouldn't, because he'd made

the decision to start the game in the rain in the first place, so he should see it through. In relating the story many years later, Ossie Bluege wondered how many owners, with their team ahead, would have taken such a stand. Griff would have done better to have kept his mouth shut.

By the top of the seventh, with Washington still hanging on to its two-run lead, the rain was coming down very hard. The Nats were doing nothing offensively against Ray Kremer, who had stepped in for Morrison to start the fifth. Johnny Moore opened the bottom of the inning with a pop fly to left which Roger Peckinpaugh dropped for his seventh error of the Series. Max Carey, 3–for–3 with two doubles, sent a Texas Leaguer down the left field line that Bluege, Goslin, and Peckinpaugh converged on. They all reacted as if the ball was foul, and had begun to return to their positions when they heard the fair call.

Carey, hampered by two ribs broken in the previous game, hustled into second with his fourth hit of the day and his third double. Moore scored, closing the gap to 6–5 in favor of Washington. With two down, Pie Traynor tripled to bring in the tying run. Traynor's smash rolled to the fence in right center and was retrieved by Joe Harris. Harris's relay to his namesake, the second baseman, found its way to the plate on time to nip Traynor, who was trying for the tie-breaking run. This ended the inning, and none too soon, as the score was knotted at 6–6.

With one out in the eighth, the harried Roger Peckinpaugh drove a ball high over the low temporary fence in left field, a magnificent moment of retribution for him. If this homer held, Peck's considerable sins would all be forgiven. His value to this club was well known — he was going through a period of incredibly hard luck at an incredibly inopportune time. In the bottom of the eighth, Johnson got two easy outs and the Senators were getting close to their second straight world championship. With two strikes on him, however, Earl Smith rapped a double to right center and Carson Bigbee, pinch hitting for pitcher Kremer, slammed the Pirates' seventh double of the day to bring in pinch-runner Emil Yde with the tying run.

Harris was going to sink or swim with his big man. Johnson, with the rain still driving and the score now 7–7 with two out, walked Johnny Moore. With men on first and second, Max Carey, 4–for–4 in this game, slapped the ball on the ground toward Peckinpaugh. It is easy to guess what happened next. Peck did manage to get his hands on the ball, and to field it cleanly even. He went for the force-out at second to end the inning. His short relay was off line. All baserunners were safe. This eighth error, the most costly of them all, set a World Series record that has withstood the test of time and kept the name of Peckinpaugh, a truly outstanding player, in ignominy as we enter the 21st century.

With the stations all occupied, Walter Johnson worked the count to 2–and–2 on the next batter, Kiki Cuyler, before pouring a ball down the middle which appeared waist high. Walter walked off the mound and catcher Ruel hoisted his mask off as if the inning was finally over. But the pitch was called a ball. The debacle was complete a moment later when Cuyler smoked a ground-rule double, the Pirates' eighth two-bagger of the game, into the crowd in right field. Two runs scored, and hearts were sinking in the Nats' dugout. The sounds of celebration reverberated all around them in raucous Forbes Field. Before anyone knew it, the Nats had gone down in order against Pirates reliever Red Oldham, with both Rice, who hit .364 for the Series, and Goslin, who hit .308, taking called third strikes. The unthinkable had happened. The Nats had dropped an unprecedented three World Series games in a row and lost the World Series.

It was Goose Goslin who had been the closest human being to Kiki Cuyler's game-winning hit. Goslin said that the umpires couldn't see the ball at all, it was so dark and foggy. The ball had fallen two feet foul, Goose maintained. How could he be so sure? The ball, he insisted, had fallen in the mud and stuck there! As Goslin was to point out many years later, the good Lord took, in the 1925 World Series, what He had given in 1924, and what the Goose was talking about was just plain old Lady Luck.

Roger Peckinpaugh, who'd committed eight of the club's nine errors in the Series, wept. He would have to wear the goat's horns, and he knew it. Walter Johnson, who'd shown what kind of man he was when he embraced Peck on the field following the game, would refuse to make excuses for his 15-hit performance, insisting instead that his arm and bandaged leg had felt fine all the way.

Bucky Harris, who'd batted only .087 for the Series, was criticized by many, including the ostentatious American League president, Ban Johnson, for having stuck with Walter Johnson until the bitter end. Harris had done so for reasons of "mawkish" sentimentality, according to Johnson, thereby costing Ban's league a world championship.

Bucky did have cause to reflect. A batting hero in 1924, he had been a bust in this Series, managing but a puny 2–for–23. Perhaps the spike wound to his hand had been more detrimental to his performance than he had thought possible. He did admit that he shouldn't have waited until the eighth inning of the sixth game to send someone to bat for him. Also, Harris would have forever to reflect on the way he had handled his pitchers. There is much to wonder about. The American League's best lefthander in 1925, Dutch Ruether, had not been handed the ball at all. Experienced Tom Zachary only appeared briefly in one game. It could well be that in attempting to crush Pirates' appetite for southpaws, Bucky Harris had simply outsmarted himself.

Adding insult to injury, Harris, along with Roger Peckinpaugh and Muddy Ruel, was hauled onto the proverbial carpet by Commissioner Landis because of derogatory remarks the Senators had allegedly made about the quality of the umpiring. The loss had to be tremendously disappointing. It would be 1958 before such a turnaround recurred — with a team with a 3–1 lead blowing it — in the World Series.

Twenty-four Nats players shared a World

Series booty amounting to about $3,800 apiece. The suddenly magnanimous Clark Griffith awarded $1,000 bonuses on top of this "windfall" to Coveleski and Marberry for performances during the season which he personally deemed outstanding. This ballclub, which Griffith himself had molded, had won a world championship and should have had a second consecutive one. Those two World Series would, as the passing of time bore out, continue to stand among the most dramatic of all time. Now was surely not the time to implement any changes, but rumors persisted throughout the off season that Goose Goslin would be traded. Griffith kept trying to dispel them, indicating that he would not be cajoled into giving up Goslin, not even for the entire roster of the New York Yankees.

Walter Johnson started the Nats out on the right foot at Griffith Stadium on Opening Day, 1926, as he had with victories in nine previous opening games. This one was a marathon, 15 innings, and Barney yielded a measly six hits, walked three, and struck out nine Philadelphia A's in staying the distance. No one reached second base against the Big Train throughout the entire contest. Of all his games and masterpieces, this was the one Walter Johnson considered his greatest, and it came as he was starting his 20th big-league campaign. It was another one of those lifetime-record 38 1–0 wins which Walter would chalk up by the end of his career, and was the last of his 13 home openers, ten of which he won, six by shutout.

However, age was beginning to catch up with the Washington Senators' pitching staff in 1926. Johnson, now 38, slipped to 15–16 on the heels of his 20–7, 3.07. It was an up-and-down year, as he went from a 6–1 record in mid–May to later losing seven in a row as the Nats fell to the second division. Barney's 3.61 ERA was the worst of his career, but in fairness to the great one, eight of his defeats were by a one-run margin, and five others were by two runs.

Stan Coveleski, a year and a half Johnson's junior, had his last useful season but nonetheless diminished to 14–11, 3.12. It had

been seen fit prior to the start of the season to dispatch Tom Zachary and Win Ballou, who'd pitched briefly but well in the '25 Series, to the Browns, for over-the-hill "Bullet Joe" Bush (1–8 for the Senators) and Jack Tobin (.212 average for Washington), an outfielder whose better days were also decidedly behind him. The trade can be categorized as a calamity, considering that Zachary won 14 for the Browns. While the Nats did not completely wilt in 1926, they did not win with enough regularity.

A respectable 81–69 record, enhanced by some strong play in the final six weeks of the campaign, landed the Senators in fourth place, but just barely. Joe Judge had to hit a home run against the White Sox on the last day of the season to vault Washington into the first division. The Yankees regained control of the league in '26 by edging the A's by three games at season's end. The Nats finished eight games out, two games behind third-place Philadelphia. The Senators led the league with a .292 team batting average, but the Yankees slugged 121 homers, the Nats 43.

Nineteen twenty-six was the year Roger Peckinpaugh became a part-time player. He hit .238 while participating in just 57 games. Following a year spent as a sub with the White Sox, Peck would take over the managerial reigns of the Cleveland Indians for 1928. Buddy Myer, whose eight at-bats in the World Series had matched his career regular-season total, took over Peck's spot right from opening day 1926 and hit a commendable .304 in 132 games. Earl McNeely played a bit more and managed a stellar .303, up from .284 in 1925. Sam Rice led the league in hits in posting an excellent .337 mark. Goose Goslin rounded out an all–.300-hitting outfield, finishing with a .354 average, a 20-point improvement, with 17–108 power numbers comparable to the previous season's.

Despite the hoopla, the Goose was suspended indefinitely at the end of August for what was termed indifferent play. Nevertheless, he was named by *The Sporting News* as leftfielder on the publication's Major-League All-Star team, a compilation inaugurated the previous season, when Walter Johnson was chosen as the Nats' only representative. Goslin placed fifth in the league in slugging percentage with .543, just six one-thousandths of a point behind Lou Gehrig. But Gehrig's teammate, Babe Ruth, slugged at an incredible .737 clip.

The Babe's 47 homers in 1926 placed him first in the league by a margin of 28 over Al Simmons of the A's. The Babe had regained top billing following the year of the famous bellyache, but the Yankees dropped the World Series in seven games to the St. Louis Cardinals. This was the Series in which Old Pete Alexander, wracked by age but especially by alcoholism, came in to relieve in game seven to strike out Tony Lazzeri with the bases loaded to end the seventh inning. It was also the World Series which ended when Ruth, who had been walked with two down, his 11th pass of the Series, got thrown out attempting to steal second base.

Very early in 1927, Walter Johnson signed what was to be, he said, his last contract to pitch for the Washington Senators. It called for his same $20,000 salary for the one year. Bucky Harris's plan was to work Walter and Stan Coveleski in spots, and then only when the two graybeards would feel like pitching. When Johnson was hit in the leg by a line drive off the bat of his roommate, Joe Judge, during spring training of 1927 at Tampa, coach Al Schacht, the clown, reportedly stood over Johnson and gave him the ten-count. The comedian didn't know that he was counting down the days left in the Big Train's career. Johnson's leg was broken (officially a fracture of the fibula, about 3½ inches above the ankle). The Big Train would be sidelined for six weeks, and this injury would precipitate the end of his scintillating career in 1927.

The Senators did have another most distinguished player in their midst for the first time at their training camp at Tampa. Tris Speaker, soon to be 39, seventh all-time in batting average as the 21st century begins, had been signed to a $35,000 contract on January 31. The Cleveland Indians had replaced Speaker as manager and had then cleared him

to sign with any team. Speaker had recently been embroiled in controversy. Pitcher Dutch Leonard (this was the lefthanded Dutch Leonard, who was about 17 years older than the righthanded Dutch Leonard who would later pitch for Washington) had accused both him and Ty Cobb of conniving to fix a game between the Indians and the Tigers back in September 1919.

Leonard's charges were never substantiated, but the resulting investigation had a lot to do with finally bringing down Ban Johnson, whose grip on the league's operations had been slipping. Johnson would resign in October after 27 years as president, rather than risk being fired at a general meeting requested by the team owners. Clark Griffith took advantage of the brouhaha surrounding the investigation of the two star players, enticing Speaker with the hefty one-year contract in return for outfield insurance. The pact was sealed four days after Commissioner Landis absolved the two star players of involvement in any wrongdoing. Speaker hit .389 in 1925, but had slipped to .304 in '26.

Griffith could always make room for a .344 career hitter, though. Speaker played a role in shaping the Senators' long-term future in 1927 but, unfortunately, not in a positive sense. "Spoke" was high on a 30-year-old shortstop named Emory "Topper" Rigney, of the Red Sox. Speaker contended that with Rigney, a .270 hitter in '26, at short instead of Buddy Myer, Ossie Bluege could move to second and the Nats would be much improved as a result. Bucky Harris got talked into this and in turn coaxed Clark Griffith into making the trade with Boston.

This, Griffith would admit in later years, was the worst deal ever made under his administration. Within a year and a half, the Nats would give up five players to get Myer back. Topper Rigney batted only .253 in 150 at-bats in 1927, and it was his major-league swan song. He was released after just 45 games with the Senators, while Myer continued to improve and would lead the league in stolen bases in 1928.

Walter Johnson made his first appearance

of the 1927 season on Memorial Day. He was pleased to find that he still had good speed, and upon his return, like on so many of his first starts of previous years, he was superb, allowing just three hits, walking no one, and blanking Boston 3–0 at Griffith Stadium. This was the 11th and final time that fewer than 30 batters (29 in this instance) came up to the plate to face him in a complete game.

More significant than all of the above, however, may have been the fact that Barney struck out just one batter. He fanned six in his next start, a 5–3 loss to the Browns, but was then bombed 7–1 by Cleveland in an outing where no speed was evident. Johnson was held back from a couple of turns in mid–June, and when he did come back, he was the victim of an 8–2 drubbing at the hands of the Athletics.

Walter Johnson had been in the major leagues for 20 years, and August 2, 1927, was the precise anniversary date of his big-league debut. Coincidentally, he would be facing the Tigers on this day as well. Tributes were delivered by both clubs at Griffith Stadium — Walter was handed the day's receipts of $14,476.05, and gifts from fans included over $1,500 in cash. Secretary of State Frank Kellogg spoke before the crowd of 20,000 and declared that the name Walter Johnson exemplified what was best about sports. The man stood as a shining beacon whose example the youth of America could follow.

Unfortunately, on this day, the Big Train surrendered four runs in the fifth on the way to a 7–6, incomplete-game loss. The defeat was debited from reliever Garland Braxton, although under modern rules Walter would have been the pitcher of record. This was poetic justice in the sense that his first loss, 20 years earlier, would not have been charged to him under the revised rules. The end came quickly for Walter Johnson in 1927, given his 31 decisions the previous year. His ERA ballooned to a surreal 5.10, and as a result his workload diminished to just 107⅔ innings. That was it.

Tris Speaker, five months younger than Johnson, whose career was very nearly over,

did earn his 30 grand, upping his average to .327 in 1927. It was to be his only year in Washington — Spoke's final year in the majors would be spent in the company of Ty Cobb with the Philadelphia A's in 1928. Goose Goslin, still only 26, hit .334 in '27, as he had in the Nats' last pennant-winning year, and tied for third in ribbies behind the Yankees' fearsome Ruth-Gehrig tandem. These were the highlights for a club, not far removed from a position at the top of the baseball world, which won 85 games. Regrettably, these Senators were at the same point in the continuum of time and space as were the 1927 New York Yankees.

The '27 Yankees are considered by many to have been the best team ever. They won 110 games and left the Nats in third place, but groveling in the dust, a full 25 games out of a pennant position. On July 4, 74,000 had turned up at Yankee Stadium for a doubleheader which the Yankees swept from the Nats by embarrassing 12–1 and 21–1 scores. Babe Ruth went 5–for–7 and Lou Gehrig hit two homers on the day, enabling him to pass Ruth momentarily in the home-run derby. The previous day, back in Washington, Ruth had hit what came to be considered for years as the longest drive ever seen at Griffith Stadium. The Babe had, quite naturally, tipped his cap for the fans while rounding the bases with the little steps that he took.

Going into this disastrous doubleheader, the Senators had been on a 10-game winning streak. Walter Johnson was summoned for mop-up duty in the first game after the Yankees had slapped around Washington starter Hollis "Sloppy" Thurston (the nickname was a misnomer — Thurston was a very flashy dresser). A former 20-game winner but only 13–13, 4.47, for the Nats in '27, Thurston was abused to the tune of eight runs in four innings. Despite giving up four runs in the eighth in relief, Johnson struck out both Babe Ruth and Lou Gehrig in the inning. This might just perhaps have been an indication that he would be able to help the Nats mount some sort of threat to the Yankees for the title.

Johnson's July 9 start was a success, a 3–2

win over Cleveland with eight strikeouts. He pitched a second complete game in a row in his next start over the White Sox, the only complete games produced by the pitching staff in three weeks. Then, on July 28, 1927, Walter Johnson allowed just one earned run in a 12–2 pasting of the White Sox. This win, which brought his record to 5–4, was the last of his 417 wins in the major leagues. He would be used sparingly until the end of the season, as Bucky Harris stuck more and more with youngsters. On August 22, Walter lost 7–3 to the Tigers at Detroit, fixing his season's record at 5–6. For the great one, this was the last decision and last defeat of his unparalleled career.

Walter Johnson's final pitching appearance in the big leagues occurred on September 22, 1927, the same day that heavyweight fighter Gene Tunney took the long count and came back to defend his crown against ex-champion Jack Dempsey in Chicago. Former Nats teammate Frank "Blackie" O'Rourke, the Canadian, was the last big leaguer to get a hit off Walter, and he also was the last man to be struck out by him. On September 30, Barney played in his final game. He pinch hit for Tom Zachary, his 110th official pinch-hit appearance, in the very same game in which Zachary surrendered Babe Ruth's 60th home run. In Walter Johnson's final appearance in a major-league game, he hit a flyball to the outfield: to Babe Ruth ... who else!

On October 15, 1927, with no contract yet tendered, Johnson walked into Clark Griffith's office to ask for his release. The old man specified that Walter hadn't received a contract because none had been issued to any of the players yet. Barney felt his broken leg had taken the zip off his fastball, however, and that the time had finally come. At the time of his retirement, Walter Johnson held just about every 20th-century pitching record. His 110 shutouts and 3,509 strikeouts were seemingly out of the reach of any subsequent assault. Most of the newspaper tributes, however, focused on the quality of the individual and what he had meant to the game.

Two days following the announcement,

on the 17th of October, another of the Old Fox's old associates, league president Ban Johnson, finally stepped down. Many team owners felt it was time, after 27 years, that he do so. The last straw for the autocrat had been the tongue-lashing he had endured from Commissioner Kenesaw Landis for his handling of the aforementioned Cobb-Speaker affair. It turned out that Johnson had tried to keep the affair secret by offering Dutch Leonard $20,000 for his silence. Landis had instead insisted upon bringing the entire sordid matter into the public realm.

The Senators became even more indelibly linked with the Yankees when, at season's end, they arrived at Yankee Stadium for the last three games. Babe Ruth was three home runs shy of breaking his record of 59, set in 1921. Lord knows he'd been trying, but the closest he'd been to approaching 59 in the six years since was 47. Until now. On September 29, Ruth chalked up number 58 when he got hold of a curveball that submariner Hod Lisenbee tried to sneak by him.

What followed may well be one of the most dramatic beginnings to any major leaguer's career. Young Paul Hopkins, graduated four months earlier from Colgate University, had been working out with the Nationals for three weeks when Bucky Harris, with the bases loaded, finally called upon him. Hopkins had no idea whose turn it was to bat. Seventy-one years later, he still recalled standing on the mound wondering who the first batter would be.

When Paul Hopkins found out the first man he would face in the major leagues would be none other than Babe Ruth, he was nervous, he admitted later, but not scared, since he felt he was capable of getting anybody out. The youngster threw nothing but curves, most of them slow. The Babe ripped foul balls down both lines, and the count got up to 3–and–2. Then Hopkins threw yet another curve, extra slow, and Ruth had to pull up a bit before launching a rocket toward the right field stands, a grand slam for his 59th homer of the year. Paul Hopkins may never have recovered from the blow, although he would always remember striking out the next batter, Lou Gehrig. When he got back to the bench, his self-image shattered, he said he sat down and cried because he couldn't get Babe Ruth out. Hopkins' major-league journey lasted all of 27 innings.

The next day, with the score knotted at two runs apiece in the eighth inning, Tom Zachary had the task of keeping Ruth from driving in the potential game-winning run, which was standing on third in the person of Mark Koenig, who had tripled. Zachary, reacquired by the Nats from the St. Louis Browns at midseason and 4–7 the rest of the way for Washington, hadn't done too well thus far this day, yielding a walk and two singles to the Bambino. The Babe unleashed a mighty wallop on a 1–1 pitch, a low inside fastball that barely stayed fair. "Foul ball!" yelled Tom Zachary, but fair it stayed.

There was never any doubt about the distance on home run number 60, and the sphere came to rest way up in the bleachers, about 15 rows from the top. The game ended with the score still 4–2 Yankees a few minutes later, when pinch hitter Walter Johnson flew out to the Babe in right field. "Let's see some other son of a bitch match that!" challenged the Babe, as the Yankees prepared for the beginning of the World Series five days later against the Pirates in Pittsburgh.

Gentle Tom Zachary, when pressed later on in life to give his impressions of surrendering Ruth's 60th homer, declared, "If you really want to know the truth, I'd rather have thrown at his big, fat head." Zachary was just 4–7 for the '27 Nats. The Senators' best pitchers that year were a pair of rookie graduates of the Southern Association. Irving Darius "Bump" Hadley went 14–6 with a sparkling 2.85 ERA, and Horace Milton "Hod" Lisenbee was 18–9, 3.57. While Hadley would twice win 15 in the future, this season would really be the high-water mark for both pitchers. A Yankee refugee, Garland Braxton, set a then record for appearances with 58 outings with the '27 Nats. The toothpick-shaped Braxton finished at 10–9 with a very respectable 2.95 ERA. Fred Marberry went 10-

7, but his ERA mushroomed from exactly 3.00 the previous season to 4.64.

The Senators nearly placed second in the league in pitching, but were far inferior to the Yankees in that department. Washington was now two years removed from its appearance in the World Series, and was obviously no match for the Bambino and the rest of that New York ballclub. Neither, by the way, were the Pirates, who returned to the World Series after a one-year hiatus. Baseball lore has it that when the young Waner boys, of whom Lloyd was the tallest at 5'9" and Paul the heaviest at about 153 pounds, first caught a glimpse of the giant Ruth and Gehrig, their hearts sank right then and there. The Pirates couldn't win a single game.

There is some sort of irony in the fact that the game's greatest active pitcher made his last appearance as a pinch-hitter (he hit .235 lifetime with 24 home runs), and that the ball was caught by the greatest hitter the game had ever known. Walter Johnson would stay in the game as a manager, and within 11 days of announcing his retirement as a player, he revealed he'd just signed a two-year contract to be playing manager at Newark of the International League. Infections to both kidneys would keep him hospitalized for the first month of the 1928 season and, his strength affected and doctors recommending only gradual rehabilitation, he faced only one batter all year. Newark, a team comprised of a number of former big leaguers but riddled with dissension, finished seventh. It turned out that Walter would not serve his full term in Newark. Regardless, for the moment the Senators would have to get along without him.

The standards established by Johnson during his 21-year journey through the American League remain a tribute to the man. He had pitched in more games than any pitcher in A.L. history (802). He had won the most games in the league, a figure adjusted over the years and which seems to stand for all eternity at 417, which is safely second on the all-time chart, and first for a pitcher who played his entire career during the 20th century. Johnson still holds the American League record for most shutouts (113), and he pitched the most consecutive shutout innings in league history (55⅔).

Walter Johnson's 3,509 strikeouts were the most in history until surpassed in 1983 by Nolan Ryan, Steve Carlton, and Gaylord Perry. His mark remained an A.L. record until broken by Roger Clemens in 2001. When his career ended, Barney held marks for most innings pitched, most games started, and most complete games. In a slew of years, he had led pitchers with perfect fielding averages in most chances accepted. Walter Johnson was as dominant a pitcher as any in the history of baseball.

If the Big Train's retirement was not sufficient a setback for the Washington Senators of 1928, then there was the matter of Goose Goslin's arm. The Goose, who hadn't hit below .334, with no fewer than 108 RBIs, in the past three years, had a habit of getting into some sort of hot water every spring training. This year, he had strutted over to the Tampa Fair Grounds and, to amuse himself and members of a high-school track team, had shown off at shot put. As the story goes in baseball, his arm was so sore the next day that he couldn't even comb his hair.

The baseball club Bucky Harris was forced to take north to open the season might have made a good football team. The shortstop, who had taken over from Peckinpaugh the previous season, was Bobby Reeves. Better known for his work on the gridiron at the Georgia Institute of Technology, Reeves had an outstanding throwing arm and bore the appropriate nickname of "Gunner." His backup at shortstop was Grant Gillis, who had thrown the winning pass for the University of Alabama in the 1928 Rose Bowl game. The receiver of that pass, Red Barnes, made the Senators as a reserve outfielder. Reeves and Barnes would play in most of the games in 1928, and both would hit over .300.

Goslin's sore arm meant that poor Reeves had to cover as much ground as possible at short, which he did ably, earning the unwanted designation of being Goose's caddy. This arrangement worked well for Goslin,

who hit a hefty .379. For Bobby Reeves, however, the long season became exhausting physically. The Senators had a need for a shortstop and they went out and acquired a 21-year-old former bank clerk, Joe Cronin, from the Pirates — the Pirates still had Glenn Wright. Cronin hit only .242 as a part-timer but Bucky Harris, in particular, was impressed. Happily, Harris's opinion prevailed over that of Clark Griffith, and Bobby Reeves was gone from the roster by the time the calendar year ended.

Harris's keen baseball instincts would stand the Senators in good stead. In Joe Cronin, Bucky had made the acquisition of a Hall of Famer. *The Sporting News* would name Joe Cronin the top major-league shortstop for seven of the ten years of the 1930s. For his services, Washington had paid a paltry $7,500 to the Kansas City club of the minor-league American Association. Cronin always felt that one doubleheader versus the Yankees at the end of the '28 season sealed his fate with the Nats. He went 6–for–8 with three triples that day, all the while overhearing Yankees manager Miller Huggins imploring his pitchers "coive the busher!"

The regular centerfielder when spring training broke in 1928 was Sam West, a rookie from Longview, Texas, who had come from Birmingham with good credentials the previous year, but who'd hit just .239 for the Nats in 38 games. West would click and bat .302, and would average an even .300 during a six-year stay in the capital. He would finish with .299 for a 16-year career.

Another presence, initially more auspicious, on the Washington Senators' roster in early 1928 was George Sisler, a great first baseman since 1915 who had now just passed his 35th birthday. He had been purchased from the Browns in December for $25,000, but Bucky Harris was worried about his fielding. After Sisler hit just .245 in 20 games, he was sold to the Boston Braves for just $7,500. Adding salt to the wound, Sisler hit .326 over three more seasons with the Braves.

Despite the failure of the Sisler experiment, and the fact that the Senators had more position players sharing playing time than in recent memory, it was the team's pitching that told the story for 1928. Hod Lisenbee, who'd defeated the '27 Yankees' "Murderers Row" five times on the way to a slate of 18–9, fell to 2–6 and was never again a top pitcher. Firpo Marberry, who led the A.L. in appearances, and Bump Hadley, were only ordinary, logging records of 13–13 and 12–13 respectively. Hadley did gain a place in posterity when, on September 3, he allowed what turned out to be the great Ty Cobb's very last hit, his 4,191st. The hit also happened to be Cobb's 724th double.

For the Senators' staff, the revelation may have been Garland Braxton, who was 13–11 with a sparkling 2.51 ERA that led the league. The acquisition of veteran righthander Sad Sam Jones did yield huge results. Jones of the World Series heroics earlier in the decade was traded from the Yankees, following the World Series, in exchange for Earl McNeely. Named "Sad Sam" by writer Bill McGeehan, who felt Jones looked dour on the field (Jones believed this was because he wore his cap down low near his eyes), he was the Senators' big winner, and one of three workhorses along with Hadley and Braxton in 1928. He finished at 17–7 with a neat 2.84 ERA.

Another portsider who'd also come over from the Yankees, Milt Gaston, did not fare so well, managing only a 6–12 record. In the second game of a doubleheader at Griffith Stadium on July 10, Gaston had his day in the sun, however, pitching a very unconventional shutout against the Indians. He permitted 14 hits, but only three extra-base hits and no homers during a 9–0 Washington romp. Nonetheless, Gaston's atrocious 5.51 ERA would earn him a ticket out of town before the start of the 1929 campaign.

One of the highlights of the social season at Griffith Stadium occurred on September 1, when President Herbert Hoover showed up to pose with Babe Ruth. "Nothing doing," responded the Babe, "I'm for Al Smith." The Babe would again denigrate President Hoover a couple of years later when reminded that he, a mere baseball player, was earning more than

the President. The Babe retorted that he had had a better year than Hoover, too.

When all was said and done, the 1928 edition of the Washington Nationals was no better than a fourth-place club, coming in with a sub–.500 record of 75–79. They started off poorly, and before the end of May were already 20 games off the pace set by the Yankees. They climbed into the second division thanks to a strong finish. The batting race in which Goose Goslin was involved was more entertaining for Washington fans than the pennant race. Goslin was challenged early in the season by Al Simmons, and then later by Lou Gehrig. When both of those future immortals dropped off, Heinie Manush took up the chase. Indeed, Manush took over the lead a week before the end of the season, and the race finally came down to a two-game series scheduled between the Senators and Manush's St. Louis Browns to close out the season.

The two went into the very last day of the season tied for top spot, and what happened on that day has been seen by baseball historians as calling Goose Goslin's integrity, as well as the integrity of all of major-league baseball, into question. The batting race came down to a final at-bat, with Goslin's final appearance to decide the championship. If he made a hit he would win the title; if he didn't, he wouldn't. It was that simple.

For Lawrence Ritter's *The Glory of Their Times,* published in 1966, the Goose admitted that he was not at all inclined to take the at-bat. Bucky Harris offered to send someone up to hit for him, and Goslin was ready to take him up on the offer. He reasoned that this was his one crack at a batting crown, and by golly he was going to take it, even if it meant sitting down. Goslin recalled years later, however, that his decision prompted quite a discussion among the players on the bench. Joe Judge was the central figure in pointing out the obvious to Goose — what was Heinie Manush, out there in left field, going to think of him if he backed out of this challenge? Everyone in baseball would call him yellow! Exasperated with the bickering around him, Leon Goslin grabbed a bat and strode to the plate determinedly.

Before he had a chance to compose himself, the Goose had two strikes on him. He conceded to Lawrence Ritter that he then devised a second devious plot that might bring him the batting title. He turned toward umpire Bill Guthrie and began calling the ump every name in the book for signaling two strikes on pitches the Goose hadn't bothered to wave at. Goslin was not shy about telling Ritter that he had stepped on the umpire's shoes, had pushed him, had done everything he could think of to get himself tossed out of the game. Guthrie had been on to him, however, and had stated emphatically that yes, Goose was going to bat, and that he better not leave his bat on his shoulder anymore.

Goslin did scratch out an infield hit, his seventh safety in his final 15 at-bats of the season, to win the championship fair and square anyway. This chase for the title remains the closest batting race in history. Leon Goslin became the first Washington Senator to win a batting crown since Big Ed Delahanty had done so back in 1902.

The mediocre overall finish prompted Clark Griffith to fire Bucky Harris on October 1, 1928. Harris had slowed tremendously as a second sacker and his batting average had plummeted to .204. By the end of the season, he had voluntarily turned over his position to rookie Jackie Hayes. Bucky was finished as a player, an old 32, his legs no longer able to support him through the wars. He was held accountable for the ill-advised trade which had sent Buddy Myer to the Boston Red Sox. It was also a popular conception that Harris's marriage into high society in 1926 to the daughter of a West Virginia senator had not served him well, that maybe he was living a little too "high off the hog."

It was with true remorse that Clark Griffith sent the still-game Harris packing. Loyal to the end, Griffith took the approach that he was merely inviting Bucky to leave. The old man, after all, had a job already pre-arranged — no less a position than that of manager of his old buddy Frank Navin's Detroit Tigers. Minutes after being fired, Harris had the Tiger's job. Griffith was big on re-cruiting and hiring his own men, and Harris had been a man in his image, a leader, a scrapper. The Old Fox must have thought of his own veterans, Sam Rice and Joe Judge, as potential replacements, but did not think either one had the stuff to lead a team of men.

It was perhaps inevitable that the man Clark Griffith should settle on was Walter Johnson. The Big Train signed a three-year contract at $25,000 a year to manage the Senators, on October 15, 1928, a year to the day following his retirement as a player. Griff had succeeded in convincing Newark owner Paul Block to give Walter his release. Block acknowledged that Griff had been instrumental in delivering Johnson to Newark in the first place, and reluctantly agreed to grant the Old Fox the favor.

Walter Johnson, Griffith realized, may well have been too nice to manage a big-league ballclub, particularly in these more promiscuous times. But Walter, who did not drink nor smoke, definitely had the respect of his peers. And he had shown how tough he could be by suspending some of his Newark players in his one season as a manager. The Big Train had known no equal as a player and, by anyone's scorecard in the game of life, very few as a person, and the hopes of baseball fans around the nation were with him. In hiring Walter Johnson, Clark Griffith scored a public relations coup and absolved himself of a great deal of criticism for having dropped Bucky Harris.

All good wishes aside, things would not go well, as Johnson himself was not pleased with the team he had inherited for 1929. This displeasure proved well founded when the Nats became firmly ensconced in the second division. The youngsters touted as replacements for Harris at second, Jackie Hayes and Stuffy Stewart, were unimpressive to Johnson, and the Big Train did not think Bobby Reeves was the long-term answer at short. The new manager proposed moving Ossie Bluege to short and benching young Cronin, a future star. He wanted the ballclub to reacquire Buddy Myer, who'd been transformed into a top-notch third baseman with the Red Sox, to patrol the hot corner. Barney figured second base could be handled by committee for the time being, but the sooner Myer was brought back, the better.

Buddy Myer, who'd played at shortstop during his two seasons at Washington, would not come without a high price tag. On December 15, 1928, Myer, who had been traded two years earlier for the unproductive Topper Rigney, was let go by Boston for five players. The Senators were to get the better of this exchange. The price appeared steep, however, and it pained Griffith to give up his two gridiron stars, Bobby Reeves and Grant Gillis. The Nats also turned loose pitchers Hod Lisenbee and Milt Gaston, both busts in '28, and rookie outfielder Elliott Bigelow, who would play just one year at the major-league level.

Considering the fact that he had refused to pay him that paltry $1,000 bonus for his signature on a Senators contract back in 1925, Griffith could bemoan the fact that Myer had cost him roughly $125,000 in money and players. However steep the price tag Griffith had to pay, this would be one of the old flesh trader's grandest coups. While Myer was to star for the Senators for another 13 years, perhaps the most important aspect of the deal was that the Red Sox had insisted that Bobby Reeves, rather than Joe Cronin, be the shortstop coming the other way.

Walter Johnson's charges dropped three games lower in the standings and their fate was once again sealed early, when they lost an appalling 13 of 14 games with the Philadelphia A's in the opening six weeks. One of those was the season opener, attended by President Herbert Hoover, a 13–4 debacle. Following a tongue-lashing administered by the normally placid manager, who made the players attend morning drills to sharpen their minds and make them think about the dumb plays some of them were making, the ballclub won 14 of 20 on the road, and 35 of their last 58 to edge Bucky Harris's Tigers by two games in the quest for fifth place in 1929. Nevertheless, this marked the first time in seven years that the Nats found themselves out of the first division.

Firpo Marberry, the rough tough Texan, was the workhorse with an outstanding 19–12,

3.06 season. For Marberry, in fact, 1929's rebound represented the high-water mark of a very fine career. The new chief fireman, Garland Braxton, was the only other pitcher to win more than nine games for the Senators in '29. But Braxton's ERA was a high 4.85 in a league which averaged 4.24. Sad Sam Jones joined the ranks of the merely mortal at 9–9, and Bump Hadley finished with a horrible 6–16, 5.65. Compounding an already bad situation, over in New York, Tom Zachary, who had given up Babe Ruth's 60th homer and was now the Babe's teammate, finished the season at 12–0 with a sparkling 2.48 ERA.

Washington's offense rated below average, chiefly due to an unproductive outfield, with only Sam Rice having a good year among the flychasers with a .323 mark. Goslin slipped to .288 (in a league which hit .284) with less than 100 ribbies. Young Sam West, who had yet to find his stride, produced .267 in center. Buddy Myer played at both third and second, where Johnson felt he should stay because of the club's weakness at that position, and finished at .300. Joe Cronin, who displayed a fine arm, hit .281 with eight homers. Joe Judge, at 35, continued to field steadily and hit a resounding .315, and 23-year-old Jackie Hayes spent the most time at third and chipped in with .276. Ossie Bluege, 28, saw less action than in any previous season, but still contributed a .295 batting mark.

On the organizational front, Clark Griffith had purchased the Chattanooga Lookouts franchise, planning to make it a minor-league showpiece, complete with a new stadium. His old friend and scout Joe Engel became president and part owner, and the new ballpark carried Engel's name. A promoter extraordinaire, Engel's most famous gambit would be to employ a 17-year-old girl, Virne "Jackie" Mitchell, to pitch to Babe Ruth and Lou Gehrig in a 1931 exhibition game. Both sluggers were struck out by the girl in a scenario which may well have been orchestrated by Engel.

Chattanooga aside, the big club returned to the second division in 1929 with a sub–.500 season for the second year in a row. The Nats were a mixture of veterans and youngsters, with few in-betweeners, and the statistics showed that Washington was below average in all important categories: hitting, fielding, and pitching. As the stock market came crashing down on Black Thursday, October 24, so apparently were the fortunes of the Washington Senators at the dawning of the century's fourth decade.

1930–1939:
Peaks and Valleys

Since the Washington Senators of 1930 distinguished themselves by having five pitchers with 15 or more wins (a record not to be tied for 68 years), it is readily understandable that they were able to make a remarkable turnaround. The Nats won 94, against just 60 losses. The 22-game improvement nevertheless landed the Senators a full eight games out of first place at the end of the year, second to the defending world champions, the Philadelphia A's. With the bats of young players Jimmie Foxx, Mickey Cochrane, and Al Simmons supplementing the veteran arms of Lefty Grove, George Earnshaw, and Rube Walberg, the Athletics were on their way to a second straight world championship.

The Senators roared through a terrific 17–2 preseason, and won ten of their first 12 to start the 1930 campaign, including six of seven against Philadelphia. But this Washington team could not win with any kind of regularity on the road, and by mid–June the club was already well off the pace set by the A's. At this time, a murderous rivalry between the two clubs, more specifically between big Firpo Marberry and Al Simmons of the A's, came to a head.

Marberry was not afraid to pitch batters tight. It came out in print that Simmons was accusing him of trying to bean him, a charge that Marberry would not deny. Every game played against the A's thereafter featured a dustup, with Simmons having to pick himself off the ground. On several occasions, the eventual Hall of Famer took off after Marberry, his bat brandished high. Firpo wasn't backing off, and on each occasion, players from both clubs had had to restrain the two from coming to blows.

Al Simmons did show the Senators what a Hall of Famer is made of in the Fourth of July doubleheader in Philadelphia, and many Washington baseball observers felt that the season turned on that day. Hobbled by a lame ankle, Simmons sat out the first game, which in those days was played in the morning. In the ninth inning, however, he was called upon to pinch hit with the bases loaded and homered off Bump Hadley to win the game. In the afternoon, he again came off the bench to hit a home run off Ad Liska to beat the Senators.

The ax fell in Washington at the mid–June trading deadline. Clark Griffith dropped a bombshell on June 13, announcing that Goose Goslin, the greatest power hitter in team history, had been traded to the St. Louis Browns. In return, Washington got Heinie Manush, whom Goslin had edged out in the celebrated batting race of '28, and pitcher Alvin "General" Crowder. The involvement of Goslin and Manush in this transaction signifies the only time in major-league history that former batting champions were traded for one another. This deal would tilt heavily in Washington's favor, and was proposed to the Nats by Browns owner Phil Ball, who had had personal differences with both of the players he disposed of.

General Crowder, who owed his nickname to General Enoch Crowder, who had devised the World War I draft lottery, was coming back to Washington after a three-year absence. Crowder had served nearly three years in the army during World War I, including a stint in the Philippines and 11 months in Siberia. He didn't, however, come even remotely near attaining the rank of General. Clark Griffith had erred by swapping the General (7–4 as a rookie with the Nats in 1926) to the Browns three years earlier. During that time, Crowder had won 21 and 17 games in his two full seasons with St. Louis, but was only 3–7 in 1930 when the big trade happened.

There seems to have been a pattern to Clark Griffith's madness in terms of his constantly wishing to re-enlist men who'd played for him before. For one thing, he was never perceived as being hard-headed about admitting poor decisions. Buddy Myer had been brought back to the capital and Goose Goslin, for that matter, would eventually find his way back as well. In Heinie Manush, the Senators got an outstanding hitter. Hot at the time of the trade, his stats at the end of the year were 7–65–.362. Goslin hit .330, but with 30 homers and an even 100 ribbies. Sam Rice, who had turned 40 before the season began, showed no sign of a diminished batting eye, hitting .349, just a shade less than his .350 career high set in '25. Rice became the oldest player to score 100 runs, and he counted 121.

A third Senator hit over .340. Joe Cronin had his breakthrough year, becoming the first Washington player named to the prestigious Major-League All-Star team by *The Sporting News* since Goose Goslin four years earlier. (No Washington player *other* than Cronin would be named to this very exclusive club between 1926 and 1941.) His .346, a .104 increase in two years, featured some excellent power numbers which certainly compensated for the loss of Goose Goslin over the second half of the season. Among Cronin's 203 hits were numbered 41 doubles, nine triples, 13 homers, and 126 RBIs.

Although Cronin would hit the magic .300 mark for his career (.301 to be exact), he would never hit as high as .346 again. He would duplicate the runs-driven-in total of 126 the following year, but never top that figure. In 1930, he scored one more run than he drove in — 127. At the beginning of the 21st century, only nine major-league shortstops had scored 100 runs and driven in 100 in the same season (including Alex Rodriguez, 1996 and 1998, and Nomar Garciaparra, 1998). By 1930, Honus Wagner had accomplished this feat on three occasions. Joe Cronin would do it four times. Vigorous and modest to a fault, Cronin, without a doubt, made his mark on the strength of his hitting; while not one of the smoother fielders, he was able to make all the plays.

The Senators finished third in the league in batting with an impressive .302. But the league as a whole hit .288 — the National League average was .303. In support of the "big three" of Manush, Rice, and Cronin, centerfielder Sam West hit .328 and second baseman Buddy Myer .303. Ossie Bluege was the only regular under .300, at .290. The catching was split in this season. Veteran Muddy Ruel hit .253 and gave up most of his playing time to Roy Spencer, who managed .255 in 93 games.

This year's staff was, as mentioned, very deep, and led the league in earned run average in an era in which batting figures were way up, and never more so than in the year 1930. Walter Johnson's contingent led with a 3.96 staff ERA. Alvin Crowder made up for some of the difference in the Manush-Goslin power exchange. He went 15–9 for Washington to ring up 18 wins for the year. Three others won 15 on the 1930 squad: Fred Marberry 15–5, Sam Jones 15–7, and Bump Hadley, who led the club in innings pitched, as he had two years before, 15–11. Topping them all was Lloyd "Gimpy" Brown, 16–12 with a mediocre 4.25 ERA and a fat 220 hits allowed in 197 innings. Brown would improve on these figures the following year. He is chiefly remembered, though, for surrendering more home runs to Lou Gehrig over the Iron Horse's career than anyone else, 15; he is also the only pitcher to allow two of Gehrig's lifetime-record 23 grand slams (only one as a Senator, on August 31, '31).

On the same day as the "Big Deal" in which the Senators parted ways with Goose Goslin, Griffith had traded reserve outfielder Red Barnes (who hadn't hit well since his .302 in 1928) to the Chicago White Sox for Dave "Sheriff" Harris. It seemed there was never a shortage of players named Harris on the Senators of this era. A .310 batter as a pinch hitter over his career but hitting only .244 with the White Sox prior to the trade, Harris produced at a .317 clip for the Senators over the rest of the season. He would continue to pay dividends over the next two seasons with robust averages of .312 and .327 logged as a part-timer.

On the Fourth of July, the Nats swept a twin bill from the Yankees at home. Hot since the Goslin-Manush deal three weeks earlier, the Nats had now won 13 of 14, and three days later pulled half a game ahead of the Athletics. A disastrous road trip which ended in St. Louis three weeks later, however, dropped the Nats 6½ games out of the top spot. The pitching, bereft of a reliever because Garland Braxton had been traded away, had collapsed. Except for Sam Jones, all the starters were used in relief, with disastrous results. Walter Johnson considered pitching himself, but was dissuaded by Clark Griffith.

Walter lost his beloved wife Hazel on August 1, but was back with the club within four days of her funeral. The Nats won 21 of 30 in the month and left the Yankees far in their wake. They got to within 5½ games of the Athletics during the first week of September before fading into a .500 pattern over the rest of the month. They finished eight games behind the A's, and eight ahead of the Yankees. Their 94–60 record was two games better than that of the Washington team which had won the World Series six years before.

Near the end of the season, on September 17, the Nats were the victims of an outstanding performance by second-year Cleveland outfielder Earl Averill (Hall of Fame,

1975). In the first game of a doubleheader, Averill homered in three consecutive at-bats, and could have had a fourth, if not for an apparent bad call. He led off with another home run in the second game, which the Senators won 6–4 to salvage a split of the doubleheader. Averill drove in a record 11 RBIs on the day.

A mere three days after Griffith had engineered both the trade for Manush and Crowder, and the deal for Harris, he had also bartered for one of the truly original characters to have graced the baseball firmament. Art "The Great" Shires, a self-proclaimed superman, was brought over from the White Sox in exchange for the fast-fading lefty, Garland Braxton, and Bennie Tate, who had done most of the catching for the Senators in 1929. The blond Shires came complete with a huge luggage trunk which proclaimed him as Art 'The Great' Shires — The Knockout Kid of Baseball. His gimmick was to boast that he could outbox any boxer and outwrestle any wrestler. Shires did have true talent for the game of baseball, but in the end not quite enough to justify his egotism.

There is evidence, however, that Shires once knocked out his manager with the White Sox, Lena Blackburne. In fact Shires had two celebrated run-ins with Blackburne in 1929. The first confrontation arose because Shires had refused to remove a ridiculous-looking red felt hat that he'd been wearing while taking batting practice. The second row took place when Blackburne surprised Shires drinking bootleg whisky in his hotel room while the team was in Philadelphia.

The Great Shires' career in the majors had begun the previous year with four hits in his very first game. While a decent hitter, as his .291 career mark seems to prove, Shires fancied himself as an even greater fighter. During the first winter following the stock market crash, he earned cold cash by lining up a number of boxing matches involving himself. He had quite a bit of success, reportedly losing only to George Trafton, center of the football Chicago Bears.

When Shires challenged Hack Wilson of the Chicago Cubs to fight, Commissioner

Kenesaw Landis put his foot down, insisting he give up his pugilistic career. Shires, coming off a .312 season in 100 games for the White Sox in 1929, was demanding the then unthinkable salary of $30,000 for 1930. Charles Comiskey responded by shipping him to Washington. While he participated in just 38 games for the Senators in 1930, he hit a mighty .369. Two years later, however, the redoubtable Art Shires would be out of the big leagues for good.

Shires had been obtained by Clark Griffith so that the old man could keep the pressure on Joe Judge. It was Griffith's firm belief that Judge needed competition in order to keep himself at the top of his form. Indeed Shires could have learned a lot about fielding the first base position from Judge, who was tops in fielding for the sixth time (leading or tied) in eight years. In addition, the 36-year-old veteran batted .326 for the season, his best mark in ten years.

Clark Griffith made a key move in August in preparation for the day when Judge would fade. Solid-hitting Joe Kuhel of Kansas City prompted Griffith to part with the princely sum of $65,000. Griff must have been thinking that even if this transaction was to prove a bad one, the acquisition of Joe Cronin from the same club two years before would more than make up for it. As it turned out, the move would be a key ingredient in terms of bringing the Nats back to the top of the American League standings. Less heralded than the acquisition of Art Shires was Griffith's decision in April to claim a slow-footed 31-year-old outfielder named Earl Webb, who'd been placed on the waiver wire by the Cincinnati Reds. Webb had seen part-time duty with the Cubs in 1927 and '28, and had hit a composite .286 and shown good power, with 14 homers in '27.

The Senators hung on to Earl Webb for less than four weeks, never played him in a game, and then shipped him to Boston for "Whispering Bill" Barrett, who really was soft-spoken, and whose six games with Washington would be the last of his big-league life. Webb went on to bat .323 for the Red Sox,

and followed that up with a .333 average and a miraculous (considering his lack of speed) 67 doubles in 1931. This is still the all-time single-season record for two-baggers. While he continued to make good contact, Webb's career lasted only two more years after that, his age and physical limitations finally getting the best of him.

Walter Johnson fielded another excellent ballclub for 1931. Johnson was gaining a reputation as a winning manager as a result of the about-face the team had done in 1930, and the '31 season enhanced the perception that most observers came to have of him as a manager. Once his career came to an end, though, it would be generally felt that someone else might have accomplished more with what he had had to work with. Johnson was not perceived as a great communicator.

For 1931, the Big Train had basically the same material as in '30, and the Nats finished at 92–62, the exact same record as in their 1924 championship year. But being in the same league as the Philadelphia A's would again be their downfall. The Nats won 12 in a row on the road and stood at 37–17 after two months, but were still three games behind the Athletics.

The only major roster change in 1931 involved the demise of Joe Judge. Johnson had grown disenchanted with Judge, who had saved his no-hit game with his glove work back in 1920. He felt Judge was a little too prone to injury and otherwise missed too many games. Johnson did like the new guy, Joe Kuhel, who, like Walter himself, had a self-effacing type of personality. What Kuhel lacked in flamboyance, he made up for with great style around the first-base bag. With Joe Judge at that position for 15 years, this had come to be expected in Washington.

To Johnson's dismay but to Clark Griffith's glee, Joe Judge had a better training camp than the 24-year-old Kuhel, so the latter was farmed out to Baltimore in late April. Four days later, Judge had an appendicitis attack at Fenway Park and was hospitalized. Kuhel was summoned and took over as the first sacker, fielding brilliantly. While he hit a merely creditable .269 with eight homers, Kuhel drove in 85 runs.

During the same week in late April that Kuhel was dispatched to the minors, Lou Gehrig, at this early juncture in the season, actually lost the home-run title right at Griffith Stadium. With Lyn Lary on first with two out, Larrupin' Lou hit a monster shot a dozen or so rows beyond the center-field fence. The ball bounced off a bleacher seat, and Lary somehow concluded the ball had been caught. Manager Joe McCarthy was making wild gestures from the third base coach's box, and Lary figured that meant that the third out had been made.

These misjudgments were compounded by the fact that Gehrig remained oblivious to what was going on. Confident that he'd indeed hit a home run, Gehrig passed Lary on the bases, thereby becoming the third out. The Iron Horse's home run was scored a triple. At season's end, Lou Gehrig and Babe Ruth tied for the home-run title with 46. Ruth and Gehrig had finished 1–2 in the home-run derby for four years running, and Gehrig would have to wait three more years, when the Babe would be on his downslide, before he could at once overtake the Babe in homers and also lead the league in that category.

While Goose Goslin's loss would be felt in the power department in Washington, the Senators of 1931 were an exciting offensive ballclub which placed near the top in doubles, and far ahead of the pack in three-base hits. Joe Cronin's average dipped 40 points to .306, but he drove in the exact same number of runs as in 1930, 126, and hit 12 homers, compared with 13 the previous year.

Ossie Bluege had an especially productive season, his 98 RBIs far surpassing his previous high of 79 in 1925. Second baseman Buddy Myer scored over 100 runs (114) for the first of four times in his career while batting .293. Heinie Manush, while no slugger in the Goslin mold, nevertheless gained acceptance among the fans and scored an even 100 runs, hitting .307. Youthful centerfielder Sammy West was third on the Senators in runs driven

in with 91, and his .333 average put him among the league leaders. Sam Rice may have been slowing down a tad in right field, but at the age of 41 he still hit .310, and rounded out an outfield with Manush and West that was far superior to what it had been when it included Goose Goslin.

Lloyd Brown led the league's second-best pitching staff in innings and earned run average while logging an unimpressive 15–14. General Crowder, particularly adept at the cerebral part of the game and at keeping runners on, came in at 18–11. Firpo Marberry, who, like Crowder and Gimpy Brown, pitched over 200 innings, had another strong year with a sparkling 16–4. This was the third straight year that Marberry was used more frequently as a starter than as a reliever.

However, it was neither Brown nor Marberry who grabbed the biggest headlines among the Griffithmen in 1931. A 24-year-old beanpole named Bobby Burke, who already had four years and a composite 14–18 record with the Senators under his belt going into 1930, threw one of the American League's two no-hitters on August 8 at Griffith Stadium. Burke, 7–2 going into the game, struck out eight Red Sox and walked five, but his fielders never had a real tough play to make all day, and there were no miscues, in a 5–0 shutout. Buddy Myer and Joe Cronin both tripled, with Cronin's blow driving in two runs.

Bobby Burke claimed to have thrown just six curveballs in accomplishing the no-hitter. Amazingly, his feat still stands as the only no-hitter in the entire history of the Senators apart from Walter Johnson's in 1920. Just as amazing is that Burke didn't win another game over the final two months of the 1931 season. He managed to hang on with the Nats for another four seasons, largely on the strength, many believed, of that one game in August '31. He left the big leagues following a failed attempt at making the Philadelphia Phillies in 1937. The Senators' old field boss, Bucky Harris, dubbed Burke "the kid who got an eleven-year tryout."

Ultimately, pitching did win the 1931 pennant, but it was the Athletics who were the best. While the Yankees had re-established themselves as the offensive force in the A.L., outscoring their chief rivals, Philadelphia and Washington, by more than 200 runs, the A's had a complement of pitchers that was marginally better than the Senators', and far superior to the Yankees'.

Lefty Grove of Philadelphia had the first 30–win season in the big leagues since Jim Bagby's 31 wins for Cleveland in 1920. (No one won 30 in the major leagues in the years between 1934 and 1968.) Grove won 31 games against just four losses, with a scintillating 2.06 ERA, which led the league. In fact, no one else in the majors had more than 21 victories except Wes Ferrell of Cleveland. Grove's teammate, George Earnshaw, won 21. A third Philadelphia hurler to log more than 280 innings was Rube Walberg, who led the league in that department and finished at 20–12. Jimmie Foxx hit 30 homers, Al Simmons 22, and Mickey Cochrane 17, and the A's won an astounding 107 games to finish the season 13½ games up on their nearest rivals.

The Senators were in the running for second until the last weekend, when they were edged out by the Yankees and settled in third, a full 16 games behind the Athletics. Despite having dropped a rung in the standings, Clark Griffith still felt that the eight men he could put on the field could match the more powerful lineups in the league, namely New York and Philadelphia. Griff decided not to do much tinkering with his ballclub for 1932, a year which would prove to be another exciting one for his team. The Nats had, above all, a terrific infield. Joe Cronin drove in 116 runs, batted .318, and led the league's shortstops in put-outs, assists, double plays, and fielding average. The Senators as a team were once again at the top of the league in fielding in 1932, in a virtual tie for top spot with the A's.

Offensively, Joe Kuhel improved to .291 in his second full year, although he shared first base with Joe Judge, who hit .258 in his 18th and final season in Washington. Third baseman Ossie Bluege hit .258, and his production returned to normal, with 64 ribbies, compared to his anomalous 98 RBIs the pre-

vious year. Buddy Myer dropped to .279, the second-lowest mark of his career, but, ironically, scored a career-high 120 runs.

Preparing the outfield for the '32 campaign presented a bit more of a challenge to Griffith, who decided to trade for outfielder Carl Reynolds of the Chicago White Sox. Reynolds, solidly built but viewed as temperamental by Chisox manager Donie Bush, had slipped to .290 in 1931 after finishing third in the batting race in 1930 with .359. That season, during which he bashed three homers in consecutive at-bats in a game at Yankee Stadium, Reynolds accumulated 22 homers and 100 RBIs, but those figures dipped to 6–77 in '31.

Griffith figured the righthanded Reynolds would counterbalance the lefty-hitting Sammy West and Heinie Manush. Manush hit a resounding .342, fourth-best in the league, and exactly matched Cronin's RBI output of 116. West slipped to .287 from .333, but had 15 outfield assists, just one short of the tally of the league leader in that department, Goose Goslin of the Browns.

Griffith's plan worked well, as Reynolds, who would end up hitting .302 for his career, was having a great season until Independence Day, 1932, when he crashed into Yankee catcher Bill Dickey in a close play at the plate. This triggered one of the rowdiest incidents in Griffith Stadium history. Dickey, a tough 25-year-old already on his way to the Hall of Fame, was incensed by the way Reynolds barged into him, which had caused him to drop the ball. Unbeknownst to anyone but the Yankee players, the same thing had happened to Dickey a few days before in Boston. Furthermore, Reynolds, a 200-pounder, was known for being one of those players who slid particularly hard, which may endear a player to his manager, but not to enemy fielders.

As Reynolds trotted toward the dugout following the collision, Dickey came running from behind, got in front of him, and socked him in the mouth, breaking his jaw in two places. Dickey was suspended for 30 days and fined $1,000 for his one-punch decision. Carl Reynolds, who had been hitting for the Nats like he had for Chicago during his great season in '30, did not regain his batting eye when he returned following a six-week layoff. Underweight after having his jaw wired during the convalescence, his average slumped over 50 points to .305 for the season.

It must be said that Sam Rice, at 42 years of age, performed admirably while Reynolds was absent, managing .323 in 106 games. Rice, who would have to wait until age 73 to be inducted into the Hall of Fame, was performing at a high level at an age when most Hall of Famers were either on the coaching lines or enjoying a more leisurely lifestyle back in their hometowns.

David Stanley "Sheriff" Harris was a fifth important contributor to Walter Johnson's outfield in 1932, and he was at the center of a couple of truly unusual occurrences involving the Senators in this year. Not related to and not to be confused with Stanley "Bucky" Harris or Joe "Moon" Harris, heroes of earlier days, the Sheriff was one of those original baseball types common back in the thirties, but extinct today. He was essentially an uneducated hillbilly from North Carolina who had explained in his best drawl upon joining the club that he really was no sheriff at all. Harris had the demeanor of a sheriff, but insisted that the real story was that he'd been deputized once only, so that he could help chase mule thieves down in the Carolinas.

All Dave Harris had done since coming to Washington in 1930 as a journeyman 30-year-old, with less than two years of mediocrity in the big leagues behind him, was hit well over .300. In 1932, he came off the bench to pinch hit a league-high 43 times and bat .326 in that role. His status on the club, however, was limited by his erratic fielding. But, as Sheriff Harris liked to say, he could drive in more runs than smarter guys could think across. While this opinion was not shared by all, and in fairness to him this Senators outfield was stacked with talent, Harris hit .327 for the season and drove in 29 runs in only 156 official chances (a rate good for 90–100 RBIs over a full season).

At spring training 1932, held in Biloxi,

Miss., Sheriff Harris, an easygoing country bumpkin if ever there was one, had drawn as a roommate the man who was likely the brightest ever to play professional baseball. Catcher Moe Berg, a New Yorker, had been kicking around the majors since 1923 with little success. Known as an able handler of pitchers with an exceptional throwing arm, he had hit only .240 over that span. In 1929, Berg had played more and hit .288 for the White Sox. The Senators would not get much offense from the catching position in '32 — Berg would hit .236, and Roy Spencer, who played twice as much, only .246.

Moe Berg was much more than a competent defensive catcher. The man was an alumnus of three universities — a lawyer, mathematician, and linguist. He reputedly spoke as many as 17 languages and by the time he joined the Senators, his thesis on Sanskrit was listed in the Library of Congress. Nonetheless, coach Al Schacht, Berg's best friend on the team, referred to him regularly as "just an educated imbecile." With respect to Berg's poor hitting, it was often said that he could speak in many languages, but could hit in none.

Casey Stengel, the "old perfesser," once said that Moe Berg was just about the strangest bird he'd ever come across in baseball. Still active as a player with the Giants when Berg broke into the National League with the Brooklyn Dodgers in 1923, Stengel had not been the only one to hear stories about him. Berg would carry piles of books and newspapers to his dressing-room stall. Not only did this mystify his generally poorly educated teammates, they were amazed that they were not permitted to touch any of Berg's stuff. Berg believed the printed page to have "life," and should his papers be read by anyone else, they would "die." He was known to go out to get copies of newspapers to replace those that someone had "killed."

His eccentricities aside, Berg would eventually become one of America's most important atomic spies. When teams of major leaguers visited Japan in the early thirties, baseball fans might have been amazed that a third-string catcher like Berg had been sent along. He was actually there to take photos for the government. During World War II, he was assigned to the OSS, the forerunner of the CIA. During the war, he was parachuted behind enemy lines to kidnap atomic scientists and bring them back to America.

For his heroism, Berg was to have been awarded the Medal of Merit, but he turned it down. Dark and highly refined in manner, attractive in the eyes of many highly placed ladies, Berg was also honorable and forthright whenever it was suggested that he was wasting his intellect on baseball. He always answered what the most bright-eyed of American youths would have — that he would rather be a ballplayer than a U.S. Supreme Court Justice.

What a pair Moe Berg and Sheriff Harris made! Berg respected the coarse Harris for what he could do — come up to the plate in any situation and perform with confidence. Berg reasoned that Harris owed this skill to what actually boiled down to a lack of mental acuity. Harris' brain was totally devoid of outside encumbrances, and with nothing else on his mind, he was better able to focus on the pitcher and the task at hand. The Sheriff, who thought Berg was the smartest man ever to grace the planet, would respond that, with runners on base, what the Senators needed was "a genius like me."

It was in such a situation that Dave Harris made the most memorable hit of the season for the Senators, albeit in a woefully pitiful cause. On August 5, with the score 13–0 in favor of Detroit, Tommy Bridges was just one out away from a perfect game. Due up was pitcher Bobby Burke, but Walter Johnson, tough competitor that he was, was going to do everything in his power to prevent Bridges from attaining immortality at the expense of his boys. Johnson summoned Harris, who for years had been saying that Tommy Bridges was one of the main reasons why he had managed to survive as a big-league hitter. Sure enough, Harris, a remarkably good curveball hitter, rapped a clean single to center, sparing the Senators the embarrassment of being victimized by a perfect game.

The Nats were themselves able to subdue other A.L. teams more often than not in 1932, and this was largely thanks to a pitching staff that allowed fewer runs than any other in the league. General Alvin Crowder had a career year, 26–13, 3.33. He led the league in wins and was also the number-one workhorse in the loop, with a whopping 327 innings (Dizzy Dean was first in the National League with just 286). Crowder's 26th win was his 15th in a row, a 2–1 decision over the A's at Griffith Stadium. Philadelphia's only run resulted from Jimmie Foxx's 58th home run, which turned out to be his last of the year in the first serious challenge mounted on Babe Ruth's 1927 standard. In this season, Foxx had had two home runs canceled because of rainouts in the early innings of games.

Rookie righthander Monte Weaver, purchased from Baltimore the previous season, spun a very gratifying 22–10 record for Clark Griffith in 1932. In later years, Weaver recalled how he'd been greeted upon his arrival in '31, when he won his first big-league decision. While he was shagging flies in the outfield, Walter Johnson went up to him and said that if Weaver pitched like he had in Baltimore, everything would be fine. The fact was, however, that Weaver had been pitching, to quote him, "lousy" in Baltimore at the time of his purchase. Being a brainy guy who later earned a master's degree in mathematics, he knew that Walter was just being nice. In addition to Weaver's phenomenal rookie year, Lloyd Brown contributed a 15–12 slate, and Firpo Marberry, used primarily as a reliever for the first time in four years, went 8–4 with a league-leading 13 saves.

All added up, the Senators had another great year — 93 wins, third-highest in club history, against 61 losses. It was a better record than that of the National League champions, the Chicago Cubs. However, Washington only gained two games in the standings, winding up a disappointing 14 lengths behind New York, winners of 107 games, who finished 13 ahead of the defending champions, the Athletics. While Babe Ruth and Lou Gehrig drove in 288 runs between them, it was with pitching—courtesy of Gomez, Ruffing, Pipgras, and Pennock—that the Yankees were able to outclass the A's.

Despite an outstanding ballclub and another profitable year for the club coffers, a pennant seemed no closer in sight. A hot September, in which the Nats had won 24 of 28 games, had left them one game out of second place. This was not good enough for the assembled talent, and Clark Griffith was not going to stand for it.

The Yankees won the World Series in four straight. That Series would long be remembered for something which may or may not have happened in the third game. Babe Ruth made a gesture which some interpreted as a sign that he was going to belt one over the fence, which he promptly did. The pitcher, Charlie Root, maintained until his death in 1970 that he would have decked Ruth if the Babe had really been calling his shot, and that Ruth had merely been indicating that he had but one strike left.

It is very likely that Clark Griffith had other things on his mind at this particular time. As soon as the 1932 season ended, he asked Walter Johnson—the *great* Walter Johnson—whether he was set financially and whether he could have his permission to dismiss him as an employee. In other words, he was firing the Big Train. This came as no surprise to Barney, who'd been working on a one-year contract after his initial three-year deal to manage had expired. The writing had been on the wall, and 1932 was a crucial year for him if he was to continue on as field boss of the Senators. A relationship begun 26 years earlier was severed, but the two parted on amiable terms. After all, for most of the period between 1912 and 1928, Griff had made Johnson the highest-paid pitcher in the American League.

By the following summer, a third of the way into the 1933 campaign, Johnson would be hired to manage the Cleveland Indians, replacing his old teammate, Roger Peckinpaugh, who'd been field boss of the Tribe since 1928. (Peck would later serve as the Indians' president and general manager.) Wes Ferrell, a North Carolina farmer and banjo picker who was to pitch his way into the Hall of Fame, was then with the Indians. Ferrell said he'd never been able to get along with Peckinpaugh, who he said was surly and uncommunicative.

Ferrell preferred Johnson, although he thought the Big Train's idea of managing was to give inane rah-rah speeches punctuated by plenty of "dadgummits" and "doggonnits." Barney brought the Indians in fourth in '33 and third in '34, when he had Sam Rice and Moe Berg on the squad, but was relieved of his duties after a 46–48 start in 1935. There exist varied opinions as to his proficiency as a manager. There is support for the school of thought which holds that Johnson should have had more success, especially in light of what was to transpire in 1933. To the charge that he was not a good handler of pitchers, the Big Train answered that, having been a pitcher himself, he felt that no one could know how any pitcher was going to do on any given day. All a manager could do in terms of deploying pitchers was to hope for the best.

There is no doubt that chopping Walter Johnson's $25,000 salary was a key consideration for Clark Griffith when he politely showed Barney the door. Attendance at the stadium had plummeted from 614,000 two years before to 371,000 during the throes of the depression in 1932. The intelligent guess was that Griff would again dip into the ranks of his own club to find a replacement for Johnson. Since he'd given up managing in 1920, he'd followed this pattern on five successive occasions, hiring George McBride, Clyde Milan, Donie Bush, Bucky Harris, and Walter Johnson. There was also widespread speculation that Griffith wanted to purchase Al Simmons's contract from Connie Mack and make him the manager. The old man added fat to the fire by reminding members of the media that he'd once *himself* managed an American League pennant winner, and that he wasn't too old to do so again.

On October 8, 1932, just four days before his 26th birthday, Joe Cronin was named manager of the Washington Senators, making him at the time the youngest man to be appointed manager of a big-league team before the start of the season. (Roger Peckinpaugh still holds the big-league record as the youngest manager to ever end a season, having guided the Yankees for the final 17 games as a 23-year-old in 1914.) Cronin was more than a year younger than Bucky Harris had been when he was hired to skip the Nats back in '24.

Cronin had first been spotted by the Pirates as a 17-year-old playing semipro ball around his hometown of San Francisco. After impressing many in his first season by hitting .313 at Johnstown of the Middle Atlantic League in 1925, the Pirates brought him up to the big team to sit on the bench during the hard-fought World Series against the Senators. He got to pose for the team picture with the world champs. But Cronin hit only .257 in brief tryouts with the Pirates over the next two seasons, and was batting only .245 for Kansas City of the American Association in midsummer 1928 when Joe Engel came calling.

Washington's ace scout had been "beating the bushes," looking for a good shortstop the likes of whom the Nats had not had since the departure of Peckinpaugh. As the story goes, the owner of the Kansas City ballclub was entertaining a number of scouts in his brewery one night and proclaimed with disgust that a week before, he could have gotten $15,000 for Cronin's contract, but that he'd stupidly turned the offer down. Now, he said, he'd accept $10,000.

Joe Engel, not quite sure he had the authority, nonetheless immediately chimed in with an offer of $7,500. The deal done, he reached Griffith by phone and the old man exploded, wondering very loudly whether Engel had lost it completely by agreeing to pay such a large sum for a minor-league shortstop batting .245. So furious was the old man that Engel thought it best to keep Cronin with him for a week or so while he continued his scouting trip. This seemed far preferable to

sending the youngster to Washington right away, and thereby possibly exposing him to Griffith's wrath firsthand.

If Griffith was not smitten with Cronin at first, finding him awkward in the field and with an open stance that showed little likelihood of any power in his batting stroke, he of course came to realize that Joe Engel's purchase had been as good a deal as he'd ever made. Now he'd be making even more money with that investment. Cronin was getting a raise of $2,500 for managing as well as playing in 1933. Griff could thereby pocket the rest of Walter Johnson's $25,000 salary. But what the Old Fox had come to like beyond all else about his perennial all-star shortstop was the man's combativeness. The handsome, square-jowled Irishman had a temper that came to the surface quickly on the field. *That* was why Clark Griffith made his great shortstop his manager.

A couple of months after being hired, in early December 1932, Joe Cronin arrived in Washington from San Francisco to meet with Griffith and plot strategy for the coming campaign. The owners of the major-league clubs would be meeting the following week in New York for the annual trading sessions. Cronin would come to that meeting with his owner, and he would come prepared. Based on his own experiences as a batter, and on a hunch that the men involved could be acquired by Washington, Cronin announced to Griffith that he had a short list of pitchers that he just had to have. He boldly challenged Griff to get these men for him, emphasizing that from all accounts he'd heard, if there was any baseball man who could make a deal for these men, Clark Griffith was that man. The acclamation may well have helped Cronin's cause.

The three pitchers Cronin named were lefthanders Earl Whitehill of the Tigers and Walter Stewart of the Browns, and righty Jack Russell* of the Indians. It was Cronin's opinion that the Yankees were the team to beat, and that what separated the Yankees from the

---

This is the same Jack Russell for whom the Phillies' spring training facility in Clearwater, Florida, was named — in his later years, Russell was City Commissioner of Clearwater and instrumental in getting the facility built.

Senators was pitching, particularly of the left-handed variety. Whitehill and Stewart were two who matched up well against the Bronx Bombers. As for Russell, Cronin wanted him for quite another reason — he had owned the Senators the previous season, and that had to mean something.

Griffith decided to accede to Cronin's demands, possibly spurred on by vanity after Cronin expressed confidence in his skill as a shrewd negotiator. When they got to New York, Cronin was dispatched to the hotel lobby to accost some of the officials of the three teams the Senators wanted to deal with. Their first move was to reverse a trade they had made on June 9 by reobtaining southpaw Carl Fischer (who had had one good year with the Senators in '31 when he went 13–9) in exchange for Dick Coffman. Fischer had gone 3–7 for the Browns after the June deal, but the Detroit Tigers had some interest in him. Coffman, a lefthander, had registered a 1–6 record on a strong Washington club.

On the following day, Fischer became part of a trade that also brought Earl Oliver Whitehill to Washington, but the cost was much higher than just Fischer. The Tigers insisted on Firpo Marberry, the starter-reliever who'd recorded a stunning 39–13 record over the past three years. However, Marberry had passed his 34th birthday two weeks earlier. Earl Whitehill was only two months younger, but he'd been logging a lot of innings for the Tigers for ten years and was considered a reliable starter and a fierce competitor. Whitehill took a back seat to no one on the field — he was a win-at-all-costs type of player, as evidenced by his arguments with his manager at Detroit, Ty Cobb, whenever the abrasive Cobb came to the mound to tell him how to pitch.

Dubbed the "Earl" for his dazzling wardrobe, good looks (he was married to the model who gained perpetual life by posing as the original Sunshine Raisin girl), and temperamental air, Whitehill wasn't afraid to tell off teammates or umpires, depending on the particular game situation. While Marberry would have a good year for Detroit, posting a 16–11

record, Earl Whitehill, who'd never won more than 17 for the Tigers, would win 22 games and be the Senators' best pitcher in 1933. Whitehill would eventually retire from baseball with 218 wins, but with the highest ERA (4.36) of any 200-game winner in history. He regularly walked more batters than he struck out in a season, and as late as the 1980s he was still on the top-ten all-time list for bases on balls given up over a career.

The trade for Whitehill appeared relatively insignificant, however, compared to the other deal swung by the Senators on the same day, December 14, 1932. Since the firing of Walter Johnson, Goose Goslin, who didn't get along with Johnson, had put the word out to Clark Griffith that he would love to come back to the capital. As Griffith negotiated with the Browns for Walter "Lefty" Stewart in exchange for Sammy West, he kept Goslin's plea in mind. He offered Carl Reynolds if the Browns would include Goose, who'd hit .299 with 17 homers and 104 ribbies in the last campaign. The Browns didn't think that was quite equitable, and asked Griffith about Lloyd Brown, the lefty who'd won 15 in '32. (Brown would never again win more than nine games in a season and would be gone from St. Louis after just eight games at the start of the '33 campaign.) To make it a three-for-three transaction, the Senators settled on righthanded outfielder Fred Schulte, who'd enjoyed what was for him a typical .294 season in '32.

The loss of centerfielder Sam West had to be seen as leaving the biggest void on the Washington side, and he would indeed hit an even .300 and nearly double his home run output for St. Louis in 1933. But the Browns would finish last. The mild-mannered Schulte, truly a fine fielder, kept right on hitting and would drive in nearly twice as many runs for the Senators as West would for the Browns while batting .295.

President Alva Bradley of the Cleveland Indians was the next to be brought in by Cronin to talk turkey with Griffith at the late 1932 New York meetings. The Senators were playing on Cleveland's desperate need for a first baseman. Secure in his belief that Joe

Kuhel would be around for a long time (which would prove to be correct), Washington would part with promising Harley Boss from its Chattanooga farm club and an undisclosed amount of cash for Jack Russell, the third pitcher Cronin had requested for his team. Russell at this time had an atrocious 46–98 record in the big leagues, but the 27-year-old had spent most of his career in the National League with the sad-sack Boston Braves. Griffith even managed to wrangle an outfielder, Bruce Connatser, from Bradley as part of this exchange. This would prove of no consequence, as Connatser, a part-timer with the Indians the two previous years, never again appeared in a single major-league game.

The trade with the Indians may have been incomplete, for at the end of the first week of January, another deal was struck. The Senators sent their most regular catcher, Roy Spencer, to Cleveland, for Luke Sewell, an experienced veteran receiver. Sewell, a year younger than Spencer and at least his equal as a hitter, had turned 32 two days before the trade was made. He had hit .253 in 300 at-bats for the Browns in '32, and was a good defensive catcher, as demonstrated by the fact that he'd led American League backstops in assists three straight years, 1926–28. He had already spent 12 years in the American League, all with the Indians, and was the younger brother of future Hall of Famer Joe Sewell.*

Joe Cronin now had all he had asked for, and more. In addition to the three pitchers, the Senators were better set behind the plate with the reliable Sewell. Goose Goslin's lefthanded power and Fred Schulte's righthanded bat were expected to round out an even better outfield with Heinie Manush, the high-percentage lefthanded-hitting left fielder for whom Goslin had been traded 2½ years earlier, being the third flychaser.

At the Biloxi training camp, the young manager sought to enlist the support of the veterans the way Bucky Harris had during the Senators' salad days in the midtwenties, and he

got it. One day, however, General Crowder, yanked out of a game by Cronin, hurled his glove all the way from the mound to the dugout. When fined $25 on the spot, Crowder yelled at Cronin that $25 amounted to a bush-league fine. To which Cronin retorted that Crowder's outburst had been exactly that — bush. There was nothing bush about General Crowder's results in 1933, however, as he went on to win 24 games, best on the staff.

It was indeed, as Joe Cronin had expected, the Yankees, and not the A's, who represented the Senators' main adversary in 1933, and the rivalry was exacerbated by the unforgotten incident involving the departed Carl Reynolds and Bill Dickey the previous year. The Yankees leaped out of the starting gate and won their first seven in a row before coming to Washington. Things got hot when Joe Cronin challenged Babe Ruth to a fight after Ruth came into him hard while Cronin was covering third. But all hell broke loose at Griffith Stadium a few days later, on April 25, when outfielder Ben Chapman of the Yankees, who ran the bases like a wild goose, came in with spikes high on Buddy Myer at second in order to break up a double play. Myer, who the Yankees were accusing of having spiked Lou Gehrig on a play at the first base bag, bounced right back to his feet and began kicking Chapman — some onlookers estimated Chapman might have absorbed as many as a dozen kicks. The benches emptied and some fans came out of the stands to attack the Yankees as well.

Yankees ace Lefty Gomez brandished a bat and waved it around, reportedly striking a policeman. Dixie Walker, a rookie outfielder with New York who would later star in the National League, as would his younger brother Harry, managed to reach Myer, jumped him, and began punching him repeatedly as Myer lay on the ground. Someone decked Yankees manager Joe McCarthy. Police had to be called in to bring some order to the proceedings, and arrested five fans who had gotten involved.

*The same Joe Sewell who had begun his career under a microscope as the replacement for star shortstop Ray Chapman of the Indians, the victim of the majors' only on-field player fatality, in 1920.

Myer, Walker, and Chapman were thrown out of the game, but Chapman's woes weren't over. On the way to the dressing room, he had to pass by the Senators' dugout, where the belligerent Earl Whitehill began berating him. Chapman, who would in the future, on two occasions, join the Senators, took a swing that connected with Whitehill's left eye, knocking Washington's ace pitcher back. More Senators players and the police stepped in. Perhaps what infuriated the Nats most in this game was the final score: 16–0 Yankees.

Lost in the shuffle was the performance of New York's Russ Van Atta, who gave up just five hits in posting a shutout in his big-league debut. A few days later, Clark Griffith was angered again when suspensions were announced by league president Will Harridge. Both Myer and Whitehill drew five-day suspensions and $100 fines, while only Chapman of the Yankees incurred the same fate. Dixie Walker got nothing.

Joe Cronin had been right in terms of how the pennant race would go. The A's were out of it early and never really posed a threat. There was an obvious reason. Owner Connie Mack, engineering a fire sale reminiscent of what he'd done 20 years earlier to keep his operation afloat, had gotten rid of Al Simmons, Mule Haas, and Jimmy Dykes at the end of the previous season. The whole lot of them were sold to the White Sox for a cool $100,000.

In terms of competing with the Yankees, Earl Whitehill and Lefty Stewart were indeed the answer for Washington. On Independence Day, exactly a year after the Dickey-Reynolds dustup, Whitehill and Stewart pitched a doubleheader at Griffith Stadium with the Nationals going into the day with a scant half-game lead. The Senators took the first game in ten innings, 6–5, when Cronin singled to drive in Manush.

Walter "Lefty" Stewart went all the way in the second game and the Senators prevailed 3–2 to sweep the twin bill. Stewart, born in 1900 in central Tennessee, nearly died in 1927 when his appendix burst while he was out hunting. Told he'd never play baseball again,

Lefty persisted and eventually proved the experts wrong. Nevertheless, he was only 24–26 over three years with the Browns, who had been enjoying relatively good years over that same period. Then, in 1930, Stewart came into his own, sounding the death knell for the Washington Senators in the process. Lefty beat the second-place Nats five times that year on his way to a breakthrough 20–12 season during which the Browns made a swift return to mediocrity. While he remained the Brownies' ace in '31 and '32, he recorded a composite 28–36 over those two seasons.

Lefty Stewart shared the bulk of the mound chores on the '33 Senators with General Crowder, who finished with 15 losses to go along with his 24 wins, and with Earl Whitehill, 22–8 with a superior (for the inflationary times) 3.33 ERA. Stewart contributed a 15–6 slate. Jack Russell, the third pitcher added before the season, led the league in saves with 13 and posted a 12–6 record with a stingy 2.69 ERA

The pitching arsenal was stacked. Monte Weaver, coming off a 22-win campaign, pitched much less but showed much-improved mastery of the strike zone, culminating in a fine 10–5 year for him. Alphonse "Tommy" Thomas, a veteran righthander who had once won 19 games for the White Sox and led the A.L. in innings pitched, was only 7–7. Thomas had simply pitched his arm out for the White Sox and his career had been on a downslide since 1930. In '33, his first full season in Washington, his ERA was a characteristically high 4.80.

Backed by the best-fielding club in the league, the pitching staff as a unit allowed fewer runs than any other A.L. club in 1933. Nats hitters combined for the best batting average in the league, .287. All of these factors have a good chance of spelling success of course, and 1933 would in fact stand forever as the best season in Washington Senators history. Lead-off man Buddy Myer raised his average 23 points to .302 and scored 95 runs. Young Joe Kuhel topped anything he'd done previously and hit .322 with 117 RBIs. Manager and shortstop Joe Cronin showed leadership in the most tangible of ways with another stellar year, batting .309 with 118 ribbies.

Ossie Bluege, a fixture for 11 years at third and at 32 in his last season as a full-fledged regular, enjoyed a typical year for him, with .261 and 71 runs driven in. On May 16 of this season, the Nats introduced for the first time a lefthanded-hitting third baseman who would take over the hot corner and eventually prove himself to be one of the great Washington Senators. His name, Cecil Travis, became known to all serious readers of the sports pages on the morning of May 17, 1933.

In his debut, Travis, a lefthanded slap hitter who at this point in his development drove nearly everything to the opposite field, had on the previous day connected for five hits in his first five big-league opportunities. Travis was put out in his final two at-bats in a 12-inning game at Griffith Stadium won by the home side 11–10 over the Indians. Incredibly, Joe Kuhel also rapped out five hits in the same 12-inning game. Travis got into only 17 more games during the course of the regular season, batting .302. In the minors with the Chattanooga Lookouts, the Senators' affiliate in the Southern Association, Travis, himself a Southerner from Riverdale, Georgia, posted an ominous .352 bat mark.

The 1933 Washington outfield, predictably potent, did not really disappoint, with Goslin, Schulte and Manush averaging .297, .295, and .336 respectively. Goslin's power numbers, however, did diminish significantly, and he hit just ten homers and produced 64 runs. On the way to placing second in the league in batting to Jimmie Foxx, who won the triple crown with gigantic figures of 48–163–.356, Manush hit in 33 consecutive games. This established the still-standing team benchmark, which eclipsed the record of 31 games set by Sam Rice in 1924.

By the second week of September, this best-ever version of the Washington Senators had opened up a nine-game lead, and the pennant was wrapped up by the end of the third week, against the St. Louis Browns. The Senators recorded 99 wins in a year in which they played only 152 games. (It was more common

back then to leave some games unplayed at the end of the schedule if those games were to have no bearing on the final standings.)

The Yankees were in fact involved in two games fewer than the Senators, but when play stopped the Nats finished seven full games ahead of New York, spelling the end of the heyday of Murderers' Row. While Babe Ruth still hit .301 with 34 homers, his production was down and his career was petering out fast. It would be nearly three years before the Yanks would be able to regroup around a rookie named Joe DiMaggio and once again dominate the American League.

The Senators influenced firsthand New York's demise, and Lady Luck was on their side at crucial times during the season. Back in April, Washington was ahead by three runs when Tony Lazzeri, with Lou Gehrig on second and Dixie Walker on first, launched a bullet which ricocheted off Yankee Stadium's rightfield fence. Gehrig thought Goose Goslin might catch the ball, so he tagged up. The much-faster Walker did not, and so here they both came, one behind the other, barreling toward third.

Coach Art Fletcher, confused, couldn't stop one baserunner and not the other. Joe Cronin's relay was on time for Luke Sewell to tag Gehrig out, and then to spin around and tag Walker also. Later in the season, in a game in which the Senators trailed 1–0 in the ninth, with a man on first and two out, Buddy Myer fouled one to the screen which Bill Dickey went back on and caught. Umpire Bill McGowan ruled the ball had grazed the screen, just barely, and Myer had a reprieve. He hit the next pitch out of the park to win the game, one of his four homers of the 1933 campaign.

In the final game of the season, coach Nick Altrock was given a chance to become the oldest player to participate in a major-league game up to that time by being allowed to pinch hit. Unsuccessful in the attempt, against Rube Walberg of the A's, Altrock had played at the age of 57 years, 16 days, a record now held by Satchel Paige, who pitched for the Kansas City Athletics in 1965 at the age of 59 years, 2 months, 18 days. Minnie Minoso fell just a few months short of Paige's record when he appeared for the Chicago White Sox in 1980 so that he could become the second player in history to appear in five decades as a player. The first had been Nick Altrock.

If the Senators dominated the league in 1933, Bill Terry's New York Giants did the same in the rival loop, emerging as clear-cut champs with a five-game edge over the Pittsburgh Pirates. The upcoming World Series would pit two "boy managers" against one another. At 34, Terry had taken over from John McGraw early in the 1932 campaign, marking the end of the Lil' General's 30-year reign as the Giants' field boss. Cronin, eight years Terry's junior, became the youngest manager in World Series history, a distinction he still held at the beginning of this century.

So it would be, as in 1924, a confrontation between the Giants and the Senators. However, unlike the '24 Giants team, which was built around hitting, this outfit centered around an outstanding pitching staff. Its ace was Carl Hubbell,* a lanky, floppy-eared, 30-year-old lefthander who'd been pitching in the National League for six years with some success.

Carl Hubbell's specialty was the screwball, and he delivered it with a slow, cartwheeling movement toward the plate. Until this season, his best showings had been a pair of 18–11 efforts in '29 and '32. But in 1933, Hubbell occupied another stratosphere, leading all National League pitchers in wins (23), ERA (an overpowering 1.66), innings pitched, and shutouts. His ten shutouts were three more than were posted by his teammate, Hal Schumacher, second best in the league in that category. "Prince Hal," a righthander who threw a heavy ball and had a very good overhand curve, went 19–12 with a 2.16 ERA, third best in the league. Hubbell and Schumacher were 1–2 in the N.L in allowing the fewest number of hits per nine innings, and third on that list was another Giant, Fat Freddie Fitzsimmons, 16–11 with another ERA under 3.00.

Giants manager Bill Terry wasted no time making known who his starter would be for the first game — Carl Hubbell. The lefty's screwball was said to be even more effective against left-handed hitters, and of those, Washington had plenty in its starting lineup — Myer, Goslin, and Manush, who would be penciled into the 1–2–3 slots in the batting order in game one, and Joe Kuhel, who would bat sixth.

It was the Washington Senators, a truly balanced ballclub, who were considered runaway favorites to win the 1933 World Series. As the first contest at New York's Polo Grounds, slated for October 3, approached, Joe Cronin remained mum regarding who would start the first game for the Senators. Terry had already declared that Carl Hubbell would win the first and fourth games, and this may have contributed to Cronin's determination to remain silent. After dallying for a week, he settled on a lefthander as well, but baseball observers were shocked that it wasn't Earl Whitehill, the 22-game winner. Instead, Lefty Stewart, loser of only six games all season, got the nod.

The day of the first game started off very badly for the Senators ... even before play even began. On his way to the Polo Grounds, lead-off batter Buddy Myer was reportedly a witness to a traffic accident in which a pedestrian was killed. Myer, visibly and understandably shaken by the experience, would make three errors in the field on this day. He was easy prey for Hubbell leading off the game, and struck out. Goose Goslin and Heinie Manush both struck out as well.

In the field, right away Myer had to handle a ground ball off the bat of lead-off man Jo-Jo Moore (not the same player as *Eddie Moore,* the second baseman who'd played for the Pirates against Washington in the 1925 Series). Myer booted the play, and the error would be costly. Lefty Stewart got the next two batters but then Mel Ott, the Giants' most powerful hitter, propelled a drive into the lower rightfield stands.

Hubbell would be forever remembered in baseball lore for something that would happen during the following year. In the 1934 All-Star game, he struck out, in succession, no less a group of sluggers than Babe Ruth, Lou Gehrig, Jimmie Foxx, Al Simmons, and Joe Cronin.

Stewart, Cronin's "hunch," pitched just two innings. He was lifted after giving up three singles, one of them off the wall, and a run, without getting anyone out in the top of the third. Jack Russell came in and got three straight outs, but another run came in when a shot off the bat of Travis Jackson, a 1924 World Series alumnus, went off Kuhel's glove to Myer, who relayed to Russell covering first.

The Senators scored single runs in the fourth and ninth, both unearned, off Hubbell, who went all the way and gave up just five hits. Buddy Myer opened the fourth with a single, advanced on an error by second baseman Hughie Critz, and scored on Fred Schulte's single. In the top of the ninth, with the Nats still down 4–1, New York shortstop Blondy Ryan muffed a Manush grounder to start the inning. Joe Cronin and Fred Schulte then singled, both of them for the second time in the game. Here were the makings of a rally. Joe Kuhel grounded to short for the first out. Manush scored. The next batter, Ossie Bluege, struck out for the third time, proving that Hubbell was no picnic for righthanded hitters either. Luke Sewell then grounded to third to end the game.

The events of game two would in no way inspire any second-guessing about Joe Cronin having picked Lefty Stewart as his starting pitcher in the Series opener. This is because of what happened when the Nats' top winner, General Alvin Crowder, was handed the ball for the second game. With two down in the third, Goose Goslin, hitless in his first five at-bats in this Series, belted a Hal Schumacher pitch into the upper right field stands. The ball sailed over a sign sponsored by the NRA proclaiming "We Do Our Part." Crowder was doing his part, coasting through the first five innings, giving up just one walk and two harmless singles.

In the sixth, however, the roof caved in. In the top half, the Nats had men on second and third with one out when Goslin, the lead runner, got caught in a rundown when Fred Schulte grounded toward third. Joe Kuhel walked to load the bases, but Ossie Bluege struck out for the fourth time in five official at-bats so far in the Series. In the bottom of the inning, the Giants sent 12 batters to the plate, bunching seven singles, a double by Terry, and an intentional walk, to score six runs and chase Crowder. The tying and winning runs were driven in by pinch hitter Lefty O'Doul, a pitcher who had been transformed into an outfielder while already in his thirties. O'Doul had proceeded to win the National League batting championship in 1930 with a .398 average.

Tommy Thomas came in to relieve Crowder with two out and the score 6–1, and gave up an inconsequential infield single before getting Bill Terry to ground into a force play to end the slaughter. The score remained as it was at the end of New York's six-run sixth, 6–1. The Giants, who had ten hits in each of the first two games to the Senators' five in each game, were well positioned now with a 2–0 lead with the sixth and seventh games, should the Senators succeed in rendering them necessary, to be played at the Polo Grounds.

One aside to this unhappy story from the Nationals' perspective was that Sam Rice, owner of a .290 career batting average in the World Series, got one last crack at the bat. The 43-year-old was brought in as a pinch hitter for Tommy Thomas after the sixth-inning debacle. With one out in the top of the seventh, Rice singled to center to raise his World Series batting average above the magical .300 barrier (.302) for all eternity. As things would go, this was Sam Rice's final at-bat with the Senators after having donned a Washington uniform over a span of 19 consecutive years.

The weather may have matched the mood at Griffith Stadium for the third game on October 5. The teams had traveled by train from New York, and there were still no off days scheduled during the fall classics of this era. It rained hard before the game, drenching a relatively sparse crowd of under 26,000 which included President Franklin D. Roosevelt and a large congressional retinue — the largest, it was said, ever to see a baseball game. President Roosevelt threw out the first ball, and the custom then in vogue was for the players to scramble to catch it. On this occasion, a wild melee ensued, and it was lucky no one was injured. For the record, it was Heinie Manush who finally emerged from the scrum with the ball.

A short while earlier, Joe Cronin had a few choice words for his troops. As manager, but also as their shortstop, he told them that he hoped every man in the room was as ashamed as he was about what had happened in New York. He told them that they were a better team than the New York Giants, and now was the time to show that.

Cronin's words didn't hurt. As the Giants had done in the first game, the Senators struck for two runs right off the bat in this one. After Earl Whitehill mowed New York down in order, lead-off man Buddy Myer, who up to this point was a dismal 1–for–7 with three errors on only ten fielding chances in the first two games, singled off Fat Freddie Fitzsimmons. Goose Goslin, up next, unloaded on one of Fred's fat ones, propelling it off the top of the fence in right field. Mel Ott gamely retrieved it, keeping Myer from scoring.

After Heinie Manush popped up, Cronin hit a bouncer back to the mound. Myer had moved quickly, however, and Fitzsimmons had no choice but to go for the easy out at first, making the score 1–0 Washington. Fred Schulte kept the rally going, tagging a double to right to bring in Goslin with the second run of the inning. The rally ended moments later when Schulte got caught in a rundown after Kuhel had hit a ground ball toward Travis Jackson, the former shortstop who was just recently starting to play some at the hot corner.

Like Myer had done in the Washington half of the first inning, Ossie Bluege gained a measure of redemption in opening the second. Like Myer, Ossie needed it. He was 0–for–6 with four strikeouts in the Series to date, but this time he banged a double down the third-base line. The veteran Luke Sewell hit expertly behind the runner, and Bluege was quickly moved up to third with one away.

What happened next was thrilling, although it would end up being unimportant.

Pitcher Earl Whitehill drove a bouncing ball toward the mound and Fred Fitzsimmons made a split-second decision to try and nab Bluege off third. He didn't, and there were now runners on the corners. The beleaguered Buddy Myer promptly doubled down the first-base line, bringing in a third run and putting Whitehill on third. The next batter, Goslin, drove a fly to left on which Whitehill was given the go-ahead to try and score, but Jo-Jo Moore's relay to Gus Mancuso got Whitehill at the plate and the inning was over. But it was 3–0 Washington.

The flashy Whitehill would allow but six hits on this day and only one for extra bases — a harmless fourth-inning two-out double which resulted in Travis Jackson being stranded on second. With the score unchanged in the bottom of the seventh, Buddy Myer singled to right, his third hit of the day, off reliever Hi Bell, who'd been brought in after six innings to relieve Fitzsimmons. The hit brought in Luke Sewell, who had beaten out a grounder to short, stolen second, and made it to third when Whitehill grounded to second.

Whitehill, winner of 22 games, the Senators' best lefthander and ace of the staff, completed the shutout, the only one there would be in this Series. He kept hitless the trio of Moore, Terry, and Ott, who between them had made eight hits in the first two games. That Whitehill had had to wait until the third game for his chance, particularly in light of the fact that it was Carl Hubbell's turn again, was an issue that was at this point certainly gaining importance in the psyche of many a fan of the Washington Senators. By Heinie Manush, Whitehill was presented with the hard-earned "game ball" President Roosevelt had thrown out. But would he get another start? The likelihood that Whitehill would pitch again seemed reduced all the more by Cronin's choice of Monte Weaver as his fourth-game starter. If the Senators kept winning and Lefty Stewart and General Crowder did not miss their turns, Whitehill would have to wait until a seventh game.

Weaver and Carl Hubbell were responsible for making game four the jewel of this

World Series. With one out in the fourth and Weaver having allowed but a walk and a weak single in the first inning, Bill Terry catapulted a rocket far into the Griffith Stadium centerfield bleachers. It was still 1–0 when the Senators, who had but two singles and a walk off Hubbell after five frames, threatened in the sixth. Buddy Myer, batting first in the inning, had beaten out a base hit into the hole behind second base, and had made it to second courtesy of a Goose Goslin sacrifice.

Up next was Heinie Manush, the American League's second-leading batsman in 1933. Manush knocked the ball on the ground between first and second, and first baseman Bill Terry thought he had a chance to make the play. Carl Hubbell saw that as well, and scooted toward first to cover. It was a good thing for the Giants that he did, because it was second baseman Hughie Critz who made a sensational grab in the hole and relayed to Hubbell.

Charley Moran, a National League umpire, motioned that Manush was out, at which time Heinie began gesticulating to indicate to everyone in Griffith Stadium that he could not believe what he was seeing and hearing. Not only did manager Cronin leap out of the dugout, as managers are still wont to do many decades later, but the whole Senators bench was out there to argue the call as well. But players didn't win arguments with umpires back in the thirties either. What happened next got Manush thrown out of the game. As he passed by Moran while retreating unhappily back to the dugout, he brushed or wiped his hand on the nape of the umpire's neck. Moran wheeled around suddenly and gave Manush the old heave-ho.

Heinie didn't abide by the order, though. After Joe Cronin struck out, leaving Myer to die on third, Manush trotted back to his position in left field. Moran would have none of that, but when he began waving for Manush to get off the field, he got an uncomplimentary gesture back. The chief of the umpiring crew, George Moriarty, had to make the long walk to retrieve the outfielder. Following a lengthy discussion, Manush started the long

walk back. All the while, the partisan home crowd was screaming for him to stay in.

With Goose Goslin moved over to left field and the more defensively uncertain Dave Harris now guarding right, the Senators were not only weaker in the field, but without their best hitter as well. Monte Weaver allowed a one-out double to left center by Jo-Jo Moore, but then got an infield out and a pop-up to the mound to get out of the seventh inning. The Nats then tied the score. Joe Kuhel made it to first safely when Hubbell messed up on his bunt attempt with one out. Cronin opted to go for the sacrifice, which Bluege promptly delivered. Luke Sewell then took the mail all the way home, singling to knot the score at one, bringing immense relief to the assembled partisans.

The Senators nearly took the lead in the eighth following a Myer walk and a Texas League single off the bat of Cronin, but Fred Schulte, who would tie Mel Ott for most RBIs in this Series, couldn't do it this time. His pop-up to the infield ended the inning. The ninth was entirely uneventful from an offensive standpoint, except for New York shortstop Blondy Ryan's single just past Joe Kuhel's head to lead off the inning. In the tenth, Weaver, being kept in the game (a very unhappy move in retrospect), struck out. Buddy Myer continued his torrid hitting, with his second single and third appearance on the bases. He advanced to second on Goslin's groundout, and Dave Harris walked. Cronin then squandered another chance to put his boys ahead, hitting the ball to short for the force at second.

Would this be another 12-inning World Series game, as there were on not one, but two occasions, between these two teams back in '24? With two of the next three games slated for New York, one thing seemed sure—the Nats could not get down 3-1 in games and realistically expect to come back. Travis Jackson surprised the Senators with a bunt to start the 11th. Jackson was quickly sacrificed to second and Blondy Ryan singled to left to break the tie and the hearts of the Washington faithful. Weaver then yielded a single over Cronin's head to Carl Hubbell, a .183 hitter during the regular season. Cronin had finally seen enough of Weaver and brought Jack Russell into the ballgame. Russell threw four pitches and got the side out, fanning Jo-Jo Moore on three pitches and enticing Hughie Critz to fly out to center on his first offering.

Fred Schulte, who'd had four hits in the first three ballgames but none in this one, restored hope with a single over shortstop for the Senators' seventh hit of the ballgame to start the bottom of the 11th. Joe Kuhel, up next, made it eight with a bunt that hugged the first-base line. Bill Terry let the ball roll, hoping it would go foul. Bluege sacrificed an out for the second time in the game, putting the tying run on third and the winning run on second with only one out. With the table set, Luke Sewell wasn't allowed to partake in the banquet. The Giants' brain trust dictated that Sewell be walked, loading the bases with pitcher Jack Russell, who wouldn't bat of course, up next.

The next player called into this high drama was Cliff Bolton, a young reserve catcher who nearly never caught, as the Senators still had Moe Berg to back Sewell behind the plate. Bolton was with the club for one purpose only — to come off the bench and drive in some runs. He hit .410 during the season, but was given just 39 at-bats (he was 9-for-22 as a pinch hitter, for a .409 mark in that role). But Bolton was a lefthanded hitter, and one might have wondered about the wisdom of letting him face the great lefty, Carl Hubbell. The Senators, after all, had a capable gentleman on the bench who just happened to swing from the right side. He also happened to be the owner of a .323 career batting average over 19 big-league campaigns. We refer, of course, to Sam Rice.

Oh, but for what might have been! Bolton did make solid contact, sending a shot toward second. Blondy Ryan, who'd driven in the tie-breaking run in the top of the inning, moved in and scooped up the ball, instantly flipping it to Critz, who completed a game-ending double play by relaying to first on time to nail the slow-footed Bolton. Cronin's failure to drive in runs despite opportunities in the fourth, sixth, and tenth innings, his decision to let Weaver bat for himself in the tenth and to continue pitching, his reluctance to send in the illustrious Rice, or Manush's rash behavior to get himself thrown out of the game — these were all points the second-guessers would be able to mull over forever. But it was really all academic now. The fact of the matter was that the best team in this World Series was but one loss away from elimination.

Joe Cronin would observe many years later that he wished he'd never agreed to play and manage at the same time. Having had to deal with players, management, and the press, while maintaining a high calibre of play on the field was an exceedingly tall order. After this season, Cronin would nearly reconsider and ask to step down, but would decide not too. *That* would be something he would always regret.

For the fifth game of the World Series, the New York Giants would evidently be going with Hal Schumacher, winner of game two. Cronin, who'd used four starters, as opposed to Bill Terry's three, opted to break his own pattern and bypass Lefty Stewart, the starter of the first game, and to go instead with General Crowder, the righthander. This seemed, in the eyes of more than a few keen observers, to defy logic. Firstly, Cronin would be playing right into his opponent's power — the Giants' two best hitters, Bill Terry and Mel Ott, were both lefthanded hitters. Secondly, Cronin had thought enough of Walter Stewart to start him in the all-important first game.

While it was true Stewart had gotten shelled early in the first game, Crowder had hardly done any better in game two. Given that he had been handed the ball less often than had Crowder during the regular season, Stewart had done just as well. Nonetheless, Cronin had more confidence in Crowder during the year, and regardless of the righty-lefty matchup, it would be the General who the Senators would follow into this last battle at Griffith Stadium.

The very first batter of the game, Jo-Jo Moore, singled off Crowder and made it to third on a Bill Terry single. Crowder, though, got out of the inning by striking out the deadly Mel Ott and inducing Kiddo Davis to hit the ball on the ground for an infield force-out. When the General again gave up a lead-off single in the second inning, to Travis Jackson, the Giants, for the fourth time in five games, were the first to score. After Gus Mancuso walked and Blondy Ryan sacrificed for the first out by advancing the runners, pitcher Hal Schumacher, not a particularly good hitter even for a pitcher, singled to center to drive in both runners.

After a 1–2–3 Washington second, Bill Terry opened the Giants' third with, predictably, another single. But Alvin Crowder got nine straight outs and surrendered just a walk in the fourth. The Nats, however, were not generating any kind of offense in support of him. Until the fifth, the only one to get on base was Goose Goslin, who singled past short in the first inning and walked in the fourth.

With two out in the fifth, the Nationals did mount what looked like a serious threat, getting the first two batters on. Fred Schulte had opened with a single, beating a slow roller toward Travis Jackson at third. Schulte quickly found himself on second when Joe Kuhel singled cleanly to left.

With nobody out and the fans entranced now, Ossie Bluege followed the book and attempted to bunt the runners ahead. When Hal Schumacher got two strikes on him, the Nats decided to try again anyway. The bunt attempt went foul, and Bluege was out. After Luke Sewell lined to left, failing to advance any runner, Prince Hal let a pitch slip off his fingers and Schulte made it to third while Kuhel held first. With two out and baserunners on the corners, it was the pitcher's turn to bat, and Joe Cronin let General Crowder take his turn.

In the manager's defense, it was less common in this era to pinch hit for starting pitchers in the middle innings. Nevertheless, Lefty Stewart was on the bench, and so was Jack Russell, who'd already pitched very well in his two appearances, and obviously, the Senators were in desperate need of some runs. In fact, they'd scored but one run since the seventh

inning of the third game. The options were Sam Rice, a .294 hitter during the regular season, or Cliff Bolton, a super hitter in a pinch in '33, as the batter in Crowder's stead. But Cronin stuck with his man Crowder, decidedly a poor-hitting pitcher. The Prince got the General to ground out to short.

Again in the top of the sixth, with the Giants still ahead 2–0, New York's first batter, outfielder Kiddo Davis, got a hit off Crowder, this time a double down the leftfield line. Travis Jackson sacrificed Davis along, but it was unnecessary because Gus Mancuso then slammed a double beyond Schulte's reach in Griffith Stadium's very deep center field. This put New York up three runs and knocked Crowder out of the game. Second-guessing aside, everyone in the park then knew that the Senators really had squandered an opportunity to get on the board in the previous half inning.

Jack Russell, who'd allowed but four hits and no walks in 5⅔ innings so far in the Series, was brought in. He threw seven pitches and struck out Blondy Ryan and Hal Schumacher to put an end to the Giants' festivities. The downcast crowd was soon upbeat again. In the bottom of the sixth, after Myer and Goslin made routine outs, Heinie Manush and Joe Cronin hit back-to-back singles. Fred Schulte, 1-for-2 and batting .294 for the Series as he stepped up to the plate, then crunched a Schumacher offering and sent it sailing into the left field pavilion for a three-run homer. It was 3–3, just like that.

Now it was anybody's ballgame, and the Nats were showing signs of wanting to make it theirs. Joe Kuhel followed Schulte with a hard smash along the ground that rattled off second baseman Hughie Critz's legs. The ball was hit solidly enough for Kuhel to be credited with a base hit by the official scorer. Ossie Bluege then shot a hot potato toward third that sent Jackson scrambling, but the veteran came up with it. His throw to first was wild, pulling Bill Terry off the bag and allowing Joe Kuhel to bring the tie-breaking run as far as third.

Terry had seen enough, as Prince Hal had

given up five consecutive hits, with the latter three crushed particularly hard. A new player was introduced into this Series. Terry called in 43-year-old Cuban Dolf Luque. A caucasian, Luque had been a big star in American baseball in the 1920s. Having first come to the States in 1912, he'd had a couple of unsuccessful trials with the Boston National League club before catching on with the wartime Cincinnati Reds. He'd won 189 regular-season games since that time, and had shown consistency despite winning 20 or more only once — in 1923, when he won 27 and led the league in earned run average, which he did again in 1925.

In 1933, Luque still had a very good curve, and retained the meanness and guile which allowed him to last 20 years in the major leagues. Luke Sewell, who would hit just .176 in these games, was the first to toe in against the 5'7" portsider. Kuhel and Bluege were left stranded at their stations, as Luque got Sewell to ground out to Critz at second. But the Senators were so much better off than they'd been minutes before.

Jack Russell continued to pitch well, and so did Luque. They coasted through the next three innings, with Russell yielding three inconsequential singles and Luque one. For the second day in a row and the fourth time in 12 games dating back to 1924, a World Series game between these two clubs would be decided in extra innings — and decided suddenly.

After Russell obtained two easy outs, he served up a pitch to Mel Ott that "Master Melvin" expelled on a long arc toward deep center field. Fred Schulte, the Senators' man of the hour, had a bead on the ball, tracked it, and got his glove on it. Just as he did, he came into collision with the wall and when he did, the ball plopped into the first row of the bleachers. It was a home run. Or was it?

The umpire at second base, Charles Pfirman, thought the ball had bounced off the ground and over the fence, and when Ott reached second, Pfirman stopped him there. Bill Terry came storming out of the Giants' dugout, and Pfirman was coerced into consulting with the plate umpire, who happened

to be the crew chief, Charley Moran. With the approbation of Moran, who'd been much further from the play than Pfirman, the call was reversed. It was the right call, though, and the Nats faced elimination as never before in this game.

Joe Cronin, the major leagues' best shortstop, who'd given no evidence in this World Series of being anywhere near that status as a manager, came up to bat with two down in the bottom of the tenth and, worse still, with no one on base. Luque had already disposed of Goslin and Manush, but Cronin got his second straight hit off him, the only Washington player to get on base against The "Pride of Havana." Fred Schulte, who'd gone from hero to goat in a single inning, looked at four straight pitches and bumped Cronin along to second. Everything would rest on the shoulders of the lefthanded-hitting Joe Kuhel, a potent .322 slugger with 107 runs driven in during the season. Kuhel had entered the game batting .067 but had managed two hits in this contest. It wasn't to be his moment, though. He struck out, and the season was over.

For the old Giants manager, John McGraw, who'd been in professional baseball since 1891, the victory of the young manager, Bill Terry, was also his. Not well enough physically to continue to occupy his place in the dugout, McGraw nonetheless thought of this Giants team as his own. Before the beginning of the next season, he would be dead at age 60. As for the Senators, the players received their losers' share of $3,019.86 per man (it was $4,256.72 for the Giants), as receipts were the lowest for a World Series since 1922. The Series had been witnessed by fewer fans than any since 1918 despite the fact that, since that time, four Series had gone just four games.

As for the supporters of the losing side, they knew in their hearts that the favored team, the Washington Senators of 1933, was indeed the *best* team in all of baseball and *should* have won the World Series. The everlasting sentiment among the fans of the nation's capital was that the Nats had been victimized by bad breaks, ill-advised decisions, and worse umpiring. It was a cruel fate for what history shows was the best Washington Senators' baseball club ever.

In the real world, FBI chief J. Edgar Hoover's G-men (short for Government Men) made significant inroads into bringing down a criminal element that had become increasingly prevalent in American life during the desperate depression. As for Bonnie and Clyde, John Dillinger, and Pretty Boy Floyd, the fate met by baseball's G-men (short for Griffithmen) in 1934 was a miserable one. While the gangsters paid with the price of their lives, our Senators incurred physical injury on such a widespread basis that the club dropped further in the standings in just one year than any other pennant winner in major-league baseball history.

Bad luck struck in spring training when catcher Luke Sewell, who was coming off one of his best offensive years, broke his finger. The Senators improvised with Eddie Phillips, formerly a highly sought athlete at Boston College. Phillips' career in baseball had been that of a journeyman, however. In 1932, the Yankees called upon his services when their receiver, Bill Dickey, was injured. In 1935, Phillips would fill in for the injured first-stringer Frankie Pytlak at Cleveland. He was unable to make the best of his opportunity in Washington, his fifth chance with a big-league club in 11 years. Phillips hit a pathetic .195, and as soon as Luke Sewell could play again, in mid–June, he was back in the lineup.

The regular third baseman from the outset in 1934 was rookie Cecil Travis, he of the five hits in his first big-league game, who was showing that he had the right stuff. First spotted on the sandlots of Atlanta by Kid Elberfeld, the old Washington shortstop of 1910–11, Travis had incited the Senators to shell out the modest sum of $300 to acquire his services, and he'd been a star his first two years in the Southern Association at Chattanooga, batting .356 and .352.

When Travis, a lefthanded hitter who slapped everything to the opposite field at this point in his career, took over as the team's third baseman, Ossie Bluege's days as a regular ended. While Bluege had shown up at the Biloxi training camp sporting eyeglasses for the first time, his tenure with the Nats was by no means over, and he would stay on as a valuable sub for another half dozen years.

Cecil Travis, who was beaned in the preseason, had a hand in another unlucky injury beside his own. He and pitcher Jack Russell collided as they converged on a bunted ball. Russell came out of it with a spike wound and could never get untracked in this season. Given the outstanding year he'd had in '33, he was a major disappointment with a final 5–10 won-lost record with an ERA of well over four runs per game in 1934. Buddy Myer was also spiked, by Indians' shortstop Hal Trosky, and was out of commission for two weeks as a result. In June, first baseman Joe Kuhel broke his ankle while sliding and trying to avoid a collision with Detroit's Charley Gehringer. Kuhel missed more than half the season and drove in only 25 runs on the heels of his 107–RBI campaign the previous year.

The harassed Joe Cronin had more challenges in the outfield. There had been trouble before spring training even began. Goose Goslin had complained vociferously during the '33 season about being sat down against certain lefthanded pitchers. The Goose was just a stubborn old-timer who refused to acknowledge that there was a discernible difference between lefty and righty flingers and that southpaws were a greater challenge for him. The constant repartee between Goslin and management caused Clark Griffith to make his first player transaction in nearly a year. A few days before Christmas, Goslin got what he had hoped for, and was traded away by the Senators for the second time in his career. The Detroit Tigers were the recipients of an early Christmas goose.

The exchange was one–for–one, and outfielder John Stone, who like Goslin batted lefthanded, came to Washington. Stone had hit .280 the previous season and had modest power, having produced 38 homers over the previous three campaigns. He would indeed hit over .300 in four seasons for Washington but he was not in Goslin's class as a power hitter and run producer. Stone drove in 67 for the Nats, while Goslin produced an even 100 for the Tigers. The Tigers finished first, the Senators ... seventh.

Stone did not escape the injury bug either, sustaining a sprained ankle. In addition, late in the season, when Joe Kuhel returned to play after a three-month convalescence, Heinie Manush sprained his ankle. Manush had been enjoying another stellar season, driving in 89 runs and raising his average to .349 for the year, good for third–best in the American League in 1934.

The litany of injuries involved the club's other outfielder, Dave Harris, as well. Harris was hampered by a charley horse and hit an atypical .251 for the season. Catcher Moe Berg was also sidelined by a charley horse, forcing Cronin to go with Phillips on a steady basis, with the regular catcher, Sewell, out with the broken finger. Berg was soon released to Cleveland but prior to that, on April 21, 1934, the enigmatic scholar-athlete set an American League record by participating in his 117th consecutive game sporting the tools of ignorance without committing a single error.

The Senators needed, and acquired from the Indians in May, an experienced infielder to help plug some of the vacated spots. But Ralph "Red" Kress, a good-natured, wise-cracking sort, hit just .228 until mid–August, when he broke his thumb and was shelved for the rest of the season. A couple of weeks later, the standout Buddy Myer, as tough a competitor in the field as at bat, aggravated spike injuries that had sidelined him earlier. This time, Myer was out for nearly all of what was left of this lost season. In his 139 games, though, he'd walked what would remain a career-high 102 times and scored 103 runs on what was a very unlucky ballclub. Myer's .305 average was his second consecutive over .300, and his fourth in six seasons with the Senators to this point. To lose players like him, Joe Kuhel, and Heinie Manush for long stretches of time might have crippled any ballclub.

All of these tribulations had to weigh heaviest on Joe Cronin, who was hard-pressed to pencil in a decent starting lineup every day,

let alone fulfill his duties as a shortstop. Cronin's average dipped to .284, but he led the club once again with 101 RBIs. For the fifth straight year, he was selected the top player at his position in all of baseball. Cronin did, unlike his subordinates, manage to stay healthy, at least until early September, when he broke his wrist in a baserunning mishap. His season was over, his hand in a cast for the duration.

Ossie Bluege played some shortstop and then found himself in the outfield for the first time in his 13 seasons. Luke Sewell, who'd been a catcher in all but two of the 1,103 big-league games he'd taken part in prior to this horrible season, was called upon to fill in at all three bases and in the outfield. In Joe Kuhel's three-month absence, the first baseman over the last third of the season was Pete Susko, a one-year big leaguer who hit well (.286), but who would be out of a job permanently when Kuhel returned.

The pitching staff didn't walk away from the 1934 season unscathed either. Apart from the aforementioned spike injury sustained by Jack Russell, Lefty Stewart, who'd been told by doctors seven years before that he had no chance of ever playing baseball again, was most affected. Stewart's face had gone numb, paralyzed completely. As a follow-up to his 15–6 pennant-winning season, he got into only 24 games and had only a 7–11 record and an ERA of over four runs per game to show for them.

General Crowder was lost on August 4, not through injury, but because Cronin had had enough of him. Crowder had been vocal with Cronin about Cecil Travis replacing Ossie Bluege, who he considered was able to provide more reliable defense. The General was having an awful year and was 4–10 when Cronin ditched him, selling him to the Tigers. Thus ended the General's time in Washington for good. Each time the Senators got rid of him, however, it was a bad move (the first time was the trade to the Browns for Tom Zachary in 1927). On the 1934 pennant-winning Tigers, Crowder would go 5–1 the rest of the way. The following year he would win 16 with another Detroit championship club, one which won the World Series.

A righthander the Senators had been grooming, Ed Linke, became, like Lefty Stewart, somewhat of a medical oddity in 1934. Linke's pitching hand went numb, the result of circulation problems in his fingers. This kept him out for practically the entire year, but was nothing compared to what would happen to him the following season. A line drive bounced off Linke's skull back toward the plate far enough to be caught by the catcher, Jack Redmond (he played in just 22 games in the majors), who gunned the ball to second to catch Ben Chapman off the bag for a rally-snuffing double play.

As for Linke, he was hospitalized but made a full recovery. As a matter of fact, he never pitched better and won every one of his next eight starts that year, 1935, when he finished at 11–7. Just for the record, Linke, who gave up way too many hits, would only win eight more games in the majors and would bow out with a 22–22 record, impressive considering his nightmarish 5.61 career earned run average.

The entire Washington staff was ineffectual, plagued even more by high ERAs than by injuries in '34. As a staff, Cronin's moundsmen surrendered nearly one more run per game than they did the previous year, dropping the Nats from second to a telltale sixth in the league pitching hierarchy. Earl Whitehill was the biggest winner with 14–11, but every starter except Bobby Burke allowed more runs than the league average of 4.50 per game. In 1934, Burke, "the kid who got the eleven-year tryout" and who had been reliable in a limited role during the pennant-winning '33 season, posted a sparkling ERA, for the era, of 3.21, despite a mundane 8–8 ledger.

Monte Weaver was, apart from Whitehill, the only other starter to win in double figures, finishing with a dismal 11–15, 4.79 slate. The scoop on Montgomery Morton Weaver, who would later become a mathematics professor at Emory and Henry College in Virginia, is that he'd been less effective ever since embarking on a vegetarian diet following his rookie year. While his control had improved, he had lost 20 pounds *and* the zip on his fastball. For a time in '35, he would be banished to the minors. It was said of Weaver that he didn't find his fastball until he found beefsteak again. Even worse than Weaver at surrendering runs, at 5.47 per game, was Tommy Thomas, who was lucky not to finish worse than 8–9.

All added up, it is little wonder that the Washington Senators, the proud defending champions of the American League, finished 34 games out of first place in 1934. They'd gone from 99 wins to 66 in one year. How bad had things gotten? Bad enough that Allen Benson, a member of the House of David baseball team, was signed by Griffith in an effort to boost fan interest in his sagging franchise. The House of David team consisted of good amateur players who toured the country, playing teams of local all-stars wherever they went. Their gimmick, apart from playing good baseball, was that every member of the club wore a long beard.

Griffith thought that might work well at Griffith Stadium, and Benson, known as "Bullet Ben," attracted a large Sunday crowd on August 19, 1934. He was battered about by the league-leading Tigers, but apparently not so badly that Griffith wouldn't give him another shot. Slated to next appear against the St. Louis Browns, Benson begged the owner to let him shave his beard so that he wouldn't feel like he was making such a spectacle of himself. Griffith insisted that if the beard went, Bullet Ben would have to go too. So the pitcher relented and was trounced by the Browns as well.

So ended an ill-advised career in the major leagues, with Allen Benson having allowed 19 hits in 9.2 innings, for a 12.10 ERA that lives on in infamy. These same words could be used to describe the '34 season for the Washington Senators. The injured Joe Cronin turned over his managing chores toward the end of the season to Al (the Clown Prince of Baseball) Schacht. This somehow seemed fitting — Schacht had already made his mark in baseball as a comedian.

The history of the Senators became once again intertwined with that of the Yankees during this campaign. Lou Gehrig's consecutive-games streak, begun against the Senators on June 1, 1925, was placed in jeopardy on June 29, 1934, when he was hit in the head by a pitch during an exhibition game with the Yanks' Norfolk affiliate. As Gehrig was taken to hospital, manager Joe McCarthy moaned that the pennant was surely lost. Diagnosed as a concussion, not a fracture, the injury did not keep Gehrig down. He traveled to Washington by steamboat and made it on time for the next game against the Senators. Equally amazing is the fact that the Iron Horse hit three triples in three at-bats, one to each field. Happily for the Senators, who were trailing as a result of this onslaught, the game was washed out by heavy squalls before it became official. Gehrig of course kept the streak going until it reached 2,130 games, an all-time record no one thought would be broken. But it was, of course, by Cal Ripken, Jr., on September 6, 1995.

On September 29, 1934, Babe Ruth hit his last American League home run at Griffith Stadium. The 708th of his career was off Sid Cohen, a rookie and younger brother of Andy Cohen, a middle infielder with the Giants in the late twenties. The following day marked the last time Babe Ruth appeared in the pinstripes that he, more than anyone, had made famous. With Ruth's wife and daughter on hand, Senators fans presented him with a scroll of appreciation. The band from St. Mary's Industrial School in Baltimore, where Ruth was raised, provided music for the occasion. With 0–for–3 on the day, the Babe flew out to Nats prospect Jake Powell in center to end the game. He left the field crying. In this way, an era drew to a close.

If the season had been nothing but disappointing for Senators' fans, the greatest calamity was yet to befall them. The bombshell came 2½ weeks after the conclusion of the World Series, which the Tigers of Goslin and Crowder lost in seven games to the St. Louis Cardinals. Clark Griffith had always maintained that, his reputation as a flesh

trader aside, he had never sold a player outright for a large sum of cash. Sure, he had sold bit players at times, but never anyone who could, by his absence, have drastically impacted the ballclub's fortunes.

All of this changed on October 26, 1934, when Griffith stole some headlines from Hoover's G-men. Just four days earlier, federal agents had gunned down Charles "Pretty Boy" Floyd, the bank robber and murderer who'd been dubbed the "most dangerous man alive," when he attempted to flee from them in Ohio. With *his* news, Clark Griffith was to get a lot of attention not only in the baseball world, but with Americans in all walks of life.

Joe Cronin, already Griffith's best player and manager, had become part of the family a month earlier, in late September, 1934. Three weeks after he'd broken his wrist, he had married Mildred Robertson, who was not only Griffith's secretary, but also his niece. The Cronins had met shortly after Joe was first assigned to the Senators on Friday the 13th of July, 1928.

Joe Cronin had come to Washington highly recommended not only as a shortstop, but as a prospective beau for Mildred, who'd received a note from scout Joe Engel that he was bringing her "a real sweetie." When Cronin walked into Griffith's office on July 16, there was Mildred, the girl of his dreams, something Joe said he immediately recognized. She, apparently, didn't recognize the boy of her dreams right away, and in fact it would be a number of years before she would even pay any attention to him, according to Cronin. Mildred Robertson was a fount of baseball knowledge — Cronin once said he would have put her up against anyone in terms of the wealth of baseball information her brain contained.

It is not difficult to imagine, then, Clark Griffith's dilemma when he got a phone call from Tom Yawkey of Boston during the 1934 World Series. Yawkey said that he had a check made out in Griffith's name in the amount of $250,000, and that he would part with it in exchange for Joe Cronin. To provide some idea of what this sum meant, Babe Ruth, already a superstar when he was sold by the Red Sox in 1920, had fetched only half that amount. Nothing of the kind had been seen since. Now, in much harder times, here was an offer of a quarter of a million dollars!

The Senators' owner was incredulous, thinking that not even Cronin could be worth that much. He was very emphatic in stating that there was no chance that he would sell the rights to his nephew, the majors' premier shortstop. Yawkey was not deterred and called again a couple of weeks later. Griffith once again told him that he was not selling, and politely requested that Yawkey please consider the matter closed. Another week passed and Yawkey called again, more insistent than ever. The heir to a lumber and iron empire worth millions kept making the point that he could do a darn sight more for Griffith's new nephew than Griff himself could. Griffith was no millionaire. His club's nosedive in 1934 had cost him dearly, and he owed the banks about $125,000. Tom Yawkey was requesting a meeting in New York, and he expected Clark Griffith to be there.

Now Yawkey had the Old Fox really wondering. Was he doing the best thing for young Joe? Cronin would be the manager at Boston, just like he was in Washington. Besides, Griffith had taken a lot of heat during the year, as it had become popular, unfairly so, to poke fun at Cronin's marriage into the family. Unfair charges of nepotism, Griffith envisioned, would never go away. He agreed to at least listen to what Tom Yawkey had to say.

The negotiations did not go smoothly. Griffith thought the exchange might be done if the Red Sox would include shortstop Lyn Lary in the transaction. But Yawkey had just paid $35,000 for Lary, and balked at including him in the negotiations. That appeared to be the end of the discussion, and Griffith and his business manager, Ed Eynon, got up to leave. The old man was likely not bluffing, and mentioned to Eynon that they didn't have much time if they were to catch the train for Washington that night. Yawkey turned abruptly to his general manager, Eddie Collins, and

asked what Collins thought of giving up Lary. Collins indicated that it would be okay with him as long as the boss, Yawkey himself, didn't have any objections.

Tom Yawkey grabbed a bill of sale, made it out for $225,000, which had been agreed upon as the adjusted price following the inclusion of Lary, and signed it. There were some final conditions. Griffith requested a healthy raise for his nephew, and Yawkey would go along with a five-year pact, unheard of in this period. The contract would stipulate that Cronin could not be released, which would thereby guarantee his salary. There was one last proviso — Joe Cronin would have to be agreeable to all this. When he got back to Washington that night, it was with great trepidation that Griffith phoned Cronin, who was in his hometown of San Francisco, having just arrived there on a honeymoon trip that had taken him and his new bride through the Panama Canal.

Whatever apprehension Griffith might have had was quickly dispelled by Cronin, who took it all in stride, like a fat pitch right down the middle. This was the Depression, and his uncle needed the money. Joe and Mildred decided to consider the matter overnight. When he called back the next day, Cronin told Griffith not to worry about what he thought of the proposal, and that he should immediately call Boston and tell them that they had themselves a deal. Cronin reportedly cut the conversation short by insisting that he should hang up, joking that long-distance telephone charges were going to eat up all the profits. Unlike the decision he'd taken to be a player-manager at Washington, this was something Joe Cronin would never regret.

Cronin's passing from the local baseball scene prompted at least one contemporary columnist to write that he thought Clark Griffith really had something there — that he sure wished he could have sold his own son-in-law for a quarter of a million dollars. The Washington Senators Baseball Club would never, arguably, have a star player of the caliber of Joe Cronin again. For Cronin, this move began an association with the Red Sox organization which would last a quarter of a century, and which would someday lead to the position of President of the American League.

While replacing his shortstop would be another matter entirely, Clark Griffith knew all along who would be taking Cronin's place as manager — Bucky Harris. Harris had just completed a one-year term as manager of Tom Yawkey's Bosox and had led them to a .500 record in '34, an improvement of 11½ games over the previous campaign. Bucky had known no real success, however, since his salad days with the Senators. His Tiger teams from '29 to 33 had usually been buried in the league's second division. But Griffith's feelings about Bucky Harris ran deep.

The old man had often freely admitted that Harris had not been the disciplinarian he would have preferred to have seen in the late twenties. On the other hand, Griffith liked to say, there was no one who in his mind could get as much out of a baseball team during the crucial afternoon hours as Bucky could. The 39-year-old Harris, who hadn't played on any kind of regular basis since his last year with the Senators (1928), praised the old man as well. Bucky told the press he was flattered to be hired by the likes of Griffith. The Old Fox wasn't just any baseball owner, but a former player, a man with a profound understanding of the game. If Clark Griffith wanted you as his manager, Harris contended, that ought to be considered an honor.

Joe Cronin the shortstop, however, would not be replaceable, and certainly not by "Broadway Lyn" Lary, whose Senator career would amount to just 39 games and a .194 average before Griffith got rid of him in exchange for another shortstop, Alan Strange of the Browns. Strange would do even worse, with .185, and wouldn't play in the majors again until 1940. Lary did go on to lead the league in stolen bases with the Browns in '36 and, transferred to the Indians in '37, had a good year there as well. His failure in Washington, though, and that of Strange, meant the Senators had yet to obtain anyone useful with the cash Griffith had collected from the Red Sox when he'd sold Cronin.

That deal, incidentally, was the second large transaction involving cash in which Lyn Lary had been included. Back in 1928, the Yankees had paid too much when they shelled out 125 grand to the Pacific Coast League's Oakland Oaks for Lary and his double-play partner, Jimmy Reese, who played in only parts of two seasons for the Bronx Bombers.

In late November 1934, the Yankees made a much better deal with another Coast League club, purchasing the rights to a terrific outfielder, just turned 20, who was a cinch to be a star. The youngster had injured his knee while getting out of a cab the previous June, and, given his age, the New York brain trust felt it might be a good idea to leave the phenom, a fellow named Joe DiMaggio, in the minors another full year. The Yanks had just come off a 94-win season, which in most years is enough to win a pennant. In '34, however, the Bombers fell seven games short of the Tigers. The rumors flying about in the New York newspapers were to the effect that the Yanks, badly in need of a left fielder, were about to close a deal with Washington for Heinie Manush. What's more, the Yankees might even land Buddy Myer, too.

None of that came to pass, and a good thing indeed that was for the Senators. Nineteen thirty-five was to be Buddy Myer's big year. He stayed injury-free, rapped out 215 hits, and hit .349. Defensively, he led all American League second basemen in put-outs and double plays. Going into the last game of the '35 season at Philadelphia, Myer, now 31, trailed Cleveland outfielder Joe Vosmik by one point in the batting race. Vosmik, just 25, was having the season of his life, leading the league in hits, doubles, and triples. The Indians were sitting Vosmik down for the first game of their doubleheader, protecting his lead for the time being. But at Shibe Park in Philadelphia, Myer was having a terrific day. When news reached Cleveland of his three singles, one of them a bunt (Myer was an expert drag bunter who, it was estimated, had gotten as many as 60 bunt singles in 1935), the Indians had to play Vosmik in their second game. He went 1–for–4.

Buddy Myer needed a hit in his last at-bat

against the A's to win the batting title. As related by Shirley Povich in *The Washington Senators,* Myer had found a pin on the sidewalk that day on his way to board a morning train that was taking the team from Washington to Philadelphia. He'd remarked to his wife, in these more superstitious times, that this was a sign of a two-base hit. He got it in his last at-bat of the season, and his .349 won the batting crown.

Myer thus became the third Washington Senator, after Ed Delahanty (1902) and Leon Goslin (1928) to win a batting championship. The margin over Vosmik went down in the books as .3490 to .3483. Some Senators fans would have considered Myer's title particularly sweet simply because of the fact that he had edged out a Cleveland player. The Indians had ditched Walter Johnson as their manager on August 5, two weeks after Walter Johnson Day at Griffith Stadium, where he had been showered with gifts and adulation by his old fans. As it turned out, this brought the Big Train's managing career to a permanent end.

Walter Johnson settled on the farm he had purchased in Germantown, Maryland, the previous winter. For the rest of his life, which was to be only another 11½ years, he farmed and raised purebred cattle and prize birds, and hunted with his beloved dogs. Sam Rice had a chicken farm at nearby Rossmor, and visited frequently. Walter's retirement was punctuated in early 1936, bringing great pride to supporters of the Washington Senators, when he was one of the five former baseball stars who received 75 percent of votes necessary for enshrinement in the new National Baseball Hall of Fame. The other initial inductees were Ty Cobb, Babe Ruth, Honus Wagner, and Christy Mathewson.

In 1937, Barney became a spokesman for the Dr. Pepper soft-drink company and, carrying his easygoing magnetism even further, was employed as the Senators' radio broadcaster during the 1939 season, doing the whole show by himself during much of the campaign, and acquitting himself quite well. Johnson dabbled in politics, was Commissioner of Montgomery County, Maryland, and went so far as to run for Congress, winning the Republican nomination for Maryland's 6th District. Walter had no agenda and made few speeches but nearly won anyway — he was narrowly defeated in the practically wholesale sweep by the Democrats which carried Franklin D. Roosevelt to the White House for a third term.

Buddy Myer's batting title was the best thing to happen on the Washington baseball landscape during the summer of 1935, unfortunately. The team never got untracked. It lost exactly the same number of games as in '34, 86, and won one more game, 67. It stayed reasonably injury-free, but of course, there was no 100-RBI producer at the shortstop position either. There was no ready solution there, with Ossie Bluege, now 34, given some of the work at the position. If Bluege's range was not what it had once been, it certainly didn't hurt the Nats to have him at short.

Red Kress, the old Browns shortstop who hadn't played short with any regularity in five years, ended up with Bluege's job by year's end. This was quite a turnaround for Kress. He had hit poorly after coming over to the Senators during the '34 season, and at mid-season 1935, he was demoted to Chattanooga. While packing his bags, he got a phone call. Buddy Myer had been ejected from the first game of a doubleheader and would not be allowed to play the second game. Kress got four straight hits against Cleveland that day and, with Myer obviously a fixture at second, was promptly installed at short for the rest of the season.

Kress hit .298 for the year, and sophomore Cecil Travis followed up a .319 season with .318. But Travis, almost strictly an opposite-field hitter, had zero homers. Kress had two all year, Bluege none. Buddy Myer had five. The other infielder, first baseman Joe Kuhel, showed some rust after missing half the previous season with his broken ankle. Kuhel had just two homers in 633 at-bats and batted just .261, the lowest mark of his career. Cliff Bolton, always a hitter and given a chance to catch almost regularly, responded predictably well but he too had only two home runs. Joe Cronin, out in Boston, hit nine home runs and drove in 95, while batting .295. However, the Red Sox, like the Senators, didn't improve, winning only two more games than they had in '34.

The lack of power hitting on this edition of the Washington Senators was so pronounced as to be laughable. Rookie Jake Powell was able to wrest the centerfield position away from incumbent Fred Schulte, who'd been one of the few Senators to play in nearly all the games the previous season. A true gentleman in an era when ballplayers were, in the main, rambunctious country boys, Schulte was 34 years of age and would be out of the big leagues for good within two years.

Young Powell, a native of nearby Silver Spring, Maryland, who had been plucked off the local sandlots, doubled Schulte's home-run output. That meant he hit only six all year, however, but it led the club. The Senators, playing half their games in the vast expanse of Griffith Stadium, hit only 32 as a team, the lowest collective total in the majors in four years. Rightfielder John Stone, who had eight hits in a doubleheader on June 16, contributed a .315 average, but with only one homer. Heinie Manush slumped badly and his .273 mark was by far the worst of his career.

An old rookie at 27 whose years exceeded his maturity, Jake Powell hit .312 and produced 98 runs, just two short of Myer's output of exactly 100. Powell wouldn't be kept on, though, and by mid–June of the following season would be traded to the Yankees. After starring in the 1936 World Series, his life would unravel quickly. Daring on the ballfield and prejudiced off it, Powell had a reputation of not getting along well with his teammates. In 1938, he was suspended for slurring black people during the course of a radio interview. In 1948, at the age of 40, while being detained in a Washington police station on a charge of passing bad checks, Jake Powell shot himself to death.

In terms of the discussion of the 1935 Senators, we have saved the worst for last. The pitching staff continued its slide, allowing an appalling 903 runs. The team ERA was an eye-popping 5.25, an iota better than the 5.26 of the Browns. Southpaw Earl Whitehill was by far the best of the starters, at 14–13, 4.29. Stocky curveballer Bump Hadley followed up his 10–16, 4.35 totals in '34 with 10–15, 4.92. A year after leading the league in saves and appearances, Jack Russell's days as an effective reliever seemed pretty much over. He wound up 4–9 with an abhorrent 5.71 earned run average. Ed Linke did manage his 11 wins, but with an ERA over five.

To sum up the 1935 season for the Washington Senators — teams with lousy pitching and no power don't go anywhere in the game of baseball. The pitching staff did provide, however, the best comic relief in an otherwise relatively dull season. This came in the person of one Norman Louis "Bobo" (or "Buck") Newsom. The brash Bobo, a tall chunky fellow from Hartsville, South Carolina, had seen limited action with the Dodgers and Cubs before winning 30 games in the Pacific Coast League in 1933. Bobo liked to say he'd actually won 33 in '33 and, when challenged and told the record books said 30, he'd respond "Who are you going to believe?"

His 30-win campaign earned him another shot at the big time with the St. Louis Browns. With the Brownies, a team on the level of the Senators, the rookie led the entire league in losses (20) and walks (149) in 1934. Newsom also regularly led the league in outrageous remarks and sheer color. The man had a flair for exaggeration and a cheerful disposition, and could always be counted upon to vehemently uphold any outrageous declaration he might make. Clark Griffith liked the barrel-chested, boastful Bobo.

The nickname evolved from the fact that Newsom seldom bothered to learn anyone's name. This was understandable, considering that he was the most celebrated baseball traveler of his time. Eventually, Bobo Newsom would make 17 stops along the major-league trail, and Clark Griffith would acquire his services on five different occasions. The old man's best explanation for that would be that he rather enjoyed playing pinochle with the fellow.

Buck Newsom's career would span 26 years and include ten different minor-league stops as well.

Another nickname Bobo earned was the "Hartsville Squire," because he told tall tales of owning a 13-room mansion on a plantation back home, where he hunted with hounds and made more money growing cotton than he made playing baseball. Vexed once with a Washington baseball writer who had labeled him "a $14,000-a-year pitcher," Newsom admonished the reporter for making him look bad, insisting he would never have signed for less than the $18,000 he was earning at the time. In actual fact, he was making $13,000.

Money and all of its trappings were what Bobo liked to show off most. As a Detroit Tiger in 1940, he arrived at training camp in a car which had "BOBO" in neon lights on the door, and a horn which played "The Tiger Rag." In 1942, a rookie invited for a drive in Newsom's convertible was astonished when Bobo insisted on paying double the fine after getting pulled over for speeding. He wanted to pay double, he told the officer, because he certainly intended to drive just as fast on his way back.

Bobo Newsom made a habit of holding out at the beginning of many a spring, and was ahead of his time in that he might be considered one of the first player reps in baseball. He had become known as "The Voice" around St. Louis because of his willingness to tangle with management whenever he felt a teammate was being slighted. Despite the man's nature, Bucky Harris went along with Griffith's plan to purchase Bobo from the Browns on May 21, 1935. The Old Fox had decided to parlay some of his "winnings" from the sale of his nephew, and Bobo was as good a $40,000 investment as any other.

Bucky Harris, in despair over the disarray of his pitching staff, recognized that Newsom was a blowhard, and said as much, but reasoned that he could handle the headaches if the hard thrower could win Washington some games. Newsom was off to a bad 0–6 start when acquired, and he went 11–12 for the Nats to finish with a very ordinary 11–18, 4.52

slate for the season. But it didn't take him long to get attention with the Senators. In one of his first starts, Earl Averill conked the big guy on the knee with a line drive. Bobo made a show of it, delaying proceedings while he went to the bench for a while, but it wasn't until after the game that he was taken seriously. He had, after all, pitched until the end, and won. It was discovered later that his kneecap was broken.

Newsom would again show uncommon courage in 1940, while a member of the Tigers. After witnessing his son start and win the first game of the World Series, Bobo Newsom's dad died suddenly. A distraught Bobo dedicated his next game to his father and, with all of America's baseball fans except for a few Cincinnati dissenters behind him, won that one as well. Nonetheless, the Cincinnati Reds insisted on deviating from the consummate script, and handed Newsom a very tough 2–1 complete-game loss in game seven.

Bobo was also in the spotlight, right where he wanted to be, when Bucky Harris selected him as starting pitcher for the 1936 season opener against the Yankees. Always up to a challenge, later in this season, with a start against the Yankees forthcoming, Newsom, unwisely, publicly vowed to find a weakness in rookie Joe DiMaggio's batting eye. Following the game, much hay was made of the fact that he had indeed uncovered something. It was obvious that Dimaggio had a penchant for doubles, having hit three of them off Bobo.

On opening day, 1936, Newsom got to exchange autographs with President Franklin Delano Roosevelt. With the President, his Cabinet, the Army Band, and 31,000 faithful in the seats, Bobo may have been a little overwhelmed. He wasn't very alert when Yankees outfielder Ben Chapman bunted to the left side of the infield. Newsom made a move toward the ball, and then decided to let Ossie Bluege field it. For some unknown reason, Bobo made no attempt to get out of the way of what had to be a strong throw to nip the swift Chapman. Bluege's missile traveled all of 15 feet or so before it conked Bobo right on the coconut.

Instead of falling, the 6'3" Newsom embarked on a stagger which took him toward the presidential box before veering back toward the mound. He was steered to the bench by his teammates, and, revived with nothing more than a cold towel, proceeded to pitch a complete-game 1–0 shutout. The Nats got the season off on the right foot. Newsom was a horse for Harris all year, won 17 games against 15 losses, and, with 286 innings pitched, was just 15 short of league leader Wes Ferrell of Boston.

Ossie Bluege was surprised to find himself starting at third base to open the 1936 season. Bucky Harris had intended to go with John Kelly "Buddy" Lewis, a 19-year-old stringbean from Gastonia, North Carolina, who had once traveled to New York for a tryout only to be passed over by Bill Terry and the Giants. Joe Engel spotted Lewis in Gastonia, and the youngster did very well at Chattanooga in '35, batting .303 with good power.

Called up at the tail end of the previous campaign, Buddy Lewis managed but a feeble .107 in eight games, but Bucky Harris was expecting big things. He would be right to have those expectations, but for the moment, the hubbub surrounding the Presidential Opener was giving Lewis cold feet. He begged out of the starting lineup, and Harris understood. Within a few years, with the world plunged into war, Buddy Lewis would be flying dangerous missions over India.

Lewis did well with the Senators in '36. The rookie led the club in at-bats, hit .291, and scored an even 100 runs, quite an accomplishment, as he was still a teenager over the course of most of the season. Lewis would score more than 100 times in three of the next four seasons, and the Nats had themselves a successor to Bluege, who was freed up to play mostly at second base. Ossie once again got an opportunity to render himself useful, as Buddy Myer, coming off his batting championship, was nagged by injuries and out of action practically all season. Bluege was playing a position entirely new to him, and he did admirable work in his 15th season, filling in as

needed at short and third as well, and batting .288, his best mark since 1930.

Myer's follow-up to his batting championship was a frustrating blow. Injuries had finally caught up with him. Throughout his career, Myer had been the ultimate baseball schizophrenic — a serene type off the ballfield, he instantly became belligerent, even reckless, the minute he stepped onto it. Now he and the team were paying the price. At age 32, he ended up missing over 100 games and his batting average dropped 80 points, to .269, in just 156 at-bats. Red Kress filled in at second and enjoyed good offensive success for a second consecutive year, batting .284. Kress had shown good power with the Browns and White Sox in the early thirties, and this year contributed eight homers and 51 ribbies in his part-time role.

The Senators were much improved in the power department in 1936, but that wasn't necessarily due to good planning. Eight days before Christmas 1935, Clark Griffith parted ways with Heinie Manush, whose numbers, as mentioned, were way down from his '33 figures, when he'd led the league in hits and triples, and had finished second in the batting race. The Old Fox was correct in his assessment that at age 35, Heinie's batting eye wasn't as true as it had once been.

Manush was dispatched to the Red Sox. Unlike so many stars who had left Griffith's employ in the past, the battling .330 career hitter would not be back before the end of his playing days. By 1938, Manush would be playing in the minors, hanging on for dear life at age 37. The Pirates purchased his contract from the International League's Toronto Maple Leafs, but after going 1–for–12 to start 1939, he was released and never played again. He did, however, return to Washington as a coach in 1953 and '54, and as a scout in 1961 and '62.

In return for Manush, Griffith acquired, in mid–December 1935, two outfielders — Carl Reynolds, who had played for the Senators in '32 until being knocked out of commission by Bill Dickey's fist, and Roy Johnson. Both would turn 33 before the next season began, and neither had shown much power lately. Reynolds was destined to play only about half the time and hit .276. Johnson, a half-Cherokee and brother of the more famous slugger "Indian Bob" Johnson of the Athletics, never did play for Washington.

On January 17, 1936, exactly a month after obtaining his rights, Griffith shipped Johnson to the Yankees, along with pitcher Bump Hadley. In return, the Nats made the acquisition of a notoriously wild 26-year-old righthander, Jimmie DeShong, and Jesse Hill, a little 28-year-old outfielder who was lightning-fast and had once challenged for a spot on the U.S. Olympic track team. While Hill did well, batting .305 while sharing some of the work in the outfield with Carl Reynolds, it was DeShong who was the real find. He made Clark Griffith look like a genius, winning even more often than Newsom, with 18 victories and just ten losses. While DeShong's 4.63 ERA was higher than Newsom's 4.32, it was still well below the league average. While things had remained stable in the National League, American League hitters established an unprecedented dominance in 1936, and the league ERA mushroomed to 5.04, as opposed to just 4.02 in the senior circuit.

In this context, Earl Whitehill's 4.87 ERA reflects an ordinary season for him. He wound up 14–11, the third year in a row he'd won 14 following his career year on that great '33 Senators club, when he'd won 22. Whitehill's tenure as an effective big-league pitcher was effectively over. Clark Griffith and Bucky Harris got rid of him at the right time at the end of the season but failed to get anything useful in return. The veteran righthander obtained from the Indians, Jack Salveson, didn't even make the team and did not play in the majors again until World War II was half over, at a time when major-league talent was seriously depleted.

Besides Jimmie DeShong, there was another surprise performer on the 1936 pitching staff. Pete Appleton (born Peter William Jablonowski), a 32-year-old who'd won 17 big-league games up until then, spun 14 victories for the Senators, against nine losses. Apple-

ton's 3.53 ERA was sterling in these inflationary times. An accomplished pianist who had been bandleader at the University of Michigan, he had chosen to go into baseball instead of music upon graduation. It was possibly not a good career move. Appleton, who actually played in the major leagues under his real name of Jablonowski until obtaining a legal name change in 1933, would never replicate his successes of 1936, despite the fact that the Senators would give him plenty of chances over the course of the next three seasons.

In mid–June, the club bade farewell to a player who, like Heinie Manush who had departed six months earlier, had served them extraordinarily well. As in Manush's case, Jack Russell's better days had come and gone, and he was sent to the Red Sox for Joseph Thomas "Crooning Joe" Cascarella. Cascarella might have formed a duo with Appleton, for he had a wonderful tenor voice and a personality to match. These types of personal talents, however, don't always translate into success at throwing a baseball. Cascarella's big-league journey would span just five seasons. He did a creditable job in '36 for the Senators, achieving a 9–8 record, but would be so ineffective the following year that he would be sold to Cincinnati by midseason.

In sum, the Nats had the third-best pitching staff in the league in 1936, and that was a monumental improvement over the previous year, when they had been practically tied for dead last. The club got an offensive boost also, when on June 14, Jake Powell, the angry young outfielder, was moved to the Yankees for Ben Chapman, a fine but temperamental veteran outfielder who'd led the American League in stolen bases for three consecutive years in the early thirties. Griffith had grown tired of Powell's shenanigans on the field, which culminated in an early-season incident at Griffith Stadium. Powell broke Hank Greenberg's left wrist in a collision caused by yet another reckless baserunning escapade.

Greenberg, the most prominent player in baseball the previous year (he led the majors in homers and RBIs in '35), only appeared in 12 games in 1936. Jake Powell's involvement in his injury was the straw that broke Griffith's back. Back in the spring, Griff had endured the ultimate insult from Powell. After having already been fined for breaking curfew, the outfielder missed a train in Florida, but mysteriously reappeared on time for an exhibition game in Georgia the next day.

Clark Griffith had once been asked to name the one figure he admired most in America. He answered "the Lone Ranger," revealing that he considered the masked marvel his "guiding star" and "the sort of man I wanted to be." Indeed, Griff kept a picture of the caped crusader in his office. Now, the guiding star of the Senators needed to call upon all of his virtuousness not to throttle Jake Powell. The boss found out that the young man had rejoined the team so quickly because he had come from Florida *by airplane,* and had billed the ballclub for the flight.

Gradually, the extreme dislike in Washington for local boy Powell, a .312 hitter as a rookie in '35, spread to the fans. Upon his return to the capital following the trade with the Yankees, Powell was booed vociferously whenever he took his leftfield position. When he responded in kind, he was showered with empty bottles. Instead of running for cover, Jake threw the bottles back. The police had to step in and break things up.

The man Washington got in exchange for Powell, Ben Chapman, also had an interesting, but much longer, career in baseball. Born in Nashville, Tennessee, on Christmas Day, 1908, the 27-year-old Chapman was a converted infielder who'd been moved to the outfield so that New York could maximize the benefit from his outstanding speed and throwing arm. Chapman went on to rack up great numbers on some very good Yankees teams of the early 1930s. With the arrival of Joe DiMaggio in the spring of '36, however, he had outworn his welcome. Moving him to Washington meant the Yanks could open up centerfield for DiMaggio, who'd been playing in left. But Chapman was certainly a welcome addition in the Washington outfield, scoring an awesome 91 runs in just 97 games, and batting .332.

Ben Chapman would last only one year with the Senators, though, and would be through as a regular by 1940. A couple of years later, while managing and trying to revive his playing career as a pitcher at Richmond of the Piedmont League, he slugged an umpire and was suspended from playing for a full year. He made it back to the majors as a pitcher, going 5–3 for the wartime Dodgers in 1944. Traded to the Phillies in '45, Chapman was, within a couple of weeks of his arrival, named manager of a bad ballclub which ended up losing 108 games. When Jackie Robinson of the Dodgers broke baseball's racial barrier in 1947, Chapman made some ill-timed comments which further tarnished his reputation and frustrated owner Bob Carpenter, who fired him in '48.

Along with Ben Chapman, Johnny Stone, who had moved over to left field in Griffith's reworked outfield for 1936, also picked up some offensive slack by socking 15 home runs, up from just one in '35, and batting at a .341 clip. Despite placing seventh in home runs as a team, the club total of 62 nonetheless nearly represented a 100 percent improvement. Top man was Joe Kuhel, the comeback player of the year, who had 16 round-trippers, 118 runs driven in, and a .321 average in this, the best season of his career. While Kuhel and the rookie Buddy Lewis kept the infield corners anchored, the middle infield remained less settled, with Ossie Bluege and Red Kress sharing some time at those positions with Cecil Travis.

With Bluege and Kress hitting so well, Travis appeared in 53 games in the outfield. The experiment was never pursued following 1936, as Travis would never again play so much as a single game in the garden. While displaced from his regular shortstop position for more than half the season, Travis produced 92 runs. Still an opposite-field hitter, he hit the second and third home runs of his stellar three-year career, during which his batting averages had been .319, .318, and .317.

The catching workload was also split, between Cliff Bolton and Wally Millies, a 29 year-old who, except for seven at-bats for the

Dodgers, had been a career minor-leaguer. The better of the two offensively, Bolton hit .291, but Millies was far from a slouch, attaining a .312 mark in the 74 games in which he participated. Millies made his presence felt late in the season when Jake Powell, with the Yankees now, tried to barge into Joe Kuhel, like he had into Greenberg when he'd broken the superstar's wrist. The usually mild-mannered Kuhel managed to get out of the way but became incensed with Powell. Millies, who already disliked Powell, sprang off the bench and jumped Powell from behind. When Powell punched him in the head, Powell was the one who got hurt. Millies had kept his catcher's mask on.

This club put forth a much more spirited effort. There was leadership from old champions Harris and Bluege. There was some slugging, provided primarily by Kuhel and Stone. There was a newfound cohesion after the trade of Jake Powell, and plenty of team speed (the Senators led the league in triples for the sixth consecutive year) supplemented by the addition of Ben Chapman. Young players Travis and Lewis made enormous contributions, and of course there was the constant presence of the raucous Bobo Newsom.

The Senators in 1936 were a winning ballclub again, finishing with 82 wins, 11 games above .500. This was good for a tie for third place with the White Sox, but a long way from the World Series. The Nats finished an even 20 games behind the Yankees, who defeated the Giants in six games in the fall classic. The previous year's World Series hero was Goose Goslin, who had singled in the winning run in the sixth and final game with two out in the ninth. (It was during this Series, as well, that umpire Bill Klem was sharply rebuked and fined by Commissioner Kenesaw Landis for dressing Goslin down as a result of a heated on-field discussion.) This year's hero was none other than Jake Powell, who had ten hits and batted .455.

The 1937 Washington Senators' batting lineup was bolstered by the addition of a man destined for the Hall of Fame, Al Simmons. (See Appendix B for records of all Hall of Famers who played for the Senators.) Known as "Bucketfoot" because of his open stance and movement toward third as he took his righthanded swing, Simmons was simply one of the greatest batsmen to ever come down the pipe. Just coming up on his 35th birthday, he had enjoyed a terrific 13–112–.327 year with the Tigers in 1936, his first season in Detroit. In 1935, however, he had experienced an off year for the first time in his illustrious 12-year career. He'd been Connie Mack's all-time favorite, and the revered McGillicuddy said as much at the end of a 50-year career during which he had performed double duty as both A's owner and manager. When asked to name his all-time favorite players, the octogenarian wistfully replied that he wished he could have "nine players named Simmons."

The presence of a two-time batting champion in Washington was exciting for the fans. But which Al Simmons had Clark Griffith just spent $15,000 for? If he could replicate what he'd done last season, and if the Yankees let up, who knew! It was thought that just about every hitter in the lineup had the ability to hit .300. Pitching had been the Nats' strong suit in '36 and this continued early in '37. Unfortunately, the offense sputtered horribly, resulting in a 2–7 start. That's where the team sat when a transaction was made to shore up the weakest position on the squad, that of catcher. Clark Griffith unloaded the bulky Shanty Hogan on Indianapolis of the American Association. Hogan had been, once, one of the finest receivers and hitters in the National League. Oft criticized for his weight, he'd come to spring training a changed man, having shed a reported 51 pounds. But when he started the season off by batting .120, he was gone.

Bucky Harris obtained from Indianapolis a catcher he thought would be able to be a very good big-league backstop. His name was Johnny Riddle and he came highly recommended by Clark Griffith's trusted bird dog, Joe Engel. Griff had to throw in cash rumored in the neighborhood of $5,000 to sweeten the deal for Riddle. If he seemed to be the answer to the catching "Riddle" early on, the solution was illusory. After eight games, Riddle's arm got so sore that he couldn't throw at all. He kept insisting that the soreness was just something that came up every spring, and that it would work itself out, but Griffith had a hunch that x-rays should be taken. When two chipped bones and a growth in Riddle's elbow were detected, the Old Fox cried foul.

Washington wanted the Riddle deal declared null and void, and Commissioner Kenesaw Landis agreed. By default, Wally Millies got the first-string catching job and, for a while, was driving in key runs. But he couldn't hold his own offensively over the long haul, and, while a capable backstop, he did not have a particularly strong arm. Cliff Bolton was not considered even adequate defensively, and was waived off the club on June 10. The following day, Griffith pulled off a much more important coup, landing the celebrated Ferrell brothers from the Red Sox in exchange for Bobo Newsom and centerfielder Ben Chapman. Bobo was allowing nearly six runs per nine innings in 1937, and Chapman had only 12 RBIs in 35 games and his average was a puny .262.

In return, the Senators were getting a sibling battery the likes of which has not since been seen in the major leagues. Catcher Rick Ferrell, a .296 career hitter (Hall of Fame, 1984), still just 31, had hit .312 in '36 and was at .308 this season. He was known for his good eye at the plate and was a crackerjack receiver. The brothers were North Carolina farm boys and Rick Ferrell, one of the best catchers of his time, was the more mild-mannered of the two. Three years younger than Rick, Wes Ferrell was as handy with a guitar and a banjo as with a pitchfork or a baseball. Younger than Bobo Newsom (who'd won 47 big-league games to this point), Wes Ferrell had already racked up six 20-win seasons in the majors. Included were two 25-win years, in 1930 and '35, when he led the league.

Wesley Cheek Ferrell seemed to have a lot more cheek than his older brother. He was a hothead who would at times fly into rages even if he was just having a bad day at the card table. Teammate Billy Werber told of how he'd seen him stomp on an expensive watch after some setback on the field. In 1932, Wes's manager at Cleveland, Roger Peckinpaugh, fined him for refusing to come out of a ballgame. In '36, Wes had a run-in with another old Nat, Joe Cronin, his manager at Boston, who fined him for doing exactly the opposite and leaving a game without permission. Later, while managing in the minor leagues, Wes would be suspended for smacking an umpire, and on another occasion for pulling his team off the field.

Apart from the fact that he'd won 20 or more in six of eight seasons, Wes Ferrell also arrived in Washington carrying the reputation of being the best-hitting pitcher in the history of baseball. His lifetime .280 average and 38 home runs are still all-time records. In one memorable contest involving the Senators in late July 1935, he slammed two homers off Bobo Newsom while pitching the Bosox to victory — remarkably, he hit two home runs in the same game on five different occasions. A week before he had victimized Bobo, he had pinch hit for the immortal Lefty Grove in the ninth inning with two men on base and the score 6–4. The pitcher was Tommy Bridges, who had 21 wins, four shutouts, and who led the league in strikeouts that year. Wes homered, for the victory.

The price of obtaining the Ferrells was a weakened outfield, but Mexican Mel Almada, who also came over from the Red Sox, filled the breach left by Ben Chapman remarkably well. While Chapman went on to regain his batting eye with the Red Sox, Almada, who didn't have Chapman's power, batted .309 over the rest of the season for the Senators. He distinguished himself on July 25, in particular, as the Nats swept two from the Browns by inflated 16–10 and 15–5 scores. Almada set a record by scoring nine times in the one day. Rightfielder Johnny Stone had a great year, batting .330 and driving in 88. Al Simmons was a major disappointment — he did produce 84 runs, but batted only .279, which was also what the Senators managed as a team in a league which as a whole hit .281.

A former Most Valuable Player of the Southern Association, Fred Sington, got his first opportunity to play semi-regularly after batting .319 on a limited basis in '36. Singston was a gifted athlete, a member of the College Football Hall of Fame in fact. A lad of 6'2" and 220 pounds, he had turned down offers from pro football and wrestling to pursue a career in baseball. Originally a pitcher, he had converted to the outfield to take advantage of his speed and arm on a daily basis. Singston hit only .237 for the Nats, and never got as good a chance to show his stuff again, despite hitting .358 in 17 games for the Brooklyn Dodgers the following season.

Buddy Lewis and Cecil Travis, like Johnny Stone, both batted over .300 for the Senators in 1937. Lewis improved on his impressive rookie-year numbers, and with his league-leading 668 official at-bats, he knocked in 79 runs. His ten homers were best on an outfit once again woefully short on the long ball. Lewis did have his trials in the field, and his .938 fielding average was the worst in the league among regular third basemen. Four of his 29 errors, however, occurred in the same game on August 10, tying a league record. (Within three days in 1990, Mike Blowers of the Yankees and Edgar Martinez of Seattle both had four blunders in one game, becoming the 21st and 22nd A.L. third basemen on the list of the temporarily inept.) Cecil Travis, growing into a role of leadership on this club in just his fourth season, broke out of his enviable .319–.318–.317 cycle. Despite tearing some ligaments in his right knee on April 28, at a time when he was batting .553, Travis lost just three weeks and registered a loud .344 for the year.

Buddy Myer bounced back from his injury-ridden season with a .293 bat mark, but he did lead all second basemen in errors. As a group, however, the Nats led the league in double plays. First baseman Joe Kuhel had more of an ordinary season. His homer output dropped from 16 to six, and his ribbies from 118 to only 61.

The club's pitching took a step back in '37, despite the addition of the Ferrells. Both were disappointments, as was Simmons, the team's other important acquisition. Coming off two straight seasons in which he'd hit over .300, Bucketfoot Al faltered to .229 in 104 games for Washington after the June trade. Wes Ferrell went 11–13 the rest of the way as Harris's stopper, and was 14–19, 4.90 overall. At 29, Ferrell had already passed his prime, and he would be gone from the roster before the end of the following campaign.

The staff as a whole was mediocre in '37, with no one standing out. Jimmie DeShong bloomed in the spring, winning four in a row in one stretch, but then wilted badly. Shelled repeatedly, DeShong was lucky to finish with the 14–15 record he earned while allowing nearly five runs a game. Monte "Prof" Weaver, having taken up red meat again, did have a decent comeback year with a 12–9 slate and a good 4.20 ERA (the league average was 4.62). Pete Appleton, as in the case of all of the previously mentioned Nats pitchers, was also on the decline. He never did get back to the standards of his one good year, and in this season he did not get good support and finished 8–15. Ed Linke had an incongruous record of 6–1 with an appalling 5.60 ERA.

The main focus of the baseball season was the All-Star game, the annual event inaugurated in 1933. Clark Griffith, always decked out in dazzling clothing for these occasions, had promised at the 1936 event in St. Louis that the one at Griffith Stadium on July 7, 1937, would be the best yet. When the proud day arrived, Griffith, dressed all in white and grinning from ear to ear, led a presidential parade staged before the game. The Old Fox was the first out of the gate, and was followed by Boy Scouts, and then by two vehicles carrying President Roosevelt and his entourage.

Not a single member of the Senators got into the game, and Joe McCarthy of the Yankees, the manager of the A.L. squad, got plenty of local criticism for that. Both Ferrell boys and Buddy Myer were chosen for the team, but McCarthy was bent on winning at all costs and employed Bill Dickey and Charley Gehringer for the entire game at Rick Ferrell's and Myer's positions. Win McCarthy did, by a margin of 8–3, with Gehringer getting three hits and Dickey two. Only three pitchers appeared for the A.L.—Lefty Gomez, Tommy Bridges, and Mel Harder.

The starter for the National League, Dizzy Dean of the Cardinals, who had won 24 in '36 and seemed headed for just as good a season this year, had begged off pitching in this game because his arm was tired. He did finally accept the starting assignment, however, at the urging of Cards owner Sam Breadon. This was the turning point of Dean's career. He took a line drive off the bat of Cleveland's Earl Averill off his toe. When he attempted to return to action too early after the mishap, favoring the bad foot and compensating for the injury with changes in his delivery, Dean caused irreparable harm to his career. Soon, Ol' Diz would be earning a living with his comedic talents, which he came by very naturally.

Another highlight of this baseball season in Washington took place on April 30, 1937, when the Senators were mired in their early slump. They had just dropped a pair of games at Griffith Stadium to the Yankees (Cecil Travis had suffered his ankle injury in the first game), and in the final game of the series, Joe DiMaggio made his first appearance of the season. DiMaggio was already the hottest ticket in baseball. At age 22, he was coming off a 46–167–.346 sophomore year.

Enlightening as to just how good a season "Joltin' Joe" had just had is the fact that his totals for home runs, runs scored (151), and slugging percentage (.673) were figures he would never surpass in the 11 years of his golden career still ahead of him. DiMaggio had been a member of a world championship club in each of his first two years. In his first appearance of 1937, he connected for a pinch single in the seventh inning off Bobo Newsom, but Newsom won his first game of the year with a complete-game five-hitter as the Senators salvaged their only win of the three-game set.

The highly promising roster of players Clark Griffith had assembled, seemingly enhanced by the addition of the Ferrell boys and Al Simmons, was a major letdown for the old man. His ballclub dropped three places in the standings, managing only to place ahead of some of the most infamous teams in the entire history of both the Philadelphia A's and St. Louis Browns. Surprisingly, however, it was a quiet winter, and Griff did not begin addressing the club's shortcomings until spring training was nearly over.

On March 18, 1938, Joe Kuhel was traded to the White Sox for the antithesis of Kuhel, a big lummox with the rhyming name of Zeke "What a Physique" Bonura. A classic good-field, no-hit first baseman, the muscular Bonura (also affectionately called "Banana Nose" for obvious reasons) was a fan's delight but a manager's nightmare. He held out practically on an annual basis, and Jimmy Dykes, the White Sox pilot, was of the opinion that Bonura was the worst first baseman who had ever lived, and said so publicly.

Bonura, in actual fact a college man, was so slothful a fielder as to often make himself look ridiculous on a ballfield when he didn't have a bat in his hands. When he mysteriously led the league's first baseman in fielding in '36, Dykes was quick to discredit Bonura, pointing out that players don't get errors on balls they don't touch. What's more, Bonura wouldn't just wave at ground balls, he would give them the "Mussolini salute" with his glove. Opposing fans in particular loved this, but it is not hard to imagine what his manager thought of the behavior.

There are several versions of the following apocryphal story. Chisox manager Jimmy Dykes had decided that it would hardly be worth the trouble of changing his signals just because Bonura was now on the opposing team. Dykes told coach Bing Miller that Bonura had never been able to remember the signs when he was with Chicago anyway. As the story goes, the dreadfully slow-footed Bonura had made it to third on behalf of the Senators against his old team. At this point, Dykes began waving his scorecard to shoo away some flies which had been buzzing around him on the bench. Bonura, forgetting which side he was on, took Dykes' motions to be the steal sign, and he took off for the plate.

He barged into the catcher, the ball was shaken loose, and he was in there. While this makes one hell of a good story, it indeed could not have happened in a regular-season game — Bonura stole home only once in his seven-year big-league career, and that had happened when he was a member of the White Sox, in the 15th inning of a game against the Yankees.

Zeke Bonura did bring the anticipated bat the Senators had been banking on, however, and slugged 22 homers for them in 1938. Despite a terrible start which had him hitting just .190 in mid–June, Bonura batted .289 and drove in 114 runs, which tied him for sixth best in the league with Lou Gehrig. Once again, his lack of range enabled him to lead all American League first basemen in fielding. Jimmy Dykes may have had a point when he'd said that at Chicago, Bonura let in three runs for every one he batted in. Coupled with the resurgence of Al Simmons, who banged out 21 dingers in 1938, the Senators nearly doubled their home-run output.

Cecil Travis seemed on his way to a Hall of Fame career. (One could think in these terms by 1938, as the Hall of Fame at Cooperstown, New York, had been created in '36.) Travis batted .335 with 96 runs scored, and his keystone partner, Buddy Myer, exceeded his remarkable performance of the previous comeback campaign and hit .336. Buddy Lewis rounded out a highly productive infield, knocking in 91 runs with 12 homers and a .296 mark.

When Mel Almada, the "California Spaniard," hit only .244 in nearly 200 at-bats, Griffith engineered a deal with the Browns which brought Sammy West back to the Senators after a 5½-year separation. This exchange would be the first one in a while to turn heavily in the Nats' favor. West, still a dependable centerfielder at 34, hit .302 in 92 games after coming on board. The trade was consummated on June 15, 1938, an important date on baseball's timeline. On this day, Johnny Vander Meer, 23-year-old lefthander of the Cincinnati Reds, hurled a second consecutive no-hitter.

Vander Meer's feat remains unique in baseball history. The second of the no-hitters took place in the first night game played at Ebbets Field in Brooklyn. (Cincinnati's Crosley Field had been the scene of the first night game in the big leagues, back on May 24, 1935.) Clark Griffith had said that there was no chance night baseball would ever catch on in the majors. The game, the Old Fox reasoned, was meant to be played "in the Lord's own sunshine."

It was longer still before baseball began to see another kind of light. On the same day John Vander Meer tossed his second no-hitter, Billy Leo Williams was born in Whistler, Alabama. Williams, a sweet-swinging left-handed hitter who would make the Hall of Fame, was black. To baseball's eternal shame, it would be nearly ten more years before a black man would be allowed to participate in a major-league game.

In the 1930s and 40s, Griffith Stadium was home not only to the Senators, but to the Homestead Grays of the Negro National League. Clark Griffith therefore had occasion to reflect prophetically on the future of blacks in baseball. The Grays, who played some home games at Forbes Field in Pittsburgh and the rest in Washington, had a catcher who was on the way to winning the home-run and batting titles of Negro baseball in 1938 (and he would win the home-run title again in 1939). His name was Josh Gibson, and Griffith knew darn well that Gibson was hitting more home runs into the distant left-field seats than the entire white American League combined.

In March of this year, Griffith told the *Washington Tribune* that the time was not far off when black Americans would be playing in the big leagues. He wasn't sure, however, that the time had arrived yet. He did talk about the subject often, but never did anything about it. In 1944, he was polled by sportswriter Wendell Smith of the *Pittsburgh Courier*, a black newspaper, who wanted to know what Griffith thought of Commissioner Landis's statement that the major leagues were not actively excluding blacks.

The commissioner had made the pronouncement in reply to the troublesome Leo

Durocher, outspoken manager of the Dodgers, who had stated during an interview published in the Communist *Daily Worker* that he felt it was Landis who was really the one keeping blacks out of the majors. The Old Fox may have come across as somewhat evasive to Wendell Smith. His idea, Griffith told Smith, was that the Negro Leagues needed to *continue* to develop so that *someday*, when they were good enough, the best black players might play for a world championship against the best the big leagues could offer.

Once, Clark Griffith had reportedly called Josh Gibson and the Homestead Grays' other great hitter, Buck Leonard, into his office to tell them the only reason he wasn't signing them to big-league contracts was because of the hardships they would encounter due to racial tensions. Of Gibson, the great Walter Johnson once said, "There is a catcher that any big-league club would like to buy for $200,000. I've heard of him before. His name is Gibson. He can do everything. He hits that ball a mile. And he catches so easy he might as well be in a rocking chair. Throws like a rifle. Bill Dickey isn't as good a catcher. Too bad this Gibson is a colored fellow."*

Clark Griffith did predict that the player who would eventually break baseball's unwritten color ban would have to be a martyr, impervious to the taunts and insults contrived to show the black man unworthy of playing with whites. In this Griffith was right, but by the time that chosen man, Jackie Robinson, came along, Josh Gibson was dead. He was just past his 35th birthday when he died of a stroke on January 20, 1947, just 85 days before Jackie Robinson graced the field among white players — one of the greatest moments in the history of baseball and, because of what it symbolized for so many, one of the greatest moments in the history of America.

The trade that brought Sammy West back to patrol centerfield at Griffith Stadium was not the only ray of sunshine for the club in 1938, what with Al Simmons' resurgence and Zeke Bonura's ability to knock in some runs. Poor Johnny Stone, the Nats' rightfielder who by now had enjoyed four consecutive seasons of hitting well over .300 for the Senators, was no longer an important contributor, however. Following a .244 start in 56 games, Stone contracted tuberculosis and was not able to play baseball again. While he survived the disease and scouted for the Detroit Tigers later on, he was barely 50 when he passed away in 1955.

Johnny Stone's decline did open the way for a couple of outstanding performers on the 1938 Washington Senators. A 22-year-old speedster named George Washington Case, who had led the New York-Penn. League in stolen bases and had hit .338 while playing in his hometown of Trenton, New Jersey, got his chance and made the most of it. Case had done well in a September call-up in '37, and would remain a fixture in Washington's outfield for eight years. Destined to lead the A.L. in stolen bases five straight years, he batted .305.

Another recruit, Taft Wright, named after the President who had been the first to throw a ceremonial pitch on opening day in Washington, made a tremendous impression. The broad-shouldered Wright turned 27 in August of his belated rookie year, and hit a poetic .350. When he didn't make it into Bucky Harris' starting lineup, which was often, he rendered himself useful in a pinch, pacing the league with 13 hits in 39 tries. Under rules in effect at this time, Wright should have won the batting title — he participated in the requisite 100 games, playing in exactly that number. But because of his many pinch hit appearances, the commissioner's office decided to step in and hand the batting crown to Jimmie Foxx. Even Washington fans had to admit that Foxx was somewhat more deserving of the honor — the "Beast" hit 50 homers and also led the league in RBIs, with 175. It was an MVP year for Foxx, his third, but first in five years.

While the offense had improved marginally, there was a letdown on the mound for

*Washington Post, *April 7, 1939.*

Washington in 1938 which resulted in an advancement of only one place in the standings, from sixth to fifth. The unlikely ace of the pitching staff was Emil John "Dutch" Leonard, a 29-year-old lefthander who had compiled a mediocre 18–23 ledger over four seasons with the Brooklyn Dodgers. Leonard was one of the first pitchers in baseball to rely on the knuckleball as his main pitch. He would go on to win 191 games, mostly for the Senators, and his success would encourage the likes of Hoyt Wilhelm and Phil Niekro, who would ride the knuckleball right through the portals of the Hall of Fame.

Leonard savored one good year with the Dodgers, in '34, when he went 14–11 for a sixth-place club. But a sore arm had resulted in banishment to the minors, where he had revived his career with the Atlanta Crackers of the Southern Association. While just 12–15 for the Nats in '38, Leonard usually had pinpoint control of the knuckler, and also threw an occasional fastball or slip pitch for strikes.

Everyone else on this pitching staff failed abominably. Pete Appleton produced a 7–9, 4.60 slate and his days as a spot starter were numbered. Hard-throwing lefthander Ken Chase walked nearly twice as many as he struck out and wound up 9–10 despite a sky-high ERA of 5.58. Wes Ferrell's performance was even worse, and his record even more unlikely. Ferrell was 13–8 with a grotesque 5.92 ERA when Clark Griffith got rid of him and his big salary. Within a couple of days of his release, Ferrell figured he got Griff's goat when he was picked up by the World Series–bound Yankees, who would win their third World Championship in four straight over the Cubs in a Series in which Ferrell would not pitch. Ferrell got a great kick out of beating the Senators at a time when Griffith was paying him — he was still collecting ten days' salary Washington owed him following his release when he beat the Nats in extra innings.

Brother Rick's tenure as the Senators' catcher was to be much longer, and he hit .292 in 135 games while leading the loop's catchers in double plays, but also in errors. Among the other pitchers Rick Ferrell was given to han-

dle was Harry Kelley, who'd lost 21 games the previous year for the A's, and who went 9–8 with a 4.49 ERA after being claimed on waivers.

Monte Weaver was 7–6, but his sorry 5.24 ERA was a warning sign that he'd have to turn to college teaching to make a living, which he did following a brief stint with the Red Sox at the beginning of the 1939 season. Jimmie DeShong, who'd pitched well until early in the previous season, continued a fatal downward spiral with an ugly 6.58 ERA. When DeShong, hopelessly wild, got off to another disastrous start in '39, the Senators waived him and he disappeared from the big-league scene, at age 29, forever.

One low point of the 1938 campaign happened on Independence Day. During the first game of a doubleheader at Griffith Stadium, play was held up for 15 minutes when fans became enraged about a call on the field and littered the grounds with glass bottles and vegetables. When play resumed, the Nats were thrashed by the Yankees, 10–5. The Senators didn't play their full complement of games in '38, and had they done so, they might have finished at an even .500. As it was, they wound up 75–76, 23½ games behind the conquering Yankees.

One nice touch to this year was that Clark Griffith was able to bring Leon Goslin back for one final go-round. Goslin hit only .158 in 38 games, putting the cap on an outstanding career. Quite likely the best hitter in the team's history, he finished his big-league journey with an even 500 doubles, 173 triples, 248 home runs, and a .316 batting average. Clark Griffith had a job for him the following year, and the Goose returned to his home state of New Jersey to play for the Nats' Trenton farm team, where he hit .324.

On the Washington club of 1939, the revelation was second-year outfielder George Case. Indeed, Case caused a sensation throughout baseball, stealing 51 bases, the highest total in the majors since Ben Chapman's 61 eight years earlier. Case would become the greatest basestealer of his time; in the 40-year period from 1921 to 1961, no one would pilfer more than the 61 he would swipe in 1940. For five straight years beginning in 1939, Case would lead both major leagues in steals, a feat unprecedented in major-league history. He did incur numerous injuries while sliding, but in 1946, hobbled by pains which were bringing his career to an abrupt end at age 31, he would win a sixth league title.

George Washington Case's association with the Washington Senators was the product of a business relationship which had existed between Clark Griffith and a Baltimore laundryman named Joe Cambria since 1934. Originally from Messina, Italy, but brought to America around 1890 when he was just three months old, Cambria was to become the Bobo Newsom of baseball club owners. Raised in Boston, his baseball travels began in 1910 as an outfielder with Newport of the Rhode Island State League. He hung on to a career as a minor-leaguer until 1916, when he fractured his leg. Cambria nevertheless did serve in World War I and, after the war, got into the laundry business, once sponsoring a boys team on which Clark Griffith's young nephew, Calvin, played.

For ten years beginning in the late twenties, Joe Cambria furthered his career as a nomadic minor-league operator. He successively bought clubs in various leagues in outposts like Hagerstown (Blue Ridge League); Youngstown (Middle Atlantic League); Albany (International League); Harrisburg (New York-Penn. League); Salisbury, Maryland (Eastern Shore League); St. Augustine (Florida State); and Greenville (Sally League).

In 1934, Cambria ran into some difficulty in meeting his payroll. It was then that he introduced himself to Clark Griffith for the first time. Needing $1,500 to stay afloat, Cambria was able to coax the sum out of the Old Fox, who would over the years reap a return worth many times his initial investment. At first, Cambria began beating the bushes for Griffith as a scout on a part-time basis only. He had no license to spend Griff's money, so as a result, he did his bird-dogging in locales less frequented by other scouts, generally in the lower minor leagues.

This approach led Joe Cambria clear out of the country to explore talent in Puerto Rico, Panama, and Mexico. In 1911, he had played in Cuba and recalled having been impressed with the agility of the players and the overall quality of play. He would eventually sign a great number of Cuban players for the Washington Senators on behalf of Clark Griffith.

The first of those was Bobby Estalella, a powerful hitter who packed 185 pounds on a 5'6" frame. Discovered by Cambria in the Havana winter league while in his early twenties, Estalella could hit the ball a long way, when he connected. Unfortunately, his fielding average at third base risked dropping to the level of his batting average. In his debut with the Senators, in 1935, he got into 15 games and hit a couple of homers. In the field, he was knocking balls down any way he could, and the Griffith Stadium fans loved him. He faded back to the minors, but nearly four years later, Estalella was brought back to spend the better part of six seasons in the big leagues. In '39, the Nats made use of him in about half their games, but only in the outfield, and he managed to hit a creditable .275 with eight homers. Estalella was not destined to ever become a star, however.

A more pronounced flop was Cuban pitcher René Monteagudo, whom Cambria had had on his Greenville, South Carolina, club. Monteagudo beat the Senators in an exhibition game and Griffith took him on, but his career in the big leagues was very brief. In 33 games with the Nats over two years, he was 3–7 with an atrocious earned run average of six runs per game. It had been said that Monteagudo's chief asset in terms of pitching in the big leagues was that he could speak English. This would have made him easier prey for Joe Cambria who, surprisingly, knew very little Spanish. On one occasion, after Clark Griffith had been unsuccessful in attempts to elicit some information from a Latin player, he asked Cambria to speak for him. Cambria went up to the player and asked the same thing Griffith had, in English, but he asked *louder*.

Next on the Cuban prospect list, and

considerably more successful, was Alejandro Alexander Aparicio Elroy Carrasquel, a name which might possibly have been rendered even more elegant had his parents left out the "Elroy." Certainly, Alex Carrasquel was an elegant pitcher. His age was officially given as 27 when he joined the Nationals for the 1939 season, but some Cubans who had played with him during a tour of Florida insisted that he was more like 35. At his first training camp, all Carrasquel could say in English was, "Me peetch goood."

What Alex Carrasquel was for sure was a man fond of the rumba and the night life, and the owner of a fine fastball. Following his rookie season in 1939, in which he went 5–9 for another underachieving Washington ballclub, Carrasquel would find his niche with the Senators as a reliever throughout the war years. His fastball became a prized commodity on a staff which would eventually be comprised almost entirely of knuckleballers, and his 50–39 career record, amassed on losing clubs, attests to his competence. Eventually, like Bobby Estalella, Carrasquel would be banned from baseball for jumping to the Mexican League, but would later make a brief return to the majors, with the White Sox, in 1949.

Joe Cambria's most heralded Cuban prospect, brought up for the 1941 season, would be a flop. Roberto Ortiz was a 6'4", 200-pounder who, according to Cambria, threw harder than Walter Johnson and could hit a ball farther than Jimmie Foxx. None of that was ever placed into evidence, however, and Ortiz hit a grand total of eight homers in a career spanning just 659 at-bats, mostly on weakened wartime teams in the early forties. Later on, Joe Cambria would have better luck with his recruits. Eventually, he would have a hand in bringing to the Senators' organization such Cuban stalwarts as Connie Marrero, Sandy Consuegra, Mike Fornieles, Pedro Ramos, Camilo Pascual, Zoilo Versalles, and, last but not least, Tony Oliva.

While other clubs began scouring the Pearl of the Antilles, Cambria remained the most popular scout with the Cuban people. He headquartered at the American Club in Havana, and in fact became so well known that a cigar was named after him — it was called the "Papa Joe." Cambria earned a reputation as a man genuinely concerned for the Cuban players he did sign, but in the first few years of his association with Clark Griffith, he had more success recruiting Americans. Among these, George Case was already a star. There would be others, like Eddie Yost and Walter Masterson, but never again would Cambria help promote players of the calibre of a pair of rookies who first appeared in the big leagues with the 1939 edition of the Washington Senators. These two Cambria protégés were Mickey Vernon and Early Wynn.

Two weeks before Christmas 1938, the Senators cast adrift Zeke Bonura, getting a couple of minor-leaguers and more importantly, $20,000, in return for the counterproductive first baseman. Within a year and a bit, however, Clark Griffith would turn right around and return the money to the Giants in exchange for old "Banana Nose." In the meantime, there was a void at first base.

At spring training 1939, Griffith declared that two players were in a position to "make or break this club." Both failed to "make" the club, and the Senators were indeed broken. One of two mentioned by Griff was Bobby Estalella, who played badly enough to get himself demoted to Minneapolis the following season. The boss's other key to a successful season was Jimmy Wasdell, a first baseman called upon to fill Bonura's shoes, but who so far had hit only .244 in 85 games with the Nats over the two previous seasons. Wasdell was at .303 for 29 games, but with no power, and he was on his way to Minneapolis, even more hastily than Estalella was, not even finishing the year with the big club.

This was the year that possibly the best hitter of all time made his debut in the league, with the Boston Red Sox. Later in the season, on August 19, 1939, Theodore Samuel Williams smashed his first career grand slam against the Senators in an 8–6 Red Sox victory. Williams would go on in his rookie season to hit 31 homers, drive in a league-leading 145 runs, and bat .327. The league's great star, Joltin' Joe

DiMaggio, would lead the junior circuit in batting with .381, which would hold as the highest average of his career. DiMag did miss five weeks of the season, though, as a result of a muscle tear in his leg sustained on Griffith Stadium's muddy outfield grass while chasing a Bobby Estalella liner on April 29.

Players of the caliber of Joe DiMaggio and Ted Williams may come along once in a generation, but not likely twice, as they did. While the Senators didn't have a DiMaggio or a Williams, they did unveil some future standouts of their own in 1939. On July 8, a 21-year-old first baseman made his first appearance in a box score. Mickey Vernon would remain at the position for a period spanning four decades, most of which he would spend in Washington. Vernon's debut year was relatively inauspicious, as he hit just .257 with one home run the rest of the way. By season's end, the native of Marcus Hook, Pa., had played in 76 games, and before his career ended, he would hold the major-league record for most games played at first base. Quiet, consistent, and blessed with a good deal of charisma, Vernon would win the batting title twice, lead the league in doubles three times, and hit 490 career doubles. As a fielder, he was outstanding as well, the best at his position four times, twice pacing the entire majors.

On September 13, another Joe Cambria protégé, Early "Gus" Wynn, a 19-year-old righthander from Hartford, Alabama, started on the trail to Cooperstown. Unfortunately, Wynn would not find the right fork in the road until he left Washington, but eventually he too, like Mickey Vernon, would extend his career beyond the 1950s. He managed to play long enough to earn his 300th and final win, thereby guaranteeing immortality in the Hall of Fame, into which he was inducted in 1972. A scowling type on the mound, Wynn had a live fastball, but indeed never assembled the complementary pitches required for consistency until the Nats traded him to Cleveland at the end of 1948. In retrospect, that deal may well have been the worst the Senators made in their entire history, but for the time being, Wynn lost both his late-season decisions, and

he would spend the better part of the next two years in the minors before resurfacing in Washington in 1941.

The player of the year on the '39 Senators was no doubt the stout knuckleballer, Dutch Leonard, who managed to accumulate 20 wins, no small accomplishment on a club which dropped a notch in the standings and finished sixth, a full 21 games below the .500 level of semi-respectability. The pitching staff as a whole placed where the team did — sixth-best in the loop. The two main starters were Ken Chase and Joe Krakauskas. Chase, who hailed from Oneonta, N.Y., near the Hall of Fame in Cooperstown, had world-class velocity. But his atrocious control would not permit him to have a long career, let alone one that would lead to Cooperstown. While greatly improved in the control department in '39, Chase's record slipped to 10–19.

Joe Krakauskas was a big, 24-year-old Canadian who'd done well, amassing an 11–6 composite record in '37 and '38 for the Nats. Given lots of work, Krakauskas faltered in this year, which would prove the most active of his entire career. His numbers at the end were 11–17, 4.60. Besides Alex Carrasquel's 5–9 record, the other main contributors to this staff were rookie righthander Joe Haynes, 8–12 with an awful 5.36 ERA, and Pete Appleton, 5–10, 4.56, who had by now pitched himself right off the team.

One of baseball's most moving dramas unfolded right before the Senators in 1939. On April 30, the day after Joe DiMaggio tore up his leg at Griffith Stadium, Lou Gehrig appeared in his 2,130th consecutive game, the last one of his streak, which had begun against the Nats 14 years earlier. The Iron Horse went hitless against Joe Krakauskas, and upon making a routine play, was congratulated by Yankees pitcher Johnny Murphy. Two days later, after traveling to Detroit, Gehrig would take himself out of the lineup, suffering from unexplained sluggishness. His replacement, a rookie named Babe Dahlgren, homered and doubled and the Yanks won 22–2. (Coincidentally, pitcher Fred Hutchinson of the Tigers, later a World Series manager and well-loved figure, made his big-league debut in the same game, and it was a disaster for him. Hutchinson surrendered five walks, four hits, and eight runs in two-thirds of an inning.)

On June 20, Gehrig was diagnosed at the Mayo Clinic in Rochester, Minn., as suffering from amyotrophic lateral sclerosis (ALS), an incurable form of paralysis which became known as Lou Gehrig's Disease. When he appeared in front of nearly 62,000 fans at Yankee Stadium for Lou Gehrig Day two weeks later, the visitors were the Washington Senators. Gehrig gave his stirring "luckiest man on earth" speech, during the course of which he reflected on the courage and support displayed by his wife and family throughout his ordeal, and the good fortune he had had to be associated with some of the finest men in baseball. "I might have had a bad break," he concluded, "but I have an awful lot to live for." Less than two years later, a few days short of his 38th birthday, Lou Gehrig was dead.

The young Washington Senators of 1939 could already hit for average at the big-league level. This team was, however, sorrowfully short on power. The main sources the previous season, Zeke Bonura and Al Simmons, were both gone, Simmons having been sold to the Boston Braves two days before New Year's 1939. He had fallen out of favor in a big way with Clark Griffith on the very last day of the '38 season. Having had enough of the abuse which showered down on him from the Griffith Stadium box seats, Simmons walked over and unleashed a torrent of expletives. Griffith fined him, and this was the origin of the bad blood between the two. When Simmons expressed the opinion that the old man was only fining him so that he could recoup bonus money Simmons had earned by batting .300, he was a goner, Hall of Fame credentials notwithstanding.

Buddy Lewis was the club's best hitter in

'39. His 12 homers had placed him third on the club the previous year, but this year he led the team with 10. Lewis hit .319 in this, his fourth full season, and led the league with 16 triples. The young Nats were tops in the A.L. in that department, and bolstered by George Case's coming-out, were now a fast, aggressive crew. Third baseman Cecil Travis missed some games due to injury and finished below .300 for the first time in his seven-year career, but still managed .292.

Veteran Sammy West hit .282 and still played an excellent center field. George Case hit over .300 again (.302), as he had in his rookie season in '38. In addition, Taffy Wright proved his .350 average as a rookie had been no fluke. With increased work, the leftfielder hit .309 and drove in a team-high 93 runs. Buddy Myer, hobbled by infirmities rendering him incapable of playing full time now, participated in about half the games and hit .302. Yet another rookie, Jimmy Bloodworth, was brought in, and held up his end of the bargain in sharing time with Myer. Bloodworth batted .289, a figure he would unfortunately never even approach again in a big-league career which would last another ten years.

Bucky Harris, surviving on one-year contracts, had by now managed five years into his second term with the club, and had just gone through the most disillusioning season of all with a sixth-place finish. But there was a great future in the personnel on this club, embodied in the likes of Lewis, Travis, Case, and unbeknownst to anyone for the moment, Vernon and Wynn.

This young nucleus seemed to bode well for the early years of the new decade. But parts of the world were already at war. The conflict would mean an upheaval in baseball, not to mention the entire world, of a magnitude that no one at this point could even begin to imagine.

1940–1949:
THE DESCENT

The decade of the forties, destined to become the darkest of the century for major-league baseball, got off with the biggest kind of a bang. On April 16, 1940, 21-year-old "Rapid Robert" Feller of the Indians pitched a no-hitter on Opening Day, the first time this had ever happened. The command performance was given in 47-degree weather at Comiskey Park in Chicago. The final out registered when Feller induced Taft Wright to ground out.

The 29-year-old Wright had been a Washington Senator until recently, when he'd been traded to Chicago, with Pete Appleton, in exchange for a powerfully built 31-year-old outfielder named Gerald "Gee" Walker. Walker had slipped below .300 the previous season for the first time since 1933, but had slugged 13 homers, with 111 ribbies, as compared to just four homers for Taffy Wright. As for Appleton, he had not been an especially effective pitcher since 1936, and would not be again.

Gee Walker had hit as high as .353 in 1936, and had followed that up with .335 in '37. He had been immensely popular in Detroit before moving on to the White Sox prior to the 1938 campaign. While Walker often made up for his deficiencies with his bat, his frequent mental lapses when dealing with other phases of the game had earned him the unflattering nickname of "Ironhead." Once, he tried to steal a base while the batter was being walked intentionally. On another occasion, he was picked off base twice in the same inning.

At Detroit, Walker had been on the outs with manager Bucky Harris for two seasons because of something which happened in 1933. He had hit a line shot directly to the second baseman, who made a nifty stab on a hard skip. Walker, disgusted, flung his bat and headed for his defensive position. His playing time was curtailed after that. Then, during the 1934 World Series, while busy arguing with some of his enemies on the St. Louis Cardinals bench, he was picked off first base.

At Washington Gee Walker would not disappoint Bucky Harris, under whom he'd played for three years in Detroit; this time he produced of 13–96–.294 numbers for the Senators on what was ironically the most anemic offense in the American League in 1940. Second baseman Jimmy Bloodworth was the only other player on the club to hit more than six homers. In terms of home run production, the Nats finished dead last in the league, by far, with their total of 52. They scored the fewest runs in the process.

By way of contrast, the Yankees, who would finish third, but a mere two games behind the pennant-winning Tigers, slugged 155 home runs. Clark Griffith raised a few eyebrows at the 1940 winter meetings of baseball's owners by sponsoring a motion prohibiting trades between the pennant winner and other clubs in the league. In actual fact, it had been years since the Yankees had obtained a player in a trade who had made a critical difference in a pennant race. When the Yanks wound up third, the whole no-trade notion was permanently scrapped.

Mickey Vernon, the 22-year-old first baseman, was going to be given the 1940 season to sharpen his skills at Jersey City, where he would hit .283 with nine homers. After a 16-month absence, Zeke Bonura, who'd lasted just the one year in Washington before being sold to the Giants because of his defensive inadequacies, was brought back to help shore up the offense and fill the vacuum at first base. But Bonura was again converted into cash on July 22, when the Cubs came inquiring about his services. He had managed exactly three homers in three months for Washington.

Despite his modest power surge, Jimmy Bloodworth hit only .245 from the second base position, and shortstop was a trouble spot for Bucky Harris all year. The decision had been taken before the season to install Cecil Travis at third base, where his range would better suit the position, and to move Buddy Lewis to right field, where the value of his throwing arm would be optimized.

Another part of the reasoning was that Clark Griffith, at significant expense, had purchased a shortstop who he announced would be a dandy. His name was Jimmy Pofahl, and he turned out to be a dud. Pofahl reported with a throwing arm that had no zip at all. Griffith tried to get the deal he'd made with Minneapolis canceled, but Pofahl admitted he'd hurt his arm when a taxicab door had accidentally slammed shut on it. Griffith was stuck with a financial loss of serious proportions, estimated at as much as $40,000. It certainly wasn't that Pofahl was not given a chance — there really was no one else. He hit only .234, and had it not been for the oncoming war, he likely would never have played again.

Cecil Travis and Buddy Lewis remained the pillars of the organization, and despite playing new positions, hit .322 and .317 re-

spectively. George Case, moved to center field to replace the aging Sammy West, led the league in stolen bases for the second consecutive season, and hit .293. But between them, Lewis, Case, and West managed just 13 homers, matching the number Gee Walker hit by himself. West hardly played, getting just 99 official at-bats and batting .253. Buddy Myer hit .290 as the part-time second baseman and was nearing the end of the road. He closed out his career the following year by participating in just 53 games, settling on a .303 batting average for his career. In his analytical tome *The Bill James Baseball Abstract,* James compares the career of contemporary second baseman Billy Herman with Myer's. How in the world, James wonders, can one (Herman) be in the Hall of Fame, and not the other?

If the Nats were to finish near the bottom, then their young guys were going to get some experience. Finish near the bottom they did in 1940, winding up seventh with just 64 wins, saved from tenancy in the cellar by the Athletics, who lost exactly 100 times. Seventh place was the lowest Washington had finished since 1934, when the club also placed second from the bottom. The pitching was at least decent. Dutch Leonard, despite a very good 3.49 ERA, wound up 14–19 due to lack of support. Ken Chase, with a 3.23 ERA that was well over a full run lower than the league average, finished at 15–17.

The staff was also bolstered by the top rookie pitcher of the American League for 1940, who the Senators had plucked from a Class-D League, the lowest rung on the professional baseball ladder. Sid Hudson, a gangly 6'4" native of Coalfield, Tennessee, at age 25 led the Nats in wins with 17, against 16 losses, despite an ERA slightly below the league average at 4.57. This was particularly impressive in light of the fact that Hudson had struggled early, getting knocked out of the box in every one of his first seven starts. While he would never win as many again, he would enjoy a long stay with the Nats.

So would Walter Masterson, a tall (6'2" was tall by big-league standards in 1940), bespectacled 20-year-old from Philadelphia.

Masterson, who had seen some action with the big club in '39, suffered with his control, and the result on this punchless team was a 3–13 record. Another big righthander, sophomore player Joe Haynes did bring some winning ways to Washington. He won the hand of Thelma Griffith, Clark Griffith's adopted daughter. The two would be married in October '41, but by then Haynes had been out of the organization for nearly a year, sold to the White Sox following a 3–6, 6.54 output in 1940. The marriage did begin a longtime association between Haynes and the Washington Senators, but it would be many years before the old man would bring him back as a player.

Other off-season activity following the last game of 1940 involved the reacquisition of Ben Chapman, who'd performed at a .290 clip for Cleveland. But Chapman was on his way out as a big leaguer — after a 28-game looksee, the Nats would move him to the White Sox in '41. In exchange for him, the Nationals gave up lefty Joe Krakauskas, who had racked up a 1–6 mark for the 1940 Senators while permitting a ghastly 6.08 runs per nine innings. Plagued by wildness throughout his career, Krakauskas would be unable to break into a deep Cleveland rotation and his major-league career, virtually over, left a lot of early promise unfulfilled.

The year 1941 was wonderful for American League baseball. Little more than half a decade after Clark Griffith made his prophecy about night baseball and gave his personal endorsement of "the Lord's own sunshine," the lights were turned on for the first time at Griffith Stadium, on May 28, 1941. (The Nats had played their first night game nearly two years earlier, on July 6, 1939, at Philadelphia.) The Yankees were the visitors for the occasion and winners by a 6–5 count. As usual this season, it was the Yanks, and more specifically Joe DiMaggio, who were generating most of the magic. In every game New York played between May 15 and July 17, 56 of them, DiMaggio got at least one hit to set a mark yet unbroken.

The Senators did not, of course, escape the wrath of DiMaggio during this period. At Griffith Stadium on May 27, he went 4–for–5 to extend his streak to 12 straight games with a hit. On the 28th, in a night game, DiMag tripled off Sid Hudson. The Nats lost that one in a manner that was particularly heartbreaking, beaten by a pinch-hit grand slam by George Selkirk, who one day would become General Manager of the Washington Senators.

On June 29, 1941, it was against the Senators that the Yankee Clipper tied and then broke George Sisler's all-time American League record of hitting successfully in 41 consecutive games. In the first game of a doubleheader, DiMaggio doubled off Dutch Leonard in the sixth inning to tie Sisler's record, and in the second game, he singled in the seventh off big Red Anderson (who totaled 36 big-league appearances) to set a new standard. Joe D was only 2–for–9 on the day, but the Bombers still battered the Senators, 9–4 and 7–5.

Joe DiMaggio eventually broke Wee Willie Keeler's all-time mark of base hits in 44 straight games, at Yankee Stadium on July 2. The record-setter was a three-run homer off Dick Newsome of the Red Sox, and came after Joltin' Joe had been robbed of hits in his two previous at-bats that day. The skein reached 56 games, and the final hit was a long double surrendered by Joe Krakauskas. On the following day, "the streak" was halted by Krakauskas's new teammates, pitchers Al Smith and Jim Bagby, but especially by third baseman Ken Keltner, who made two sensational diving stops on DiMaggio rockets. After that game, Joltin' Joe, who, incredibly, had hit in 61 straight contests as an 18-year-old in the very tough Pacific Coast League, had safeties in 16 more games in a row. He led the league with 125 runs batted in, and the Yankees went on to their fifth World Series triumph in six years, reclaiming for the league the championship lost by the Tigers in seven games to the Cincinnati Reds in 1940.

At the time, DiMaggio's streak garnered much more media attention than another accomplishment which has since gained greater prominence. Nineteen forty-one was the year that Ted Williams hit .406, the first time the

.400 barrier had been surpassed in the league since 1923, when Harry Heilmann reached .403 for the Tigers. Bill Terry had been the last to bat .400 in the majors, posting a .401 mark in 1930. Williams' on-base percentage of .551 achieved in this season will likely stand as a record forever. But in 1941, much more was made of DiMag's streak, which, after all, had shattered a mark which had stayed on the books for 44 years. Over the entire season, however, Ted Williams' batting average was just two points lower than DiMaggio's had been during the 56-game streak.

Ted Williams was a young man who did not lack in confidence, and this quality was exemplified on September 28, when manager Joe Cronin offered him the possibility of sitting out both games of a doubleheader on the last day of the season. Ted's average stood at .39955, which would round out to an even .400. Ted's answer was to the effect that he didn't care to become known as a .400 hitter with a lousy average of .39955.

The true hero that he was (he would become one in the military sphere during World War II, and again in Korea, as a Marine flier), Williams, just 23 years old, went 6–for–8 and finished the season at .4057. The Splendid Splinter asked writers following that last game, "Ain't I the best hitter you ever saw?" Nearly 30 years later, Ted would write in his book *My Turn At Bat*, "I want people to say, 'There Goes Ted Williams, the greatest hitter who ever lived.'"

But it was neither Joe DiMaggio nor Ted Williams who led the American League in base hits in 1941. The distinction went to Cecil Travis of the Washington Senators, who managed 218 safeties. Travis placed between the Splendid Splinter and the Yankee Clipper in batting average, with .359. His 316 total bases, only 32 behind DiMaggio, were the result of seven homers, a huge improvement, and 19 triples, which placed him just behind Jeff Heath of Cleveland, who led the league in that department with 20.

The third-base experiment had ended for Travis, and his wonderful offensive year brought the 28-year-old's career batting aver-

age to .327. He was named to the Major-League All-Star team at shortstop by *The Sporting News*, the first Washington player to be named among the elite since Joe Cronin had been designated, at the same position, seven years before. Despite Travis's presence, the Senators' infield still looked makeshift. Jimmy Bloodworth led all A.L. second basemen in both put-outs and assists, and cracked seven homers. But he hit .245 for the second straight year, and had had his last chance with the Nats.

The infield corners were the real question marks. Cecil Travis's vacated spot at third eventually fell to George Archie, a 27-year-old drafted by the Senators for the purpose. Archie's big-league experience prior to 1941 amounted to all of three games. He hit .269 in 105 games, but his fielding was found wanting, and his .936 percentage, perilously close to being the worst in the league, resulted in the Senators casting him adrift near the end of the '41 season. Archie was picked up by the Browns and hit .379 for them in nine games. But the war, and a bad showing with the Browns in '46 in a brief trial, would bring his career to its conclusion.

A terrific big-league career did begin as a result of Bucky Harris's precarious infield situation in 1941, however. Mickey Vernon, fresh from his one-year exile for further apprenticeship at Jersey City, met all expectations. Vernon hit for a sparkling .299, and was right behind Cecil Travis in RBIs, with 93.

Everyone knew the Nats had a solid outfield. Buddy Lewis, unlike Travis who was back at short, did remain at the new position he'd been assigned the previous year, and was third on the club in batting, right on Vernon's heels, with .297. George Case, last year's centerfielder, was moved over to left, his third outfield position in three years. Despite his great speed, Case was erratic in the outfield, but he, more than any player in the big leagues, was responsible for bringing the art of the stolen base back to baseball. For the third year in a row, he led the league in thefts, with 33, but his average dropped 22 points to .271. Case's speed did help him score 95 runs, and to lead the league in outfield assists with 21.

It was two weeks before Christmas, 1940, when George Case found out his one-year incumbency as centerfielder for the Senators was over. The Nats on that day swapped the unpredictable Gee Walker to the Boston Red Sox for Doc Cramer, one of the best fly-chasers in the business. Cramer was going to turn 36 in July, but had tied for the league lead in hits, with 200, during the past season. Nicknamed "Doc" for his actual interest in medicine, and "Flit," after the insecticide, because he was death to fly balls, Cramer was the ultimate ping hitter who could bang out a good number of doubles each year. Fast and agile, he had missed batting .300 only twice in the past nine years. Unfortunately, he picked 1941 to do that, and slipped to .273 with Washington while leading the league in at-bats for the sixth time in his career.

On December 12, 1941, exactly one year to the day after the Nats had traded Gee Walker for him, Doc Cramer was on the move again, traded to the Tigers along with Jimmy Bloodworth for second baseman Frank Croucher and outfielder Bruce Campbell. Croucher, a .254 hitter and regular the past year with the Tigers, had 65 at-bats left in his big-league career. He would miss almost the entirety of his only season with the Senators due to a sore arm, and military service would take care of the rest.

Campbell was a journeyman outfielder whose career in the majors would last just a few more months. Less than a week before the trade, the Japanese had bombed Pearl Harbor. Nearly all able-bodied professional ballplayers (and they were nearly all able-bodied) were soon conscripted, and big-league baseball as it was previously constituted became a thing of the past in the years during which the global conflict raged on.

One always gets a good sense of how a baseball season turns out for a club by glancing at the pitchers' won-loss records. Dutch Leonard pitched just as well in 1941 as he had in '40, and turned his record around to a very tidy 18–13, with a 3.45 earned run average. Sid Hudson's ERA was 3.46, and he wound up 13–14. Ken Chase remained wild, and his horrific 6–18, 5.08 performance, bought him

a ticket out of town one day after Doc Cramer and Jimmy Bloodworth were sent packing to Detroit.

The Senators traded with the Browns in May '41, parting with subsequent Hall of Fame catcher Rick Ferrell, now 35, in exchange for Vern Kennedy, a 34-year-old right-hander who'd been a regular starter in the league since 1935. This would leave the catching up to Jake Early, who'd been the backup since the previous year. Early responded well and batted .287 with ten homers in '41, but unfortunately this would be his best year.

Following a so-so start with the Browns, Vern Kennedy was downright incompetent with Washington, winning just one and losing seven with an ERA of nearly six runs per game. The Nats' other starter besides Leonard, Hudson, and Chase, was a refugee from the Yankees named Steve Sundra who showed good control but gave up way too many hits (203 in only 168⅓ innings.) Sundra had run off a string of 11 straight victories for the Yankees in '39, but just two years later with the Nats, he posted a 9–13, 5.29 record that soon had him beating a path to baseball oblivion, sometimes also known as the roster of the St. Louis Browns.

So bad were the Brownies of this era that following the '39 season, during which they had performed at a level which earned them 43 wins and 111 losses, A.L. president Will Harridge besieged every other club in the league to "go a little socialist for their own good." Harridge meant that by sharing some baseball talent with the Browns, all clubs would be better off, as attendance figures might improve in St. Louis and at other parks in the league whenever the Brownies appeared. As a result, several teams sold players to St. Louis.

The Senators, however, could scarcely participate in this generous plan, for they were really no better than the Browns, as their 1941 record attests. The two clubs finished in a dead heat for sixth place with identical 70–84 records, a six-game improvement over the preceding season for Washington. The gap between them and the pennant winners, again the Yankees, was a full 31 games. The cellar-dwelling A's improved by a full ten games, but still finished 37 games out. While the outlook for the entire world, let alone for baseball and the Washington Senators, was bleaker than ever, the fortunes of the St. Louis Browns would soon improve dramatically.

Two days following the bombing of Pearl Harbor, the American League's number one pitcher, 23-year-old Bob Feller of the Cleveland Indians, enlisted in the navy. Throughout the 1942 season, baseball's best players were answering the call, leaving their spots to marginal players who were either being rejected for military service, or were too old to get the call from Uncle Sam. There was real doubt for a time at the beginning of 1942 as to whether major-league baseball would even be allowed to continue during wartime. Clark Griffith, a pretty good friend of President Roosevelt's, told everyone within earshot that it would.

Griff was right, and within the baseball community, the old man got a lot of credit for convincing the President of the cause. Griffith had stressed the appeal of night games, which would permit more workers to see baseball played; this was ironic coming from the Old Fox, who had previously campaigned vociferously against lights in league stadiums. On January 15, 1942, President Roosevelt gave his famous "green light" speech, reasoning that if baseball players were able to provide entertainment for 20 million of their fellow citizens involved in the war effort, then baseball as a wartime endeavor could be considered "thoroughly worthwhile."

Despite the loss of Bob Feller, it was still baseball pretty much as usual for 1942, but such was not the case for the Washington Nats. The club lost its two best players, Cecil Travis and Buddy Lewis, right away. Lewis became one of the first big-league players to join up when he enlisted in the Air Corps to become a pilot.

The war would take four years off Cecil Travis's baseball career, the years between the ages of 29 and 32. These were years that Travis could have possibly maintained or bolstered that already impressive .327 career batting average. Instead of carving a niche for himself in the hallowed Hall of Fame, Travis endured hardships overseas. His feet froze in the Battle of the Bulge, and when he finally did return, at age 31 in 1945, his skills had eroded. Cecil Travis would play another season and a half, and retire at age 34 in 1947.

Due to the absence of their two on-field leaders and an injury which kept their top pitcher out all year, the Washington Senators in 1942 experienced their worst year since 1919, winding up in seventh place at 62–89. Ace Dutch Leonard broke his leg in April on an unusual play, particularly for a pitcher, as it happened while he was sliding into first base. For the third straight year, only the A's saved the Nats from free-falling into the league basement.

Cuban Bobby Estalella, acquired from the Browns for third baseman George Archie near the end of the '41 season, did a decent job at the hot corner. Estalella's 8–65–.277 offensive numbers complemented the work of the young man at the other corner, Mickey Vernon, whose average dipped to .271, but who managed nine homers and drove in 86 runs. Vernon also stole 25 bases, placing second in the league to leftfielder George Case (who batted .320, the best average of his career), and scored 101 runs. Case's 44 stolen bases won the base-stealing crown for the fourth year in a row.

The new rightfielder for 1942, in Buddy Lewis' absence, was the fly-hawk the Nats had obtained from the Tigers in December, Bruce Campbell. He hit .278 and drove in 63 runs on just five homers. Between Campbell and Case was Stan Spence, who'd been with the Red Sox previously. On December 13, 1941, the day after the trade with the Tigers in which the Nats had surrendered Jimmy Bloodworth and Doc Cramer, Spence, along with pitcher Jack Wilson, came over from the Bosox in exchange for the hard-throwing Ken Chase, who never would get his act together, and Johnny Welaj (a good baseball name, pronounced "well-eye"), a part-time outfielder who'd hit .254 for the Nats since joining them in '39.

This would be a very good deal, for Spence was impressive enough to be selected for the midseason All-Star game. He led the league with 15 triples, and batted a cool .323, third best behind his two ex-teammates, Ted Williams and Johnny Pesky of the Red Sox. Williams won the Triple Crown but, evidence of his often bumpy relationships with some members of the media, was, to the astonishment of most fans, not selected the American League's Most Valuable Player. The honor went instead to second baseman Joe Gordon of the world champion Yankees.

The Senators were particularly weak at the middle-infield positions in 1942, as those jobs were assigned to a pair of rookies from the Southern Association. Jimmy Pofahl got another chance to take the shortstop position, which he had failed to do a couple of years earlier. His weak bat produced a .208 average and only nine extra base hits in more than half a season, and his big-league career was over at 25. The assignment was then handed to a 21-year-old from Chicago, John Sullivan, who struggled defensively and hit just .235. Despite the fact that he showed little improvement (in fact leading the league in errors and batting only .208 in '43), Sullivan would remain for another two seasons.

The second baseman the Nats had thought would replace Bloodworth, Frank Croucher, developed a sore arm and was of no use. He participated in only 26 games and military service effectively brought his baseball career to an end. The job fell to Ellis Clary, a journeyman who would have a short big-league career as a player, but a long association with the Washington Senators as a coach. Clary performed well for the time being, batting .275 in half a season as the regular second baseman.

Twenty-four-year-old Bob Repass was the other main player in the middle-infield mix. He was one of those who had escaped the vast minor-league network maintained by the St. Louis Cardinals, and had been drafted off the Columbus club by Washington. In spring training, Repass evoked visions of the second coming of Marty Marion, the great Cardinal

shortstop of the era. It soon became apparent, however, that Repass's performance on the field was more akin to something like the first coming of Marty Perez.

The young shortstop had taken to keeping fast company, hanging around with some of the veterans on the club who were prone to partying and staying out late. The main members of this group were pitcher Jack Wilson, outfielder Roy Cullenbine, obtained from the Browns in early June, and pitcher Bobo Newsom. Ah yes, Bobo was back! Bucky Harris, entrusted with a losing club for the sixth straight year, had no patience with the revelers, and wanted Clark Griffith to get rid of them all.

This was gradually done. Wilson, a 30-year-old who had once won as many as 16 with the Red Sox, was the first of the rowdy contingent to go. When he started the season 1–4 with a 6.64 ERA, he was traded to the Tigers in mid–July for a commodity the team desperately needed, a shortstop. But the shortstop in question, veteran Eric McNair, to the Nats' great consternation, would hear nothing of reporting to the lousy Senators. Clark Griffith decided to accept $5,000, less than the waiver price, just to get rid of Wilson anyway. As for Cullenbine, he batted .286 in less than three months, and was then waived to the Yankees just prior to the deadline for World Series eligibility, August 31.

Bobo Newsom returned to the Nats on March 31, 1942, as a result of Clark Griffith paying what was reported to be as high as $40,000 for his contract. Following his excellent 21–5 season in 1940, which was punctuated by his tear-jerking World Series heroics, Newsom had decidedly had an off year in '41, his ERA expanding by nearly two runs per game. He remained in this slump in '42, racking up 11–17, 4.93 figures for the Nats. Despite finishing the season in a different league, Bobo did lead the American League in strikeouts (tied), but with a modest total, even for the times, of 113. On August 30 he took his boastful, blustery personality to Brooklyn, having been sold to the Dodgers for $25,000. His value had apparently dipped by 15 grand in five months. Unfazed, Bobo sent off a telegram to Brooklyn upon hearing of the transaction. In it, he congratulated the Dodgers upon buying themselves the pennant (which, incidentally, they hadn't).

The staff workhorse in '42 was young Sid Hudson, 10–17, 4.36. The youngster Early Wynn, a 22-year-old rookie getting his first chance as a regular starter, was going through growing pains and was almost perpetually in trouble, as attest his 5.12 ERA and 10–16 won-loss record. At this point in his career, the future Hall of Famer, an intimidating type of pitcher, threw only fastballs. These three main starters for Washington constituted the principal reason why the pitching staff was the worst in the league in '42.

Not even the return of the great Walter Johnson was able to inspire Griffith's pitchers. On August 23, before a crowd of more than 69,000 souls at Yankee Stadium, the 54-year-old icon agreed to be an accessory in an event featuring the appearance of Babe Ruth, then 47, organized to raise money for the benefit of the Army-Navy Relief Fund. Johnson was to pitch to Ruth between games of a double-header, the first of which was won by the Senators. This was a much-ballyhooed event, as it was only the Babe's second appearance at Yankee Stadium since he had left the club eight years earlier. (The first time had been for Lou Gehrig's tragic 1939 farewell.)

The Big Train had promised the Babe, according to writer Tom Meany, that he would lay it in there for him, and on the fifth easy toss, the out-of-shape Bambino drove a home run into the lower stands in right field. On the next 14 pitches, Ruth could manage only a couple of deep outfield drives but then he lofted a towering fly into the upper deck. Although the ball was hit foul, the Babe rounded the bases for the adoring masses anyway, and the event raised $80,000. Walter Johnson did not mind at all that Ruth, who had hit ten homers off him during their careers, was the focal point of this day.

Those who followed the exploits of the "big three" of Hudson, Newsom, and Wynn — the pecking order in the Nats' pitching rota-tion during this season — realized they were really no better than those who were handed the ball on a less frequent basis. Venezuelan Alex Carrasquel had a second consecutive fine season, going 7–7, 3.43, in relief and as a spot starter. Sinkerballer Bill "Goober" Zuber, another righthander, improved appreciably, finishing at 9–9, 3.85. A native of Middle Amana, Iowa, Zuber was the only Amish player in all of major-league history. Walter Masterson, who like Carrasquel got 15 starts, was a disappointing 5–9, but with a very impressive 3.34 earned run average. Four of Masterson's five victories were complete-game shutouts.

The catching was once again in the capable hands of Jake Early, a fine defensive receiver who was a real asset on a ballclub, a chatterbox who loved trying to distract hitters. He usually did a running play-by-play broadcast as the game went along. Early had progressed steadily at the plate in the big leagues following his promotion from the Piedmont League, where he'd hit .316 at Charlotte in 1938. Initially groomed as the heir apparent to Rick Ferrell, he came into his own in 1941 and enjoyed his career year, but he sank to a miserable .204 in 1942. He was going to bounce back a bit in '43, but like many others, the combination of the war and advancing age would prove a devastating one-two punch.

Bucky Harris was the one who, at the end of the season, took it right on the chin. It had been an unhappy eight-year stretch for Bucky, the man who had managed this franchise's only world championship team. Of those eight years, the second, 1936, had been the only one in which the Nats had been able to boast a winning record. Bucky had grown distant and was often glum, and Benny Bengough, a coach with the club since 1940, often acted as go-between for the manager with the players. Now Clark Griffith was unhappy, and he suggested that Harris might want to manage the farm club up in Buffalo. Bucky took the hint, and was accorded the right to preserve some dignity by announcing his own resignation.

Bucky Harris would be back in the American League, and to manage a World Series champion, no less. For the time being, though, he landed on his feet, albeit with a terrible ballclub, as manager of the Philadelphia Phillies. Harris wouldn't even last the year in Philly, having inherited a team coming off a 42–109 record. He was taking on even more troubles than he could have bargained for, as we shall soon see.

Not one to break with tradition, Clark Griffith, for the ninth consecutive time, delved into the ranks of men who had played for him previously. As his new manager, he chose as reliable an employee as he had ever had, the old third baseman, Ossie Bluege. Bluege, who had last appeared in a game in '39, was a true organization man. He had coached under Harris over the past three seasons, and would one day become director of the farm system (1948–56). In 1957, he became comptroller for the Griffiths' major-league operations.

This is not to say that Bluege and the old man had not had their spats. An accountant in his spare time during his playing career, Ossie had counted some of Washington's best hotels as clients. Always eager to protect his own interests, Griffith was afraid that straining over figures would ruin his third baseman's batting eye and had ordered Bluege to let go of his side job. Bluege replied in no uncertain terms that considering what he made as a baseball player, he had to have two jobs.

Clark Griffith's eldest nephew, Calvin, got his first taste of a front-office job in 1942, when he was named vice-president of the ballclub. Calvin and his sister Thelma had been taken in by Clark Griffith when they were very young. Their parents, the Robertsons, were having a difficult time making ends meet with a houseful of children. Thelma, of course, eventually married Joe Haynes, the ex–Senator righthander now with the White Sox. Joe Cronin's wife, Mildred, was another one of Calvin's sisters. While he did eventually change his name of Calvin Griffith Robertson to Calvin Robertson Griffith, Calvin never was legally adopted by the old man. The boy was too old by the time Clark had applied.

One of Calvin's brothers, Sherrard (Sherry) Robertson, was a professional ballplayer who appeared in 11 games with the Senators in 1940 and '41, and who would hang on until the next decade as a reserve outfielder. Like Calvin, brothers Sherry, Jimmy and Billy would eventually become administrators in their uncle's baseball enterprise.

In 1943, the war, which had quickly claimed casualties in the Senators' lineup, caught up to the rest of the league. While the rosters of most teams were being depleted, Clark Griffith, who was politically well-connected and met regularly for dinner with military draft officials in Washington, was able to stem the damage to his team by obtaining temporary deferrals for his players. Griff would further supplement his available pool of players with a number of Cubans and other Latin Americans, who were not draft-eligible until late 1944. Starting this season, training camps were no longer being held at the customary warm-weather sites in Florida and California. Travel requirements would have to be curtailed because of the war, and the Senators would train at nearby College Park, Maryland, home of the University of Maryland.

Ossie Bluege took what looked to be, at the beginning of the 1943 season, essentially the same ballclub to a second-place finish. The Ted Williamses, the Joe DiMaggios — those fellows were now gone too, and the Nats, once more on an even, albeit diluted, playing field, won 15 more games than they lost. This occurred despite the absence of the club's two best position players before the war, Cecil Travis and Buddy Lewis.

There never was any real pennant race in '43 — the Yankees, like the Cardinals in the National League, were runaway champions. But 13½ games out of first still represented a 26-game improvement for the Washington Senators. The Nats scored only three fewer runs than the league leaders in that category, the Yankees. They were in a three-team scramble for third-best in pitching, and this combination, despite the absence of a single .300 hitter, yielded an 84–69 won-loss record. Early Wynn, at 23, showed the first consistent signs of brilliance, amassing a record of 18–12, 2.91, while leading the league with 33 starting assignments. While Wynn had four more years left with the Senators before moving on to Cleveland and better things, this would be his best year in the capital. During the season to follow, he would slip to 8–17 despite a workmanlike 3.38 ERA.

Wynn was third in the league in innings pitched with 256⅔, but not far behind him on the staff was the knuckler, Dutch Leonard, now 34 and making a comeback from the broken ankle which had resulted in his missing nearly the entire summer of '42. Leonard completed half of his 30 starts to lead the team in that department, gave up the least number of walks per nine innings of any starter in the league (1.88), and fashioned a tidy 3.28 ERA despite an unlucky 11–13 slate for 1943.

Clark Griffith had, the previous winter, pulled a few strings designed to bolster his pitching. Some of the moves had not worked out so well, but others turned out to be remarkably insightful. Much was made of the purchase of Lefty Gomez, winner of 189 big-league games and a 6–0 World Series record (the best ever) with the great Yankees teams of the thirties. But Gomez was washed up. He made one start for Washington and got rocked. The Nats released him and he never played in the big leagues again. Another trade, though, engineered with the Yankees on January 29, paid huge and immediate dividends.

The deal probably had something to do with the fact that the Nats had let the Yankees have the troublesome Roy Cullenbine before the trade deadline passed the previous summer. The Yanks now accepted side-arming Goober Zuber, age 30, who had but 24 wins left in his sinkerball. In exchange, Washington obtained from the talent-rich Yankees 23-year-old second baseman Gerry Priddy and 25-year-old righthanded pitcher Milo Candini.

Priddy enabled the Senators to plug one of their leaks in the middle of the infield. Priddy had teamed up with Phil Rizzuto in the Yankees' farm system, and the two came up together to the big club in 1941. While Rizzuto hit .307 while playing full time, Priddy was the understudy to Joe Gordon, which he remained while with New York. Gordon

slugged 24 homers in '41, and 18 more while batting .322 and winning what may have rightfully been Ted Williams' MVP title in '42. Priddy managed a composite .248 over those two seasons with the Yankees, batting less than 200 times each year.

The Nats thought they just might have snagged a future star. A native Californian, Gerry Priddy had in the late thirties played with Babe Herman's All-Stars, a touring troupe of big leaguers who staged exhibitions against all-stars from the Negro Leagues. Charlie Biot, a black outfielder who many contended was at least Joe DiMaggio's defensive equal, recalled in old age how impressive a ballplayer Priddy was in those games. Priddy became one of the bright lights on the '43 Senators, batting .271 and driving in 62 runs. This would be his best year with the Nats, however, and he would be off to war before the start of the next season.

Following two more years with the Senators after the war, which included a miserable .214 offensive output in 1947, Priddy would enjoy fine years with the St. Louis Browns in '48 and '49, batting .296 and .290. He followed up with .277 in 1950, when he scored 104 runs for the Tigers. Later in life, Priddy got himself into serious trouble with the law. He was found guilty of attempted extortion for placing a bomb on a ship and demanding $250,000 ransom from the shipping company.

Milo Candini also experienced tragedy during his life, only he didn't wait as long as Gerry Priddy — his baseball career was a tragedy in itself. A hard thrower given to fits of wildness, Candini was a hit in the capital right off the bat. He won his first seven decisions in the big leagues and coasted to an 11–7 record with an exceedingly impressive 2.49 ERA. He would slip to 6–7, 4.11 in '44, however, and after spending all of '45 in the army, Candini was never effective again, winning a grand total of nine games in six more seasons.

There was a second find on the pitching staff in '43 which contributed to the club's tremendous rebound performance. Mickey Haefner, a 5'8", 31-year-old knuckleballing lefthander, was purchased from Minneapolis for a reported $20,000. Especially at a time when Americans were being asked to tighten their belts, this could have been considered an awful lot of money for a pitcher who had managed a record of 18–17, 4.22, in the minor leagues. But Haefner responded wonderfully, finishing the year at 11–5 with a minuscule 2.29 earned run average, which would have been good for third in the league had he pitched enough innings to qualify for the honor.

A fourth 11-game winner on the squad was fastballer Alex Carrasquel, who started and relieved and lost seven. Catcher Jake Early, always a plus defensively, experienced a resurgence with the bat, producing 60 runs while hitting .258 and earning a trip to the 1943 All-Star game. Early's output somewhat made up for Mickey Vernon's temporary developmental delay in becoming a premier offensive producer. Vernon's average dropped only three points, to .268, and he drove in 70, 16 runs fewer than in '42. Mickey was a base-stealing threat, swiping 24, fifth best in the league. The previous season, he had placed second to George Case, who in '43 pilfered 61 bases, his career high and a mark which led the league for the fifth straight year. Military duty, however, would keep Mickey Vernon completely out of the picture for the next two years.

George Case was the Washington player of the year. His .294 average placed him fifth in the A.L. in a season in which the league batting average as a whole slipped eight points to .249, the lowest ebb since 1917. With wartime attendance sagging during the season, Case was offered $1,000 by Clark Griffith to circle the bases as fast as he could. The object of the pregame promotion was to see if Case could beat the documented record of 13.8 seconds set by Hans Lobert (National League third baseman, 1903–17). He did, by three-tenths of a second. Case also frequently ran races for promotional purposes during the war years, as many as five in a season according to his own estimate. The only man who beat him was track star Jesse Owens.

Centerfielder Stan Spence had a second successive productive year for the Nats in 1943, driving in 88 runs, although his average tumbled an appalling 56 points to .267. The third regular outfielder was "Indian Bob" Johnson, a former star with the A's who had passed his 36th birthday in November, and whose home run production had slipped from 31 in 1940 to 13 in '42. Johnson put up 7–63–.265 numbers and was sold to Boston in December. With the Red Sox, Indian Bob's production shot up to 17–106–.324 in 1944, his last good season.

The Nats also traded Bobby Estalella, who hit .298 and .299 for the A's in '44 and '45, but after that, the 34-year-old's career was practically over. Suspended for three years for having jumped to the Mexican League, he would bat only 20 more times in the majors. Shortstop Johnny Sullivan batted only .208 but was adequate defensively, and so would not be replaced. To Sullivan's credit, he would have a much better season the following year.

The third baseman for most of '43 was Ellis Clary. On April 24, Clary led off a game with a double off Spud Chandler of the Yankees. It was the last hit the Nats got all day off Chandler, who went on to have the year of his life, an incredible 20–4, 1.64 performance which won him Most Valuable Player honors. Chandler was the first American League pitcher to capture the M.V.P. award since its inaugural season of 1931, when the Baseball Writers of America had established it permanently and Lefty Grove was its first recipient.

Ellis Clary had been brought up to the big leagues by Clark Griffith during the previous season strictly because of on his spirit and combativeness. He had managed only .255 in parts of two seasons with Chattanooga of the Southern Association, which wasn't even at the highest level of minor-league baseball. Stories of Clary's toughness abound. One time in the minors, when two consecutive pitches came too close to his head, he went up to the mound and knocked the pitcher out cold. On another occasion, he took care of a fan who had been giving the business to his teammates (who had been sitting in a parked bus), but the punch on the heckler's nose landed him in jail. When Clary came up to the majors, Birdie Tebbetts, the Detroit Tigers' catcher, predicted that Clary would get hit in the head if he kept crowding the plate and sticking his neck over it.

Sure enough, this happened, and Clary was down for about half a minute. Then, he got up as if unhurt and pranced to first base. When asked how he had been able to recover so quickly, Clary replied that he had just wanted to make sure the umpire realized he'd been hit. Back in the minors, he had been beaned and had brushed it off. Seeing Clary's undisturbed reaction, the umpire had thought he hadn't been hit at all, and had ruled the ball had come into contact with his bat instead.

Ellis Clary didn't last the season. On August 18, 1943, he was packaged with a big 28-year-old pitcher, Ox Miller, whose career in the bigs would be inconsequential, and a hefty load of cash, said to be $35,000, in a deal with the Browns. The exchange brought to Washington another knuckleball pitcher, Johnny Niggeling, and a third baseman to take Clary's spot, Harlond Clift. Clary would not be forgotten by the Griffith family, however. In the midfifties, he was brought back as manager of the Charlotte, N.C., farm club, and then as coach with the big club for four years.

Harlond Clift was one of the best third basemen in the league, but at age 30 his power numbers had already diminished significantly. A member of the Browns since '34, Clift would unfortunately miss out on the Brownies' only pennant in the next year, 1944. After batting just .232 in 105 games for St. Louis, Clift got off on the right foot with the Nats, hitting at a .300 clip in his first eight games before coming down with the mumps. He caught them from his daughter, while visiting his family in St. Louis, and it ended his season. That winter, he was riding a horse on his farm when he was thrown onto his right shoulder. As a result, Clift played very little in '44, and after the following year faded out of the picture altogether.

Johnny Niggeling, the pitcher acquired

with Clift from the Browns, was by now 40 years old. He was 35 when he'd first made it to the majors, and had enjoyed a stellar 15–11, 2.66 season with the improving Browns in '42. With the Senators, he won four of his six outings and finished 10–10, 2.59 for the season. Niggeling would be an important contributor again in '44 (10–8, 2.32). He was moved to the Red Sox in '46, where his career petered out. Niggeling's life ended in suicide at age 60 in 1963.

There were several highlights to a highly successful 1943 season for the Washington Senators. On May 21, the Nats were shut out by the White Sox, 1–0, at Griffith Stadium, in just one hour, 29 minutes. This was the quickest nine-inning game ever in American League history. In June, Buddy Lewis, who had flown dozens of dangerous missions during the war, transported some VIPs to Washington and dropped by the stadium to visit with the boys before the start of a doubleheader. Lewis promised his teammates he'd be flying over the flagpole in center field before the end of the day. Sure enough, later on in the afternoon, a low-flying DC-3, wings wiggling, came zooming down from above the stands. John Kelly Lewis would not be back with the Senators before the end of the war, and at age 25 his best baseball years were already all behind him.

One old Senator who came back much more frequently was the irrepressible Bobo Newsom, who was around for his third tour of duty. Washington was Bobo's third team in 1943. This in no way posed a hindrance to Newsom's supreme self-confidence, which no doubt contributed to his resilience. Here was the man who had won 20 or more three years in a row but who, before it all ended, would lead his league four times in losses. Bobo is one of only two pitchers in history to win over 200 games in the big leagues, but to lose even more often than he won (final numbers: 211–222).

Newsom had been with the Dodgers until mid-July, and pitched well. However, he unwisely became embroiled in a player rebellion and was traded to the Browns, a team he was joining for the second time, for a couple of nondescript pitchers. Bobo went 1–6 for St. Louis, and his sale to Washington followed on August 31, exactly one year and one day after Clark Griffith had sold him to Brooklyn for $25,000. Bobo went 3–3 and was traded to the Philadelphia A's a couple of weeks before Christmas in return for yet another knuckleballer, Roger Wolff. The Senators thus became armed with pitchers who would compose baseball's first, and last, all-knuckleballer starting staff— Haeffner, Leonard, Niggeling, and Wolff!

Bucky Harris's stay at the helm of the Phillies did not last long. The worst club in baseball the previous year was much improved under him, but at 40–53, the Phillies' owner, lumber baron William D. Cox, fired him. The players threatened to go on strike over the dismissal, but Harris appealed to them to keep playing. He was replaced by Freddie Fitzsimmons, the same Fat Freddie who had taken the Giants' only loss to the Senators in the World Series ten years before. While Bucky Harris did help keep the Phillies on the field in the aftermath of his firing, he went after William Cox's jugular. He told newspaper reporters that Cox, on a regular basis, had been placing bets on his team to win games. Commissioner Kenesaw Mountain Landis launched an immediate investigation.

Four months after Harris's dismissal, William Cox admitted during a radio interview that he had indeed made bets of a small and sentimental nature, involving things like dinners, hats, and cigars, before he'd been made aware of the rules forbidding them. Judge Landis's iron hand clamped down on Cox— the Phils' owner was banned from baseball for life for his trespasses. On the very day of the expulsion, November 23, 1943, the Phillies were sold to Robert R. M. Carpenter, Sr., chairman of the board of DuPont, for $400,000. This purchase, resulting from Bucky Harris's intervention, began a long association between the Carpenters and the Philadelphia Phillies. Robert Carpenter, Jr. was immediately installed as board chairman, the position he held until he passed the torch on to his son Ruly following the 1972 baseball season. As for the man who had managed Washington's one-and-only world championship club, the baseball world had not heard the last of him.

For the 1944 season, Clark Griffith's luck with the draft board had run out. First baseman Mickey Vernon, second baseman Gerry Priddy, and catcher Jack Early were all lost to the war effort. Al Evans, an adequate backup receiver, was also in service. Rick Ferrell was brought back after a three-year absence and performed creditably, batting .277 as a 38-year-old following his acquisition from the Browns in a minor trade. Ferrell's backup was Mike Guerra of Havana, an old rookie at 31, who hit .281 in 75 games. Third baseman Harlond Clift was unavailable due to his winter horseriding accident, and veteran outfielder Bob Johnson had been unwisely sold to the Red Sox. For the first time in 35 years, and for the very first time under Clark Griffith's leadership, the Senators fulfilled the prophecy of being "last in the American League."

Home run production was down by a third in the American League from ten years before. The Nats were found particularly wanting in this area. Stan Spence was the club's offensive bulwark in 1944— his 18 homers were three more than the rest of the club's combined. Spence tied for third in the league in roundtrippers, and his 100 RBIs were fourth best. He placed fifth in the batting race with .316. Joe Kuhel, now 38 and back following a six-year absence, was purchased from the White Sox to play first base and hit .278.

All 4–Fs, players rejected by Uncle Sam because of physical shortcomings, were now a valuable commodity in baseball, and so were Clark Griffith's Cubans. In the spring of 1944, Griff had a dozen of them at training camp. Of the group, only 28-year-old rookie third baseman Gil Torres would play regularly, batting .267 with 58 ribbies, but without a single home run. Johnny Sullivan was once again the shortstop and, as mentioned a little earlier, improved offensively, batting .251. Sullivan, however, led the league's shortstops with an appalling 50 errors.

Gerry Priddy was replaced at second by George Myatt, a Giants farmhand with the reputation of possessing an erratic arm and a weak bat. Myatt indeed was one of the worst in the league at fielding his position, but was somewhat of a revelation offensively, batting .284. He also stole 26 bases, third best in the league, but had no homers — in fact, the entire infield had four homers the entire year, all by Joe Kuhel.

Cuban Roberto Ortiz finally got a shot at regular play. He was one of only three Cubans, along with Torres and Guerra, among the 12 at training camp who stuck with the club. Ortiz appeared in the Senators' outfield in 80 games but did not do much with the opportunity (his one legitimate shot as it would turn out), batting .253 with only five homers.

At midseason, the Selective Service came down with a ruling that would be very detrimental to the Senators — all Cubans then in the U.S. would have to register for the military draft. Torres, Guerra, and Ortiz quickly beat a path back to Cuba, where they would remain temporarily, leaving Clark Griffith desperately strapped for players. So desperate was he that he signed Eddie Boland, who'd had brief flings with the Philadelphia Phillies ten years earlier. Boland had been playing baseball for the N.Y.C. Sanitation Department when he came calling for a tryout, but he didn't do too badly, posting a .271 bat mark in 19 games.

At age 28, leftfielder George Case's string of five consecutive seasons leading the league in stolen bases was broken. The wear and tear incurred from his rambunctious style of play was taking its toll, and he missed 35 games. His runs scored fell from 102 to 63, and his batting average took a tumble from .294 in '43 to .249. Case swiped 49 bases and finished second to Snuffy Stirnweiss, sophomore shortstop of the New York Yankees, who also led the league in hits, runs scored, and triples, as well as in putouts, assists, and fielding average for second basemen. Despite Stirnweiss's contributions, the Yankees, an unrecognizable group of ragamuffins, fell to third place. By now, all teams were composed primarily of "has-beens, never-wases, and grass-green rookies."

While the Nats were never out of the second division following the early weeks of the '44 season, the St. Louis Browns, saddled with the same reputation as the Senators, but much more justifiably so, took advantage of the wartime disarray to capture the first pennant in their history. Managed by ex–Washington catcher Luke Sewell, St. Louis was no longer "First in shoes, first in booze, and last in the American League," but, finally, first in the American League. St. Louis was also first in the National League in 1944. For the N.L.'s Cardinals, this was hardly a new trend — the Redbirds were taking their third straight pennant. For the Brownies, though, first place was an entirely unfamiliar perch. They had finished dead last on six occasions since the Senators had last done so back in 1909, and they had wound up seventh on seven other occasions during that 34-year period.

The Senators and the Browns had a feud going during the 1944 season. Its origins could probably be traced to a July game in which George Case was hit by a pitched ball. Case went to the mound to retaliate and slugged it out with pitcher Nelson Potter. Later, the Nats' Roger Wolff, who would end up 4-15 this season with a pathetic 4.99 ERA, hit Browns shortstop Junior Stephens on the leg with a pitch. St. Louis manager Luke Sewell, the old Senators catcher, yelled at the opposition bench that Washington's "lousy eighth-place club is always trying to cause trouble."

Matters were brought to a head in St. Louis later in the season. The Browns' third-string catcher, Tom Turner, was heckling the Senators' Cubans unmercifully. Mike Guerra told Turner to shut up, only to have his ears assailed with another unsavory epithet. "I fight for you," declared big Roberto Ortiz, who took off for the Browns' bench, bat in hand. No one came to Turner's aid, as the catcher was not popular with his teammates. Ortiz came away with the decision, but also with a broken thumb, so, as in the pennant race, the Senators were the big losers. A long-standing friendship between Ossie Bluege and Luke Sewell, who had been roommates on the last pennant winner in Washington, came to an end. Bluege warned Sewell: "Lay off my Cubans, or you and I are going to fight."

The pennant race involving the Browns and the Detroit Tigers did go right down to the wire. Ironically, it was the Senators who enabled St. Louis to win it all. The Nats' last game of the season was a very important one. With the Tigers and Browns in a dead heat on the very last day, Washington's starter, Dutch Leonard, reported that he got a $10,000 bribe from an anonymous telephone caller to lose the game on purpose.

Leonard, who along with Mickey Haefner (12–15, 3.04) was the Nats' best pitcher this season, chose the high road and knocked off the Tigers, 4-1, to even his season record at 14–14, with a 3.06 ERA. Stan Spence, who had murdered the Browns' pitching all year, ironically won the pennant for St. Louis with his two-run homer. Leonard, author of a four hitter, said after the game that he had considered the bribe to be a hoax, anyway. The Browns were unable to parlay their one and only pennant into a world championship. They lost the all–St. Louis World Series (the last World Series involving two teams from the same city before the 2000 classic) in six games to the Cardinals.

In mid–March, 1945, Clark Griffith received a phone call from soon-to-be U.S. Secretary of War, Robert Patterson. Patterson had recently asked to be introduced to some ex-prisoners of war, and one of those he met had told him that he intended to pursue a career in major-league baseball. Patterson wanted to know if Clark Griffith would be willing to help this man achieve his goal. The old man no doubt saw the great publicity value of such a story. Griff would have no problem at all with the new man coming out for a tryout, as soon as he wanted to — after he got his new leg!

The amputee in question was Robert Earl "Bert" Shepard, a 24-year-old fighter pilot from Dana, Indiana, who'd had his right foot blown off while flying a bombing mission over Berlin on May 21, 1944. Shepard, a minor-league pitcher before the war, had originally taught himself how to pitch in 1938, as an 18-

year-old, by studying photos in *Life* magazine depicting the delivery of Cincinnati's John Vander Meer, who had pitched his two consecutive no-hitters that summer. Shepard had been squeezed out of a job because of the war and the resultant shrinkage of the minor leagues. Rejected following stints with the White Sox and Athletics organizations, he'd still been looking for a place to play at the time he was drafted, in May 1942. He had been at Walter Reed Hospital in Washington to get fitted for an artificial leg when he met Robert Patterson.

Shepard was dead serious about resuming his career, and here, because of his amputation, he was being offered the opportunity to do so. He showed up at training camp a mere four days after being fitted with the artificial limb, and he threw very hard. For the newsreel cameras, he also demonstrated that he could field bunts. Because he threw lefthanded, Shepard had to rely less on his missing leg, as a pitcher of course throws off his back foot. On one occasion later in the summer, when the Bert Shepard story was still unknown to the public, fans at Boston's Fenway Park were in utter shock when they saw the batting-practice pitcher's foot dangling from his leg. The artificial limb had broken. Some of the players were bent over laughing, but those among the crowd who'd been paying attention were aghast.

Clark Griffith was impressed with what Shepard could do on the ballfield, and saw what a great opportunity it was to have himself and his ballclub associated with a morale-boosting drama at a time when patriotism was surely running at an all-time high. Shepard had become the club's only lefthanded batting-practice pitcher. When Griff decided to give him a pitching assignment, however, Shepard was nowhere to be found. Larry MacPhail, soon to become General Manager of the Yankees, had lured him to Atlantic City to work out with the Yankees in front of war amputees hospitalized there. If the Senators didn't sign him, then the Yankees would, MacPhail promised. Clark Griffith was enraged by this turn of events, and it took the future Secretary of War to calm him down. Griff signed Bert Shepard to a coaching contract and, upon doing so, made a public statement to the effect that Shepard was a symbol of courage for the youth of America, and that he carried the same spirit onto the baseball field that he had into combat.

Bert Shepard did not get a chance to carry that spirit into actual big-league combat throughout most of the summer. This was no doubt primarily due to the fact that the Washington Senators had done another complete about-face. The roller-coaster ride that had seen them sink to last place from second spot the previous year had now reversed. One of the reasons was that the Old Fox had been living up to his nickname. Once the furthest thing from a proponent of night baseball, Griffith had since come around and had wheedled out of the American League the right to stage 21 night games per season, seven more than any other team was allowed. Griff won approval because of Washington's peculiar situation, in that wartime work was being done exclusively during daytime hours.

The concept certainly suited Griffith's ballclub, which had a starting staff of knuckleballers whose assortment of flutterballs would become that much more difficult to hit. Batters would be swatting at butterflies while depending on relatively poor illumination. The brightest light on the ballclub was Roger Wolff, who got himself turned around and won 20 games while losing just 10. The Senators had the league's best pitching staff in 1945. The club's league-best ERA was 2.92. Wolff's 2.12 was third best in the league, and he placed in the top three in fewest hits, and also fewest walks allowed, per nine innings.

The customary ace of the staff, southpaw Dutch Leonard, by now a 36-year-old knuckler, enjoyed an outstanding season at 17–7, 2.13. Mickey Haefner, the other starting lefty, posted a decent 16–14, 3.47. The record of John Niggeling, the last member of the knuckleball quartet, would seem to indicate that he had a bit of hard luck, as he finished at 7–12, 3.16.

There was one revelation on the pitching staff as well, in the form of 5'7" Italian-born Marino Pieretti, who wound up 14–13, 3.32, in what for him would be a banner season. Pieretti worked in a slaughterhouse in the off season, and it was said that he actually killed cattle with a baseball bat. It was he who would eventually be slaughtered — his career as a big-league pitcher would go the way of many wartime players. Pieretti would manage to stick around for five years following the return of the big boys after the war, but his best season would be 8–12, 5.47, for the Senators and White Sox in 1948.

The Nats were hardly contenders throughout the early part of the 1945 season, and nearly two weeks into June were firmly ensconced in the depths of seventh place. The club got a terrific boost when Buddy Lewis returned to the club following an absence of 3½ years. The fighter pilot played like a trooper and hit an amazing .333 over the second half of the season. Along with Lewis, outfielder George "Bingo" Binks helped make up for the loss of last year's best player, Stan Spence, who was now in service. Binks was another typical player of the era, getting his first crack at the big leagues at age 30. He had speed, hit .278, and drove in 81 runs to lead the team.

The other top run producer was Joe Kuhel, the old standby who at age 39 drove in 75 and hit .285. Third baseman Harlond Clift, playing out the string, paced the Senators with a modest eight homers, but batted .211 and would not play again. Joe Kuhel had only two homers, but then again the club managed only 27 for the year, which wasn't even lowest in the league (the distinction belonged to the White Sox, who had 22). Even more appalling, one of Kuhel's two roundtrippers was the Nats' only one at home all season. The ball didn't even leave the expansive stadium, as it was an inside-the-park job off Bob Muncrief of the Browns on September 7. For the record, the opposition got six home runs at Griffith Stadium in '45, with Detroit's Rudy York connecting for two.

Joe Kuhel also provided the type of sure-handedness expected from the line of first sackers in place on the club since Joe Judge arrived on the scene in 1916 (and for that matter, Chick Gandil before him). Judge made a return to the Senators in 1945 and '46 to serve as coach. This was his only hiatus from a position at Georgetown University, where he was coach during all other years from 1937 until 1958.

Like Kuhel, Lewis, and Binks, George Case was another key factor in '45, batting .291 with 30 stolen bases. Also stealing 30 bases was second baseman George "Stud" Myatt, who delivered a second consecutive strong season, with .296, and 81 runs scored, right up there among the league leaders. Myatt had earned his nickname in the minors when, as a young player, he'd been the clubhouse caddy, or "boy friday" of ex-big-leaguer Smead Jolley, whose nickname was "Big Stud." Following the war, Stud Myatt would bat a grand total of 41 times in the major leagues.

By mid–July the club had been red-hot for a month and had vaulted into second place, within striking distance of the Detroit Tigers. With the pressure on in August, the Nats swept doubleheaders against the Red Sox and A's. Ossie Bluege was using a short pitching staff, and it was against this backdrop on August 4, 1945, during the second game of a doubleheader at Griffith Stadium, that Bert Shepard got to realize his dream of pitching in the big leagues. Shepard, signed as a coach, had been placed on the active roster earlier in the summer, before the Nats made their move in the standings, following an impressive outing in an exhibition game versus the Brooklyn Dodgers. On that occasion, he had surrendered just one hit in three innings before getting rattled by four consecutive singles which had produced two runs. He left the game with the lead and was declared the winner.

In the second game of the August 4 twin bill, the Senators were getting rocked. A rookie named Joe "Fire" Cleary, making his big-league debut, was brought in to douse the fire. Instead, it was Cleary who was getting torched. He got one man out while allowing five hits and three walks. Because he would never participate in a big-league game again,

Joe Cleary would take away, from this solitary experience, a career earned run mark of 189 runs per game, an all-time record for any pitcher who got at least one man out, and who has, therefore, an earned run average better than infinity.

Knowing the game was already lost, manager Ossie Bluege called upon Bert Shepard, about to become a hero in the eyes of the American public. There had been cases similar to his in recent history. Monty Stratton had won 15 games in both 1937 and 1938 before shooting himself in the right knee in a hunting accident in November 1938. Stratton's leg was amputated the next day. When the White Sox sponsored a charity contest in 1939, Stratton valiantly took to the mound to show the fans that he could still throw. It was apparent, however, that he had a good deal of trouble transferring his weight onto his artificial limb. Stratton never did pitch in the majors again, but in 1946 won 18 games in the lowly East Texas League. By 1949, his would be a household name, as his life story was fictionalized that year in a hit Hollywood movie, *The Stratton Story,* starring Jimmy Stewart and June Allyson.

Baseball fans all across America were also familiar with the name Pete Gray, a one-armed outfielder with the St. Louis Browns in 1945. A natural righthander, Gray, born Peter Wyshner, was a truly gifted athlete who had lost his right arm in a childhood accident. He learned to throw and bat from the opposite side and became a star at the semipro level in the coal towns of his native Pennsylvania. Gray opted for professional ball at age 25 in 1942, and batted .381 in 42 games at Three Rivers of the Canadian-American League. At a higher level the following year, he hit .289 in a full year at Memphis. In '44, he caught everyone's eye by batting .333 with five home runs and stealing 68 bases, tying a Southern Association record. The one-armed man was named Most Valuable Player. In the major leagues, Gray was a little overmatched, but still hit .218, better than a lot of two-armed competitors. In one particularly stirring game at Yankee Stadium in May, he rapped out four hits, scored twice, and drove in two.

So the world at large was ready for Bert Shepard, but was Bert Shepard ready for the big leagues? He had been waiting for the opportunity for a month, and he felt confident. The first batter he faced was a young left-handed hitter, George "Catfish" Metkovich. The count went to three and two, and then Shepard struck Metkovich out on a waist-high fastball. That was the third out. Bert Shepard had struck out the first batter to face him in the major leagues, and pridefully strode off the mound basking in the mad applause of the Griffith Stadium faithful.

There's more. Shepard pitched another five innings, completing the game. He allowed only three hits and a walk, struck out two, and threw out two batters who hit ground balls back to the mound. It was a stellar performance, but with the club on its ascendancy in the standings, Ossie Bluege would not see fit to use him again. A mere 11 days following these heroics, World War II ended. Like Joe Cleary, Bert Shepard would never pitch in the big leagues again. But unlike Cleary, he would leave the scene with a very attractive 1.69 ERA. Shepard pitched professionally, often as a sideshow act as late as 1955, and then became an outstanding golfer, winning the National Amputee golf championship in both 1968 and 1971.

The 1945 pennant race remained a close one through mid–September when, with a half-game lead, the first-place Tigers arrived in Washington for a five-game series. The Tigers won three of the first four, with Roger Wolff beating Tiger ace and eventual MVP Hal Newhouser, 3–2, for the lone Nat triumph. Things looked grim indeed as the Tigers surged to a 5–0 lead in the final contest. The Senators then scored 12 straight runs, and escaped the series trailing the Tigers by only a game and a half.

On September 23, in another key game, Walt Masterson, who'd just resumed pitching following his recent return from service, was toiling in a critical situation. It was the 12th inning of a tie game with the Philadelphia A's at Shibe Park. During the previous half-inning, outfielder Sam Chapman of the A's had asked for a delay in order to call for his sunglasses, as the late-afternoon sun had become very bothersome. Centerfielder Bingo Binks of the Senators failed to take the hint. With two out and no one on, Ernie Kish of the A's lifted a lazy pop fly toward Binks. Binks, sans sunglasses, nearly got bonked on the coconut by the ball. He didn't catch it, thereby incurring the wrath of his teammates, some of whom threatened to vote to cut his share of what everyone would earn for finishing in second place.

Finish second they did, and in the end the flyball lost in the sun could have cost the Senators the chance of playing the Tigers to break a dead heat. The season came to a halt in a particularly anti-climactic fashion. Because Clark Griffith never would have guessed that his Nats would be contenders at this late stage in the season, he had rented Griffith Stadium to the Washington football team for a week. To make the deal work, he had consented to some extra doubleheaders for his baseball team earlier in the month. This meant that the Senators had finished their schedule when the Tigers still had four games remaining on theirs. The quirky scheduling had been particularly hard, needless to say, on the Nats' pitching arms.

The players literally hung around Griffith Stadium with their bags packed. The suspense lasted until the third game of the Tigers' four-game set versus the St. Louis Browns. Word came from St. Louis that Hank Greenberg, just out of the army, had hit a grand-slam home run to win the game. The dream was over — there would be no play-offs. For the record, the Nats were 87–67 in 1945, a mere 1½ games behind the Tigers, an unbelievable turnaround from their last-place finish the previous year. *The Sporting News* named Ossie Bluege "Major League Manager of the Year."

With the war now ended, the nation's capital was a wonderful place for a baseball team in 1946. The immediate economic boom resulted in the Senators drawing a million fans to Griffith Stadium for the one and only time. Within ten years, however, drawing even half a million would be unrealistic. Many of the people attending Senators' games in the years to come would be out-of-towners either living in Washington because of their involvement in some facet of government work, or tourists passing through. Because of that, and in some measure also because of the nature of future Washington ballclubs, the crowd was just as liable to root for the opposition as for the home team, or to not show up at all.

A wonderful promotion was held at Griffith Stadium on August 20, 1946, prior to a game with the Cleveland Indians. The U.S. Army's "Sky Screen Chronograph" was brought in to clock Bob Feller's fastball. This machine was deemed accurate to one ten-thousandth of a second. Feller's hard one was measured at 98.6 miles per hour, shattering the previous known record established by Atley Donald of the Yankees, who'd been clocked at 94 mph.

A couple of months earlier, Clark Griffith had been involved in proceedings that were much more elaborate, and certainly closer to his heart. The largest class ever — 11 new members — were inducted into the Baseball Hall of Fame on June 13, and he was among that number. It was the old man's finest hour since becoming a professional player back in 1888.

Before the '46 season even began, the Senators had missed a chance of acquiring the services of a man whose fame, on another stage, would eclipse that of even Clark Griffith. He was a skinny 20-year-old pitcher from Cuba whom scout Joe Cambria had wanted to bring to Griff's attention. The youngster was not signed and returned home to Cuba. Eventually, he became a star at Belen College and the University of Havana, and the New York Giants would think enough of his curveball to offer him a $5,000 signing bonus. The youngster turned the Giants down, opting to pursue a law degree. After that, he became a leader in Cuba's revolutionary movement. His name — Fidel Castro.

While the Senators dropped to fourth, and below .500 at 76–78, the 1946 season produced the club's first batting champion in 11 years. Mickey Vernon joined the select company of Delahanty, Goslin, and Myer, by staving off the challenge of Ted Williams of Boston, who had a phenomenal .342–38–123 campaign. Williams' performance very closely duplicated the results of his last season, before the war had interrupted his career, four years before. In fact, Williams, with one swing of the bat, showed very early in the season, on April 16 at Griffith Stadium, that he had lost none of his great power despite an absence of three full years. On the other hand, Mickey Vernon was in the .380s at midseason and, while certainly not a hitter of Williams' magnitude, maintained a steady pace thereafter, aided by his speed and ability to hit to all fields.

Vernon was the best performer in the all-new 1946 infield. Second sacker Gerry Priddy and shortstop Cecil Travis were also back from military service, but the pair hit just .254 and .252 respectively. Travis was but a shadow of his former self because of his slow feet. After batting just .216 in half a season in '47, he retired for good as a player shortly after his 34th birthday. A scout for the Senators from 1948 until 1955, he then left the game to devote his energies to raising cattle in his native Georgia.

The third baseman on the '46 club, most of the time, was Billy Hitchcock, a 30-year-old who hadn't played in the big leagues since his rookie 1942 season, when he'd hit .211 for the Tigers. Hitchcock improved to .212 for the Nats in '46, and would understandably be sold to the Browns before the beginning of the following season.

The Senators hit only 60 homers all year. By contrast, Hank Greenberg slugged 44 all by himself to lead the league in that respect. Clark Griffith had tried to rectify the obvious power shortage following the '45 campaign when he parted with George Case (who had enjoyed one of his better years) in exchange for Cleveland slugger Jeff Heath. Heath hit just four homers in 48 games before being dumped in a deal with the Browns at the trading deadline which brought over Joe Grace, who batted .302 for the Nats as the starting leftfielder during the second half of the season.

As for George Case, he had his last hurrah when, upon his return to Washington, he was asked to participate in a crowd-drawing promotion dreamed up by Clark Griffith. The Senators had a rookie named Gil Coan whom they'd promoted from their Chattanooga farmclub. There, in 1945, he had led the Southern Association in just about every offensive category, including hits, doubles, triples, home runs, and batting average (.372). Coan was also now being touted as the fastest man in the American League. In a promotional race at Griffith Stadium, George Case put an end to that talk by beating coan. In 59 games, Coan would bat just .209. While he would have a couple of good seasons for the Nats later on, Coan's career would never take off as expected. Buddy Lewis and Stan Spence were the other outfielders, and they had themselves good seasons in '46, both batting .292. Spence had 16 homers and 87 ribbies to lead the club in both categories. Rightfielder Lewis led all players at his position with 16 assists, and Spence had 15 in center field.

The chief impediment to any success for the Senators in 1946 was the pitching staff, handled for the most part by Al Evans who, in his seventh year with the club, finally got the bulk of the chores behind the plate and hit .254. Little Mickey Haefner, the lefty, was the Nats' most consistent pitcher, winding up at 14–11, 2.85. It was Haefner's best season since his outstanding '43 rookie campaign and, as it would turn out, his last really solid year in the big leagues.

The team's other top pitcher this season was no stranger to the capital baseball scene, seeing he was returning to it for the fourth time. Following a 3–5 start during which he pitched pretty well for the A's, Bobo Newsom talked Connie Mack into giving him his release. Bobo preferred Washington and knew that Clark Griffith would have a place for him. His old pinochle partner, it was said, would always be able to win back from Bobo whatever it was that he was paying him to play baseball. Bobo went 11–8 for the Nats with a highly respectable 2.78 ERA the rest of the way.

Dutch Leonard chalked up a 10–10 mark and was sold to the Phillies at the end of the season, ending his stellar nine-year stay in the capital. The other starters, Ray Scarborough and Sid Hudson, were 7–11 and 8–11 respectively. The club's third knuckleballer besides Haefner and Leonard, Roger Wolff, had no luck and won just five and lost eight despite a 2.58 ERA. Early Wynn, who'd skipped a year for military duty, came back on time to start 12 ballgames and responded well, finishing at 8–5, 3.11. Walter Masterson, the dark-spectacled hurler who had done so well at the tail end of the previous season, was a disappointment at 5–6, 6.01. This nucleus of pitchers, minus Leonard and Wolff, would be around again for 1947.

Walter Johnson, however, would not. A pall fell on the baseball community and on the whole country when it was learned on December 10, 1946, that Johnson had died at age 59. In the spring, the Big Train had experienced some numbness in his left arm. A brain tumor was discovered, and its ravages were quick and deadly. Walter spent the period until his death drifting in and out of prolonged comas. The man many say epitomized the qualities of modesty, dedication, and moderation, left behind two daughters, three sons, and his mother. Clark Griffith brought to the funeral flowers which he had planted in dirt taken from the pitcher's mound at Griffith Stadium.

The pallbearers at Walter Johnson's funeral included a plethora of teammates, including Muddy Ruel, Joe Judge, Sam Rice, Roger Peckinpaugh, and Clyde Milan. Clark Griffith, the fellow Hall of Famer, had been with him until the end. The Very Reverend John Suter, conducting the services in the magnificence of the Washington Cathedral, might have been speaking metaphorically of the Washington Senators (although in all likelihood, he wasn't) when he gave thanks for all that Johnson's life had brought to the world.

Author Henry W. Thomas, in his excellent biographical work *Walter Johnson* discusses in depth the question of whether Johnson was the greatest pitcher ever. For all the reasons mentioned elsewhere in this book, there is plenty of support for that contention.

When, in December 1999, a six-member panel of experts assembled by the Associated Press announced its choices for the top ten baseball players of the 20th century, only one pitcher appeared on the list — Walter Johnson.

The baseball records speak for themselves, but with the death of Walter Johnson passed a man of a depth of character as difficult to contemplate as the very source and meaning of life itself. He had been to multitudes of people what he had been to ballplayers — an eminently decent man, reserved, but with a sense of humor, gentle, kind ... and the best pitcher of his time, of any time perhaps. In our world, it is not likely there could ever be another Walter Johnson.

Ossie Bluege had a disastrous year in 1947, and, doubtless partly as cause and partly as effect, the Washington Senators suffered as well. Bluege, who as a player had been dependable and subdued, was turning snippy in the face of tremendous challenges, not the least of which involved a rumored insurrection by some of his players. The pitchers, in particular, complained of too often being deployed out of turn, a situation which had begun festering the previous fall when all those games had been bunched up in the early part of September because of the scheduling fiasco. The players also had reason to gripe when, all too frequently, the Senators would arrive in a city and discover that no hotel rooms had been booked for them. Bluege was seen as not being firm enough with old man Griffith and his irregular travel arrangements.

When the sports pages began criticizing him and adding fuel to stories of an impending revolt, Bluege took the unconventional measure of insisting that his players sign a petition. It would state that there was no shred of truth to the newspaper stories that he had lost the confidence and support of his men. Only one player wouldn't sign the petition. Gerry Priddy had been feuding with Bluege and had been bawled out by the manager in front of everyone. No use kidding ourselves, Priddy told Bluege, neither one of us likes the other. Priddy had once criticized the revered Joe McCarthy in 1942 for failing to play him

enough, which had hastened his departure from the Yankees. Priddy's batting average dropped from .254 to .214, and the animosity between him and the manager certainly shortened his stay in Washington. A big mess resulted.

Clark Griffith traded Priddy in November 1947 to the St. Louis Browns, who, from their lofty status of pennant winners three years earlier, had tumbled to the more familiar confines of last place in '47. In return for the 28-year-old Priddy, the Nats would get Johnny Berardino, 2½ years older than Priddy, who had hit .261 in the campaign just completed, roughly his career average for five full seasons. Berardino, an aspiring actor, instructed Clark Griffith to get in touch with his agent to discuss contractual terms for 1948.

Griffith blew a gasket, and so did Berardino, who, totally unimpressed with the Old Fox's negotiation tactics, told Griff to take a hike. Berardino wouldn't come to Washington, and would go into acting full time instead. (Eventually, he settled into a longtime role as Dr. Steve Hardy on television's daytime drama, *General Hospital.*) Griffith wouldn't back down. Okay, Berardino could stay with the Browns, but Washington was going to have no part of taking Gerry Priddy back. The Browns could keep him too. Griffith was that piqued by Priddy's insolence that he accepted cash for him. The fact that this left his ballclub without a competent second baseman did not seem an undue concern for the time being.

By the end of the season, manager Bluege had also fallen into disfavor with Griffith, who fired him. His five-year regime had been an up-and-down one to say the least, with two second-place finishes sandwiching a last-place season in 1944. Then came the nearly .500 '46 season. But in '47 the Nats dropped 12 more games and three more places in the standings to place seventh with a humiliating 64–90 slate.

Walter Masterson emerged as a dependable starter in '47, and placed third in the league in strikeouts while registering a 12–16, 3.13 record. Masterson started the season strongly — he blanked the White Sox in 16 innings, and posted two other early season shutouts — but did not keep up the pace. Early Wynn was not always outstanding but won 17 games (against 15 losses), his best win total since '43. Wynn was a horse, completing 22 games, and had a knack for beating the league's MVP of the past two years, lefty Hal Newhouser of Detroit, in head-to-head matchups.

Wynn was the staff stopper, extinguishing losing streaks on an almost regular basis during the course of the season. The Nats had also acknowledged his hitting prowess, and began to use him increasingly in a pinch hitting role, something they had begun doing with him in '44, when they were particularly desperate for good players. Based on his .319 hitting mark in '46, Wynn's at-bats nearly tripled and he managed a highly commendable .275. Lefty Mickey Haefner pitched well in spots, with four shutouts, which tied him for second best in the league with teammate Masterson, just one fewer than Cleveland's Bob Feller. Curiously, the seventh-place Senators got 15 shutouts from their pitchers, tying them for best in the league in that category with the second-place Tigers. Haefner wound up 10–14, and exactly matched Wynn's 3.64 ERA.

Curveballer Ray Scarborough had another disappointing year in '47 with 6–13, 3.41. Veteran Tom Ferrick, a 6'2", 220-pound reliever, had no luck at all, leading the league in relief losses, and winding up 1–7 despite a respectable 3.15 earned run average. Following a rocky 4–6, 4.09, start, Bobo Newsom hit the road again, waived to the Yankees on July 11. That was a good move for Bobo, who went 7–5, 2.80, the rest of the way and got a chance to pitch in his second World Series, his first in seven years. (He started game three and got bombed.)

Senators fans could take solace in the fact that not only could they follow Bobo Newsom in the World Series, they could also root for Bucky Harris, who had been hired to manage the Yankees for the '47 season. Harris took the Yanks from third to first and to a World Se-ries conquest over the Brooklyn Dodgers; even in victory, however, he could not escape controversy. Following the sixth game, which New York lost 8–6 at Yankee Stadium, the Yankees' co-owner and president Larry MacPhail — who had a terrible mean streak when he drank, which was frequently — berated outfielder Johnny Lindell. Lindell had been forced to come out of the game because of a cracked rib. When the Yanks won it all the following day, Harris stood up to MacPhail and barred him from the team's post-game victory celebration.

Harris's retributive action may have been the catalyst for the events that followed. At the victory dinner at New York's Biltmore Hotel that night, a seemingly crazed MacPhail threatened to punch media members if they got too close to him. He did punch his former road secretary from his days at the helm of the Dodgers. He also fired his farm director, George Weiss. Finally, he was pulled into the kitchen by Dan Topping who, like MacPhail, owned a third of the club. When the two re-emerged, Larry MacPhail announced that he was resigning as president, treasurer, and general manager of the New York Yankees. The next day, he sold his one-third share for $2 million to Dan Topping and his partner, Del Webb.

All that was happening at the top of the league, however, and the Senators lived near the bottom during 1947, nestling into seventh place in May and staying there. The most glaring disappointment stemmed from the performance of Mickey Vernon, whose batting average tumbled nearly 100 points. All year, poor Mickey heard that his 1946 batting championship had been a fluke, and nothing seemed to go right for him. Clark Griffith may have had misgivings about turning down Larry MacPhail's offer the previous spring of outfielder Lindell, third baseman Billy Johnson, a pair of pitchers, and some cash, in exchange for Vernon. At the time, Griffith had a very adverse reaction to MacPhail's offer, and went so far as to accuse the Yankees' executive of trying to disrupt the stability of the Washington ballclub.

The truth was that the Washington ball-club was growing old. With both catchers, Jake Early and Al Evans, having poor years at the dish, 42-year-old Rick Ferrell, who hadn't played in two years, came out of retirement to lend a hand. Ferrell hit an unbelievable .303 in 99 at-bats, thereby putting the cap on his Hall of Fame career. When Cecil Travis reluctantly gave up on the game, riding off with his .314 career average, 33-year-old Mark Christman, who had been the Browns' shortstop in their championship year but had been sold to the Senators at the start of the '47 season, became the regular. Christman hit .222, teaming with Gerry Priddy to compose by far the most anemic middle infield in the league.

The third-base job was handed over this season to a 20-year-old from Brooklyn, New York—Eddie Yost. Yost was considered a blue-chipper, and so much so by the Senators that he never spent a single day in the minor leagues, graduating to the bigs straight from the Brooklyn sandlots and the campus of New York University. After being passed over by the Red Sox following a tryout, Yost came to the Nats as a 17-year-old third baseman-shortstop in 1944. He then joined the Coast Guard and was not discharged until late '46.

When Yost came to the Florida camp in the spring of '47, he fully expected to be farmed out. When the Nats tried to do just that, they found out they couldn't. Under the strict interpretation of the G.I. Bill passed by Congress, Commissioner Happy Chandler ruled that Yost, like every other returning soldier, was entitled, for at least one year, to the same job he had held before going into the service. He would hold a big-league job for 16 more years. A participant in 115 games in '47, Yost hit only .238, drove in only 14 runs in 428 at-bats, and walked just 45 times, a figure he would more than triple in the future. But he would be a fixture at third base in Washington for a dozen years.

Yost would have one prominent souvenir from his first game in the major leagues as a fresh-faced 17-year-old back in August 1944. Instructed in the manner by Ossie Bluege, Yost, in anticipation of a bunt, sprang toward the plate from the third base position. Unfortunately, the pitcher, Bobo Newsom, still had his back to the plate and hadn't yet begun his delivery. Embarrassed, Yost began trotting back to his position when the veteran Newsom called him over. The vet told the youngster to take it easy, that Old Bobo was right there beside him, and that no one was going to shove a ball between the two of them. But best to stay back a little more, Newson told his rookie third baseman, lest Yost get up to the plate faster than Bobo's fastball.

Eddie Yost's youth was an exception on this club. The outfielders — Buddy Lewis, Stan Spence, Joe Grace — were all in their thirties. Spence led the club with 16 homers, but in December, when Clark Griffith decided to do something about the fact that he'd gotten rid of Gerry Priddy without obtaining a warm body in return, Spence was shuffled off to the Red Sox for Al Kozar, age 25, a career minor-leaguer who might be able to play second, and Leon Culberson, a 28-year-old utility outfielder whose big-league experience so far had been garnered as a member of the mighty Bosox.

Veteran rightfielder Buddy Lewis hit .261, bringing his career batting average down to an even .300, with exactly 1500 hits. Not as spry as he'd once been, perhaps the result of crouching in fighter planes, Lewis announced at the end of the '47 season that he was retiring. He had started an auto business in his hometown of Gastonia, N.C., was doing well with it, and pronounced himself ready to make selling cars his full-time occupation. But Lewis would get the bug again. After sitting 1948 out, he attempted a comeback with the Nats in '49. It was probably a mistake. He would add a meaningless 63 hits to his career total, and his .245 mark would bring his .300 average down to its eternal resting place of .297. At risk of getting ahead of ourselves, Lewis would earn himself the distinction of playing on one last lousy ballclub.

One notorious low point of the '47 season occurred on September 3, when Washington was embarrassed by the obscure Bill McCahan of the Philadelphia A's, who gave up no hits and no walks in shutting them out

3–0. The Nats were spared the ignominy of being the victims of a perfect game only because rookie first baseman Ferris Fain, who would eventually become the best-fielding first sacker in the business, committed a throwing error. McCahan had ironically been on the losing end of a no-hitter thrown by Cleveland's Don Black less than two months earlier. (McCahan won a grand total of 16 big-league ballgames; Black 34.)

Adding to the turmoil in the Senators' clubhouse was the tenuous position held by Sherry Robertson, Clark Griffith's nephew, who'd been brought up to the big club straight from the lowly Piedmont League the previous year. There were grumblings of nepotism as Robinson continued to struggle. He had hit just .200 as a utility infielder the previous year, and now this year, as an outfielder, he improved, but barely, to .233 with just a single home run in 95 games.

After Ossie Bluege was fired as manager and moved into the newly created position of Director of Farm Clubs (where his accounting background might serve the club better), Clark Griffith was a little mystified as to who he would get to manage for 1948. There was only one man on his roster that he might consider, Rick Ferrell, but Griffith had, not at all surprisingly, an ex-employee of longer standing in mind. After obtaining permission from the White Sox, Griff talked to Joe Kuhel, who had just retired as a player with a .277 lifetime average after four pinch-hitting appearances for Chicago in '47. He had most recently been managing a White Sox farm team at Hot Springs, Arkansas.

Joe Kuhel came to terms with Griffith and got the job to manage the Senators, the team he had played for during his first seven years in the majors in the early thirties, and for another two seasons in the midforties. With the hiring, the gag making the rounds was that Kuhel was a magician of the sleight-of-hand variety. Indeed, Kuhel, a gentlemanly type who'd been literally fearless on a baseball field, was a member of the American Society of Magicians and had apprenticed with a famed card magician named Cardini. The running joke of

course was that he would need all of the smoke-and-mirrors action he could get if this year's version of the Washington Senators was to fare any better than last year's sorry bunch.

They didn't. Clark Griffith had predicted early on that things would get worse before they got better, and he was absolutely right. After getting off on the right foot, this ballclub would keep losing all year long. Washington won eight fewer games, winding up an indecent 56–97, and stayed stuck in a seventh-place rut for a second straight year. Joe Kuhel (whose name sounded like "Joe Cool," and indeed, he was cool, perhaps too much so) didn't convince the old man to do much to improve the club, however.

Following the acquisition of Al Kozar and Leon Culberson for the previous year's best hitter, Stan Spence, the club made just one significant move for 1948 — veteran catcher Jake Early was purchased from the Browns. Early, always solid defensively, was returning to the team he'd played for during his first six years in the majors, but he hadn't improved as a hitter during his one-year stop with the Browns. He would bat only .220 while doing most of the catching.

At spring training at Tinker Field in Orlando, Florida, perhaps one of the game's oddest pregame promotional attractions was showcased. As an opening act preceding an exhibition matchup with the Athletics, two famous baseball men were to engage in a footrace. While one of them gave up eight years to the other, the race, a short one by most standards, ended in a dead heat. There must have been something perverse about enjoying such a spectacle as this one, featuring the 86-year-old Connie Mack and the redoubtable Clark Griffith, who'd turned 77 in November, trying to beat each other from third to the plate. Not a good idea, but there were no casualties.

In mid–May, Griffith and the Senators did make an anticipated move to shore up their outfield, paying a reported $15,000 for Ed "Bud" Stewart of the Yankees. Perhaps because it was felt that someone should carry the money to New York, the Nats threw in Leon

Culberson, who'd hit .172 during his one month as a member of the club. Culberson, not yet 29, had breathed his last big-league air, as the Yankees did not call on his services. He is forever remembered as the Red Sox outfielder who picked up the ball and relayed it to the infield following Harry Walker's single in the seventh game of the 1946 World Series. Shortstop Johnny Pesky took Culberson's throw but then paused, allowing the Cardinals' Enos Slaughter to score from first, on his "mad dash," the run that won the Series for St. Louis. Ted Williams, the greatest hitter of his time, batted .200 in that Series and never got another chance.

A lefthanded bat who turned 32 a month after he came to Washington, Bud Stewart drove in 69 runs and batted .279 with seven homers to bolster the outfield. The trouble was, these figures were the highest in each category on the '48 ballclub. Stewart, who in his sophomore year had blamed his lack of success with the Pittsburgh Pirates on the constant nagging to which he had been subjected by manager Frank Frisch, was making a return to the big leagues after a six-year absence. Another veteran, 30-year-old Carden Gillenwater, who'd gone from being a .288 threat to being a .228 hitter after the war, proved much less useful than Stewart. Gillenwater managed only .244 while playing mainly against lefthanders, and his major-league career ended as a result.

Stan Spence and the retired Buddy Lewis were sorely missed. The leftfielder this year was Gil Coan, a perennial sensation down on the farm who was being handed his big chance. Coan was coming off an impressive 22–92–.340 season at Chattanooga. With the Nats in '48, he drove in 60 runs and stole 23 bases, but he struck out too much, 78 times, and batted only .232 as a result.

Another farmhand, Junior Wooten, who like Coan was a native of the Carolinas (the Senators, you may have noticed, traditionally drew most of their players from the South or mid–South), played primarily against righthanders and hit .256 with little power. The other outfielder was Sherry Robertson, Clark

Griffith's nephew. Blessed with a gun for an arm and with good running speed (he would never steal more than ten bases in a season, however), it was just a matter of time for Sherry, his uncle felt. But Sherry was already 29, and the best he could manage was .246, his career best, although he hit at a .412 clip as a lefthanded pinch hitter.

The Senators had no power whatsoever. Coan's seven homers were by far the most on the team. Mickey Vernon and Gillenwater were next with three. Vernon's average dropped again, to .242, reinforcing the notion that his .353 mark in '46 had to have been a monumental fluke. The 31 homers the Nats hit for the year were a joke and, excluding wartime, the fewest hit by a major-league team since the White Sox back in 1931. (Coincidentally, that club finished with the same 56–97 record as did the '48 Nats.)

Second baseman Al Kozar, replacing Gerry Priddy, drew spring predictions in the media that he would be no better than a .250 hitter. Admitting later that he did let the press distract him, Kozar, to his great consternation, hit .250 right on the nose. He later related an interesting anecdote to Danny Peary for Peary's *We Played the Game.*

Throughout 1948, Kozar had been complaining to manager Joe Kuhel about how calls rendered by veteran umpire Bill McGowan were always going against him and the ball club. Kozar felt Kuhel ignored his complaints about McGowan all year. Until, that is, one day when McGowan ejected Kuhel and the whole coaching staff for razzing him from the bench. At that point, Kozar was approached to sign a petition against McGowan and offer some corroboration as to the umpire's earlier behavior, as the Senators were launching an official protest about the arbiter. Kozar, nicknamed "Mumbles" because of the way he spoke due to his shy demeanor, wouldn't do it. This, perhaps as much as his playing, hastened his departure after one more season.

At shortstop, Johnny Sullivan, the team's incumbent during most of the war years, had managed .256 on an irregular basis in '47, and the Nats still felt he would be the answer defensively if only he could hit. He couldn't, batting .208 in '48, and had to be replaced again by the veteran Mark Christman, who hit .259 and fielded respectably. The 21-year-old New Yorker at third base, Eddie Yost, was the only position player on this club who offered any real hope for the future. He raised his average from .238 to .249, a modest improvement, but nearly doubled the frequency of his walks, earning 82 passes, and he drove in 50 runs. Yost would only start reaching the seats with his pokes the following year, but he showed good doubles and triples power, knocking out 32 and 11 respectively. The Nats tied for the league lead in triples, a telling sign in terms of team speed. Bud Stewart led the club with 13.

With an offensive attack like this one, even superior pitching could not have won. No one hit as high as .280, and the team batting average of .244, way below the A.L.'s .266, was the worst in the league. The truth is, mediocre would be a polite term to describe the pitching staff, which allowed an overly generous 4.65 runs per game. The league average was 4.28 and, unbelievably, the White Sox and Browns were even worse than the Nats, with the Browns settling just above the five-run barrier at 5.01 at year's end.

For Washington, only the crafty Ray Scarborough had a good year among pitchers in '48, his first good one, with 15–8 and a sterling 2.82 ERA. Walter Masterson was second best at 8–15, 3.83. The others were terrible. Mickey Haefner went 5–13 in his last full year as a Senator, and Sid Hudson, of whom so many nice things had been said prior to the war, hit rock bottom at 4–16, 5.88. For the second year in a row, Hudson was allowing nearly six runs per nine innings, and it didn't look at this point as if he'd last much longer. In fact, he was to lead the entire league in losses in 1949, and yet would keep himself employed in the majors until 1954.

Early Wynn got the most work of any member of the starting crew, and, looking at his stats, it is easy to see that Washington had a very poor aggregation of pitchers. After two somewhat encouraging seasons, Wynn regressed to 8–19 with a frightening 5.82 earned runs per game. Wynn's inability to harness his great talent and competitiveness — or perhaps better put, the Nats' inability to get the most out of him — led to what might easily be considered the worst deal in the entire history of Washington Senators baseball. On December 14, 1948, the Nats agreed to send Early Wynn and Mickey Vernon to the Cleveland Indians in a desperate attempt to shore up their pitching.

This trade would come to be ridiculed in baseball circles, going down in history as "Thelma's Deal." Thelma Griffith, Clark's adopted daughter, was the wife of Joe Haynes, who'd pitched for Washington during his first two years in the majors back in 1939–40. Haynes had performed for the White Sox since then, with only moderate success, but over the past two seasons, he had gone 23–16. Thelma preferred living in Washington, so, as legend has it, her daddy brought her and her husband back, along with pitcher Ed Klieman, like Haynes a righthander, and big Eddie Robinson, who'd swatted 16 homers and driven in 83 for the world champion '48 Indians.

As it turned out, Mickey Vernon had plenty of good baseball left in him, despite his two-year slump, and bad as this trade was, it would have been much worse if, as with the Buddy Myer trade more than 20 years before, the Nats hadn't reacquired Vernon from the Indians after just one and a half seasons. But the crux of the matter is this — Clark Griffith's son-in-law and Ed Klieman would win a grand total of 12 more games in the major leagues, ten of them for the Washington Senators (Haynes ten, Klieman none).

Early Wynn would go on to win 228 more games in the major leagues (see Appendix B for a comparison of Wynn's lifetime record and Washington totals). He would rack up 20 or more in a season five times, and would also enjoy 18– and 17–win campaigns. Under pitching coach Mel Harder at Cleveland, Wynn would learn how to throw a host of pitches to complement his fastball: curve, slider, changeup, even knuckleball. For anyone who cared about the Washington Senators, the trading of Early Wynn became a blunder the significance of which would be too enormous to contemplate.

"What we're trying to do here is make chicken salad out of chicken shit," proclaimed manager Joe Kuhel, in an eloquent pronouncement on what he thought the 1949 season might yield for supporters of the Senators. Following a bad start, the club hit the road and enjoyed great success on a western swing. When the Nats' train pulled into Washington, the players were met at the station by a crowd of 5,000 people.

There was a motorcade up Pennsylvania Avenue. Fans were carrying placards with catchy phrases such as "Drink a Toast with Eddie Yost" and "We'll Win Plenty with Sam Dente." Yost continued to walk a lot (91 times) and began reaching the seats (nine homers), but hit only .253 and brought home only 57 runs all year. Dente was this year's regular shortstop, acquired from the Browns right after the '48 season in exchange for pitcher Tom Ferrick, shortstop John Sullivan, and a sum reported to be a hefty $25,000. Dente hit .273 but led the league's shortstops in errors, and the rhyme of "We'll Win Plenty…" would be recalled with derision by fans long after Dente had departed from the local scene.

Nineteen forty-nine would be another long year. Little wonder. On the one hand, the farm system was less than bountiful, and had come up with nothing better than Gil Coan (.218–3–25). But there was no doubt that bad personnel decisions were being made at the big-league level, with the trade of Wynn and Vernon but the most extreme example. Tom Ferrick was another case in point. While the veteran reliever pitched well, he was seldom used by the Nats when they had him in '47 and '48. In '47, Ferrick had led the league in relief losses, but that happened because he never got any support in tight ballgames. He responded well (6–4, 3.88) with an increased workload with the Browns in '49, and by the middle of the following season, when Casey Stengel lost confidence in his ace Joe Page, Ferrick took over as the main man in the

bullpen for the eventual world champion Yankees. Ferrick would win eight and save nine more in 30 appearances down the stretch for New York, and would win the third game of the World Series.

Then there is the astonishing story of Dick Welteroth. Signed as a teenager three years earlier, before he'd been eligible for the armed forces draft, Welteroth had gotten his feet wet the previous season. In 65⅓ innings, he had come away with a 2–1 record despite a 5.51 ERA. Joe Page led the league in appearances with 60 in 1949. He saved 27 ballgames for the Yankees, and posted an ERA. of 2.59. Second in the league in appearances was … Dick Welteroth, who earned this distinction despite a gaudy 7.36 ERA. If this doesn't say all about the sorry state of the Washington Senators' pitching staff, it would be hard to imagine what would! Welteroth appeared five more times in a major-league uniform with the Nats in 1950, and that was it for his big-league career.

Another pitcher who was handed the ball frequently by Joe Kuhel in 1949 was Paul Calvert, a 31-year-old French Canadian and graduate of the University of Montreal. The bespectacled righthander, who had pitched briefly for the Indians during the war years, rewarded his manager's confidence by leading the league in losses; he tied with teammate Sid Hudson, who was 8–17, and with Ned Garver of the Browns, who won twice as many games as Calvert with an equally lousy club. Calvert wound up with a 6–17 ledger and an exaggerated 5.43 ERA. He suffered through 14 consecutive losses this season, and this, as the century ended, would still stand as the fourth-longest streak in American League history.

As a staff, Nats pitchers let in 5.10 earned runs per game (again the Browns were even worse at 5.21). Lefty Mickey Harris went 2–12, 5.16, after coming over from the Red Sox with outfielder Sam Mele for Walt Masterson in mid–June. Dick Weik, a 6'3" righthander with a blazing fastball but no control (103 walks in 95⅓ innings) finished at 3–12, 5.38. Worst of all was Thelma Haynes' husband, righthander Joe, who rang up a despicable 2–9, 6.26.

While Haynes' performance may have been the best example of nepotism at its finest, another conundrum concerned the continuing role of Sherry Robertson on the club. In deference to Clark Griffith's nephew, Al Kozar, who was becoming a competent hitter (.269) and who was already a dependable fielder, was getting less time at second base. Robertson did hit 11 homers, but he was no second baseman. In all fairness, Robertson had been tried all over the ballpark since his arrival with the Nats nearly ten years before. This year would be his last big chance and, despite the 11 homers, he hit just .251. Sherry would play much less in the two remaining years he'd spend in uniform with his uncle's ballclub.

By August 1949, the Nats had tumbled into last place, where they finished despite the fact that the St. Louis Browns lost 101 games. The Senators dropped 104, winning a mere 50 times. There were very few pluses on this club. Eddie Robinson, the new first baseman, injected some badly needed home run power, posting 18–78–.294 figures. Mickey Vernon finally got himself back on track at Cleveland, and had a season similar to Robinson's — 18–83–.291. Early Wynn, meanwhile, went 11–7, 4.15, for the Indians. It would be another year before he started winning big. The other main contributor to the Nats' attack was Clyde Vollmer, who hit 14 homers to go along with his .253 percentage. Early in '50, Vollmer would be squandered in a trade with Boston, where he played an important role on a pennant contender.

The Senators did have a place in the collective consciousness of American baseball fans in 1949. The Red Sox and Yankees were involved in one of the best pennant races ever, and had the Red Sox been able to beat the Senators and Ray Scarborough in their final series before a two-game showdown with the Yankees, they would have had a good chance of taking the flag. But Scarborough, the Nats' ace in '49 with a 13–11 record, was a smart pitcher. He had beaten the Red Sox three times in '48, including in one crucial game at the end of the year. If the Red Sox, who had come within an eyelash of the pennant, had

been able to beat him on that occasion, the World Series would have been an all–Boston affair.

Scarborough was again hard on the Red Sox on this day. Forty years hence, Ted Williams would pay him the ultimate compliment by admitting that Scarborough had caused him to chase more pitches out of the strike zone than any other pitcher he'd ever faced. The Red Sox got but four hits off him, but Chuck Stobbs, a big young righthander (of whom much more would be heard later) was just as good. Boston took a 1–0 lead into the bottom of the ninth. But Roberto Ortiz, Eddie Robinson, and Al Kozar all singled, with Kozar's drive bringing in pinch runner Gil Coan with the tying run for Washington. After Robinson got tagged at the plate for the second out, Mel Parnell came in to relieve Stobbs.

The batter was Buddy Lewis, making his one-year comeback attempt. With the count 1–and–2, Parnell bounced one low and wide of the plate. Catcher Birdie Tebbetts reacted slowly, acting as if he had the ball. Al Kozar didn't think Tebbetts had it, and took off on his own. He made it. Had the Red Sox won this game, they could have lost the two games they had remaining against the Yankees, which they did, and still forced a play-off. This way, there were no play-offs and the Red Sox were once again bridesmaids. The Washington Nationals, of course, never did get to the banquet, and Clark Griffith had had enough of Joe Kuhel, who had done him the ultimate dishonor of bringing in a last-place entry. This was only the second time this had happened to Griffith in his 38-year association with the Washington Senators, a franchise he had governed as supreme commander for 30 years.

It was a challenge to this hegemony, the first Griffith had ever faced, that presented him with his biggest test yet. As if things weren't bad enough on the field, the old man learned threatening news one fall day from the mouth of a visitor to his office. The unexpected guest, John J. Jachym of Jamestown, New York, a perfect stranger to Griffith, announced that he was his new partner. With the backing of Pennsylvania oilman Hugh Grant, Jachym had purchased a 40 percent share in the team. He had paid $550,000 for stock which had been held by the heirs of William V. Richardson of Philadelphia, who had been Griffith's faithful silent partner. The old man was furious. After 30 years as the boss, he wasn't about to give up control to this johnny-come-lately, to whom he took an instant dislike.

By all other accounts, Jachym had the hallmarks of a fine gentleman. He was a retired Marine Corps captain who'd earned the Silver Star for bravery, a graduate of the Missouri School of Journalism, a scout for the St. Louis Cardinals, and later an owner of the Jamestown franchise. But Clark Griffith had news for him, and began scurrying about. He had never bothered buying a majority ownership in the club (his family held only 44 percent of the stock), so he set out to acquire more in order to guarantee control. The Old Fox already had plenty of support among the stockholders, which assured that he could always outvote Jachym.

At the shareholders' meeting in December 1949, John Jachym was not voted to any official position with the team, let alone to a place on the board of directors. Jachym argued that he had never had any intention of usurping the old man's authority, but Griffith didn't even give him a season's pass. Jachym gave up on any designs he might have had six months later, and sold his entire 40 percent to H. Gabriel Murphy, a Washington insurance man, at a tidy profit reported to be $85,000.

Gabriel Murphy was an old friend of Griff's, the two having conducted business with one another for years. As manager of athletics at Georgetown University as a young man, Murphy had negotiated the rental of Griffith Stadium for Georgetown football games. He had no qualms at all about selling Griff the 300 shares he needed to gain control of the operation. In return, Murphy was guaranteed a stock option should Clark Griffith or his heirs ever decide to sell.

The old man may have been breathing a little easier, but he had heard the rumble on the street and in the press. There was dissatisfaction with his ballclub, and with good reason; it had finished seventh and eighth in the last two years. His new field boss, unlike the last two, would not be a rookie manager, but neither would he be a stranger. Manager of the world champs in 1947, Bucky Harris had been rudely dumped by the Yankees the following year after a 94–60 third-place finish, unacceptable in New York. From there, Bucky had taken over as manager at San Diego of the Pacific Coast League.

In September, Clark Griffith called on Harris to ask his opinion of outfielder Irv Noren, a slick-fielding ballhawk and contact hitter Griffith ended up purchasing from the P.C.L.'s Hollywood Stars on Bucky's recommendation. When Griff broached the matter of Bucky returning to Washington for a third go-round as manager, Harris was not opposed to the idea. He wrangled a reported $65,000 for a two-year deal beginning in 1950. Twenty-six years after first taking the job, Bucky Harris was once again manager of the Washington Senators.

1950–1960:
THE ROAD TO OBLIVION

As had been the case the previous year, the American League was divided into two very distinct tiers in 1950, and the Senators, while coming in fifth, were again one of the league's inferior ballclubs. Bucky Harris could do no better than produce a 67–87 record, which positioned Washington a full 25 games behind fourth-place Cleveland. Nineteen fifty was the year that the Red Sox were awesome offensively. While Ted Williams played in just 89 games because of an elbow fracture sustained in the All-Star game, the Bosox were buoyed by rookie Walt Dropo and shortstop Vern Stephens, who tied one another for the lead in RBIs, with 144. Because of an inferior pitching staff, Boston finished third, a game behind the Tigers and four behind the Yankees, who went on to win it all for the third time in four years.

Near the end of the season, there were a couple of noteworthy events when the Senators had the misfortune of being the reigning world champions' opponents. On September 10, 1950, Joe DiMaggio became the first player ever to hit three home runs in cavernous Griffith Stadium in a single game. Each shot traveled 400-plus feet, and the Yanks won 8–1. On September 25, Yankee rookie Whitey Ford beat the Nats for his ninth consecutive win since being called up from the minor leagues. These were the first nine wins of a career that would eventually qualify Ford for enshrinement in the Hall of Fame.

The record shows the Nats had better pitching than the Red Sox in 1950, and were right around the league average, but this was a club which again lacked power and was sub-par defensively. The main addition to the pitching staff was Conrado "Connie" Marrero, a Cuban knuckleballer who reported his age as 33, although many ex-players swore they had faced him in Cuba as many as 20 years before. Relying on a vast repertoire of off-speed stuff, Marrero had a pitching delivery which seemed to have originated in his home country. The media made reference to its resemblance to the swinging of a machete cutting sugar cane.

No Cuban player had ever really been one of the boys, but Connie Marrero did more than any of his predecessors to break down social barriers. He did so without showing even the slightest interest in learning the English language. Shaped like a Kewpie doll, Marrero just loved to chomp on Havana cigars and had no lack of confidence. He became something of a media darling in Washington but his teammates bore him no resentment for his pronounced individuality, and he became a popular member of the club. Despite the all too frequent losses, there was always good camaraderie on the Senators. The Griffiths contributed to this, often hosting barbecues at Beverly Beach on Chesapeake Bay, where the beer would flow freely. On other occasions, there were parties at the Copacabana and other popular venues when the club visited New York.

Bucky Harris was hardly enamored with Marrero at first sight in the spring of 1950. Harris figured that this was just another one of Joe Cambria's Cuban projects destined to flop. Hardly blessed with a deep roster, however, Bucky, who'd envisaged Marrero as at least a relief possibility, ended up using him primarily as a starter. No less a hitter than Ted Williams became an admirer of Connie Marrero, telling writers that Marrero threw everything toward the plate but the ball. Hitters would be salivating, anxious to get a crack at his knuckler, but once Marrero got ahead of you, Williams said, you were dead. It was after Marrero struck out the Kid with the bases loaded at Fenway Park one day that it became obvious to everyone on the bench that all was well with Marrero and Harris. Connie walked off the field, proudly plopped his glove right in Harris's lap, and proclaimed, "More money now."

While Marrero was just 6–10, 4.50, during this campaign, he would be useful to Harris for a few years to come. Another Joe Cambria recruit, Sandalio "Sandy" Consuegra, made belated beginnings in the majors with Washington in 1950, starting 18 times for a 7–8, 4.40, record. These figures must be considered in the context of the league ERA, which was a whopping 4.58, up from 4.20 in '49. Sid Hudson was by far the horse on this staff, bouncing back with a respectable 14–14, 4.09.

Mickey Harris, the lefty whose arrival with the Red Sox ten years earlier had been considered akin to the second coming of Lefty Gomez, was the designated bullpen ace. Despite a very ordinary 5–9, 4.78, showing, Harris supplanted the Yankees' Joe Page as the league's leader in saves, with 15, at a time when complete games were still much more commonplace than they would be over most of the half-century to follow.

On the last day of May 1950, Bucky Harris engineered a trade with the Chicago White Sox which may well have been perceived by Washington fans as one in which the home side gave up too much. The team's lone power hitter, Eddie Robinson, and its winningest pitcher from the previous year, Ray Scarborough, as well as scrappy second baseman Al Kozar, were turned over to Chicago. In return, Washington added second baseman Cass Michaels (real name — Casimir Eugene Kwietniewski), who had hit .308 while participating in every game for Chicago in '49, as well as a hard-throwing pitcher named Bob Kuzava. The Nats also acquired John Ostrowski, a young reserve outfielder who would never amount to anything with them, or anyone else in the big leagues for that matter.

This was indeed another stinker of a deal for Washington. Kuzava did fashion a winning record as a dependable starter, going 8–7 in '50, but his stay in the capital was brief, lasting just a year. Kuzava would be traded to the Yankees for a tremendous young talent, and *that* deal could have been one of the franchise's best, had the Senators not spoiled things by making yet another poor trade. As for Cass Michaels, he never again approached his 1949 offensive numbers. After roaring off to a .312 start with the White Sox in 36 games in 1950, he managed a mere .250 in 106 games the rest of the way with Washington. While Ray Scarborough had seen better days (he did win 12 games after finding his way back to the Red Sox for 1951), Eddie Robinson would be a dependable fielder and hitter in the league for a few more years, and would average nearly 24 home runs per year from 1950 to 1953.

The Nats were fortunate to replace Robinson within two weeks. Perhaps still overconfident as a result of their steal of Early Wynn in the transaction which had taken place precisely a year and a half before, the Cleveland Indians decided they would take a chance on a rapid 22-year-old righthander who had struggled to a composite 5–17 record in three trials with the Nats. There was some poetic justice here, as Dick Weik won exactly one more game in the major leagues. In return, in a straight one-for-one swap for Weik, Washington fans were elated to welcome back

Mickey Vernon, who batted .306 and drove in 65 runs from mid–June until the end of the season. At the time he rejoined the Senators, the 32-year-old Vernon still had ten more years left as a player, during which he was to win another batting championship and lead the league in doubles twice more.

From an offensive standpoint, there were some other encouraging signs. Eddie Yost and rookie Irv Noren both hit .295. Noren led with 14 homers and 98 ribbies, and Yost chipped in with 11 dingers and scored 101 runs. Noren would play ten more years in the majors, but would never have a season nearly as good as this one. As for Yost, who would never hit .295 again, he began a practice which he'd replicate six more times in the decade — walking more than 100 times. He led the league with a whopping 141 bases on balls (Ted Williams, obviously a much more dangerous hitter, had regularly topped that figure in preceding years), and Eddie would soon be universally known as the "Walking Man." His .440 on-base percentage in 1950 would stand as the best of his career, which spanned 18 campaigns. Yost's emergence as a quality player, coupled with Mickey Vernon's strong showing upon his return to the capital, had to be extremely gratifying for Joe Cambria, the much-maligned bush-beater who had signed them both.

There were more revelations in the outfield. So much had been expected from Gil Coan since his dreamy 1945 season, when he'd led the Southern Association in nearly every important category, but he had hit just .235 in a little over 1,000 at-bats with the big club. Coan finally broke out of his slump in 1950, batting .303 in 104 games, and seemed on the verge of becoming a productive regular player. Another find was Sabath Anthony ("Sam," from his initials) Mele, who had come over from Boston along with Mickey Harris in the Walt Masterson deal in mid-'49. Mele had hit .302 as a Red Sox rookie in '47, but had then faltered and been relegated to the bench. He drove in 86 runs, would top that in '51, and hit .274 both years in Washington. Those would be his best years in the big show as a player but when, one day, this club again found its way to the World Series, Sam Mele was the man who guided it.

It was obvious by 1951 that the Nats had plenty of talented offensive players on their squad. Twenty-four-year-old Ed Yost scored more than 100 runs for the second straight year, walked 126 times (and was second to Ted Williams, who usually led the league), and led the team in home runs, with 12. The fact that a lead-off type of hitter could lead the team in homers underlined the Washington ballclub's persistent offensive miseries. The Nats hit only 54 homers all year long, an average of about two a week. Yost was becoming the team's star. He smashed 36 doubles, enough to share top billing in the league in that department with teammate Sam Mele and Detroit's perennial Major League All-Star at third base, George Kell.

Eddie Yost further distinguished himself by leading the league's glovemen in put-outs at the hot corner for the third time in four seasons. By the time his career ended in 1962, he had led his league in put-outs a total of eight times, a *major-league* record still standing at the beginning of this century. On July 3, 1951, Yost began a string of appearances in consecutive games at third base which lasted nearly four seasons, until May 11, 1955. His 576 straight games at third was another major-league standard yet unmatched when the 21st century began. (It is illuminating to compare this record to the National League mark of 364 games, set by Ron Santo of the Cubs, April 1964–May 1966.)

Counting pinch-hit appearances, Yost put together a consecutive-games streak of 838 which stretched from July 6, 1949 to 1955, when he was sidelined by tonsillitis. Other records he held when he called it quits were most career games played at third, most chances, and most assists. His best-known stock in trade, however, consisted of earning free passes to first base. No player with fewer than 200 career homers has matched Eddie Yost's 1,614 career walks.

There were a number of good batsmen with the club in 1951, but unlike Yost, none of them reached double figures in home runs.

Sam Mele drove in 94 runs, an incredible accomplishment considering he had only five roundtrippers and batted .274. Mickey Vernon (.293) and Irv Noren (.279) were also solid contributors, with 87 and 86 RBIs respectively. Gil Coan continued to improve, driving in 62 while batting .303 for the second consecutive year.

The catching was by committee. Mickey Grasso, so named because of his facial resemblance to Mickey Cochrane, showed he had little in common with the Hall of Famer except that he played the same position. On the heels of an encouraging .287 bat mark as Al Evans' backup in '50, Grasso tumbled to .206 and would do no better than .216 in a semi-regular role over the next couple of seasons. Mike Guerra, a Cuban signed by Joe Cambria during the war, ended up doing most of the catching, as Evans was waived to the Red Sox during the winter to make way for Grasso. Guerra hit a pitiful .201.

The other member of the catching triumvirate was Clyde Kluttz, who, as his name might suggest, was not gifted defensively. A major leaguer since 1942 and a much better hitter than the other two receivers, Kluttz hit .308 in 53 games. With his lack of mobility a factor at age 34, however, he could not be counted on as a regular the following year. Much later, Kluttz would stake his claim to fame when, as a scout for the Yankees, he played a major role in enticing free agent pitcher and fellow North Carolinian Jim "Catfish" Hunter to sign with New York for 1975. At the time of his death in 1979, Kluttz was Director of Player Development for the Baltimore Orioles.

Washington's middle infield in 1951 included second baseman Cass Michaels, who had to be classed as a disappointment. He batted just .258, 50 points below his '49 average with the White Sox, when he'd also led the league in double plays and assists. With the Senators, Michaels led in errors instead. By early '52, he would be unceremoniously unloaded on the Browns in return for left-handed pitcher Lou Sleater and shortstop Freddie Marsh, neither of whom panned out

in Washington. Sleater would go 4–2 for the Nats in '52 before disappearing from the big-league scene for more than two years. During his short stay in Washington, however, he had the distinction of putting an end to Walt "Moose" (from Moosup, Connecticut) Dropo's unbelievable streak of hitting safely in 12 consecutive at-bats.

At short, Sam Dente had hit just .239 in '50, and stayed at that level in '51, with .238. On July 1, 1951, the Nats introduced for the first time a ping-hitting 23-year-old native of East Texas named Pete Runnels. Two short years earlier, Runnels had belatedly begun his baseball career at the outpost of Chickasha, Oklahoma, and had led the Sooner State League in hitting with .372. Still tentative defensively, he was batting .356 at Chattanooga when the Senators called him up. While playing a very tough position in the big leagues proved a challenge (18 errors in half a season — Eddie Joost of the A's and Chico Carrasquel of the White Sox had 20 each all season), Runnels acquitted himself very well with the bat, with a promising .278 in 78 games.

What Bucky Harris needed more than anything at this point was some mound help. The pitching staff, decent in '50, was horrible this season, second worst in the league and the reason Washington dropped five more games, and two positions in the standings, and finished seventh. Only the Browns, who lost 102 games, were worse. It was only logical that Harris, who'd managed the Yankees in '47 and '48, should turn his attention to the best organization in all of baseball for help.

Coincidentally, it was the Yankees who came calling for the Nats' quick lefthander Bob Kuzava. Big Kuzava, 6'2", 202 pounds, known as "Sarge" because he had risen to the rank of sergeant in World War II, was struggling at this time, at 3–3, 5.50. New York was offering a couple of veteran pitchers who might be of short-term help, Tom Ferrick and Fred Sanford, and lots of cash, a reported $50,000. When Washington showed reticence, the Yankees let it be known that they might include another player from their farm system. Harris certainly knew who he would like to have — a righthander named Bob Porterfield, who had unwittingly played a role in determining Bucky's longevity, or lack of it, with the Yankees. Back in '48, when Harris had committed the cardinal sin of failing to win the pennant in New York, he petitioned Yanks' G.M. George Weiss to bring Porterfield, then 24, up from Newark, where he had a 15–6 record and led the International League with a 2.17 ERA.

Porterfield was eventually brought up, at Harris's behest, and contributed five wins to the Yanks' drive in '48, but not before a considerable amount of bad blood had developed between Harris and his G.M., a situation which the media dubbed "L'Affaire Porterfield." Weiss initially had resisted bringing the hurler up to the big club on the pretext that he was needed in Newark, and that he was unwilling to jeopardize that club's chances for a title. When the newspapers also began howling for Porterfield's callup, George Weiss blamed Harris for inciting those demands and undermining his authority. At season's end, Bucky Harris was fired.

Since that time, Porterfield had suffered from arm problems and had won a grand total of two games for the Yankees in three years. He wasn't pitching particularly well at Kansas City either, when Bucky Harris called to inquire about his arm and whether he would be interested in coming over to Washington. Porterfield said his right arm felt fine and that he would love to get a real opportunity. The deal was made in mid–June 1951, and the Nats also got Sanford, Ferrick, and all the money.

The Yanks gained in Kuzava a hurler who closed off two victorious World Series for them. But in Bob Porterfield, the Washington Senators gained a pitcher who within two years would lead the American League in wins, complete games, and shutouts. It was not surprising, then, that Bucky Harris would go to the well very soon again to see what he could draw up from the deep reserve of New York Yankees talent.

The Yankees were always trying to strengthen themselves at every position, avoiding the risk of injuries or a sudden decline,

weakening their chances of once more repeating as world champs. By 1952, they had won four world championships in five years, with Bucky Harris's last year at the helm, 1948, being the only season since '47 that they had failed to capture baseball's ultimate prize. By May, they were looking for more outfield depth. Young Mickey Mantle, a rookie the previous year, was faltering. New York put an offer in to the Nationals for Irv Noren, an excellent lefthanded contact hitter and a superior outfielder. Noren, however, had chronic knee problems and was hitting just .245 after 12 games.

The Yankees indicated they would be willing to part with their golden boy — not Mickey Mantle but Jackie Jensen, the blond Californian who just a couple of years earlier had been hailed by the New York press as the heir apparent to Joe DiMaggio. Blessed with a robust physique, Jensen was an All-American footballer at the University of California before turning to professional baseball as a more lucrative career. He signed a bonus contract with the Yankees for $75,000, but hit just .261 in his only minor-league season, at Oakland of the Pacific Coast League, in 1949. Following that campaign, he married Olympic diving champion Zoe Ann Olsen.

Since that time, Jensen had been used strictly as a fill-in by Casey Stengel on the big club, but had come through, at .298 with eight homers in just 56 games in '51. He bemoaned the fact that whenever he went hitless, Stengel would jerk him out of the lineup, and with the Yankees, it wasn't easy to get back in. Jensen's wish of being able to get up in the morning knowing that he'd be in the starting lineup was about to be realized. But typically, Clark Griffith insisted that Bucky Harris hold out for more when the Nats and Yankees began discussing the possibility of a trade involving Irv Noren and Jackie Jensen. Rumors were abounding in the relentless New York press when the Nats arrived for a series at Yankee Stadium. As the story goes, it was Yogi Berra, who was a rookie under Bucky Harris in '47, who accosted the Washington manager and gave him what turned out to be a very valuable tip.

Frank Shea, Berra told Harris, was the man Washington should go for. Stengel wasn't using him, and Berra felt Shea had more stuff than anyone else on the Yankees' staff, the league's best. On May 3, 1952, the Senators consummated an extremely favorable deal, bringing over Jensen, Shea, outfielder Archie Wilson, and infielder Jerry Snyder, in exchange for Noren and a skinny shortstop, Tom "Muscles" Upton, obtained from the White Sox the previous November for Sam Dente. While the inclusion in the deal of Upton, Wilson, and Snyder proved of little consequence (although Snyder would be able to hang on as a reserve player with the Senators through 1958), the others would play influential roles in determining their respective teams' futures.

On the very day the deal for Jensen and Shea was made, the Nats shipped Sam Mele, arguably their most reliable hitter over the past couple of years, to the Chicago White Sox, for Jim Busby, an outstanding outfielder who, at 25, was four years Mele's junior. Busby would man center field now that Noren was gone, and it would take a while for his offense to kick in (.244 in '52), but considering his enormous outfield skills, his would prove a valuable acquisition. The outfield was thus reorganized around Busby, with Jackie Jensen, whom Ted Williams would one day call the best outfielder he ever saw, in right, and Gil Coan, for the time being, retaining his spot in left. Coan would crash and burn at .205 following his two successive .303 campaigns, and his tenure as a full-time player was ending. Ken Wood, previously with the Browns and Red Sox, spelled Coan in left and drove in 32 runs in 61 games, but hit only .238 and fielded unreliably.

Not surprisingly, however, the Nats became one of the league's top fielding units in 1952. Jim Busby led all centerfielders in percentage and total chances per game, catching everything hit his way and then some. Jensen threw out 17 baserunners who dared challenge his arm, to lead the league in outfield assists. At bat, he had ten homers and 80 ribbies, matching Mickey Vernon's home run and RBI

totals exactly. Jensen hit .286, but Vernon a disappointing .251. Mickey was great in the field as usual, and posted the best fielding average at his position in the A.L. The banjo-hitting shortstop, Pete Runnels, gave every indication at age 24 that he was already a true big-leaguer, batting .285 and driving in an amazing 64 runs.

Runnels' fielding percentage was superior to those of established shortstops Chico Carrasquel of the White Sox and Eddie Joost of the A's. Both he and third baseman Eddie Yost led the loop in put-outs at their positions, and Yost again paced the club in homers with 12, but drove in only 49 runs, in large part a consequence of batting only .233. At second base, the Nationals employed a twosome after dispatching Cass Michaels to the Browns in May. "Silent Floyd" Baker, an inordinately quiet man obtained from the White Sox the previous fall, would likely have won a Gold Glove hands down had he played enough games; as it was, he hit a creditable .262 while sharing time with 29-year-old rookie Mel Hoderlein, who managed a .269 mark in his only serious big-league shot.

If the Washington Senators were obviously an improved club in the field, their batting averages, when taken collectively, amounted to a miserable .239, a drastic dip from 1951's .263, and to boot, they hit even fewer home runs — only 50. Both marks were the American League's worst. These were Washington clubs that, typically, if they got behind in a ballgame, rarely came back. If they were able to win more games than they lost in '52, winding up in fifth place at 78–76, it was due to a dramatic improvement in the club's pitching. The staff ERA went from 4.49 to 3.37, only fourth–best in the circuit, but less than a quarter of a run per game more than the league-leading Yankees.

Bob Porterfield gave Bucky Harris well over 200 innings and posted a 2.72 ERA. The Nats were obviously not scoring a lot of runs for him, as he won 13 and lost 14. Spec Shea, a clubhouse cutup, made the best of his reunion with Bucky Harris, for whom he'd won two World Series games for the 1947 world champs. Nicknamed the "Naugatuck Nugget" by Yankees broadcaster Mel Allen, the right-hander, more commonly known as Spec because of his freckles, had not pitched well since '47 because of a neck injury. It was finally a chiropractor in his hometown of Naugatuck, Connecticut, who cured him during a 15-minute visit in the winter of '51. Shea went 11–7, 2.93, for the Nats in '52.

In June, the Senators brought back Walter Masterson, a pitcher seemingly possessing all the required tools of the trade, but who generally had a tough time getting the job done. Since his departure three years earlier, the big righthander had won a grand total of 21 games for the Red Sox. In '51 he struck out Mickey Mantle five straight times, which resulted in the Yankee rookie's demotion to the minors. Mantle nearly quit baseball altogether before his father talked him out of it.

In exchange for Masterson and veteran righthander Randy Gumpert, who ironically had served up Mickey Mantle's first major-league home run, the Nats parted ways with Sid Hudson, in his tenth year with the club. Hudson put up a composite 10–13, 3.34, for the season. Masterson posted a respectable 9–8, 3.70, and Gumpert completed his big-league swan song by going 4–9, 4.24, for Washington following the early season trade with Boston.

The Cubans got their act together during the 1952 campaign. The rotund Connie Marrero went 11–8, 2.88, and had his best big-league season. Likewise for Julio Moreno, a 30-year-old rookie with the Nats in '51 who'd gone 5–11, 4.88. In '52, Moreno improved to 9–9, 3.97. A third Cuban righthander, 32-year-old Sandy Consuegra, who'd registered a 7–8 slate for the Nats in both '50 and '51, was a perfect 6–0, 3.05. Consuegra was inexplicably sold to the White Sox early in the '53 season. Not a good idea. With the exception of 1956, his worst ERA in five more years in the big leagues would be 2.86. In '53, Consuegra went 7–5 for the Chisox, and in '54, he put together a remarkable 16–3, 2.69, year, leading the American League in winning percentage.

On September 2, '52, the Nats introduced another Cuban, this one a youngster, Mike Fornieles. The 20-year-old fashioned a one-hitter in his first big-league appearance, whitewashing Philadelphia 5–0, and his ERA for 26⅓ innings at the end of the season was a microscopic 1.37. Fornieles' one-hit debut tied a 50-year record for the modern era established by Addie Joss of the Cleveland Indians (Hall of Fame, 1978), who had last turned the trick, back on April 26, 1902.

Following the season, Mike Fornieles was shipped to the White Sox, sacrificed for a much-needed lefthander, Chuck Stobbs, a big hard thrower who'd gone 7–12 for the Chisox. Both hurlers would go on to experience ups and downs in their careers, and Fornieles was unable to fulfill his early promise. He would finish a 12-year stay in the majors with a 63–64 record and a 3.96 ERA. In his best year, in 1960 with Boston, he was named recipient of the inaugural Fireman of the Year Award as top relief pitcher in the American League.

Five days after Fornieles pitched his gem, Johnny "The Big Cat" Mize, a former National League great winding up his career as a premier pinch hitter and part-time first baseman with the Yankees, attained a milestone at Griffith Stadium by knocking one out of the park. As it happened, the dinger was a grand slam over the right field wall off Walt Masterson, and a particularly hurtful one at that, as it provided the margin of victory in a 5–1 decision over the Nats. The homer meant that Mize had finally homered in every ballpark in the big leagues, and it was only fitting that immense Griffith Stadium should be last on the list of conquests. Playing at Grand Old Griffith certainly did not help the Nats' homer totals, but in terms of wins and losses, the dimensions were less important.

There were several other footnotes to the 1952 season. For the fifth and final time, Bobo Newsom joined the club. Signed to a contract just before the start of the season, Bobo hadn't pitched in the majors since 1948, but had remained active with the farm team at Chattanooga, where he'd averaged 15 wins per season since then. He won one and lost one for the Nats before being sent to the A's, where he hung around long enough to pitch in his 20th big-league season in '53. Bobo's last big-league win, his 211th, was his 200th in the American League and came at the ripe old age of 46 years, three weeks. In that game, which he won 10–4 over the Tigers, Newsom became the oldest pitcher to throw a complete game. Thus came to an end the career of a most original character, who was, incidentally, the only player whose big-league career spanned the period from the 1920s to the 1950s.

At about the same time in the spring of '52 that Bobo moved on to Philadelphia, the Nats finally parted ways with Sherry Robertson, Clark Griffith's nephew. The club's primary second baseman in '49, Sherry's career had taken a turn for the worse with Bucky Harris's arrival in 1950. Harris would not even let him take ground balls at second base at spring training, and when Robertson hit .189 in 62 games as a reserve outfielder in '51, his fate was sealed. He caught on with the A's following his release but hit just .200, mainly as a pinch hitter, and didn't play again. He would be well taken care of in the Griffith baseball empire, becoming a coach, farm director, and eventually vice-president before his untimely death in an auto accident at age 51 in 1970.

On May 15, '52, the Nats were no-hit at Briggs Stadium in Detroit by a chunky fastballer, 33-year-old Virgil Trucks. Trucks drew the most appropriate nickname of "Fire," as that is exactly what he threw up there. He walked only one on this day but could not have had any aspirations of tossing a perfect game, as his mates committed three errors behind him. The Nats might even have won the game — with two out in the bottom of the ninth, Bob Porterfield gave up a gopher ball to Vic Wertz for the only run of the game. There are two more relevant facts here: the second much more surreal than the first. Firstly, Fire Trucks, on August 25 of the same season, pitched another no-hitter, this time versus the team with the best batting percentage in the league, the Yankees. Secondly, in this same season, Trucks finished with an atrocious 5–19

won-loss record. This dubious accomplishment was attained despite the fact that he allowed fewer hits than innings pitched, and that he gave up well under four walks per nine innings. His Tigers had to be a lousy club, and they truly were in 1952, finishing dead last at 50–104.

The Washington Nationals of 1952 and 1953 were very good ballclubs. The main strike against these teams was a crippling lack of power. In addition, the American League was very unbalanced, listing as a result of unbelievably strong clubs in New York, Cleveland, and to a lesser degree, Chicago and Boston. The Red Sox dropped 11 games in the standings in '52 as a result of being without Ted Williams, who was off fighting in Korea for practically the entire year. (He recorded only four hits, including a home run, in ten at-bats.) On February 19, 1953, Williams crash-landed his F–9 Panther jet fighter after it was hit by enemy fire. He escaped from the burning plane, and it exploded moments later.

In only 91 at-bats in '53, Ted Williams smoked 13 homers and batted .407. At that pace, he would have needed only 427 at-bats to break Babe Ruth's home-run record. Since Williams walked so much, however, he never did record that many official at-bats in any of the seven campaigns which followed his return from Korea.

Nineteen fifty-three also began on a sour note for the Washington Nationals. Clyde Milan, the great player who had coached for the club since 1937, collapsed and died of a heart attack while hitting fungoes at the start of spring training. He was just three weeks short of his 66th birthday at the time of his death on March 3.

The season also had an ominous start. In an early game, on Saturday, April 17, at Griffith Stadium, Mickey Mantle smashed what was possibly the longest home run ever. The blow came in the fifth inning off the Nats' new lefty, Chuck Stobbs, who had served up a fastball. The ball flew over the 50-foot fence at the 391-foot marker in left centerfield, and was deposited in the backyard of the house at 434 Oakdale Street. When Chuck Stobbs saw the ball take flight, he thought that it would land in the Potomac River. It was retrieved by a ten-year-old boy named Donald Dunaway, who turned it over to Mantle for a cash settlement and the 21-year-old star's autograph on another ball. Yankee publicist Red Patterson got out a measuring tape later and came up with the guesstimate on the distance — 565 feet!

Despite these early setbacks, the Nats had a good year. Within a couple of days, the Red Sox were in town and Walter Masterson shut them out and the team got on track. When the Bosox left town, they left behind Clyde Vollmer, who was returning to the Nats following a three-year absence. Vollmer had done well during his time in Boston. He enjoyed a 22-homer season in '51, and in July of that summer was baseball's hottest hitter, clubbing 13 dingers and driving in 30. On July 28, '51, he hit what still stands as the latest grand slam in major-league history, a blast in the 16th inning.

Now, though, Clyde Vollmer was being squeezed out of Boston by younger, faster men like Jim Piersall, Tommy Umphlett (more on these two later), and Gene Stephens, for whom the Red Sox were intent on providing more playing time. Vollmer played regularly for the Nats in 1953, hit .260, and drove in 74 runs in only 408 official at-bats. His purchase from the Red Sox resulted in Ken Wood getting his outright release, extinguishing his major-league career. Also as a consequence of Vollmer's presence, but precipitated by his woeful .196 bat mark in 68 games, Gil Coan lost his job as a regular player.

The golden-haired Californian, Jackie Jensen, had another good year for the Nats, although his average dipped a bit, to .266. Jensen again managed ten homers, and drove in 84. Jim Busby was really the star of the outfield. A vacuum cleaner out there, it was Busby's hitting, particularly during the last couple of months of the season, that had Bucky Harris raving about the fact that Washington now had the best centerfielder in the league. Busby hit .312 (fifth-best mark in the junior circuit and quite a jump from his .244 in '52) and drove in 82 runs.

Like Busby, Ed Yost led all players at his position in put-outs and, hovering in the low .240s on the heels of a poor offensive showing in '52, he turned on the juice in mid–August and wound up at a respectable .272. The Walking Man earned 123 free passes, and with Ted Williams out of the way, led the league in that category for the second consecutive year.

The second baseman was new, the third regular at the position in three years. National League transplant Wayne Terwilliger, purchased from the Dodgers the previous September, began a long association with Washington Senators baseball by providing some reliable defense while batting an adequate .252 with 46 ribbies. Shortstop Pete Runnels suffered a relapse, however, after his fine showing in '52, his first full year. His bat mark fell from .285 to .257, and his defense was the most porous among the league's regular shortstops. Runnels became the team's biggest question mark, but doubts about him would, eventually, prove unfounded.

To don the "tools of ignorance," a sound gloveman, Ed Fitz Gerald, was obtained in mid–May from the Pittsburgh Pirates. He hit .250, but that was much better than the anemic Mickey Grasso's .209. Fitz Gerald's fielding percentage was second best among the league's catchers (behind one of the all-time greats at the position, Sherman Lollar of the White Sox). He also turned a rare unassisted double play during the season, and drew attention as one of seven brothers who barnstormed as the "Traveling Fitz Gerald Basketball Team."

Unrivaled as player of the year for Washington in 1953 was Mickey Vernon. He hit 15 homers, the team high on a club which was again at the bottom in that department, and drove in 115, which would stand as the high-water mark of his illustrious career. Vernon's involvement in a neck-and-neck race for the batting title with Cleveland third baseman Al Rosen resulted in a most unusual, not to mention unfortunate, set of circumstances on the season's final day. Word came down to the dugout from the press box after the seventh inning that Rosen had collected three hits in

Cleveland, and had finished the year at .336. This meant that if Vernon, who was 2–for–4 on the day and stood at .337 for the season, came back up to the plate and made an out, he would lose the batting title.

Six more batters were due up before Mickey would once again come up to the plate. If they were all put out, obviously, he would not have to hit again. The game was already out of the Athletics' reach, important to the Senators, who evened their record at 76–76 for the year. In the eighth inning, Mickey Grasso had the temerity to slug a double. Perhaps realizing the foolhardiness of this, Grasso ventured so far off the bag that the A's really had no choice but to pick him off, which they did. There were no other threats to Mickey Vernon's batting average in the eighth.

In the ninth, the first man up, pinch hitter Kite Thomas, obtained from these same A's on waivers three months earlier, singled but then rashly decided to stretch the hit into a double. He was out by a country mile. The next batter was Eddie Yost, the shrewd judge of pitches, who struck out on a pitch over his head. Pete Runnels, an excellent contact man, was next, and also struck out, although it was not so blatantly obvious that he was trying to do so. It was only Pete's 36th strikeout in 486 at-bats.

Mickey Vernon won the batting title by one one-thousandth of a point over Al Rosen. This was regrettable, in the minds of most baseball fans, because Rosen was the loop's best offensive player, leading in home runs and runs batted in. Those among the Washington fans who noticed, and the players too, probably, might have rationalized the audacious acts by pointing to the importance of standing solidly by a teammate held in high esteem by all, and deservedly so. Collusion or not, shameful or not, the record stands, and Mickey Vernon, for one, could not blame himself for what transpired.

While not quite as good as in '52, the pitching staff was way better than average. Bob Porterfield had what would easily be the best season of his career, setting the pace in the A.L. for wins (22), shutouts (9), and complete games (24). *The Sporting News* named him American League Pitcher of the Year. His 255 innings were the most by a Washington pitcher in ten years (Early Wynn, 257 innings, 1943). Big Walter Masterson was also effective, racking up a 3.63 ERA despite 10–12 won-loss totals. Unfortunately for the Nationals, Masterson, at age 33, decided to retire during the off season. The other starters, Spec Shea and the lone lefty, Chuck Stobbs, rang up 12–7, 3.94, and 11–8, 3.29, totals respectively. Connie Marrero won eight games in a starting role, although his starts were generally limited to one a week.

Attendance had been declining steadily throughout the early 1950s, and at the end of 1953, fans were given yet one more reason to stay away from Griffith Stadium. If the American League gave its assent, the St. Louis Browns would be moving to nearby Baltimore, the first franchise shift in league history. Clark Griffith favored the move, feeling it was vital to that club's survival. His emissary at league meetings by now, however, was his nephew Calvin, who he considered his son. Calvin, meanwhile, was secretly, as far as the Old Fox was concerned, and vehemently opposed to shifting the Browns—Washington fans would then have the choice of attending ballgames in Baltimore. When the 84-year-old owner found out what was going on, he was predictably furious, and personally attended the session that gave the go-ahead for the formation of the present-day Baltimore Orioles.

In December, the club's administration gave the impression that it had given up on the idea of obtaining the slugging necessary to enable the Nats to rank with the league's elite. The sure sign came when, horror of horrors, the team's best athlete, Jackie Jensen, was traded to Boston on December 9, 1953—yet another dark day in Washington Senators history. The prevailing opinion was that Jensen was more trouble than he was worth, and there is evidence that Bucky Harris really worked hard to move him to the Red Sox. Jensen had a phobia of flying. Later in his career, he would at times disappear before team flights and resurface a thousand miles away, having made the long trip by car. Jensen also had a tendency to ground into double plays — in fact, on average, he hit into one every 28 at-bats for his career, an inordinately high frequency.

But ... Jackie Jensen became, in 1958, the American League's Most Valuable Player. Moving him was a real rock of a move. As soon as Jensen left Washington and was able to take aim at the alluring Green Monster, the left field wall in Boston, he never hit fewer than 20 home runs in six seasons, and averaged 26 a year. He led the league in runs driven in for three of those six years and had less than 100 only once in those seasons, in 1956, when he drove in 97. Jackie Jensen was also, as Ted Williams would testify, an outstanding outfielder with a gun for an arm.

In 1960, Jensen, then 33 and not able to handle the grind of constant travel, called it quits. He wanted to spend time with his family, he said, but his marriage didn't last, and neither did his retirement. He came back with the Red Sox in '61, the year following Ted Williams' retirement, but he was not as spry and managed 13–66–.263 numbers before hanging them up for good, just one home run shy of the magic 200 circle. His was a somewhat tragic career, at least from a baseball perspective, since Jackie could have been an even greater player than he was. He died on July 14, 1982, at age 55.

Clark Griffith wholeheartedly approved of the Jensen deal when it was made. After all, his ballpark was too big to think of stocking the team with home run hitters who wouldn't be able to hit the ball out for half the games anyway — might as well get another top-flight pitcher! The arm selected had to be left-handed, and the Nats thought Mickey McDermott, a garrulous, uninhibited sort, would be a good bet to bolster their chances.

McDermott had just enjoyed a terrific 18–10, 3.01, season, in Boston of all places, where everyone knew it was very tough for a lefty to be successful. McDermott arrived at spring training proclaiming himself a "triple-threat" as a ballplayer: he could pitch, hit

(nine homers and a career .252 B.A.) ... and sing! He did some crooning in nightclubs during the off season, but as it turned out, the Nats might have done better to invest in Perry Como or Pat Boone. McDermott had 17 wins left in his wing, and it took him six years to get them.

Compounding this monumental blunder was the inclusion of outfielder Tommy Umphlett in the deal. A rookie in '53, Umphlett had taken over Boston's vast center field for the retired Dominic DiMaggio. His defense was almost impeccable and he hit .283. It's no wonder that Ted Williams, who had never heard of Umphlett before going to Korea, wanted to know all about this guy. Well, Bucky Harris and Clark Griffith thought they knew all about him, and how sorely wrong they were. The best reason they should have come up with for acquiring Umphlett was that he was from North Carolina, traditional Senators country.

Umphlett had to be given every chance to make good, but he failed, and miserably. He hit .219 and .217 while playing in over 100 games in both 1954 and 1955. After that, it was adios. To make matters worse, the Nats got rid of Jim Busby two months into the 1955 season, still deluding themselves that Umphlett was going to be the man. The Jackie Jensen trade was one nightmarish incident in the history of Washington baseball, rivaling the Early Wynn fiasco for sheer boneheadedness.

The Nats did get lucky in the winter and spring, however. On February 18, 1954, they peddled Gil Coan, whose market value by now was close to zilch, to the St. Louis Browns, for a former Rookie of the Year (1949), Roy Sievers, age 27. The Browns had somewhat soured on Sievers, a victim of the so-called sophomore jinx in 1950 who ran into some incredibly bad luck soon afterward. On August 1, '51, he separated a shoulder making a tumbling catch, causing him to miss the rest of the season. He reported early the following spring, but dislocated his arm at the shoulder and didn't play again until September. Having sat out more than a full year, he drove in only 35 runs in 92 games in '53. But in Washington, Roy Sievers would enjoy some wonderful seasons, particularly in 1957 and '58, and would be a star for the Nats for six years. Gil Coan had but two years left in the majors, and as a part-time player at that.

Barely a month into the '54 season, the Nats purchased the contract of Jim Lemon, a lanky 26-year-old 6'4" outfielder with all of 28 games' worth of big-league experience. Lemon would have to be sent down for seasoning, but by 1956 he would be an important cog. As for Roy Sievers, he paid dividends right away. Nicknamed "Squirrel" because, as a high-school basketball player, he had hung around the "cage" all the time, Sievers batted just .232 in his first year in Washington, but poled 24 homers and drove in 102 runs. No Washington player had hit 20 homers in a season since 1938, when both Zeke Bonura and Al Simmons did so. Then lo and behold — or, as Yogi Berra said, "You could look it up"— Roy Sievers hit 24 in his first year with the club. Nobody, in the 54-year history of the Washington American League baseball club, had ever hit that many home runs in a season.

As if invigorated by Sievers' presence, Mickey Vernon turned it up a notch and hit 20 homers himself, for the one and only time in his 20-year career. Vernon also drove in 97 runners and, as reigning batting champion, hit at a .291 clip. For all that, however, the Nats were not a better ballclub in '54. Fewer runs were scored because of a team batting percentage which plummeted from .263 to .246, next to last in the A.L. They scored 55 fewer runs and dropped 11 games and one rung in the standings, down to sixth place.

In June '54, positive things were happening more off the field than on. The Nationals were courting a sturdy, athletic teenager from Payette, Idaho, as were all the teams in the majors but one. Harmon Killebrew wanted nothing more than to play big-league baseball for a living, but, just turning 18, he figured he would go to the University of Oregon on a football scholarship first. Killebrew's sister, however, had been in the employ of Idaho Senator Herman Welker for a while,

and it was Welker who sought to bend Clark Griffith's ear with regard to this kid, who could really hit a baseball a long way.

The old man listened, and an offer was made that no other team bothered to top. All along, it was the Red Sox who had shown the most interest in Killebrew. Boston scout Earl Johnson had told him not to sign anything before checking with him first. But Boston did not counter when Washington offered a $4,000 signing bonus and a total of $10,000 for each of the next three years. Of course, in 1954, this was tantamount to making the player Washington property forever. Harmon Killebrew rationalized his decision, reasoning that with the Senators, he stood a better chance of making it to the major leagues.

Killebrew was the diligent sort, having had a job since the age of 12 and being orphaned at 16. He was a confident young man who felt he could adjust to anything, including facing pitchers at the very highest level of professional baseball. Rooming with Johnny Pesky, the longtime Red Sox shortstop the Nats obtained in mid–June from the Tigers, wouldn't hurt Killebrew either. The bonus contract he signed guaranteed him a spot on the roster for two years, this being the "bonus-baby rule" in effect in baseball at the time.

Despite joining the Nats in June, Killebrew got up to bat on only 13 occasions all year, striking out three times, walking twice, and banging out an encouraging four hits, including a double. But it would take Harmon Killebrew a full five years to become a force on the major-league playing field, and the Nats needed help right away. None of the regulars besides Roy Sievers, Mickey Vernon, and Jim Busby (who hit .298 and enjoyed a second successive excellent year before being traded away) had particularly good campaigns in 1954.

In baseball lingo, the term "career year" means an uncommonly productive season for a player, one which posterity shows was not duplicated. Jim Busby had *two* career years during his 13-year journey through the major leagues, and he had them both while in a Washington uniform. Considering that he only played two full seasons with the Senators (and parts of two others), the Nats were pretty lucky to have him when they did.

Third sacker Ed Yost did score 101 times and walk 131 times in '54, and led the league in put-outs and assists, but hit no better than .256. Pete Runnels' .268 was a long way off his earlier promise, and his defense was very wobbly, his .953 percentage way down the list in that category among the league's shortstops. Second baseman Wayne Terwilliger, suddenly average defensively, disappointed with an anemic .208. The ex-marine's fielding percentage would rebound the following year, and he would hit much better (.257). By then, however, Terwilliger would be a part-timer in the National League, where he would be a teammate of the player he later said was the best he ever saw, a 24-year-old kid named Willie Howard Mays. After that year, 1955, the slender Twig had fewer than 100 games left in the big leagues, but he would spend much of the 1960s as a Senators coach.

Catcher Ed Fitz Gerald was a surprise offensively, chipping in with a fine .289 average in 1954. The pitching staff was certainly decent when taken as a group, but lacked an outstanding contribution from anyone, including Bob Porterfield, who would never come close to replicating his successes of 1953. Porterfield had a solid 13–15, 3.22, season. The new southpaw, 33-year-old Johnny Schmitz, a veteran spot starter formerly with the Cubs who'd been unable to pitch on a regular basis since 1950, was the top hurler at 11–8, 2.91. Mickey McDermott, the easygoing righty the Nats had traded Jackie Jensen for, was saddled with hard luck and wound up a miserable 7–15, 3.44.

The other starters were the power lefty, Chuck Stobbs, at 11–11, 4.10, and rookie Dean Stone, another lanky southpaw, who delivered a promising 12–10, 3.22. Stone had the privilege of being named the winning pitcher in the 1954 All-Star game. An honor indeed, because he didn't face a single batter. With two down in the eighth and the American League trailing 9–8, Stone came into the game with Red Schoendienst, a ten-year St. Louis Cardinals veteran, on third base. Schoendienst tried to steal home on the rookie, and got nailed. The A.L. scored three runs in the next half-inning.

There is an apocryphal story of Dean Stone's young son having a discussion with another player's son in the locker room of the Houston Colts, a new National League entry, in the early 1960s. Dean's boy insisted his father was not a baseball player, but a boxer, and when challenged offered as evidence the fact that whenever he heard a radio announcer speak of his father, he would always end up saying, "There goes Stone, he's been knocked out again!" Stone never won more than six games in a season again, and compiled a grand total of 29 decisions in eight years in the big leagues.

Spec Shea's fastball wasn't so fast anymore, his change wasn't changing, his slider wasn't sliding, and a 2–9, 6.18, slate resulted. The other main player on the '54 staff was a rookie Cuban righthander blessed with a blazing fastball, Camilo Pascual. The slender Pascual had been recommended to the Nats by his brother, Carlos, nicknamed "Big Potato" because of his roundish stature (listed at 5'6½", 172 pounds). Big Potato had pitched 17 innings with good results for the Senators back in 1950.

Just 4–7, 4.22, in his rookie 1954 season, 20-year-old Camilo, "Little Potato," would struggle for four more years, amassing an appalling 28–66 big-league record before coming up with a wicked sidearm curve to complement his fastball and, ultimately, his pinpoint control. Pascual would eventually win 20 games twice in a row and become the league's strikeout king. Cool and confident, it was he who, when reached by phone at the team hotel early one morning by an intruding reporter who asked whether he spoke English, replied just before hanging up that yes he did, but not at seven o'clock in the morning.

Another Cuban, outfielder Carlos Paula, joined the ball club on September 6, 1954. This was a very significant occurrence because Paula became the first negro to play for the Washington Senators. The next day, 460 fans — 460! — showed up for a game with the

A's at Griffith Stadium. Despite early consideration of the concept of improving the Senators by signing black players more than a decade earlier, the Nats became one of the last teams to incorporate them. The Red Sox became the very last club in the league to do so when they added infielder Elijah "Pumpsie" Green to their lineup on July 21, 1959.

The 6'3", 195-pound Carlos Paula, who, like Camilo Pascual, was from Havana, brought a lot to the plate as a hitter, and would do well in '55 as a quasi-regular. Paula also had a tremendously strong throwing arm, but unfortunately that did not compensate for the fact that he often threw in the wrong direction. Despite a .271 major-league average, he was gone, never to return, by early 1956. Harmon Killebrew and Camilo Pascual, the two main ingredients of a club that would eventually win a pennant, were also both a long way from stardom, but they were now onboard. The Washington Senators, 66–88 in '54, were better off than anyone could have known.

Bucky Harris was fired following the season, a decision which Calvin Griffith urged his 85-year-old uncle to make. The real change was that for the first time since 1911 (when Jimmy McAleer was appointed), a pilot was hired who had never played for the club. The man picked this time was Charlie Dressen, a 56-year-old, 5'6" pepperpot who ironically had coached for the Yankees under Bucky Harris in 1947–48. Dressen, an inveterate gambler on the horses, would establish himself as a player's manager with the Nats, the third major-league club he directed.

Back in 1933, Dressen, a third baseman, had ended his eight-year playing career, virtually all of which was spent with the Cincinnati Reds. He was a coach with the Giants by the time they beat the Senators in 1933 in that last World Series for Washington. Dressen had coached or managed, mainly in the big leagues, since then, and had recently led the Brooklyn Dodgers to pennants in two of the last three years he managed there. He missed in '51, but it took Bobby Thomson's "shot heard around the world" in the last inning of a three-game

playoff to do it. When the Dodgers replaced Dressen with Walter Alston for the 1954 season, they lost the pennant to the New York Giants by five games.

Following a '54 season during which he guided the Oakland Oaks of the Pacific Coast League to a modest 85–82 record, the effervescent, extroverted Dressen brought his boundless enthusiasm to Washington. Charlie had a strong ego and never lacked confidence. Among the oft-repeated warcries heard by his players were, "Hold them, boys, I'll think of something," and "I'll steal enough games to put us well into the first division." Despite the bravado, with the Nats his seemingly contagious attitude wasn't translating into gains in the win column. Two seasons after piloting Brooklyn to 105 victories, he found himself at the helm of an outfit which lost 101 games.

Things went sour very early. After winning their home opener, 12–5 over the Orioles, the Nats suffered the most lopsided Opening Day defeat (it was the *Yankees'* season opener) in history. Whitey Ford twirled a two-hitter, had more hits himself (three singles) than the entire Washington team, and drove in four runs. Mickey Mantle, Yogi Berra, and sophomore player Bill Skowron all homered. Mantle and Bob Cerv each drove in four runs. Final score — New York 19, Washington 1.

In 1955, the Nationals (the name had regained popularity by the midfifties) gave credence to the current broadway hit, *Damn Yankees*. This was the musical adaptation by Richard Adler and Jerry Ross of the book by Douglass Wallop published the previous year entitled *The Year the Yankees Lost the Pennant*. The Nats hit rock bottom in '55, the club's first last-place finish since 1949, but only its third in 46 seasons. The play was about an aging Washington Senators fan, long thirsting for a pennant, who sold his soul to the devil so that he could be transformed into a superstar named Joe Hardy who would lead the Nats to glory. By finishing last in this year, of all years, the Nats reinforced the notion, rather an unfair one, that they were indeed the league's doormats. As the nickname "Nats" was employed extensively in the musical fantasy, the team's administration, namely the Griffiths, began insisting that the club be exclusively referred to as the "Senators."

The new outfielder, Carlos Paula, was very nearly the team's best hitter in 1955, at .299, but his ten outfield errors led the league and contributed to Washington placing very near the bottom of the league in that department. Mickey Vernon, at age 37, enjoyed his third consecutive fine year with the bat, just making it beyond the magical barrier at .301, with good power, clubbing 14 homers and driving in 85.

Roy Sievers topped both those figures, with 25–106, and improved his batting average dramatically, upping it nearly 40 points, to .271. Tom Umphlett failed to hit, and some of his time was taken up by a pint-sized (5'4", 145 pounds) lefthanded outfielder named Ernie Oravetz. Oravetz came through, batting .270 in 100 games despite a puny .171 percentage as a frequent pinch hitter (35 official at-bats). Like Paula, little Ernie Oravetz would not be as successful the following year and would depart the big leagues during the '56 season.

When ironman Eddie Yost missed 32 games because of his tonsillitis in '55, Harmon Killebrew, just turning 19, stepped into the breach. The youngster saw his first big-league action at third base (his three appearances in the field in '54 had been at second), a position he had never played before. Reporters and fans alike in Washington were already comparing Killebrew to Joe Hardy, the fictitious country hick who had become a big-league slugger in *Damn Yankees.* If the comparison was premature, it was certainly prophetic.

On June 24, 1956, Killebrew, five days short of his 20th birthday, hit his first big-league homer at Griffith Stadium during the course of a lopsided defeat at the hands of the Tigers. With a 2–2 count, Tiger catcher Frank "Pig" House told the kid that Tiger lefty Billy Hoeft was about to throw a fastball. Killebrew didn't know whether House was being truthful, but found out that he was, and the result was a very long blast. While he would hit

many more home runs at Griffith Stadium, he came to consider his first one as perhaps the longest he ever hit there. Frank House told Killebrew as he crossed the plate that this was the last time he would ever tell him what was coming. Harmon hit three more homers for his 80 at-bats, including the longest shot in Baltimore all year. At season's end, his forced servitude on a big-league bench came to an end — he had served the two-year apprenticeship warranted by the bonus rule.

Killebrew hit .200 in '56, an inauspicious debut for a man who would eventually rank second only to Babe Ruth in American League homers, and whose rate of hitting one out every 14.22 at-bats would place him third in major-league history. But Killebrew would spend the better part of the next three seasons toiling in the minor leagues at Charlotte, N.C., and Chattanooga, Tenn. The youngster felt some minor-league experience would do him good, and in the equivalent of half a season at Charlotte of the Sally League in '56, he hit .325 with 15 homers.

One asterisk to this season belongs against September 17, when the Senators were the visitors at Baltimore as another future great third baseman made his major-league debut. He went 2–for–4 in a 3–1 decision over the Nats. His name — Brooks Robinson, a name which would become synonymous with fielding excellence.

Within a month of the end of a very dismal last-place 53–101 season, only the team's second 100-loss debacle since 1909 (1949 was the other), Clark Griffith died. The Old Fox breathed his last on October 27, 1955, on the 44th anniversary of the signing of his first contract to manage the ballclub. He was 24 days short of his 86th birthday. Griffith's career in professional baseball spanned 67 years, and the Old Fox had lived the last nine years of his life with the status of a member of the National Baseball Hall of Fame. Aside from having been the patriarch of the Senators, his legacy includes the development of relief pitching as a strategic part of the game. The succession of relievers Griff employed during the seventh game of the 1924 World Series forced the

Giants to pull Bill Terry from the game, and eventually set the stage for Walter Johnson's, and the Washington Senators', most triumphant hour.

Sadly, scarcely more than two months following Griffith's death, his old friend, Connie Mack, passed away, on February 8, 1956. The Tall Tactician, who had given up managing only five years earlier after leading the A's from the bench for exactly 50 years, was two weeks short of his 94th birthday at the time of his death.

Under the terms of Clark Griffith's will, both Calvin and Thelma acquired 26 percent of the franchise. "Twenty-six percent what?" was the key question. Operating on a shoestring budget throughout these many years, Calvin Griffith revealed there was barely $25,000 in the club's account at the time of his uncle's death. While this was still an era when major-league teams had farm clubs scattered all over the country, Washington had only three — at Charlotte, Chattanooga, and Orlando, Florida. More money was being made from concessions and renting Griffith Stadium to the football Redskins than from actual attendance at baseball games. The team had fallen into last place, and *Damn Yankees* was every Washington Senators fan's nightmare.

Minority stockholder H. Gabriel Murphy presented another obstacle for Calvin Griffith, who assumed control of the ballclub because his sister Thelma was happy to rubber-stamp everything. With Clark's passing, Murphy had hoped the franchise, on which he had gained first option in 1950, would pass into his own hands. When he discovered the Griffiths weren't prepared to cooperate, he began disparaging Calvin Griffith's ability to govern a ballclub. Murphy harped hard and long about the family-run front office, which included Thelma's husband, Joe Haynes, as vice-president, brother Sherry Robertson as farm director, and two other brothers as head of concessions and stadium operations. Throughout the rest of this decade and well into the next, Murphy filed various lawsuits aimed at gaining control of the franchise. Try as he might, he would never be successful.

Meanwhile, the Nats were desperate to improve themselves on the field for 1956. On November 8, '55, less than two weeks after Clark Griffith's death, a nine-player deal was struck with the Red Sox. The Nats were giving up veterans for youth, and Mickey Vernon was traded away for the second and last time. Vernon would produce at a .310 clip as a 38-year-old in '56, but it would be his last full season. The Nats also parted with two members of their starting staff, Bob Porterfield, 10–17, 4.45, in '55, and lefty Johnny Schmitz, 7–10, 3.71. They threw in Tommy Umphlett, their prodigy of two years before, obtained in the catastrophic Jackie Jensen trade. Jensen had just led the American League in runs batted in for 1955, with 116.

While Porterfield had a dismal year and the veteran Schmitz's career was all but over, the Washington Senators struck out on all counts with their new acquisitions. Righthander Tex Clevenger, 23, would win the grand sum of 29 games over five years for them, and Dick Brodowski, also 23, had three big-league wins left in his right arm, none at all as a member of the Senators. A third pitcher, minor-leaguer Al Curtis, never made it to the show at all.

With Roy Sievers having moved to the infield, there was not one outfield position which wasn't up for grabs in '56. Karl Olson, a big lad who'd been on the Red Sox bench over parts of most years in the early fifties, would squander the one good chance the Nats were willing to give him. During spring training, Olson voiced the opinion that the Green Monster, the invitingly close left field wall at Boston's Fenway Park, had been his ruination as a hitter. According to him, the Red Sox had tried to make him a pull hitter, spoiling his previous proclivity for spraying his hits all over the place. But Olson never did recover from whatever it was that Boston did to him, and hit just .246 with four homers for the Senators.

Carlos Paula and the other outfielder obtained from the Red Sox along with Olson, Neil Chrisley, had been expected to fight it out for the rightfield spot. Paula could muster only .183 in 33 games, and that's when he found himself back in the minors permanently. As for Chrisley, he wouldn't even make the team before 1957, and would hit just .204 over parts of '57 and '58. Mickey Vernon's .310 average for the Red Sox would have tied him for best on the club in Washington in 1956. The mark belonged to Pete Runnels, enjoying a second fine year in succession with the bat (.284 in '55), who drove in 76 runs.

The Nats were marginally better offensively in 1956, banging out 112 homers, 32 more than the previous year, thanks to the exploits of Roy Sievers and the club's new longball threat, Jim Lemon. When Calvin Griffith assumed the club presidency in time for the '56 season, he had ordered a six-foot screen placed 55 feet in front of Griffith Stadium's left field stands, reducing the distances for the likes of Lemon, Sievers, and later, Harmon Killebrew. The new 350–408–320 dimensions from left to right would not, however, improve the club's standing during the old ballpark's few remaining years.

Roy Sievers, playing first following Vernon's departure, produced 29–95–.253 numbers. Jim Lemon came to spring training fresh from having led the Mexican Pacific Coast League in homers during the winter. He had slammed 40 in a season and a half in the minors, but had a reputation of striking out often. While certainly no gazelle defensively, Lemon became the answer to the right-field predicament and produced a solid 27–96–.271 '56 campaign to take the team RBI title in his rookie year.

The only other real fixture in the lineup aside from Roy Sievers as the season got under way was Eddie Yost. (It was believed at the time that Pete Runnels was being seriously challenged at second by Herbie Plews.) Yost, always stellar in the field, led the league in put-outs, assists, and double plays at the hot corner, but experienced an off year at the dish. He hit just .231, but on September 6, 1956, he walked twice, and the second free pass was his 142nd of the season, which broke the team record he already held. Yost finished the season with a career-high 151 walks, still the all-time Washington Senators record.

Chuck Stobbs' slate was 15–15, 3.60, which qualified him as the ace on a pitching staff on which he got no competition. Stobbs missed his 16th win, and instead got debited with a loss, when the Yankees scored two unearned runs on an error committed by Eddie Yost, of all people. This was a fine comeback effort by the 27-year-old lefty, who had been a huge disappointment with a 4–14 record and an even 5.00 ERA in '55. The cool Cuban, Camilo Pascual, who seemed to have all the right stuff, got hammered often for the second straight season, and finished a dreadful year at 6–18, 5.87. This was a slight improvement, considering Little Potato's 2–12, 6.14, performance in '55. Pascual had an uncommonly good breaking ball but was wild on occasion. He often pitched his best when extricating himself from jams for which he had only himself to blame. His penchant for giving up the long ball resulted in his setting the new unenviable record for home runs allowed in a season: 34.

Pascual's roommate, at least until Charlie Dressen split the pair up so that they would learn English more quickly, earned the nickname the "Cuban Cowboy" during this season. Pedro Ramos, just 21 and a native of Pinar del Rio, Cuba, had debuted in '55 with a decent 5–11, 3.88, campaign. Highly sought after by the Dodgers organization as a high schooler, Ramos had instead signed for $150 a month with Joe Cambria, correctly calculating that his chances of reaching the big leagues would be better with Washington. Three years later, he was earning $6,500 a year as a 20-year-old rookie in the big leagues. As Ramos's 5.27 ERA attests, he was lucky to wind up 12–10 in 1956. He and Chuck Stobbs were the only two pitchers on the club with more than six wins.

On one particular trip to Kansas City, Ramos, who loved the smell of anything western, had tagged along with catcher Clint Courtney, who was shopping for cows for his farm. Ramos ended up buying a complete western wardrobe in a supply store, including guns — real ones — and a gun belt. The Cuban Cowboy paraded around downtown Washington in full regalia, including the guns. He did *not* bring the pistols to the ballpark, but he did show up at Griffith Stadium in stetson hats, fringed jackets, and black Hoppalong Cassidy–style suits.

It took a lot to dampen Ramos's spirit, and it *would* be tested. By 1958, the flashy Cuban would begin a string of four seasons during which he would lead the entire league in losses each year. A confirmed bachelor known for dating a bevy of girls, Ramos nonetheless never got himself in trouble by missing curfew. But later in life, trouble would find him. In 1979, he was arrested for possession of cocaine in a drug bust that reportedly netted authorities two million dollars. For that, the Cuban Cowboy got a three-year prison term.

Washington's pitching staff, far and away the American League's worst, kept the team in the headlines throughout most of the '56 season. The late Clark Griffith had been known to say, tongue in cheek when things weren't going well, that baseball fans loved home runs, and the Washington Senators had rounded up a bunch of pitchers capable of keeping them happy. The truth was, however, that the Nats were generally among the leaders in fewest home runs allowed (during the preceding 15-year period, 1941–55, the Senators were nine times tops in fewest homers given up). The reason for that, of course, was the sheer vastness of Griffith Stadium and the advantage it represented for pitchers who played half their games there.

The Old Fox would have been spinning in his grave had he been around for 1956. Now in smaller confines at home, Nats hurlers, who'd surrendered only 99 home runs in '55, served up 171 gopher balls, better only than the dreadful last-place Athletics. The trend began in the home opener, April 17, on the third anniversary of Mickey Mantle's 565-foot blast at Griffith Stadium. Mantle, starting off a Triple Crown campaign in fitting style, hammered more than a thousand feet worth of home runs off Camilo Pascual. It only took two shots, so they were evidently prodigious, both traveling over 500 feet. The second one was proclaimed the longest ever hit into Griffith's rightfield bleachers. Mantle's .353–52–130 season would justify the stunning $10,000 salary increase,

to $30,000, which he had been awarded during the previous off season.

A month into the campaign, Camilo Pascual lost a game in a most unorthodox fashion against the Indians. Pascual allowed just two hits, but surrendered 11 walks, three of which came with all the bases occupied, and dropped a 5–1 decision. It didn't help that Herb Score was striking out 15 Nats while surrendering just three hits. The very next day, much was made of a pitch delivered by Chuck Stobbs at Briggs Stadium in Detroit. With Bob Kennedy batting with the bases loaded, Stobbs fired a missile which may well have been the wildest pitch in history. Laterally, it was about 30 feet off the mark, toward the first base side. Vertically, it was something else again — the ball landed in the seventeenth row of the stands! Stobbs admitted later that at the very moment he released that ball, he would have liked to have dug a hole right then and there on the mound and crawled into it.

On May 30, 1956, Pete Ramos incurred the wrath of the rampaging Mickey Mantle. There was some history involving the two. Ramos, a terrific athlete, was the hardest thrower on the Senators, and perhaps in the league at times, but he was also a fine hitter for a pitcher. He slugged 15 lifetime homers, and twice got two in a game. He was also fast afoot, and proud of it to the point that he challenged Mickey Mantle to a footrace on several occasions. Mantle never took him up on the offer, but he did meet Ramos's fastball squarely on this late May day.

The Mick had worked the count to 2-and-2, and Ramos at this point wanted him to hit the ball. But the result was astounding. The ball came within 18 inches of clearing the famous Yankee Stadium facade and leaving the park. It was the closest anyone ever came to hitting a ball out of the Stadium. It was also estimated that this one would have traveled 600 feet had its trajectory not been obstructed. The blow came during the first game of a doubleheader. Following a 12–5 drubbing of Pascual in the nightcap, Mantle, who had homered again, had 16 dingers for May and was batting .425 with 50 ribbies.

Then on July 1, following a 3–2 Yankee win in the first game of a twin bill at Yankee Stadium, Mantle hit switch homers in the same game for the fourth time in his career. The first shot, which had Mantle batting righty against the Nats' fourth starter, Dean Stone, was number 28 of the season. Stone went 5–7 for the year, with a sad 6.27 ERA. Home run number 29 came with Mantle turned around against Eldred "Bud" Byerly, a tall 35-year-old who hadn't pitched with any regularity in the big leagues in five years. While he pitched in only 25 games, all in a relief role, Byerly had by far the best ERA on the staff, 2.96, winning two while losing four.

A week after Mantle's switch-hitting exploitation of the Senators' pitching, it was the All-Star break, and the baseball world focused on Washington for the game of July 10. It would have been a proud time for Clark Griffith, who had had his one opportunity to host the game back in 1937. While the A.L. had triumphed on that occasion, it was to be a different story this time. The game was entertaining, and never had so many upper-echelon stars homered in the same game. Willie Mays had a two-run shot and Stan Musial homered in the All-Star tilt for the second straight year. For the A.L. side, Ted Williams and Mickey Mantle hit back-to-back homers in the sixth. But by then, the National League, powered on this day by St. Louis third baseman Ken Boyer's three hits and three outstanding fielding plays, was leading 5–0 on its way to a 7–3 verdict.

The summer got a lot longer in Washington after the break. A number of hurlers got their one big crack at the big leagues with the Washington Senators in '56, and none made good. Bob Wiesler, a big righthander plucked from the Yankees farm system, finished with a disastrous 3–12, 6.44. Wiesler was one of five players the Senators finagled out of the Yankees on February 8 (the day Connie Mack died) in exchange for Mickey McDermott, the third starter traded out of the rotation since the end of the '55 season, and shortstop Bobby Kline, who had hit just .221 in what was to be his one shot at the majors with the Nats in '55. The ballclub was at least able to add quantity to a thin lineup as a result of this transaction. Lou Berberet became a capable backup catcher. Veteran minor-leaguer Herbie Plews brought infield versatility and a .270 average. Pete Runnels was often moved to first against righthanders in order to make room for Plews' bat.

The other middle infielder in the picture was Jose Valdivielso, a 22-year-old from Matanzas, Cuba, who had hit .221 as a half-timer for the Nats in '55. At this time, Chuck Dressen was hailing Valdivielso as the best defensive shortstop in the league, and declared the kid would be the "all-everything" in the American League if only he could hit as high as .270. Pete Runnels, moved over to second as a result of Valdivielso's arrival, proceeded to have a much better season in '55, from both offensive and defensive standpoints. In Dressen's mind, the shortstop position had gone from being the most vulnerable in the infield, to the strongest position.

Valdivielso, who had weighed about 160 pounds in 1955 before adding another 15 pounds or so during the winter, had a tendency to swing from the heels. The astute Chuck Dressen attempted to correct this by painting a white mark above the knob of the shortstop's bat and threatening a fine if Valdivielso put his hands below that line. Valdivielso improved, but minimally, to just .236, and thereafter his time in the major leagues was curtailed to almost nothing before he briefly resurfaced again in 1960.

Another prospect the Nats had taken off the hands of the talent-laden Yankees roster in the McDermott trade was Whitey Herzog, a 24-year-old rookie outfielder. Herzog played in 117 games, which would remain his career high for a season, and batted .245. Most of his baseball heroics, however, were still far in the future. Herzog would eventually manage major-league clubs to five division championships and one World Series conquest (St. Louis Cardinals, 1982).

As for Mickey McDermott, for whom Jackie Jensen had been traded, it would soon be time for the nightclub crooner to sing for his supper. Just 28 years old, McDermott would win just four more games in the big leagues. If the Yankees had much the better of the Senators on the field in '56, the Nats were best in their own boardroom on the day McDermott passed out of the organization. Aside from Bob Wiesler, among the many mound misfits with the Nats in '56 was one Veston Goff "Bunky" Stewart, a skinny rake of a left-hander, who got his first big break with the club since being called up in 1952. Stewart had fives and sevens going for him, but that resulted in a 5–7, 5.57, record, and that was the last he knew of life in the big leagues.

Another lefty, an ex–Dodger farm hand with the somewhat unfortunate name of Conrad "Connie" Grob (which rhymes with "probe"), went 4–5, 7.83, in his one kick at the can. Righthander Bob Chakales, one of three players obtained from the White Sox for Jim Busby the previous June, was better, at 4–4, 4.03, as a reliever, but within a year it would be all over for him as well. Perhaps Grob and Chakales had set the tone for the entire season when, while enjoying some time off on the golf course during spring training, they went off a narrow bridge with their electric cart and took a dunking in the lake below. That, and Chuck Dressen falling into the water while fishing, provided some early laughs in a season that turned out to be no laughing matter.

Other than Bob Chakales, the players Washington obtained when they parted with Jim Busby made that trade a palatable one, for a change. Busby, as intimated earlier, never had another good offensive year after leaving Washington, despite hanging around in the majors for the better part of seven more seasons. Johnny Groth, one of the players the Nationals got for him, turned out to be a very useful player, but not for the Nats, as he was unwisely sold to the A's early in the season.

The third player the White Sox had banished to Washington for Busby was a catcher, Clint Courtney. Besides being a farmer, Courtney was also a catcher and a hitter, and he did a decent job at both. Immediately taking over for Ed Fitz Gerald, who'd been slip-

ping offensively, Courtney hit .298 over the second half of the '55 season, and was a bulwark again in '56, batting an even .300 with 44 runs driven in. He was the first catcher to wear eyeglasses, but if that made him look like a professor, mild-mannered he was not. It was Courtney who his ex-teammate with the St. Louis Browns, the renowned Negro League pitcher Satchel Paige, had called "the meanest man alive."

Due to his combative nature, Clint Courtney was nicknamed "the "Toy Bulldog" by either his manager with the Browns, Marty Marion, or broadcaster Dizzy Dean, Courtney's most celebrated altercation came as a member of the Browns, in a game against the Yankees on July 12, 1952. He had originally come up in the Yankees' system but had been pushed out of the picture by Yogi Berra, and was now pushing back. In the second inning, Courtney kicked the ball out of second baseman Billy Martin's glove. In the sixth, he slid hard into Berra at the plate. In the eighth, the Toy Bulldog tried to steal second, but was beaten by a tag applied to the face for his trouble. He sprang to his feet to go after Martin, but Billy decked him, not once but twice, sending Courtney's glasses flying. The dugouts emptied and two umpires were knocked down in the ensuing confusion. When the dust cleared, Courtney was ejected; Martin was not.

Very early the following season, Courtney became angry when Gil McDougald of the visiting Yankees, who had come in to score standing up on a play that wasn't even close, needlessly barged into him and knocked the ball out of his glove. When the Browns came up, Courtney drove an Allie Reynolds offering off the right field screen, and kept right on going to second base. When he got there, he slid high into Yankee shortstop Phil Rizzuto. All hell broke loose, with several Yanks chasing Courtney and Reynolds getting in the first good shot.

The benches cleared, and with only three policemen on duty, fans threw bottles at the Yankees. Umpire John Stevens suffered a broken collarbone during the course of a 17-minute donnybrook, and amidst the pandemonium,

Clint Courtney lost a shoe. He also lost $250, the fine imposed by league president Will Harridge, who called Courtney the instigator who had "violated all rules of sportsmanship" during the course of his shameful Sportsman's Park display.

Clint Courtney was definitely a plus on a team lacking leadership, especially following Mickey Vernon's departure. Following his playing career, he would coach in the Astros' and Braves' chains, and two years to the day after being hired by the Braves to manage their top farm club at Richmond, he died at age 48. While a nice guy off the field who liked to drink beer and talk about cows, Courtney, a Hall of Famer as far as heart and competitiveness were concerned, was the furthest thing from nice on the field.

One of the best things to happen to Washington baseball followers during this summer was the election to the Baseball Hall of Fame, the legitimate one, on July 23, of Joe Cronin, who served the Senators as star shortstop and then player-manager during his seven-year tour of service, 1928–34. Within two weeks of his ascendancy to the Hall, Cronin, who at this stage had spent eight years in the Red Sox front office, found himself embroiled in an ugly scenario which featured Ted Williams in the leading role.

In a game at Fenway Park versus the Yankees, Williams took heat from the fans after misplaying a fly ball on a windy day. When he made a nice over-the-shoulder catch a little later in the game, he spat twice toward the section which had been jeering him the hardest. The Yankees bench was also on the Great One's case, so he lurched back out of the dugout and spat twice toward them. With the bases loaded in the bottom of the 11th, Williams drew a walk from Tommy Byrne and flung his bat about 40 feet in the air. General Manager Joe Cronin took a dim view of his star player's antics and fined him $5,000, but Williams was unrepentant. He had returned to baseball in 1954 and hit .345, after having missed practically all of the '52 and '53 seasons because of the Korean conflict. He asserted that some of the fans he had spit at were among the worst fans in the world. When, the following night, he cranked a homer at Fenway, Williams made a grand gesture of clapping his hand over his mouth as he crossed home plate. He again hit for a .345 average, sandwiching between .345 seasons a .356 mark in 98 games in '55.

Since being sold by his father-in-law, Joe Cronin had put the cap on an outstanding career by appearing as a player in another 11 seasons before hanging up the spikes with a .301 average after breaking his leg early in the 1945 season. He had managed the Red Sox all those years, but it wasn't before he quit as a player that he won his first pennant in Boston, in 1946, only to lose the World Series as a result of Enos Slaughter's "mad dash" in the seventh game. Following a disappointing third-place finish in '47, Cronin, still just 41, moved into the Boston front office for 11 more years.

Another great honor followed Joe Cronin's election to the Hall of Fame. In 1959, he was named President of the American League, the first former player elevated to that office. Under Cronin's stewardship, the American League would expand twice, but he drew criticism at times as well, particularly when he showed the door to two umpires after he found out they were trying to form a union. On another occasion, he came under fire for blocking Yankees owner George Steinbrenner's attempt to hire Dick Williams, while at the same time allowing the Tigers to sign Ralph Houk away from Steinbrenner's club.

By season's end, the Senators had lost 95 games, a six-game improvement, and they were spared last place only because the A's, who seemed better than the Nats in most areas, lost more close games and wound up with 102 defeats. The quality of play on the field was obviously not doing a whole lot to allay the perilous financial position the team was in. Washington fans first heard rumors their team could be moved in October 1956, when former baseball Commissioner Happy Chandler came to a Senators board meeting to announce that the city of Louisville, Kentucky, was prepared to build a 50,000-seat stadium. Louisville would also underwrite guarantees for at least a million fans a year for three years if the Senators would be willing to move there.

Similar offers poured in from San Francisco and Minneapolis. Happy Chandler's namesake, *Los Angeles Times* publisher Norman Chandler, began acting as a go-between with Calvin Griffith for the mayor of Los Angeles, Norris Poulson, who started exploring the possibility of bringing big-league ball to the west coast as early as 1957. Poulson, a former Congressman, was never impressed with the Griffiths and their ragtag ballclub during his time in the capital, and had already begun negotiations with owner Walter O'Malley to pull the Dodgers, the heart and soul of their community, out of Brooklyn, New York. Former California governor Earl Warren, Chief Justice of the Supreme Court, was meanwhile involved in attempting to hook Cal Griffith up with some San Jose businessmen. Those efforts came to naught when New York Giants owner Horace Stoneham agreed to move and rename his team the San Francisco Giants in time for 1958.

In response to mounting pressure in Washington, Senators president Calvin Griffith declared in the *Washington Post* in mid–January 1957, that neither he nor his team were going anywhere. The City of Washington was also under the gun, and the municipality applied enough pressure for Congress to agree to look at the possibility of financing a six million-dollar venue to replace creaky Griffith Stadium. The new facility, however, would be built in the predominantly black northeast section of town, and Cal Griffith objected to that. Griffith had no confidence that a new stadium would be the answer to his problems anyway. To the contrary, he was of the opinion that the new park would be run by government types who would rob him of the concessions and rent profits from the football team, the Redskins, which had been keeping his operation afloat in the first place.

By the middle of the decade, attendance had declined to well below a half million per season in Washington; by 1955, it had sunk to 425,238. On the field, the tenants of the 46-year-old structure were now mired in a horrible stretch of 15 years during which, for the period ending in 1960, they would reach the .500 level only twice. The Senators had not finished higher than fourth since the end of World War II, and they were getting worse.

On April 21, 1957, at Griffith Stadium, for the first time in major-league history, a game was called (suspended after five innings) on account of a power failure. Shortly afterward, the plug was pulled on Chuck Dressen after he got the squad away to a 5–16 start. His third base coach, Harry "Cookie" Lavagetto, took over from the man Jackie Robinson had called the best manager he'd ever played for. Lavagetto, however, was a good baseball man as well, as evidenced by the fact that Dressen, an expert sign stealer, had turned over the third base coaching reigns to him. Lavagetto was a direct sort who laid down the rules, and he gave his men no grief if they followed them.

It mattered little who was steering this vessel. The pitching staff was again by far the league's worst. Pete Ramos was the only one to win more than eight games, finishing at 12–16, with a disturbing 4.79 ERA. Before the season, Ramos had been denied a $1,000 raise to $7,500 by Calvin Griffith, despite his winning record in '56. This was two decades before the advent of free agency, and Ramos revealed later that Griffith had told him that if he didn't like the offer, he could go back to Cuba and cut sugar cane.

Camilo Pascual, in particular, made great strides, but occasional wildness and lack of support brought him no better than an 8–17 slate and a 4.10 ERA in 1957. Last year's ace, Chuck Stobbs, was this year's bum, tumbling to an 8–20 mark, which led the league in losses. His ERA was a wretched 5.36. Russ Kemmerer, a hard thrower, was obtained from the Red Sox at the end of April in a deal that saw Dean Stone and Bob Chakales go the other way. Kemmerer, who had gone 5–3 down the stretch for Boston as a rookie in '54, began a string of three losing seasons in Washington's starting rotation with a 7–11, 4.96, effort.

In relief, Bud Byerly had another good

year, at 6–6, 3.13. A bespectacled submariner named Dick Hyde appeared in 52 games, coming out of the bullpen in all but two of them, and went 4–3, 4.12. The 6'4" Ted Abernathy, who threw all the way underhand and whose curveball consequently shot up rather than sank, was terrible, and his record also sank, to 2–10, 6.78. This resulted in a two-year banishment to the minors, but when Abernathy returned, he had a largely pleasurable 11-year stay in the majors.

There was little offense, apart from that provided by Roy Sievers, to supplement the Senators' mound woes. The Squirrel had the best year of his career, not only setting a Senators record for home runs in a season with 42, but leading the entire league in '57. His 114 ribbies were also tops in the A.L. Sievers had begun spending more time in the outfield the previous year, and to compensate for the lack of talent in the garden, played left field almost exclusively in '57. Jim Lemon was second to Sievers in production, but with 50 fewer RBIs. He rapped out 17 homers and hit .284. Once again, Lemon led the league in strikeouts, but cut his total from 138 in '56 to 94 this season. In '58, he would make it three strikeout titles in a row by whiffing 120 times.

Bob Usher, sometimes a National League outfielder for various periods during the forties and fifties, played between Sievers and Lemon in the outfield. Usher managed a .261 bat mark in 96 games and became another in a long line of one-year players for the Washington Senators during the course of the 1950s. Eddie Yost jacked his average up by 20 points, but that was still only good for .251 with a paltry 38 runs driven in.

At short, the Nats introduced one of the game's great comedians, Rocky Bridges, who was snagged off the waiver wire from the Cincinnati Reds on May 20. Now nearly 30 years old, Bridges had been bounced between the majors and minors in the Dodgers' and Reds' organizations for more than ten years. As he put it, he had had more numbers on his back than you find on a bingo card. He used to say that he was moved so often between the majors and the bushes that his wife would

write to him in care of the Commissioner of Baseball. About batting .196 in limited opportunities on a great Dodger club in 1952, Bridges was quoted as saying that the more he played for Brooklyn, the more he found out that no one on the Dodgers could take a joke — the joke being his own batting average.

One of Bridges' best lines was delivered as he struggled with his weight. He told writers he was on a diet that called for two jiggers of scotch to one jigger of Metrecal, and to that point, he had lost five pounds ... *and* his driver's license. As had been the case in Brooklyn, there was nothing funny, however, about Rocky's .228 batting average for the Nats in '57. On the plus side, he was sure-handed defensively, and led the league in chances per game as a rookie.

Despite the output of Sievers and Lemon, the Senators were tied for last in batting percentage in the league, were near the bottom in homers, and seventh in runs scored. The club embarrassed itself by proving to be the most slothful in all of baseball history, managing a seemingly preposterous total of just 13 stolen bases all year, a shameful record not likely ever to be broken (the St. Louis Cardinals came closest, swiping 17 in 1949). For the second time in three years, the Nats were last, with the worst composite record in the league over that span.

On their way to their 55–99 status at the 1957 finish line, the Senators were no-hit: the season's only such example in either league. Bob Keegan of the White Sox, on August 20 at Comiskey Park, walked only two in blanking Washington 6–0. Keegan, a beefy righthander who was 32 when he made it to the majors, would only win 40 games in the big leagues. His moment in the sun coincided with poor Chuck Stobbs' 20th loss. Stobbs did not recover from this season and was never again the workhorse and dominating hurler he had once been.

Back on May 8, it was the same Bob Keegan who had surrendered three homers to Ted Williams, the first time in 11 years, surprisingly perhaps, that the Splendid Splinter had turned that particular feat. The bombastic

Williams, never one to mince words, had over the previous winter openly criticized the U.S. government for not having gone all out to win the war in Korea. Teddy Ballgame went so far as to call President Harry Truman and Senator Robert Taft "gutless politicians." (When Truman later met Williams, he told Teddy Ballgame how much he enjoyed watching him play, and that he didn't blame Ted for speaking out — that he himself had said a few things in his day.)

As a hitter, Williams had, over the past four years since his return from overseas, merely been solidifying his status as one of baseball's premier batsmen of all time. His lowest average over those four years was his .345 in both '54 and '56. This year, he was on his way to a batting title, and would fall, incredibly at age 39, just five hits short of .400. By now, it was 16 years since Williams had hit .406, the last mortal to do so in the majors. In September '57, the Senators called up Hal Griggs, who had won 21 games at Chattanooga and provided some reason for hope for 1958. On the 24th, Griggs got Williams to ground out, the first time Williams had made an out in a week. This incredible string had stretched over 16 consecutive official at-bats.

Next year, one of Williams' teammates would be Pete Runnels, who, following a move to first base to make way for Herbie Plews at second, was a disappointment in '57, batting .230 with a mere 35 runs batted in, which spelled the end for him in Washington. Plews hit .271 with little power, and within a year would already lose his status as a semiregular player. On January 23, 1958, the Senators traded Pete Runnels to the Red Sox for two players, little Albie Pearson, a 5'5" outfielder, and Norm Zauchin, a muscular 28-year-old first baseman who had once slugged 27 homers in a season. Pearson, only 23 but a gung-ho character, would be able to compete very well, and was named the '58 Rookie of the Year, the first time a Washington Senators player had been so honored since the award's inception in 1947.

Pearson's exploits, however, would be overshadowed by those of Pete Runnels, who

was about to shed the shackles of inconsistency that had so far characterized a good part of his seven years in Washington. The 30-year-old began hitting everything the other way and raised his average by nearly 100 points with the Red Sox, good for runner-up to Ted Williams in the batting race at .322. Williams, with .328, won a second straight batting title, at age 40.

Pete Runnels was to embark on a period of consistency that saw him hit well over .300 over a stretch of five years; his lowest mark during that time would be .314. He is remembered today because he won two batting titles during those years with the Red Sox, in 1960 and 1962, with .320 and .326 respectively. Unlike longtime Senators of earlier years, the lefty line-drive hitter never would return to Washington.

Harmon Killebrew spent nearly the entire '57 season down on the farm at A.A. Chattanooga, where he produced encouraging numbers — .279–29–101, with his home run total the Southern Association's best. The Senators had a top-notch baseball mind, Cal Ermer, later a big-league manager, expend long hours helping young Harmon learn the intricacies of playing the third-base position. At bat at this stage, Killebrew had a natural inclination to hit the low fastball but had trouble with high heat. Ermer took the time to pitch to him every day himself, before batting practice. When recalled briefly, Killebrew hit two homers and batted .290 in just 31 official plate appearances with the Nats.

Killebrew got exactly 31 official at-bats once again in '58, and he would admit later that this time, it was very disappointing for him to be sent back down to the minors. The Senators recognized his progress, but didn't have a AAA-level club to send him to. The White Sox affiliate at Indianapolis was able to take some Washington players, and that's where Harmon ended up. His fielding was atrocious (.907 percentage) and he hit just .215 with two homers in 38 games, whereupon the Nats got him another ticket on the Chattanooga Choo-choo. In 86 games there, he socked 17 homers and hit .308. At the end of the season, Killebrew was brought back up and produced no homers with his 31 at-bats, and hit just .194. Nonetheless, he was just on the verge of becoming one of baseball's greatest sluggers of all time, and would never see the minor leagues again for the duration of his professional baseball career — another 17 years.

In the meantime, Eddie Yost continued to patrol third base for the Washington Senators. At the beginning of the season, Yost, now 31½ years old, had indicated that whenever management felt that Killebrew was ready to move in, he would agree to relocate to the outfield. Since the ballclub was in dire need of pitching, as well as help at shortstop and in the outfield, a trade might have seemed a more likely solution. Ed Yost helped precipitate that solution when, in his 14th season with the Nats, he hit only .224 with 37 runs driven in. On December 6, '58, his long association with the Senators as a player came to an end when he was traded to Detroit. There, he underwent a wonderful rejuvenation, bashing a career-high 21 homers and scoring 115 runs, another personal summit.

At the other infield corner in '58, big Norm Zauchin drove in the same number of runs Yost did, only 37. His 15 homers and .228 average would not be enough to merit full-time work in '59. Herbie Plews saw plenty of action at both third, where he spelled Yost, and at second, his primary position, where he shared time with a new man, Ken Aspromonte. Plews hit .258 but with only two homers. The Brooklyn-born Aspromonte, whose brother Bob was on the brink of becoming a big-leaguer with the Dodgers, was acquired on May 1 of this season in exchange for catcher Lou Berberet. Aspromonte hit only .225, but could play short and third, making him a commodity worth keeping around for next year. Rocky Bridges got most of the work at short and hit a respectable .263, good enough for the Tigers to insist he be included in the deal that brought them Eddie Yost.

Lou Berberet's departure left the catching in the capable hands of Clint Courtney. Courtney was a very good receiver who led the entire league in assists at the position in

'58, besides batting .251 with eight home runs and 62 ribbies. Besides the "Toy Bulldog," Courtney had another nickname — "Old Scrap Iron." That moniker had apparently been applied when he banged himself up after stumbling during a footrace with his teammate on the '52 St. Louis Browns, pitcher Duane Pillette, and Buddy Blattner, an ex-infielder turned broadcaster (who had quite a surprising handle for one who made his living with his mouth).

Given the anemic infield, it's no wonder that once again the Senators had the league's worst team batting average in '58, not to mention its worst record. This despite the accomplishments of Roy Sievers, who didn't let up one bit following his terrific performance in '57. Sievers smashed 39 homers, third-best in the circuit, and drove in 108, also good for third. Rightfielder Jim Lemon hit only .246, primarily because of his high strikeout total; he did send 26 drives out of the park and produce 75 runs.

The man in the middle, little Albie Pearson, settled on .275 for the year. The outfield seemed set, but in fact by next year only Lemon would be playing there with any regularity. For the time being, Pearson was doing so well that in mid–May, Whitey Herzog, a spare part since the end of his rookie year of 1956, was sold to the K.C. A's. Herzog hit just .240 as a reserve and would not play even semiregularly until 1961, when he enjoyed his best year and managed .291 for the Baltimore Orioles.

The Senators picked up six games in the standings in 1958, but once again wound up as the league's doormat at 61–93. As if the general public needed any reminder of how bad they were, the film version of *Damn Yankees*, starring Tab Hunter and Ray Walston, was released. For the second straight year, the team's pitchers, collectively, were the league's worst. Individually, however, there were occasional flashes of brilliance.

Pedro Ramos, aided by a pitch he referred to as his "Cuban Palmball," again led the club in wins, finishing with a decent 14–18, 4.23. Ramos was tops in the entire league in innings pitched. The Cuban Palmball was actually a spitter, but whenever Pete was accused of illegally wetting the ball, he would deny it, attributing the movement on the ball to what he said was a palmball. Truth was, Ramos admitted later, that he never did throw a palmball. He recognized that his curveball wasn't always effective, and he needed something to keep hitters off balance rather than having them sit on his fastball. Like so many other pitchers who greased or scuffed the ball, Pete Ramos was never caught doing it.

More and more, his sidekick, Camilo Pascual, was showing signs of the pitcher he was to become. Little Potato finished 8–12 with a very tidy 3.15 ERA. He also led the entire league in strikeouts per nine innings, at 7.41. Pascual's control allowed him to put the ball where he wanted to most of the time, and he wasn't afraid to keep the hitters honest so they didn't get too good a toehold at the plate. This may even have been a boost to team morale, as the Senators often found themselves involved in bench-clearing brawls as a result. Over the next six years, Pascual could generally be counted among the loop's top hurlers. By the early sixties, he was arguably the best pitcher in the league, leading the A.L. in strikeouts three years running.

When Chuck Stobbs, still reeling from his 20 losses the previous year, got off to a dismal 2–6, 6.04, start in '58, he was waived right out of the league to the St. Louis Cardinals in early July. Big Russ Kemmerer pitched only 25 fewer innings than Pete Ramos, but ended up 6–15, 4.61, for his efforts. Tex Clevenger, obtained in late '55 in the Mickey Vernon deal, topped the league with 55 pitching appearances, all but four of which were in relief, and earned a 9–9, 4.35, slate. Clevenger had never won nine games before, and never would again.

The marvel of the pitching staff in 1958 was Dick Hyde, another underhand pitcher in the Ted Abernathy submarine mold. On this club, he finished with a miraculous 10–3 record and an equally sparkling 1.75 ERA. He ended up second in saves, behind the Yankees' Ryne Duren, who was on a team which won 31 more games than the Nats did. After this campaign, though, Dick Hyde became Mr. Hyde and won only three more games in the major leagues.

By the end of September, the Nats' only role in the grand scheme of things was to decide who among their opponents would win the batting championship. Would it be Ted Williams, or their erstwhile castoff, Pete Runnels? It was bad enough that Jackie Jensen, with his .286–35–122 totals, would earn league MVP honors. On September 28, the Nats held Runnels hitless in four turns, while Williams homered and doubled, securing the batting title by the .328–.322 margin over his teammate. Runnels' turn would come.

A week after the end of the World Series, which the Yankees won in seven over the Braves (avenging their seven-game loss to Milwaukee in '57), the owner of the Indians, William Daley, whose franchise was being wooed by interests in Houston and Minneapolis, announced that his club would stay in Cleveland. Moving a ballclub, something which hadn't been done in the first half of the century, was a concept now perceived as entirely within the realm of practicability. Earlier in the decade, the Braves had gone from Boston to Milwaukee, the Browns from St. Louis to Baltimore, and the Athletics from Philadelphia to Kansas City. The Dodgers and Giants had just completed their first campaigns on the west coast, and sod was turned in October to begin construction of San Francisco's Candlestick Park.

In May '58, the Commissioner of Baseball, Ford Frick, expressed sympathy for Senators owner Calvin Griffith. While moving out of the capital would not be good for baseball, Frick averred, he could not ignore the plight of the "poor devil" who ran the operation. Minneapolis and Houston would now be concentrating their efforts on enticing the Senators to uproot and come to their cities, as it had become clear that the Indians weren't budging. Toronto, Dallas, and Louisville would also enter the bidding at various times. With attendance continuing to dwindle and his ballclub offering so little encouragement to potential fans, Griffith's declarations to the effect that the Senators would stay were sounding less and less convincing. He admitted being especially impressed with the Minneapolis delegation, spearheaded by lobbyist Gerald Moore.

There was certainly strong opposition to any eventual move out of Washington. The main fear of American League owners was that the politicians might take umbrage at the displacement of this ballclub in particular. Many of them were already upset enough that the Dodgers and Giants had left New York. In 1958, Brooklyn Congressman Emanuel Celler introduced a bill that would bring all sports under antitrust laws. Such legislation would have reduced the owners' tyranny over the players and precipitated a chain of events which would have granted the players more freedom of movement. This is what the owners feared more than anything, and they would manage to stave it off for more than another decade and a half. No significant progress was reported on Congressman Cellar's bill, and the departure of the Senators from Washington seemed more of a possibility as a result.

Some of the American League's elite players in 1959 were members of the Washington Senators. The club's fans, while not growing perceptibly in numbers, had much to cheer for, uncharacteristically, in a season punctuated by remarkable individual accomplishments. From a team perspective, it was the usual story. In a nutshell, the Nats had four outstanding position players and four mediocre ones. The press began referring to the top tier as the "Fearsome Foursome."

The heretofore punchless Nats were suddenly among the deadliest offensive machines in the big leagues, likely to smack one out of the park at any given moment. Washington very nearly led the A.L. in four-base knocks, finishing the season with only four fewer than the league-leading Indians. Harmon Killebrew burst onto the scene with enormous impact. He shared the home run title, during what should logically have been considered his rookie season, with another young slugger (who was nonetheless three years his senior), Rocky Colavito of Cleveland.

The "Killer," as he could now be called, had never gotten discouraged despite his three demotions to the minors. He always believed that his chances of performing in the big time were enhanced by the fact that he belonged to a baseball club that needed help. He certainly still needed help himself, particularly from a defensive standpoint. Maligned by many for being something less than a fielding star throughout his career, Killebrew would in fact be a tremendous asset to his team. Aside from his prodigious output as a hitter, he would play three different positions for long stretches of time, filling a void wherever his team was weakest.

In '59, Killebrew amassed 105 ribbies, which placed him third in the league behind Jackie Jensen and Colavito, despite batting just .242. The fans, who he felt had always supported him in Washington, loved him now. And Harmon loved playing in Washington. One of the highlights of his year occurred when President Dwight Eisenhower called him over to his seat one day to request an autographed baseball for his grandson David. An even greater thrill was Killebrew's participation in the first All-Star game on July 7 in Pittsburgh (beginning in '59, and for the next three years, two All-Star games were played each year instead of one). Killebrew had the impression that his manager that day, Casey Stengel, didn't even know his name. He did play, though, but went hitless in three at-bats.

Leftfielder Jim Lemon placed second in the league in roundtrippers, with 33, drove in 100 runs, and improved to a very respectable .279, a 33-point improvement. Lemon still struck out 99 times, but that represented a cutback of nearly 20 percent, and he went from top strikeout man in the league to second on the team, to Killebrew, who whiffed 116 times. The Senators led the league in striking out, accounting for their league-worst .237 batting average and their characteristically poor finish in the standings. They won only 63 times for Cookie Lavagetto, an improvement of only two games in the standings

In 1959, for the second year in a row, the Nats could boast of having the league's best rookie. Young centerfielder Bobby Allison, a handsome, rugged, former college fullback who had never hit more than 12 homers in the minors, hit 30 taters. This was the first of five campaigns during which he would hit 29 or more in his career. Allison drove in 85 runs, the result of a big swing and pure doggedness. He also struck out 92 times, supporting his assertion that hitting a baseball was the toughest thing he had had to learn in life.

Now 32 years old, Roy Sievers was moved back to first base, where the Nats had been vulnerable and where Sievers had spent about half his time three years earlier. Squirrel chipped in with 21 homers while sharing time with the lefthanded Julio Becquer. Becquer, a Cuban, had been the club's pinch hitter extraordinaire since '57, leading the league in appearances in both '57 and '59, despite batting only .248 in that role during those years.

The rightfielder in 1959 was Faye Throneberry, the less illustrious older brother of the great minor-league slugger, "Marvelous Marv" Throneberry. "Fabulous Faye" was not as colorful as his younger sibling, and had nowhere near his power. Still, Faye managed ten homers and a .251 average. After just 31 more at-bats in '61, however, his big-league journey came to an abrupt end. The rest of the Senators' lineup, the middle infield and the catching spot, were in utter disarray, occupied by a hodgepodge of never-wases and marginal big-leaguers.

Reno Bertoia was the main piece obtained in the transaction that forced the departure of Ed Yost, Rocky Bridges, and spare flychaser Neil Chrisley to Detroit in December. Born in St. Vito Udine, Italy, and raised in Windsor, Ontario, Canada, Bertoia was a highly touted $10,000 bonus baby for the Tigers. A major-leaguer at 18, he broke in for good in '57 and for a while early that season led the league in batting. Eventually, though, it would be found out that Bertoia just didn't hit enough to keep a full-time job in the majors. In 1959, however, with his .237 average

and eight homers, he was the best of the lot outside of the "Fearsome Foursome" of Killebrew, Sievers, Lemon, and Allison.

Ken Aspromonte was the second man at second, but hit only .244 with considerably less power than Bertoia. Along with Bertoia from Detroit had come Ron Samford, a 29-year-old 155-pounder who'd originally broken in with the New York Giants during their championship 1954 season. Samford had a career year with the Nats in '59. Unfortunately, all he had to do to achieve that was hit .224 with five homers. The third player the Nats got from the Tigers was Jim Delsing, a long-time American League reserve outfielder and defensive stalwart whose main claim to fame was that he was the only man ever to pinch run for a midget. Eddie Gaedel was recruited to stand in as a pinch hitter in a spontaneous publicity stunt devised by Browns owner Bill Veeck in 1951. The 3'7" 65-pounder, not surprisingly, drew a walk.

On June 11, 1959, the Senators, moving to replace a shortstop who wasn't hitting or providing adequate defense, dealt sputtering submariner Dick Hyde to the Red Sox along with Herbie Plews, who had been getting practically no playing time. In return, the Nationals acquired utilityman Billy Consolo. Consolo had played in the same high-school infield as Sparky Anderson, future manager of world champions, and went from there directly to the Cincinnati Reds after signing for a stunning $60,000 in 1953. Ultimately, Consolo's main claim to fame would be that he was born on the very same day as the great Roberto Clemente. Consolo bore no resemblance to Roberto at the plate and hit just .213 as the regular shortstop the rest of the way in '59. He stuck around the big leagues for ten years, but averaged only .221 by the time all was said and done.

The young team, despite all its might, agonized through an insufferable 18-game losing streak. Changes were made in midstream to offset the weaknesses. They didn't help much. Clint Courtney, age 32, was nowhere near the hitter he had been in the midfifties and batted just .233. Backup Ed Fitz Gerald, who hit into a triple play on opening day, the first big-leaguer ever to do so, was not the answer. In late May, Fitz Gerald's six-year sojourn in the capital was interrupted, when he was traded to Cleveland for two guys named Hal, pitcher Woodeshick and catcher Naragon. Woodeshick (2–4, 3.69) proved useful out of the bullpen, and would show some major-league staying power, lasting 11 years, mostly with National League clubs. Naragon played most of the time the rest of the year but hit only .241, without power.

On the day following the deal for the two Hals, May 26, 1959,* the Senators made another move to deepen their outfield. In a trade with Baltimore, Washington obtained a speedy flyhawk, Lenny Green, in exchange for last year's brilliant rookie, Albie Pearson, still just 24.

Pearson had started the season off by hitting .188 in 25 games. Like Ernie Oravetz before him and longtime big-league shortstop Fred Patek later on, there was a feeling that had Pearson been bigger, he would have been better. Green had hit .311 in the tough Pacific Coast League in 1957, and had won the batting championship of the Sally League in '56. He hit only .242 as a 25-year-old for the Senators in '59, but the next three seasons would be very good for him. Pearson, on the other hand, would languish a while longer in Baltimore, but would eventually carve a niche for himself with the Los Angeles Angels in the early sixties; his tenure with them culminated in an appearance in the 1963 All-Star game.

Given the increased offensive output, it would seem logical to expect it to be reflected in the club's won-loss record. Overall, the pitching was much improved as well. The staff as a whole was fifth best in the league. Camilo Pascual, 17–10, 2.64, established himself as a top-of-the-line pitcher in '59, leading the league in complete games and shutouts, and finishing runner-up for fewest earned runs and most strikeouts. Pedro Ramos led the league in losses with 19, and won only 13, with a 4.16 ERA. Ramos was working on another out pitch, a sinker, to go along with his fastball and Cuban Palmball, and the following year would enjoy possibly his best season as a starter, going 11–18, 3.45. In '61, he would lose 20 to lead the league in losses four years running.

Another hard thrower, Russ Kemmerer, still didn't have his act together in '59 and went 8–17, 4.50. The fourth starter was Bill Fischer, a righthanded former marine drill instructor claimed from the Tigers on waivers late in the '58 campaign. Fischer was 9–11, 4.28, and Tex Clevenger managed a respectable 8–5, 3.91, primarily, as usual, in a relief role.

On the other side of the ledger stood Hal Griggs, 2–8, 5.25, as a follow-up to his 3–11, 5.52 in '58. Griggs had been a 21-year-old bellhop in a hotel in Miami when the owner of a minor-league team invited him to come out and try for a spot on his team. He lost 21 games in his first year of pro ball at Hickory, North Carolina, in 1950, but the worst was yet to come. By now, his big-league record was 6–26, and he would never get another chance to improve on that, his ineffectiveness bringing an end to his time under the big top. Chuck Stobbs' record was also skewed toward the debit side, despite a creditable performance. Re-signed by the Senators after being released by the Cardinals in January, Stobbs, now employed in relief, went a luckless 1–8 despite a 2.98 ERA.

In spite of the most powerful display in the club's 59-year history, there was not enough contact hitting for the club to make appreciable gains. The aberrant long losing streak certainly did not help. What might have been if Jack Jensen (league RBI leader), Pete Runnels (third in the league in hitting), and Eddie Yost (tops in runs scored and walks), had still been

*This date is famous in baseball history because Harvey Haddix, a veteran lefthander in his first year with the Pirates, threw a 12-inning perfect game, a feat never approached before or since. Perhaps even more incredibly, Haddix didn't even win the game. The first man up in the 13th made it to first on an error and was sacrificed ahead. Haddix walked Henry Aaron, never a bad move, but allowed a home run to another slugger, Joe Adcock. Adcock passed Aaron on the basepaths, and the homer — but not Aaron's run — was nullified.

in Washington is anyone's guess. For the first time in a long time, however, things were definitely looking up between the white lines.

A chaw-chewing veteran infielder, Billy Gardner, steadied the infield for the '60 Senators after coming over from the Orioles in a swap for Clint Courtney and Ron Samford at the beginning of the season. The acquisition of Gardner, who had led the league in doubles (tied) as recently as 1957, meant that Reno Bertoia, a good fielder, would take over at third for Harmon Killebrew most of the time. Killebrew began to learn the intricacies of the first base position, which he had never played at any level of professional baseball. For his part, Clint Courtney went on to some unique accomplishments in Baltimore in this year. In a game in late May, at the urging of his manager, Paul Richards, Courtney caught knuckleballer Hoyt Wilhelm with a catcher's mitt 50 percent larger than the standard. He had no passed balls, but the mitt was later banned. In September, Scrap Iron became the first major-league receiver since 1918 to record two unassisted double plays in his career.

Senators fans' heads were sent spinning as the team rose to the dizzying heights of fifth place in 1960. This happened despite the fact that Killebrew lost time due to injuries and had 100 fewer at-bats. The Killer made more adjustments — he still stood close to the plate but employed a more compact swing. The result was an appreciable improvement in batting average from .242 to .276. Conversely, Harmon still struck out a lot, only ten fewer times than in '59, despite the reduced playing time. He did belt 31 homers, though.

In '61, the year of the homer in the American League, Killebrew would slam 46. Then, over the next three seasons, he would cement his place as one of baseball's greatest sluggers, averaging better than 47 home runs per season and winning three straight home run championships. Killebrew would lead the league six times in that category. His election to the Hall of Fame, after belting 573 career homers, the most by a righthanded hitter in the history of the American League, was as automatic as his home run trot.

Harmon Killebrew had to make an even greater adjustment as a fielder than as a hitter during what proved to be his last year in Washington. First base is an easier position to play than third from a mobility standpoint, and was a spot the Nats were weakest at. After Vic Power was acquired and played at first base, and Don Mincher played well enough to take over there, Killebrew became an outfielder for the better part of three years. After that, he would alternate between first and third for most of the rest of his career, until 1971, when he was 35 years old.

In the years ahead, it would become clear that the roster of the 1960 Washington Senators was stocked with a number of future big-league stars. Bobby Allison, who slipped to 15–69–.251 in his sophomore year, eventually hit 256 home runs in the majors. Earl Battey took over the catching job and hit .270 with 15 homers of his own. Don Mincher became a reliable 20-homer man throughout most of the mid to late sixties. All these players made the American League All-Star team at various times during the 1960's.

Zoilo Versalles, a shortstop the Senators had signed out of Cuba and who appeared with the Nats for a cup of coffee in '59, became a great success. While Versalles weighed less than 150 pounds, he was a dangerous power hitter, clubbing 17 as a 22-year-old shortstop as early as 1962. He had 20 round-trippers in '64, and in 1965 had his career season at a time when everything was coming together for the team as well. That year, Versalles led the league in at-bats, doubles, triples, runs scored (as well as strikeouts) and led the Washington Senators, alias the Minnesota Twins, to their first pennant in 32 years.

There was also a young Cuban outfielder Joe Cambria had scouted for the Senators who was about to come to America with two dozen of his young countrymen for tryouts. His name — Tony Oliva. He won the American League batting title in his first season, 1964, when he was named Rookie of the Year. Oliva won the batting crown again the following year, the only player in history to do so in his first two campaigns. He copped a third batting title in 1971, and hit .304 for a 15-year career.

Pitchers Jim Kaat, Camilo Pascual, and Jack Kralick were other long-term assets already on the big-league club in 1960. The left-handed Kaat was coming off an 8–8 season at Chattanooga, where he had struck out 19 Nashville batters in a 1959 game. He won only one game as a Washington Senator, but by '62 he was winning 18 as a Twin. Kaat would go on to pitch in the majors for a record 25 years, during which time he won nearly 300 games, 283 to be exact, and won an astonishing 16 consecutive gold gloves, a fielding mark for pitchers not likely to be matched.

Camilo Pascual gave a command performance on Opening Day, 1960, at Griffith Stadium, on April 18. He struck out 15 Red Sox and the Nats came away victors, 10–1. The only run given up was a home run to Ted Williams, the 493rd of the great one's career, which tied him with Lou Gehrig. A solid 12–8, 3.03, in '60, Pascual hit his stride in his late twenties, overcoming the recurring arm problems which had plagued his career until then. He parlayed his fastball, pinpoint control, and devastating sidearm curve into 20 wins in 1962, and 21 in '63. He was likely the best pitcher in the American League during those two seasons, leading the loop in complete games and strikeouts both years. In 1964, he came within four K's of leading the A.L. for four straight years.

Jack Kralick, 8–6 and a highly respectable 3.04 as a rookie during the team's last year in Washington, won between 12 and 14 games for the Twins each year during the early sixties. On August 26, '62, he flung a no-hitter at the Athletics, the first for the franchise since Walter Johnson's gem back in July 1920. Kralick's stock was high enough that early in the '63 season, the Twins were able to trade him to the Cleveland Indians for a future Cy Young Award winner, Jim Perry.

Beyond the white lines, there may in a sense have been more optimism about the Senators' future in 1959. Joe Cronin was named League President in January, and it is true that he and his former owner, Tom Yawkey of Boston, were not in favor of a league without the national capital in it. Apart from the sentimental reasons Cronin may well have had, the Red Sox had just moved their affiliate in the high minors to Minneapolis, the city which seemed to hold the most appeal for Calvin Griffith. As well, the influential New York Yankees had good reason to want to keep the politicians' noses out of their business — owners Dan Topping and Del Webb certainly didn't want their tangled business affairs in the spotlight. The Cleveland Indians had a motive for wanting to keep the baseball Senators in Washington and the nonbaseball senators out of the picture as well — they were, at various times, considering moves to cities that Calvin Griffith also had his eye on.

In midsummer, the major leagues were warned by Senator Estes Kefauver that their actions with respect to the formation of the new Continental Baseball League would be closely monitored. The new league, the brainchild of Branch Rickey, owed its genesis to the fact that there was now just one team in New York, instead of three. New York City, Denver, Houston, Toronto, and Minneapolis, would be among the new franchises. Big-league owners occupied a tenuous position as feudal lords in a fiefdom where slavery was condoned by the government. That was a good position to be in, and not one to be jeopardized by leaving Washington out in the cold.

In the end, subscription to the "if you can't beat 'em, join 'em" approach provided a way out for Calvin Griffith. On June 28, 1960, Senator Kefauver's challenge to baseball's exemption to antitrust regulations was defeated, but narrowly, by four votes only. It was evident that big-league magnates could not confront the Continental League venture without raising further antitrust concerns. Owners of American League teams recognized they should immediately grab the lucrative Los Angeles market for themselves. In addition, while they questioned the existence of a professional league outside the realm of "organized" baseball, there was no doubt in their minds that their compatriot, Calvin Griffith, had every right to pursue a means of making a living someplace else. Calvin could take his team to Minneapolis-St. Paul, and outrage regarding the absence of a team in the capital could be easily countered. At the same time, the league would award an expansion charter to Washington. The fans wouldn't care, league owners believed; there didn't seem to be too many of them left, anyway.

The dastardly plan became reality on October 26, 1960, when American League owners, meeting at the Savoy Hilton in New York, approved an expansion to ten teams. The National League had taken a similar decision nine days earlier, which rendered the path the A.L. would take all the more evident. The N.L.'s expansion would occur within an expedient period of time, 17 months, prior to the start of the 1962 season. There would be no such dillydallying in the junior circuit. The Washington Senators were to be moved immediately to Minnesota. There, to underscore the proximity of Minneapolis and St. Paul—the "Twin Cities"—the Senators were to be rechristened the Minnesota Twins.

On November 17, 1960, the American League gave its approval to a group of ten investors, hastily brought together, to give birth to an organization with the ominous name, "Senators, Inc." Washington's new club would therefore retain the old nickname. The investment group was headed by Elwood R. "Pete" Quesada, an administrator with the Federal Aviation Authority. Within two days, a general manager and field manager for the new Senators were in place. G.M. Ed Doherty and Manager Mickey Vernon were going to be responsible for making good on the $2.2 million Quesada and his group had paid the league for its entrance fee and the right, along with the Los Angeles Angels, to select a group of 28 players left unprotected by the A.L.'s eight existing member clubs. Doherty had previously been the president of the Triple-A American Association, while Vernon had served as coach with the Pittsburgh Pirates, who had just beaten the New York Yankees in an improbable seven-game World Series in which the Yanks outscored the Pirates 55–27.

This collection of culls would have to supersede the pretty good baseball team which had just left town. Unbeknownst to all but the most enlightened at the time, the Senators, henceforth known as the "original Senators," had lost the last game of their 60-year life. On October 2, 1960, Milt Pappas and the Orioles shut out Pete Ramos and the Senators, 2–0. The defeat dropped Washington to eight games below .500; yet this was a considerable improvement, and represented a ten-game climb in the standings. The club's talent base had been further solidified at the very start of the season when the aging slugger, Roy Sievers, was transferred to the Chicago White Sox for two younger players. Both of these, catcher Earl Battey and first baseman Don Mincher, would play important roles in eventually helping the club achieve on-field success.

Instead of enjoying a ballclub of the caliber of the Minnesota Twins, who would be in contention nearly every year from the middle to late sixties, fans in Washington would once again get stuck with a loser. The player draft was set for December 14, 1960, but Senators, Inc. began putting together a roster more than two weeks earlier. The first acquisitions were pitchers John Gabler, who would win three more big-league games, and Roman Semproch, a veteran of the National League, who would never win so much as one more game. Those two were taken at the first minor-league draft, held November 28, 1960. The following day, there was a free-agent signing—Danny O'Connell, a veteran National League infielder, would play regularly at second and third for the Senators in their inaugural year.

The expansion draft, which took place in Boston, yielded some players many baseball fans had never heard of (see Appendix C for the full list). If today names like Dutch Dotterer, Joe Hicks, Coot Veal, Chester Boak, and Carl Mathias hold any meaning for someone, then they are more than a casual student of baseball history. Some other names had a more familiar ring—Gene Woodling, Dale Long, Bobby Shantz, Dick Donovan, Mike Garcia, and Jim King were among those.

The Los Angeles Angels picked first on December 14, 1960, and took nearsighted Eli Grba, a righthander who was to start and win the Angels' first ever game. The Senators then chose as their first pick Shantz, who, like Grba, was selected from the roster of the league champion Yankees. Shantz was traded two days later, to the team which had defeated his Yankees in the World Series two months earlier, the Pittsburgh Pirates.

In this first trade in the history of the second franchise, the Senators obtained a 28-year-old righthander who would lead their pitching staff in victories (12) in 1961, Bennie Daniels. Daniels came along with a pair of infielders who would not have his longevity. One, Harry Bright, was a veteran who could play the infield corners. The other, R C Stevens, nicknamed "Cola" for an obvious reason, was a behemoth, a first baseman the Pirates had taken on as a project but had gained no satisfactory results from. The same would apply for R C in D.C.

Toward the end of the 1950s, Washington was not generally considered a desirable place for any major-leaguer to play. Despite the opportunity to cavort with statesmen and famous entertainers, this was a losing club with too little fan support and a ballpark located in a slum area. The clientele always included an unusually high percentage of rowdies and troublemakers with no better place to be. Most fans, many of them displaced government employees, seemed ambivalent in terms of who won or lost. Attendance had not increased appreciably despite repeated rumors that Calvin Griffith would someday take his team away. In effect, this city had not been adequately supporting a big-league franchise and had lost it as a result. Solely because of its status as the nation's capital, Washington was getting another chance.

1961–1971:
THE END OF THE LINE

Because there had never been such a thing as expansion in the history of the major leagues, no one quite knew what to expect of Washington's bunch of rejects. There were comments made that the team might barely be able to win 40 games. The schedule would run 162 games in 1961, up from 154, which had been the standard since 1904.

Manager Mickey Vernon, just 43 years old and fresh from his tour of duty as coach with the world champion Pirates, felt the club could at least be competitive. Vernon had a good handle on most of the players, he felt, having recently played in the American League and played and coached in the National. (See Appendix C for the list of players drafted.) For a while, it looked as if he was right. The new Nats posted the best record of any American League team during the exhibition schedule at 15–10. Maybe this team would even be better than the old one in its first year. Five hundred fans waited four hours, in the rain, at Washington Airport to give the group of baseball orphans a heroes' welcome when they arrived in the city for the first time.

It was a gathering of 26,725, a modest figure by most yardsticks but impressive by Washington standards, which witnessed the first game in the history of the second franchise. It was played on April 10, 1961, and was the first ever by a major-league expansion team; the Los Angeles Angels, in deference to

the Presidential Opener, were scheduled to begin play the following day. Among those gathered was President John F. Kennedy, and this season opener featured the Chicago White Sox as guests. Jungle Jim Rivera, Chicago outfielder, caught the opening-day presidential toss, but after the President autographed the ball for him, Rivera told JFK he'd have to do better because what the President had scratched on the ball was barely legible.

The Senators' starting pitcher, Dick Donovan, had been chosen in the expansion draft from the Chisox, with whom he had struggled in 1960. The starter for Chicago would be Early Wynn, who had first pitched for the Washington Senators way back in 1939. The Senators had a 3–2 lead in the seventh when a misplay by veteran outfielder Gene Woodling on a flyball, and an error by another veteran, first baseman Dale Long, allowed the tying run to come across. In the next inning, Senators catcher Pete Daley's wide throw to second on a steal attempt by Minnie Minoso allowed Minoso to take third and score the winning run. In throwing away the game, the new Nats made four errors.

Four days later, following two rainouts, the Senators won their first game and evened their record at .500, with a 3–2 verdict over Cleveland. The attendance for this second game—a telltale 10,126. Joe McClain, one of three players the new Senators had drafted from the old Senators in a special minor-league draft for the expansion teams, pitched splendidly, allowing just seven hits and no walks while going the distance for the new franchise's first win. By the All-Star break McClain's record stood at 7–7, and he led the staff in wins. After the break, the 28-year-old rookie went 1–11. And so went the fortunes of the Washington Senators in 1961. They were sitting at .500 as late as June 15, when their record was 30–30. A highlight of the early season came in late May when the old Senators, disguised as the Minnesota Twins, showed up at Griffith Stadium for the first time. The fans threw eggs at their former favorites, and the home team swept all three games. After the middle of June, the Senators, like the bunch of castoffs they were, proceeded to disintegrate like a watermelon dropped from the top of the Washington Monument.

Following its .500 getaway after 60 games, the expansion ballclub went into a 10-game tailspin, losing every time out. From August 1 on, the Nats played the worst ball in the league, winning only 12 of 58. In one stretch, they dropped a gut-wrenching 24 of 25. The Senators were a pathetic 31–70 from June 15 on, thereby winning exactly 61 in '61. That combination of numbers somehow had a more lasting impression after Roger Maris broke Babe Ruth's 34-year home run record with 61 in '61. With allowances made for the added number of games, there were about 25 percent more homers hit in the American League in 1961 than in the previous season. There were 20 more pitchers, which caused a dilution in talent serious enough to account for the difference.

For the record, Roger Maris hit nine of his dingers off Washington pitching, but only four against the Angels, so at the pace he set against expansion teams, he would have hit 58.5 home runs on the season and not broken Ruth's record. The main reason his detractors cited in support of the retention of Ruth's mark on the books, naturally, was the increased number of games. Poor Maris had to endure much grief as a New York Yankee trying to break an icon's record in the icon's town.

When the season and the record went into the books, an asterisk next to Maris's accomplishment went in along with them.

The Senators finished dead last in a dead heat with the Kansas City Athletics, with the A's winning the last game of the year between the two clubs, thereby avoiding the ultimate disgrace of finishing behind two expansion teams. But more disillusioning than the club's performance on the field, to those who might have cared about Washington baseball, were the poor turnouts. In what would end up being Griffith Stadium's last season, the Nats couldn't draw flies, with less than 10,000 showing up for games on a regular basis, even on weekends. The club reported operating losses of a quarter of a million dollars in the first season. Last in the league in attendance (597,287), the new Nats attracted about 150,000 fewer fans than had the dear departed ballclub the previous year. To bolster attendance, the club announced a promotion in June during which a new automobile would be won by a fan at every game the Senators won. The club went through a long losing streak, and it was suggested that if it continued, "The Senators, Inc." might wind up in the car business.

Calvin Griffith's strong hunch had been correct — his team drew in excess of a million fans to his new home in Minneapolis–St. Paul. This figure was a quarter of a million better than had *ever* come to see the Senators play during 60 years of American League baseball in D.C.

The Angels won nine more games than the Senators, and finished just half a game out of seventh place in the inaugural year of post-expansion play. (Finishing seventh were the Minnesota Twins, who were actually worse than they had been during their previous incarnation as the 1960 Senators.) It would soon be increasingly apparent that the Angels had done a better job of scouting baseball players than had the Senators. Shortstop Jim Fregosi, taken from the Red Sox in the expansion draft, would be a top performer for many years. Bob (Buck) Rodgers, a stellar defensive catcher, was drafted from the Tigers. Pitcher Dean

Chance, selected from the Orioles, would be the best pitcher in the league and win the Cy Young Award by 1964.

The Angels' gigantic first-base combination of vets, Ted Kluszewski and Steve Bilko, hit 35 homers between them in the team's inaugural year. Leon Wagner, an outfielder obtained in a trade with St. Louis at the beginning of the season, slammed 28 homers, batted .280, and became a league All-Star. Albie Pearson, the pint-sized former Nat, hit .288. Ray Gillespie wrote in *The Sporting News* that no one in baseball got so much out of so few pounds and so few muscles as Los Angeles' Albie Pearson.

The Senators had certainly not shown a bent for sentimentality in the expansion draft, letting the Angels claim Ed Yost, but Yost's contributions were minimal in '61 and '62. He then retired and took up coaching with the Senators. Ken Hunt, an outfielder the Angels drafted from the Yankees, and Lee Thomas, another picket obtained in an early-season trade with New York, pounded 25 and 24 homers respectively for the first Angels squad in '61.

Washington's main threat and only .300 hitter was Gene Woodling, a veteran who had played on some of history's greatest teams. Woodling began with the Yankees in 1949 after a few cups of coffee with the Indians and Pirates. He was then on board for five straight Yankees world championships. In later years, Woodling stated that 1961 was the first year he hit .300 (.313) but didn't enjoy himself. Gene Green, a catcher in name only who swung the bat hard, led the Senators in homers with 18. In all fairness, Green had not played behind the plate very much, and wasn't very fast. Despite having already shown that he could hit in the National League, he was a man without a position; the future designated-hitter role would have been just perfect for him. First baseman Dale Long and outfielder Willie Tasby both chipped in with 17 homers as part of the league's worst offensive unit, and batted only .249 and .251 respectively.

Long is always remembered for his home runs in eight consecutive games in 1956, a record which Don Mattingly of the Yankees tied 31 years later. Tasby, an outfielder who played regularly with the Orioles and Red Sox in previous seasons, once had a friend who was killed by lightning, and he was afraid of it. On one occasion in Baltimore, he wanted to play the outfield with no shoes on, afraid lightning would be attracted to the metal in his cleats. On another occasion he asked to be removed from a game in Detroit. Tasby, Long, and Gene Green were at the center of controversy during the season when they were publicly chastised by team president Pete Quesada, manager Mickey Vernon, and G.M. Ed Doherty. Accused of indifferent play and not hustling, all three were fined. Long, as well as Green, it should be noted, was slow afoot.

Like the L.A. Angels' Dean Chance, the best player the Senators selected in the expansion draft came from the Baltimore Orioles. Chuck Hinton had been left off the Birdos' protected list despite the fact that he'd just won a batting title in the California League. After his good start at Indianapolis, the Senators called Hinton up and he batted .260. Chuck Cottier, a defensive star at second, was obtained in a trade with the Tigers in early June, but hit .234. Cottier's presence allowed veteran Danny O'Connell to be moved to third, which had been a particularly troublesome spot. O'Connell hit .260.

Dealt to the Tigers in exchange for Cottier was Hal Woodeshick, who basked for all of two months in the luxury of not having had to change addresses during the previous off season. Woodeshick, along with infielder Johnny Schaive and pitchers Rudy Hernandez and Hector Maestri, none of whom had any impact in '61 or later, had been drafted from the Twins. These four became the first to wear the colors of both 20th-century Washington clubs. In the ensuing years, only five more original Senators joined the new franchise — they were, chronologically in terms of their reappearance in Washington, Roy Sievers, Camilo Pascual, Zoilo Versalles, Pedro Ramos, and Don Mincher.

The opening-day pitcher, Dick Donovan,

was the team's lone representative at the first All-Star game. Donovan was arguably the best pitcher in the league, going by ERA. His mark was 2.40, and his record was 10–10 despite his 0–5 start and not winning his first game before June 2. He also missed most of September because of a sprained right toe. Success in the big leagues was nothing new for Donovan, a late bloomer whose mastery of the slider had helped him win 15 games twice and 16 once for the White Sox from the middle to the late fifties.

Dick Donovan provided the team's highlight performance of the year on September 24 when, in his first game back since being injured on August 29, he spun a one-hitter against the Twins, of all teams. The lone hit came in the seventh inning off the bat of Joe Altobelli, a future big-league manager who had a very brief playing career at the major-league level. In 1962, Donovan at age 34 would win 20 for the first time. Unfortunately, he would do so as a member of the Cleveland Indians. At the end of the new ballclub's first season, the Nats shipped him to the Indians along with Gene Green and shortstop Jim Mahoney (.241 in 43 games) for one man—outfielder Jimmy Piersall. This was not a brilliant idea, something the Washington brass would have to acknowledge after Piersall hit .244 with four homers for them in 1962.

The last games ever played at Griffith Stadium fittingly involved Calvin Griffith's Minnesota Twins. No one came to salute the passing of the old ballyard, or just about no one. Since the previous fall, a new 45,000-seat multipurpose facility, District of Columbia Stadium, had been home to the National Football League's Washington Redskins. Located at East Capitol and 22nd streets, D.C. Stadium was the first of its kind in that it was conceived as a multisport venue. Built by the federal government at a cost of something between $22 and $24 million, it featured a section of moveable stands on the third-base side which could be swung around in order to convert the playing area into the more regular shape of a football field. An extra 3,000 seats could be installed for football games.

Only 1,980 faithful witnessed a 3–1 Senators loss in the first of three games of the last series at Griffith Stadium. It was Joe McClain's 18th defeat, despite a strong showing. The second day's game was rained out, and in the final engagement at the magical old ballyard, on September 21, '61, the Twins won again 5–1. This may have been as appropriate an ending as any for an expansion team which, needing to win six of its last nine games (all on the road) in order to avoid losing 100 games, fell just short and won five. Only 1,498 people turned up for the grand finale. Four years later, Griffith Stadium would disappear without a trace, with not even a marker erected in its memory. The site is now occupied by Howard University Hospital.

Manager Mickey Vernon's take on the first year was that the potential of an average, or even less-than-ordinary, ballclub, can rise with good pitching. His team had not gotten that type of pitching in '61, and G.M. Ed Doherty's decision to trade away a front-line pitcher, the club's *only* front-line pitcher at this point, seemed to go against the grain of Vernon's assessment. Doherty would quickly begin making amends by acquiring some talent. Before the first season was even over, he had traded Dave Sisler, son of Hall of Famer George Sisler, a 31-year-old righthander who had put in some mediocre seasons with the Red Sox in the late fifties, to the Cincinnati Reds. In exchange, the Nats obtained a 23-year-old lefty from Caney Springs, Tenn., named Claude Osteen. Sisler had four wins left in his right arm. Osteen had 196 left in his left.

Doherty let go of Marty Keough, an outfielder drafted from Cleveland who had been penciled into the number three slot in the lineup earlier in the season. Keough hit .249 with just nine homers and played himself out of a regular spot. Doherty also packaged righthander Johnny Klippstein, a D.C. native, to Cincinnati in exchange for catcher Bob Schmidt, a veteran National Leaguer who would catch semi-regularly during the upcoming season, and pitcher Dave Stenhouse. Stenhouse, a veteran of seven years in the

Reds' minor-league system, was ready for his big chance, and how. He would become Mickey Vernon's best pitcher, going 11–12, 3.65, and would be chosen to represent the Senators at both 1962 All-Star games.

In early May, Doherty parted with Willie Tasby to shore up the supply of left arms on the pitching staff, and acquired portsiders Don Rudolph and Steve Hamilton, a reliever, from the Indians. After several failures in the big leagues, Rudolph had won 18 games in the PCL and another crack at the big time. The Senators benefited from a fine season from him — 8–10, 3.62. Rudolph threw fast and worked fast, and was often involved in games lasting less than two hours. This prompted jokes that he was likely in a hurry to get home to his wife, Patricia Hardwick, aka Patti Waggin, a striptease dancer. Rudolph was something of a showman himself, adept at the piano and manager of his wife's "career." His life came to a tragic and premature end at age 37 as a result of an auto accident in Encino, California, in September 1968.

The season opener and first game at D.C. Stadium drew Washington's largest crowd for a baseball game up to that time, 42,143, on April 9, 1962. President John F. Kennedy was on hand to throw out the first ball as rain clouds gathered. The new stadium would eventually be renamed RFK Stadium in honor of the President's brother, Senator Robert F. Kennedy. The fans were drenched by an April shower in the second inning, but otherwise the new season got off on a positive note. The Senators beat the Detroit Tigers 4–1, as Bennie Daniels tossed a nifty five-hitter. Bob Johnson, a utility infielder taken from the A's in the expansion draft, homered. Johnson had hit .295 as a part-timer for the Nats in '61 and, handed a chance to prove himself this year, playing regularly at either short or third, responded with a .288 performance with 12 homers. The Senators would proceed to deal him away in December '62 in a poor trade, acquiring infielder Marv Breeding and outfielder Barry Shetrone from the Orioles.

After the Nats went 12–10 in exhibition play and won their first two games of the '62

season, the prevailing mood soured. They managed to lose 13 straight, and 16 of their first 20, and tumbled into the cellar where they remained, by themselves, for the rest of the year. There were enough high jinks going on off the field, however, to keep things percolating. With the Senators crawling along at a 42–70 clip and on a six-game losing streak, club president Pete Quesada indicated that both manager Mickey Vernon and G.M. Ed Doherty were skating on thin ice. Quesada told the *Washington Star* that he would make sweeping changes, despite the fact that replacing Vernon and Doherty would be his toughest decisions yet. He was looking at a list of ten replacement candidates for each job.

Following the declaration, Quesada was not the most popular man about town, as most sympathies rested with Mickey Vernon, the closest thing to a baseball idol in D.C. Quesada attempted a semidenial the following day, saying he would be glad to retain Vernon and Doherty, but in the same breath wondered whether Vernon would consider accepting a different assignment within the organization. Quesada's treatment of Tasby, Green, and Long, the previous year was rehashed. He had gotten rid of all three players, eventually.

As fate would have it, both Willie Tasby and Gene Green were in town with the Cleveland Indians on August 12, the day Quesada's ominous pronouncement was published. Between the two of them, they accounted for all the runs, Green with two homers and Tasby with an RBI single in a 5–3 Cleveland win. Tasby gleefully waved his cap at Quesada from the Indians' dugout. This particular game did have some positive implications as far as the Senators were concerned. A turnout of over 9,500 meant the club had passed its previous year's attendance with 18 home dates to spare.

President Quesada had not restricted his early–August tirade to just Mickey Vernon and Ed Doherty. He remarked that the team had suffered in '62 due to a lack of punch at traditional power positions, first base and the outfield. The first baseman happened to be Harry Bright, who was having the time of his life, flirting with a .300 average all season long.

On the day Bright read Quesada's comment, he hit a home run in the 5–3 loss to the Indians in Washington. In the dressing room, he fearlessly approached Quesada and made clear exactly what he thought of him and his opinions.

The following night, Bright homered in both games of a doubleheader sweep in Cleveland. His 17 homers for the season tied him for the club lead, and he batted a very creditable .273. Needless to say, though, telling off Pete Quesada was not that bright a move, especially if he wanted to stay in Washington. Bright was a goner at the end of the season, traded to the Reds for a righthanded Cuban first baseman who would never play for Washington, Rogelio Alvarez. As for Harry Bright, he was moved by the Reds to the Yankees, and made it with them to the World Series (he became Sandy Koufax's record 15th strikeout victim to end game one of the '63 Series). To all intents and purposes, though, his career in the majors was over when the '63 Series ended.

Leftfielder Chuck Hinton, who like Bright had 17 homers, placed third in the '62 A.L. batting race with .310, as 34-year-old ex–Senator Pete Runnels ran away with his second batting crown in three years. For Hinton, there was a 50-point gain in batting average, and the graceful flychaser drove in 75 runs. Despite the fact that he'd play 11 years in the show, this would be his best year by far. On disappointing centerfielder Jim Piersall's other flank in right field during the first half of the year was original draftee Jim King, who rang up 11 homers for the second year in a row while hitting just .243. The outfield picture did improve considerably with the arrival of Don Lock from the Yankees at the All-Star break in a straight-up trade for Dale Long. After a good start, Long's production had diminished, and the Senators were gaining ten years in this deal.

Tall and lanky and subscribing to the Jim Lemon school of hitting, the 26-year-old Lock had obvious power, but a propensity for striking out. In the minors, Lock had had a bad habit of overstriding, which his manager at Richmond, Cal Ermer, attempted to cure by tying a rope around his waist in batting practice. Every time Lock spread his legs too wide when moving into the pitch, Ermer would lock up his stride by tugging on the rope. An earlier attempt at a remedy had involved tying Lock's feet together with sweatsocks. Predictably, that hadn't worked either.

Don Lock struck out in 28 percent of his at-bats in '62, and despite the fact that he would deposit the ball over the fence with regularity over the next couple of years for the Senators, he would continue to strike out at a rate as alarming as that during his rookie season. His first-year numbers for the last half of '62, however, were 12–37–.253 in 71 games. His arrival resulted in Chuck Hinton being moved over to right field, where he adapted well. Lock was also reliable defensively.

Lock had joined a team which had just closed out the first half of its second season by losing seven straight. The Senators were firmly entrenched in last place, a seemingly insurmountable 11½ games behind ninth-place Kansas City. Although the ballclub stood at 26–54 at the break, Lock would be the last player brought into the mix from outside the organization before the end of the season. The Nats were to improve to 34–47 in the second half, but first, in tribute to D.C. Stadium's first year, came the All-Star game. Nineteen sixty-two turned out to be the last of the four years during which two All-Star games would be contested. The classic would be played in the nation's capital on the sixth anniversary to the day of the last one played at Griffith Stadium.

It was the first of the two All-Star games, and President Kennedy and Vice-President Lyndon Johnson were among a capacity crowd of 45,480, to witness D.C. native son Maury Wills of the Dodgers literally steal the show. Wills entered a scoreless game in the sixth to pinch-run for 41-year-old Stan Musial. He promptly stole second and scored on Dick Groat's single up the middle. Leading off the eighth with a base hit, Wills hustled to third on a single to short left field when Rocky Colavito threw to second base. He subsequently scored the game's final run in a 3-1 National League victory.

To the disappointment of the partisan crowd, the Senators' representative on the All-Star team, Dave Stenhouse, did not get to play. Ironically, Stenhouse was named starting pitcher when the second All-Star game was played at Wrigley Field in Chicago 20 days later. He looked jittery in that one, but gave up just one run despite surrendering three hits, a walk, a wild pitch, and a hit batsman in two innings of work. Pete Runnels, the old Senator, who hit a grand total of 49 homers over 14 seasons in the majors, cracked one of three A.L. homers as the junior circuit prevailed 9–4 in the last "second All-Star game."

After splitting four games at Minnesota and Los Angeles immediately following the All-Star break, the Nats rattled off five road victories in succession, taking two from the Angels and sweeping the White Sox. The trip continued in New York, where Whitey Ford and Ralph Terry put a damper on the newfound ways with narrow 3–2 and 4–3 decisions. On the following day, Sunday, July 22, 1962, it was Yankees be damned! Poor Joe Hardy, who had sold his soul to the devil so the Senators could beat the Yankees, was redeemed on this day as the Nats swept a doubleheader, and at Yankee Stadium to boot.

Harry Bright homered for the second straight day in the lid-lifter to eke out a 3–2 verdict and boost Dave Stenhouse's record to 9–4. In the nightcap, Jim King, Chuck Hinton, and winning pitcher Bennie Daniels all homered as the Nats drubbed the reigning and eventually repeating world champs 8–3. Joe Hardy would have been as proud as manager Mickey Vernon. Although he'd played on much better Washington clubs, Vernon marveled at this feat, unable to recall having ever beaten the Yankees twice in one day.

Along with Dave Stenhouse and Don Rudolph, the Nats' top starter this season was Tom Cheney, a 27-year-old righthander picked up in a trade for original draftee Tom Sturdivant in June '61. The best Cheney had managed so far in his 10-year pro career was a couple of 14-win seasons in the minors. Mickey Vernon knew Cheney from the '60 Pirates, for whom Cheney went 2–2 during limited time

in the regular season and appeared in the World Series. On the way to a highly respectable 7–9, 3.17, slate for the Senators, he accomplished what can be considered the greatest single-game achievement in the abbreviated history of this franchise.

On September 12, '62, Tom Cheney struck out 21 Orioles in a 16-inning night game at Baltimore. As the century drew to a close, this still stood as a single-game record. Of course, Roger Clemens (twice) and Kerry Wood later fanned 20 in regulation-length games, but Tom Cheney's record would continue to have its special place in the history books. At the time of his feat, the record of 18 strikeouts in an extra-inning contest was shared by Jack Coombs and Warren Spahn. Amazingly, Coombs did it twice: in a 24-inning game for the A's in 1906, and in 16 innings (like Cheney) in 1910. Spahn, the game's greatest lefthander, had 18 K's in just 15 innings for the Boston Braves in 1952.*

Cheney's evening included 13 strikeouts in nine frames, and he surpassed Spahn's mark with his 18th in the 14th inning. Washington rookie Bud Zipfel hit a home run in the top of the 16th off reliever Dick Hall for a 2–1 lead. At this point, Cheney had not allowed a hit since future batting guru Charlie Lau's game-tying single in the seventh. With one out in the bottom of the 16th, free-swinging Dave Nicholson, of all people, singled. Cheney then retired Jackie Brandt, and sealed an amazing triumph by fanning the last man to face him, future big-league manager Dick Williams, for strikeout number 21, seconds before the midnight curfew.

Exactly two weeks after Cheney's masterpiece, the axe fell on General Manager Ed Doherty. Doherty would spend 1963 as G.M. at Nashville of the Sally League, and at the end of the year would be appointed by Commissioner Ford Frick as liaison between professional and amateur baseball organizations. The Senators' 101 losses had been magnified by the L.A. Angels' terrific 86–76 third-place finish in '62.

*Cheney's record was seriously threatened on May 8, 2001, by Arizona's Randy Johnson, who fanned 20 Reds in nine innings. The game went into extra frames, but Johnson did not pitch beyond the ninth.

When the Angels swept the visiting Nats in a July 4 twin bill, they climbed briefly into first place, a remarkable accomplishment at that stage of the season. L.A. finished ten games out of the top rung, occupied once again by the Yankees; right between the two in second spot at the end were the original Washington Senators. Harmon Killebrew led the league in home runs (48) and ribbies (126). Bob Allison also drove in over 100 runs for the Twins. In one memorable July game, Killebrew and Allison both smashed grand slams in the first inning of a romp over Cleveland.

Pete Quesada announced Ed Doherty's firing at the same time as he endorsed Mickey Vernon's work, tendering Vernon a one-year contract. Doherty, ironically, had previously suggested to Quesada that Vernon should be fired for what Doherty had termed "indifference." By now, baseball people were recognizing that Doherty had put together one of the finest young pitching staffs in the game, and had done so without expending anyone who had become a first-stringer anywhere else. In fact, just one day before Doherty was dumped by the board of directors, Ralph Houk, the New York Yankees' manager, verbalized exactly that sentiment. On the other hand, one of Quesada's concerns with Doherty's regime was that his development philosophy had excluded young black players; there were only two in the entire farm system at this time.

The club's directors met less than a week prior to the announcement of Doherty's dismissal. When Pete Quesada was asked if the board had considered firing *him*, he curtly responded that he would not dignify that question with an answer. As opposed to the loss of a quarter of a million dollars the previous year, the club was reporting a 22 percent attendance increase and earnings of $140,000 at the new ballpark in 1962. To replace Doherty, the Senators signed George Selkirk to a two-year contract on November 21. A former outfielder on world champion Yankees teams, Selkirk had been supervisor of player personnel at Kansas City, and more recently had served as field coordinator for the Baltimore Orioles. Assistant G.M. Joe Burke was retained, with the new title of Business Manager, for an additional two years. Hal Keller, the director of the farm system, resigned near the end of the season to take a job with his former associates with the Minnesota Twins, as scout and assistant under farm director Sherry Robertson.

With a pitching staff which had ranked near the middle of the pack in the club's second season, the Nats nevertheless wound up a hopeless 11½ games out of ninth place. The club fell one run short of 600 for the year, by far the lowest in the league. The middle infield had offered little offensive support; the quartet of Danny O'Connell, John Schaive, Ken Hamlin (an original Angel draftee), and Chuck Cottier, combined for a grand total of 17 homers, and O'Connell's .263 average was highest among the group. This turned out to be O'Connell's last year as a player, although he was to stay on as coach with the Senators for two more seasons. Like Don Rudolph, he perished in a car accident at a young age, 42, in 1969.

Other personnel changes worthy of mention in 1962 involved a major-league veteran moving on, and some longtime future Nats moving in. On June 14, Gene Woodling drew a base on balls against his original big-league team, the Indians, to keep a rally going. It was his last appearance in a Senators uniform, as he was sold to the expansion New York Mets following the game. Woodling, a couple of months short of his 40th birthday, would later joke about how the majors had conspired to expand for the sole purpose of prolonging his career. In New York, he was reunited with the manager who had constantly platooned him on the great Yankee teams of the fifties, Casey Stengel. Stengel announced that "Old Faithful," as Woodling was known, would now be given as much playing time as he wanted.

Four days after Woodling's departure, the Nats called up a slender shortstop who was batting .324 at Raleigh of the lowly Carolina League. Ed Brinkman, not yet 21, had attended Western Hills High School, the same Cincinnati school as Pete Rose. He was an outstanding fielder but not yet ready to face big-league pitching. Brinkman got into 54 games as a rookie and hit a meager .165. He was retained for 1963 as the regular shortstop, and continued to struggle with a .228 average. While leading the league's shortstops in double plays, he also committed the most errors, 37. It was an inauspicious debut for a young man who would become the best in the league at the position.

During the first month of the '63 campaign, president Pete Quesada issued a three-part report on the state of the Senators, and about a week after delivering the third installment, he resigned as president and sold his shares in the club. Four other original stockholders also bailed out, and the franchise passed to a group headed by investment bankers James M. Johnston and James H. Lemon (not the ex–Washington player). Johnston was named chairman of the board in the reorganization, and no successor to Quesada, as president, was deemed necessary.

During spring training 1963, George Selkirk continued to wheel and deal. Among his principal acquisitions were veteran right-hander Ron Kline, purchased from the Tigers, and Minnie Minoso, an accomplished veteran of the American League who had just completed an unhappy stint with the St. Louis Cardinals. Kline would assume the role of closer and was to save 17 games while recording a 2.79 ERA. Minoso, on the other hand, would be a bust in '63, batting just .229 in 109 games.

The star of the exhibition season was Tom Brown, who had starred in both football and baseball at the University of Maryland. He was a first baseman, and the Senators were desperate for one. Rogelio Alvarez, obtained from the Reds for Harry Bright, was stuck in Cuba because Fidel Castro wouldn't let him leave. Brown was ticketed for the minors, but when he led the team in hitting during the exhibition season, he got the call on opening day. The lineup in fact had only one holdover from the previous season's opening-day lineup, outfielder Chuck Hinton.

The Nats lost the 1963 opener to the Orioles, and when Tom Brown went hitless in his first 14 at-bats in the early season, he was benched in favor of Dick "Puppy Dog"

Phillips, a 30-year-old rookie with San Francisco the previous year, who would carry the bulk of the load the rest of the way. Phillips would hit ten homers but bat .237 and end up sharing first base with Larry "Bobo" Osborne, a powerfully built lefthanded hitter who had spent parts of five seasons as a sub at Detroit. With Washington in '63, his big-league adieu, Osborne cracked 12 homers, but hit .212.

As for Tom Brown, he managed only ten base hits in 80 at-bats, and by July was banished to York of the Eastern League, where he should have started in the first place. He was brought back up in September, when he hit his one and only major-league homer off Phil "The Vulture" Regan of the Tigers. In his 61 big-league games, Brown hit just .147. While he had once been quoted as saying that baseball was preferable to the "head-knocking" involved in football, his demise as a baseball player was likely a blessing. He signed with the Green Bay Packers at the end of the year, and eventually became the first big-leaguer to appear in the Super Bowl, which he did twice with the Packers.

The Nats held up pretty well over the first six weeks of the season. Tom Cheney adopted the stopper role, winning his first four decisions, with each of the four following a Washington loss. The first of these came in the season's third game, on April 11, 1963, when Cheney collared the Red Sox with a one-hitter, giving up only a single to shortstop Ed Bressoud in the fourth inning. The club was ambling along at a 13–18 pace following a doubleheader split in Boston, but everything began unraveling at that point. A loss in the second game of that doubleheader, in which the Senators were victims of a one-hitter by 19-year-old Bosox rookie Dave Morehead (Chuck Hinton slugged a home run in the first inning), began a skein of nine losses in ten games. Attendance waned.

At this point, one quarter of the way through the season and with his most powerful ally, Pete Quesada, no longer there to support him, Mickey Vernon was fired. So was coach George Case. Both would be offered jobs within the organization, however, and

Case remained as special assignments scout. Vernon accepted a job as Selkirk's administrative assistant; but after 23 years in a big-league uniform, he found the drudgery of office work rather not to his liking, and quit after two weeks. To replace him, the Nats swung a deal with the New York Mets in which they relinquished the services of the erratic and unproductive Jim Piersall (.245 in 29 games thus far) in exchange for the venerable National Leaguer, Gil Hodges.

A veteran of seven World Series with the Brooklyn and L.A. Dodgers, Hodges was a man's man, the type who walks softly but carries a big stick, as the expression goes. Nonetheless, the Senators continued their freefall. They lost their first five and nine of their first ten games under Hodges; by then they had been on the losing end in 17 of their last 19. Finally, a modest four-game winning streak was manufactured during the first week of June, and Tom Cheney won his first decision following six straight losses. But the Nats lost 21 of 25 during the rest of the month, including ten in a row, and by season's end Gil Hodges, a winner all his life, admitted the team he had piloted had on many occasions looked more like an American Legion team than an American League entry.

Toward the end of this most dismal period of the '63 season, George Selkirk pulled a couple of strings, which helped tremendously. He purchased infielders Don Zimmer and Don Blasingame and this paid off with seven straight wins during the first week of July. Incredibly, it had been 14 years since a Washington ball club had won that many in a row. Zimmer, who had also attended Western Hills High School in Cincinnati (before Ed Brinkman and Pete Rose), took over at third base after coming over from the Dodgers, and bopped 13 homers in three months. Second baseman Blasingame, a veteran who had recently lost his job at Cincinnati to the rookie Rose, hit .256 the rest of the way.

The loss of Tom Cheney for a prolonged period was particularly costly. He had registered his career-high eighth win, against nine losses, on Independence Day, but in his next

start hurt his elbow and was gone for the entire second half. His ERA for the year was a sterling 2.71. Last year's ace, Dave Stenhouse, was just 3–9, 4.55, when he was shelved for the final 12 weeks of the season due to bone chips in his pitching elbow, which necessitated surgery. Don Rudolph, who had been handed the opening-day assignment, was a depressing 7–19, 4.55. The staff bulwark was lefty Claude Osteen, 9–14, 3.35.

Slim 6'4" righthander Jim Duckworth got his baptism of fire in 1963. He had been chosen in the minor-league draft in the off season, and while eventually less successful than two others drafted at the same time, outfielders Brant Alyea and Lou Piniella, he was the first among them, at 24, to get his feet wet in the big pond. Things did not go at all well, and Duckworth's slate for the year read 4–12, with an inflated 6.04 ERA.

Complicating matters was Duckworth's fear of flying. With shades of Jackie Jensen, he once stepped off a plane during a stopover and refused to get back on. He was placed on the disabled list at his request at one point so that he could seek therapy. Duckworth never did get cured, although he did go so far as to take flying lessons. He won three more games in three years before fading into the mist, leaving a lifetime 7–25, 5.26, ledger in his wake. Duckworth apparently did not mind excitement, as long as his feet were planted on the ground, because he eventually became an instructor at the California Highway Patrol Academy.

Ken Retzer was, for the second year in succession, the team's most regular receiver, but his average plunged from .285 to .242. Don Leppert, acquired from Pittsburgh for a minor-league pitcher during the off season to add punch to the catching position, hit just .237 with six homers while participating in nearly half the games. Testimony to this team's anemic offense is the fact that it was one-hit four times, half the league total, over the course of the season. The Nats were victimized of course by Dave Morehead of the Red Sox in May. Pete Ramos, now with the Indians, came close to a perfect game versus the Senators on June 15. In his first appearance since having sustained an arm injury three weeks earlier, the "Cuban Cowboy" mowed down the first 20 batters before Jim King doubled with two down in the seventh. Another old Nat, submariner Ted Abernathy, took the mound for the final two innings and allowed no hits.

Don Blasingame saved the Senators from eternal shame on the other two occasions. Blazer's third-inning double on August 6 kept New York's Stan Williams, who walked just one, from achieving a no-hitter. Exactly two weeks later, Moe Drabowsky of the Kansas City A's was robbed of a no-hitter in the fourth inning when Blasingame bunted on him. Drabowsky, three years away from World Series glory, walked only two, keeping the bats silent as he went the route in a 9–0 dousing of the Senators.

Washington was also subjected to two-hitters on five occasions in 1963. These were authored by Sudden Sam McDowell of the Indians, Robin Roberts of the Orioles (weak-hitting Ed Brinkman had both hits), strikeout pitcher Dick Stigman of the Twins, Al Downing of the Yankees, and Joel Horlen of the White Sox (in this one, the Senators won on a single in the ninth by Hinton and a homer by King). The Nats' best-pitched game, apart from Cheney's one-hitter in the third game of the season, was Bennie Daniels' two-hit, complete-game, 10–0 whitewash on August 17. Better yet, Daniels worked his wonders against the despised Minnesota Twins.

Whatever offensive punch the Senators had came from the outfield positions. Don Lock and Jim King had 27 and 24 homers respectively, but Lock hit just .252 and King .231. The club's leading batsman, Chuck Hinton, was beaned in the head by a pitch thrown by the Yankees' Ralph Terry in early September and missed the next two weeks. When he came back, his vision was impaired and his average fell from .280 to .269, but he was the closest thing the Nats had to a .270 hitter. On September 6, '63, the day following the Hinton beaning, the Senators participated in the 100,000th game in major-league history and, what's more, they won. Bennie Daniels, 5–10,

4.38, for the year, subdued Dick Donovan and the Indians 7–2.

The third-year Nats were last in the league in runs scored, runs allowed, fielding, and pitching. The club had gotten progressively worse each year of its new existence, dropping 106 games in '63, the most by an A.L. club in 26 years, against only 56 victories. Home attendance was a major-league low of 535,604, a drop of nearly 200,000. The new owners lost an estimated half a million dollars on the year's operations. There was precious little that this ballclub could offer to prospective baseball fans, but old-time followers were able to take solace in the fact that on August 5, Sam Rice, one of their favorites, was named to the Baseball Hall of Fame.

Although he had disappeared into the sunset with a hefty .322 career average and had batted .349 at age 40, Rice had gone on record in recent years as having said that he wouldn't vote for himself for the Hall of Fame. To Sam, only people of the ilk of Babe Ruth, Ty Cobb, and Walter Johnson belonged in the Hall. He was also of the opinion that Firpo Marberry, the old Senators relief ace, should have gotten in ahead of him. Rice and Goose Goslin are the only Washington Senators in the Hall of Fame who played on all three of the team's pennant winners.

Sam Rice was the Senators' longest-serving position player of all time, having put in 20 years in the uniform. He died at age 84 in Rossmor, Maryland, in October 1974. Following his death, a letter he had sealed and entrusted to Baseball Hall of Fame president Paul Kerr nearly ten years earlier was opened in Cooperstown, N.Y. In it, Rice stated that Earl McNeely had grabbed him by the back of his shirt and had pulled him onto the field after he had made his famous catch during the 1925 World Series. At no time, Rice wrote, had he lost control of the ball.

No one could have accused the Senators of setting outlandish goals for the upcoming season. The slogan was "Off the Floor in '64," indicating that an escape from tenth place would be considered a major accomplishment. Room had been made on the roster for players made available by other clubs. Obtained for cash were outfielder Fred Valentine, who had hit .309 as a part-time outfielder in the Oriole chain at Rochester, and Mike Brumley, a catcher and Dodger farm hand who had been a minor-league all-star for three consecutive years. Brumley took over the regular catching chores in '64, but hit just .244 with a mere two homers. The Nats also purchased Bill "Moose" Skowron, the longtime Yankee slugger, now 33 years old, from the Dodgers. Reliever Marshall Bridges, who had seen limited action over the past two seasons, was acquired from the league champion Yankees. He would bomb for the Senators in '64 at 0–3, 5.70.

Moose Skowron was considered an important addition, seeing that he would bolster a lineup whose only semi-dangerous hitters were Jim King, Don Lock, and Chuck Hinton. Ironic in light of the assassination of the President the previous November, the Nats would be going with John Kennedy at third base in '64. Kennedy, who also shared JFK's May 29 birthday, was pretty much handed the job in spring training, when incumbent Don Zimmer reported with a broken wrist incurred while playing handball. Kennedy had been on the scene as a sub since '62, when on September 5 of that year he became just the second player in big-league history to hit a pinch home run in his first major-league at-bat.

The Senators' brass figured that with Kennedy and Ed Brinkman covering the left side, half the infield was set for perhaps another ten years. They were only half right. Kennedy hit just .230 and Brinkman .224 for the Senators in 1964, and they contributed to what was once again the league's most punchless offense. Bill Skowron did hit 13 homers by mid–July, but was then traded to the contending Chicago White Sox along with pitcher Carl Bouldin, who never pitched in the big leagues again. Coming to Washington were first baseman Joe Cunningham, a veteran who could hit for average but who didn't have Skowron's power, and Frank Kreutzer, a lefty destined to win two games for the Nats in both '64 and '65.

The offense was an absolute joke. Not a single player on the club would manage to hit as high as .275, and for more than a month in midseason, it was looking as if the Nats getting off the floor in '64 was nothing more than a pipe dream; Beginning in the last week of June, the club lost 16 of 19, and then 32 of 45. The Senators would wind up dead last in hitting with a collective .231, and would strike out a major-league high 1,124 times. The club was blanked 22 times, and shut out over four straight home games in early September.

Chuck Hinton was actually the league's top hitter for much of the first half. At the end of July, however, he was struck on the right wrist by an errant pitch and was out of the lineup for ten days. He wasn't the same after his return, driving in just three runs during the entire month of August, and wound up with a .274 mark. Don Lock was the offensive standout, slugging 28 homers, a record for the second franchise, but he struck out 137 times. Jim King, on May 25, became the new Senators' first player (and as it turned out, its *only* player) to hit for the cycle. Only a handful had turned the trick for the old Senators — Otis Clymer (1908), Goose Goslin (1924), Joe Cronin (1929), and Mickey Vernon (1946).

In early June '64, Jim King also bashed three homers in one game. Each roundtripper was a solo effort, however, and the Nats contrived to lose the game, as they had when King hit for the cycle. No wonder King always had a glum look about him. His final totals were nothing to rejoice over either — 18 homers, 56 ribbies, and a .241 bat mark. One of the great sluggers in Washington baseball history, Roy Sievers, was purchased from the Philadelphia Phillies in mid–July in an effort to alleviate the lack of righthanded punch off the bench. Sievers did manage four homers in 58 at-bats in this role, and appropriately hit the last four of his big-league career with Washington, where he had lived his best baseball moments. His average for 33 games was .172.

The brightest light in a fourth dismal year was Claude Osteen, the lefthander the Nats had obtained for next to nothing in late '61 from the Cincinnati Reds. Osteen became the first pitcher to win more than 12 games for the new Nats, and the 25-year-old lefty did so in grand style by going 15–13, 3.33. Over the next nine years, Osteen would record fewer than 15 victories in a season only twice. Ron Kline contributed an outstanding campaign in a relief role, recording 12 saves and a 10–7 record in 61 appearances. It was Kline's first winning season in 11 big-league years, while supported by a downtrodden cast of ballplayers who were losers 100 times.

Dave Stenhouse and Tom Cheney, former staff aces, were both again beset by arm ailments. Stenhouse went on the disabled list in late May and upon his return, Cheney encountered the same fate due to what was finally diagnosed as epicondylitis, more commonly known as tennis elbow. Cheney would sit out all of 1965, and would start one more game for the Nats in '66 before calling it quits. Stenhouse, 2–7, 4.81, in '64, never pitched in the bigs again. Two promising careers were snuffed out on a team that sorely needed pitching arms.

The mound problems had been anticipated in the winter, as both Stenhouse and Cheney were coming off elbow surgery. This prompted G.M. George Selkirk to deal with the Orioles for Leslie "Buster" Narum, a chunky righthander who'd achieved a less than sparkling 6–12, 4.88, slate with the Orioles' Rochester farm in '63. For Narum, who got lots of work and turned in a 9–15, 4.30, performance as the Nat's third-best winner in '64, the Senators had given up a 20-year-old outfielder then serving a six-month tour of duty in the army. His name — Lou Piniella. Bennie Daniels was another casualty on this pitching staff, although of a different kind than Tom Cheney and Dave Stenhouse. Daniels won five of his first seven decisions, but then made 13 starts before winning again, and by then he'd been relegated to a relief role. He wound up 8–10, 3.70.

While the Senators did manage to get off the floor in '64, there was nothing to take pride in. The club improved by six games in the standings, but still lost 100. The Nats climbed into ninth place because the Kansas City A's had dreadful pitching and won just 57

ballgames. Attendance went up, but was still the lowest in either league. The club again reported losses in the vicinity of half a million dollars.

In January 1965, James M. Johnston, chairman of the board, became the undisputed head honcho when he and James H. Lemon, his partner in investment banking, bought the 30 shares held by George Bunker, president of the Martin Marietta Corporation, and the ten shares owned by Floyd Akers, president of a local automobile company. Johnston and Lemon paid an estimated two million dollars for the 40 percent interest they had needed in order to assume complete control of a still-unprofitable property. The pair would take yet another financial dousing in 1965. D.C. Stadium attendance would decline by 40,000 and rank third from the bottom in the majors.

The catchphrase for the new season was "On We Drive in '65." The Senators would be resting their hopes on the outcome of two trades completed during the first four days of December. In the first exchange, Chuck Hinton, the best hitter in club history, was sent packing to Cleveland. Hinton may well have fallen into disfavor with the deceptively serene Gil Hodges early in the '64 season when, confused about the number of outs and under the impression that he had just caught a ball to retire the side, he had allowed a run to score easily from third.

The Nats took two players in return, both of whom had good power. Bob Chance was a 24-year-old first baseman coming off a fine year with the Indians during which he'd driven in 75 runs. Chance was a solid physical specimen who'd knocked out 14 dingers for the Indians, and there was every reason to think he could do a lot better than that. In reality, however, he would hit eight more home runs in the majors over the next four seasons. The other player obtained from Cleveland, Woodie Held, had been in the big leagues since 1957 and could play second, short, third, and the outfield, although not particularly well anywhere. Held had surprising power for a man his size and was usually good for 20 home runs per season despite filling a utility role. He would bang out 16 roundtrippers for the Senators in '65, getting his name in 122 box scores, mostly as the starting rightfielder.

A much more significant transaction occurred three days later, on December 4, 1964. The Senators acquired their franchise player on this day, a man who, over a span of three years yet to come, would hit enough home runs to lead the entire majors. The deal with the Los Angeles Dodgers for Frank Oliver Howard had its roots in the fact that the Dodgers, always strong in pitching, were most concerned about the health of their lefthanded ace, Sandy Koufax. An injury in '64 had brought about arthritis in Koufax's left elbow. The Dodgers did well to anticipate further problems, because following another stellar season in 1966, when he went 27–9, Koufax decided to retire. The best medical advice he had been getting was that he was risking crippling his arm permanently if he kept on throwing.

The Dodgers were interested in the talents of the Nats' 15-game winner, Claude Osteen. Nicknamed "Gomer" because of his resemblance to television's Gomer Pyle, Osteen would continue to win in double figures right through 1973. In L.A., he joined a rotation composed entirely of eventual Hall of Famers — Koufax, Don Drysdale, and rookie righthander Don Sutton. In the upcoming World Series, Osteen would get the Dodgers back on track after they dropped the first two games.

Infielder John Kennedy was also turned over to the Dodgers, but in return the Senators knew that from an offensive standpoint, they were bound to get men who would bang a few more balls out of the yard. Moving to Washington in this 5–for–2 exchange along with Frank Howard were third baseman Ken McMullen, first baseman Dick Nen, and pitchers Pete Richert and Phil Ortega. The Nats also transferred $100,000 to the Dodgers to complete the arrangement, which was finalized 11 days later when Nen's contract was transferred to Washington. Nen was the "player to be named later" in the deal.

Frank Howard, a powerplant of a man put together like NFL linebackers would be a decade or more hence, was from a Washington perspective the most valued asset involved in this transaction. Standing 6'7" and tipping the scales at about 260 pounds (by the end of the 1970 season, he had ballooned to a reported 302 pounds), the Dodgers signed him out of Ohio State for $108,000 in 1958. However, Howard was not always a regular player after joining L.A. for good in 1960, when he was selected National League Rookie of the Year. He lacked dexterity and speed in the outfield, and had a propensity for striking out, something he did more than once a game on average.

In 1962, Howard put it all together for the first time on a consistent basis in the majors, throwing big numbers on the board — 31–108–.296. In '63, he drove in 116 runs on the power-starved Dodgers and hit a game-winning home run off Whitey Ford in the fourth and final game of the World Series. In the first game of that Series, Howard had slugged a drive which no less an authority than Mickey Mantle claimed was the hardest he'd ever seen. The screaming liner, also off Ford, had caromed off the centerfield wall, and he was held to a double.

In the season just completed, though, Howard batted only .226 and drove in a mere 69 runs. He was seen as expendable by the Dodgers, who were proving that pitching, fielding, and speed, were all a team needed to win a pennant. Howard, who had turned 28 the previous August, was characteristically not at all disappointed to be coming to Washington. He admitted not knowing much about the town where he would earn the wonderful nickname the "Capital Punisher," but figured it had to be a decent place, what with all its history and prestige. He knew what type of ballclub he was coming to, but saw that as a bonus. For Howard, it would be a chance to play regularly without worrying so much about lapses which would relegate him to the bench — lapses which he had made so often on the other coast.

Kenny McMullen, another potential power source, was a third baseman, and he moved right into Kennedy's place and, pegged in the eighth hole in the lineup much of the time, slugged 18 homers and hit a respectable .263 in 1965. McMullen was not particularly quick or agile, but he was especially adept at moving in on bunts and slow rollers, a skill for which he would acquire quite a reputation around the league in years to come.

First baseman Dick Nen, father of future big-league reliever Robb Nen, shared time with the veteran Joe Cunningham but never became a solid major-leaguer. In the interim, he helped out with six homers and a .260 average in his first year in Washington. The Senators had insisted on Nen's inclusion in the Howard trade, and George Selkirk was lauding him as late as August as the Nats' first baseman of the future. Selkirk was wrong. This would be the only year Nen hit above .218 in four seasons as a part-timer with the club.

Even before he struck out the first six batters he faced in the big leagues, lefthander Pete Richert was considered a tremendous major-league prospect. (The six batters included four in his first complete inning — one made it to first when the third strike got away from the catcher.) Since that unforgettable debut in April '62, however, Richert had wallowed in near anonymity in the pitching-rich Dodgers' system. Given his first real shot by the Senators, the 25-year-old won six of seven decisions during the second half of the season before being forced to the sidelines by an infected foot. Richert replaced Claude Osteen's 15 wins by gaining 15 of his own, against 12 losses, and his 2.60 ERA was fifth best in the league among qualifiers.

Pete Richert was the Nats' representative in the '65 All-Star game, played in Minnesota, and he pitched two scoreless innings, allowing one hit and whiffing two. His work permitted the A.L. to come back from a 5–0 deficit to tie the score in a game eventually lost 6–5. The other star of the Nats' pitching staff was the reliever, Ron Kline, who once again came up with an outstanding season. He appeared in 74 games, shattering the Senators' record of 64 set 39 years earlier by Firpo Marberry. Kline won seven ballgames and saved 21 more in his rescue role.

Skinny Phil Ortega had amassed a 7–9 ledger with the Dodgers in '64. Twenty-two days older than Richert, Ortega earned the nod from Gil Hodges to start the season opener (which the Nats lost to the Red Sox 7–2 at D.C. Stadium) on the strength of his spring performances. He did pitch well for much of the first part of the season, and stood at 11–8 with a week left in July. Ortega's effectiveness then vanished. He ended up as the Nats' second-biggest winner at 12–15, but with a less than flattering 5.11 ERA.

Most frequently employed by Hodges, next to the two acquisitions from the Dodgers, was holdover Buster Narum, who won just 4 and lost 12 with an ERA way over four runs per game for the second straight year. This spelled Narum's demise, and he would be handed just five more starts over the next two years, his career virtually over before age 25. Bennie Daniels remained an enigma, and his 5–13 record spelled termination — he would never pitch in the bigs again. Mike McCormick, a fancy lefthander plagued by arm trouble, made a rebound of sorts with the Nats in '65. The hot-tempered southpaw had once won 15 for the Giants (1960, when he led the N.L. in ERA) and had been obtained from the Orioles in April for cash and a minor-leaguer. He went 8–8, 3.36, with better days ahead. Unfortunately, McCormick would be out of Washington by the time he put it all together.

One of McCormick's old teammates on the Giants was burly outfielder Willie Kirkland, who had shown promise as a slugger, but had been squeezed out of the picture, and understandably so, by the likes of Orlando Cepeda, Willie McCovey, and Felipe Alou. Following two years in Cleveland, where Kirkland hit 27 and 21 homers, he had languished with the Orioles before being purchased by the Nats in August '64. He knocked out 14 homers in 123 games for Washington in '65, but hit just .231.

Kirkland's presence, along with that of Frank Howard, Woodie Held, and holdover Don Lock (who kept on striking out, hit only 16 homers, and batted a moanful .215), created a congested atmosphere which resulted in the release of a man who may have rivaled Mickey Vernon as the greatest baseball icon in Washington since the Second World War. Roy Sievers was released, and when apprised of the news, expressed his incredulity to manager Gil Hodges. Here was a team with little home run power, and he was the one being cut loose? Sievers had hit but .180 in '64 and his average stood at .190 for 21 at-bats when the decision was made on May 11,—a decision taken solely by G.M. George Selkirk, Hodges explained. A major-league career begun in 1949 which had produced 318 home runs came to an abrupt end, and Roy Sievers went home.

Having swept Baltimore twice during a two-week period during the latter part of August, and split a four-game set with the Red Sox, the Nats sat at 60–75. If they won just three of their remaining 27 games, the Senators would avoid 100 losses for the first time in the history of the new franchise. The historic win came on September 10, 1965, with Pete Richert registering a 4–1 decision over the Angels in Washington to boost the club's record to 63–80.

Two days later, a rookie outfielder brought up from the top farm club in Honolulu, Hawaii, made his debut in the big leagues. He was Brant Alyea, a young slugger seized in the minor-league draft following the 1962 season. It is virtually impossible to make a bigger splash than did Alyea. Summoned to the plate as a pinch hitter with two men on, he faced another rookie, Rudy May of the Angels. May had himself made quite an impression in his first big-league game back in April when he'd given up just one hit in nine innings to the Tigers. Brant Alyea drove the very first pitch he ever saw in the big leagues over the fence, the first pinch hitter in league history to do so. It was the big blow in a 7–1 win.

Another, more recent, Washington draftee had an even greater impact. The Senators had been assigned, because of their ninth-place finish the previous year, the third overall pick in the first-ever free-agent draft, held in New York on June 8–9, 1965. With that pick, they selected Joe Coleman, Jr., a 17-year-old right-hander from Natick, Mass., and son of a former major-league pitcher. Coleman had failed to turn any heads at Burlington of the Carolina League in the last two months of that loop's season, having compiled a 2–10, 4.56, ledger. G.M. Selkirk had professed all season long that he felt it was better to leave the Senators' best young arms down in the minors, where they could develop naturally. Still, with nothing at risk late in the season, Selkirk was anxious to see what the youngster could do at the highest level.

Joe Coleman made his debut in Washington against the Kansas City A's in the first game of the second-last series of the year. His opponent on this day was James "Catfish" Hunter, who, at 22, was completing his fourth major-league campaign. Coleman was tagged for a first-inning triple by Jose Tartabull, father of future star Danny Tartabull, but got out of the inning by fanning Ken "Hawk" Harrelson. He gave up just one more hit until the ninth, when back-to-back doubles produced a run, but that was it, and Coleman wrapped up a 4–1 four-hitter in his first game. The A's won the second game but Jim Hannan, a righthander who'd seen spot duty with the Nats since back in '62, stopped K.C. on five hits in the third tilt for his ninth big-league win and first shutout, as the Nats romped 9–0.

That win brought the club's record to 69–90. Eighth place had long since been secured, and the Nats had made good, although precariously, on their preseason vow of driving on in '65. Youngsters Denny McLain and Mickey Lolich of the Tigers won the first two games of the season's final series, and it fell upon Joe Coleman to win the 70th game for the Nats. He did so, holding the Tigers to five hits and prevailing by a 3–2 margin. While the Nats wound up eighth, they might have taken some solace in the fact that they finished only seven games out of sixth. The club now had a legitimate power threat in big Frank Howard, who had many pitchers' knees knocking at the very sight of him. Facing a whole new set of pitchers, Howard hit 21 homers, despite missing time in August because of an elbow injury.

He hit for an inspiring .289, and drove in a record number of runs for the new franchise, 84.

On the other side of the ledger, team batting was once again the worst in the league. The culprits were the middle infielders. Ed Brinkman hit for an awful .185, and Don Blasingame .223. Ken Hamlin ended up spelling both at various times and doing much better, batting .273 in 117 contests. Catchers Mike Brumley and Doug Camilli batted .208 and .192 respectively. The hard-boiled Don Zimmer, an underrated talent and extraordinary competitor, had been asked, at age 34, to learn how to catch in the Florida Instructional League. Zimmer was a quick study, but the wheels fell off at the plate, and he finished below what would one day be called the "Mendoza Line," with a season bat mark of .199. For Don Zimmer as a major-league player, it was, after 12 seasons, the end of the line.

Contributing to the dim outlook for the fans was the fact that their ex-favorites, the Twins, won the pennant and very nearly won the world championship. Had it not been for last year's top pitcher, Claude Osteen, now of the Dodgers, the old Nats would have. But the trade with the Dodgers was, from Washington's point of view, an unequivocal success, and now there seemed to be fewer holes to fill as the Nats attempted to keep the drive alive after '65.

President Lyndon Johnson was enjoying his Easter vacation at the LBJ Ranch in Texas so much that he decided to keep enjoying it and forgo an appearance for the baseball season opener on April 11, 1966. Vice-President Hubert Humphrey threw out the ceremonial first pitch in his stead, but this did not change the Nats' luck in opening games, as they lost their fifth in six years. In the sixth, with a man on and the hometown team trailing 1–0, Indians' starter "Sudden Sam" McDowell delivered a hummer under Frank Howard's chin. Hondo (Howard's favorite and most commonly used nickname, derived from the 1953 John Wayne movie *Hondo*) got back in the box and cranked the very next offering against the left field foul pole for a 2–1 lead.

Pete Richert was stellar until the ninth when he put men on second and third with one out. Reliever par excellence Ron Kline was brought in, but a soft single to left by banjo-hitting Vic Davalillo made both runs count. Wilfred "Sonny" Siebert, a righthander who would this year replicate last year's 16–8 record, was brought in to quiet the Senators' bats in the ninth, which he did. This was nothing compared to what Siebert inflicted on the Senators later on in the season, on June 10, at Cleveland's Municipal Stadium. Scheduled to start that night, Siebert had been needled by his wife about how he'd been manhandled by opposing batsmen of late. Sonny told her that he would do anything to get her off his back, and that he was willing to pitch a no-hitter if that was what it would take.

That's what he did. There was only one no-hitter in the big leagues in 1966, and the Senators were the dupes, the first time the second franchise had been so victimized. Siebert, who got the benefit of three major-league-caliber plays behind him, faced only two batters more than the minimum. Dick Nen drew a walk in the fifth, and rookie catcher Paul Casanova was safe on an error in the seventh. Poor Phil Ortega tossed a magnificent game for the Nats, allowing only five hits, but as was so often the case, it was all for naught. That defeat was the fifth of seven consecutive losses, which put a damper on a decent start to the season. The Nats had at one point won ten of fifteen in May, and climbed to fifth place exactly a week before succumbing to Siebert's magnum opus. Alas, the heady heights of the first division were too much to handle. By the end of June, despite some more roster changes, the Senators had tumbled to the more familiar climes of ninth place.

Utility infielder Bob Saverine had been purchased from the Orioles and was playing, somewhere, most of the time. Nicknamed "Rabbit" for his speed on the basepaths, Saverine had been the second-youngest player, next to Tim McCarver, to have appeared in a big-league game in the 1950s. He had kicked around with the Orioles since that time. Elevated to the bigs, Saverine managed .251 for the Nats, but stole only four bases. Still, this was preferable to keeping Don Blasingame, who hit .215 in 68 games, at second. Blasingame was pawned off on the much-improved Kansas City Athletics, which was just about the only club the Nats dealt with in '66.

Baseball's flower child, Ken Harrelson, arrived in the nation's capital from the A's in late June as a result of a one-for-one exchange for Jim Duckworth, still racked by his fear of flying. Adorned with long blond hair, beads, bell-bottoms, Nehru jackets, and all the other trappings of the sixties, Harrelson had slugged 23 homers for the A's in '65, but had only five homers and was batting .224 for K.C. at the time of the trade. Dick Nen was turning out to be a bust and would bat just .213 for the season, and the Nats were hoping Harrelson, dubbed "Hawk" because of his protruding proboscis, would regain his batting eye. Hawk didn't do that, and managed only .248 with just seven dingers over the last three months of the campaign. When he got off on the wrong foot again in 1967, the Nats sold him back to the A's, exactly two weeks short of the one-year anniversary of the original transaction.

More damaging than Harrelson's mediocre output was the fact that the A's cried foul about the original acquisition of Duckworth. The Senators agreed to take him back six weeks later in return for another righthanded pitcher, Cuban native Diego Segui. Segui, whose son David would become a big-league star, had been struggling with a 3–7 record and an ERA of 5.00 at the time. He had shown flashes of brilliance, though, particularly when he tossed a complete-game shutout at the Yankees just before the All-Star break, the first such achievement by a Washington pitcher in nearly two and a half months. The A's demoted Segui to the minors, but would call him back up in late '67 after he'd compiled a brilliant 1.29 ERA at Vancouver of the Pacific Coast League. He became one of baseball's most reliable firemen over the next seven years. In 1970 and '71, the A's, by then in Oakland, began using Segui as a starter as well, and in '70 he led the entire league in earned run average.

The Nats did for the time being have the advantage of carrying one of the league's top relievers on their staff. Ron Kline placed second in the running for the Fireman of the Year Award with an outstanding 6–4, 2.39, campaign punctuated by 23 saves. In a setup role, Bob Humphreys, previously a journeyman minor-leaguer obtained from the Cubs by George Selkirk in April, was a pleasant surprise, posting 7–3, 2.82, numbers. Canadian Dick Lines got into 53 games and put up excellent figures as well — 5–2, 2.28.

The starting pitching was pretty decent as well for the '66 Senators. The ace was again Pete Richert, who for the second year running was the club's lone representative in the All-Star game at St. Louis. Unfortunately, Richert was the loser. Called into the game at the start of the tenth inning with the score knotted at one, the lefty threw just eight pitches, yielding a lead-off single to Tim McCarver and another single to Maury Wills. Richert's slate for the year was 14–14, 3.37. Portsider Phil Ortega also won half his decisions, winding up at 12–12, 3.92.

Both Richert and Ortega made historically significant contributions in an oddly similar manner during the 1966 season. At this time, the American League record for consecutive strikeouts stood at seven and, incredibly, both Washington hurlers matched it during the year. Both did it in D.C. Stadium and, adding an additional twist, a third pitcher, Jim Merritt of the Twins, also accomplished the feat in '66, and it was *against* the Nats at D.C. Stadium. Richert's spree occurred early in the season versus the Tigers, against whom the Nats were terrible this year, winning just five of 18. Richert actually lost that game, on April 24, 4–0.

Ortega fanned seven straight on May 29 versus the Red Sox, who were to finish behind Washington in the standings, in ninth place. Ortega won his game, 3–2. The other club, aside from the Tigers, that the Nats had most difficulty with in '66 was the Twins, as they took just four of 18 from the old Senators. On July 21, Minnesota's Merritt whiffed his seven Washington batters in a row, and 12 in all, in going the route and shutting out the Nats on just three hits.

Washington still didn't have the pitching to challenge the big boys, but the staff had done nothing but improve steadily in the past year. Lefty Mike McCormick continued his comeback from arm woes earlier in the decade. With the encouragement of coach Rube Walker, the southpaw began employing the screwball, which many had blamed for his problems in the first place. McCormick always disagreed, and, with the screwball added to his arsenal, hurled three of the Senators' six shutouts this season. He registered a record of 11–14, 3.46, despite eight attempts at winning his eighth game.

The other significant pitchers on the club this year were here for the longer term. Jim Hannan, now 26 and a big-leaguer on an intermittent basis with the Nats since 1962, won just three games and lost nine; but within a couple of years, he would finally be a factor. Casey Cox, a big Californian and eventually a starter, took part in 66 games in his rookie campaign, winding up with a serviceable 4–5, 3.50. At the end of May, the Nats called up Dick Bosman, a hard-nosed righthander from Wisconsin who arguably would become the most important pitcher in the second franchise's history. The 22-year-old Bosman made his debut at Fenway Park in Boston and came away with a 6–3 verdict over Jim Lonborg. It would be his only win, as he lost six and wound up with a scary 7.62 ERA.

Prior to Pete Richert's misfortune in the All-Star game, the Nats had sailed into the All-Star break with five games in three days at Yankee Stadium. They won four, and the Yanks' lone victory was achieved by surmounting a 4–0 deficit, thanks in part to a Mickey Mantle home run. The Mick pulled a hamstring in the same game, however, and was to be sidelined after the break. Finally, the Washington Senators had the Yankees' number, and won the season's series for the first time since the '33 Nats, likely the best Washington team ever, had done so. These, of course, were hardly the same Yankees. Mantle's knee ailments limited him to 108 games.

The club's top home run hitter, Joe Pepitone, batted only .255. Roger Maris, totally disenchanted in New York, was in a season-long slump, and at age 32 hit just .233. Young Mel Stottlemyre went from 20-game winner to 20-game loser, and Whitey Ford's arm flared up and he underwent another operation in September. Regardless, the Washington Senators were better than the New York Yankees, finally!

On the last weekend of the season, the Senators made history by introducing to the game the first female public-address announcer in major-league history, Joy Hawkins-McCabe, daughter of the club's traveling secretary, Burt Hawkins. The Senators responded by committing a team-record seven errors, losing to the White Sox 6–2. The next day, the Nats swept two games, and on the following day, September 26, the Red Sox strode in for a make-up doubleheader, a crucial one in terms of determining the order of standing among the lower-echelon clubs. Ballplayers do take games like these seriously.

Fans, however, do not. Only 485 souls showed up at D.C. Stadium on the Monday afternoon, with their favorites clinging to eighth place with a half-game lead over the Bosox. Boston rookie Darrell Brandon pitched a shutout in the first game. No one knew at this point that the last series of the year against the Yankees would be washed out completely; the second game of the twin bill versus Boston turned out to be the last game of the year. Joe Coleman, the 18-year-old who'd won his first two big-league games in impressive fashion at the end of the previous season, was nominated by Gil Hodges to start for Washington.

Joe Junior gave up just six hits and two walks, and Don Lock slammed a two-run homer in the seventh to put the game away. The Nats won their 71st game, bettering their previous record of 70 set the previous year. With the weather cooperating, the Senators found themselves a half-game ahead of Boston and a full game up on the Yankees who, astonishingly, finished dead last.

Don Lock hit only .233 for the season, with 16 homers for the second consecutive year. He split more time in the outfield with Jim King, and starred mostly in a pinch-hitting role. In one noteworthy performance on July 2, '66, Lock went 5–for–5, with a home run and two doubles, as the Nats applied a 10–4 pasting to the Yankees. He led the league with three pinch homers, but this was primarily a reflection of the fact that he was no longer a regular player. Lock was striking out, in his fourth full year with the Nats, at a rate more alarming than ever. His counterparts in the outfield were Frank Howard and Fred Valentine. Big Frank, plagued all year long by his nagging elbow injury, led the club with a .278 average, although his power numbers were down and he hit only 18 homers, none after September 2. Valentine, coming off an excellent .324, 25-home run campaign at Triple-A Hawaii, connected for 16 roundtrippers and batted .276 in '66. It would, by far, be his best year in baseball.

Following the season, it was the wildly inconsistent Lock, often mentioned as trade bait, who was dispatched to the Philadelphia Phillies for lefthanded reliever Darold Knowles, a deal which turned out to be an excellent one for Washington. This set up the trade of bullpen ace Ron Kline three days later. Kline went to the Twins for Bernie Allen and an old favorite in Washington, Camilo Pascual, the ex-strikeout king who had been plagued by arm troubles for two years. But Pascual wasn't quite 35 yet, and G.M. Selkirk was hoping he could regain some of his old form.

Darold Knowles would likely be able to step into Kline's role as stopper and if not, Bob Humphreys would be waiting in the wings. Bernie Allen, a second baseman, had burst onto the scene by winning A.L. Rookie of the Year honors back in '62. A couple of years later, he was injured in a collision with Don Zimmer of the Senators and never regained his previous offensive form. He was very good defensively, though, and would fill the most gaping hole.

There was no reason for great encouragement on the left side of the infield either. One sad comment on the offensive state of the club was the fact that Ed Brinkman was by the end of the year the lead-off man despite his .229 batting percentage. Brinkman was by now, however, peerless among the league's shortstops, although his fielding percentage was not fully reflecting his outstanding range and throwing arm. Kenny McMullen at third suffered from the sophomore jinx, his average plummeting 30 points in '66 to .233 with 13 homers, five fewer than during his rookie season.

Ten days after the 2–for–1 trade with the Twins, the Senators turned around and engineered a similar transaction with the San Francisco Giants. Mike McCormick would be returning to his old club, and this did not turn out so well for Washington. McCormick immediately transformed himself into the National League's best pitcher, copping the Cy Young Award. In return for him, the Senators obtained Cap Peterson, an outfielder who had hit .236 over four years as a reserve outfielder with the Giants, and Bob Priddy, a 27-year-old righthander who'd amassed 6–3, 3.96, totals in an understandably limited role on a Giants club which had finished the season just a game and a half out of first place. Priddy would go 3–7, 3.44, in long relief for Washington in '67 before moving on. Cap Peterson got his big chance as a professional ballplayer, but flubbed it by batting just .240 with eight homers.

It was thought by the administration that these changes would finally be enough to pull the Washington Senators up among the elite clubs in the league in 1967. The Nats had just finished in the second division for the 20th consecutive year. Small wonder that the turnstiles continued to turn too infrequently. The season attendance of 576,260 was by far the lowest in the majors — 60,000 less than the next most pitiable figure, counted at Wrigley Field in Chicago.

Nineteen sixty-seven was indeed a breakthrough year for the Washington Senators. They managed to finish in a dead heat with the previous year's pennant winners, the Baltimore Orioles. The Orioles, however, slipped from their lofty perch to sixth place. This season was a topsy-turvy one throughout the majors. The pennant winners were the Red Sox, who had wound up behind the Nats in ninth place the previous year. In the other league, the Cardinals placed first following a sixth-place finish in '66, and the Dodgers slipped to an ignoble eighth on the heels of a pennant-winning season.

Gil Hodges, well-liked and certainly re-spected, continued to improve his record year by year, and his '67 ball club posted a 76–85 mark. This was the first time a Washington team had won this many games since 1953, when the Nats played at a .500 level back in the days of the 154-game schedule. The fans showed a willingness to show up in greater numbers if the club was going to be compet-itive, and an increase of more than 194,000 flocking to D.C. Stadium represented an at-tendance of over 770,000, a record for the new franchise.

Out of the gate, Pete Richert, Phil Or-tega, still with the club despite constant trade rumors over the past year or so, and Camilo Pascual, were perceived as the big three in the rotation. Joe Coleman, only 20 years old, ap-peared to be the incumbent for the fourth spot. The Nats also had at their disposal Barry Moore, a North Carolinian who had split six decisions and pitched well for them in '66. Moore, they hoped, would supply some sup-port from the left side, as Richert was the only accomplished southpaw among the starters. Moore's control would suffer somewhat, and he posted a 7–11, 3.75, slate in his role as fifth starter. He did author the club's best-pitched game of the year, though — a complete-game 3–0 one-hitter over the Twins on April 30.

Phil Ortega finally distinguished himself, not losing in a single outing through 16 starts from late May through late August. The sup-port Ortega got throughout the season was surely not overwhelming, and his final stats were 10–10, 3.03. The heat and humidity must have agreed with Camilo Pascual. Pitching for Washington for the first time since 1960, Lit-tle Potato led the staff in wins, with 12, lost 10, and recorded a 3.28 ERA. He might have won 15 or so had he not broken a bone in his right ankle while sliding back into second base, with more than three weeks left in the season. Joe

Coleman, who'd won his first three big-league starts as an 18- and 19-year-old, won his first two '67 outings but eventually struggled in a rookie campaign in which he managed a slate of 8–9 with a high 4.63 earned run mark.

The staff ace, Pete Richert, got off on the wrong foot on opening day, permitting the mediocre Yankees to score seven times in the third inning. By the fifth, President Lyndon Johnson had seen enough and vacated his seat as the Nats succumbed 8–0. On May 29, Richert, although impressive in his last few starts, sat at 2–6, 4.64, and was traded to the Baltimore Orioles, where he would recover and complete a composite 9–16 campaign. Pete Richert was to pitch seven more years in the big leagues but would not start another game, as the pitching-rich Orioles could afford the luxury of deploying his left wing out of their bullpen. In the Orioles' pennant-win-ning years of 1969 and 1970, Richert was 7–4, 2.20, and 7–2, 1.96, respectively.

The trade with the Orioles was precipi-tated by circumstances which made major headlines at the time. Baltimore had in its farm system a promising young slugger named Mike Epstein. Optioned to Rochester by the Orioles in '66, Epstein had set the Interna-tional League on fire, leading the circuit in home runs (29), runs batted in (102), and bat-ting .309. For those heroics, he was named Minor League Player of the Year. But Balti-more was coming off a world championship, and Epstein couldn't dislodge either Boog Powell from first base or Curt Blefary from left field in early '67.

On roster cutdown date, May 10, Balti-more General Manager Harry Dalton in-formed Epstein that he was being optioned to Rochester once again. Under regulations in force at the time, Epstein could have been sent back to the minors again the following season, at the Orioles' option, which would have made it three years in a row. Only after that would they have been forced to either keep him or trade him.

Mike Epstein decided to buck the sys-tem. He told Harry Dalton that if the Orioles wouldn't trade him, he was going home. And he did. The Orioles did trade him, less than three weeks following the ultimatum, insisting that they were not yielding to the sitdown strike, but to the necessity of reinforcing their pitching staff before first place got too far away from them. In the big picture, Epstein's defiance was encouragement for the burgeoning Major League Players' Association. Before the end of the year, the players would win concessions from the owners on a number of points in a new agreement. The minimum player salary, for example, increased to $10,000 per year from $7,000, which had been the standard in the majors since 1957.

The acquisition of Mike Epstein and lefthander Frank Bertaina, on whom G.M. George Selkirk had had his eye since his own days in the Baltimore organization, also improved the outlook on the field for the Senators. The lefthanded Bertaina — nicknamed "Toys in the Attic" by ex-teammate Moe Drabowsky for his daffiness — paid immediate dividends. He went 6–5, 2.92, but among those six wins were four shutouts, and another of his wins was a shared shutout.

In the long run, Epstein would prove more valuable. For the present, his arrival did help unclutter the first-base glut, with the likes of Ken Harrelson, Dick Nen, and Bob Chance all still on the roster. Epstein, nicknamed "Superjew" by rival manager Rocky Bridges for his 1965 batting exploits in the California League, hit just .229 with nine homers in '67. But he would become an important component in future years.

Eleven days after the trade, the Nats divested themselves of one of their first basemen by selling Ken Harrelson back to the A's. This started another portentous chain of events which made major news during the summer of '67. Following the Hawk's return to the A's, maverick owner Charles O. Finley fined youthful pitcher Lew Krausse as a result of an incident during a commercial airline flight. The players rallied against Finley, who got no support from his manager, Alvin Dark. Finley subsequently fired Dark. The A's players stood up for their manager, and Harrelson was widely quoted as having said that Finley was

a menace to baseball. Finley phoned Harrelson to ask if the reports had been accurate, and Harrelson said not exactly — what he had actually said was that *Finley's actions* over those last few days had been bad for baseball.

The events which transpired next made Hawk Harrelson a very happy man. Finley decided he didn't want him on his ballclub, and instead of trying to trade him, the most conventional and beneficial way of getting rid of a ballplayer, he decided to give Hawk his unconditional release. Had Finley at least put Harrelson on waivers, he likely would have gotten $50,000 for him. There were reports that the humiliated Harrelson was considering the idea of making a public retraction.

Then Hawk began receiving a lot of phone calls — phone calls from other teams. He realized he was in an unheard-of bargaining position for a big-league ballplayer. He was free to make his own deal. And a sweet one he made, too, with the Boston Red Sox. It included a bonus estimated at $75,000, and a salary package covering the rest of the season and 1968 as well. To top it all off, Harrelson went with the Red Sox to the World Series. It was still nearly a decade before the advent of free agency, and this entire matter was seen in a very negative light by the lords of baseball.

A rule change was engineered in December to prevent a similar type of incident from reoccurring. It would no longer be possible for a player to be placed on the customary $1 waivers before going through irrevocable waivers. In plain terms, this meant that the player in question would have to go to the team that claimed him first, and many teams could and certainly would have claimed Harrelson ahead of the Red Sox. The price for making such a waiver claim at the time was $20,000. Whether a player in Harrelson's shoes would have agreed to join whichever lower-level team had claimed him was a secondary matter to club owners. What really mattered to them was that no player be allowed to cut his own deal with whichever club he chose.

The Senators, incidentally, did become

factors in the Charlie Finley controversy, and in a peculiar way. Finley had brought some pretty bizarre innovations to the game. In the early sixties, he traded for sluggers Rocky Colavito and Jim Gentile, and then brought his outfield fence closer in to increase home-run production. Finley paraded a mule he had named "Charlie O," which was the official team mascot, onto the ballfield, and even into cocktail parties and hotel lobbies. He introduced orange baseballs to the game. He had at least one intelligent idea, advocating night World Series games to help boost fan interest. In protest of many of Finley's colorful concepts, the Senators began wearing white caps and white stockings for their games versus the Athletics. These may have helped, as the Nats went 11–6 over the A's on the season.

But what truly distinguished the Senators' year in 1967 was their propensity for playing in long ballgames — *very* long ball-games. The trend was set early. After winning in 11 innings in their third game of the year, the Nats were the losers the very next day in a 16-inning contest, the second game of a doubleheader, in Chicago. Then on June 4, having fallen behind 4–0 in the second inning, the Nats became entangled in a marathon at Baltimore. The Senators stormed back with five runs in the third, but the Orioles notched a tying run in the seventh following a valiant effort by Fred Valentine, who dove and got his glove hand on the ball but then dropped it. The score remained the same for 12 more innings, until Oriole catcher Andy Etchebarren cranked a home run off Bob Priddy in the bottom of the 19th inning.

This was not nearly as exciting, particularly from a Washington fan's perspective, as what happened at D.C. Stadium just over a week later on June 12, in the first game of a nine-game homestand. The Nats were in sole possession of last place, which they would occupy during much of June and early July, as the night began. Cap Peterson homered twice and Frank Howard once during the first six innings to power them to a 4–1 lead, but the White Sox responded by scoring three times in the seventh. In the top of the tenth, Chicago took the lead on a walk and a couple of broken-bat singles to apparently wrap things up.

In the bottom of the inning, a single by Ken McMullen, a couple of wild pitches courtesy of reliever Bob Locker, and a sacrifice fly by pinch hitter Jim King* once again knotted the score. Over the next nine innings, the Senators managed just four more hits, without incident, against Chicago relievers Locker, Hoyt Wilhelm, and John Buzhardt. The Nats' two relief aces in this campaign, lefty Darold Knowles (6–8, 2.70, with 14 saves) and sidearming righthanded rookie Dave Baldwin (2–4, and an eye-popping 1.70, with 12 saves) permitted just five hits and three walks over that span. Counting force-outs and double plays, the Nats had left just two men on base in those first 19 frames.

There had been some close calls. In the 13th, Chicago's Tommie Agee was called out at home after attempting to score from third on a grounder to shortstop Bob Saverine. In the 16th, swift Ken Berry was unsuccessful in a daring attempt to steal home with the bases loaded and two out. In the bottom of the 20th, Fred Valentine opened with a single off John Buzhardt and moved to third on Cap Peterson's one-out single. Mike Epstein was walked intentionally, but catcher Paul Casanova, the club's lone All-Star representative the following month (he would not play), grounded into an inning-ending third-to-home-to-first double play.

In the 22nd, Casanova, a receiver with an outstanding arm and an extended-leg catching style which served as a prototype for future stars like Tony Pena and Benito Santiago, got a second opportunity. Hank Allen, perpetually and unfortunately known as Richie Allen's brother, opened the inning for Washington with a walk. Allen advanced to third on

---

*This was one of Jim King's last good deeds for his longtime team. Three days later, he would be joining these same White Sox, with a younger, speedier flychaser, Edwin Marvin "The Creeper" Stroud, coming Washington's way. King's departure marked the extinction of original 1961 draftees with the Washington Senators' second ballclub.

Cap Peterson's fourth hit of the night (he went 4–for–9, the only player on either side with four hits). With eery similarity to what happened in the 20th Mike Epstein was again passed intentionally by John Buzhardt, who pitched eight innings of relief on this long night, to load the bases. Again, with one out, up came Paul Casanova, 0–for–8 for the evening, who had caught 268 pitches so far and cut down three runners who'd foolishly challenged his gun. The lanky 6'4" refugee, who'd hit .254 with 13 homers for the Nats as a rookie in '66, came through with a single to bring in the winning run. Of the original 7,236 spectators who had paid to get into the park, an estimated 1,500 were still around to see the end of the 22-inning epic.

A number of records were set. The game was the longest night game in all of baseball history up to that time, both from a standpoint of innings played and actual time expended. The longest previous night games had gone 19 innings — there had been five. On the clock, the game used up six hours, 38 minutes, obliterating the old mark by one hour and 25 minutes. Neither team made an error, and this established another record. Mike Epstein set an American League fielding standard by handling 34 chances without an error, including an A.L.–record 33 putouts. The longest game by innings, incidentally, has been on the books since 1920, and was a National League contest involving the Boston Braves and the Brooklyn Dodgers. Played during baseball's dark ages, nearly two decades before lighted stadiums came into vogue, that one was called on account of darkness, after 26 innings, still tied 1–1.

Before the 22-inning game, manager Gil Hodges was presented a trophy by the B'nai B'rith Society for being their Sportsman of the Year. Seven hours later, he joked that the game was so long the trophy had become tarnished. Hodges forgot to give a break to the next day's starting pitcher, Barry Moore, who charted every single pitch that night. Hodges had meant to send Moore home to catch come shut-eye, but his intentions were lost in the excitement.

There were two more marathons for the Nats later on in 1967 — a 20-inning 9–7 triumph over the Twins at Minnesota on August 9, and eight days later, a 16-inning 8–3 loss to the Indians at home. In July, more excitement was generated among the local fandom when eight straight wins were strung together, the first two as a result of a doubleheader sweep at Cleveland just prior to the All-Star break. The Nats established the club record eighth win in a row on July 17 in Washington, as Darold Knowles hurled four scoreless innings and drove in the insurance run in a 4–2 decision. Before the streak, the Senators had been languishing at 13 games below .500. By the time it was over, the club was only six games out of first place, and Washington went baseball-mad.

Of course, the streak, and the madness, didn't last, but now there seemed to be some reason for optimism in terms of the future. Frank Howard, finally recovered from the pain in his elbow which had hampered his swing for nearly two years, slugged 36 homers and drove in 89, leading the club in both departments once again. The homer total represented a career high, and the RBI output was his best in five years. Aided principally by Hondo's slugging, it was the pitching staff, however, which carried the club through most of the campaign.

The team batting average of .223 was the worst in the league, and the Nats were very nearly last in slugging. Ken McMullen had continued his rapid development early on, and was the Senators' hottest hitter when his hand was ripped open by a line drive off the bat of the Twins' Bobby Allison in early August. At that point, McMullen had 12 homers and 54 driven in, already matching his RBI total of the previous two years. He had also embarked on a 19-game hitting streak, the second-longest in the American League in 1967. Following his return to action, McMullen hit only four more homers and drove in only 13 more runners to finish with a .245 batting mark.

Shortstop Ed Brinkman was terrible at the plate during a season disrupted by stints in the military. Brinkman did get into 109 games, despite a .188 batting average, because of his impeccable fielding. Bernie Allen, obtained from the Twins in the Ron Kline deal, showed no signs of resuscitating his career and compiled a pathetic .193 mark. Tim Cullen, a 25-year-old righthanded batter also known for his glove work, ended up spelling both Allen and Brinkman, and earning more playing time than either of them. At least, Cullen's batting average was better than the team's (the team, of course, included pitchers in the pre–DH era): .236, with two homers. In the outfield, aside from Cap Peterson's eight homers and .240 average, Fred Valentine had an awful start and finished at .234 with 11 homers. Hank Allen had .233–3–17 figures.

The '67 season ended on a high note. This was the year that four clubs had a shot at first place on the final weekend. One of those clubs, the Chicago White Sox, the modern-day version of the Hitless Wonders, lost three straight to the Senators on that last weekend. Chicago finished fourth by exactly that margin of three games, despite having held onto first place for a total of three months during the regular season.

Ten days after the end of the campaign, manager Gil Hodges confirmed rumors which had begun to circulate two years earlier when Casey Stengel, then nearly 75 years old, had resigned as manager of the New York Mets. Hodges had been immediately seen as a fitting replacement, a former star already established as a manager, returning to the town where he'd spent his glory days. But Hodges had proceeded to sign a contract extension with the Senators good through 1968. He had done as well as anyone had a right to expect, winning more games each and every year since his hiring in 1963. The players admired him because of his ability to match wits with anyone in the opposing dugout, and loved him because he respected them, expecting only 100 percent effort in return.

In exchange for the rights to their manager, the Senators accepted $100,000 and a stout righthanded pitcher named Bill Denehy, who had cultivated a 1–7, 4.70, record with the last-place Mets in '67. Denehy's claim to fame remains the fact that he appeared on the same rookie bubblegum baseball card as Tom Seaver, who went on to great things. Denehy didn't, and his career with the Senators consisted of two innings in 1968, during which he gave up two runs. The Nats lost more than just their manager to the Mets. Gil Hodges dragged his entire coaching staff to New York along with him — Eddie Yost, and his old Brooklyn chums, Rube Walker and Joe Pignatano. Within two years, that crew would guide the Mets to a frenetic world championship. But the toll Hodges paid was enormous. He suffered a heart attack on September 24, 1968, and within four years was dead, two days short of his 48th birthday.

Washington General Manager George Selkirk wasted little time in picking a successor for 1968. He chose Jim Lemon, well known to the local baseball citizenry, who'd retired as a player in '63 and had been coaching for the Twins during the past three seasons. Lemon quickly assembled a coaching staff. Sid Hudson, the old Washington twirler, would return as pitching coach. Hudson seemed the right man for the job, coming off a three-year stint as roving minor-league pitching instructor within the organization.

The others brought in were ex–New York Giants infielder Bobby Hofman, and recent Senator catcher Doug Camilli, son of ex–Brooklyn star Dolph Camilli. There was also future Hall of Famer (inducted in 1997) Nellie Fox. So proud was Fox to be associated with the Senators that when he died prematurely in 1975 at age 47, his epitaph proclaimed he had been a member of the Chicago White Sox *and* the Washington Senators. Fox played 14 of his 19 years with the White Sox, but never once appeared in uniform for the Washington Senators as a player.

Meanwhile, the new manager's namesake, James H. Lemon, took over as Board Chairman after current chairman James M. Johnston succumbed to cancer on December 28. But there weren't that many lemons on this club anymore, and whenever asked, Chairman Lemon insisted that the Senators were not for sale. The ballclub seemed finally, realistically, poised to make a move into the first division.

In January 1968, Leon "Goose" Goslin, likely the best hitter the Washington Senators ever had, was inducted into the Baseball Hall of Fame. Goslin, unlike many others, was still living and able to enjoy the thrill of becoming a member of such a revered fraternity. He came to the Senators in late 1921 and had eight productive seasons with them, peaking at .379 in 1928. The Goose was brought back to participate in the capital's third pennant winner in 1933. With Detroit later, he won a couple more A.L. championships, and left behind a .316 lifetime average.

The focus was soon back on the upcoming season, and indeed talk, while cheap, was decidedly upbeat in regard to the Washington Senators and their aspirations for 1968. For a change, this wasn't the case just around Washington. Contention was perceived to be a definite possibility. Given the mix of youth and the untapped potential of the pitching staff in particular, there was no telling how far the Nats might be able to climb. An indication of the feeling pervasive in the organization was the fact that G.M. George Selkirk made just one trade in the off season, besides the Gil Hodges deal. Pitchers Buster Narum and Bob Priddy, neither of whom was heavily counted upon for the future, and slick-fielding but weak-hitting middle infielder Tim Cullen, were allowed to go to the White Sox. In return, the Nats took righthanded reliever Dennis Higgins, lefthander Steve Jones, and Ron Hansen, a 30-year-old vet who would be counted on to take up the slack at short should Ed Brinkman continue to be absent because of military obligations.

The Senators, clad in new uniforms which featured red in their caps and socks, rather than the traditional blue with piping on the caps, ran roughshod over their opponents during the 1968 Florida Grapefruit League season. The Nats finished ahead of all other teams, in either league, and were particularly hard on National League opponents, winning all 11 meetings against them. In Memphis, Tenn., on April 4, four days before the scheduled Presidential Opener, Dr. Martin Luther King, Jr., the leading civil rights advocate in the nation, was gunned down. Riots erupted in major cities across the U.S. Out of respect for the slain martyr, the season opener was delayed two days, until after Dr. King's funeral. When it did take place, just over 32,000 fans showed up in Washington, 10,000 or so fewer than normal, due to the fear of further rioting.

Vice-President Hubert Humphrey was the one to do the honors this time. President Johnson, who'd announced ten days earlier that he wouldn't be seeking nomination for another term, was unavailable at this highly charged time. The National Guard was visible everywhere in D.C. Stadium and in fact, in one of their uniforms was shortstop Ed Brinkman, who had started every opening day for the club since 1963. "Casper," as he was nicknamed by his mates for his thin, ghostly appearance, was the club's best prankster, and on this day he had to be content with antagonizing Frank Howard from beyond the left-field fence.

The Nats lost their sixth consecutive opener, as the Minnesota Twins prevailed 2–0. Harmon Killebrew and Bob Allison hit solo homers and the Twins were off on a six-game winning streak to start the '68 season. The Nats did pick it up, however, and before the end of the month attained the level of three games over .500 for the first time in the new club's history.

The Senators went 11–7 for the month, but then lost six straight games. Chief among the culprits during this debacle was Mike Epstein, who'd enjoyed a sensational spring but injured his right arm just before the start of the season. In early May, he was hitting only .085 for his first 71 at-bats when Jim Lemon decided to let Frank Howard play first base. Epstein was demoted to the minors three weeks later, but returned after two weeks, having seemingly regained his batting eye with the top farm club at Buffalo. Howard, who'd played four games at first base for the Nats in three years, responded with homers in his first two games as an infielder.

Hondo then embarked on a ferocious home run spree the likes of which has not been seen before or since. On May 12, he blasted a sixth-inning two-strike offering by Mickey Lolich off the wall way up over the visitors' bullpen at D.C. Stadium. Two innings later, he reached the fourth row of the upper deck off reliever Fred Lasher as the Senators doubled the Tigers 6–3. Following an off day during which the club traveled to Boston, the Senators dropped a 5–4 decision in ten innings. Big Frank drove in three of the runs. With a man on in the first inning, he slugged a liner into the net above the Green Monster off the righthanded Ray Culp, for his third roundtripper in as many at-bats. In the third, Howard would have tied a big-league record had he homered again. Instead, he grounded into a force-out. But he was right back at it in the fifth, arching a shot into the faraway centerfield bleachers off Lee Stange, making it four dingers in five at-bats.

Howard added a single later on and the next day, in the first inning, he smashed a high one into the screen atop the Monster in left off Jose Santiago. In his subsequent trips, he grounded into a double play, struck out, and doubled, and fell one homer short of tying the all-time record of six in three games. The Nats had been victors in just one of those contests.

Hondo and his entourage took their act to Cleveland for a single game on May 16. Barry Moore and Dennis Higgins combined on a four-hitter and the Senators beat the Indians' ace, Sam McDowell, 4–1. Howard drove in all the runs with a pair of two-run homers. In the third inning, he unloaded a mammoth shot which landed 14 rows behind the 435-foot sign in the leftfield stands, an estimated 455 feet from home plate. Two innings later, he outdid the first moonshot, again off McDowell, with a missile which crash-landed an estimated 480 feet away on the runway beyond the gate in left field. With that blast, Hondo very nearly became the first player to hit a ball into the remote centerfield bleachers at vast Cleveland Stadium.

By now, "The Capital Punisher" had the attention of every baseball fan in America. The biggest man in the big leagues, for whom a breakfast of six to eight eggs and a couple of

steaks was customary, now had a total of seven homers for four consecutive games. This equaled the all-time American League record established by both Tony Lazzeri of the Yankees in 1936, and Gus Zernial of the Philadelphia Athletics in 1951.

On to Detroit for a three-game series. In the first game, with Joe Sparma on the mound (he was always a tough solve for the Nats), the Tigers clung onto a two-run lead from the first inning until the seventh, when Ken McMullen socked a solo homer. In the ninth, with the Tigers still ahead 2–1 and everyone aware that Hondo's streak was in jeopardy, the big man came up with a man on. He had previously bounced out twice and struck out on a full count. The giant swung mightily and sent one sailing over the lower stands in left. Big Frank had snatched victory from the jaws of defeat, but that was temporary. In the bottom of the inning, Jim Northrup connected for a grand slam off Steve Jones to ice the game. But what had became known simply as "the streak" had taken on a life of its own, and was still living — eight home runs in five games and counting.

On May 18, '68, during a day game at Tiger Stadium, Frank Howard smashed two more home runs. He didn't need them to set the record for most homers in six consecutive games, however — he already held it before coming to bat. The previous record had been only seven. In the third inning, he skied a Mickey Lolich pitch into the upper stands in right field, a solo shot. In the fifth, with two men on, and in his 20th at-bat since slugging his first homer off Lolich six days earlier, Hondo unleashed his mightiest drive yet, possibly the longest tater of his career.

The ball hooked near the foul line, struck the top of the 82-foot barrier above the 346-foot marker in left field, and hopped out of the park onto an unfinished highway on a single bounce. The entire distance traveled was guesstimated at 550 feet. Only Harmon Killebrew, back in 1962, had ever managed to hit a ball clear out of Tiger Stadium. This smash certainly rivaled the one Mickey Mantle had crushed off the Nats' Chuck Stobbs at Griffith

Stadium back in '53. Ten homers in six games remained an all-time record when the 21st century began, as did Frank Howard's ten homers in one week, which surpassed the previous record of nine, held jointly by Babe Ruth and Hank Greenberg.

Frank Howard is a modest man, an "aw shucks" kind of guy who learned to take the good with the bad in his career. His ascendancy as a premier slugger in the big leagues contrasted with the fact that, to prove himself, he had to be relegated to a perennially losing ball club. The Capital Punisher ascribed some of his incredible performance of hitting one out every second time up to good fortune. But he also knew that sometimes, a batter just sees the ball well and can hit it hard nearly every time he swings at it. He gave most of the credit to his new manager, Jim Lemon, who had taken Gil Hodges' previous instruction just a little further. Lemon, who ironically had been a strikeout king himself in his heyday with the Nats in the late fifties, had implored the big guy to move closer to the plate, with his legs spread out just a little more to cut down on his stride into the pitch. This all contributed to Frank Howard becoming a more selective hitter.

Jim Lemon needed all the praise his slugger could heap on him. Despite Howard's heroics in May (15 homers during the month), the Senators won only six of 27 games and crashed into the league basement. This would easily be the most disappointing year in the second franchise's history. Hondo could not be expected to maintain the pace he'd set over the first couple of months of the season, but it was unthinkable that he would not hit at least 50 homers (by the end of his streak, he was on a pace to hit 84) and perhaps even win the triple crown. He was batting .346 following the sixth game of his streak, and leading the league in home runs and RBIs with no one even close to him in any of those categories.

Frank kept warning anyone who'd listen, though, that he was no .300 hitter, that things would even out eventually. His hitting did tail off and he wound up at .274, one point above his eventual lifetime average, but his RBI production was second best in the league. Hondo led in homers with 44, his career high at age 32. His .552 slugging percentage led both leagues. Although he limped for weeks on a badly sprained ankle, in 1968 — long remembered as the "Year of the Pitcher" — Frank Howard was doubtless the most exciting player in the American League and helped the Nats draw over a million fans on the road.

At D.C. Stadium, where a number of seats were painted white to indicate where some of Hondo's most prodigious shots had landed, it was quite another story. Howard was booed there early in the year on a few occasions when he made bad plays and dropped balls in the outfield. Proud as any pro, he acknowledged that he was not a complete player and that the fans certainly had the right to boo. Frank guessed that he deserved the razzing, but he certainly didn't relish looking like a big dummy out there.

The subject of Frank Howard's salary was suddenly foremost on everyone's mind. It was true that Howard was highly paid, and he had held out for a salary reported to be $50,000 for 1968. But on a club on which opposing pitchers had little to fear from those behind him in the batting order, Hondo frequently had to press and found himself making less contact. He struck out 141 times.

The Senators found themselves in all-too-familiar territory at the end of the season, having won fewer games than any team in either league. The 65–96 record was their worst since 1964. Attendance at home games was correspondingly the lowest in the majors, just under 550,000, and the least in Washington since the 106-loss season in 1963. The club was struck particularly hard as a result of players fulfilling military obligations — Ed Brinkman and lefthander Frank Bertaina were the most frequent absentees. Brinkman played in less than half the team's games and hit below .190 for the second consecutive year. Whenever it seemed that Bertaina was about to settle into a groove, he was called back to his unit. He pitched only 127.1 innings, but his 7–13, 4.66, output when he was around was a letdown for this club.

Perhaps even more important was the loss of crack reliever Darold Knowles, undoubtedly the best lefthanded fireman in the league in 1967. No other club lost a player of Knowles' caliber for so long a time. He got only 41.1 innings of work all year (1–1, 2.18), was in and out of military service early in the summer, and then was called into active duty by the Air Force and dispatched to Japan in July. Without Darold Knowles, there was no stopper out of the pen.

The young phenom, Joe Coleman, or "Boy Blunder" as he was sometimes derisively called because of his rookie mistakes, blossomed into a very good pitcher at the tender age of 21, winning 12 against 16 losses, with a respectable 3.27 ERA. Veteran Camilo Pascual registered his 2,000th strikeout during the season, and went 13–12, 2.69, in what would turn out to be his last hurrah. The talent was spread too thin, however, and the staff ERA of 3.64 in a year when pitchers dominated was by far the worst in the league. The only other bright spot was Jim Hannan, Senator since '62, who finally took advantage of his chance to shine, posting a 10–6, 3.01, mark. On June 2, Hannan retired 26 in a row after giving up a double and a homer in the first inning at Cleveland.

Besides Frank Howard's memorable hitting frenzy during the third week of May, there were some other high points. Hondo made an All-Star team for the first time in his career and became the first member of the second Senators to be picked as a starter in the midsummer classic. He finished second in voting for A.L. outfielders behind eventual batting champion Carl Yastrzemski (whose .301 was the lowest bat mark for a champion in modern history). In the actual game, Hondo was 0–for–2, striking out once against Juan Marichal. The National League scored an unearned run in the first inning, the only run of the 1968 All-Star game.

The best addition to the club was centerfielder Del Unser, a sure-handed 23-year-old with just one full year of minor-league experience, during which he'd batted an uninspiring .231 in the Eastern League. Unser started

off well but did not have the stamina for the long season; he tailed off at the plate to finish at .230 for the year. On August 20, he hit his first major-league homer in his first at-bat of the first game of a doubleheader at Oakland, and proceeded to tie a team record with five hits in the game. Speedster Ed Stroud saw most of the action in right field, but hit .239 with just nine stolen bases.

Catcher Paul Casanova, whose .248 average with nine homers in '67 had been considered adequate, in view of his defensive abilities, slipped badly at the plate and was demoted to the minors, along with lefty Barry Moore, near the end of June. Cazzie batted .196 for the year and his replacement, scrappy Jim French, .194. Around the horn in the infield from left to right — Ken McMullen hit 20 homers but for a while early in the season was lamenting the fact that he was hitting more homers than singles. As a result, he batted .248 and his 62 ribbies were, sadly, second best on the club to Frank Howard's 106. Shortstop Ron Hansen batted just .185 before being traded. Bernie Allen made only five errors in 110 games at second base and was the leader at his position. However, he batted .241, and that batting mark was third best among the club's regulars. To some extent, Mike Epstein did manage to salvage something from this season, finishing with 13 homers, but only a .234 average.

Ron Hansen went through a most bizarre period in the span of three days as July crept into the dog days of August. In the first inning of the July 30 game at Cleveland, the Indians had men on first and second with no outs. On a 3–2 pitch with the runners moving, Joe Azcue of the Indians lined to Hansen, who caught the ball and stepped on second. The lanky shortstop then tagged Russ Snyder ambling down from first for the first unassisted triple play in the big leagues in 41 years. Two days later, Hansen hit a grand slam at Detroit in a 9–3 win. Despite these heroics, however, he was batting below .200, and the Senators sent him back to the Chicago White Sox. Oddly enough, Hansen was traded for a player included in the original February deal which had brought him to the capital, second baseman Tim Cullen. The story gets stranger still.

The Senators were about to start a four-game series against Chicago, but the first game was to be played at County Stadium in Milwaukee (the White Sox, attempting to bolster their sagging home attendance, played 20 games at County Stadium in 1968–69). Tim Cullen was notified of his involvement in the trade that same morning by Chicago G.M. Ed Short. He asked Short about how he was going to get to Milwaukee for the game. Short told him that the deal would not be announced until just before game time. Cullen could therefore travel with the club, since the news would still not be known by his teammates.

Cullen took advantage of the situation by boarding the bus early and choosing a seat next to the evening's starting pitcher, left-hander Gary Peters. All the way to Milwaukee, he quizzed Peters about how he was going to pitch to each Senator. When he got off the bus, he went straight to the visitors' clubhouse, taking a dark tunnel to get there. Along the way, he met someone in the shadows. It was Ron Hansen. Cullen celebrated his return to his old team by having one of his best days in a major-league uniform, stroking three hits. Hansen played third base for the Chisox and had a two-hit game for the first time since June. What Cullen had not counted on was having to board the White Sox team bus to get back to Chicago after the game. No one would share space with him, and he had to sit up front by himself. Such is the life of a major leaguer.

The Washington Senators finished dead in the water in 1968, in tenth place, where they were guaranteed never to end up again. For 1969, major-league baseball would cross international frontiers, expanding by two more teams in each league and splitting each league into two divisions. Even greater, more ominous, changes were in store for the national capital. In December, attorneys representing the estate of the late James Johnston accepted a bid of $9 million for majority ownership of the Washington Senators. The new man in control was Robert E. Short, a Minnesota

trucking magnate who also happened to be treasurer of the Democratic National Committee. Short named himself team president, and James H. Lemon remained Chairman of the Board, with a minority interest in the team. Short's first official move was to withdraw G.M. George Selkirk's authority to make unilateral decisions regarding personnel.

Bob Short had made millions as a result of his personal traits of enthusiasm and stubbornness. He also had a track record, a dubious one, in pro sports. He purchased the Minneapolis Lakers of the National Basketball Association in 1957, and thanks to him, that franchise was moved to Los Angeles three years later. In 1965, Short sold the Lakers to Jack Kent Cooke, having realized a value appreciation of a cool $5.2 million. Did he have a similar fate in mind for the Senators? He parodied great men with his response, maintaining that he hadn't bought the franchise just so he could preside over its dissolution. No greater falsehood was ever spoken.

Within two days of the announcement of Bob Short's purchase of the Washington Senators, a small caption appeared in the *Washington Star* quoting him to the effect that he was not making any promises about keeping his baseball team in Washington. The stadium would have to be made safer for the fans. No, he hadn't bought the club to move it, but he was thinking of *other possibilities*. A month later, Short told the same newspaper that if his team was not wanted, and if he did not get the requisite broadcast and box office revenue, then there were other cities, like Dallas and Milwaukee for example, which might suit him just fine. It was no coincidence that Bob Short was already making many people nervous about the future of Washington's baseball team.

For the time being, an American League baseball club represented a tremendous tax write-off for Short, who ran a network of trucking operations nationwide, as well as three hotels in Minneapolis. His trucking empire alone grossed $40 million in 1967, and he hopped around the country in a $700,000 Lear Jet. Owners of professional sports teams had an advantage granted them by Congress that allowed depreciation of their clubs to the full purchase price, and this could be done over a five-year period. This was the sort of corporate tax shelter that other businessmen could only dream of.

When in late January 1969, Bob Short took official control of the Washington Senators' operation, his first move was to completely usurp the authority of those who had been making the on-field decisions up until that time. When he had taken over the basketball Lakers in 1957, he had fired a successful nine-year coach, John Kundla, and a long period of mediocrity followed. Now, he fired both George Selkirk and the one-year manager, Jim Lemon. From now on, there would be no G.M. — Short didn't have any for his other businesses, and he didn't see why he should need one here.

The second franchise's first G.M., Ed Doherty, was brought in by Short to lend a hand, but Doherty's unofficial role would breed confusion. Short also had his own promotions guru and friend, a man by the name of Oscar Molomot, seize some of the authority held by traveling secretary Burt Hawkins, who had previously been in charge of media relations. John Welaj, the ex-player, lost his title in promotions and advertising to the same Molomot. Quite naturally, bitter rivalries would develop between these men.

Bob Short also immediately proceeded to raise ticket prices at D.C. Stadium, henceforth known as Robert F. Kennedy Memorial Stadium in honor of the presidential candidate slain by an assassin's bullet the previous June. The new boss insisted prices had to go up in order to finally begin to show a profit, so he turned reserved seats into box seats, and changed seating previously designated as general admission to reserved status. There would be no general-admission (unreserved) seating downstairs anymore and, understandably, there would be considerable grumbling on the part of the average fan as a result.

Ticket prices to Senators games would rise between 50 and 100 percent over two years, making them the most expensive in all

of baseball. But the fans would understand in the end, Short felt certain. After all, the new boss amazingly contended, Washington, along with New York and Los Angeles, was one of only three great baseball cities in the nation. Fans quickly tired, however, of poverty pleas from a man able to jet-set across the country in his own private airliner.

Bob Short was in need of a field manager, and his first choice was Bob Kennedy, who had just led the Athletics to their first winning season since 1962, only to be fired by Charlie Finley. But Kennedy had no interest in Short's offer. The next name brought up was that of Ted Williams, the Hall of Famer who'd been in virtual exile from baseball, apart from some brief spring-training coaching duties with the Red Sox, since taking his leave as a player in 1960.

Ted had been fishing, mostly, living on deferred baseball earnings for eight years. Red Sox owner Tom Yawkey, revered by Williams, had not been able to convince him to come back to Boston to manage. Many would have contended that the concept was perhaps not a sensible one, given Ted's reputation for rudeness — the "Great Expectorator" was one nickname favored by detractors. (The players on the Senators would come to call him either "Number Nine" or "TW." There is no doubt that Ted's personal favorite pet name was "Teddy Ballgame," which he would frequently employ to refer to himself in the third person.)

Bob Short managed to somehow coax the Splinter back into uniform, but Williams didn't come cheaply. He reportedly got $65,000 a year in a five-year contract, although Short leaked to the press that the figure was actually $100,000 a year. There were also some major perks — a $15,000-a-year apartment in Washington, and an unlimited expense account. Williams was also granted an option to buy as much as 10 percent of the ball club if he wanted to, and was handed the title of vice-president to go along with his field manager's hat. Furthermore, if he found that he didn't like managing after all, he would be allowed to move into an administrative position in the front office.

It was a sweetheart deal which not even the single-minded Ted Williams could turn down. There were other motivating factors for Teddy Ballgame, however. He knew he was inheriting the worst team in baseball, and Ted had a yearning to teach. In his self-assessment, Williams admitted that he would need a lot of help from his coaches on matters of strategy, infield play, and making out lineups. But what *he* excelled at was sharing what he knew best — how the batter should play "the game within the game" with the pitcher. With that, Ted was sure, he would be able to help the Washington hitters. His decision to return to baseball was the game's biggest story of 1969 — until, that is, the New York Mets' unthinkable World Series conquest.

The contract was signed on February 21, 1969, and a press conference was held that very day. Bob Short also unveiled another new slogan for the club for '69: "It's a Whole New Ballgame." Club owners delayed the start of spring training by one week because of haggling over the Major League Baseball Players' Association pension fund. After that week passed, some of the veteran players were still taking their time to report, so mostly young players were in camp when Teddy Ballgame took the field for the first time as manager of the Senators on February 25. Media from all over the U.S. followed his every move.

Infamous for his relations with the press as a player, Williams spent the main part of that first day patiently fielding questions from reporters. There was considerable skepticism expressed during the spring as to whether the Splinter could possibly continue to get along with the "Knights of the Keyboard," as he had once referred to them. For the most part, his relationship with the press would remain cordial throughout the season, as he made himself readily accessible for the customary interview sessions before and after games. Following games, however, Williams insisted on a 15-minute clubhouse ban, a concept held over from his playing days with the Red Sox. The scribes would take exception to this cooling-off period and the Baseball Writers' Association of America would go so far as to make an appeal, which went nowhere, to the new commissioner, Bowie Kuhn.

Williams was predictably a no-nonsense manager right from the start. It was no secret that he could talk about hitting until the cows came home, and he would have no recriminations about jumping all over anyone who was not concentrating at the plate and not putting his instructions into practice. Ted was optimistic in his dealings with the players, something he said he had picked up from his first big-league manager, Joe Cronin. The man in the best position to make the most of Williams' availability was the Nats' best hitter, Frank Howard. Hondo had held out, as he did most years, for a salary boost. For his 44-HR season, he demanded a cool one hundred grand, and got it.

Frank Howard would become an even better hitter by heeding Williams' oft-repeated advice to take strike one, and even strike two, if a pitch was not to his liking. It had always been felt that Howard, who had worn fairly strong glasses since his early years in the majors to correct nearsightedness, would have been a better hitter had his eyes been better. All of a sudden, Hondo became much more selective, nearly doubling his base-on-balls total in '69. His season average rose to .296 (a career-high, which he managed three times), and he hit more home runs than ever.

There was a presaging event during the 1969 exhibition season (not a successful one on the field for the Senators), but hardly anyone, except perhaps Robert Short, likely took notice. The last two preseason games, against the Pittsburgh Pirates, had been scheduled for Louisville, Kentucky. When the field there was judged unsatisfactory for play, the Pirates agreed with Short's suggestion that the games be contested instead at Arlington, in the Dallas-Fort Worth, Texas, area.

The Senators certainly had their work cut out for them. With the new divisional format, they ended up in the East Division with the five clubs who had placed in the first division the previous year. Most pundits concurred that not even Ted Williams would be able to work the miracle it would take for the club to finish out of last place. Well, everyone was in for a big surprise. Teddy Ballgame had said in Florida that his goal was to see every man on the squad show improvement. That is pretty much what would be accomplished. By the end of the season, Williams would be able to boast that he had brought that about without tampering with batting styles — hitting, he insisted, was dependent on what happened from the neck up, and that's where he concentrated his efforts.

President Richard Nixon, a knowledgeable baseball fan who'd been in his new job exactly 11 weeks, sent the Senators off on what would be a magnificent season by throwing out the first pitch on April 7 before a packed house of over 45,000 faithful. The visiting Yankees laced into Camilo Pascual for four runs in the first three innings and led 8–0 in the fourth. Pascual, now 35 and the club's best pitcher in '68, seemed to have a difficult time adapting to changes in the game aimed at shifting the balance of power back to the hitters. The smaller strike zone, and particularly the lower mound, contributed to a horrible three months, after which the longtime Senator was sold to Cincinnati. Little Potato would win just two more big-league games.

Frank Howard began defending his A.L. home run title right away, with roundtrippers in the club's first three games of the year. Nineteen sixty-nine would be an exciting year for Hondo and his fans, as he became embroiled in a neck-and-neck race for the home run title with the great Harmon Killebrew and a newcomer, Reggie Jackson of the Oakland A's.

The first month of the season was a resounding success, with the Nats leaving on a protracted road trip sporting a 16–11 record. That trip was disastrous, however, as the club dropped nine of the first ten games. On May 10, the Nats led 11–3 at Seattle and wound up on the losing end of a 16–13 score at the hands of the expansion Pilots. At the end of the season, the Senators would feel the sting of their poor record against both the Pilots and their expansion cousins, the Kansas City Royals: Washington won just five of 12 versus each of those clubs.

During the early part of the season, righthander Dick Bosman, just 2–9 the previous year, came out of the bullpen to perform extremely well in long relief. Pretty soon, Bosman found himself in a starting role and became the club's most dependable hurler. Bozzie won eight in a row at one stage, wound up 14–5, and by year's end was duking it out with the Orioles' Jim Palmer for the ERA title, which he won with a scintillating 2.19.

The Nats finally bid their goodbyes to Phil Ortega at the beginning of the season. They were glad to get the $20,000 waiver price paid by the California Angels, because all indications pointed to their releasing the righthander if the Angels hadn't shown interest. Ted Williams had not been at all impressed with Ortega's work habits. As a member of the Angels, Ortega was badly roughed up in a bar fight, incurring a concussion and broken jaw. When he was reactivated, he was discovered in the lobby of a Kansas City hotel dressed only in his undershorts, and that was his final undoing (no pun intended). He was fined $500 by the Angels, and manager Lefty Phillips called Ortega a disgrace not only to the ballclub, but to himself. He was demoted, never to resurface at the big-league level.

The Senators made another good decision when they acquired righthander Jim Shellenback from the Pittsburgh Pirates in exchange for journeyman Frank Kreutzer. Shellenback was lucky just to be in the big leagues, as he had been left with a permanent limp as a result of an automobile accident in October 1967. He had suffered a compound fracture of the right leg, as well as rib and internal injuries. Doctors had predicted he would never play baseball again, but he was back by June of the following season. With the Senators, Shellenback would have a checkered existence, pitching in a manner alternately brilliant and horrible. He was 4–7, 4.04, in 30 games for the Nats in 1969.

Apart from Dick Bosman, the other pitcher on the squad who appeared to benefit most from Ted Williams' continued emphasis on off-speed stuff and mixing up pitches was Casey Cox. Following Bosman's lead, Cox earned 13 starts after some excellent work in a long-relief role. He placed sixth in the league in ERA, at 2.78, and won 12 against seven losses. Manager Williams would later delight in telling how, in spring training, he had asked the writers on the beat to name the club's best pitchers. The names which surfaced were Camilo Pascual, Barry Moore, Jim Hannan, and Joe Coleman (Darold Knowles was not included because he was still in service in the spring). "So who are our best pitchers?" Williams would ask with obvious relish later in the season before providing his own punch-line — "Dick Bosman and Casey Cox!"

Williams and Joe Coleman, a veteran with three years under his belt at age 22, already knew one another. As a youngster, Coleman, whose dad had also been a big-league pitcher, had attended some baseball camps supervised by Williams. Ted expected a lot from Joe, Jr., but didn't always get his co-operation. Ted's pet pitch was the slider, which had given him the most trouble as a hitter, and he wanted all of his pitchers to use it. Coleman would have no part of the slider and he was frustrated, as the other starters were, by Ted's insistence that five or six strong innings were all that was expected of them. By 1972, Dick Bosman would be arguing with Ted about being pulled too early, but this wouldn't change TW's mind. That year, Williams' club would set a major-league record for fewest complete games by its pitchers (11).

There was no doubt about young Joe's competitiveness, but the rift with "Number Nine" likely contributed to an eventual trade which would have dire consequences for the Nats. With a strong finish, Coleman in '69 won the same number of games, 12, with exactly the same earned run figure, 3.27, that he'd had in '68. He had four shutouts, tops on the squad and fourth best in the loop.

Righthander Jim Hannan did not blossom as anticipated on the strength of his output in '68 — he slipped to 7–6, 3.64. Lefty Barry Moore had a so-so year, in and out of the starting rotation, finishing 9–8, 4.30. Dennis Higgins had a good season seconding Darold Knowles in the bullpen, racking up respectable 10–9, 3.48, numbers, with 16 saves. In December, however, Higgins and Moore were packaged to Cleveland in exchange for reserve middle infielder Dave Nelson, along with a pair of seldom-used pitchers with the Tribe, Horacio Pina and Ron Law.

Darold Knowles returned to the club at the end of May '69, having spent nearly a year in the air force. Three and a half weeks later, the club made another important addition, acquiring veteran outfielder Arthur Lee Maye from the Indians in exchange for Bill Denehy, the pitcher obtained from the Mets for Gil Hodges. Proving he was the extra lefthanded bat Ted Williams had been searching for, Maye hit .290 with nine homers in 71 games. As for Knowles, he ended up 9–2, with a minute 2.24 ERA, over the last four months of the season. He pitched so well so quickly following his return that for the first time in the history of the second franchise, the Senators placed two players on the All-Star squad — Knowles and Frank Howard.

With baseball observing its centennial year in 1969, the nation's capital was a natural for the 40th All-Star game. The game was almost not played at all. Washington was drenched by heavy rains and the resultant flash flood forced postponement for one day. The National League won its seventh straight All-Star encounter, by a 9–3 score. The host American League lost the third of four tilts played in Washington, but there were dramatics in the early innings courtesy of the local hero, Frank Howard. The first run of the game was scored in the first inning when Hondo misjudged and then dropped a pop fly off the bat of Hank Aaron for a two-base error. He got that run back in the second when he came up to face Steve Carlton of St. Louis and smashed a home run to straightaway center. Already ahead 3–1, the National League piled up five runs off John "Blue Moon" Odom in the top of the third. Darold Knowles was called in to face two batters, and got them both to ground out harmlessly. Frank Howard appeared at the plate once more and walked, in the fourth, setting up the American League's third and final run for the day.

However, it was the events *surrounding* the '69 midseason Classic which were the harbinger, in the eyes of many observers, of baseball's resurgence as the premier sport in America. This was in no small part due to Commissioner Bowie Kuhn, who arranged for a lavish black-tie dinner hosted at the White House by President Nixon. Nearly 500 people had received engraved invitations, and the President was a big hit. He spoke as if the Washington Senators, then 51–50 (the first time the new Nats had been over .500 at the break), were already well established as a winning club. In reference to the string of losing years and the recent upturn, the President declared that someone really had to be a strong fan to continue to root for the Washington Senators back in "those days." Nixon shook hands with hundreds of baseball luminaries, including Casey Stengel, Mrs. Babe Ruth, Mrs. Lou Gehrig, Joe DiMaggio, and Joe Cronin, making an appropriate comment or asking a perceptive question in every case.

Baseball's reputation as the National Pastime seemed restored. A weighty editorial which appeared in the *New York Times* pointed out that this occasion in Washington, which had captured the attention of fans and nonfans alike, was surely a sign that baseball was not only alive and well but also, contrary to the opinion of many, still ahead of football as the true national pastime.

There was no disputing the fact that the Washington Senators were an improved ballclub, a notion they further perpetuated during the second half with a 35–26 record. September was full of benchmarks for the second Washington Senators team. On the 13th, the Nats scored four runs in the seventh versus the Tigers to reach six games over .500 for the first time in the second franchise's history. On September 24 at Detroit, Frank Howard connected for his 47th homer of the season, tying him at that moment with Harmon Killebrew and Reggie Jackson. It was a race Hondo should have won, but he reached the fences only twice after September 10. To maximize his chances, Ted Williams slotted him in the lead-off spot in the final game of the year, but

to no avail, and Howard's total of 48 fell just one short of the Killer. In the manner so typical of him, Hondo was still insisting many years later that he had been privileged even to be involved in a quest for the home-run crown with two sluggers of the magnitude of Killebrew and Reggie Jackson.

On the day following Hondo's 47th, Dick Bosman won the seventh of eight straight, and the Senators sat at 81–75 — Washington was guaranteed a .500 record. Lee Maye's grand slam at home against the team he had started the season with, the Indians, accounted for all the runs Joe Coleman needed the next day. It was a winning year. The Nats swept the Indians and had now won six in a row. The last series of the season was key in the brilliant mind of Ted Williams. The Red Sox were coming in, and if the Senators could take all three, they would pass Boston for third place. That hope evaporated quickly as Sonny Siebert, the noted nemesis, prevailed 8–5 over Casey Cox, although the Senators did win the last two games of the year for a final record of 86–76, fourth in the division but within two wins of placing fourth overall in the entire league. The club won eight of the season's last nine, a high note that did bode well for the start of the new decade.

It was only on the very last day of the season that Ted Williams allowed the baseball writers to come into the clubhouse before the mandatory 15 minutes had elapsed at the end of the game. Earlier in the day, TW had gotten a standing ovation from the Fenway Park crowd when he took the starting lineup to home plate, and he acknowledged it with a wave. Ted had a thing about never tipping his cap and he maintained he never would. He had refused to do so in 1960 when he had homered in his last game at Fenway Park. (That game turned out to be his last anywhere because he opted not to make the season-ending road trip to New York.) Ted finally did tip his cap to the Boston fans, by the way, but not until May 12, 1991, "Ted Williams Day" at Fenway Park.

Williams was named American League Manager of the Year for 1969 by the Associated Press. He had nearly succeeded in attaining his stated goal of aiding just about every hitter on the team to improve his performance. Most noteworthy among them was the great gloveman, Eddie Brinkman. With enhanced concentration, and constantly held under the gun by Williams to hit the ball "line-drive down," Casper raised his average by 79 percentage points to wind up at .266. That mark was 20 points above the league average, which itself had risen 16 percentage points from 1968's .230, demonstrating that the rule changes had had an influence.

Frank Howard, already a star, set career bests in 1969 for hits (175), home runs (48), RBIs (111), and runs (111). For the first time in a season in which he'd participated in at least 100 games, he struck out less than 100 times (96), and walked more than 60 times (a remarkable leap, to 102). Most prominent among the other regulars who made the most startling progress were Mike Epstein, Ken McMullen, and Del Unser. Epstein hit 30 homers, drove in 85, and raised his batting average 44 points to .278. Like Howard, Epstein continued to strike out just as much but nevertheless became much more selective, thereby nearly doubling his number of walks. Del Unser learned how to study pitchers while not in the batter's box, and he credited Williams with his dramatic improvement—he raised his average from .230 to .286 in his sophomore year, and also led the league with eight triples. Kenny McMullen made much better contact, boosted his average by 24 points, and drove in 87 runs, second on the club to Frank Howard and 20 more than ever before for him.

There were some others who did not fare so well under Ted Williams. Brant Alyea showed his power early in the season and led the league with three pinch homers, but failed to add to his homer total of ten reached by the fourth of July. The pair of second basemen, Bernie Allen and Tim Cullen, more or less stayed at their levels, batting .247 and .209 respectively. Paul Casanova had a second consecutive horrendous year with the bat (.216), and rugged Jim French hit under .200 for the second year in a row (.196).

At the end of the season, some of the more successful Washington players became highly sought commodities. The Oakland A's wanted Mike Epstein at all costs, and offered a number of scenarios. One of those would have seen Jim "Catfish" Hunter coming to Washington for Epstein, straight up. Even more astonishing in retrospect were the great lengths the world champion New York Mets were prepared to go to in order to finally solve their perpetual deficiency at third base. For Ken McMullen, Washington could have had their pick of two highly promising pitchers, one of whom was Tug McGraw. The other one, who'd appeared in the World Series just completed, had a frightening fastball but questionable control. His name—Nolan Ryan. Of all the past bonehead deals the Senators had swung, and would yet swing, it is likely that those they did *not* consummate at the end of the 1969 season hurt them the most.

In December, Bob Short announced that he was jacking up ticket prices again. Baseball, after all, was turning out to be a winning proposition in Washington. Over 918,000 turned out to see a winning ball club in 1969, which was the sixth best result among the league's 12 clubs and represented a whopping 68 percent jump. The numbers proved that Washington fans would indeed show up if they had a competitive team to watch. There was cause for encouragement, as this was the second-highest paid attendance in 69 years of American League baseball in the city. There was a winning baseball team in D.C. for the first time in 17 years, and loyal fans were being rewarded with the highest ticket prices in the American League.

Revenues had reportedly gone up threefold (Bob Short didn't open his books to anyone) and yet, within months Short would be imploring the broadcasters of Senators games to literally intimidate people to come to the park. If people didn't turn out, the message was that there soon would be no team to support. The turnstiles would click 825,000 times in 1970, and there was good reason for the decline, as far as the ballclub's performance was concerned. This would still be one of the better years in terms of turnout, especially in light of the fact that ticket prices were the highest in the league.

Nineteen seventy ended up being a long season for the Washington Senators — precisely, in fact, 14 games too long. The Nats certainly didn't set the league on fire during the first 148 ballgames either, but the ending was particularly disastrous. The continued improvement that had been expected this year under Ted Williams did not materialize. Frank Howard was an exception. Hondo led the league in home runs with 44, and runs batted in, with 126, and hit a solid .283. He set the pace in the A.L. in *walks* for the first and only time in his career, something which would have been entirely unthinkable before Ted Williams' time.

In late April, with the Nats in the middle of a 15-game homestand, their longest of the year, Howard delivered one of his more remarkable tape-measure shots. He connected off Andy Messersmith of the Angels and the ball went sailing through an exit ramp, about halfway up the right field upper deck. This one would stand as the longest home run ever hit at RFK Stadium, traveling an estimated distance of 500 feet as the crow flies. Ted Williams had seen most of the great sluggers, going back to Jimmie Foxx, who'd been a teammate of his during his first three years in the big leagues, and there was never anyone, according to Ted, who could hit monster shots with regularity like Frank Howard.

Dick Bosman and Ed Brinkman were the others among the more important players who continued to blossom. Bosman for a time had realistic sights set on winning 20, but because of a tough September settled on 16–12, 3.00. Brinkman hit .262 while supplying the usual yeoman work in the infield — he led all A.L. shortstops in put-outs and assists, while continuing to benefit from the fact that Ted Williams was right on top of him whenever he got back into his old habit of hitting too many flyballs. Outfielder Ed Stroud was the only position player who clearly demonstrated progress in 1970, doubling his playing time and participating in 118 games in the outfield. Stroud

batted .266 (.316 in a pinch in 19 official appearances), and was a threat as a runner, pilfering 29 bases.

However, Ted Williams' philosophy of players hitting with their head — knowing what they want, having the patience to make the pitcher pitch, and then pouncing on that pitch — did not seem to work as well on the other guys. It was tough on Ted Williams too. Here was a genius who had always been able to solve any baseball problem before him. As a player, he was one in a million, which is not to say that everything came easily. Blessed with a wonderful batting eye, he'd nonetheless had to figure tough pitchers out. Now he was nearly 52 years old and his job was more trying on his patience. Ted was certainly unwilling to relax the 15-minute ban he had introduced for the writers. In midsummer, he became especially irritated by what he felt was excessive second-guessing. After a few days, however, he greeted the writers in good cheer and all was well again.

The 1970 season once again started with another loss, the eighth consecutive one in the Presidential Opener, a 5–0 setback at the hands of Mickey Lolich and the Detroit Tigers. The ceremonial first pitch was tossed, in Richard Nixon's absence, by son-in-law David Eisenhower. The grandson of former President Dwight Eisenhower was also an employee of the ballclub now. A keen baseball fan, David had requested a summer job as statistician, and was keeping tabs on all the major-leaguers, plus about 120 players on the Senators' five minor-league clubs.

The President was at the White House, kept there on this day because of a pending Supreme Court nomination. Nixon did make an appearance in the fifth inning, and got a few boos from the crowd, having presumably committed no crime greater than having shown up late for a baseball game. The President had missed the first American League appearance of Morganna the Kissing Bandit. Frank Howard became the junior circuit's first victim of the hugely endowed lady, whose main thrill in life seemed to be to prance onto baseball fields and plant generous kisses on ballplayers. Morganna had leaped over the railing near the dugout on the third base side as Hondo prepared to hit in the third inning.

The Nats had once again concluded the Grapefruit League calendar with games in Arlington, Texas, playing right up to the deadline and flying back to Washington for the season opener the very next day. No one could have surmised that this odd scheduling had any significance.

Nineteen seventy turned into one big letdown for Ted Williams, who had seemingly had every reason to think that the Senators would be better. Having won just eight of their 15 games on the early homestand, the Nats embarked on a nine-game loss string three days later which set the tone for the entire season. They fell into last place and were constantly behind the eightball from then on, never reaching the .500 level again. They finished last in the division. Negativity surfaced often. At one point, enraged by what he had perceived to be a lack of hustle from a teammate, Dick Bosman, who always competed hard, was quoted as having told the player that he would kick his ass if he didn't put out while he was pitching. In a stirring address by Williams at the end of the season, he implored some of the players to go home and do some soul-searching during the winter.

The cleanup spot in the order was a main weakness, and one Williams did not try to gloss over. Ted frequently pointed out this deficiency to media men. Mike Epstein drove in just 56 runs on 20 homers, and his average slipped to .256. Williams was unable to make a hitter out of Paul Casanova. Cazzie did improve, but not enough, winding up at .229 with six homers. When he did no better than .203 in '71, the Nats ended his six-year stay, during which he never again attained his rookie mark of .254.

In April, Ken McMullen, who'd been off to a slow start, was sent to the Angels in a swap for Rick Reichardt and Aurelio Rodriguez. This contributed 34 homers to the offense, 19 by Rodriguez, a third baseman with a golden arm, and 15 by outfielder Reichardt, a golden boy. Reichardt, once a high-priced bonus baby, fashioned an 11-year career but never quite lived up to his advance press. There was still too little support in the lineup for Frank Howard. Reichardt hit just .253 and drove in 46 runs for Washington. Rodriguez had 76 ribbies, but batted .247. The defensive upside that Rodriguez brought to the club, however, meant that the trade, for the time being, was a good one for the ballclub.

In late July, Bob Short insisted that the Senators bring up a 19-year-old slugger, Jeff Burroughs, from the top farm club in Denver. Burroughs, who would eventually become the club's first MVP (1974), was not ready. The youngster had been signed right out of high school in Long Beach, California, for a sum of $88,000. The Nats had made him the number one pick in the country the previous year. In the big leagues too quickly, Burroughs' timing was thrown off terribly and, once returned to the minors, he remained disoriented at the plate. Another promising outfielder, Tom Grieve, was given a chance over the last half of the season but hit only .198 and would not become a regular in the big leagues until the midseventies. Grieve, father of future big-leaguer Ben, eventually became an executive at the major-league level.

The precocious Joe Coleman, now all of 23, failed to develop into a 15-game winner as anticipated, and Casey Cox, projected as perhaps even a 20-game man given his imposing physique and encouraging work in '69, also disappointed. Both went 8–12, and Jim Hannan, loser of his last six decisions, dropped to 9–11, 4.01. For a time, Pedro Ramos, the workhorse from the fifties, was on the squad. Ramos had asked for a tryout and did as well as anyone in spring training. But with a 7.88 ERA in eight innings of work, he was cut at the end of April to make room for the extra man following the Ken McMullen trade.

George Brunet, a 35-year-old righty who had been acquired from the expansion Seattle Pilots in exchange for Dave Baldwin, won eight games. Brunet changed teams 31 times in 18 years of professional baseball, and despite his contribution, soon hit the road again, traded on the last day of August to Pittsburgh.

In return, the Nats acquired Denny Riddle-berger, a righthander who would have little impact, and $50,000 that Bob Short insisted he needed in order to meet the payroll at the end of the season.

Darold Knowles, the wunderkind reliever, in 1970 registered one of the more lop-sided records to be found in the annals of baseball. The ballclub scored practically zero runs whenever Knowles pitched. As chief fireman, he was brought into games when the Nats were either tied or leading. His ERA for the year was an admirable 2.04, which would have led the league by more than half a run per game had he pitched enough innings to qualify for the distinction. Knowles saved 27 ballgames, nearly 40 percent of the team's victory total. All season long, though, it seemed that if he gave up even one run, he lost. Consequently, poor Knowles' won-loss record was a satirical 2–14!

When Dick Bosman won his 16th game on September 17, setting a record for the new franchise, the Nats' record improved to 70–78. Then, the club stopped hitting. In the very next game, Frank Howard set the trend by striking out five times, and fanned in his first appearance in the next game, setting a major-league record by fanning six consecutive times. Dick Bosman had three more chances to win his 17th, but came away with two defeats and a no-decision. The Nats were swept in three-game sets in Boston and New York before returning home for a final four-game home-stand with the Red Sox. Owner Bob Short stated that he needed to draw 50,000 fans for the final series to have a chance of breaking even financially. All he got was an average of 5,215 per game. At the turnstiles, top prices and a poor entry on the ballfield do not a winning combination make.

The Senators lost all four games to the Red Sox. They moved on to Baltimore to finish off the season and lost four more. The losing streak ended when the season did —14 consecutive losses to close the year. The 14 setbacks tied a highly dubious team mark set in the expansion season of 1961, and the Senators' final record of 70–92 earned them a last-place

finish, six games behind Cleveland. Ted Williams did not have much to say when the season mercifully wound down. He refused to comment publicly with regards to what Dick Bosman had said about players not putting out, but he did send the boys home with that appeal to each one's conscience. In light of later developments, many of those closest to the club felt the year-end blast bred more malcontentedness for 1971, and in the end did more harm than good.

Before the All-Star break in 1970, when the Nats were ten games back, Williams had predicted that the Senators would top .500 by year's end. When they did, he promised, he would ram the words back down the throat of a television announcer who'd predicted the Nats would never see .500 again. Well, they didn't, and it was Teddy Ballgame who ate crow. As the season droned onward to its dismal conclusion, widely read columnist Dick Young wondered about the purpose of Ted's infamous 15-minute ban — if it was supposed to be so important, then how come the Senators had finished last? That's what Bob Short wanted to know. By the time all was said and done, Short was insistent that he had lost one million dollars on his ballclub in 1970. The attendance drop ranked Washington eighth among the league's 12 clubs.

The owner had a plan to grab headlines, and to do so during the World Series besides. Short lusted after Denny McLain, the highly controversial Detroit Tigers pitcher. McLain had won 31 games in 1968, more than any major leaguer had in 37 years. In '69, he'd won 24 more. But between starts, he'd found time to get himself into lots of trouble. By 1970, McLain was baseball's bad boy and biggest newsmaker, and not because of his exploits on the field where, for the record, he was 3–5, 4.65, and did not pitch a complete game until his 13th start. He didn't pitch much because he was given three suspensions during the '70 season, two of them meted out by Commissioner Bowie Kuhn himself.

The first was for allegedly consorting with gamblers and getting involved in a 1967 bookmaking operation run out of Flint, Michigan.

That suspension was for the first half of the season and ended July 1, when his dramatic return drew Tiger Stadium's largest crowd in nine years. The opinion widely held in the press at the time the suspension was imposed was that the sentence was too lenient. Commissioner Kuhn reasoned that McLain had been duped by his accomplices and in a sense was a victim in the affair. When a reporter asked Kuhn, a lawyer, to explain the moral difference between attempting to become a bookie, as McLain had done, and actually being one, Kuhn's response was a memorable, and widely quoted one: "I think you have to consider the difference is the same as between murder and attempted murder."

Two months following his return to the active list, McLain doused a pair of Detroit writers with a bucket of ice water. For that stunt, Tigers General Manager Jim Campbell suspended him for a period "not to exceed 30 days" and fined him at the rate of $500 a day.

McLain drew his third suspension for carrying a gun and breaking probation. This one, imposed by Commissioner Kuhn, stemmed from information Kuhn had received to the effect that McLain had packed a pistol during the Tigers' August 6–19 road trip, which, needless to say, was "not consistent with his probationary status." On at least one occasion, Kuhn stated, McLain had removed the gun from its holster in a Chicago restaurant and shown it to several of his teammates.

Yet, there was something about this man that intrigued Robert Short. The bomb was dropped on October 9, one day before the beginning of the 1970 World Series, in which Baltimore was to prevail in five games over the Cincinnati Reds. A deal was announced by Bowie Kuhn, and it was believed this was the first time a commissioner had announced a trade. There were special circumstances. A suspended player cannot be traded, so Kuhn announced that he had taken McLain's name off the suspended list. The gun-toting incident was explained away as having been a mere manifestation of McLain's flamboyant personality, and a result of the emotional stress he'd been under. In mid–September, Kuhn re-

vealed, an eminent psychiatrist had declared McLain to be sane, a point that many in baseball had doubted, although Bob Short, obviously, was not one of them.

Around World Series headquarters where the deal was announced, the general consensus was that the Washington Senators had made the worst trade in the history of the game. Short declared that he took full credit for it, and that McLain was the greatest pitcher in baseball. It certainly wasn't Ted Williams' trade, and the great one made no bones about it. Williams stated flat out that the Senators had given up way too much talent for Denny McLain. Bob Short acknowledged Ted's opposition to the idea at the press conference called to announce the trade.

And boy, was Ted Williams ever right! This was a real groaner, indeed the worst trade the new Nats would ever make. The Detroit Tigers got the Senators' excellent left side of the infield — Ed Brinkman and Aurelio Rodriguez. They also obtained the services of the 23-year-old righthander with the still-bright future, and who indeed would begin fulfilling all his promise with the Tigers, Joe Coleman. The Bengals also landed righthander Jim Hannan, who would last one more year in the majors. These players contributed to a 12-game improvement in the Tigers' fortunes in 1971. Coleman was to win 20, 19, and 23 games over the next three seasons. Brinkman became a leader with his new team, and together with Rodriguez solidified the left side of Detroit's infield defense, which had been found sorely deficient in 1970. Tigers manager Billy Martin had the highest praise for Rodriguez, rating him right up there with Brooks Robinson as the best he had seen at the position. Together the trio contributed to a division championship for Detroit in 1972.

In return, along with McLain, the Nats got a weak-hitting 32-year-old third baseman, Don Wert, and Elliott Maddox, a young utilityman who'd hit .248 for Detroit in 1970. The Nats also added a pitcher, Norm McRae, who had never won a game in the big leagues and never would. There were some in the

Washington camp who may have taken some solace in the fact that Frank Howard was not sacrificed in order to bring Denny McLain over, but in retrospect it would have been better if he had been. Hondo was 34 and would never again hit even 30 homers or drive in even close to 100 runs.

It would come out later, and bears mentioning, that there may have been more to the Detroit deal than baseball followers were originally given to understand. Part of the financing Short had required in order to purchase the Senators in the first place had been in the form of a loan of $2.2 million from the Fruehauf Corporation of Detroit, with which he had previously done business through his trucking interests. Some media sources suspected that the Detroit Tigers had in fact stepped in to facilitate the transaction, and Short began talking with the Tigers about obtaining McLain in early 1970, not that long after the loan was negotiated.

Short had gotten himself in hot water outside the baseball world with that loan, which had actually been disbursed to Admiral-Merchants, a trucking concern he ran. When money was eventually transferred to the Washington Senators' account with the American Security and Trust Company in Washington, it drew Uncle Sam's attention. The Interstate Commerce Commission launched an investigation to see if the carrier company had engaged in business dealings, without offering competitive bidding, with a company with directors and officers in common, namely the Senators' ballclub. Short was eventually acquitted following lengthy administrative delays and a longer investigation.

There were trades the Nats failed to make which in retrospect proved to be decisions just as asinine as the Denny McLain fiasco. In '69, the Atlanta Braves had offered Joe Torre for Mike Epstein and Paul Casanova. Cal Griffith wanted the Senators' promising slugger, Brant Alyea, and was offering a little-known infielder-outfielder for him. His name — Graig Nettles. Bob Short, in his infinite wisdom, turned down both of those opportunities. Had he chosen those personnel changes instead of the

McLain deal, his club would surely have been transformed into an instant contender.

Short, however, had another trick, again a controversial one, left up his sleeve. Three and a half weeks following the McLain deal, he swapped three minor leaguers to the Philadelphia Phillies for the right to negotiate with outfielder Curt Flood. Flood, now nearly 33, had been traded to the Phillies by the St. Louis Cardinals a year before, but had refused to report. He was a .293 career hitter at the time, and had batted .285 for the Cards in his last season, 1969. He refused to accept the trade to Philadelphia, unwilling to relocate his family and business (Flood was a portrait artist). He sat out throughout 1970, at considerable cost to himself, as he was turning down at least $90,000, his season's baseball salary.

Curt Flood wanted to challenge in a court of law major-league baseball's reserve clause, the part of a player's contract that tied him to one team and denied him the right, exercised by all other free men, to seek employment wherever he wanted. However, if the Washington Senators were going to sign Flood, Commissioner Bowie Kuhn was going to insist that the standard reserve clause be included in his contract. Kuhn would agree to the inclusion of an additional condition stating that the contract would not prejudice any issue being disputed in court.

So Bob Short made his own deal with Curt Flood. He secretly told Flood that if at the end of the 1971 season the two could not come to terms for the following year, he would grant Flood his wish: he would make him a free agent so that Flood could deal with other teams just as if there were no reserve clause in his contract. The owner promised that the outfielder could not be traded in 1971, and that he would get a full year's pay no matter what. Short would not put any part of this agreement in writing of course — that would mean doing something illegal. According to Flood, Bob Short told him that if word ever got out that he had agreed to these conditions, he would deny it.

The Senators' owner went to the league at the winter meetings and claimed near bankruptcy. The D.C. Armory Board was pestering him for back rent on RFK Stadium, and Short asserted that he didn't even have enough money to finance the upcoming spring training. He was desperate, he said, and to show he meant it, he put star reliever Darold Knowles on the auction block for half a million dollars. He received no bids at that level.

Bob Short wanted a stadium deal similar to the one the Seattle Pilots received when they moved to Milwaukee to become the Brewers — that is, no rent at all (a token $1) until admission reached a million. He would pay a percentage on attendance over one million only. When the Armory Board turned him down, Short reiterated that he could not continue to operate under the present scheme and that if something wasn't done, he was going to take his baseball team elsewhere. He mentioned that Dallas-Fort Worth seemed like the ideal destination.

Short was also wheeling and dealing baseball players, and in another ill-timed move sent outfielder Rick Reichardt to the White Sox. In return, the Senators obtained Gerry Janeski, a righthander who'd just completed a 10–17 rookie season with the hapless Pale Hose, the worst team in all of baseball in 1970. Janeski was to win one more big-league game, while Reichardt, who'd been unhappy in a platoon role in Washington, hit 19 homers for Chicago and enjoyed what was probably his best year in the majors in 1971.

At the end of spring training, the club's fastest man, Ed Stroud, was traded back to the White Sox for veteran first baseman-outfielder Tom McCraw. McCraw would serve as backup first baseman for Mike Epstein — the plan was for Frank Howard to patrol left field on a permanent basis. There was no clear-cut winner in this exchange. Stroud, who had his jaw broken during his strong '70 season, never regained his batting stroke and his career fizzled out after he hit .177 in brief trials with the Chisox in '71.

McCraw, on the other hand, hit .213 in 122 games for the Senators and would soon be gone from the organization. He ended up sharing first base with Don Mincher, who had played with the old Senators in 1960. Aside from being one of the nine men to play for both Washington franchises, Mincher is the one and only player to have been a member of the original and second Senators, as well as of both the Minnesota Twins and Texas Rangers. He had slammed 27 homers for Oakland in 1970, his career-best output, but came at a price. In yet another logic-defying maneuver, the Senators traded both Mike Epstein and Darold Knowles to Oakland. Along with Mincher, Washington accepted lefthanded reliever Paul Lindblad and reserve catcher-outfielder Frank Fernandez. The catch was that Oakland was throwing in $300,000 to sweeten the deal for cash-strapped Bob Short.

Epstein helped Oakland to a division championship with 18 homers. A reflective Epstein pointed out how expectations had never been very high in Washington, and that one could take more pride in a first-place club. Lefty Darold Knowles lasted ten more years in the big leagues doing exactly what he'd always done for the Senators, providing effective short relief. When he retired, Knowles ranked in the top-ten all-time in pitching appearances. Don Mincher, on the other hand, played only until the end of the following season. He hit .291 in 100 games for the Senators in '71, and the next year he went out in the finest style. Having been reacquired by Oakland at midseason 1972, he drove in the tying run in the ninth inning of the fourth game of that fall's World Series, which the A's won. It was his last plate appearance in the big leagues. Following the season, he retired, a world champ, at age 34.

Frank Fernandez was never a factor as a big-leaguer, but the other player obtained for Knowles and Epstein, Paul Lindblad, did enjoy a successful career as a reliever. However, most of that success was following a return to Oakland, where he made solid contributions to two world championship teams. As a matter of fact, Mike Epstein, like Mincher and Lindblad, also eventually ended up back with his original team. Ted Williams favored the Epstein trade because he believed Don Mincher to be a better team player. By the time Epstein came back to this club, Ted Williams would be long gone.

There was yet another youth movement afoot in Washington in 1971. Youngsters Toby Harrah and Jim Mason were vying for the shortstop job. Rookie flychasers Larry Biittner and Jeff Burroughs would both approach 200 at-bats during this season. Another newcomer was Joe Foy, once minor-league player of the year but now, six years later, cast adrift by a third major-league organization. Foy would fight it out with Don Wert for playing time at third.

A key piece in the trade with Detroit, if one presumes that there was one for the Nats, Wert turned out to be a bust in Washington. He suffered a strained back during the spring and was a pitiful 2-for-40 after being reactivated. With the Senators off to another bad start at 21–36 in mid–June, it so happened that both Wert and Joe Foy were demoted to the minors on the very same day. Wert refused to report to Denver and was granted his release. Infielders Dave Nelson and Lenny Randle were called up, and Nelson hit .280 as the regular third baseman the rest of the way. By this time, however, it was obvious the Senators were going nowhere in the American League East race.

Yet, the season had gotten under way with no diminished optimism. In the absence of President Nixon, who was tied up at the western White House, Dick Bosman and the Nats polished off the A's 8–0 in front of 45,000 fans at RFK. The defeated pitcher on Opening Day, Vida Blue, would rhyme off ten wins before he lost again, and the A's would sail to a division championship. Curt Flood scored two runs in the opener and was impressed with Toby Harrah. The 22-year-old shortstop was on base three times and scored twice, and was on his way to a fine 17-year career in the majors.

The Senators were sporting a won-loss mark of 11–8 on the night of April 27, when Denny McLain hurled what was already his second shutout of the season. This was overshadowed by the news that Curt Flood, recently platooned against lefthanded pitching, had jumped the team, leaving behind a 22-word note for Bob Short which stated that he

had tried, but a year and a half out of the game was too much. Flood added that he had "very serious problems" piling up every day, and he thanked Short for his confidence and understanding in their dealings. He then left his .200 batting average behind and flew off to Denmark by way of Barcelona, Spain, not to be seen on a big-league playing field again. It was reported at the time that the "very serious problems" Flood referred to in his note had to do with financial difficulties related to his photographic business. There were reports he had already collected half his $110,000 pay for the year by the time he bolted.

Flood's case against baseball's reserve clause, which he, a black man, had compared to the slavery of his ancestors a hundred years before, became in the short term a setback for him and all baseball players. The Supreme Court upheld earlier District Court and Appeals Court decisions rendered in favor of organized baseball. In the long term, however, the debate was the antecedent of the eventual emancipation of the player and the creation of a new breed of baseball businessmen — the men actually playing the game — during the last quarter of the 20th century.

The fall guy in this scenario, as it played itself out in Washington, was Bob Short. He had generally been perceived as a victim of circumstances beyond his control, but this sympathy was not going to last any longer. Short was now making it abundantly clear that he would sell the Senators to the highest bidder, provided his rock-bottom price of $12 million was met. This was $2.6 million more than what he'd paid three years before, but he pointed out that the profit would only cover his losses over that period. The dean of Washington sportswriters, Shirley Povich of the *Post*, deemed Short's asking price analogous to a situation where a man paid $9,000 for a car, abused it and spent $3,000 on repairs, and then reasoned that he had a car worth $12,000. Others pointed out that Short had really only paid $7.9 million for the franchise, because there had been cash equity in the corporation when he bought it. Short had also sold 10 percent of his stock to minority holder

James Lemon at the time of his purchase of the ballclub.

Comedian Bob Hope was approached by Bill Veeck, the famous baseball owner and promoter, about putting up $7.5 million toward the purchase price, but Hope thought that too risky an investment. No one bid more than 70 percent of what Short was looking for. The president of Giant Food, Inc., Joseph Danzansky, entered the picture on September 9, 1971, offering a figure reported to be as high as $8.4 million. However, when the owners examined Danzansky's plan at a meeting convened in Boston less than two weeks later, they found it too flimsy. In fact, Danzansky did not have financing arranged, and would put up only $50,000 of his own money for the time being in order to purchase the option to buy. He would then negotiate a loan of $6.6 million which the league, he unabashedly explained, would underwrite. In other words, the owners of the American League clubs would be liable for his losses. Those owners soured on the idea at the very moment they realized what sort of scheme Danzansky had in mind and what it would cost them.

Nonetheless, the owners could no longer ignore the albatross in Washington. Back in June, Short began pestering Commissioner Bowie Kuhn and league president Joe Cronin to hear his plea. The Senators' owner was stating there was now no way that he could continue to operate in Washington. An eight-hour meeting was held in secrecy in Detroit on June 30, and Short emerged still contending that he hadn't purchased the Washington Senators to move them. In reality, behind those closed doors, he threatened his fellow owners with a lawsuit should he not be allowed to move. (He was big on threats to sue — in the past he had directed similar menaces at broadcast outlets, owners of training facilities, and even the Washington Redskins football team because they tore up the turf at D.C. Stadium.) All that was revealed publicly was that a resolution had been passed which authorized league president Joe Cronin to begin exploring all avenues and to recommend some solution to the financial situation in the capital.

Short admitted that he had been talking with an interested group from Dallas just four days prior to the owners' Detroit meeting, and that he'd also been in touch with contacts in Toronto and New Orleans. His most quoted line was to the effect that he never intended to move to Dallas, but he also cautioned that there was no guarantee that it couldn't happen. Short had been aware ever since he purchased the ballclub that the stadium lease would not expire before the end of the '71 season, and that it would be impossible to take the Senators elsewhere prior to that. The Armory Board began vigorously pursuing more than $160,000 which the Senators owed in back rent. Short blasted the board for sending copies of their demanding letters to the commissioner and the league office. The board, meanwhile, made it public knowledge that its letters to Short were going unanswered.

The feud escalated when the Armory Board threatened to turn off the lights in RFK Stadium. Short's retort was, if that happened, he would take his major-league outfit to a high-school field and play there, in the daytime. A fight, indeed, was exactly what Bob Short needed at this point — the town didn't want him, he could argue, and no one there had any desire to buy the team. But he would be damned if he was going to go broke in Washington. If evicted, it was being reported, Short would seek immediate permission to move to Dallas. He would do so despite possible lawsuits brought by concerns representing season-ticket holders and radio and TV stations. There would also be the matter of indemnity to the Texas League for the harm the arrival of a big-league club would bring upon that organization's Dallas-Fort Worth entry.

From Minneapolis-St. Paul was heard the booming voice of Calvin Griffith, former owner of the Washington Senators. Keeping these Senators in Washington, Griffith intoned, would be, in a word, stupid. Washington, Cal barked, did not deserve a team.

With chaos all around him, Bob Short did keep his eye on the ball — some of the time. On June 9, the Senators had the first pick in the special phase of the free-agent draft. They chose a 21-year-old Dartmouth College pitcher, Pete Broberg. Despite his supposedly cash-strapped situation, Short peeled off $150,000 to sign Broberg right away. The youngster was immediately activated and made his first start on Sunday, June 19. He held the Red Sox scoreless for six innings, baffling them with a wicked fastball and an array of breaking stuff. He allowed only two hits and struck out seven but left a scoreless deadlock in a game the Nats eventually lost.

For the youngster, the key was to throw breaking stuff for strikes in order to complement his explosive fastball. Broberg would never completely master that, and would win a high of 14 games (against 16 losses) for Milwaukee in 1975. Except for his final year of 1978 with Oakland, he would never win more than five games in any other season. Nevertheless, Broberg fashioned a commendable 5–9, 3.46, first-year effort for the '71 Washington Senators. On Independence Day, in just his fourth start, he earned his first win, a 9–4 six-hitter over Cleveland. Ted Williams raved about the fact that he had never seen a pitcher improve as much in four games as had Pete Broberg.

Williams himself had been getting a little less attention in this year. Besides the fact that the novelty was wearing off, there was the presence of Curt Flood early in the season, and also of Denny McLain. Following the strong start, McLain, who had obviously lost a lot off his fastball in the short span since his salad days with the Tigers, fell on hard times, mostly of his own making. He wasn't blessed with a lot of offensive support either. Guile was no longer enough to get McLain by, and his record following his two April shutouts was 2–12.

When asked if he thought he might lead the league in losses, McLain replied that it wasn't likely, since Ted Williams wouldn't let him pitch every fourth day, as he was accustomed to doing. By early September, McLain would be demanding a trade because of his continuing disagreement with Williams about how often he should pitch. He wasn't the only one grumbling either — many of the veterans on the ballclub were unhappy over their reduced playing time. Williams was going with youngsters because it had become obvious early that this team, which wound up at 63–96, 11th out of 12 teams and 38½ games out of the top spot in its division, was going nowhere.

Still only 28, Denny McLain maintained that he was pitching as well as ever, but felt pressured to pitch a shutout every time out. Well, he did lead the league in losses, with 22, with only ten wins and a 4.27 ERA. He gave up more hits than he pitched innings, a stat he had never even approached as a starter with the Tigers from '64 to '69. For the record, there was nothing to indicate that he would have pitched better had Ted Williams handed him the ball every fourth day instead of every fifth. Pitching with three days' rest, he went 2–7, and with four days' rest, his dossier was 5–13. McLain would merit a composite 4–7 with the A's and Braves in '72, with a bloated 6.39 ERA, and he was just as bad when demoted to Birmingham of the Southern Association by the A's — 3–3, 6.32. The former Cy Young winner was pretty much forced to call it quits, which he did. He then set himself on a path even more turbulent than before.

As with the concept of giving pitchers four days' rest between starts, Ted Williams was also a strict disciple of the righty-lefty theory. This is the school of thought which subscribes to the concept that for a team on defense it is better to have a righthanded pitcher against a righthanded hitter, or a lefty-lefty combination. For the offensive team, an adjustment is made accordingly. For adhering to percentage baseball unfailingly, Ted Williams was at times criticized. He didn't put much stock in the sacrifice bunt, calling it a lost art. He felt that only Del Unser on his club could execute it properly. Despite employing Nellie Fox — one of the most adept at the sac bunt in the game's history — to teach the players, not much progress was evident on his Senators.

Dick Bosman, often victimized by Ted's

other mania, for yanking pitchers too early, would justify his selection as opening-day pitcher by continuing to be TW's top hurler in '71; he would have to settle for a 12–16, 3.72 record. Jim Shellenback, a lefty who was at times a reliable starter in '70 and '71, would finish a disappointing 3–11, 3.53.

With the club 20 games below .500 into the third week of August, the D.C. Armory Board, unwilling to be the scapegoat if ever the Nats were to skip town, indicated it was ready to make several lease concessions. The Senators would be granted free rent for the first million admissions. In addition, Robert Short would be allowed to keep revenue from billboard advertising during the baseball season, and run the concession stands during both the baseball and football seasons. The Senators, however, would not be forgiven back debts on rent which had mounted to more than $178,000. Short's short response — it was too late!

Washington City Council then sued both the Senators and the Armory Board for failure to pay rent and to collect rent respectively. These defaults had forced the city to borrow nearly $100,000 from the U.S. Treasury to pay interest on bonds sold in 1960 to finance the stadium's construction. This is what really set the wheels spinning for baseball to do something about the Washington problem. Commissioner Bowie Kuhn, who as a boy had spent several summers working as a scoreboard operator at Griffith Stadium, took his show on the road to solicit large U.S. companies to buy the club. A corporate base in Washington, near the seat of government, Kuhn noted, would be an invaluable asset. The purchaser would project an image, as Kuhn put it, of savior of baseball for the nation's capital.

When Bob Short kept on bad-mouthing the city of Washington during this period, Kuhn put the muzzle on him, ordering the owner to keep his yap shut while a solution was being sought. By late September, though, Joseph Danzansky's feeble offer was the best one Short had received. As soon as that proposal was dismissed, the owners voted on whether or not to allow the Senators to be

moved. Short required 75 percent of the votes, or 9 of 12. Baltimore and Chicago voted against it. Support of Short meant the National League might move into Washington and provide stiffer competition for the Orioles' product. Ted Williams' appeal to his old friend and mentor, Tom Yawkey, was apparently instrumental in swaying the millionaire owner of the Red Sox to Bob Short's side. Two teams, California and Oakland, abstained. Angels' owner Gene Autry was absent from the proceedings, but had left word with the president of his board of directors, Bob Reynolds, to block the move at all costs. Now Reynolds was volunteering to track down Autry, who had been undergoing an eye operation right there in Boston, to see if he might get him to change his mind.

In the meantime, Oakland's Charlie Finley, who had also abstained, called Ed Daly, chairman of the board of World Airways, to apprise him of the latest developments. Daly had made it known to Finley and Commissioner Kuhn that he was willing to buy the Senators for nine million. Finley told him the 11th hour had arrived — would he buy now? Daly told him he couldn't decide that fast. This changed Finley's mind about how he was going to vote. Finley approved the transfer, and so did Autry, so the motion was carried by a 10–2 margin. The Washington Senators passed into history.

Commissioner Kuhn and American League president Joe Cronin looked pale and agitated when the announcement was made. Kuhn muttered something about how fine it would be if Washington could get another team, and added that Texas was deserving of major-league ball. Short admitted to having failed to do what he had sincerely wanted to do, which was to succeed in Washington, and for that he apologized to the fans.

Many Senators fans found out the bad news from the television. As he was making his way posthaste from the meeting room to another room where the press conference was to be held, Commissioner Kuhn was accosted by reporters and asked whether Washington would still have its ball club next summer. The commish shook his head in the negative.

The rage of the populace was summed up by a local sportscaster who immediately affirmed on the air that "the fink," meaning Bob Short, had moved their beloved team to Texas. Despite the well-publicized warning clouds, no one had anticipated that such a gloomy day would ever really come. This, after all, was a charter member of the American League! Those who considered themselves in the know had felt that the idea of moving the team was simply not a practicable one, as it would risk alienating Congress and jeopardize baseball's antitrust status. The prevailing feeling, now that the worst had happened, was that President Nixon had not done enough, and that his inaction, in a year preceding an election, was in the interests of his own political skin — Texas, after all, held 26 electoral votes, and the District of Columbia three.

President Nixon had earlier termed the prospect of the Senators being transferred to some other city as "heartbreaking", but within a week he announced that the California Angels were his new adopted team and that he would be attending the 1972 home opener at Anaheim. First Lady Pat Nixon showed more compassion. She told a touching story of having once written a fan letter to a baseball player. It was addressed to Bobo Newsom, whom she had seen ejected from a game for a reason the future First Lady had thought so unfair that she felt compelled to write Bobo about it. Response throughout D.C. to the news of having lost the Senators was swift and unmerciful. Local radio station WWDC, which broadcast all Senators games, aired a two-and-a-half-hour program on which fan reaction was consistent in its condemnation of the villain in this mess, Bob Short.

The politicians for their part were threatening to remove baseball's special status as an employer exempt from antitrust regulations. Another who was particularly hurt was John Allyn, owner of the Chicago White Sox, who had fought tooth and nail against Short obtaining his wish. Allyn declared that Short had not bargained in good faith when he'd repeat-edly said that he didn't want to leave D.C. Furthermore, Allyn declared that Bob Short was a man who, in his words, had "screwed up" a franchise and was now coming out "smelling like a rose." The truth was that Short had his sights set on a ten-year, $7.5 million radio-TV contract, to be paid in advance, with the Arlington, Texas, Park Corporation. In short, Allyn explained, Short was starting off with $7.5 million that he didn't have before, and it was all interest-free tax-payers' money.

On the political front, Senator John Tunney, a Democrat from California, pointed out that baseball owners didn't seem to give two hoots about the fans. Wilmer "Vinegar Bend" Mizell, a former big-league pitcher and now a Republican Congressman from Vinegar Bend, North Carolina, asked a pointed question in the House of Representatives a month after the announcement of Short's move. Mizell wanted to know how baseball owners who only cared about the almighty dollar could possibly plead exemption from some of the laws governing American business. Within three months, 13 bills aimed at ending baseball's antitrust exemption had been introduced in Congress.

Some economists in Washington later made a study of Bob Short's books and concluded that his equity in the Senators amounted to $1,000, the cost of setting up a corporation through which he had secured the loan to buy the ballclub. Short's losses, the accountants found, were simply bookkeeping entries, accounting for depreciation and amortization on property, and not representing any actual cash deficit. The owner could only respond that the first $2 million he had borrowed toward the $9.4 million purchase price in 1968 required that he put up securities of equal value.

The final episode concerning Bob Short and the Washington Senators occurred in 1972, on the Texas Rangers' first visit to Baltimore. When it was learned that Short would be there too, about 600 Senators fans made the trip determined to see if they could torment the man. An effigy, stuffed with old copies of the *Sporting News* and decorated with a Senators hat and pennant, was held up right next to him. Finally, a woman walked past Short and, pretending to lose her balance, poured a whole glass of beer over his head.

The Washington Senators had seven games left following the September 21 death sentence. They won only two of those. In the first, 24-year-old righthander Bill Gogolewski knocked off the Indians 3–2 and rounded up his figures at 6–5, 2.76, for the year. A paltry gathering of 1,450 showed up to see that game. A string of three losses in Boston followed, with the Senators' bats even more silent than usual; the club scored only four runs in those games. The boys came home one final time, for the last series in the history of the Washington Senators, which would be played against the Damn Yankees. Joe Grzenda, who was emerging as the club's most reliable pitcher, and who had saved Gogolewski's victory against the Indians six days earlier, picked up the win in relief in the first game of the series. The next day, the Senators squandered four runs in the fifth, and Mel Stottlemyre beat the Nats for the 23rd and final time of his career, 6–3.

On the night of Thursday, September 30, 1971, a crowd estimated at nearly 20,000, including about 4,000 who crashed the gate, was in a somber, and even downright ugly, mood. Two giant signs hung vertically from the upper deck: the first read "Short" and the second "Stinks." When security removed the signs, another one was soon hoisted up which read "Short Still Stinks!" and that got a huge roar of approval. One placard implored Short to, on his way to Texas, go to hell. Bob Short's initials were displayed prominently at various times during the evening.

The climax to this eerie night came in the sixth inning. The fans were hoping that Frank Howard would hit one last home run for them, and Hondo led off the bottom of the inning against Mike Kekich with the Nats trailing 5–1. His first time up, the Capital Punisher had walked on four pitches, and he had popped up to the infield on his second try. It appeared that Mike Kekich was doing his best to furnish the best possible script for

the comic tragedy which was playing itself out. Kekich offered two straight fastballs, but Howard, anxious to do what was expected of him, couldn't do anything with either one.

Just as radio announcer Ron Menchine was saying that there was still time for the Senators to come back, Frank Howard got hold of one, and the crowd went absolutely mad. The standing ovation lasted several minutes for Hondo's 26th homer of the year and 237th, and last, as a Senator. He tipped his cap to the crowd—something, incidentally, that Ted Williams had not been able to bring himself to do in *his* farewell. Like Ted, Howard had vowed in earlier years never to tip his cap to the crowd, having too often been made the brunt of boos and catcalls in his seven years in Washington. And he never did, until now. The big man, overwhelmed with sadness but also joy, cried.

Having never felt worthy of all the adulation he had earned as the majors' top slugger over the past few years, Hondo had to be coaxed by Ted Williams and others to go out and take a couple of curtain calls. He emerged from the dugout not once but twice to blow kisses to the crowd, and he threw a helmet liner for someone to keep as a souvenir. Howard was sorry for the loyal fans the Senators had, and admired how they had continued to support the club in light of its lack of success and high ticket prices.

More than any player there, Frank Howard had known his greatest success in Washington, and now it looked as if he would be the city's last baseball hero. Of the great players of the past, only Bucky Harris was at the last game. In May of this year, symbolically, two of Harris's contemporaries, Hall of Famers Heinie Manush and Goose Goslin, who had fought until the last day of the 1928 season for the batting title, had passed away, just three days apart. League president Joe Cronin was not present at the final game. Neither was Bob Short, who possibly avoided a date with a lynch mob.

Frank Howard had frequently been quoted as saying that he did not want to go to Dallas. Over the past four years, Hondo had blossomed into a superstar in Washington, had averaged 40 homers a season, and had participated in the All-Star game each year. He had earned a total salary of $400,000, the result of contracts usually negotiated following a holdout — Frank despised spring training. With the club now in Texas, he would hold out, again, prior to the next season, further enhancing his hero image in Washington. He would publicly castigate Bob Short, and also the other American League club owners for allowing Short's move.

Hondo skipped all of spring training, and when Short finally agreed to pay him $120,000 for 1972, the same as his 1971 salary, a player strike kept Frank from whipping himself into playing shape. In the first regular-season big-league game in the state of Texas, Frank Howard unleashed a 450-foot drive in the very first inning which fell far beyond the green fence in Arlington Stadium's vast center field. But Ted Williams had told Howard that the club was going to go increasingly with youth, and that Hondo would be sitting some of the time. With a month left in the season, he was traded to Detroit. In a part-time role, he hit ten homers in '72, and 12 in Detroit in '73, as his remarkable career played itself out. The trouble with baseball, Hondo later remarked, is that by the time you finally learn how to play it, you can't play it anymore.

That last home run he hit in Washington, Howard insisted, would always overshadow all his other accomplishments in the game of baseball — that one, he said, he would take to his grave. Following the emotional smash, the Senators rallied, with the tying run counting on a double by Elliott Maddox, the outfielder who'd come from the Tigers but hit just .217. By the bottom of the eighth the mood of the crowd was obviously more volatile, and many were chanting "We want Short." For the first time on this night, but not the last, a group of fans sprinted across the diamond, delaying the start of the eighth inning. The Nats scratched out a couple of runs on two singles, an error, and a sacrifice fly, and led 7–5 heading into the ninth.

More fans trespassed onto the field and once order was restored, an announcement was made that the Senators would have to forfeit the game unless the field was kept clear. Joe Grzenda, a resident of Moscow — Moscow, Pennsylvania, that is — and nicknamed "Shaky Joe" because of his nervous habits, was on the mound to try and save Paul Lindblad's eighth win since coming to the Senators. Grzenda, who would finish the year with outstanding stats — 5–2, 1.93 — got two easy outs before fans, stacked along the two foul lines, began jumping onto the field and then jumping back off.

Del Unser, completing a .255 season and playing his last game for the ball club as it turned out, fled the scene, admitting later that he feared for his safety. Ted Williams was afraid for the safety of all his players and gave the order for his pitchers to leave the bullpen and return to the clubhouse. Instead of seeking passage below the stands, which they could have done, the pitchers ran right across the field of play. That's when all hell broke loose. The fans stormed back onto the field en masse, yanking up clumps of dirt and grass which might be kept as souvenirs of Washington Senators baseball. There was a rush for home plate and the bases, and letters and numbers were being filched from the scoreboard — anything that wasn't bolted down was fair game. Veteran umpire Jim Honochick ruled a forfeit, the first one in the majors since 1954, for a 9–0 triumph for the Yankees instead of the 7–5 Washington win which had seemed likely.

It was quite a welcoming committee which greeted Bob Short in Texas less than two months after the end of the '71 season. He announced in front of about 800 business leaders that the Texas team would be known as the "Texas Rangers." Within days, cars were driving around with bumper stickers reading "Arlington, World Series '72." That wasn't about to happen anytime soon. In fact, in a season shortened slightly because of a players' strike at the beginning, the Rangers were even worse than the Senators, losing 100 of their 154 games. They were last in the Western Division, and Ted Williams, who'd seen and had enough, bowed out of his contract one year early.

Near the end, Williams had given the impression of being totally disillusioned, calling the Rangers "the worst darn team in baseball." Often he was heard commenting that his players were continually making high-school mistakes on the playing field. Some of them, he was sure, didn't have the type of dedication and curiosity that had made him the hitter he'd been. A baseball player could not develop in the major leagues, Ted contended, and continuous disagreement on this issue eroded the relationship Ted once had with the club owner. Through it all and to his credit, Williams retained his composure. He was never ejected from a ballgame in his entire career, as a player or a manager. Ted admitted that he had regrets about not moving to the front office right after the '69 season, so that he could have gone out on another high note, as he had in late September 1960, when he homered in his last at-bat. Now 54, the Splendid Splinter retired to Florida for good.

Bob Short did not find the mother lode in Texas. Attendance remained poor—the Rangers drew 8,000 more fans than had shown up in D.C. in '71. The figure of 662,974 was also 137,000 less per season than the average in Washington over the Nats' last three years. Bob Short stated repeatedly during the first year in Texas that he needed 800,000 attendance to break even, and he looked for loopholes to get out of the agreement he had signed with Arlington mayor Tom Vandegriff. In 1973, the club was again terrible, 57–105, and attendance diminished by 140 fans per game.

In 1974, the peppery Billy Martin, hired by Short following his dismissal as manager at Detroit, took over the Texas Rangers and directed a remarkable turnaround season in which the club was in the running for the Western Division title until the final weeks. Jeff Burroughs, 23-year-old outfielder, was named the league's Most Valuable Player. The Rangers drew 1.2 million and the franchise was on its

way. By the time this first taste of success came about, however, Bob Short was already gone, having sold his interests to a local group headed by Brad Corbett. Short had done exactly the same with the Senators/Rangers as he had with the Minneapolis Lakers—raised prices, moved the franchise, and sold at a profit.

Since that time, the Texas Rangers have generally featured powerful offensive clubs which have fallen short due to a lack of pitching depth (with 1977 a particularly notable exception). Many an apparent contender has wilted in the extreme Texas heat of August, so much heat that steel girders at Arlington Stadium would expand and emit cracking sounds as loud as gunshots. Ranger fans had to wait a quarter of a century, until 1996, for a playoff appearance. The club, founded in 1961, has yet to make it to a World Series as the new century begins.

Since 1971, there have been some intermittent signs that major-league baseball would return to Washington, but this has yet to happen. In 1974, the infamous Joseph Danzansky was almost set to buy the San Diego Padres and move the club to Washington, with "almost" being the operative word. Danzansky once again fell short on financing, as he had at that crucial time three years earlier.

In the running for a new charter in 1977, American League owners, instead of welcoming Washington back, opted for Seattle, for the second time in eight years, and Toronto. In 1991, National League owners selected Miami and Denver. It was the same story in 1998, with a single team, one in Tampa Bay and one in Arizona, accepted into each league. In early 1999, D.C. Mayor Anthony Williams pledged the support of his administration for the notion of attracting major-league baseball to the national capital region. Plans were unveiled to construct a $200-million, 45,000-seat stadium in the heart of downtown Washington.

EPILOGUE:
A MILLENNIUM WISH

The story of how Clark Griffith's family enterprise came to be known as the Minnesota Twins Baseball Club is the story of a business venture which never had much of a chance to compete with some of the bigger kids on the block. A lack of revenue in a relatively small market, later fragmented because of the arrival of Baltimore on the major-league scene, resulted in fewer players being developed within the organization. With a smaller number of superior players to feature in any given era, and with little by way of a winning tradition as one consequence, many potential fans stayed away. Furthermore, because of the large public-service base in Washington, many of those fans were from other parts of America and had no emotional investment in the Senators. When they did show up, they were just as apt to root for the visiting team.

As Clark Griffith, who knew no business other than baseball, had realized, and as other owners, including his adoptive son, later found out, there was that vicious cycle at work, even before the free-agency era, against economic survival in Washington. For all anyone knows, Clark Griffith may well have at least understood the logic behind his son's move to Minnesota and Bob Short's flight to Texas (the Lone Ranger admirer might well have approved of the new nickname for the Texas entry).

The losers as always were the fans, those who loved the team despite the fact that a pennant had not been brought home in nearly 40 years, or that the club had only finished better than .500 twice since the end of World War II. In other towns, the Washington Senators were considered, in most eras, to be something of a joke — just as surely as the Yankees would be at or near the top in the standings, the Senators were apt to be near the bottom. They were the accepted clumsy cousin. But there are people for whom the term "Washington Senators" holds as much emotion as "New York Giants," "Brooklyn Dodgers," and even (Damn) "Yankees" do for others.

In the context of reality, the context of change that baseball finds itself in at the beginning of the new millennium, fans of the old Nats know that things will never again be quite the same. Even so, many of us still have our hearts set on someday proclaiming about Washington ... *First in War, First in Peace, and First in the American League!*

APPENDIX A

Record of the Washington Senators — First Franchise

Year	Wins	Losses	Pct.	Position	GBL	Manager
1901	61	73	.455	6th	21	Jimmy Manning
1902	61	75	.449	6th	22	Tom Loftus
1903	43	94	.314	8th	47.5	Tom Loftus
1904	38	113	.252	8th	55.5	Malachi Kittredge & Patsy Donovan
1905	64	87	.424	7th	29.5	Jake Stahl
1906	55	95	.367	7th	37.5	Jake Stahl
1907	49	102	.325	8th	43.5	Joe Cantillon
1908	67	85	.441	7th	22.5	Joe Cantillon
1909	42	110	.276	8th	56	Joe Cantillon
1910	66	85	.437	7th	36.5	Jimmy McAleer
1911	64	90	.416	7th	38.5	Jimmy McAleer
1912	91	61	.599	2nd	14	Clark Griffith
1913	90	64	.584	2nd	6.5	Clark Griffith
1914	81	73	.526	3rd	19	Clark Griffith
1915	85	68	.556	4th	17	Clark Griffith
1916	76	77	.497	7th	14.5	Clark Griffith
1917	74	79	.484	5th	25.5	Clark Griffith
1918	72	56	.563	3rd	4	Clark Griffith
1919	56	84	.400	7th	32	Clark Griffith
1920	68	84	.447	6th	29	Clark Griffith
1921	80	73	.523	4th	18	George McBride
1922	69	85	.448	6th	25	Clyde Milan
1923	75	78	.490	4th	23.5	Donie Bush
1924	92	62	.597	1st*	—	Bucky Harris
1925	96	55	.636	1st	—	Bucky Harris
1926	81	69	.540	4th	8	Bucky Harris
1927	85	69	.552	3rd	25	Bucky Harris
1928	75	79	.487	4th	26	Bucky Harris
1929	71	81	.467	5th	34	Walter Johnson
1930	94	60	.610	2nd	8	Walter Johnson
1931	92	62	.597	3rd	16	Walter Johnson
1932	93	61	.604	3rd	14	Walter Johnson
1933	99	53	.651	1st	—	Joe Cronin
1934	66	86	.434	7th	34	Joe Cronin
1935	67	86	.438	6th	27	Bucky Harris
1936	82	71	.536	3rd#	20	Bucky Harris

Year	Wins	Losses	Pct.	Position	GBL	Manager
1937	73	80	.477	6th	28.5	Bucky Harris
1938	75	76	.497	5th	23.5	Bucky Harris
1939	65	87	.428	6th	41.5	Bucky Harris
1940	64	90	.416	7th	26	Bucky Harris
1941	70	84	.455	6th#	31	Bucky Harris
1942	62	89	.411	7th	39.5	Bucky Harris
1943	84	69	.549	2nd	13.5	Ossie Bluege
1944	64	90	.416	8th	25	Ossie Bluege
1945	87	67	.565	2nd	1.5	Ossie Bluege
1946	76	78	.494	4th	28	Ossie Bluege
1947	64	90	.416	7th	33	Ossie Bluege
1948	56	97	.366	7th	40	Joe Kuhel
1949	50	104	.325	8th	47	Joe Kuhel
1950	67	87	.435	5th	31	Bucky Harris
1951	62	92	.403	7th	36	Bucky Harris
1952	78	76	.506	5th	17	Bucky Harris
1953	76	76	.500	5th	23.5	Bucky Harris
1954	66	88	.429	6th	45	Bucky Harris
1955	53	101	.344	8th	43	Charlie Dressen
1956	59	95	.383	7th	38	Charlie Dressen
1957	55	99	.357	8th	43	Charlie Dressen & C. Lavagetto
1958	61	93	.396	8th	31	Cookie Lavagetto
1959	63	91	.409	8th	31	Cookie Lavagetto
1960	73	81	.474	5th	24	Cookie Lavagetto

* Won World Championship
# Tied for position in standings

Record of the Washington Senators — Second Franchise

Year	Wins	Losses	Pct.	Position	GBL	Manager
1961	61	100	.379	9th#	47.5	Mickey Vernon
1962	60	101	.373	10th	35.5	Mickey Vernon
1963	56	106	.346	10th	48.5	Mickey Vernon & Gil Hodges
1964	62	100	.383	9th	37	Gil Hodges
1965	70	92	.432	8th	32	Gil Hodges
1966	71	88	.447	8th	25.5	Gil Hodges
1967	76	85	.472	6th#	15.5	Gil Hodges
1968	65	96	.404	10th	37.5	Jim Lemon
1969	86	76	.531	4thE	23	Ted Williams
1970	70	92	.432	6thE	38	Ted Williams
1971	63	96	.396	5thE	38.5	Ted Williams

Tied for position in standings
E signifies East Division beginning 1969

APPENDIX B

Lifetime records of all members of
the Baseball Hall of Fame who
played with the Washington Senators
— total statistics as a Senator, and for career.

Players listed chronologically based on year of induction into the Hall of Fame.

Walter Perry Johnson

B. Humboldt, Kansas, November 6, 1887. D. Washington, D.C., December 10, 1946.
Inducted into Hall of Fame in 1936. Pitcher, threw and batted righthanded. Played entire career with Washington.

Record with Washington, 1907–27

Years	Wins	Losses	ERA	IP	H	BB	K	ShO
21	417	279	2.17	5923.2	4927	1362	3509	110

Tristram E Speaker

B. Hubbard, Texas, April 4, 1888. D. Lake Whitney, Texas, December 8, 1958. Inducted
into Hall of Fame in 1937. Outfielder, batted and threw lefthanded.

Record with Washington, 1927

Years	Games	AB	R	H	2B	3B	HR	RBI	BA
1	141	523	71	171	43	6	2	73	.327

Career Record, 1907–28

Years	Games	AB	R	H	2B	3B	HR	RBI	BA
22	2789	10195	1882	3514	792	222	117	1529	.345

George Harold Sisler

B. Manchester, Ohio, March 24, 1893. D. Richmond Heights, Missouri, March 26, 1973. Inducted into Hall of Fame in 1939. First Baseman, batted and threw lefthanded.

Record with Washington, 1928

Years	Games	AB	R	H	2B	3B	HR	RBI	BA
1	20	49	1	12	1	0	0	2	.245

Career Record, 1915–30 (did not play, 1923)

Years	Games	AB	R	H	2B	3B	HR	RBI	BA
15	2055	8267	1284	2812	425	164	102	1175	.340

Edward James Delahanty

B. Cleveland, Ohio, October 30, 1867. D. Niagara Falls, New York, July 2, 1903. Inducted into Hall of Fame in 1945. Outfielder, batted and threw righthanded.

Record with Washington, 1902–03

Years	Games	AB	R	H	2B	3B	HR	RBI	BA
2	165	629	125	230	54	15	11	114	.360

Career Record, 1888–1903

Years	Games	AB	R	H	2B	3B	HR	RBI	BA
16	1835	7505	1599	2597	522	185	101	1464	.346

Clark Calvin Griffith

B. Clear Creek, Missouri, November 20, 1869. D. Washington, D.C., October 27, 1955. Inducted into Hall of Fame in 1946. Pitcher, threw and batted righthanded.

Record with Washington, 1912–14

Years	Wins	Losses	ERA	IP	H	BB	K	ShO
3	0	0	0.00	2	3	0	1	0

Career Record, 1891, 1893–1907, 1909, 1912–14

Years	Wins	Losses	ERA	IP	H	BB	K	ShO
20	237	146	3.31	3385.2	3670	774	955	22

Aloysius Harry Simmons

(born: Aloys Szymanski). B. Milwaukee, Wisconsin, May 22, 1902. D. Milwaukee, Wisconsin, May 26, 1956. Inducted into Hall of Fame in 1953. Outfielder, batted and threw righthanded.

Record with Washington, 1937–38

Years	Games	AB	R	H	2B	3B	HR	RBI	BA
1	228	889	139	259	44	16	29	179	.291

Career Record, 1924–44 (did not play, 1942)

Years	Games	AB	R	H	2B	3B	HR	RBI	BA
20	2215	8759	1507	2927	539	149	307	1827	.334

Joseph Edward Cronin

B. San Francisco, California, October 12, 1906. D. Osterville, Massachusetts, September 7, 1984. Inducted into Hall of Fame in 1956. Shortstop, batted and threw righthanded.

Record with Washington, 1928–34

Years	Games	AB	R	H	2B	3B	HR	RBI	BA
7	940	3582	577	1090	242	72	51	673	.304

Career Record, 1926–1945

Years	Games	AB	R	H	2B	3B	HR	RBI	BA
20	2124	7579	1233	2285	515	118	170	1424	.301

Edgar Charles (Sam) Rice

B. Morocco, Indiana, February 20, 1890. D. Rossmor, Maryland, October 13, 1974. Inducted into Hall of Fame in 1963. Outfielder, batted left-handed and threw righthanded.

Record with Washington, 1915–33

Years	Games	AB	R	H	2B	3B	HR	RBI	BA
19	2307	8934	1466	2889	479	183	33	1045	.323

Career Record, 1915–1934

Years	Games	AB	R	H	2B	3B	HR	RBI	BA
20	2404	9269	1514	2987	498	184	34	1078	.322

Henry Emmett (Heinie) Manush

B. Tuscumbia, Alabama, July 20, 1901. D. Sarasota, Florida, May 12, 1971. Inducted into Hall of Fame in 1964. Outfielder, batted and threw lefthanded.

Record with Washington, 1930–35

Years	Games	AB	R	H	2B	3B	HR	RBI	BA
6	792	3290	576	1078	215	70	47	491	.328

Career Record, 1923–1939

Years	Games	AB	R	H	2B	3B	HR	RBI	BA
17	2008	7654	1287	2524	491	160	110	1183	.330

Leon Allen (Goose) Goslin

B. Salem, New Jersey, October 16, 1900. D. Bridgeton, New Jersey, May 15, 1971. Inducted into Hall of Fame in 1968. Outfielder, batted lefthanded and threw righthanded.

Record with Washington, 1921–30, 1933, 1938

Years	Games	AB	R	H	2B	3B	HR	RBI	BA
12	1361	5140	854	1659	289	125	127	931	.323

Career Record, 1921–38

Years	Games	AB	R	H	2B	3B	HR	RBI	BA
18	2287	8656	1483	2735	500	173	248	1609	.316

Stanley Anthony Coveleski

(born: Stanislaus Kowalewski). B. Shamokin, Pennsylvania, July 13, 1889. D. South Bend, Indiana, March 20, 1984. Inducted into Hall of Fame in 1969. Pitcher, threw and batted righthanded.

Record with Washington, 1925–27

Years	Wins	Losses	ERA	IP	H	BB	K	ShO
3	36	17	2.98	500.2	515	162	111	6

Career Record, 1912, 1916–28

Years	Wins	Losses	ERA	IP	H	BB	K	ShO
14	215	142	2.89	3082	3055	802	981	38

Vernon Louis (Lefty) Gomez

B. Rodeo, California, November 26, 1908. D. Greenbrae, California, February 17, 1989. Inducted into Hall of Fame in 1972. Pitcher, threw and batted lefthanded.

Record with Washington, 1943

Years	Wins	Losses	ERA	IP	H	BB	K	ShO
1	0	1	5.79	4.2	4	5	0	0

Career Record, 1930–43

Years	Wins	Losses	ERA	IP	H	BB	K	ShO
14	189	102	3.34	2503	2290	1095	1468	28

Early (Gus) Wynn

B. Hartford, Alabama, January 6, 1920. D. Venice, Florida, April 4, 1999. Inducted into Hall of Fame in 1972. Pitcher, threw righthanded, switch hitter.

Record with Washington, 1939, 1941–44, 1946–48

Years	Wins	Losses	ERA	IP	H	BB	K	ShO
8	72	87	3.94	1266.2	1359	460	386	9

Career Record, 1939, 1941–44, 1946–63

Years	Wins	Losses	ERA	IP	H	BB	K	ShO
23	300	244	3.54	4564	4291	1775	2334	49

Stanley Raymond (Bucky) Harris

B. Port Jervis, New York, November 8, 1896. D. Bethesda, Maryland, November 8, 1977. Inducted into Hall of Fame in 1975. Second Baseman, batted and threw righthanded.

Record with Washington, 1919–28

Years	Games	AB	R	H	2B	3B	HR	RBI	BA
10	1252	4717	718	1295	223	64	9	506	.275

Career Record, 1919–29, 1931

Years	Games	AB	R	H	2B	3B	HR	RBI	BA
12	1263	4736	722	1297	224	64	9	506	.274

Richard Benjamin Ferrell

B. Durham, North Carolina, October 12, 1905. D. Bloomfield Hills, Michigan, July 27, 1995. Inducted into Hall of Fame in 1984. Catcher, batted and threw righthanded

Record with Washington, 1937–41, 1944–45, 1947

Years	Games	AB	R	H	2B	3B	HR	RBI	BA
8	659	2080	218	568	100	10	3	237	.273

Career Record, 1929–45, 1947

Years	Games	AB	R	H	2B	3B	HR	RBI	BA
18	1884	6028	687	1692	324	45	28	734	.281

Harmon Clayton Killebrew

B. Payette, Idaho, June 29, 1936. Inducted into Hall of Fame in 1984. First Baseman, Third Baseman, Outfielder. Batted and threw righthanded.

Record with Washington, 1954–60

(Killebrew played 21 years for Washington/Minnesota franchise)

Years	Games	AB	R	H	2B	3B	HR	RBI	BA
7	390	1242	211	311	45	3	84	215	.250

Career Record, 1954–75

Years	Games	AB	R	H	2B	3B	HR	RBI	BA
22	2435	8147	1283	2086	290	24	573	1584	.256

Appendix C

List of players drafted on December 14, 1960, or signed
as free agents, by the second Washington Senators
franchise prior to play in the spring of 1961.

Player	POS	Drafted from...	Years with Senators	Years in Majors
Chet Boak	2B	Kansas City A's	1	2
Leo Burke	INF	Rochester (Baltimore)	0	7
Pete Burnside	P	Detroit Tigers	3	8
Pete Daley	C	Kansas City A's	1	7
Dick Donovan	P	Chicago White Sox	1	15
Dutch Dotterer	C	Kansas City A's	1	5
John Gabler	P	Richmond (New York)	1	3
Gene Green	C-OF	Baltimore Orioles	1	7
Rudy Hernandez	P	Minnesota Twins	2	2
Joe Hicks	OF	Chicago White Sox	2	5
Chuck Hinton	OF	Baltimore Orioles	4	11
Ed Hobaugh	P	Chicago White Sox	3	3
Bob Johnson	INF	Kansas City A's	2	11
Marty Keough	OF	Cleveland Indians	1	11
Jim King	OF	Cleveland Indians	7	11
Billy Klaus	INF	Baltimore Orioles	1	11
John Klippstein	P	Cleveland Indians	1	18
Dale Long	1B	New York Yankees	2	10
Hector Maestri	P	Minnesota Twins	2	2
Jim Mahoney	P	Boston Red Sox	1	4
Carl Mathias	P	Cleveland Indians	1	2
Joe McClain	P	Charleston (Minn.)	2	2
Danny O'Connell	INF	Free Agent	2	10
Johnny Schaive	INF	Minnesota Twins	5	5
Roman Semproch	P	Spokane (Detroit)	0	4
Bobby Shantz	P	New York Yankees	0	16
Dave Sisler	P	Detroit Tigers	1	7
Tom Sturdivant	P	Boston Red Sox	1	10
Haywood Sullivan	C	Seattle (Boston)	0	7
Willie Tasby	OF	Boston Red Sox	2	6
Coot Veal	SS	Detroit Tigers	1	6
Hal Woodeshick	P	Minnesota Twins	3	11
Gene Woodling	OF	Baltimore Orioles	2	17
Bud Zipfel	1B-OF	New York Yankees	2	2

BIBLIOGRAPHY

Alexander, Charles C. *Ty Cobb* (New York: Oxford University Press, 1984).

Appel, Marty. *Yesterday's Heroes* (New York: William Morrow, 1988).

Baseball Digest. *Baseball Digest* (Columbus, OH, and Highland Park, IL: various years).

Bealle, Morris. *The Washington Senators* (Washington, DC: Columbia, 1947).

Blake, Mike. *Baseball Chronicles: An Oral History of Baseball Through the Decades* (Cincinnati: Betterway Books, 1994).

Carmichael, John P., editor. *My Greatest Day in Baseball* (New York: Grosset and Dunlap, 1968).

Chieger, Bob, editor. *Voices of Baseball* (New York: Atheneum, 1983).

Cohen, Richard M., David S. Neft, and Jordan A. Deutsch. *The World Series* (New York: The Dial Press, 1979).

Connor, Anthony J. *Baseball for the Love of It* (New York: Macmillan, 1982).

Curran, William. *Big Sticks* (New York: William Morrow, 1990).

Dewey, Donald, and Nicholas Acocella. *The Ball Clubs* (New York: HarperCollins, 1996).

Dickey, Glenn. *The History of American League Baseball Since 1901* (New York: Stein and Day, 1982).

Dickson, Paul. *Baseball's Greatest Quotations* (New York: HarperCollins, 1991).

Flood, Curt, with Richard Carter. *The Way It Is* (New York: Trident Press, 1971).

Hartley, James R. *Washington's Expansion Senators (1961–1971)* (Germantown, MD: Corduroy Press, 1997).

Hill, Art. *I Don't Care if I Never Come Back* (New York: Simon and Schuster, 1980).

Hirshberg, Al. *Frank Howard: The Gentle Giant* (New York: G.P. Putnam's Sons, 1973).

Honig, Donald. *Baseball Between the Lines* (New York: Coward, McCann & Geoghegan, 1976).

_____. *Baseball When the Grass Was Real* (New York: Coward, McCann & Geoghegan, 1975).

James, Bill. *The Bill James Historical Baseball Abstract* (New York: Villard Books, 1986).

Karst, Gene, and Martin J. Jones, Jr. *Who's Who in Professional Baseball* (New Rochelle, NY: Arlington House, 1973).

Kiersh, Edward. *Where Have You Gone, Vince DiMaggio?* (New York: Bantam Books, 1983).

Krause Publications. *Sports Collectors Digest* (Iola, WI: various years).

Linn, Ed. *Hitter: The Life and Turmoils of Ted Williams* (New York: Harcourt Brace, 1993).

Marazzi, Rich, and Len Fiorito. *Aaron to Zipfel* (New York: Avon Books, 1985).

_____, and _____. *Aaron to Zuverink* (New York: Avon Books, 1984).

Nathan, David H., editor. *Baseball Quotations* (Jefferson, NC: McFarland, 1991).

Okrent, Daniel, and Harris Lewine. *The Ultimate Baseball Book* (Boston: Houghton Mifflin, 1979).

Okrent, Daniel, and Steve Wulf. *Baseball Anecdotes* (New York: Oxford University Press, 1989).

Peary, Danny. *We Played the Game* (New York: Hyperion, 1994).

Polner, Murray. *Branch Rickey* (New York: Atheneum, 1982).

Povich, Shirley. *The Washington Senators: An Informal History* (New York: G.P. Putnam's Sons, 1954).

Reichler, Joseph L., editor. *The Baseball Encyclopedia* (New York: Macmillan, 1982).

_____. *The Baseball Trade Register* (New York: Macmillan, 1984).

Ritter, Lawrence S. *The Glory of Their Times* (New York: Macmillan, 1966).

_____. *Lost Ballparks* (New York: Viking Studio Books, 1992).

Schacht, Al. *Clowning Through Baseball* (New York: A.S. Barnes, 1941).

Seidel, Michael. *Streak: Joe DiMaggio and the Summer of '41* (New York: McGraw-Hill, 1988).

Shatzkin, Mike, editor. *The Ballplayers* (New York: William Morrow, 1990).

Solomon, Burt. *The Baseball Timeline* (New York: Avon Books, 1997).

Sowell, Mike. *July 2, 1903* (New York: Macmillan, 1992).

_____. *The Pitch That Killed* (New York: Macmillan, 1989).

The Sporting News—(newspaper); *Baseball Guide*; *Baseball Register*; *Baseball Record Book*; and *Baseball Trivia Book* (St. Louis, MO: various years).

Swirsky, Seth. *Every Pitcher Tells a Story* (New York: Random House, 1999).

Tellis, Richard. *Once Around the Bases* (Chicago: Triumph Books, 1998).

Thomas, Henry W. *Walter Johnson, Baseball's Big Train* (Washington, DC: Phenom Press, 1995).

Thompson, S.C. *All-Time Rosters of Major League Baseball Clubs* (A.S. Barnes, 1973).

Thorn, John, and Pete Palmer. *Total Baseball, Second Edition* (New York: Warner Books, 1991).

Whitfield, Shelby. *Kiss It Goodbye* (New York: Abelard-Schuman, 1973).

Whittingham, Richard, editor. *The DiMaggio Albums* (New York: G.P. Putnam's Sons, 1989).

Williams, Ted. *My Turn at Bat* (New York: Simon and Schuster, 1969).

INDEX